Management

SECOND EDITION

Management
Concepts and Practices

R. WAYNE MONDY
Northeast Louisiana University

ROBERT E. HOLMES
James Madison University

EDWIN B. FLIPPO
The University of Arizona

Allyn and Bacon, Inc.
Boston · London · Sydney · Toronto

Production Editor: Shirley Davis
Manufacturing Buyer: Patricia Hart

Library of Congress Cataloging in Publication Data

Mondy, R. Wayne
Management, concepts and practices.

Includes bibliographies and index.
1. Management. I. Holmes, Robert E.
II. Flippo, Edwin B. III. Title.
HD31.M616 1983 658.4 82-22647
ISBN 0-205-07897-4
ISBN 0-205-07951-2 (International)

Printed in the United States of America.

10 9 8 7 6 5 4 87 86 85 84

To Frank and Alvora Edens
whose friendship, patience,
and understanding
have been invaluable.
R.W.M.

To Diane McKnight Holmes
for her encouragement,
love, and faith in me
R.E.H.

To my family
E.B.F.

Contents

Preface

This book was written for an audience that wants management theory to be linked with actual management practice. Although it is essentially pragmatic in approach, the text is balanced throughout with current management theory. A common theme—a real-world approach to management—exists throughout the book. Each of the managerial functions—planning, organizing, influencing, and controlling—is discussed from the standpoint of how each function interrelates to become the management process. The book puts the student in touch with reality through the use of numerous illustrations, quotes from company executives, and company material that depicts how management is being practiced in today's organizations.

Included in the text are several chapters the authors believe deserve special emphasis. Among these are—

- ***Careers in Management*** (in the appendix to Chapter 1). The student is provided with meaningful information about careers in management and career development. The authors stress the need for thorough self-understanding and an identification of career objectives before beginning the initial job search. A unique feature of this appendix is its coverage of the initial job threats one should be aware of when a new position has been secured.
- ***The Manager's Environment.*** This chapter presents the many external environmental factors the manager confronts. Major considerations include government, competitors, labor force, unions, stockholders, suppliers, customers, and the public.
- ***Management by Objectives.*** This chapter presents the importance of and the basic concepts relating to management by objectives in an

understandable format. A comprehensive example is presented to illustrate the application of MBO in a large, diverse organization. Also covered are the strengths and weaknesses of MBO.

- ***Staffing the Organization.*** The authors present a thorough discussion of a human resources system and the staffing process. There is a model of the staffing process and a section on the special considerations for selecting managerial personnel.
- ***Production and Operations Management.*** Two complete chapters are provided to expose students to production and operations management tools and techniques. Both traditional and current approaches are discussed. Each technique is described from the viewpoint of how it is currently used in industry and what knowledge a manager needs to possess in order to use the technique.
- ***Social Responsibility and Business Ethics.*** The chapter provides a clear distinction between ethics, social responsibility, and illegal activities.
- ***Managing Small Businesses.*** This chapter is full of useful information for those students who are contemplating entering business for themselves. It contains a thorough discussion of the potential problems that may be encountered in starting and managing a small business as well as suggestions for obtaining financial and managerial assistance.
- ***Managing the Multinational Enterprise.*** This chapter utilizes a tremendous amount of company material and quotes from executives of multinational firms to provide students with a realistic understanding of the significance of their operations. The chapter illustrates how different environments can affect the operations of the multinational.

We have included the following features to promote both the readability of and practice in important management theory:

- Key terms appear at the beginning of each chapter. Each key term is also presented in bold type the first time it is defined or described as well as highlighted in the margin for easy and quick reference.
- Learning objectives are listed at the beginning of each chapter to provide students with a general overview of the purpose and the key concepts of the chapter.
- Career profiles of successful managers are included to show students that corporate executives are "real people."
- Insights to success by key executives from a wide variety of firms are provided. The comments from these managers are interesting and informative and should give additional emphasis to the real-world approach of the text.
- A large number of easy-to-read figures and tables help describe the various concepts.
- Illustrations make specific points about selected topics.

- Review questions for each chapter test the student's understanding of the material.
- Exercises for each chapter permit students to become involved in the various concepts that have been discussed in the text.
- A comprehensive list of references is provided to permit students to conduct additional in-depth study of selected topics.
- True-to-life case studies are provided at the conclusion of each chapter. Longer cases are provided at the end of functional areas sections.
- Four longer experiential exercises are included in the Instructor's Manual to give students additional insights, new knowledge, and skills in solving problems and dealing with people in a variety of situations.

IMPROVEMENTS IN THE SECOND EDITION

The first edition was used by many excellent colleges and universities. We are honored by the support it received. As we worked on this second edition, we received numerous valuable suggestions and incorporated a large number of them. Although the basic format of the book remains unchanged, we have added two entirely new chapters. "The Manager's Environment" is designed to show the many factors that affect modern managers. Also, instead of having only one chapter on organizing, we now have two: "The Organizing Process" and "Authority, Responsibility, and Organizational Structures." We believe that this change will provide a much better coverage of the organizing function.

The following topics have either been added or given additional coverage.

- The history of management thought
- A real-world company example of management by objectives (MBO)
- Balanced coverage of both pros and cons of management by objectives
- The use of computers in business
- Job design and approaches to job design
- The use of committees and their impact on and importance to organizations
- Relationship of power and authority
- Laws affecting managers of human resources
- Functions of personnel management
- Expectancy theory
- Aldefer's theory
- House, path-goal theory
- Organizational development
- Role and function of a change agent

- Communication model
- Disciplinary action and progressive discipline
- Breakeven analysis
- Linear programming
- Quality circles for improved performance
- Lessons from Japanese management

Instructors may wish to supplement this text with the **Study Guide** prepared by Kathy Hegar and William Riddell; we believe that it will be of value to students.

All of the features mentioned are designed to enhance student interest and to provide students with an enjoyable learning experience. Numerous real-life situations were used as models in writing the text. We believe that certain managerial topics are easier to explain if the writers have had "firing-line" managerial experience. The managerial experience of the authors hopefully has added a touch of realism to the book. Our sincere desire is that the reader be stimulated by the book and choose to go into one of the most challenging and rewarding careers—MANAGEMENT!

Acknowledgments

The writing of a book cannot be accomplished without the assistance of many people. It was especially true in this instance. Although it would be impossible to list each person who assisted in this project, the authors feel that certain people must be credited due to the magnitude of their contributions.

Frank N. Edens of Louisiana Tech University and Jerry M. DeHay, Robert M. Noe III, and James R. Young of East Texas State University, dear and close friends of ours, provided the inspiration and moral support to see the project through to completion. A sincere note of appreciation goes to the faculty and staffs of the College of Business at Northeast Louisiana University, Southwest Texas State University, and East Texas State University for their support and encouragement throughout the preparation of the text. Dr. Ed D. Roach, dean of the School of Business, and Joyce Boeker, and the faculty in the Department of Management and Marketing at Southwest Texas State University deserve special recognition for their continued support. Dean John Owen, of the College of Business Administration, University of Arkansas, also deserves special recognition for his encouragement. Dean Van McGraw and David L. Loudon, head, Department of Management and Marketing, both of Northeast Louisiana University College of Business, provided valued encouragement and support. Ms. Barbara D. Kener, a truly professional manuscript typist at Northeast Louisiana University, did an outstanding job in preparation of the Test Bank and Instructor's Manual.

We would like to thank our wives for their tangible contribution in the preparation of the manuscript. Without their patience, understanding, encouragement, and creative editing, the project would not have been completed. They willingly made a number of sacrifices during the long process of the preparation of the manuscript.

We would also like to acknowledge the many contributions of our editors, Shirley Davis and Jack Peters, for their thoughtfulness and assistance throughout the project. Finally, we would like to thank our reviewers—William R. Bobbitt, Calvin College; Mark Hammer, Washington State University; Kathryn W. Hegar, Mountain View College; Frank N. Edens, Louisiana Tech University, and Edward B. Lee, Jr., Community College of Allegheny County—for their many excellent suggestions during the preparation of the second edition of *Management: Concepts and Practices.*

Because of the pragmatic nature of the book, it was necessary to secure the assistance of many corporate executives in its development. We sincerely thank the following firms for providing us with valuable input that significantly aided in bringing realism to a book on management:

- AMF Incorporated
- Abbott International, Ltd.
- American Broadcasting Companies, Inc.
- American Hospital Supply Corporation
- American Management Association
- Applied Management Services
- Armco Inc.
- Arthur Young and Company
- Armstrong Rubber Co.
- Avon Products, Inc.
- Ball Corporation
- Bausch & Lomb, Inc.
- Baxter Travenol Laboratories, Inc.
- Baylor University Medical Center
- Beech Aircraft Corp.
- Bell & Howell Company
- Bendix Corporation
- Burlington Northern, Incorporated
- Burroughs Corporation
- Carrier Corporation
- Champion Spark Plug Co.
- Chicago Bridge and Iron Co.
- Chrysler Corporation
- Citizens Insurance Company of America
- Colgate-Palmolive Co.
- Commercial Metals Co.
- Continental Air Lines, Inc.
- Copperweld Corporation
- Corning Glass Works

- Crown Zellerbach Corporation
- Dallas Cowboys Football Club
- The Dallas Morning News
- Dallas Southwest Media Corporation
- Daniel International Corp.
- Deere & Company
- Digital Equipment Corp.
- Direct Lumber, Incorporated
- Dow Chemical Co.
- E-Systems, Inc.
- Equifax, Inc.
- Fisher Controls Company, Inc.
- Formfit Rogers, Incorporated
- Fruehauf Corp.
- GAF Corp.
- General Electric Co.
- General Foods Corp.
- Georgia-Pacific Corp.
- Gifford-Hill & Company, Inc.
- Graniteville Co.
- Gulf Oil Corp.
- Hewlett-Packard Co.
- Geo. A. Hormel & Co.
- Howard Johnson Co.
- Hughes Tool Company
- Illinois Tool Works Inc.
- Inland Container Corp.
- Inland Steel Co.
- Institute of Certified Professional Managers
- Internal Revenue Service
- Jack Eckerd Corporation
- Jones & Laughlin Steel Corp.
- Kaiser Aluminum & Chemical Corp.
- Kaiser Steel Corp.
- Kellogg Co.
- Kemper Corporation
- Kimberly-Clark Corp.
- Lear Siegler, Inc.
- Leaseway Transportation Corp.
- Mallinckrodt, Inc.

- Maremont Corp.
- Maytag Co.
- J. Ray McDermott & Co.
- McDonnel Douglas Corp.
- Memorex Corp.
- Michigan General Corp.
- Minnesota Mining & Mfg. Co.
- Monsanto Company
- Morrison-Knudsen Co., Inc.
- Murphy Oil Corp.
- NCR Corp.
- A. C. Nielsen Co.
- Occidental Petroleum Corp.
- Oscar Mayer & Company
- PROBE, Incorporated
- Pay 'N Save Corporation
- Pioneer Corp.
- Procter & Gamble Co.
- Raytheon Co.
- Rockwell International Corp.
- SCM Corp.
- The Seven-Up Company
- Sherwin Williams Co.
- The Signal Companies, Inc.
- Signode Corp.
- Spencer Foods, Inc.
- Southern Railway Company
- Southland Corp.
- Southwestern Public Service Co.
- A. E. Staley Mfg. Co.
- Texas Instruments Incorporated
- Textron, Inc.
- Time Inc.
- Travel Host, Inc.
- U.S. Eaton Corporation
- United Telecommunications, Inc.
- Univar Corporation
- University Computing Co.
- Wal-Mart Stores, Inc.

- Washington Post
- The Washington Post Company
- Wyly Corp.

Management

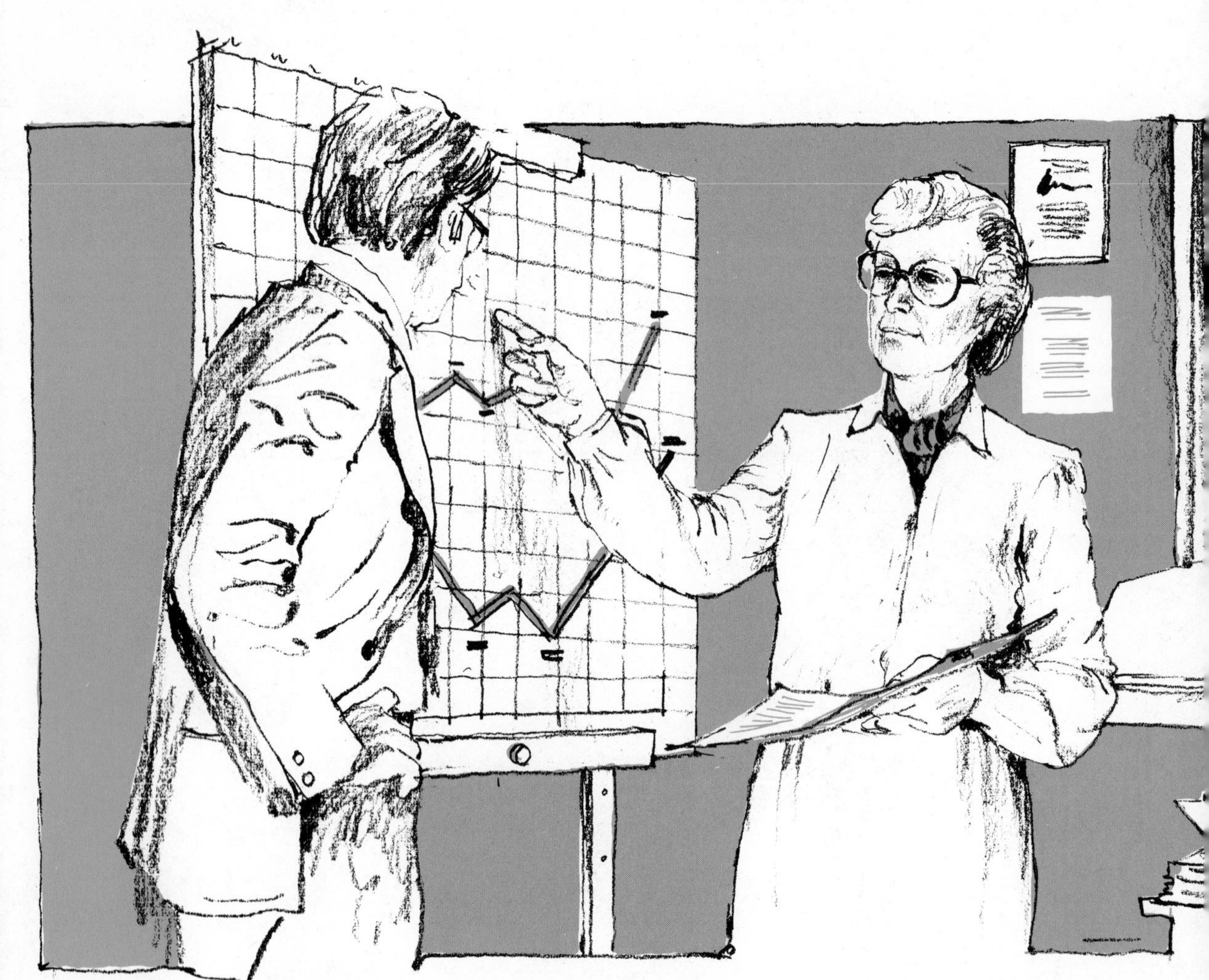

PART

I

Introduction

KEY TERMS

management
planning
organizing
influencing or directing
controlling
lower-level managers
middle managers
top management
coordination
technical skill
communication skill
human skill
analytical skill
decision-making skill
conceptual skill
classical school of management
scientific management
behavioral school of management
behavioral management science

LEARNING OBJECTIVES

After completing this chapter you should be able to

1. Define and describe management and explain the work of managers.
2. Relate the importance of service industries in today's economy.
3. Identify and describe the management functions of planning, organizing, influencing, and controlling.
4. Explain the important managerial skills: technical, communications, human, analytical, decision-making, and conceptual.
5. Describe the classical and behavioral schools of management.
6. Identify and describe the various schools or approaches to the study of management.

1

Management

As president of Centrex Corporation, a large real estate development firm, Paula Johnson is responsible for the overall success of the firm. In the five years since Paula became president of Centrex, her attitude toward managing the organization has changed considerably. Initially, she believed that if things were going to get accomplished properly, she had to make all of the decisions. It was keeping her busy seemingly twelve hours a day, seven days a week. Things have changed now. She now has five vice-presidents who report directly to her. Paula works with these vice-presidents in directing the firm toward its objectives. She thinks to herself, "At first, I was not really a manager. I was trying to do all the work myself. After I began considering myself a manager who gets the work done through other people, my job became much easier."

As office manager for Commercial Manufacturing Corporation, Wayne Thompson is responsible for supervising twelve clerks and typists. He has earned a reputation for being an excellent manager, and his work group has consistently been able to process large volumes of paperwork with a high degree of accuracy. When Wayne was asked the reasons for his department's efficiency, his reply was, "My employees do an excellent job. All I have to do is to let each person know what is expected of him or her and work with them to see that each job is accomplished efficiently and effectively."

Did you realize that 50 percent of all new businesses fail within the first two years of operation, and 70 percent fail within five years? In over 90 percent of the cases, the cause of failure can be attributed to ineffective management. The costs of poor management to individuals and to society are great. Not only are financial and physical resources wasted, but individuals often suffer psychological damage from a business failure. It's not fun to say you've failed! Many business failures can be avoided through good management practices. This is why management is a subject of increasing importance today.

We live in a society of large and small organizations. In these organizations people work together to accomplish goals that are too complex or large in number to be achieved by a single individual. Throughout life we have experiences with a variety of organizations—hospitals, schools, churches, the military, businesses, colleges, government agencies, and other types of institutions. More and more, it is being recognized that the most significant factor in determining the quality of performance and success of any organization is the success of its management.

Paula and Wayne are concerned with accomplishing a job through the efforts of other people. Why are some managers successful while others are not? The reasons for the success of managers in today's organizations are as diverse as individual personalities. Perhaps the comments of Elton H. Rule, president of American Broadcasting Companies, Inc., when he was asked the reasons for his success as a manager, best summarize the reason for success of many managers:

> Intelligence, integrity, imagination and energy: these are qualities essential to any manager anywhere. Here, though, two other qualities are equally important. A successful manager must be responsive; we serve many communities, not least among them the public at large. A manager too devoted to a single community or a single approach will rapidly become unable to function effectively. And a successful manager must be people-oriented, because human judgment and creativity are by a wide margin the most productive assets of our industry.

As Mr. Rule's comments indicate, managers must work through others to achieve success. In this book we are concerned with providing you with more knowledge about the fundamental concepts and techniques used by effective managers. Throughout the text, we will present ideas, concepts, and practices to show how important effective management is to the successful operation of all organizations. The material will be presented from the standpoint that *there is no one best way to manage.* In order to accomplish this goal, "real world" examples of how management is actually being practiced today will be presented. While our primary focus will be on the management of business organizations, most concepts and principles also apply to nonbusiness organizations such as hospitals, churches, government agencies, and schools or universities.

WHAT IS MANAGEMENT?

It is likely you will be employed by some type of organization, and, as a result, be working in a "managed environment." Therefore, an understanding of the organization and basic management concepts will be beneficial to your success as a manager. Many of you will become managers, and those who are not managers will be professional and technical personnel such as engineers, salespersons, systems analysts, accountants, market researchers, or computer programmers. Thus, it is important to address the question, "What is management?"

There are almost as many definitions of management as there are books on the subject. Most definitions of management do share a common idea—

management

management is concerned with the accomplishment of objectives through the efforts of other people. Objectives, or goals, are the final results expected. For example, your immediate objective may be to pass this course, while your long-term goals may be to graduate from college and obtain a good job. The goals of most business firms are to provide products and/or services for which they earn a profit. In order to accomplish their objectives, it is necessary for managers to do the following:

•CAREER PROFILE•

DOROTHY TIVIS POLLACK

Vice-President for Retail Merchandising and Fashion Director
Formfit Rogers, Inc.

From her first job on her home-town newspaper in Fargo, North Dakota, to her current position as vice-president for retail merchandising and fashion director at Formfit, Dorothy Pollack's career has been one big love affair—with people.

"My big love always has been meeting and talking with people," she says, and when she left Fargo for the lure of New York City, she used people-to-people contact as the basis for romantic fiction and advice to the lovelorn, which she turned out regularly for McFadden and Fawcett Publications. Jobs followed on several New York papers including the *New York Post* and, after a stint in the foreign department of United Press International, she abandoned journalism for a career as a successful fashion model. Weary of that tiresome role ("You

---

planning
organizing
influencing or directing
controlling

- Determine what is to be achieved (**planning**).
- Allocate resources and establish the means to accomplish the plans (**organizing**).
- Motivate and lead personnel (**influencing** or **directing**).
- Compare results achieved to the planned goals (**controlling**).

Thus, management may be defined as the process of planning, organizing, influencing, and controlling to accomplish organizational goals through the coordinated use of human and material resources.

WHO IS A MANAGER AND WHAT DOES A MANAGER DO?

In a sense, each of us is a manager. We manage ourselves by planning, organizing, directing, and controlling our skills, talents, time, and activities. Parents work like a truck horse!") and anxious to use the fashion expertise she'd gained by working before the cameras, Dorothy launched still a third career as the advertising director for an intimate apparel manufacturer. Later, at Formfit she added promotion and fashion merchandising, but "the best was yet to come," says Vice-President Pollack.

Retailers, and most particularly large department stores, she explains, found themselves in trouble during the 1970s as consumers turned to mass merchandisers to satisfy their needs. The big stores, feeling the pinch, needed help, especially in certain soft goods areas where marketing and merchandising efforts were lacking. Formfit already was busy establishing itself as a leader in the industry with plans to introduce a unique new product: YOU panties made of Lita, a fabric that breathes, which alone was five years in developing. Under the leadership of a bright new management team, the company employed every conceivable marketing tool to bring the concept to consumers successfully.

"As a result," Dorothy continues, "a brand new division of retail merchandising was formed and I leaped at the chance to head it." Ms. Pollack all along had been polishing her skills in people-to-people contact through "networking," a technique of giving and gleaning information and education from one's peers, which women new to the business world find especially helpful in getting ahead. No slouch in helping others herself, Dorothy has headed THE FASHION GROUP's Women in Management and Job Counseling Committees for several years and has been a seminar leader since the inception of conferences held by the American Woman's Economic Development Corp. (AWED).

Of her travels introducing new fashion concepts at stores around the country, she speaks enthusiastically: "When I prove to a sports-minded woman that a bra from Formfit's *Active Woman Collection* will give her necessary support and comfort, or watch a full-figured woman's face light up when she sees our *A Cut Above Collection,* I know that we're all on the right track." Although the division still is in its infancy, she adds, "It's booming, which is proof to us that retailers and manufacturers must join hands to make it all work."

---

manage their jobs, households, and children; children manage their allowances; and students manage their time if they expect to be successful in various subjects in school or college. Take the example of Sally Smith, an accounting major at a university. Sally's objective is a career in the public accounting field. In order to accomplish her goal, she must first complete her degree in accounting with good grades. The completion of her degree in accounting requires that she be a "good manager" of herself and her time. She must plan her course schedule, organize her time and financial resources, direct her energies toward her goal, and evaluate or control her own performance to maintain her grades.

We sometimes think of managers only in terms of top-level positions within large organizations. But actually managers operate at various levels within every type of firm, large and small, business and nonbusiness. As shown in Figure 1-1, there are three basic levels of management.

lower-level managers

Lower-level managers, usually referred to as supervisors, are responsible for managing employees in the performance of the daily operations.

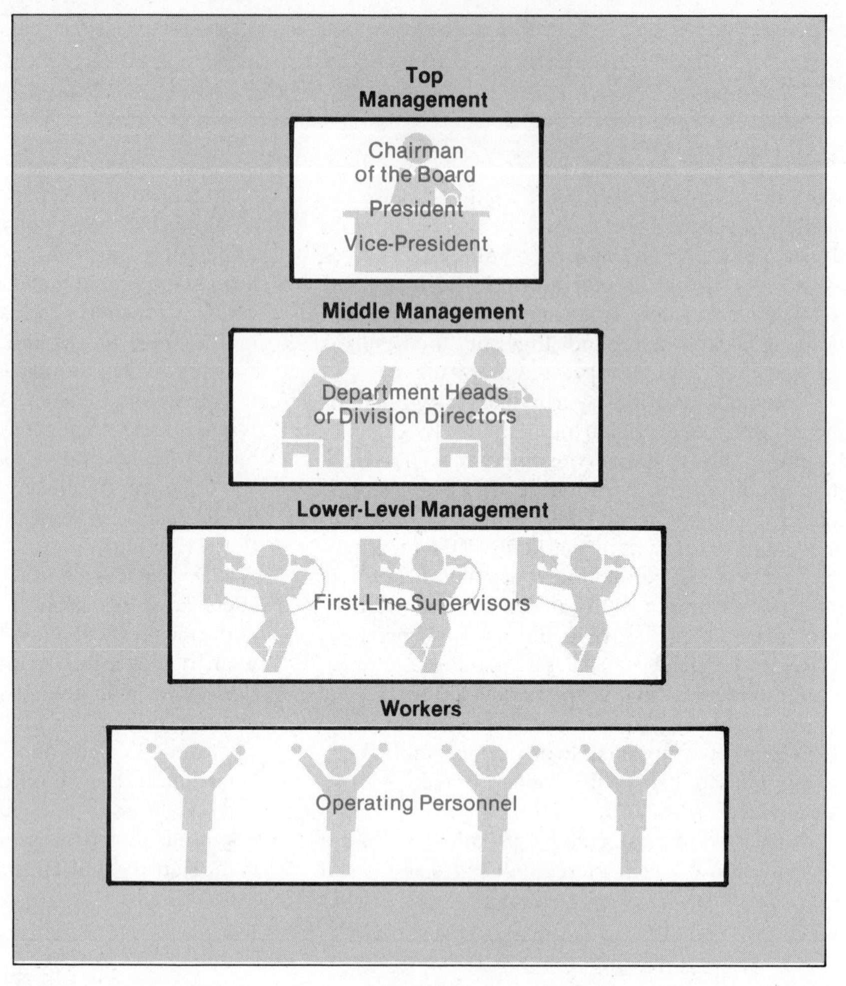

FIGURE 1-1

Managerial Levels

middle managers

Middle managers, such as department heads, are concerned primarily with the coordination of programs and activities that are necessary to achieve the overall goals of the organization as identified by top management. Finally, **top management,** referred to by such titles as president, chief executive officer (CEO), vice-president, or executive director, are responsible for providing the overall direction of the firm. In later discussions within the text, reference will be made to operating managers. Included within this category are lower- and middle-level managers.

top management

In the final analysis, *a manager is anyone, at any level of the organization, who directs the efforts of other people in accomplishing goals.* Wherever you have a group of people working together to achieve results, a manager is present. School principals, meat market supervisors, and service station operators are managers, just as the presidents of General Motors, Prudential Insurance, Gulf Oil, and Bank of America are managers. The president of the

United States is a manager, too, as are government agency heads and college deans.

A manager is the person who is responsible for making decisions concerning the use of a firm's resources to achieve results. *A manager is the catalyst who makes things happen!* He or she establishes goals, plans operations, organizes various resources—personnel, materials, equipment, capital—leads and motivates people to perform, evaluates actual results against the goals, and develops people for the organization.

Unfortunately, in many organizations, the success of a particular manager is judged exclusively on short-run output. In other words, a manager may be said to be effective if his or her unit is earning a profit, or reducing costs, or increasing the market share for the company's products, or other such measurable results. Naturally, these accomplishments are very important to a business organization. However, a major challenge and, indeed, obligation of any manager is the development of people under his or her direction, and in

The manager is the catalyst who makes things happen.

Reasons for Success and Effectiveness as a Manager

Success as a manager very seldom depends on any one attribute. Most managers have a number of pluses and a number of minuses. The objective is to have far more pluses than minuses. The pluses that I concentrate on are never to procrastinate in making a decision and never to turn down an assignment request or responsibility. And because I never turn one down or quibble in the least, perhaps I receive more assignments and responsibilities than might otherwise be the case. This improves one's opportunity to be of more benefit to the company and therefore more valuable as a manager and more deserving of promotion and pay increases. It has worked out that way for me, and I recommend it enthusiastically.

DOROTHY H. MOORE, Vice-President and Corporate Secretary, Michigan General Corporation

doing this, long-term goals may be more effectively achieved. Developing competent and well-trained people who can be promoted to more responsible jobs is a very significant part of a manager's responsibilities. This is an excellent long-run measure of the effectiveness of a manager and contributes significantly to the growth and success of the firm whether we are describing a manufacturing or service industry.

MANUFACTURING VERSUS SERVICE INDUSTRIES

In the past when management was discussed, a person envisioned buildings with smoke stacks, workers coming out of the factory with lunch pails, and assembly lines. True, the factory system is still important in our economic system, but conditions for work have changed in recent years. Service-related industries have become increasingly more important. Firms in this industry do not produce a tangible product. Rather, they create, produce, or distribute services. Examples of service industries are banks, insurance, transportation, real estate, hospitals, beauty salons, schools, and government agencies.

The importance of service industries can be illustrated by the following points:

- Approximately two out of every three working Americans are employed in service industries.
- Service industries account for over one-third of the United States's export receipts, 46 percent of gross national products, and almost fifty cents of every household dollar spent.

- In 1980, a $27.4 billion merchandise deficit existed in the balance of payments. Services offset this deficit with a $34.4 billion surplus.[1]

Service-related industries have become a major element in our economic society. As you study management, keep in mind the importance of service industries.

THE MANAGEMENT FUNCTIONS

In every organization, the work done by managers is concerned with performing the functions of planning, organizing, influencing, and controlling to achieve the objectives of the firm. Managers perform these functions within the boundaries established by the external environment and must consider the interests of such diverse groups as customers, stockholders, competitors, government, employees, unions, suppliers, and the public. Although a separate section of this text is devoted to each management function, a brief discussion of the four basic functions is presented here.

Planning

The planning function of management is concerned with determining the objectives of the firm and the means for achieving them. It is not enough to say that the objective of the company is to be the leader in the industry. The plan must be specific and provide the means for the goals to be achieved. For example, two of the primary goals of a major brewing company might be to achieve a 20 percent share of the U.S. beer market and a 15 percent rate of return on investment. In order to accomplish these goals, the firm would develop specific plans for producing and marketing their products. We discuss the planning function in Chapters 3 and 4.

Organizing

After objectives and plans have been established, management must then organize the human and physical resources of the firm. The organizing function is concerned with developing a framework that relates all personnel, work assignments, and physical resources to each other. The framework is usually termed the *organization structure* and is designed to facilitate the accomplishment of the objectives. Since each firm's goals and resources differ, a unique organization would be necessary. For instance, a university's organization structure would likely be quite different from that of a firm producing steel. The organizing function of management is discussed in Chapters 6–9.

Influencing

The third management function, influencing, is concerned with stimulating members of the organization to undertake action consistent with the plans. The influencing, or directing, function is concerned with effectively motivating, leading, and communicating with employees in the organization. These three factors have a major impact on the type of climate that exists within the firm. Topics relating to influencing are presented in Chapters 10–13.

Controlling

Ensuring that the objectives and plans of the organization are achieved is known as the controlling function. The purpose of establishing controls is to ensure proper performance in accordance with the plans. Through the establishment of controls, management is able to compare actual performance with the predetermined plan. In the event of unsatisfactory performance, corrective action can be taken. For instance, if a company's costs for producing a product are higher than planned, management must have some means to recognize the problem and take the appropriate action to correct the situation. The controlling function is discussed in Chapter 14.

COORDINATION

coordination

A number of management writers consider coordination as a separate function of management. However, in our view **coordination** involves the integration of the functions of planning, organizing, influencing, and controlling. Each management function should not be viewed as separate and distinct. For instance, the planning function is usually thought of as preceding controlling, but results of the controlling process may actually cause future plans to be altered. Coordination is necessary throughout the management process and will not be considered as a separate and distinct function of management.

The functions, physical resources, and personnel must be coordinated so that the goals of the organization can be achieved efficiently and effectively. As such, coordination represents an overall concern of all managers and is achieved when people, other resources, and functions blend together harmoniously to achieve quality results.

MANAGEMENT FUNCTIONS AT VARIOUS MANAGERIAL LEVELS

As illustrated in Figure 1-2, the basic functions of planning, organizing, influencing, and controlling are performed by managers at every level within an

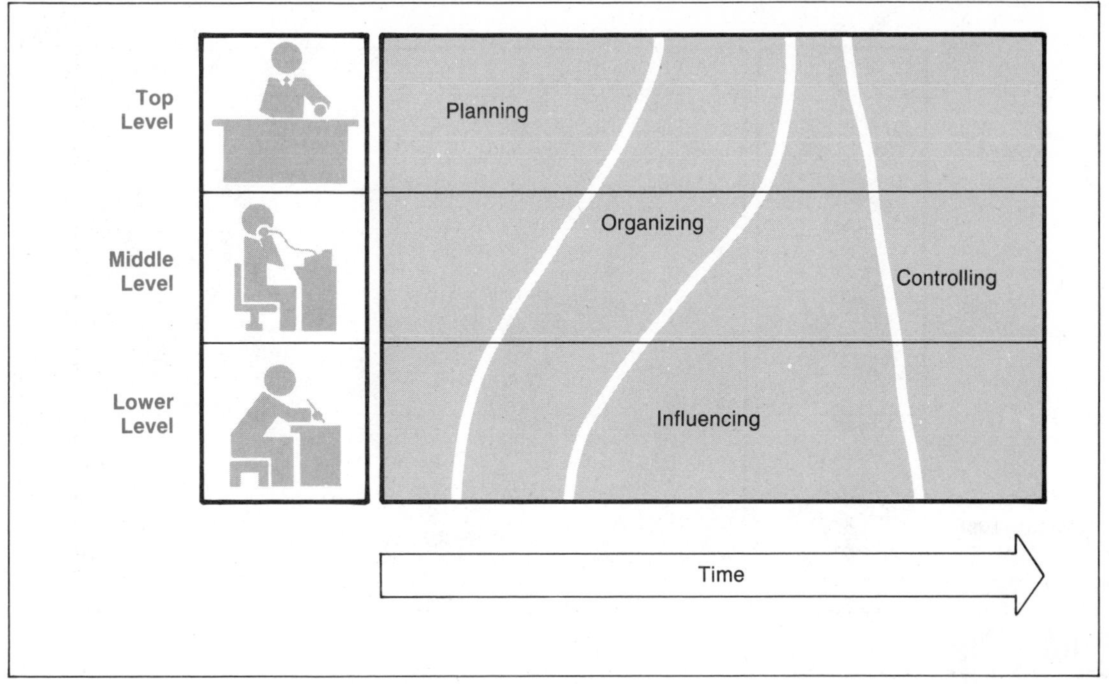

FIGURE 1-2 *Management Functions at Various Managerial Levels*

organization. The amount of time and effort devoted to each function, however, will likely depend on the level of a manager. As shown in the figure, the amount of time that lower-level managers spend on planning is much less than top-level ones. The first-line supervisor must devote considerable time and effort in influencing and controlling the work of others—accomplishing routine tasks and putting out daily fires. As managers move to higher levels in the organization, a greater percentage of their time is devoted to planning and less to influencing. The amount of time spent on the controlling function is fairly consistent at all levels of management except for the very top executive level positions such as president or CEO. At this high level, the chief executive is concerned with overall control of resources essential to the very survival of the firm. Finally, the amount of time devoted to the organizing function is fairly consistent at all levels of management.

MANAGERIAL SKILLS

In order to be effective, a manager must possess and continually develop several essential skills. Figure 1-3 illustrates a number of skills that are important to a manager's overall effectiveness. As can be seen, the relative significance of each skill varies according to the level of management an individual manager occupies within an organization.

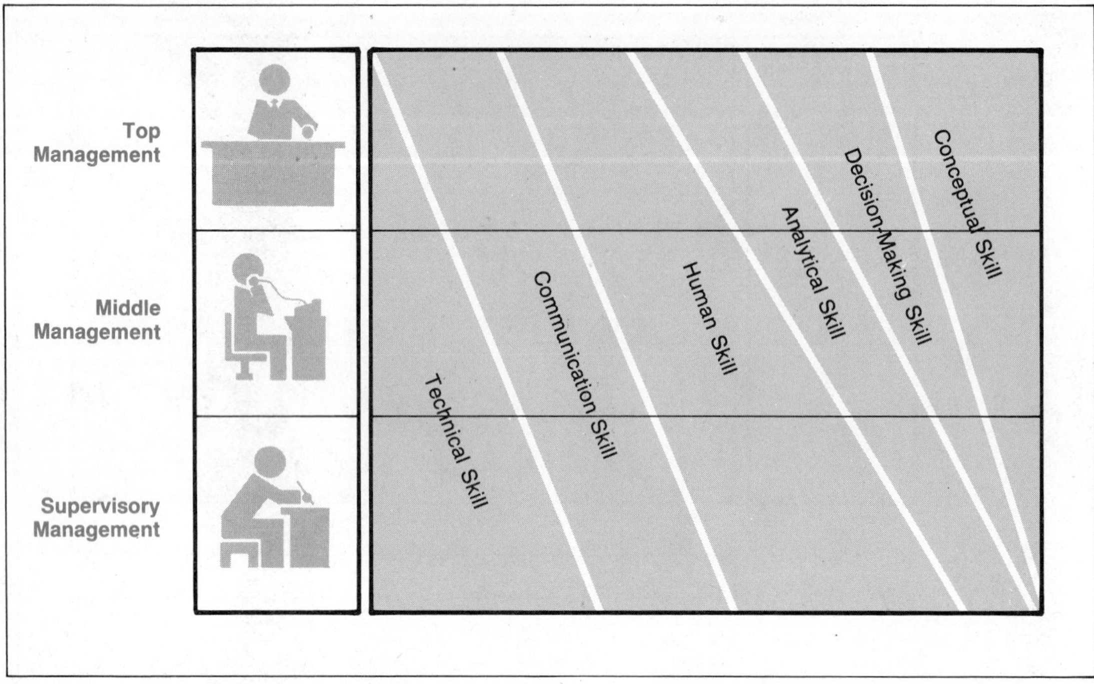

FIGURE 1-3 *Essential Skills Necessary at Various Levels of Management in an Organization*

Technical Skill

technical skill

The ability to use specific knowledge, methods, or techniques in performing work is referred to as technical skill. **Technical skill** is considered to be very crucial to the effectiveness of lower-level managers and supervisors because these individuals have direct contact with employees performing work activities within the firm. The first-line supervisor must provide technical assistance and support to personnel within the work unit. For example, a supervisor of keypunch machine operators must possess specific knowledge of the methods and techniques of operating the keypunch machines so that he or she may train newly hired operators and answer technical questions of the

---

Insights to Success

Recognize that the best management training is experience and be patient with the process of acquiring that experience. Training or academic courses are effective primarily when they accompany an opportunity to use the training.

ERNEST S. ROBSON, JR., Vice-President, Corporate Marketing, Monsanto Company

---

operators. As one moves to higher levels of management within the organization, the importance of technical skills usually diminishes because the manager has less direct contact with day-to-day problems and activities.

Communication Skill

communication skill

The ability to provide information orally and in written form to others in the organization for the purpose of achieving desired results is referred to as **communication skill.** It is a skill that is vital to the success of everyone, but most especially managers who must achieve results through the efforts of others. Communication skills are equally important at each level within the organization. Because of the importance of communication, Chapter 12 of this text is devoted to the process of communication and methods to improve managerial effectiveness.

Human Skill

human skill

The ability of a manager to understand, work with, and get along with other people is referred to as **human skill.** This skill is essential at every level of management within the organization, but it is particularly significant at lower levels of management where the supervisor has frequent and direct contact with operating personnel. Managers have "human skill" if they are able to create a climate for effective motivation and leadership. In Chapters 10–13 the importance of human skill and the ways to develop the skill are discussed in detail.

Analytical Skill

analytical skill

Analytical skill is the ability of the manager to use logical and scientific approaches or techniques in the analyses of problems and business opportunities. Although important at all levels of the organization, analytical skill tends to be relatively more significant at the upper levels of management. Lower-level managers tend to operate in a fairly stable or predictable environment with specific guidelines for their performance. By contrast, upper-level managers must function in an environment that is subject to considerable complexities and uncertainties. Some of the quantitative techniques available to assist managers in coping with a dynamic environment are discussed in Chapters 16 and 17.

Decision-making Skill

decision-making skills

The manager's skill in selecting a course of action from several alternatives is known as **decision making. Decision-making skills** are essential to managers as they perform the functions of planning, organizing, influencing,

Insights to Success

1. Develop a strong personal commitment to excellence.
2. Generate a drive and desire that will create a willingness to make personal sacrifices and do more than expected.
3. Dedicate yourself to be the "best the company has ever had" in whatever position you may be in. We move from successes.
4. Never stop studying and learning—continue to "grow."

WALTER S. BRAGER, Group Vice-President, Operations and Engineering, Oscar Mayer & Company

and controlling. Effective decision making is an important skill for managers at all levels within a firm, but it is relatively more important to upper-level managers than to lower-level supervisors. Many corporate presidents have indicated that decision making is a skill essential to successful performance. Upper management's primary responsibility is to make effective decisions, whereas lower levels of management are primarily concerned with executing or implementing decisions made by higher management. In Chapter 5 we discuss the decision-making process. Every manager, because of the fact he or she is a manager, must be a decision maker.

Conceptual Skill

conceptual skill

Conceptual skill is the ability of the manager to understand the complexities of the overall organization and how each department contributes to the accomplishment of the firm's objectives. This skill is extremely crucial to the success of top-level executives for they must be concerned with the "big picture"—assessing opportunities in the external environment and determining overall objectives, plans, and strategies. These managers must have the ability to see how each part of the organization interrelates and contributes to the primary goals of the firm. As one moves down the managerial hierarchy, conceptual skill becomes less important because other skills are more important to the success of the lower-level managers. For instance, first-level supervisors are able to refer to operating manuals to discover the capabilities of a particular piece of equipment whereas top-level managers must use their conceptual skills to determine what products will be produced with the equipment.

Professional managers recognize that they must develop and practice each of the managerial skills to be effective in accomplishing organizational and personal goals. Managers cannot concentrate their efforts on one or only a few of these skills. It is the blending of the skills in the proper proportions based on the particular level occupied by the manager that is important.

BASIC SCHOOLS OF MANAGEMENT THOUGHT

In order to improve our understanding of current management concepts, it is helpful to discuss the historical development of management thought. Most of today's management practice is based on management theory developed in this century. A look at the history of management thought is important because we must know where we have been before we can determine where we are or want to go in the future.

Classical School of Management

classical school of management

The oldest and perhaps most widely accepted school among practitioners has been called the **classical,** or traditional, **school of management.** The classical school attempted to provide a rational and scientific basis to the management of organizations. The primary contributions of the classical school of management include the following:

1. The application of the scientific method to management.
2. The classification of the basic management functions: planning, organizing, influencing, and controlling.
3. The development and application of specific principles of management.

In essence, classical management concepts have significantly improved the practice of management and have led to substantial improvements in performance within organizations.

As a result of the industrial revolution, people were brought together to work in factories. This was in marked contrast to the handicraft system where people worked separately in small shops or in their own homes. Thus, industrialization created a need for the effective management of people and other resources in the emerging organizations. In other words, there was a need for efficient planning, organizing, influencing, and controlling of work activities performed by specialized labor.

In response to changing conditions in the late nineteenth century and during the early part of the twentieth century, there was an intensified and dedicated interest in management as a process and as a science. It was apparent to many, especially Frederick Taylor, Harrington Emerson, H. L. Gantt, Frank and Lillian Gilbreth, Henri Fayol, and Chester Barnard, that management could be made more effective and efficient.

Scientific Management

scientific management

Taylor, Gantt, the Gilbreths, and Emerson were primarily interested in developing a scientific basis for the management of work. The interest and research efforts of these people gave rise to **scientific management.** Frederick

Taylor, generally recognized as the father of scientific management, was convinced that management is a process in which the scientific method should be used. The scientific method provides a logical framework for the analysis of problems. It basically consists of: defining the problem, gathering data, analyzing the data, developing alternatives, and selecting the best alternative. It was believed that following the scientific method would provide a means to determine the most efficient way to perform work. Instead of abdicating responsibility for establishing standards, for example, management would scientifically study all facets of an operation and carefully set a logical and rational standard. Instead of guessing or relying solely on trial and error, management would go through the time-consuming process of logical study and scientific research to develop answers to business problems. Taylor's philosophy can be summarized in the following four principles:

1. The development and use of the scientific method in the practice of management (finding the "one best way" to perform work).
2. Using scientific approaches to select employees who are best suited to perform a given job.
3. Providing the employee with scientific education, training, and development.
4. Encouraging friendly interaction and cooperation between management and employees but with a separation of duties between managers and workers.

Taylor stated many times that scientific management would require a revolution in thinking on the part of both the manager and the subordinate. His motives were not confined solely to advancing the interests of the manager and the enterprise. He believed sincerely that scientific management practices were for the mutual benefit of the employee and the employer through the creation of a larger productive surplus. Thus, the organization would achieve higher output, and the worker would receive a greater income.

The greater part of Taylor's work was oriented toward improving management of production operations. The classic case of the pig-iron experiment at the Bethlehem Steel Company illustrates his approach.[2] The task was simple, so much so that most managers would tend to ignore it. Laborers would pick up 92-pound pigs from a storage yard, walk up a plank onto a railroad car, and drop them at the end of the car. In a group of seventy-five laborers, the average output was about 12.5 tons per man per day. In applying the scientific method of study to this problem of getting work done through others, Taylor developed

1. An improved method of work (motion study).
2. A prescribed amount of rest on the job (fatigue study and rest periods).
3. A specific standard of output (time study).
4. Payment by the unit of output (incentive wages).

Using this approach, the average per man per day output rose from 12.5 tons to 48 tons. Under the incentive system, the daily pay rose from $1.15 to $1.85, an amount substantially higher than the going rate in the community.

Taylor's dedication to the systematic planning and study of processes pervaded his entire life. With a specially designed tennis racket, he became part of the National Doubles Tennis Championship team. When he played golf, he used uniquely designed clubs for any predictable type of lie. When he used a particular putter, his friends refused to play because of its accuracy. A famed novelist reported that Taylor died of pneumonia in a hospital with his stopwatch in his hand.

Frank and Lillian Gilbreth concentrated on motion analysis to develop *the one best way.* H. L. Gantt developed a control chart that is used to this day in production operations. Harrington Emerson developed a set of twelve principles of efficiency. Emerson's principles state that a manager should carefully define objectives, use the scientific method of analysis, develop and use standardized procedures and methods, and reward employees for good work.

General Management Theory

Henri Fayol and C. I. Barnard, in contrast to Taylor, Emerson, Gantt, and the Gilbreths, attempted to develop a broader theory concerned with general management. Fayol's thesis was that the fundamental functions of any manager consist of planning, organizing, commanding, coordinating, and controlling. He attempted to evolve empirically a number of general principles that, if followed, would improve the practice of general management.

Chester Barnard's ideas, expressed in his classic book, *The Functions of the Executive,* have significantly influenced the development of the theory and practice of management.[3] Barnard, a practicing manager, was president of New Jersey Bell Telephone. Although he made numerous contributions to the development of management thought, his concept that the most important function of a manager is to provide the basis for cooperative effort, directed toward goals of the organization, was highly significant. Barnard believed that the degree of cooperation depends upon effective communications and a balance between rewards an employee receives and contributions made by employees.

Behavioral School of Management

In the 1920s and 1930s, some observers of business management became concerned with what they felt was a shortsightedness and incompleteness in the scientific management approach. In particular, Elton Mayo and F. J. Roethlisberger began to point out that the approaches advanced by scientific management were not necessarily the most efficient, nor did they always work as intended. The human factors of business organizations had been largely ignored. The field of human relations emerged from the work of Elton *behavioral school of management*

Mayo who has become recognized as the father of the human relations movement, and, thus, the **behavioral school of management** was developed.

Human Relations Movement

The project that had the most to do with the beginning of the concern for human relations in business was the Hawthorne experiments conducted in the Western Electric Company between 1927 and 1932. In these experiments, researchers attempted to prove the validity of generally accepted principles of management. Several experiments to determine the relationship between working conditions and productivity were conducted by varying working conditions within the plant.

In one experiment, the researchers established *test groups* where changes in lighting, frequency of rest periods, and working hours occurred, and *control groups* where no changes were made. When rest periods and other improvements in working conditions were introduced to the test group, productivity increased as expected. However, the researchers were surprised when output continued to increase when the various improvements in working conditions that had been introduced, such as rest periods, were removed. As a result of these changes, the scientists expected a decrease in productivity. Contrary to these expectations, production still continued to improve in most instances. Obviously, everything had not been controlled in the experiment; the human mind was still free and uncontrolled.

The results of these experiments prompted Mayo and his fellow researchers to conclude that when employees are given special attention by management, output is likely to increase regardless of the actual changes in the working conditions. This has become known as the *Hawthorne Effect.* To gain a more in-depth understanding, Mayo and Roethlisberger followed up the experiments at the Hawthorne plant with an intensive interviewing program and an investigation of informal cliques, groupings, and relationships initiated by the members of the organization. The basic conclusion from the intensive interviewing program was that the needs of the individual and the role of the informal group have a significant impact on the performance of the work group.

Some have conceived of a total overlapping of interests between the organization and its members and contend that the objectives of both classical and behavioral approaches are identical. Much behavioral research does support the thesis that reasonable satisfaction of the needs and desires of those people who work within and contribute to the enterprise will lead to greater output. A management approach that ignores or deemphasizes the human element will often result in only partly accomplished objectives, reduced creativity, and general dissatisfaction.

Modern Behavioral Management Science

Since the early experiments of Mayo and Roethlisberger at the Hawthorne plant, there has been an increased interest in and application of behavioral

behavioral management science

science in management. The human relations approach has evolved into **behavioral management science.** In recent years, considerable research has been conducted for the purpose of developing techniques to utilize people more effectively in organizations. The contributions—theories and research applications—of such well-known behavioral scientists as Abraham Maslow, Douglas McGregor, Chris Argyris, Frederick Herzberg, and Rensis Likert have provided considerable insight into approaches for increased managerial effectiveness.

While we discuss in considerable detail the specific contributions of each of the above behavioral scientists in Chapters 10 and 11 on Motivation and Leadership, a brief mention of the basic concepts of behavioral management science will be made here.

Behavioral scientists have, in general, criticized classical management and organization theory as not being responsive enough to the needs of the employees. In essence, the behaviorists' specific criticisms include the following:

- Jobs have been overly specialized.
- People are underutilized.
- Management has exercised too much control and has prevented employees from making decisions of which they are capable.
- Organizations and management have shown too little concern about a person's needs for recognition and self-fulfillment.

Behavioral scientists argue that the design of work has not changed enough to keep pace with changes in the needs of today's employees and the working environment they confront. In today's complex, affluent, and rapidly changing society, employees cannot be treated as *interchangeable parts* within the organization. Today's worker has a higher level of education and tends to possess higher expectations for improvements in the working environment along with a desire for more diverse and challenging work. This has placed increased pressure on management to be responsive to these changes and to provide an environment designed to meet these needs.

Additional Schools of Management Thought

While our previous discussion has focused on the classical and behavioral schools of management, it should not be concluded that these two basic schools represent the only possible approaches or theories of management. Harold Koontz, in attempting to clarify what he has described as a "management theory jungle," identified eleven schools or approaches to the study of management.[4] Each of the schools in Koontz's classification is identified and briefly described in Table 1-1.

TABLE 1-1. *Koontz's Classification of the Theories of Management*

Empirical or Case Approach
In this school, management is studied through case examples of the successes and failures of practicing managers. This approach can assist managers in developing basic generalizations to support theories or principles of management. However, this method of learning about management may create illusions for current managers because the future is quite likely to be considerably different from the past. An analysis of past experiences of managers may not prove to be very helpful in solving current managerial problems.

Interpersonal Behavior Approach
According to this school of thought, management is concerned with accomplishing results through others. Therefore, the study of management should concentrate on interpersonal behavior and the study of psychology. This school focuses on the study of motivation and leadership. While the study of human behavior in organizations is important, a manager's knowledge of management is incomplete if that's all a person understands.

Group Behavior Approach
By applying research findings of sociology, anthropology, and social psychology, this approach explains management in terms of group behavior. According to this view, effective management requires a thorough understanding of behavioral patterns of group members within the organization. However, rigid adherence to this approach may cause managers to place more emphasis on organization behavior and not on other equally fundamental concepts of management.

Cooperative Social Systems Approach
An outgrowth of the interpersonal and group behavior approaches, the cooperative social systems school of management has often been referred to as the "organization theory" approach. While all managers perform in a cooperative social system, this approach does not explain complexities of modern management. Social systems is a broader concept than management, and it overlooks a number of principles, techniques, and factors that are important to effective management.

Sociotechnical Systems Approach
The sociotechnical systems approach is based on the work at the Tavistock Institute in England. It was discovered that the technical system—the machines and methods used—has a strong influence on the social system within the working environment. Personal attitudes of group members were strongly influenced by the technical system of the work place. A major task of management is to make sure that the social and technical systems are harmonious. While closely related to industrial engineering, the approach has made a significant contribution to the practice of management. It does not, however, provide an overall theory of management.

Decision Theory Approach
The major responsibility of managers is to make decisions, according to the decision theory approach to management. While many who study and/or practice management agree that decision making is an essential skill, the approach overlooks other skills and requirements of management. In some cases, the actual making of the decision may be relatively straightforward.

Systems Approach
The systems approach to management concentrates on the effective and efficient use of resources in order to produce desirable products and/or services. The systems approach requires that the physical, human, and capital resources be interrelated and coordinated within the external and internal environment of an organization.

Mathematical or Management Science Approach
This school or approach to management uses mathematical models, concepts, and symbols in solving managerial problems, particularly those requiring decisions. Ad-

TABLE 1-1 (*continued*)

vocates of the school argue that management can be made more scientific through the use of mathematical and simulation models. Many advocates argue that the mathematical or management science approach offers a complete school of management. Other theorists and practitioners believe that mathematical models are tools of analysis, not a separate school of thought.

Contingency or Situational Management

Contingency or situational management refers to managers' abilities to adapt to meet particular circumstances and restraints a firm may encounter. In other words, managerial action depends upon circumstances within the situation. That is, "no one best approach" will work in all situations. Applying a situational approach requires that managers diagnose a given situation and adapt to meet the conditions present. The difficulty with this approach is that few management writers have prescribed precisely what a manager should do in a given situation.

Managerial Roles Approach

Henry Mintzberg observed and studied what managers actually do in managing and identified the primary roles of managers.[a] He concluded that executives do not always perform the traditional managerial functions of planning, organizing, directing, controlling, but instead perform a variety of other activities. According to Mintzberg, managers have three dominant roles: interpersonal, informational, and decision making. In the interpersonal role, a manager acts as a figurehead, leader, and liaison person. In the informational role, a manager serves as a monitor, disseminator, and spokesperson. In the decision-making role, a manager acts as entrepreneur, disturbance handler, resource allocator, and negotiator. A difficulty that arises is that roles Mintzberg identifies inadequately describe managerial activities and functions. Such important roles as those of goal setting, strategy identification and implementation, developing the organization, and selecting and developing managers are not included.

Operational Approach

According to Koontz, these theories are certainly applicable to the study of management, but our interest in them must not necessarily be limited to managerial aspects and applications. The operational approach to management indicates that the foundations for management science and theory are drawn from a number of other schools and approaches. The operational approach recognizes that there are significant concepts, principles, theories, and techniques that comprise the effective practice of management. This approach draws on pertinent knowledge from other fields of study including political science, sociology, social psychology, psychology, mathematics, economics, decision theory, general systems theory, and industrial engineering. We believe that the operational approach provides a logical framework for the study of management theory and practice.

Source: Harold Koontz, "The Management Theory Jungle Revisited," *Academy of Management Review* 5, no. 2 (April 1980). Reprinted with permission of the author and *Academy of Management Review.*

[a] Henry Mintzberg, "The Manager's Job: Folklore and Fact," *Harvard Business Review* 53, no. 4 (1975): 49–61.

WHY STUDY THIS MANAGEMENT TEXT?

Effective management is essential to the success of every organization. Management influences the lives of all of us as members of an organized society. For individuals, knowledge of management is valuable as evidenced by the fact that organizations actively recruit students who have a concentration in management. It is vital for each of us to gain a better understanding of and appreciation for management if we are to function more effectively in an organization.

In this text, our study of management will provide you with the following:

- A greater knowledge of and insight into the responsibilities of managing people and other resources.
- A better understanding of the problems of operating a business organization.
- An opportunity to learn the skills essential to effective managerial decision making.
- An understanding of basic principles of management.
- Increased knowledge about production and operations management techniques.
- The ability to identify and cope with internal and external forces in the environment that affect performance.
- The skills and attitudes to continue your professional development.

In order to accomplish these objectives, this book is organized into seven sections, as illustrated in Figure 1-4. Our intent is to present fundamental management concepts and practices in a readable and interesting format. Throughout this book, we attempt to explain and provide examples of basic concepts and practices of management that have a high degree of universality among different types of enterprises, including business firms, public sector firms such as government agencies, and not-for-profit organizations such as hospitals, schools and universities.

Summary

We live in a society dominated by large organizations in which people must work together effectively to accomplish goals. The degree of success of all organizations—business and nonbusiness—is determined to a great extent by the quality and overall effectiveness of management. But what is management? Who is a manager? What do managers do? What skills are needed for good management? In answering these questions, it is important to realize that there is no *one* best approach to management that is effective in every situation.

Management is the process of planning, organizing, influencing, and controlling to accomplish organizational goals through the coordinated use of human and material resources. A manager is anyone, regardless of level within a firm, who direct the efforts of other people in accomplishing goals. A manager is the catalyst who makes things happen by *planning* what is to be achieved, *organizing* personnel and other resources to achieve the plan, *influencing* or *directing* people, and comparing results achieved to the

Part I	**INTRODUCTION**
Chapter 1	Management
Chapter 2	The Manager's Environment
Part II	**PLANNING AND DECISION MAKING**
Chapter 3	Objectives and Plans
Chapter 4	Management by Objectives: An Approach to Planning
Chapter 5	Managerial Decision Making
Part III	**ORGANIZING**
Chapter 6	The Organizing Process
Chapter 7	Authority, Responsibility, and Organization Structure
Chapter 8	The Informal Organization
Chapter 9	Staffing the Organization
Part IV	**INFLUENCING**
Chapter 10	Motivation
Chapter 11	Leadership
Chapter 12	Communication
Chapter 13	Organization Climate, Change, and Development
Part V	**CONTROLLING**
Chapter 14	Management and Control
Part VI	**PRODUCTION AND OPERATIONS MANAGEMENT**
Chapter 15	Traditional Production Management and Planning Techniques
Chapter 16	Simulation, Waiting Line, and Control Techniques
Part VII	**SITUATIONAL APPLICATIONS**
Chapter 17	Social Responsibility and Business Ethics
Chapter 18	Managing Small Businesses
Chapter 19	Managing the Multinational Enterprise

FIGURE 1-4
Organization of the book

planned performance. In order to be effective, managers need to possess and develop several essential skills, including the following: technical, communication, human, analytical, decision making, and conceptual. These skills must be mixed in the proper proportion based on the particular level occupied by the manager.

While we can agree that every organization requires good management, there is considerable disagreement as to the most effective way to manage. Historically, two basic but different schools or approaches to management have developed. The classical school, including the work of Frederick Taylor, Henri Fayol, C. I. Barnard, and others, attempted to provide a rational and scientific basis to management. Major contributions of scientific management include the application of scientific method to management and the classification of the basic management functions.

The behavioral school of management is concerned with the human element in the organization. The early "human relations" era, which resulted primarily from the Hawthorne experiments in the late 1920s and early 1930s, evolved into behavioral management science. Behavioral scientists have criticized classical management theory as not being responsive to the needs of its employees, that jobs are overly specialized, that people are underutilized and overmanaged, and that management has shown too little concern about a person's need for recognition and self-fulfillment. In today's world, management has little choice but to be more responsive to the needs of employees if improved performance is to be achieved. Harold Koontz identified eleven schools or approaches to the study of management. One of the eleven—the operational approach—indicates that the foundations of management science and theory are drawn from a number of schools and approaches.

Review Questions

1. Define management. Who is a manager and what does a manager do?
2. List some factors that may account for the success and effectiveness of a manager.
3. Why is the study of management important?
4. List and briefly describe six skills important to managerial effectiveness. How are these skills related to managers operating at different levels in the organization?
5. What is the classical school of management? Identify the basic contributions of this school of management.
6. Frederick Taylor is known as the father of scientific management. Why? What is scientific management and Taylor's philosophy?
7. Identify briefly the major contributions of the following:
   a. Henri Fayol
   b. C. I. Barnard
   c. H. L. Gantt
   d. Harrington Emerson
8. Discuss the behavioral school of management. How and why did the movement originate?
9. What specific criticisms did behavioral scientists have of traditional or classical organizations?
10. Harold Koontz coined the phrase "management theory jungle" as he described the various approaches to the study of management. What do you believe he meant and what were the various schools of management he identified?

Exercises

1. Interview three managers from different types of organizations (for example, talk to managers in a bank, retail store, manufacturer, or college/university).

Have a list of prepared questions including, but not limited to, the following:

a. How did you become a manager?

b. What does your job as a manager entail? Describe your major functions.

c. Why are you a manager?

d. What skills are necessary for success as a manager?

e. What advice would you give a person interested in a career in management?

f. Is management a profession?

g. Can one learn to be a better manager? If so, how?

2. Review the employment classified ads in *The Wall Street Journal* and a Sunday edition of a large city newspaper. Make a list of the types of managerial jobs, the companies offering employment, and the qualifications needed to obtain the positions. What is your basic conclusion after this review in terms of the availability of managerial positions and the necessary qualifications for obtaining a position?

Case Study

Promotion of an Engineer to a Manager

Jack Freemont had recently received a promotion to the position of manager of engineering within the California Manufacturing Company, a medium-sized firm producing numerous household products. Jack had an electrical engineering degree and had been with the company for nine years since graduating from the University of California, Berkeley.

Jack's record as a design engineer was excellent. He had developed three new products that had been marketed around the world and was widely respected for his many innovative contributions to a department recognized for its reputation as the industry leader in new product research and development. Not only was Jack an effective engineer, he also was popular with almost everyone in the company. Throughout his nine years with California Manufacturing, Jack had kept up-to-date in his field by reading engineering journals and by attending continuing education workshops. Because of his technical/engineering experience with the company and his ability to get along with people, top management felt very confident in promoting Jack to the position of manager of engineering.

Jack's early experience in supervising the eighteen engineers in the department proved to be a real challenge. He experienced considerable difficulties with being a manager as compared to an engineer. He continued to be very involved with research and product design and worked very long hours (sometimes up to twelve hours a day) in order to "keep up" his design engineering. As a result of this situation, Jack did not provide the overall direction and coordination of the department that top management believed was necessary in order to achieve maximum effectiveness.

Jack also began to feel pressure from some of the engineers who believed he was overly involved in performing "routine engineering" and not "managing" the department.

Since Jack wanted to improve as a manager, he decided to discuss the problems with his boss.

QUESTIONS

1. What is the basic problem confronting Jack Freemont as a manager? What is the cause(s)?
2. How does being a manger differ from being an engineer? Be specific.
3. Did top management make a mistake in promoting Jack to the position of engineering manager?
4. What skills are important for Jack as the manager? Why?
5. Does being a good engineer guarantee success as a manager? Why or why not?

Case Study

The New President

The day has finally come; Garrick Phillips is to assume the position of president of Metro Manufacturing. Metro is a widely respected producer of high-quality control mechanisms. When the previous president retired, Garrick was identified as the likely choice for assuming the post. He was respected for his competence in the field and for his ability to work with employees at all levels of operations. Garrick arrived at work early this morning, not so much to work but to think. As he sits behind his new executive desk, drinking a cup of coffee, his thoughts go back to his early days with Metro.

Twenty years ago Garrick was just a young man right out of college with no business experience and a degree in industrial management. He was hired as an assistant foreman and was placed immediately on the production line. "Oh, those were the days," he thought. "Seems like there was a problem that required solving every minute. Thank goodness for the standard operating procedures manuals (SOPs) and for a foreman who was patient enough to answer my questions. Didn't have to make too many critical decisions then but I sure was putting out a lot of daily fires."

As the nostalgia influence continues, Garrick thinks back to the time when he was taken off the production line and promoted into middle management. "Things sure did change then," he thought. As production manager, he had to think further into the future. As a foreman, Garrick was primarily concerned with meeting daily production requirements. Now he had to plan weeks and even months in advance. The human and communication problems remained although it seems like the reports he had to write were longer. But, as he remembers, the major changes occurred because he had to do more creative thinking. Laughing to himself he thought about the time he went to the files to pull out an SOP for an unusual problem he had confronted and there was none. He was frustrated because he had to handle the problem with little assistance. But as his analytical, decision-making, and conceptual ability increased, he found himself using his technical skills less and less.

Another cup of coffee provided the stimulus to think about the special promotion he made to vice-president of planning five years ago. It was a major hurdle in his life because he had been in heavy competition with five well-qualified managers. He had heard through the grapevine that he had received the position because he was able to think for himself. But even his past training did not fully prepare Garrick for the demands of the job; he had to learn much of it on his own. Rather than think months into the future, he now was required to envision years. Grinning, he remembered that at first he did not realize that there were so many people outside of production whom he had to coordinate activities with. Marketing and finance had to be tied together with production. His conceptual and decision-making skills continued to increase. A long time ago, the benefits of the "good old" SOPs lost their value.

But now, as Garrick looks at his desk plate which says "President," new thoughts run through his mind. A whole new world opens to him now. He wonders what new requirements will be placed on him. A twinge of fear moves through his body as the thoughts of the new job take hold. What skills will he now need to be successful?

QUESTIONS

1. As the president of Metro Manufacturing, what specific skills will Garrick need to be effective? Reference to Figure 1-3 will provide insight into this question.
2. How do the demands of different levels of responsibility change as a manager progresses up the hierarchy of an organization?
3. What general recommendations would you offer for Garrick Phillips?

APPENDIX

Careers in Management

People need to know much more than that they desire a career in management. The number and types of managerial positions are many. If people are to be happy in a chosen career, the best position that meets their specific needs must be obtained. This is precisely what this appendix is about—finding the right job that will lead to a career in management.

In order to do this a person should progress through a series of important steps. This appendix begins by showing how to gain valuable insight into what a person desires from a career. It is followed by a discussion of how to identify career objectives. Next, the types of careers available in management are presented, after which the actual sequence for searching for the right job is discussed. Finally, we present some job realisms. The overall purpose of this appendix is to identify what entry-level management positions are available and how a person can obtain the best match with the firm.

GAINING INSIGHT INTO YOURSELF

Successful managers come from a wide variety of experiences. Some know immediately that they want to be managers. Others believe that they want to be in management and learn later on that management is not their "cup of tea." There are individuals who may be extremely successful as a manager in one situation and a dismal failure in another environment.

The number of students who graduate from college without a clear understanding of their career goals is astounding. It is difficult to achieve a goal if you do not know what you want to accomplish. Statements such as "I want to be a manager," or "I want to be in a job where I can work with people," are not sufficient. You must be willing to go into much greater depth to gain a realistic appreciation of what you desire to accomplish in a career.

People must develop a realistic understanding of themselves. Once this has been accomplished, it is likely that individuals will be in a much better position to identify what they desire as a career. The following discussion is directed primarily toward college students who have little or no business experience and are unsure of their career goals. You need to gain critical insight into who you are and what you desire out of life.

Just as no two personalities are exactly alike, each of us has different strengths and weaknesses. People who are serious about an attempt to gain better insight into their career objectives will need to know their strengths or weaknesses. It is through the recognition of your strengths that you are encouraged toward a particular career. A knowledge of weaknesses shows a person what cannot be accomplished unless the deficiencies are removed.

Talk to Professionals

People who have gained success in their jobs are a valuable resource from which to uncover career information. It is likely that you, your parents, or close friends know individuals who would be willing to share career information with you. Most likely these people would be willing to talk to you about the demands of a particular job. However, prior to setting up an interview with such a person, it would be wise to identify some questions you would like answered. To get your mind working, some potential questions are provided below:

1. What type of entry-level position would be available to a person with my education and experience?
2. If I didn't start off in a managerial position, typically how long would it take to progress to a first-level managerial position?
3. What type of training does your firm regularly provide management personnel?
4. What is the typical salary range for a person like myself starting with your firm?
5. What would be the typical duties a new employee would be expected to perform?
6. How supportive is your firm when an employee makes a mistake?
7. Whom should I contact if I am interested in a position similar to yours?
8. What's your firm's policy regarding promotion from within?
9. What type of preparation or qualifications does a person need for a career with your firm?

The list could go on and on. The point to be stressed is that you should ask the professionals questions that concern you the most. The benefits are numerous. You are now in a position to discover if a particular job might be interesting. The professional is not under the pressure of conducting an interview and will answer questions candidly. Also, if this type of job proves interesting, you have gained valuable information that can be used in future job interviews. Confidence is built up because you can now talk intelligently about the position you are applying for. You are also able to learn the typical salary range for a specific position. This information is important because a recent college graduate can be realistic about salary expectations by not asking for too much or too little.

A final point to remember with regard to speaking with professionals is that they have progressed through the ranks and are proud of their accomplishments. It is surprising how easy it is to obtain an appointment with a person you do not know. The conversation might progress in the following manner:

Bobby Hughes: "Mr. Shudlesworth, I'm Bobby Hughes and I'm currently attending school at the university, majoring in industrial management. I have one more year to go before graduation and I have some unanswered questions that only a professional who is active in the field can answer. I recognize that your time is valuable, but I sure would appreciate your advice and counsel."

Once an affirmative reply is obtained you continue:

Bobby Hughes: "Could we possibly set up a brief appointment to discuss some questions?"

You are now off and running. This approach is used by some professional search firms in the placement of personnel. Since you are not applying for a job, the tension that may be built up in a normal job interview is reduced, and the opportunity is available to develop rapport with Mr. Shudlesworth. Once your questions have been answered, a final one such as the following may be appropriate.

Bobby Hughes: "Mr. Shudlesworth, do you know of a company that might have a need for my particular skills?"

If the discussion has progressed satisfactorily, Mr. Shudlesworth might say,

Mr. Shudlesworth: "Why don't you come back and see me when you graduate. One of my employees is retiring next year."

He could also say,

"Yes, I have several friends whom you might want to speak with."

At the very least you have gained insight into the requirements that are needed to be employed in the firm for which Mr. Shudlesworth works. There is also a potential to develop excellent contacts prior to graduation.

The University Testing Center

A resource that often goes unused by most college students is the university testing center. You might say, "Why should I use the testing service? There is nothing wrong with me?" Perhaps this myth has been built up because it has been assumed that only people who are really "messed up" should use the university testing service. Nothing could be further from the truth. The unique feature of the testing center is that you can discover many things about yourself prior to going for an interview. You can be absolutely honest because only you and your counselor will see the results. Since many companies give similar tests to their job applicants, it is likely individuals will discover that they feel much more relaxed when these tests are administered. If you wait until after graduation to utilize a similar service, it may be quite expensive. Fees up to over $5,000 are sometimes charged for these services.

The purpose of using the testing services is to gain an insight into yourself that may prove beneficial when seeking a job. Some of the topics you may desire to explore in greater detail relate to interests, aptitude, personality, and intelligence. Each will be briefly discussed from the standpoint of how the tests can be beneficial in selecting the best job.

Interest Tests

One would be surprised at the number of college students who do not know what they want to do once they graduate. One of the authors of this book in fact changed majors five times! In the "old days," he did not have the opportunity to use a modern university testing service. *Interest tests* are designed to help a person identify career fields. If the test interpretation supports the person's belief in what is desired in a career, there is a good chance that the situation has been properly assessed. A person is reinforced in the belief that the proper decision has been made. On the other hand, the individual may discover that there are other areas that were not initially recognized. Knowledge of these additional interests can provide a person with the stimulus to evaluate other alternatives.

Aptitude Tests

At times our abilities and our interests do not match up. A person may have an interest in being a brain surgeon but not the aptitude for the career. *Aptitude tests* assist individuals in determining if they have the natural inclination or talent needed for a particular job. These tests are valuable in determining a person's probability for success in a selected job.

Personality Tests

There are jobs for which certain personalities have proven to be more useful. *Personality tests* assist a person in determining if he or she possesses the proper personality for a particular job. Although it is difficult to generalize about which qualities may be beneficial on a particular job, a person should benefit from the interpretation of the test results. Corporations, like individuals, have distinctive personalities. People tend to be attracted to organizations that provide the means for meeting their goals and aspirations. A person may be quite successful in one firm and a failure in another merely because of personality differences.

Intelligence Tests

If a career field requires a certain level of intelligence, it is best to find out if you meet the minimum levels before pursuing this career. Through hard work a person may meet the entry requirements, but what will the results be in the long run? Instead, a more realistic job, with just as much challenge, may need to be considered. We cannot all be Albert Einsteins! *Intelligence tests* assist in this endeavor.

The testing service should not be expected to provide all the answers. Test results should be viewed only as indicators and should never be thought of as providing the final decision concerning the entry into a profession. However, if the results of the tests suggest an alternate career path would be warranted, it may be beneficial to reevaluate personal goals. A conference with a respected instructor may provide some assistance. You will do well to remember that we are often *pushed* into careers not of our choosing because of well-intending, but perhaps misinformed, friends.

CAREER OBJECTIVES

Once you have a thorough understanding of yourself, you are in a much better position to develop realistic career objectives. It is at this juncture that a person either enhances or diminishes his or her chances to obtain a position that will lead to a career of his or her choice. Take for instance these two career objectives, which were found on resumés of recent college graduates.

I. *Career Objective:* To obtain a position where I can work with people, perhaps in management.

II. *Career Objective:* To obtain an entry-level position in personnel management that provides the opportunities for ultimately progressing into a middle-management position.

The personnel director who showed these career objectives to one of the authors was amazed at how many college seniors are not capable of identifying what they desire in their first job. Two general guidelines are provided:

1. Be as specific as possible in identifying the type of job you would like. This point becomes quite obvious when comparing Career Objective I to Career Objective II. The company needs to know the type of job you are interested in if they are to be capable of evaluating your credentials. The personnel director is also in a position to see whether a person has given serious consideration to the type of job he or she would prefer.
2. In the objective statement provide an indication of your goals during the next five years. Most personnel directors recognize that a person does not want to stay forever in an entry-level position. But, they also want to know if prospective employees are realistic in their expectations.

Once you have clearly thought out your career objectives, you are, for the first time, in a position to evaluate the firms that have the potential for satisfying these goals. It is not a task that is accomplished overnight. Often this is the most agonizing part of the job search, but it is likely one of the most important.

ENTRY-LEVEL POSITIONS IN MANAGEMENT

Now that you have decided that you ultimately want to be a manager, the decision must be made as to what avenues are available to accomplish this goal. But now a problem arises. What types of managerial positions are available? Few first-level managerial positions are available for recent college graduates with minimal work experience. The discussion of possible entry-level positions in management will begin by gaining an appreciation of the risk factor as it applies to determining whether a person has an opportunity to secure a particular job. Next, four of the many possible avenues for obtaining entry-level management positions will be discussed. As each type of entry-level position is presented, you should consider the significance of the risk factor.

The Risk Factor

A major factor in determining the type of managerial positions that may be available to recent college graduates relates heavily to the risk factor that a company places on a particular position. *Risk* will be defined as the probability of a particular decision(s) having an adverse effect on the company. A low-risk managerial job is one in which if a mistake is made, there is a minimal potential loss for the firm. On the other hand, a high-risk managerial job is one in which a mistake by the manager may have a major impact on the organization. The types of managerial positions that are available may be viewed as a continuum that goes from low risk to high risk.

Typically, the lower the risk, the greater the opportunities available for a recent graduate with minimal work experience. A person who desires to

geology department and moved to other locations in the firm for training. He worked for several months in the human resources department, supervising a task force of three people in developing a management by objectives program. Jerry was then moved to the organization and systems development department where he again directed a task force in reorganizing a geology department. Finally, after approximately eighteen months, Jerry was transferred back into geology as a manager. Sunmark views the additional corporate exposure as vital in the career progression of a manager.

From Sales to Management

An avenue that is being used increasingly by college graduates is to progress to a management position through an entry-level sales job. A person who is in sales is in a position to learn the operations of the entire company. Thus, many college graduates have found that the quickest path to a managerial position is through sales. It is likely this situation has occurred because approximately 50 percent of all entry-level positions open to college graduates are in sales.

Some firms make it mandatory to progress through sales before any of their employees can enter management. For instance, one large insurance company has initiated a program to attract bright college graduates into their management ranks. In this program a new employee spends three months at the home office working in various departments and another three months observing in the field. He or she is then required to produce as a salesperson for one year. At this point he or she has the option of going into management or remaining in sales.

The point that should be clearly understood is that a sales position can lead to managerial positions other than in sales management. Many people have been able to go from sales to other departments, such as production. Because salespeople have been dealing with the customer who purchases the product, it is reasoned that they provide valuable input if placed in the production area of the business.

THE SEARCH FOR THE RIGHT INDUSTRY

Many college graduates begin their search for a career by first evaluating the type of job(s) available within particular firm(s). The authors believe that this is not the most advisable starting point. This became clear to one of the authors when he was a college senior interviewing a number of companies through the university placement center. After several interviews, it became somewhat obvious that companies in certain industries had considerably more potential for growth than did firms in other industries. It then began to be evident that a good starting point after a person has identified his or her career and personal goals is to identify the growth industries. Industries that are projected to grow rapidly in the future would be the target for further analysis to identify several of the *best* companies operating within the industry.

Examples of *fast*-growth industries might include: computer products, health-care products and services, electronics, energy-related, banking and financial services, various leisure-time industries, and various types of service industries. Slow-growth industries might include education, transportation (particularly railroads), and steel.

Thus, an individual should follow this recommended procedure:

1. Identify growth industries.
2. Pinpoint or select for further study and analysis the industries that would seem to fit your goals, needs or interests.
3. Determine the three or four "leading" firms in the industry—these firms may not be the largest—but they may be growing or predicted to grow at a rapid rate over the next several years.
4. Seek interviews with the companies you select from your analysis as described above. The procedure to be followed will be discussed in the following section, "The Search for the Right Company."
5. Finally, be concerned about the specific entry-level position, fully recognizing that if you perform well, you won't be in this position long—probably not more than one or two years.

Naturally, there are excellent opportunities available in some industries that are identified as slow growth. This discussion should not be taken to mean that a person should not apply to firms in the slow-growth industries. The authors merely suggest that considerable thought should be given to the selection of which industry should be pursued.

THE SEARCH FOR THE RIGHT COMPANY

You have now accomplished a thorough self-assessment, developed an appreciation of your career goals, determined companies in growth industries, and obtained an overview of the types of jobs that are available to begin a career in management. But a person cannot start his or her career until a job offer is obtained (a truism if there has ever been one). Thus, this section will concentrate on the remaining sequence of events that should be accomplished in order to obtain the management position of your choice. The importance of preparing a resume will first be presented. This will be followed by the steps necessary to match yourself with the right company.

The Resume

In many instances the first contact that a prospective employee has with the person in charge of hiring is through a resume. As such, the resume becomes an extension of an individual's personality. The resume *sells* in a person's absence. It should be designed to present an individual in the best possible perspective.

The importance of proper attention to resume preparation was vividly illustrated to one of the authors immediately after receiving his doctoral degree. He had been divorced for seven years and thought nothing of placing *divorced* in the marital status category. However, he discovered that many colleges and universities still remain quite conservative, and the placing of *divorced* in a conspicuous place often meant that the resume was not read. In addition, the author had received three degrees from one university (not extremely acceptable to many employers) and this item was placed directly following career objectives. The author had ten years of business experience with major corporations and had published numerous articles, but this fact would not be known unless the entire resume was read.

It did not take long to realize that a problem existed. The fact that the telephone did not ring and numerous letters of rejection were received contributed to this realization. This prompted a few modifications to be made, which presented the qualifications of the author in a different perspective. The ten years of business and consulting experience were highlighted immediately following career objectives. Biographical data were moved to the back of the resume and *divorced* was changed to *Dependents: one, Alyson Lynn.* The author was amazed at the change in responses. Invitations to visit campuses were received immediately, and the author was able to obtain a position of his choice.

The above illustration provides an excellent example of the importance of a clearly thought out resume. The same intensive evaluation must be made by college seniors preparing themselves to enter the job market. It must be remembered that the resume must be developed to present *you* in the best possible image. Any deficiencies can be explained during the interview, but it is difficult to accomplish this task if the opportunity to participate in the interview is not available.

Through experience and through contacts with numerous personnel directors, some guidelines have been developed that may prove to be beneficial in the preparation of a resume. They are:

1. Present your most significant accomplishments and attributes. If it is the truth, it is not bragging.
2. The order of the presentation of items on a resume is dictated by your strengths. If you have high grades, stress your grades; if you have a significant amount of work experience, it is possible that this item should receive top priority.
3. Companies are beginning to place additional emphasis upon activities outside the classroom such as membership and offices held in social and business organizations. If you have been particularly active in various campus organizations, it would be wise to highlight these endeavors.
4. The amount of college expenses that you personally paid is also receiving additional attention. A statement such as "Paid 50 percent of college expenses" is often quite helpful.

5. If you are willing to be mobile, this should be stressed. For a company that is located in cities throughout the United States a statement of geographical preference of "None" would likely receive higher attention than one that said "Butte, Montana." Naturally, if geographical preference is truly a restriction, it should be stated as such.
6. A person who has had work experience while in college should stress this fact. A firm recognizes that individuals who are working to finance their way through college will not likely have fancy titles. They are interested in determining how you performed while employed. It is highly satisfying for a recruiter to call one of your past employers and receive statements such as "He is a hard worker" or "She did not constantly watch the clock."
7. A person who has work experience should describe the functions that were performed while working. Merely listing the position titles does not give the recruiter significant insight into what type of work was actually performed. Action phrases such as "was responsible for," "coordinated the activities of," and "in charge of" are much more descriptive.
8. If references are to be placed on a resume, permission should be requested even though the reference is a good friend. A reference can assist you by tailoring his or her comments to meet the requirements of the job that you are seeking.

Matching Yourself with the Right Company

The next step in searching for the right company is to identify the firms that can afford a person the greatest opportunity to achieve career objectives. However, remember what the old philosopher said: "You can never turn down a job until an offer has been made." Identification of these firms is a task that often proves quite difficult for students seeking their first job. But it is one that must be done. Here you will be attempting to identify firms that might meet your specific needs.

There are numerous sources from which to obtain the names of the firms that will match your specific needs. A great deal of information can be found in *trade journals* that apply to the particular firm in which you are interested. Also, a large amount of useful data may be found in *Standard and Poors, Fortune, Forbes,* and *The Wall Street Journal.* A person should select only the firms that have the potential for fulfilling specific needs. For instance, if an individual's goal is to be employed by a medium-sized firm headquartered in the Southwest, he would likely not place Coca-Cola on the list (headquartered in Atlanta). Dr Pepper (headquartered in Texas and much smaller) might meet the requirements. The authors have found it beneficial to select a maximum of twenty-five companies representing several industries from which to continue the job search.

Once a list of prospective companies has been developed, a person is still not in a position to send out a resume. A certain amount of research remains. Data concerning each company should be obtained so as to send a personal cover letter to each firm. This also includes obtaining the name of a person to be addressed. In the cover letter the reason for wanting a job with this company should be stated. Remember that the *only* reason a firm will consider a person for employment is that they expect the services rendered will make money for the company.

The job search does not stop here. The waiting process begins. This also is quite difficult. But because a person has done his or her homework, it will now be assumed that an invitation has been received to visit a company. Before leaving on a trip, additional research, or at least a review of your previous research, may be necessary. Much more information than last year's sales is necessary. In addition, it may be wise to develop a list of questions that you as a prospective employee would like to know about the company. The interview is a two-way street; the interviewee is attempting to determine if this particular company is a good place to work, and the firm is evaluating the individual for potential to fit into the organization.

If the interview goes well and you believe that the company has the potential to satisfy your career objectives, it is customary to write a letter expressing your sincere interest. In this letter you should also tell them precisely why you feel qualified to take a position with their company. A comment such as, "The work that a quality control inspector with your firm performs appears extremely interesting and challenging. I am confident that I possess the type of personality to be capable of working with the people on the line, my supervisor, and top management." On the other hand, if you discover after your visit that the position is not what you expected, a courteous letter should be written thanking them for their interest, but telling the company representative that you do not believe a proper match exists.

A technique that has been quite successful in further enhancing the chances of obtaining the desired position is the follow-up phone call. Approximately one day after the follow-up letter has been received by the company, a phone call should be placed to the person who interviewed you. During this call, you should ask intelligent, searching questions as well as again express interest in the firm. Once the call has been completed, you have had the opportunity to visit with the company representatives four times: by resume, in person, by letter, and by phone.

Once an offer has been tendered, the decision must be made as to whether it should be accepted or rejected. This usually poses no problem unless several offers are received. Hopefully, since your homework has been done, this will be the case. In making a decision as to which job to take, a major point should be remembered. The job with the greatest long-run potential should be selected. Try to pick a company you can be comfortable with, including its head office location. This job is not necessarily the one with the highest starting salary. It is often tempting to take the highest salary offer without considering all other factors. But success on the first job after graduation can have a tremendous impact upon an entire career. It should be chosen with care. Congratulations on your successful entry into management!

INITIAL JOB THREATS

A recent college graduate has conquered a major hurdle in his or her life. The world's problems are now going to be solved. But from a realistic viewpoint, certain cautions should be observed. This section is not inserted to frighten or disillusion a person, but it is felt that it is needed so that the first job will be approached from a realistic appreciation of the work environment. Although a job has been secured, there are numerous initial *job threats* that a person should be aware of if long-term success is to be achieved.

The Young Brat Syndrome

All employees of a firm will not always welcome with open arms a new college graduate. Although top management may realize that it is important to bring bright, young, college-educated people into the firm, this enthusiasm may not be shared by all. Graduates may find themselves working either with or for people without a college degree. The starting salary of college graduates may be more than that of employees who have been with the firm for a long time. Some may even perceive a new college graduate as a threat. Graduates have found that out of necessity their college degree may need to be *played down.* In time people will discover that you have your degree and will likely respect you more for not bringing it to their attention.

Making Changes

After graduation, a college graduate's mind is filled with new ideas or approaches that have been learned in the classroom. But the company may have been successfully accomplishing a task in a certain manner for many years. To the graduate it may be obvious that changes need to be made, and it may come as quite a shock when his or her ideas are not immediately accepted. Although a person's first inclination may be to start making changes, it may be best to first establish a good working relationship with members of the department and gradually bring forth new ideas.

Politics

The hardest lesson a young person must learn is that hard work and long hours do not guarantee advancement. In school, most likely students were told that salary increases and promotions were a direct result of productivity. In reality, obtaining a promotion or raise may depend on whom one knows and with whom a person plays golf or tennis. While this policy is certainly not advocated, it does at times occur and an individual should be alert to the different power groups at work within the organization.

The Free Spirit

Just as each of us has different personalities, companies are also different in their attitudes toward what is an acceptable standard of appearance. If a graduate goes to work for a firm in which all of the company's managerial personnel wear suits, conformity will likely be the order of the day. Resistance to this image can only result in difficulties. If a person wants to be less conventional, there are firms that totally accept this attitude.

The Boss

Some graduates often feel that their superior is not as intellectually enlightened or supportive as they believe a person in that position should be. Assuming that a person desires to maintain that position (a reasonable alternative might be to quit or request a transfer), he or she must realize that the supervisor is still the boss. If an individual desires to progress in that firm, an overt effort must be made to support the activities of the department. Expressing doubt concerning the superior's abilities to other employees can only hurt the chances for advancement. If a person wishes to make changes, they must be accomplished within the system.

Notes

1. James D. Robinson, III, "A Full Partnership for Service," *Business Week,* June 29, 1981, p. 15.
2. Frederick W. Taylor, *The Principles of Scientific Management* (New York: Harper, 1911), pp. 41–47.
3. Chester I. Barnard, *The Functions of the Executive* (Cambridge, Mass: Harvard University Press, 1938).
4. Harold Koontz, "The Management Theory Jungle Revisited," *Academy of Management Review* 5, no. 2 (April 1980).

References

Boone, Louis E., and Johnson, James C. "Profiles of the 801 Men and 1 Woman at the Top." *Business Horizons* 23, no. 1 (February 1980): 47–53.

Cook, Curtis W. "Guidelines for Managing Motivation." *Business Horizons* 23, no. 2 (April 1980): 61–70.

Drucker, Peter F. *Management: Tasks, Responsibilities and Practices.* New York: Harper, 1974.

Fayol, Henri. *General and Industrial Management.* New York: Pitman, 1949.

George, Claude, Jr. *The History of Management Thought.* Englewood Cliffs, N.J.: Prentice-Hall, 1972.

Hay, Christine D. "Women in Management: The Obstacles and Opportunities They Face." *Personnel Administrator* 25, no. 4 (April 1980): 25–31.

Kantrow, Alan M. "Why Read Peter Drucker?" *Harvard Business Review* 58, no. 1 (January–February 1980): 74–83.

Koontz, Harold. "The Management Theory Jungle Revisited." *Academy of Management Review* 5, no. 2 (April 1980): 175–189.

McGregor, Douglas. *The Professional Manager.* New York: McGraw-Hill, 1967.

Mintzberg, Henry. "The Manager's Job: Folklore and Fact." *Harvard Business Review* (July–August 1975): 49–61.

———. *The Nature of Managerial Work.* New York: Harper, 1973.

Newman, William H., ed. *Managers for the Year 2000.* Englewood Cliffs, N.J.: Prentice-Hall, 1978.

Oliva, Terence A., and Capdevielle, Christel M. "Can Systems Really Be Taught? (A Socratic Dialogue)." *Academy of Management Review* 5, no. 2 (April 1980): 277–281.

Roethlisberger, F. J., and Dickson, W. J. *Management and the Worker: An Account of a Research Program Conducted by the Western Electric Company Hawthorne Works, Chicago.* Cambridge: Harvard University Press, 1939.

KEY TERMS

unions
stockholders
social responsibility
ethics
systems approach
system
standards
situational approach
objective
technology
structure
centralized
decentralized

LEARNING OBJECTIVES

After completing this chapter you should be able to

1. Describe the major external environmental factors that can affect a manager.
2. Explain the systems approach and describe the basic components of a business system.
3. Describe the situational approach and identify the major situational factors that must be considered.

2

The Manager's Environment

Bob Russell, president of Astro Electronics, Inc., a large computer manufacturing company, was frustrated as he arrived at his office. At a recent stockholders' meeting, Bob had heard the displeasure of stockholders as they complained about the decrease in dividends approved by the board of directors. Also, just two days ago Bob had received notification from the vice-president of personnel that the union had refused the last offer for a new three-year contract. The same day, he had been told by the vice-president of marketing that competition was cutting their prices on the minicomputers, and Astro must do the same or face a loss of sales. Additionally one of Bob's top managers had just resigned to start his own firm. And today was only Monday.

Bob Russell was experiencing pressures from some of the forces from the external environment. He was realizing that today's managers do not operate in a vacuum. They are affected by a variety of factors as they attempt to perform the various functions of management.

This chapter begins by describing some of the major external factors that can affect managers. We then present some means whereby these many interrelated factors may be studied. This is accomplished through gaining an understanding of both the systems and situational approaches, which provide a way of thinking that all managers can use to improve their performance.

THE EXTERNAL ENVIRONMENT

The manager's job is not accomplished in a vacuum. Many interacting external factors can affect his or her performance. As you can see from Figure 2-1, the external environment is comprised of a variety of factors from outside the firm's boundaries that affect a manager's performance. Major external considerations include government, competitors, labor force, unions, stockholders, suppliers, customers, and the public. Each of these separately, or in combination, can constrain today's managers. These forces themselves interact to affect management. For instance, an action by a firm's creditor might affect the firm's suppliers, which in turn could affect the organization.

Government

One of the most relevant external forces that a manager must confront relates to federal, state, and local legislation and regulations. These laws range from legislation devoted to protecting the environment (Environmental Protection Act) to a law prohibiting discrimination in employment based on

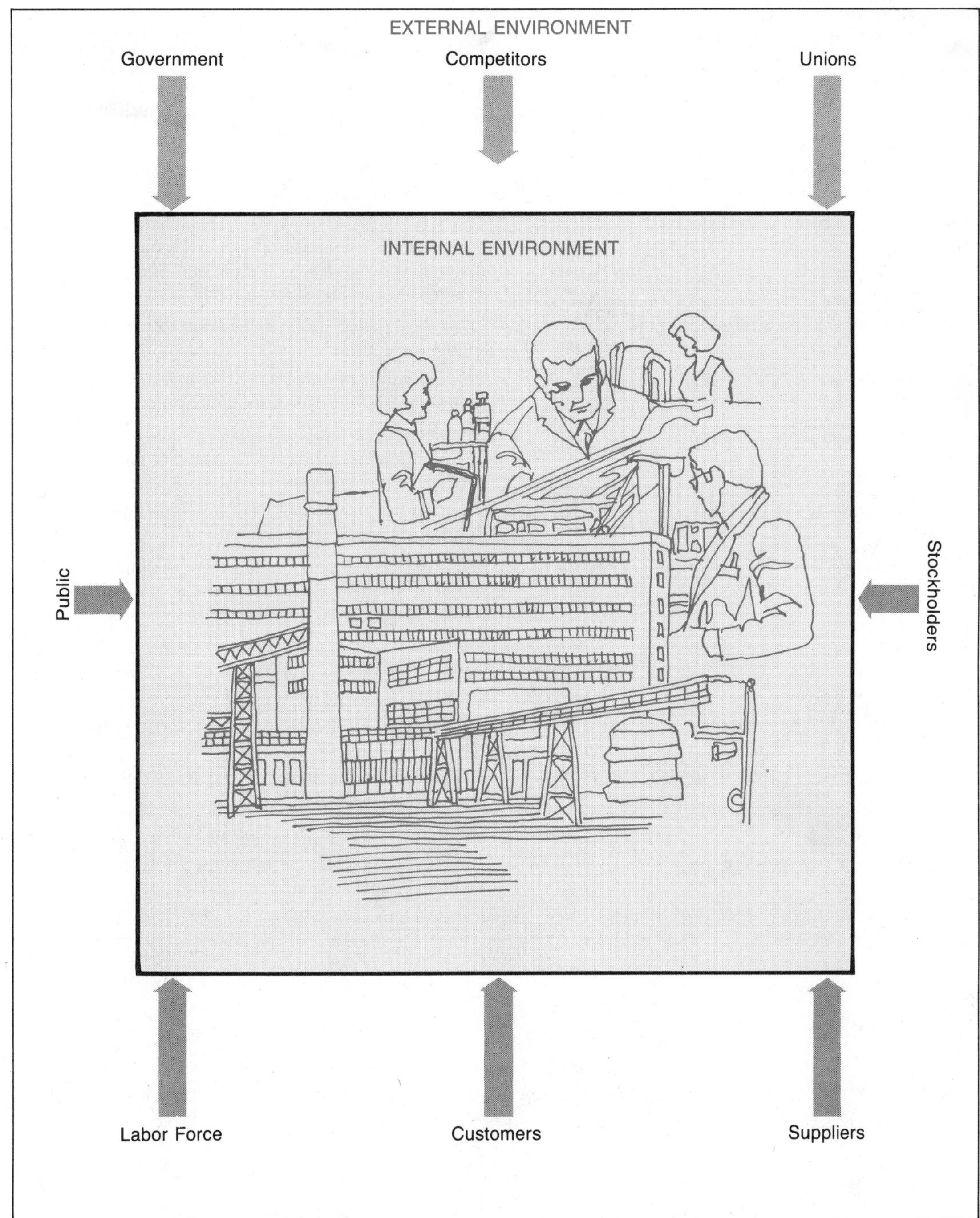

FIGURE 2-1 *External Environment Factors*

TABLE 2-1. *Samples of Federal Laws Affecting Business*

Laws	Major Provision
Sherman Act of 1890	The federal government's first large-scale intervention in private business; aimed at controlling trusts and preventing monopolies
Pure Food and Drug Act of 1906 as amended	Designed to protect consumers by requiring inspection of food and drug products
Clayton Act and the Federal Trade Commission Act of 1914	Clayton Act made tying contracts, exclusive trading, and price discrimination illegal; Federal Trade Commission Act established the Federal Trade Commission to enforce the Clayton Act
Security Exchange Commission Act of 1934	Protects investors from fraud and swindling and regulates securities markets
National Labor Relations Act of 1935	Protects rights of employees to form unions and levies bargaining responsibilities upon management
Social Security Act of 1935	Established a federal insurance program to provide retirement survivor benefits, disability payments, medicare, and unemployment insurance.
Fair Labor Standards Act of 1938	Requires firms to pay minimum wages and extra compensation for overtime
Air Pollution Control Act of 1962 as amended by the Clean Air Acts of 1970 and 1977	Established air quality standards to promote the public health and welfare and the productive capacity of the nation
Equal Pay Act of 1963	Requires that males and females on the same job get equal pay
Civil Rights Act of 1964 as amended in 1972 by the Equal Employment Opportunity Act	Prohibits discrimination in hiring, training, promotion, and pay on the basis of race, color, religion, nationality, and sex
Age Discrimination Act of 1967 as amended in 1978	Prohibits discrimination against older employees
Occupational Safety and Health Act of 1970	Sets safety and health standards and enforces them through surprise inspections and fines
Consumer Products Safety Act of 1972	Sets safety standards for consumer products and bans products that create undue risk of injury
Employee Retirement Income Security Act of 1974	Protects employee rights in private pension plans

race, color, sex, religion, or national origin (Civil Rights Act). A sample of federal legislation is presented in Table 2-1. Notice that legislation affecting management did not begin only in recent years. Whenever society perceives business as being less than responsible, legislation often is enacted.

Competitors

Unless an organization is in the unusual position of monopolizing the market it serves, other firms will be producing similar products or services. A decision made by your firm may also affect the competition and vice-versa. A decision to raise or lower prices must take into consideration the effect that it will have upon the competition.

A firm is also in competition with other companies in attracting competent employees. If a firm is to grow and prosper, it must be able to attract a qualified work force. Managers must realize that most other firms are also attempting to achieve this goal. At times, a bidding war results as firms attempt to recruit and retain employees in critical areas. Computer programmers, engineers, and accountants tend to attract considerable interest in the marketplace.

The Labor Force

The number and characteristics of individuals in the labor force is another major external factor. As these individuals enter the organization, they can affect the manager's performance. By 1990, there will be approximately 119 million persons in the civilian labor force.[1] This estimate represents an 18.5 percent increase over the 1978 figure of 87.5 million. It is expected that the labor force will grow more slowly between 1985 and 1990 (as it has since the 1960s) because of a drop in the number of young people entering the work force and a less rapid growth of the participation rate for women (see Figure 2-2). However, the figures do not tell the entire story because the labor force composition is also changing. While the participation rate for men

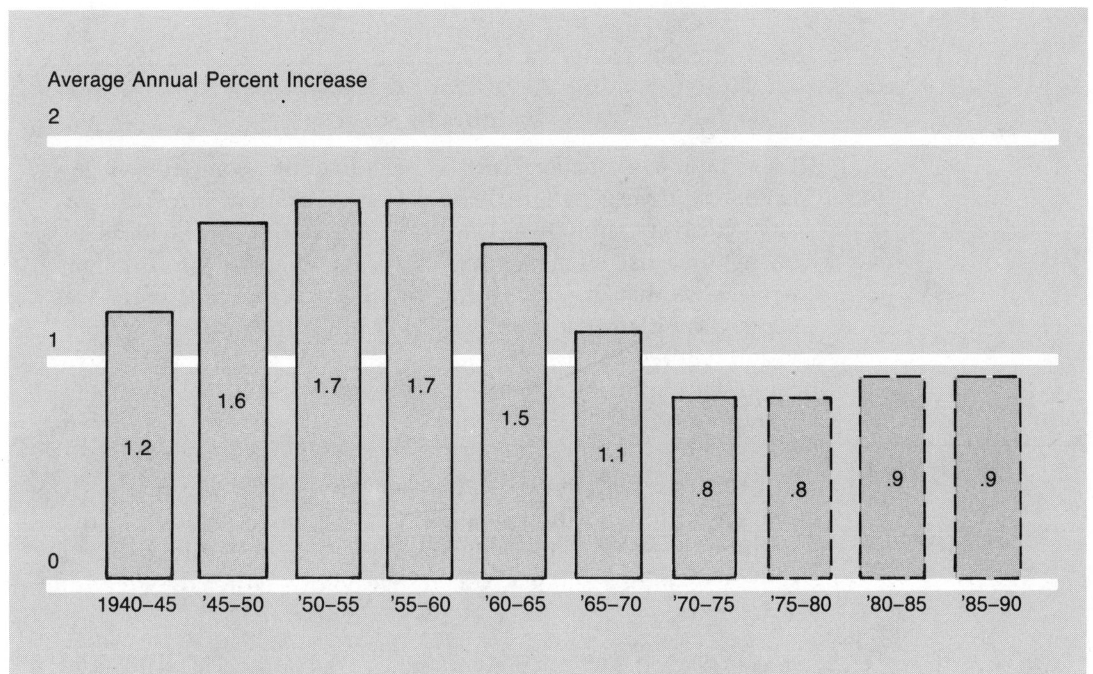

FIGURE 2-2 *Rate of Population Growth* [*Source: Bureau of the Census.*]

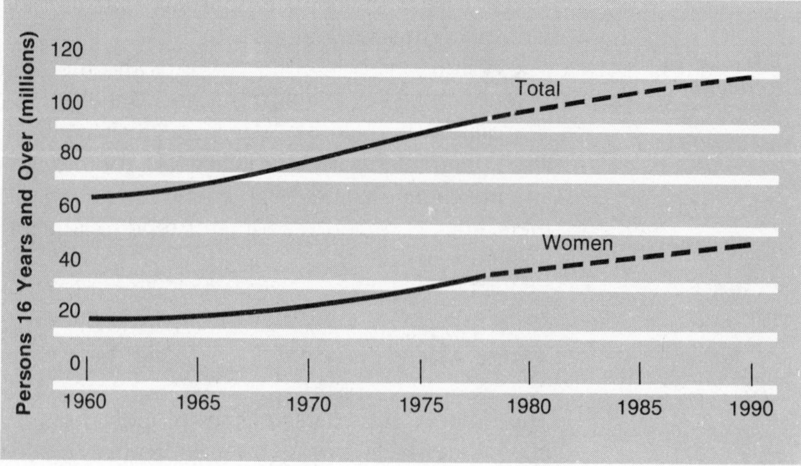

Source: Bureau of Labor Statistics.

FIGURE 2-3

Projected Increase of Women in the Work Force in the 1980s

continues to decline, that for women is rising (see Figure 2-3). Women are moving into traditionally male-dominated jobs, such as computer sales, public accounting, and management in increasing numbers. In addition, members of minority groups are gaining increased acceptance in higher-level jobs. These changes in the labor force will likely require attitude changes on the part of managers of the future.

Insights to Success

Expect to work damn hard. Expect that the competition gets keener as time goes on. Demonstrate dedication, integrity, loyalty, curiosity, humility. Don't be afraid to express ideas for change because change certainly needs to happen—but remember always that things are the way they are because there was some good reason at some point in time. Expect that the supervision will recognize competency, desire for growth, aggressiveness, with appropriate humility, and will reward achievement. Don't be too impatient, and think twice before declining potential assignments. Don't expect (at least in a company like Dow) to become a key officer of the company within the first 5–10 years, and for the individual fortunate enough to achieve that position, don't expect that the hard work, the pressure, the decisions will all of a sudden ease at that point—rather they tend to accelerate.

H. H. LYON, Vice-President—Administration, The Dow Chemical Company

•CAREER PROFILE•

MR. TEXAS E. (TEX) SCHRAMM
President and General Manager
Dallas Cowboys Football Club

Texas E. (Tex) Schramm is president and general manager of the Dallas Cowboys Football Club. While there are certainly people to argue the point, many knowledgeable sports enthusiasts believe the Dallas Cowboys to be the best organized and managed team in the league. Their success as a football power has been attained, to a great extent, because of the leadership and management ability of Tex Schramm.

When Tex graduated from the University of Texas in 1947 with a degree in journalism, little did he suspect that he would eventually become president of a highly successful football club. After working for a short time as the sports editor for the *Austin American Statesman,* he accepted the position of publicity director for the Los Angeles Rams Football Club. Before he left the Rams in 1957, he had progressed to the position of general manager. Tex next became assistant director of sports for Columbia Broadcasting System from 1957 to 1960. He joined the Cowboys in 1960 and has watched the team steadily progress from a weak expansion club to a power in the league.

Tex is, in the truest sense of the word, a manager. He says he performs the same role as any chief executive officer in that he attempts to create the proper climate within the organization so that the individuals who are specialists in their fields can perform to their maximum ability. He views his job as one of providing the resources—facilities, tools, and support—to permit his staff to perform at their maximum ability. Tex believes that the success of every organization depends upon the selection and development of quality personnel.

Tex further states that an organization should be measured on the basis of how consistently it is successful rather than, for instance, if they make it to the Super Bowl for one year. The Cowboys have certainly achieved this goal, and many teams are fearful that this trend may continue.

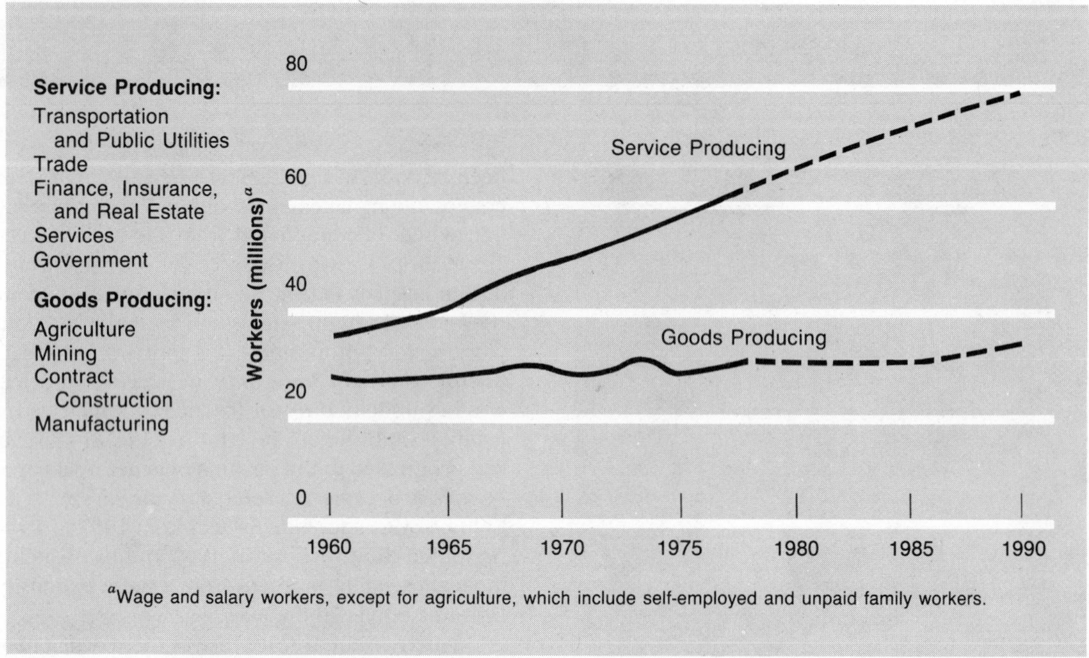

FIGURE 2-4 *Work Force for Service and Goods-Producing Industries* [*Source: Bureau of Labor Statistics.*]

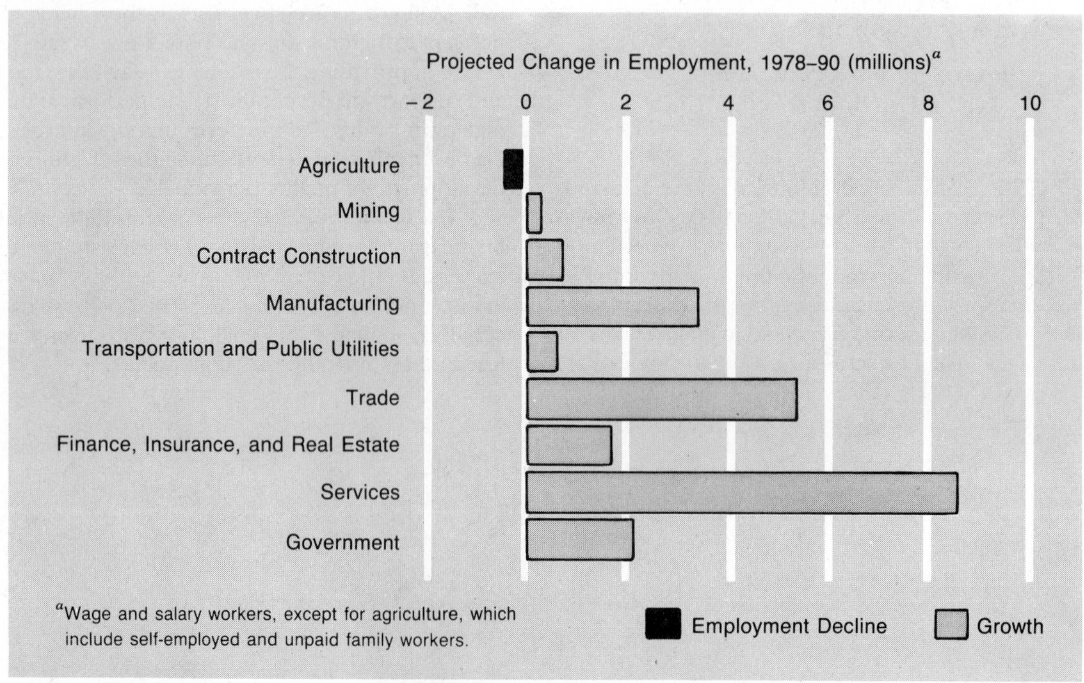

FIGURE 2-5 *Projected Changes in Employment among Industries through the 1980s* [*Source: Bureau of Labor Statistics.*]

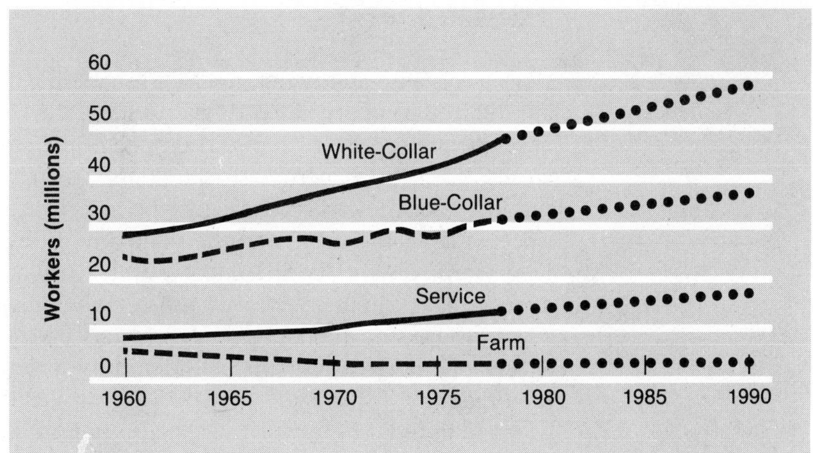

FIGURE 2-6

Projected Growth of White-collar, Blue-collar, Service, and Farm Workers through the 1980s

Source: Bureau of Labor Statistics.

The industries that will be capable of absorbing these additional employees will also likely be different from those of today. The goods-producing industries such as agriculture, construction, mining, and manufacturing are expected to remain relatively stable in terms of employment. But job opportunities in service industries such as health care, trade, repair and maintenance, government, transportation, banking, and insurance will increase (see Figure 2-4). By 1990, employment in the service industries is expected to expand by 30 percent over 1978 figures. In goods-producing industries, employment is projected to increase by only 13 percent. A projection of the employment growth by industry is presented in Figure 2-5.

The number of white-collar workers is also expected to increase through 1990, while the number of blue-collar workers should remain relatively stable. Farm workers are expected to decline by 14 percent by 1990 (see Figure 2-6).

Unions

unions

Unions consist of employees who have joined together for the purpose of presenting a united front in dealing with management. As Bob Russell realized, unions are an external environmental factor because they essentially become a third party when dealing with the company. It is the union rather than the individual employee that negotiates an agreement with the firm.

Through the process of collective bargaining, organized labor has established patterns of employee-management relations. Although union membership is only slightly higher than 20 million, or approximately 20 percent of the total labor market, this force affects many nonunion firms that strive to maintain their nonunion status. Wage levels, fringe benefits, and working conditions for millions of employees now reflect decisions made jointly by unions and management.

Stockholders

stockholders

Individuals who are owners and who share in a corporation's profit (or loss) are referred to as **stockholders.** As such, they are vitally interested in the firm's operating effectiveness. The price of the stock and the dividends paid are also of major concern to stockholders. The managers may actually operate the firm, but they must constantly be sensitive to the stockholders' needs, since in actuality, they own the company. Bob Russell, president of Astro Electronics, discovered the difficulties that can arise when the stockholders are not "sold" on the merits of a project when dividends decrease.

Because stockholders have a monetary investment in the firm, they may at times challenge programs considered by management to be beneficial to the organization. Managers may be forced to justify the merits of a particular program in terms of how it will affect future projects. For instance, if it is recommended that equipment be bought that will make the environment better, the purchase will likely have to be justified with regard to how it affects the profitability of the firm. Stockholders are concerned with how expenditure decisions relate to increased revenue or decreasing costs.

Another means by which stockholders can influence a company is through stockholder activism. Such activism was virtually unheard of in 1960, but now management has become extremely sensitive to its public image. A very small number of public interest stockholders may force a corporation to avoid bad public relations by negotiating settlements. The last thing most corporations want is criticism of the firm's performance on the front page of a major newspaper.[2]

Suppliers

A manufacturing firm cannot long operate effectively unless it is continually supplied with needed material. Lack of adequate supplies can cause the manufacturing process to be reduced or cause cessation of operations even though the firm has sufficient capital and employees. For instance, a coal strike can affect a utility firm's ability to produce sufficient quantities of electricity. Should there be another severe shortage of oil as was experienced in 1979–1980, some businesses would likely have to cease operations. And a computer services company, which provides data-processing services, would likely delay its operations if it is unable to secure the needed forms to process the customer's output.

Customers

The people who actually use a firm's products and services also must be considered part of the external environment. Because sales are critical to the firm's survival, management has the task of ensuring that its employment practices do not antagonize the members of the market it serves. There have been instances of consumer boycotts when organizations have restricted the number of minorities they employ. Legal requirements are not the only consideration when determining the firm's work-force composition.

Customers are constantly demanding high-quality products and improved services. Therefore, the firm must strive to produce products and services desired by the customers. Failure to do so will cause the firm to cease existence.

The Public

Society also exerts considerable pressure upon management. The public is no longer content to accept without question, the actions of business. The pressures that have been brought by the public with regard to the construction and operation of nuclear power plants provide an excellent example. The public has found that the pressure of their voices and votes can bring about change. Their influence is obvious in the large number of regulatory laws that have been passed since the early 1960s (refer back to Table 2-1).

Two concepts—corporate social responsibility and business ethics—must be considered when discussing the public as part of the external environment. **Social responsibility** is defined as the firm's "obligation to constituent groups in society other than stockholders and beyond that prescribed by law or union contract."[3] **Ethics** are contemporary standards or principles of conduct that govern the actions and behavior of individuals within the organization.

social responsibility

ethics

If a firm is to remain acceptable to the general public, it must be capable of satisfactorily explaining its purpose. This is a most difficult challenge. Recent surveys have indicated that the general public does not have a favorable perception of business; as many as 50 percent of persons surveyed have expressed displeasure with the actions of business. The public also has an exaggerated view of overall business profitability. When asked what a typical business firm earned on each dollar of sales, many people thought profits were almost thirty cents (30 percent) per dollar of sales when in reality profits

---

Reason for Success as a Manager

My success as a manager is based on knowing and understanding the real bottom-line objectives of my organization and unstintingly applying my time, effort, and considerable ability to advancing those goals. Only when one enjoys the integration of their own personal goals with those of the corporation can they become a success as a manager and a person.

DORIS C. ETELSON, Vice-President—Service Standards, National Restaurant Operations, Howard Johnson's

---

decreased from a median of 5.2 cents on each sales dollar in 1979 to 4.8 cents in 1980.[4]

A major point that management must consider is that the general public includes the firm's employees. For instance, if an organization has ten thousand employees, these individuals will have an influence over a larger number of people who are not connected with the firm—perhaps friends or members of an employee's family. Therefore, a firm should maintain clear communication with its employees so that the firm's side of the story is told.

THE SYSTEMS APPROACH: AN INTRODUCTION

systems approach
system

In order to be successful, managers must understand and be capable of coping with the many environmental factors that confront them virtually each day. Managers must also be able to see how the functions of planning, organizing, influencing, and controlling interrelate. A concept that facilitates a manager's ability to perform the major functions of management and to respond effectively to environmental factors is the **systems approach.** A **system** is an arrangement of interrelated parts designed to achieve objectives. Through the systems approach, a manager is better able to understand and work with the various units within the organization to interrelate and coordinate the accomplishment of the goals of the firm.

THE BUSINESS SYSTEM

Successful managers have found that the systems approach aids significantly in managing organizations. In any organization, management's job is to use resources (inputs) in an efficient manner to produce or achieve desirable products and/or services (outputs). Although the systems approach is useful in managing any type of organization—whether the firm is public, not for profit, or profit making—our illustration of its usage is applied specifically to a business firm. The basic business system components are graphically illustrated in Figure 2-7 and discussed below.

Resources

As Figure 2-7 shows, a business enterprise uses certain inputs that are processed into outputs (products and/or services). This interaction with the external environment suggests that we are operating in an open system. Essentially the organization depends upon other systems for its inputs. Just as we cannot live long without food and water, a dynamic business system cannot survive without substances (resources) that keep it alive. These items may be human (employees to run the plant) or nonhuman energies (fuel for the factory), supplies, and information. The inputs or resources needed by the system vary according to the objectives or goals of the firm. If, for

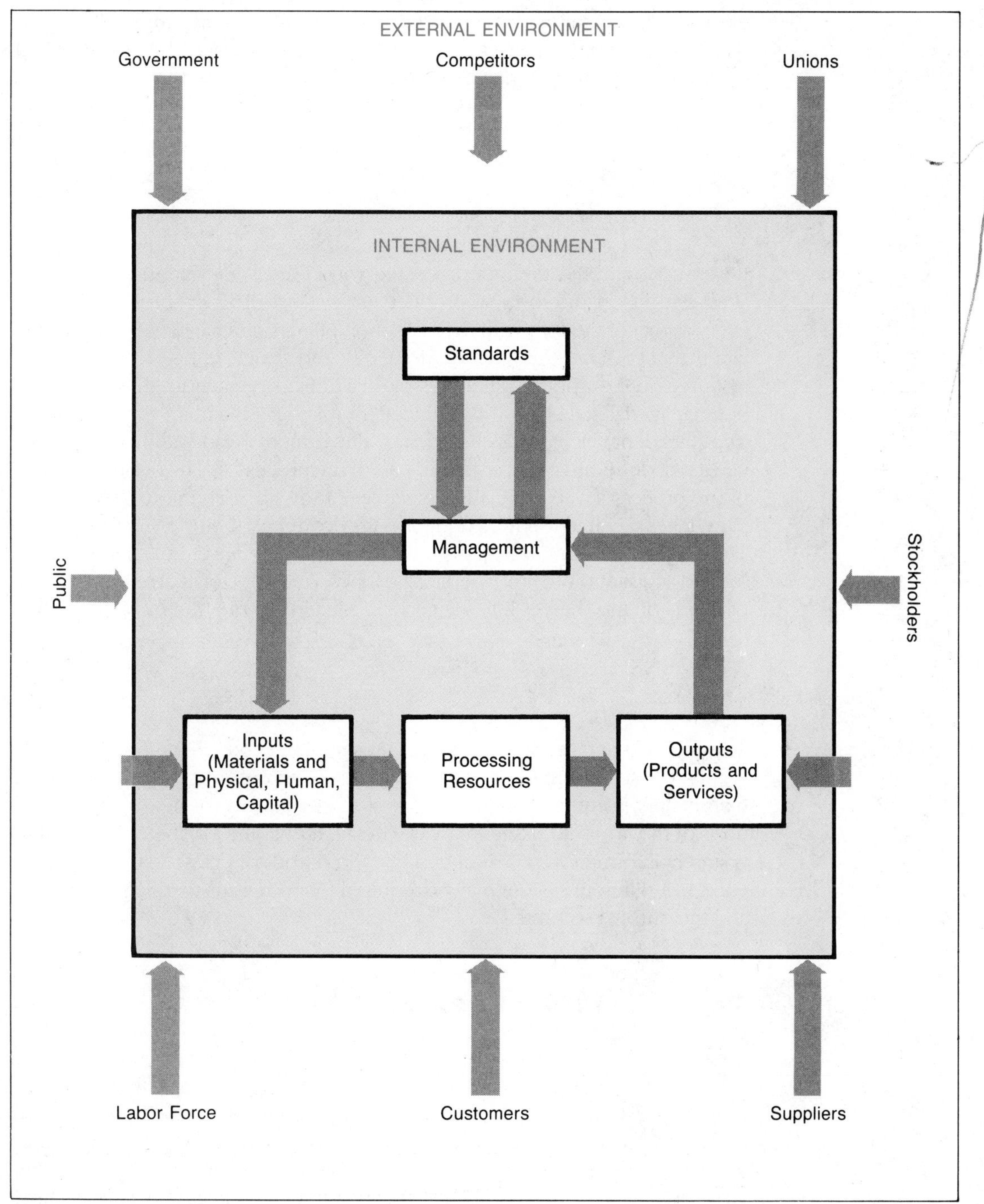

FIGURE 2-7 *The Business System*

example, a watch manfacturer has the objective of making high-quality watches, the inputs needed are likely to be highly trained craftspersons and quality equipment and materials. A manufacturer of lower-quality watches may need different inputs, such as equipment capable of mass production and less-skilled employees.

Processing Resources

Resources or inputs are next processed within the organization to create desired outputs in the form of products or services. This processing includes every aspect of the firm with the exception of managerial talent. It would contain the necessary equipment, employees, and structure needed to convert resources into outputs. The processor for a university includes the faculty, the nonmanagerial staff, and the buildings required to maintain the university. The president, vice-presidents, deans, department heads, and other managerial personnel are not considered part of the processor. The desired outputs of the processor vary with the objectives of the firm. The Ford Motor Company takes steel, aluminum, and glass and converts them into automobiles. The hospital changes ill patients into healthy ones; the school changes uninformed students into knowledgeable ones; and the retail store transforms products on the shelves into values of satisfaction in the home.

Outputs

The products and services are the end result of the conversion process. Once inputs (physical, human, capital) are converted to outputs, they return to the external environment. These outputs should conform to the objectives and goals of the firm (discussed in greater detail in Chapter 3). The output of IBM is largely information processing, while the output of Consolidated Edison is energy. A different system may be required for both firms to reflect their goals and the output required.

Management and Standards

standards

Viewing the business system still further, one notices the information feedback to management (noted by the arrow in Figure 2-7 from outputs to management). The manager uses this information to ensure that the outputs are being produced according to standard. **Standards** provide management with basic guidelines for desired performance. If standards are not being achieved, management must make changes to correct the deviation, which may be due to incorrect inputs such as defective parts or unqualified employees. As inputs are processed and transformed into outputs, a problem could result because of low morale of employees. Whatever the cause, management's task is to identify the deviation and make corrections in line with company objectives.

Dynamics of a Business System

All of the components of any firm—resources, processor, output, management, and standards—operate as a system. But it is not a closed system that fails to take into consideration the external environment. The external environment affects how the business system can operate. For instance, the union may decide to strike and shut down the processor. Suppliers may not be able to provide the material necessary to keep the processor going. Government legislation may be passed that places certain restrictions on the firm. The competition may come out with an innovative product that makes obsolete the current way that products are being processed. The business system is dynamic and constantly changing. The systems approach provides management with a means of viewing different and outside interrelationships both from within and outside a firm. Many factors must be considered if the goals of the organization are to be accomplished.

THE SITUATIONAL APPROACH

Students of management begin to recognize the many interrelationships that exist within all organizations through the use of the systems approach. Another concept—the situational approach—builds upon the systems approach and provides managers with a broader appreciation of the management process. The **situational approach** is defined as management's ability to adapt to meet particular circumstances and constraints that a firm may encounter. It is not a totally new concept; in 1512, Nicoló Machiavelli wrote,

situational approach

> Therefore, you ought to know that there are two ways to fight: by using laws, and by using force. The former is characteristic of man; the latter, of animals. . . . Therefore, since a prince must perfect his knowledge of how to use animal attributes, those he must select are the fox and the lion. Since the lion is powerless against snares and the fox is powerless against wolves, one must be a fox to recognize snares and a lion to frighten away wolves.[5]

By this statement Machiavelli was attempting to tell his prince that he must be capable of making decisions based on the demands of a particular situation; nothing is consistently either yes or no. In using this approach, the manager recognizes that many different types of situations can exist and he or she adapts to respond to them.

Although there are an unlimited number of specific factors a manager may encounter, they can be reduced to six major categories (see Figure 2-8).

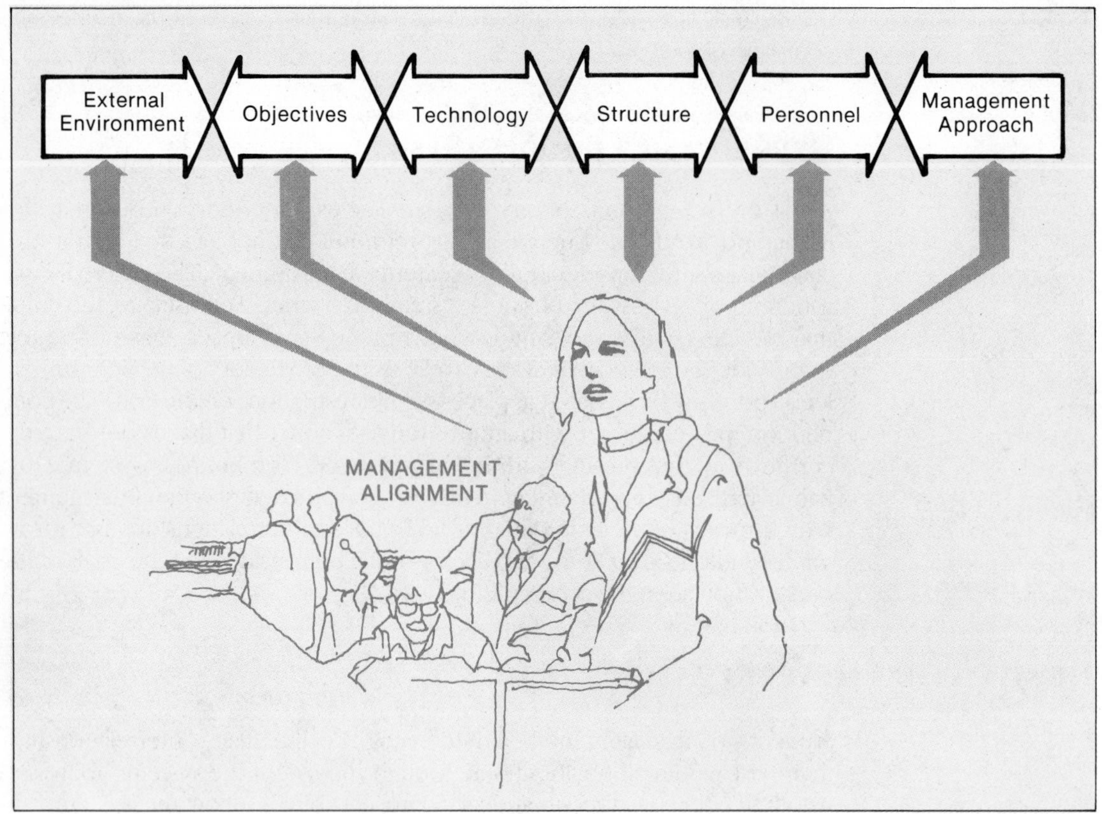

FIGURE 2-8 *The Situational Approach: Major Factors*

Not only must the manager recognize that these factors exist, he or she must be capable of aligning or synchronizing them through the help of the systems approach to achieve the best results. The situationally oriented manager must be constantly aware of these factors and the manner in which they interact. Managers should also recognize there is no one best approach to management that meets the needs of all organizations.

External Environment

Earlier in this chapter, we discussed many of the factors that comprise the external environment. These factors constantly affect the way the manager performs his or her assigned tasks.

Objectives

objective An **objective** describes the end result a firm desires to accomplish. Appropriate objectives in one firm may prove disastrous in another. These objectives may be severely affected by the external environment, which may cause a firm to alter or even completely change its direction. For instance, during the oil shortage of 1979, many plastic manufacturing firms could not obtain sufficient petroleum to maintain their operations. Some firms responded by modifying their objectives and diversifying to produce products that did not have a petroleum base. In highly uncertain environments, the objectives may be subject to rapid change. In more stable and predictable environments, management is able to establish more specific and steady objectives. As environmental requirements change, the objectives of a firm that desires to survive and prosper must also change.

Technology

technology

Technology takes into consideration all of the skills, knowledge, methods, and equipment required to convert resources into desired products and/or services. In terms of the situational approach to management, **technology** can be characterized on the basis of the state of the art. If the technology is well worked out and we know what we are doing, a routine can be developed and applied on a uniform basis. If the technology is quite complex and uncertain, the organization is more dependent on people for effective accomplishment. The technology for manufacturing hand calculators is better worked out than that for teaching college students. In turn, the technology for teaching is better developed than the technology for curing mental illness.

Structure

structure
centralized
decentralized

As used here, **structure** means the manner in which the internal environment of the firm is organized or arranged. If most major decisions are made primarily by top-level executives, the organization is **centralized.** If lower-level supervisors and managers are permitted to make significant decisions, the structure is more **decentralized.** Organizational structures are discussed in Chapter 7.

Personnel

Hire good people and let them do their thing is the general philosophy toward personnel held by many effective managers. But because we are all different in terms of our goals, aspirations, background, experiences, and personalities, some employees are a better *match* with one organization than another. It has been found that employees tend to move toward a firm that possesses an environment closely compatible with their goals and needs. If a firm has a need for individuals with skills that are different from those currently within the organization, changes may have to be made. This is a very real problem facing American workers of the future. One report estimates that technological changes will affect more than 45 million American jobs during the next twenty years.[6] For instance, robots are beginning to take the place of many automobile assembly-line workers.

Managerial Approaches

There are two fundamental *managerial approaches:* (1) the more autocratic approach and (2) the more participative style. With the autocratic approach, the manager's attitude is, "Do it my way or you are fired." With the participative style, managers encourage worker involvement in the decision-making process. Situational theory accepts both approaches as being workable under certain conditions. Management has discovered that workers who participate in the decision-making process show greater acceptance of the decision than those who do not. But at times participation in the decision-making process is not in the best interest of the firm. If a firm is in a fight for its survival, a more direct or autocratic approach may prove superior. Thus, situations often call for varying mixtures of managerial style.

BALANCING THE SITUATIONAL FACTORS

Thus far we have discussed the systems and situational approaches as if they were separate and distinct. This is not really the case since the systems approach provides the manager with the ability to balance the situational factors. It is how these factors interact, rather than any one factor taken separately, that is significant.

Insights to Success

The basic function of the plant is to convert resources (raw materials, labor, energy) into a marketable product, with maximum efficiency.

JAMES A. MACK, President and General Manager, Chemicals Division, Sherwin-Williams Company

---

Both the systems and situational concepts must be interrelated if a person is to be an effective manager. As seen in Figure 2-9, the organizational system must take into consideration the situational factors. These factors must be balanced if good results are to be achieved. As the situational factors change, the system may need to be modified. For instance, if the goals of the firm are altered (the firm decides to diversify as opposed to concentrating on producing only one product), the situational factors will likely be out of

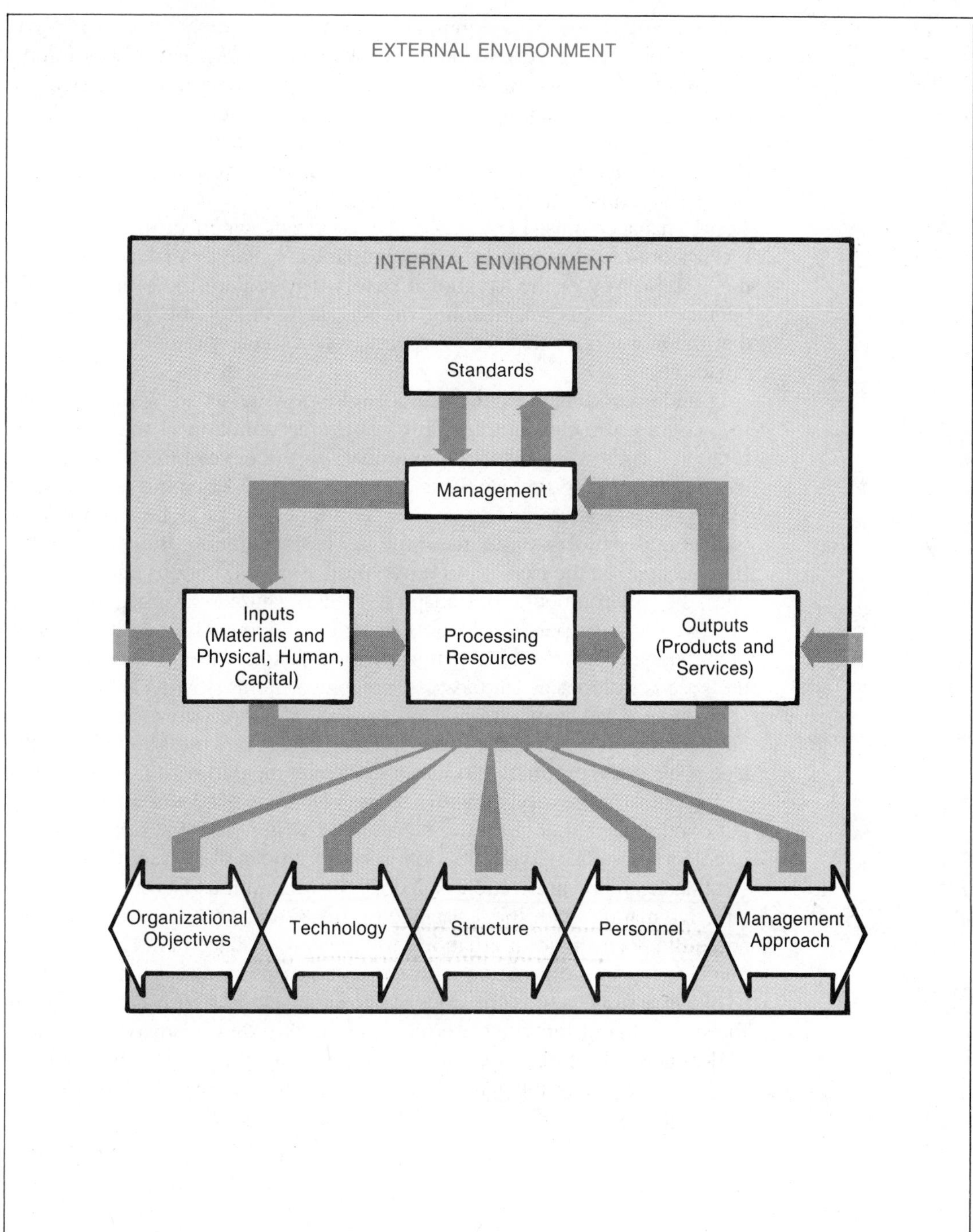

FIGURE 2-9 *Management from a Systems and Situational Viewpoint*

balance. There may be a requirement for new technologies to comply with the new objectives. New workers will likely be needed in the labor force. If the structure is not one that can accommodate these new employees or if the firm finds that it is having difficulty recruiting the type of people necessary to bring about these changes, the situational factors will likely require realignment. As the factors are altered, the system must change to adapt to the restructuring of the situational factors.

A manager must be capable of recognizing when the situational factors are out of balance and bring them back into line by making changes in the system. Any of the situational factors may require the other factors to be modified. Thus, maintaining proper alignment of the factors ensures that the firm is operating with the best system to meet the objectives of the organization.

Underwood, the leading producer of typewriters many years ago, failed to recognize the changing trends toward mechanization of the office environment. These changes were conducive to the development and sales of electric typewriters, which later became standard equipment in virtually every office. Underwood, however, continued to produce manual typewriters under the assumptions of the *old* base condition. But a competitor, IBM, recognized the trends and brought their base conditions into alignment with the environment. IBM adapted their organizational objectives, technology, structure, personnel, and management approach to meet the needs of a changing environment. The situational factors were in alignment with the base conditions as Underwood perceived them. However, the external environment had changed, and Underwood did not recognize this. IBM since has become the leading manufacturer of electric typewriters and many other electronic office products. Underwood (which merged with Olivetti in 1966 to become Underwood-Olivetti) ultimately recognized the changing market conditions and entered the electric typewriter business, but it has been unable to reestablish its former dominant position in the typewriter industry.

Management must attempt to balance the various factors in the most effective manner with the assistance of the systems approach. One can also argue the necessity for a situational approach to management by contrasting different types of organizations. It would be inappropriate to try to manage a college or university as one does a large manufacturing corporation. Though the management functions are the same in all types of organizations, their performance depends on the situation. Both the systems and situational approaches are important as managers perform their job in this dynamic environment in which we live.

Summary

The manager's job is not accomplished in a vacuum. Many interacting external factors can affect a manager's performance. Major external considerations include: government, competitors, the labor force, unions, stockholders, suppliers, customers, and the public.

One of the most relevant external forces that a manager must confront relates to federal, state, and local legislation and regulations. These laws range from legislation devoted to protecting the environment to a law prohibiting discrimination in employment based on race, color, sex, religion, or national origin. Regarding competition, a manager must remember that a decision made by another firm may also affect the competition, and vice-versa. The nature of the labor force will be quite different as more women and minorities enter the work force. In addition, the union must be considered an external environmental factor because it essentially becomes a third party when dealing with the company. Stockholders are vitally interested in the firm's operating effectiveness, and managers must be sensitive to stockholders' needs, since in actuality, stockholders own the company. Lack of adequate supplies can cause the manufacturing process to be reduced or cause cessation of operation even though the firm has sufficient capital and employees. Also, the people who actually use a firm's products and services—the customers—must be considered part of the external environment. Finally, society exerts considerable pressure upon management because the public has found that changes can be made through their voices and votes.

A concept that facilitates a manager's ability to perform the major functions of management and to respond effectively to environmental factors is the systems approach. A system is an arrangement of interrelated parts designed to achieve objectives. Successful managers have found that the systems approach aids significantly in managing organizations. In any organization, management's job is to use resources (inputs) in an efficient manner to produce or achieve desirable products and/or services (output). Standards provide management with basic guidelines for desired performance. All of the components of any firm—input, processor, management, and standards—operate as a system.

The situational approach builds upon the systems approach and provides the manager with a broader appreciation of the management process. The situational approach is defined as management's ability to adapt to meet particular circumstances and constraints that a firm may encounter. Although there are an unlimited number of specific factors a manager may encounter, they can be reduced to six major categories: the external environment, objectives, technology, structure, personnel, and the management approach. Not only must managers recognize that these factors exist, they must be capable of aligning or synchronizing them through the help of the systems approach to achieve the best results.

Review Questions

1. **Identify and describe the major external environmental factors that can affect a manager.**
2. **How is the work force expected to change by the year 1990?**
3. **Define a system. Why does a manager need to understand the systems approach?**

4. What are the components of a business system? How do they interrelate?
5. Define the situational approach to management. Identify and define the various situational factors that a manager must align or balance to achieve the best results.

Exercises

1. Consider the following objectives from two different firms:

   Firm A: Our goal is to be an innovator in the creation of new products and services.

   Firm B: Our goal is to mass produce products that have a proven record of success.

   Given these different objectives, how might the situational factors of technology, structure, personnel, and management approach be different? Are there factors from the external environment that would be different for each firm?
2. Listed below are three different managerial positions. Describe and discuss the major environmental factors that would likely affect these positions.
   - **a.** President of General Motors
   - **b.** President of a regional college or university
   - **c.** Owner and operator of Bob's Convenience Store located in a small rural community

Case Study

A Tough Decision

The setting is a grocery store in a small town of approximately 22,000 people. The grocery store chain has fifty supermarkets, and management places great emphasis on customer relations. The company strictly enforces its policy of courtesy and consideration toward all customers.

Jimmy Jones, a fifteen-year-old boy, has recently been hired. This is Jimmy's first job, and he wants to make a good impression. The older employees quickly see that Jimmy is ambitious and determined. They readily accept him as a member of the work force. Soon Jimmy becomes the friendliest and most productive member of the store's work force. He receives two consecutive raises and is also given special recognition for outstanding service.

The original store manager is suddenly transferred to the regional office, and a new manager, Louise Anderson, is sent to take over the store. Louise realizes that Jimmy is management material and that he will soon graduate from high school. Louise begins delegating Jimmy some responsibility, and Jimmy welcomes it, adjusting quite well to the idea of eventually becoming an assistant manager.

Pilferage has always been a problem at the store. One day Jimmy catches some of his fellow workers stuffing some store items into their pockets and tries to discourage them. They ridicule him for being a "goody-goody" and Jimmy decides to say nothing to Louise. It is at this time that a change takes place in Jimmy. Although Jimmy is not yet an official manager, he has the responsibility for opening the store each morning and checking in the bread and milk vendors. One day, Jimmy runs out of cigarettes and has no way of purchasing any until the store opens. He borrows a pack from the checkstand and pays for it two hours later when the store opens. Over a period of several weeks, Jimmy makes this a habit, but he does not always remember to pay for the cigarettes. Soon Jimmy is in the habit of stuffing several packs into his coat pocket each day. He even keeps some extras in his car.

Louise watches the inventory closely and soon detects the loss of cigarettes. One Saturday morning, Jimmy opens the store and gets the vendors underway as usual. While no one is looking, he takes a whole carton of cigarettes and puts the packs into his pockets, throwing the empty carton into a trash can in the restroom. Louise arrives just as the store is ready to open and relieves Jimmy. She sends Jimmy to the doughnut shop for coffee and begins to investigate the store. When Jimmy returns, he is told to report to the break area to meet with Louise. When Jimmy arrives, he immediately knows something is wrong; Louise is holding a brown paper bag and has a blank and astonished look on her face. Jimmy sits down and lights a cigarette. That begins the following conversation. "What kind of cigarettes are you smoking, Jimmy? Is it the same kind as these?" Louise asks. Then she pulls an empty carton from the paper bag and hands it to Jimmy. Louise had emptied the trash cans the night before and knows that Jimmy is the cigarette thief.

"I know that I'm in serious trouble, Louise, and I'll go along with whatever you decide to do," mumbles Jimmy as he hangs his head in shame.

"Jimmy, son, the part that kills me is that you, of all people, were the one behind this. What do you think I should do with you?"

QUESTIONS

1. List and discuss the various situational factors involved in this case.
2. Given the situation as presented above, what do you believe Louise should do regarding Jimmy?

Case Study

The New Supervisor

Bill McDonald was a mechanic at Good Job Garage. At forty years of age, Bill had worked for this garage for twenty years and had seniority on the other ten employees. His seniority provided him with the respect of his fellow workers, and they admired him for his excellent auto-repair ability. During Bill's twenty years at Good Job Garage, he maintained a spotless record. He was a model employee in every respect. His mechanical work was superior, and his attitude was excellent. Bill was helpful to all new employees, and he became an unofficial figure of authority.

Jack Smirks was the foreman at the garage. He was twenty-nine years old with a degree in auto mechanics from a technical institute. Jack had been in his position approximately two months. He was confident of himself and felt excited about his newly acquired authority. Bill liked Jack and offered him his services whenever they were needed. Jack called on Bill several times and received excellent advice.

One day, Jack arrived at work obviously irritated. At first, it appeared that Jack was upset with the entire work force, but after repeated verbal attacks on Bill, this was ruled out. Bill, being a good-natured person, took the abuse because he felt that Jack might be bothered by some personal problems.

The abuse continued for an entire month and grew progressively worse. The situation was trying for Bill. He felt the only solution was for him to continue to do his job and try to avoid Jack.

During the next two weeks, Jack placed increasingly greater demands on his workers, especially Bill. He began changing the garage around and establishing new rules. His attitude became so difficult that all the workers tried to avoid him. But, due to the size of the garage, it was impossible.

Finally, the workers went to Bill. This conversation follows:

Worker 1: Bill, we need our jobs.

Bill: I know you do.

Worker 2: But what do we do about Jack? We can't work like this.

Bill: Well, why don't you talk with him?

Worker 3: Bill, we'd like you to do it for us. He's been rough on you, too, and since you're older than we, we feel he'd respect you more.

Bill: But . . .

Worker 4: Please, Bill, we need your help.

Bill: Okay, okay. I'll talk to him.

Bill went to Jack and asked to talk with him. Jack agreed. The discussion lasted an hour as Bill explained the situation to Jack. Jack said he didn't know the employees felt the way they did, and said he would try to work with them more. Bill then shook hands with Jack and went back to work.

Jack went to the owner of the garage, to whom he reported, and told him that Bill was causing troubles where there were none. Jack had talked to the other employees individually, and they said everything was just fine. The next day, Bill, the twenty-year vet was fired.

QUESTIONS

1. What external and internal factors were involved in this case? Discuss.
2. What might have been done to have kept this situation from occurring?

Notes

1. *Occupational Outlook Handbook,* 1980–81 ed., U.S. Government Bulletin, Number 2075.
2. David Vogel, "Ralph Nader's All over the Place: Citizens vs. the Corporation," *Across the Board* 1 (April 1979): 26–31.
3. Thomas M. Jones, "Corporate Social Responsibility, Revisited, Redefined," *California Management Review* 22 (Spring 1980): 59–60.
4. Ford S. Worthy, "The Fortune Directory of the Largest U.S. Industrial Corporations," *Fortune,* May 4, 1981, p. 322.
5. Nicoló Machiavelli, *The Prince,* 1512.
6. "The Speedup in Automation," *Business Week,* August 3, 1981, p. 58.

References

Allen, Robert E., and Keaveny, Timothy J. "Does the Work Status of Married Women Affect Their Attitudes toward Family Life?" *Personnel Administrator* 26 (June 1979): 63–66.

Appley, Lawrence A. "New Directions for Management." *Supervisory Management* 26 (February 1981): 9–12.

Dam, André van. "The Future of Management." *Management World* (January 1978): 3–6.

Roy, Delwin A.; Simpson, Claude L.; and Suzman, Cedric. *Southwest Exporting: Profiles, Typology and the Role of Technology in Selected U.S. Firms.* Atlanta, Ga.: Business Publishing Division of Georgia State University, 1981.

Fram, Eugene H., and Deubrin, Andrew. "Time Span Orientation: A Key Factor of Contingency Management." *Personnel Journal* 60 (January 1981): 46–48.

Grayson, C. Jackson. "Productivity's Impact on Our Economic Future." *Personnel Administrator* 24 (December 1979): 21, 23.

Holmes, Sandra L. "Adapting Corporate Structure for Social Responsiveness." *California Management Review* 21 (Fall 1978): 47–54.

Jacobs, Bruce. "Keeping Fast-Track Managers on the Rise." *Industry Week,* November 10, 1980, p. 34.

Leslie, C. E. "Critical Issues Confronting Managers in the '80's." *Training and Development Journal* 34 (January 1980): 14–17.

Luthans, Fred, and Stewart, Todd I. "A General Contingency Theory of Management." *Academy of Management Review* 2 (April 1977): 181–195.

Marsh, Robert M., and Minnari, Hiroshi. "Technology and Size as Determinants of Organizational Structure of Japanese Factories." *Administrative Science Quarterly* 26 (March 1981): 33–57.

Mintzberg, Henry. "The Manager's Job: Folklore and Fact." *Harvard Business Review* (July–August 1975): 49–51.

Nicholson, Joan; Cooper, Toby; Peterson, Russell; Henderson, Hazel; Densen, James. "How Business Treats Its Environment." *Business and Society Review* 33 (Spring 1980): 56–65.

Rieder, George A. "The Role of Tomorrow's Manager." *Personnel Administrator* 24 (December 1979): 27–31.

Rosen, Gerald R. "Can the Corporation Survive?" *Dun's Review* 114 (August 1979): 40–42.

Stout, Russell. "Formal Theory and the Flexible Organization." *Advance Management* 446 (Winter 1981): 44–52.

Wooton, Leland M. "The Mixed Blessings of Contingency Management." *Academy of Management Review* (July 1977): 431–441.

PART

II

Planning and Decision Making

KEY TERMS

planning process
objectives
plans
strategic planning
standards
policies
procedures
rules
reactive planning
forecasting
performance results standards
process standards

LEARNING OBJECTIVES

After completing this chapter you should be able to:

1. Describe the planning process.
2. Explain the types of organizational objectives a firm must consider.
3. Explain the strategic planning process.
4. Define standards and recognize the various types of standards that may be established.
5. Distinguish among a policy, a procedure, and a rule.
6. Describe the concept of reactive planning and its importance to a business person.

3

Objectives and Plans

As production foreman for Stoner Manufacturing, Michelle Richards is responsible for ensuring that the scheduled weekly production quota she receives every Monday morning is successfully accomplished. In order to ensure that each item on the quota sheet is completed, Michelle must carefully schedule the activities of each of her workers for the entire week. Failure to plan properly the weekly activities can result in overproduction or underproduction.

As president of Duran Electronics, Rodney Odom is responsible for implementing the objectives of the organization. He recognizes that if the firm is to achieve its goal of being a leader in the industry, many projects must be planned now if they are to be implemented in the future. Today he is working on the plans for a new plant that will not go into production for five years.

As with Michelle and Rodney, all business people need to be effective planners. No matter what product or service an organization provides, the need for proper planning remains. In this chapter, the planning process is discussed first. Next, we describe organizational objectives. This is followed by a discussion of strategic planning and a description of standards, policies, procedures, and rules. The intent of the chapter is to provide students with an appreciation of the importance of the effective planner, regardless of whether the planner is a company president, a first-line supervisor, or a manager of a small business.

Insights to Success

Unless an individual has a logical, formal technique for problem solving, he will flounder in wheel-spinning.

MARVIN F. GADE, Executive Vice-President, Kimberly-Clark Corporation

THE PLANNING PROCESS: AN OVERVIEW

planning process

Determining objectives and the courses of action needed to obtain these objectives is referred to as the **planning process.** The planning process presented in Figure 3-1 serves as a guide for the entire chapter. This process is appropriate whether planning is done by upper- or lower-level management.

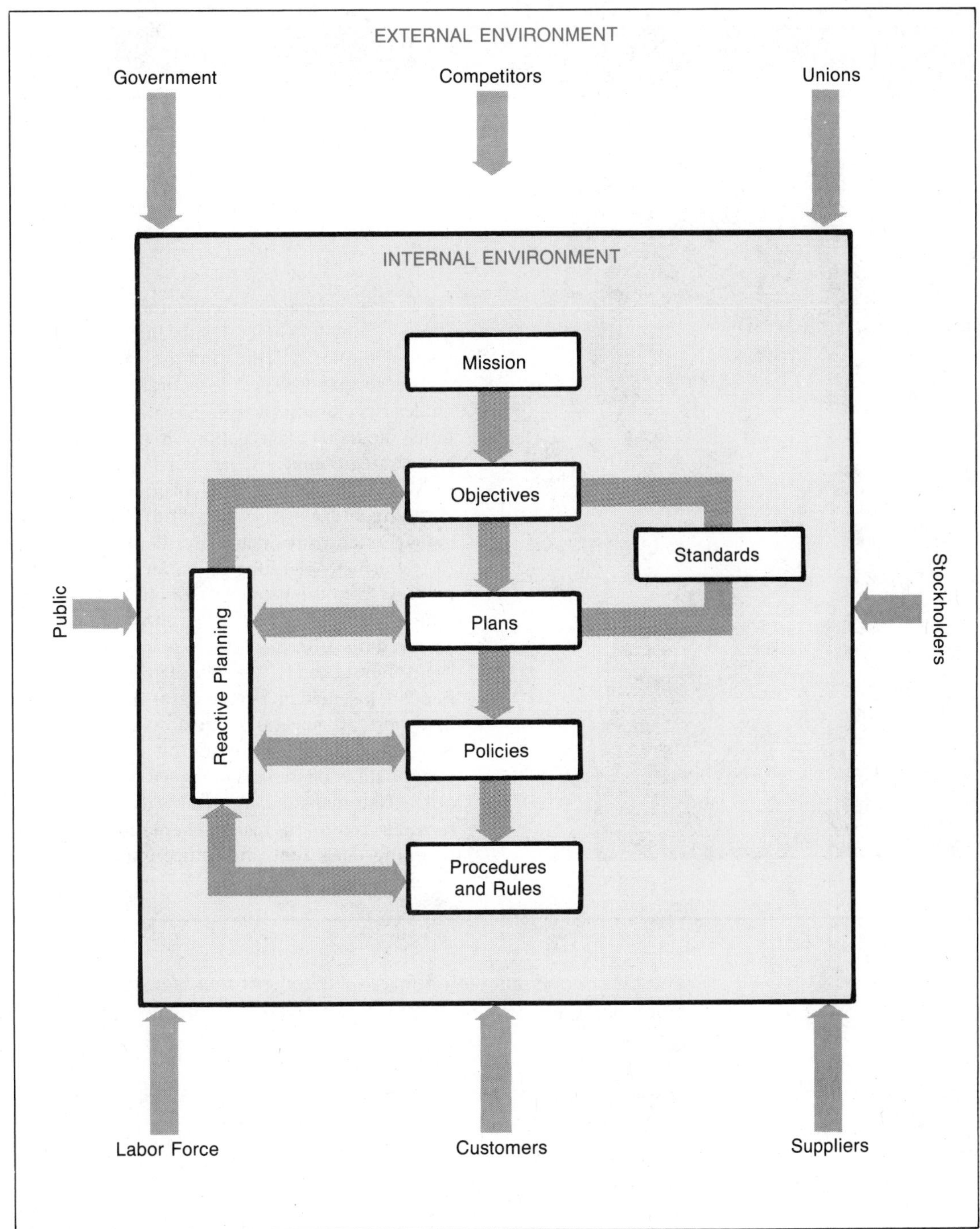

FIGURE 3-1 *The Planning Process*

•CAREER PROFILE•

JAMES F. OLSON
Manager of Corporate Strategic Planning
General Mills, Inc.

General Mills

As manager of corporate strategic planning for General Mills, Inc., James Olson is responsible for coordinating the various elements of the annual five-year corporate plan. This includes developing planning assumptions, instructions, financial aggregation, issue identification, and strategic analysis. James reports to the vice-president and director of corporate growth and planning and works closely with division general managers and subsidiary presidents of more than forty business planning units. Mr. Olson obtained his B.A. from the University of Minnesota in 1962, with a degree in industrial psychology. In 1965, he received his MBA from Kansas University.

When asked, "What is planning?" James replied, "Most managers at General Mills would agree that there are several dimensions to planning and that any definition of planning would include a combination of these factors. First, it is a philosophy. GMI management firmly believes that planning is a continuous management function. Second, planning deals with the future impact of current

The process begins with a mission statement that is a statement of the reason for being in business. The mission statement of General Motors, for example, is to provide transportation. Each managerial level in the organization has a mission—its reason for existence.

objectives

Objectives or goals that serve as the desired end results can be established once the mission statement is determined. Objectives are set at each managerial level in the organization. However, lower-level objectives must be consistent with upper-level objectives.

plans

Plans are then developed to specify the manner in which objectives are to be accomplished. Plans tell us how the desired end results are to be achieved. Determining how organizational objectives will be achieved is referred to as **strategic planning.** Planning is important at each managerial level.

strategic planning

decisions. Managers examine the current business climate and select a course of action depending upon their perception of the future environment. Third, planning is a process. The process begins with the development of objectives, defines the strategies to achieve the objectives, and develops plans to make sure that the strategies are carried out to accomplish the objectives. Fourth, it is a structure of plans. It is a structure that integrates strategic plans from areas of corporate responsibility with plans from business units, industry areas, and with the corporation as a whole."

He also says, "The fundamental purpose of GMI's strategic planning process is to provide the framework for developing a common understanding and agreement among all levels of management on basic objectives and broad strategies for each planning entity within the corporation and for the corporation as a whole. This purpose is accomplished when corporate management has achieved a relative degree of comfort with the proposed plans of the managers and when it has come to grips with such issues as:

1. Whether proper goals have been developed.
2. Whether the corporation is properly organized for achieving its goals.
3. Whether major areas of longer-term concern or opportunity have been identified and are being properly addressed."

When asked what he believed had to have contributed to the development of an effective planning process and to quality planning within General Mills, James identified these eleven aspects of strategic planning, which he regards as fundamental to effective long-term management:

1. Match planning with the organizational structure.
2. Plan continuously.
3. Identify key issues.
4. Include competitive developments.
5. Keep it simple.
6. Secure the full involvement of top decision makers.
7. Review every plan.
8. Compose the review group of top decision makers.
9. Use contingency planning.
10. Know the purpose of planning.

---

standards

Standards permit us to determine whether our own objectives in the form of plans have been achieved. Standards are norms, or criteria, to which something can be compared. A plan may be developed to enable sales to be increased by 10 percent. This 10 percent then becomes a standard by which performance can be compared.

policies

Policies are predetermined, general guides established to provide direction in decision making. Policies are based upon a thorough analysis of corporate objectives. They help in the achievement of plans. Each level of management can establish policies; however, lower-level policies must be in agreement with higher-level policies.

procedures
rules

Procedures and **rules** are created to assist in the implementation of plans. Procedures are a series of steps created to assist in the accomplishment of some special project or endeavor. Rules are very specific and detailed guides to action, set up to direct or restrict the action in a fairly narrow manner. There may be a rule that prohibits smoking in certain work areas, for example.

The successful planner does not operate in a vacuum and must be flexible enough to respond to changing external and internal conditions. When managers at any level prepare to adjust to unanticipated occurrences, they are using **reactive planning.** Reactive planning can occur at any phase of the planning process.

reactive planning

The planning process is dynamic and should be constantly evaluated and modified to conform to the current and anticipated situation.

Tex Schramm, president and general manager of the Dallas Cowboys, provides an excellent illustration of a manager who recognizes the value of planning. He states, "My team's objective is to win, and win consistently." His long-range plan involves creating an environment to accomplish this objective. Management stability is emphasized as part of the plan. Apparently this approach has worked; the Cowboys have consistently been in the National Football League playoffs, and since their beginning in 1960, there has been but one coach, Tom Landry. The player personnel director and many of the assistant coaches also have been with the team for a long period. Tex says about the Cowboys, "It is our policy to allow people to work in their area of expertise and use their initiative to gain not only team and organizational success, but individual recognition." Coach Landry provides each player with a team play book that covers in detail offensive and defensive formations as well as individual assignments. All phases of the planning process relate to the objective of winning consistently.

ORGANIZATIONAL OBJECTIVES

As described by Tex Schramm in the illustration provided above, his primary objective is to develop a team that wins consistently. This goal establishes the end result that management desires. After watching a successful team play an average team on Sunday, one sometimes wonders if the objectives of both teams are the same.

Objectives affect the size, shape, and design of the organization, and they are important in motivating and directing personnel. In order to appreciate the importance of objectives in an organization, the types of objectives that a firm may consider will next be discussed. This will be followed by a presentation of the process of establishing objectives and goal complexities that a firm must consider.

Types of Objectives

The creation of specific organizational objectives is no simple task. As we discussed in Chapter 2, numerous external factors exert their influence on a firm. These external considerations are competition, stockholders-owners, customers, unions, suppliers, the labor force, the public, and government. Because of these external factors, an organization usually has more than one objective, and the emphasis may change depending on the impact of a particular environmental factor or group of factors that is present. At least three main types of objectives can be identified for the business firm in our society:

- **Economic objectives**—survival, profit, and growth
- **Service objectives**—creation of economic value for society
- **Personal objectives**—goals of individuals and groups within the organization

Economic Objectives

The desire to survive is a basic objective of all organizations. It is the one goal common to all firms. Whether an organization is producing a desired economic value or not seems to take second place to just staying alive. It is difficult for a firm to take into account higher societal objectives when it is not known whether the next payroll can be met. As an anonymous statesman once said, "It is extremely difficult to think that your initial objective was to drain the swamp when you are up to your neck in alligators."

In order to survive, a firm must at least *break even*—that is, it must generate enough revenues at least to cover costs. But business firms want more than mere survival—they are in business to make a profit. Profit provides a vital incentive for the continued, successful operation of the business enterprise. "What is an adequate profit?" This primarily depends on the industry and the specific needs of an organization.

Growth may also be a major objective of a firm. Growth may ensure survival in the long run. In an effort to avoid failure, a company may seek unrestricted growth, and sometimes this growth can become an end in itself. When this happens, the company may become blind to the goal of economic service. There are, of course, certain economic advantages that come with size, and many companies see growth as a way of competing more effectively in the marketplace. But if the products manufactured cannot fulfill an economic value, the growth will eventually prove to be useless.

Service Objectives

Profit alone is often viewed as the primary motive for being in business. While it is true a firm cannot survive for long without making a profit, the old question, "Which comes first, the chicken or the egg?" may have meaning when discussing the profit versus the service objective. If a firm cannot consistently create economic value for society, it will not stay in business long enough to make a profit. Many firms have gone out of existence when they ceased to produce goods and services that were desired by society. To accomplish the economic objective, a firm must produce goods the consumer wants. The creation of economic value constitutes the major goal of organizations within our economic system.

TABLE 3-1. ***Possible Goal Differences between the Organization and Groups Who Have Contact with the Firm***

Groups	Possible Goal
Organization	Maximize profits
Management	Promotions, higher salaries, or bonuses
Employees	Increased wages and bonuses
Government	Adherence of firm to all government legislation, laws, and regulations
Competition	Attain a greater share of the market
Customers	Quality product at lowest price
Stockholders/owners	Higher dividends
Public	Protection of the environment
Unions	Greater influence for union members

Personal Objectives

Organizations are made up of people who have different personalities, backgrounds, experiences, and goals. Most likely, their personal goals are not always identical to the objectives of the organization. If the difference in goals is significant, the employee may choose to withdraw from the firm. However, withdrawal does not necessarily mean departure from the organization. For instance, an employee may not feel that he or she can financially afford to leave the firm. A major difference between the employee's goals and the organization's goals can result in minimum work effort, absenteeism, and even sabotage. Employees are not the only ones whose goals, when they differ from those of the organization, can affect that organization. For instance, a stockholder can cease to provide support for the organization by selling his or her stock.

If the organization is to survive, grow, and earn a profit, it must attempt to provide a match between its goals and the goals of groups who have contact with the firm. Some possible goal differences between the organization and these various groups may be seen in Table 3-1. It is not unusual for particular groups or members to feel their personal goals are in conflict with the goals of other individuals related to the organization. For instance, some customers may believe that higher wages will make the prices of products higher, while the union may believe that stockholders' profits are too high. Management has the difficult task of reconciling these conflicts, whether or not they are real.

Establishing Objectives

Objectives are established based upon the mission statement and the desires of the owners and stockholders. It is the organizational members who provide the strength of a firm, and these members are the ones who establish objectives. However, because of the wide diversity of personalities, backgrounds, experiences, and the personal goals that exist among individuals, objectives of firms may differ, even though a similar product is produced. Sometimes, it is forgotten that people, as opposed to some unknown organizational force, create these goals.

The person or persons charged with the responsibility of establishing corporate objectives vary from business to business. At times, the president or chairman of the board provides the major thrust in goal creation. At other times, a group of top-level executives are consulted in the creation of corporate goals. Whatever the source, these objectives provide the course toward which future energies of the firm will be directed.

Objectives should be well thought out and concisely stated. They should not constrain lower management to the degree that no further decision mak-

Planning is important at all levels in the organization.

Insights to Success

Be patient. Work hard. *Be a doer!* Always look for things to improve—*then improve them.* Don't sit back and wait to be told to do everything. At the end of the work day ask yourself—"What did I do today to help the company become more competitive?" Granted—the answer at times is "nothing," BUT IT WORKS.

DALE R. MCCRACKEN, Vice-President—Manufacturing, Champion Spark Plug Company

ing is possible. An objective permits the greatest possible freedom for lower-level management while still providing direction to achieve a specified end result. An example of well-thought-out objectives may be seen in Table 3-2.

Effective goal creation also requires priorities that may not be altered too frequently. Obviously, major decisions have far-reaching and drastic effects on areas such as the type of personnel required, the style of management, and the type of organizational structure. For instance, a firm dedicated to maintaining a high-quality product needs to recruit individuals capable of achiev-

TABLE 3-2. ***Robertshaw Controls Company Corporate Goals 197–***

1. Minimize historical trends in sales and profits.
   (Objective: 10 percent profit before tax is necessary to assure adequate stockholder return and reinvestment in corporate growth.)
2. Increase Robertshaw's sales and profits in the international market.
   (Objective: 10 percent minimum annual profit growth assures compounding profitability and established positive trend line.)
3. Increase utilization of stockholders' equity through return on assets and return on investment justification.
   (Objective: 10–15 percent annual sales growth is required to double the sales of the corporation every five to eight years.)
4. Review all product lines and products that cannot justify continuance based on ROA.
   (Objective: Within the broad parameters of sensors and associated controls, Robertshaw can develop adequate diversification and maximize inhouse abilities and expertise.
5. Establish corporate and divisional financial standards.
   (Objective: To evaluate and justify investments in new or old areas of opportunity to verify the potential for the corporation to achieve an industry position of no less than third.)
6. Develop improved consumer awareness and recognition of Robertshaw.
   (Objective: The criteria for growth must include favorable corporate identity at the consumer and investor levels.)

Source: Y. K. Shetty, "New Look at Corporate Goals." © 1979 by the Regents of the University of California. Reprinted from *California Management Review,* vol. 22, no. 2, p. 72, by permission of the Regents and the Company. Used also with permission of Robertshaw Controls Company.

ing the goal of quality. Also, a more participative structure may be required to keep skilled employees. Thus, once a corporate objective has been stated, the effects of the decision will be felt throughout the organization for a long time.

Problems Encountered in Establishing Objectives

Numerous difficulties can arise when creating objectives. Here are three types of conflict.

Real versus Stated Objectives

The *real* goals of any organization may be at odds with the *stated* goals. Objectives are often the result of power plays and pressures that come from circumstances in the marketplace or from internal tensions. The personal goals of the board of directors, outside creditors, lower-level managers, employees, stockholders, and labor unions are bound to be different. Because of these differences, the stated goals are at times different from the actual goals of the organizations. Goals are often significantly altered by individuals and groups who seek to adapt the organization to their narrower purposes.

To determine the real goals of an organization, one must look at the actual decisions and actions that occur day-to-day. A manager's actions speak louder than words. What functions or groups actually receive the major share of the resources? What type of behavior is accorded the greatest rewards by management? If the administration of a prison, for example, specifies its major goal as rehabilitation of prisoners but has only two counselors on its payroll while it employs five hundred guards, the facts go against the stated goal.

Multiple Objectives

At times, an organization may have multiple and sometimes conflicting real goals that must be recognized by management. For instance, what is the major service goal of a university? Is the primary objective of the university to provide education for students, or to conduct research to advance the state of knowledge, or to provide community service? In some universities, research is given the first priority in money, personnel, and privilege. In others, the teaching goal is dominant. In still others, an attempt is made *to be all things to all people.* However, given limited funds, priorities must be established in most cases. One can debate the priority of goals for such institutions as a mental hospital (therapy or confinement); a church (religion or social relationships); a prison (rehabilitation or confinement); a vocational high school (skill development, general education, or keeping young people off the streets); a medical school (training medical students for clinical practice, basic research, or academic medicine); and an aerospace firm (research information or usable hardware). At some point, choices must be made.

Goal Distortion

The more quantitative the goal, the greater the attention and pressure for its accomplishment. Production managers must meet specific quotas and schedules; personnel managers often have more subjective goals and, consequently, less pressure. If the most important goal is also the most measurable, as with the goal of winning with a professional sports team, then little distortion will take place. If the reverse is true, the organization is likely to be pushed in the direction of more quantitative, but perhaps less important, goals. In universities, research and publication are far easier to measure precisely than excellence in teaching. The primary goal of excellence in education may be replaced with the research emphasis.

PLANNING

Plans are developed to specify the manner in which objectives are to be accomplished. Referring back to the Robertshaw Controls Company corporate goals (Table 3-2), one of the objectives was to achieve a 10 percent profit before tax. Stating an objective does not mean that it will automatically be accomplished. A plan must be developed to tell managers what to do in order to fulfill the goal. New products might be added in hopes of increasing profit, or a cost-effectiveness program might be undertaken. There is more than one way to fulfill a goal. The plan states how the goal is to be achieved.

Many business people are not good planners. They are often active, energetic individuals who have become accustomed to making rapid decisions and putting out daily fires. Because of this, they often find it difficult to force themselves to think far into the future. But planning is a task that every manager, whether a top-level executive or a first-line supervisor, should perform.

STRATEGIC PLANNING

The determination of how the organizational objectives will be achieved is referred to as *strategic planning*. In essence, there are two basic stages of strategic planning—determining the strategy and developing the specific plans to implement the strategy. Long-range strategic planning has been said to cover a time frame typically extending five years or more into the future. Of course, this can vary depending on the purpose of the organization and the technology of the industry. For instance, it may be unrealistic for a professional football team to plan five years into the future. Too many factors can change: a star player can be sidelined by injury or a player may develop much faster than expected. A long-range plan for two or three years may be more realistic.

On the other hand, long-range strategic planning for some manufacturing firms may be in excess of ten years and for the forestry products industry, some thirty or forty years. Thus, long-range planning depends, to a large extent, on how far the organization can look into the future with a reasonable expectation of being accurate. What should be the strategic plan of Dr Pepper, since they have a goal of being number one in the soft drink industry? Should they diversify into other soft drinks, add new product lines other than soft drinks, add new plants, and/or expand into international markets?

Logic suggests that the firm that establishes an overall long-range strategic plan will be more effective than one that does not develop such a plan. This tends to be supported by the tendency for long-range planning to receive increased emphasis among business firms. For example, Stewart Hall, president of PROBE, Incorporated, an executive search firm, states, "More and more clients are coming to me with a priority requirement that the top-level executives they are seeking must have a strong background in strategic planning and forecasting." Another significant trend that illustrates the importance of strategic planning is the fact that numerous companies have established

TABLE 3-3. *Long-range Planning Projects*

Primary Products of Firm Studied	Type of Planning Projects
Automotive tires	Effects of energy crisis New product diversification Ailing product lines
Computers	New business markets Acquisitions Venture analysis
Aircrafts	New products
Natural gas	Acquisitions Raw materials supply Diversification
Catalog order and retail department store	Expansion of facility Corporate financing Marketing direction
Railroad transportation	Major construction project Capital expenditures Market growth
Steel	Overall industry or business capital Spending policies and trends Timing of major investment
Pharmaceuticals	Plant location planning New product development Overall business strategy
Cosmetics and toiletries	Expansion New business Resource allocation
Petroleum	Finding new energy sources New and expanded petrochemical plants Technology and personnel needs
Tobacco products	New project development Capital planning New business entry

formal planning departments for the purpose of developing three-, five-, and ten-year plans for their organizations. In fact, over 100 of the top 500 U.S. firms in sales have actually specified a position of vice-president of planning. Many of the remaining companies have top-level executives with titles relating to corporate planning and development.

The specific tasks to be accomplished in strategic planning are determined by corporate objectives and the type of business in which the firm is engaged. Gary R. Miller, director of corporate planning for Morrison-Knudsen Company, Incorporated, a construction, engineering, and real estate development corporation, says that one of the biggest tasks that an organization has is to develop an understanding of what long-range planning is and what it can do, not only for the corporation but for the individual. Specific projects for which strategic planning is actually being used may be seen in Table 3-3. As one might expect, the type of projects varies according to the company involved. As can be seen, the particular planning projects tend to be directed toward accomplishment of overall company objectives. Each phase of the strategic planning process may be seen in Figure 3-2.

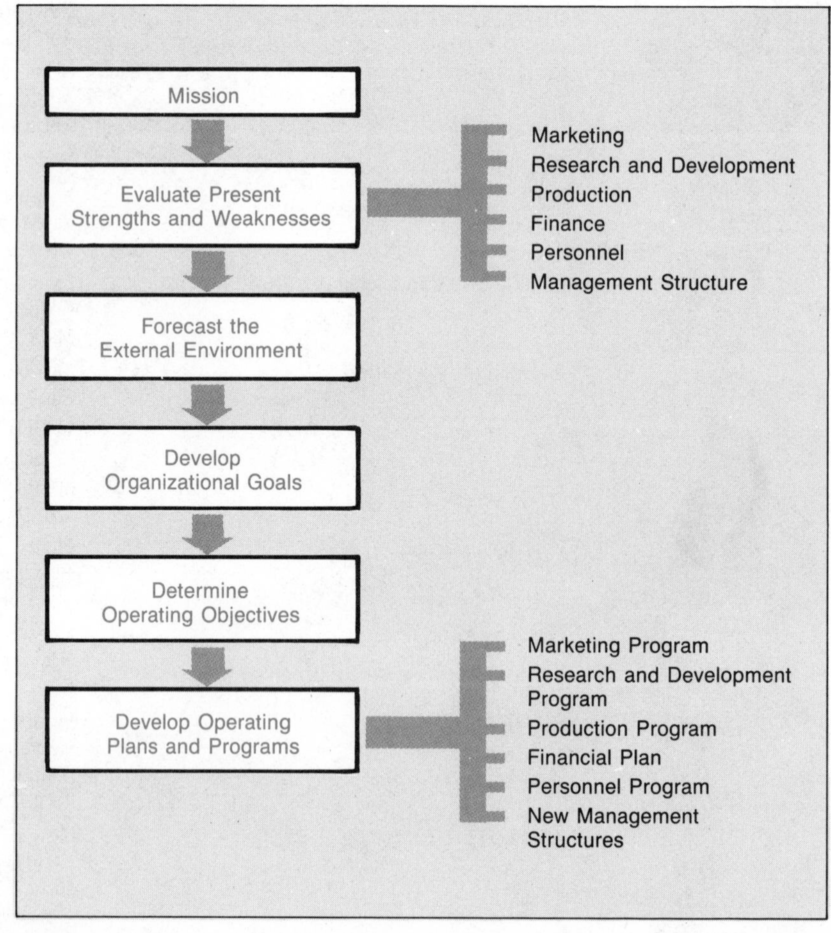

FIGURE 3-2

Strategic Planning Sequence

Mission

The starting point for all strategic planning begins with the determination of the mission or purpose for which the firm was established. The mission must be clearly understood. For instance, the mission of General Motors is to provide quality transportation. An electrical generating plant is created to provide power to the customer. This means that if a firm is to survive in the long run, it must provide some benefit to society.

Evaluate Present Strengths and Weaknesses

The next step in the strategic planning process is to analyze the present strengths and weaknesses of the firm. This involves an analysis of resources necessary for the accomplishment of these objectives—personnel, materials, money, physical plant, and machines. The strength/weakness evaluation should encourage the firm to be more reasonable in their expectations. If, for example, one of its strengths is strong management talent, this quality should be incorporated into strategic planning. For instance, E-Systems, Incorporated, has obtained numerous government contracts because it has gained a reputation of possessing strong management talent and effective planning systems. An analysis of a firm's strengths and weaknesses will permit planners to reformulate long-term goals. This competence profile may well lead to an alteration of the kind of business the firm will pursue.

Forecast the External Environment

forecasting

An attempt to project what will occur in the future is referred to as **forecasting.** It is of critical importance in the next phase of strategic planning when the long-range goals are reformulated. In this stage, an attempt to identify the external opportunities and threats to the firm is being made. Hopefully, the forecasted environment will match the strengths of the firm. At times, this is not the case, and a firm's long-term goals must be modified. For instance, it would do little good to have the strengths that are needed to manufacture a high-quality engineering slide rule (the hand electronic calculators have virtually made them extinct) when the forecast for demand for slide rules is on the downward trend. Specific forecasting techniques are described in Chapter 15.

Develop Organizational Goals

Once the firm is aware of the organization's strengths and weaknesses and has forecast the environment associated with the company, the firm is then in a position to develop its long-term goals. These goals are developed in view of both the strengths of the firm and the forecasted environment. If the strengths are not consistent with the changes predicted in the environment, certain capabilities of the firm may need to be developed in order for the objectives to be achieved.

Determine Operating Objectives

Once the long-term goals of the organization have been identified, the objectives of each of the functional departments such as marketing, production, finance, personnel, and research may be identified. If the goal of the organization is to be a leader in its field, marketing's goal, for instance, may be to increase sales by 20 percent. All functional goals must contribute to the accomplishment of organizational goals.

Develop Operating Plans and Programs

Operating plans and programs for each function are next developed. In marketing, key decisions should be made concerning such factors as product mix, sales promotion, advertising, and pricing. With respect to production, plans and programs would relate to changing technology, flexibility of present facilities, and inventory levels. Certainly research and development programs play a key part in determining the type of products the firm will be able to offer in the years ahead. Plans concerning personnel should cover needed future skills and the skill level of current employees.

Programs developed for all of the above resources obviously require financing. Perhaps the greatest restraint is the availability of money to implement the total long-range program. Profit planning, retention of earnings, and development of short- and long-range capital resources are all important elements of this plan.

Finally, the management or administrative plan must be developed. Proposed organizational structures should be designed with the emphasis on the types of decisions necessary to accomplish the tasks required by the program. In locating the appropriate decision maker, key concern is with the importance of the decision as indicated by the amount of money involved, the number of organizational units affected, the duration of the effect of the decision, and the possibility of reversing it once it is made. In addition, a control system must be designed to provide operating information so that corrections may be made when actions and environment are significantly different from the planned program.

PLANNING FOR OPERATING MANAGERS

All too often a discussion of planning is directed toward the benefits top management may derive through the use of the planning function. Sometimes we forget that all effective managers engage in planning. The planning process for both top-level and operating managers is quite similar. However, since the operating manager is lower in the organization, his or her external environment is comprised largely of company factors. A lower-level manager must develop plans that will fit within the overall company objectives and strategies, but the importance of planning remains.

As we discussed in Chapter 1, the amount of time spent in the planning function at lower levels of management may not be as great as at higher levels. For instance, a lower-level manager may devote a much larger percentage of his or her time to influencing or controlling. However, this does not diminish the importance of planning. Also, the time frame for long-range planning for lower-level managers may be shortened. Top-level management must make decisions far into the future to be successful, but to ask a lower-level manager to think five years into the future may be unrealistic. Daily, weekly, monthly, and annual quotas must be met. It is quite possible that long-range planning for some managers may encompass a relatively short time span. However, the shorter time span does not diminish the importance of long-range planning.

STANDARDS

A norm, or criterion, to which something can be compared, is referred to as a standard. Standards are created to specify what constitutes proper behavior and conditions. They permit us to determine whether our objectives in the form of plans have been achieved. As such, they provide the link between planning and controlling. Referring once again to Figure 3-1, it can be seen that standards provide a way for determining if a plan is being properly implemented. It would be foolish to establish objectives and not be able to determine if they have been achieved. But, as will be described in Chapter 14, standards provide the starting point for the controlling process.

TABLE 3-4. *Examples of Standards*

Type of Standard	Example
Performance Results	
Quantity	Forty units should be produced each day
Quality	Each part should weigh 3 pounds ± 2 ounces
Time	Project is scheduled for completion by January 1
Cost	Labor costs should not exceed $2 per unit
Process	
Function	The procedure in handbook A-1 should be followed when writing up a sales order
Personnel	The probationary period for new employees is three months
Physical factors	Only two workers at a time are permitted in the security area

performance results standards

process standards

In business, standards can be created to cover virtually every aspect of a situation. Standards can be divided into two main categories. When it is relatively simple to specify what end result is desired, they are classified as **performance results standards.** On the other hand, if we are attempting to evaluate a function for which specific standards are difficult or impossible to formulate, they are referred to as **process standards.** Examples of each type of standard may be seen in Table 3-4.

Performance Results Standards

The major topics to be evaluated regarding performance results relate to

1. The quality of work
2. The quantity of work
3. The time needed to complete work
4. The cost of work

Quality standards are usually derived from the function of product or service design. For a physical product, examples would include form, dimensions, strength, color, and durability. Often quality control inspectors are utilized to collect information from production and compare it with engineering-established requirements.

Quantity standards relate to the number of items produced during a specific time period. For instance, a time study may result in a requirement for fifty units per hour to be produced by a certain machine operator. An employment interviewer for a personnel agency may be required to place a minimum of fifteen applicants a week. In automobile assembly plants, the standard might be sixty automobiles produced each hour on the assembly line.

Standards governing *time* are often related to the quantity standards as shown in the examples above. The most common example of a time standard relates to completion of a report on a particular date. For example, a periodic accounting report will be submitted to managers by the tenth of each month.

Cost standards are established to ensure that a project is completed within set cost limits. These standards are extremely important, for it is an embarrassing situation to complete a project on time only to find that the costs are significantly higher than expected and they wipe out whatever profits might have been realized. The annual and monthly *budgets* constitute a well-known example of cost standards. Standard cost systems are also designed to enable the manager to make more effective decisions governing ongoing action.

Process Standards

Sometimes it is difficult or impossible to establish accurate standards of performance. When this occurs, process standards should be used. This type of standard relates to: personnel standards, functional standards, and physical factors standards.

Even though one may not be able to establish accurate standards of performance, one may attempt to specify and control performance through process standards. For example, a firm may try to hire a person for a particular job who possesses the highest qualifications; this would be a standard of personnel. Or the firm may develop standards for the best content (job description) and method (standard operating procedure) for executing the job. These are standards of function. Finally, standards that attempt to provide superior physical factors in terms of equipment, lighting, ventilation, privacy, and the like may be drawn up. These are physical factors standards. The operating assumption here is that the best people, using the latest in methodology and equipment, might result in maximum efficiency without having to establish specific standards of quality, quantity, time, and cost.

POLICIES

A policy is a predetermined, general course or guide established to provide direction in decision making. As such, it should be based on a thorough analysis of corporate objectives. Policies cover the important areas of a firm such as personnel, marketing, research and development, production, and finance.

To formulate policies, the manager must have knowledge of, and skill in, the area for which the policy is being created. However, there are certain generalizations that apply to the establishment of policies. The most important has already been stated: policies must be based on a thorough analysis of objectives. There are several other general principles that can help the manager create appropriate policies.

1. *Policies should be based on known principles and, as much as possible, on facts and truth.* For instance, it is a fact that Congress has passed the Age Discrimination Act. It is not a fact that a satisfied employee is a higher producer.
2. *Subordinate policies should be supplementary, not contradictory, to superior policies.* A policy for a company division should not directly conflict with a corporate policy.
3. *Policies of different divisions or departments should be coordinated.* They should be directed toward overall organization optimization instead of optimizing a particular department such as sales, engineering, purchasing, or production, to the detriment of the whole.
4. *Policies should be definite, understandable, and preferably in writing.* If a policy is to guide actions, persons concerned must be aware of its existence, and this requires creating understandable directives in a definitive written form. These sets of guides constitute the memory of the organization, which it uses to help cope with future events.
5. *Policies should be flexible and stable.* The requirements of policy stability and flexibility are not contradictory; one is a prerequisite to the

TABLE 3-5. *Armco Policies*

Ethics	To do business guided and governed by the highest standards of conduct so the end result of action taken makes a good reputation an invaluable and permanent asset.
Square deal	To insist on a square deal always. To make sure people are listened to and treated fairly, so that men and women really do right for right's sake and not just to achieve a desired result. For everyone to go beyond narrowness, littleness, selfishness in order to get the job done.
Organization	To develop and maintain an efficient, loyal, aggressive organization, who believe in their company, to whom work is a challenge and to whom extraordinary accomplishment is a personal goal.
Working conditions	To create and maintain good working conditions . . . to provide the best possible equipment and facilities . . . and plants and offices that are clean, orderly, and safe.
Quality and service	To adopt "Quality and Service" as an everyday practice. Quality will be the highest attainable in products, organization, plant, property, and equipment. Service will be the best possible to customers, to shareholders, to city, state, and nation.
Opportunity	To employ people without regard to race, sex, religion, or national origin. To encourage employees to improve their skills by participating in available educational or training programs. To provide every possible opportunity for advancement so that each individual may reach his or her highest potential.
Compensation	To provide not only fair remuneration, but the best compensation for service rendered that it is possible to pay under the changing economic, commercial, and other competitive conditions that exist from time to time. It is Armco's ambition to develop an organization of such spirit, loyalty, and efficiency that can and will secure results which will make it possible for individual members to earn and receive better compensation than would be possible if performing a similar service in other fields of effort.
Incentive	To provide realistic and practical incentive as a means of encouraging the highest standard of individual performance and to assure increased quantity and quality of performance.
Cooperation	To recognize cooperation as the medium through which great accomplishments are attained. Success depends more on a spirit of helpful cooperation than on any other one factor.
Objectivity	To always consider what is right and best for the business as a whole, rather than what may be expedient in dealing with a single, separate situation.
Conflict of interest	To prohibit employees from becoming financially interested in any company with which Armco does business, if such financial interest might possibly influence decisions employees must make in their areas of responsibility. The above policy does not apply to ownership in publicly owned companies. This is not considered a conflict of interest but, rather, is encouraged as part of the free enterprise system.

TABLE 3-5 *(continued)*

Citizenship	To create and maintain a working partnership between industry and community in this country and throughout the world. To support constructive agencies in communities where Armco people live and work in an effort to create civic conditions that respond to the highest needs of the citizens.

Used with permission from the Armco Steel Corporation.

other. Stable policy changes only in response to fundamental and basic changes in conditions. Government regulations can represent such a basic change in conditions that they can have a major impact on a firm's employment policies. The higher the organizational level, the more stable the policy must be. Changing the direction of the enterprise is a much more complex and time-consuming task than changing the direction of a department or section. The higher the organizational level, the more policy resembles principle and, conversely, the lower the level, the more it resembles or becomes a rule. The Armco Steel Corporation provides an excellent example of a firm whose policies have been remarkably stable. First formulated in 1919, these policies, outlined in Table 3-5, are still applicable today.

6. *Policies should be reasonably comprehensive in scope.* Policies conserve the executive's time by making available a previously determined decision. The manager should organize the work in such a way that subordinate personnel can handle the routine and predictable work, while he or she devotes time to the exceptional events and problems. If the body of policies is reasonably comprehensive, the cases that arise that are not covered by policy constitute exceptions.

Qualities Needed for Success as a Manager in Your Organization

- **Retain a good sense of humor. If you can't have a little levity mixed with the business, forget it.**
- **Be demanding, but be reasonable. Set a goal of being in the top 25% of your industry in terms of financial performance.**
- **Don't get in "Fool's Heaven" in times of prosperity, particularly if you are in a cyclical business. Keep the team lean and hungry in both good and bad times.**
- **Set an example of good work habits. Don't expect anybody to work harder than you do. Never "get your dauber down" in front of your people.**

GERALD L. "BUD" PEARSON, President and CEO, Spencer Foods, Incorporated

TABLE 3-6. *Examples of Policies, Procedures, and Rules*

Policy: It is the policy of the company that every employee is entitled to a safe and healthful place in which to work and desires to prevent accidents from occurring in any phase of its operation. Toward this end the full cooperation of all employees will be required.

Management will view neglect of safety policy or program as just cause for disciplinary action.

Procedure: The purpose of this procedure is to prevent injury to personnel or damage to equipment by inadvertent starting, energizing, or pressurizing equipment that has been shut down for maintenance, overhaul, lubrication, or setup.

1. Each maintenance man assigned to work on a job will lock out the machine at the proper disconnect with his own safety lock and keep the key in his possession.
2. If he does not finish the job before shift change he will remove his lock and put a seal on the disconnect. He will hang a danger tag on the control station, stating why the equipment is shut down.
3. The maintenance man who will be coming on the following shift will place his lock on the disconnect along with seal.
4. Upon completion of the repairs the area foreman will be notified by maintenance that work is completed.
5. The foreman and the maintenance man will check the equipment to see that all guards and safety devices are securely in place and operable. Then the *foreman* will break the seal and remove the danger tag from the machine.

Rules: The following rules are intended to promote employee safety.

1. The company and each employee are required to comply with provisions of the Occupational Safety and Health Act (OSHA). You will be informed by your supervisor on specific OSHA rules not covered here that apply to your job or area.
2. Report all accidents promptly that occur on the job or on company premises—this should be done whether or not any injury or damage resulted from the incident.
3. Horseplay, practical jokes, wrestling, throwing things, running in the plant and similar actions will not be tolerated as they can cause serious accidents.
4. Observe all warning signs, such as "No Smoking," "Stop," etc. They are there for your protection.
5. Keep your mind on the work being performed.
6. Familiarize yourself with the specific safety rules and precautions that relate to your work area.
7. Approved eye protection must be worn in all factory and research lab areas during scheduled working hours or at any other time work is being performed.
8. Hearing protection is required when the noise level in an area reaches limits established by OSHA.
9. Adequate hand protection should be worn while working with solvents or other materials that might be harmful to hands.
10. Wearing rings or other jewelry that could cause injury is not allowed for persons performing work in the factory area.
11. Good housekeeping is important to accident prevention. Keep your immediate work area, machinery, and equipment clean. Keep tools and materials neatly and securely stored so that they will not cause injury to you or others.

TABLE 3-6 (*continued*)

12. Aisles, fire equipment access, and other designated "clear" areas must not be blocked.
13. Learn the correct way to lift. Get help if the material to be lifted is too heavy to be lifted alone. Avoid an effort that is likely to injure you.
14. Only authorized employees are allowed to operate forklifts and company vehicles. Passengers are not allowed on lift equipment or other material handling equipment except as required in the performance of a job.
15. Learn the right way to do your job. If you are not sure you thoroughly understand a job, ask for assistance. This will often contribute to your job performance as well as your job safety.
16. Observe safe and courteous driving habits on the parking lot.

PROCEDURES AND RULES

Once broad policies have been established, more specific plans may need to be created to ensure compliance with policy. Procedures and rules might be thought of as further restrictions on the actions of lower-level personnel. They are usually established to ensure adherence to a particular policy. Although the two terms are similar, they will be defined separately.

Procedure

A procedure is a series of steps established for the accomplishment of some specific project or endeavor. For most policies, there is an accompanying procedure to indicate how that policy should be carried out.

Rule

A rule is a very specific and detailed guide to action, which is set up to direct or restrict action in a fairly narrow manner.

An illustration of the differences among policies, procedures, and rules is shown in Table 3-6. As may be seen from the illustration, procedures and rules may overlap as to definition. Taken out of a sequence of steps, a procedure may actually become a rule.

Policies, procedures, and rules are designed to direct action toward the accomplishment of objectives. If we could be assured that the persons doing the work were thoroughly in agreement with, and completely understood, basic objectives, there would be no need for policies, procedures, and rules. Moreover, it is apparent that objectives are at times unclear and even controversial. Thus, all organizations have a need for policies, procedures, and rules that can and should be more definitive and understandable than the objectives on which they are based.

REACTIVE PLANNING

Robert Burns' line, "The best laid plans of mice and men oft go astray," is certainly applicable in today's business world. Events can occur so rapidly that plans may be useless before they can be fully implemented. Even though it is properly developed, external and internal disturbances often occur that can result in a plan's being modified or even eliminated. A prudent manager recognizes that events can occur that were not planned and that he or she must attempt to anticipate these disruptions, and deal effectively with the new conditions these disruptions create. When a manager at any level prepares to adjust to unanticipated occurrences, he or she is using reactive planning.

Oliver R. Kirby, vice-president for advanced planning for E-Systems, Incorporated, summarized the use of reactive planning when he stated, "Reactive planning fills the holes that you don't initially recognize." Clearly, it entails a recognition that unforeseen events can and will occur to alter initial plans. Reactive planning therefore becomes a systematic way of modifying objectives, long-range planning, policies, procedures and rules, and standards to adapt to the real world environment. A manager who uses reactive planning is employing a true situational approach to planning.

Referring again to Figure 3-1, reactive planning encompasses all phases of the planning process. Suppose, for instance, that the competition alters their direction. This change could actually affect the plans of the firm. Reactive planning must quickly take effect, or the firm might be thrown into confusion. Changes in the plans could affect not only long-range planning but also policies, procedures, and rules, and even standards. Examples that reenforce the need for reactive planning are numerous. For instance, a government policy change may have a drastic effect on a long-range business plan; it can even change corporate objectives. Also, an unanticipated stoppage of supplies of a raw material, as with the oil embargo of 1973, certainly will bring reactive planning into play.

Reactive planning does not mean that a firm has to wait for an unanticipated situation to occur before it responds. Management should attempt to anticipate these contingencies as far as possible. Naturally, not all situations can be anticipated, but the manager who tries to anticipate possible deviations will stand a much better chance of coping with the new situation brought about by the deviation.

UNINTENDED SIDE EFFECTS OF PLANS

Few things in life and organizations are absolutely pure and untainted. Every plan is likely to have certain undesired effects, and the manager must not be blinded by all of the possible good results of a plan. Managers must attempt to anticipate the negative as well as the positive results of a plan. In many instances, a possible counterproductive effect of a plan can be headed off by appropriate action. For example, asking for weekly output figures in terms of poundage produced is likely to stimulate frantic juggling of orders to ensure high poundage runs on Thursday and Friday. This, in turn, is likely to lead to missing some delivery promises for smaller poundage orders. Rather than abolish the poundage reports, thereby harming the control function, the manager can ask for such reports on a semimonthly basis. This additional time should provide the flexibility for lower managers to meet both delivery dates and poundage standards. Looking at an important index too frequently can produce some undesirable side effects.

The fact that a plan may have negative effects is not necessarily adequate justification for its abandonment. Management needs to anticipate negative consequences and make special provision for their handling. More subordinate participation can reduce some of the adverse effects, and education, patience, participation, and more effective rewards systems can remove many more of the undesired effects. Specialization cannot be abandoned, but efforts can be undertaken to ensure that various units communicate, coordinate, and work together.

Summary

Determining objectives and the causes of action needed to obtain these objectives is referred to as the planning process. Objectives that serve as the desired end result should be established first. Then plans are developed to specify the manner in which objectives are to be accomplished. Standards are developed to determine if the objectives in the form of plans have been attained. Appropriate policies, procedures, and rules are then created to specify in greater detail the manner in which the plan will be achieved. Yet the successful planner does not operate in a vacuum and must be flexible enough to respond to changing external and internal conditions. This is referred to as reactive planning and must be designed with the system. Thus the planning process is dynamic, and plans should be constantly evaluated and modified to conform to the current and anticipated situations.

The three main types of business objectives are economic, service, and personal. If the organization is to survive, grow, and earn a profit, it attempts to provide a match between its goals and the goals of groups who have contact with the firm. Some of the problems encountered in establishing objectives include conflicts between real and stated objectives, multiple objectives, and goal distortion.

The determination of how the organizational objectives will be achieved is referred to as strategic planning. There are two basic stages of strategic planning: determining the strategy and developing the specific plans to implement the strategy. The distinction made regarding planning by lower-level management as opposed to upper-level management is largely one of degree. A primary difference between the two situations is the external environment in which the two managers operate.

Policies, procedures, and rules are available to assist in implementation of plans for this purpose. A policy is a predetermined, general course or guide established to provide direction in decision making. A procedure is a series of steps established for the accomplishment of some specific project or endeavor. A rule is a very specific and detailed guide to action that is set up to direct or restrict action in a fairly narrow manner.

Review Questions

1. What are the steps involved in the planning process?
2. What are the main types of objectives that can be identified for business firms in our society?
3. Describe and briefly discuss the strategic planning sequence discussed in the text.
4. Define standards. Why is it important for a manager to develop clearly defined standards?
5. Distinguish by definition policies, procedures, and rules.
6. What is meant by the term *reactive planning* as it relates to the planning process?
7. What are some unintended side effects of plans? Discuss.

Exercises

1. It has been stated in the text that a firm can have multiple objectives. What do you feel would be the objectives of the following firms and organizations with regard to their interrelationship with society?
   a. Ford Motor Company
   b. American Airlines
   c. Peat, Marwick, Mitchell & Co. (a Big-8 CPA firm)
   d. New York Yankees
   e. Girl Scouts of America
   f. Internal Revenue Service

2. Assume that you determine your objective is to obtain a 4.0 grade point average the following semester. Develop a plan, policies, procedures, rules, and standards that could help you achieve this goal.

Case Study

Objectives and Plans for a Financial Career

Barbara Williams has been attending State University for the past two years. Until now she has regarded school as a means of passing away four years, and her grades generally reflect this attitude (her 2.2/4.0 keeps her in school but it is nothing to write home about). Barbara studies when she absolutely has to and enjoys the very active social life that is available at the university. Her college grades are quite different from those in high school, where she was one of the top students earning very high grades. However, since she began going to college, she has not been able to decide what she wants to concentrate on as a major. Her attitude has been one of "I just haven't found the career that turns me on."

At least the above situation existed until Barbara enrolled in Dr. Edens' finance class this summer. She had intended to spend the summer getting a good suntan and meeting as many young men as possible (a hidden goal for which many students aspire). However, a strange thing happened; Barbara was "turned on" to the field of finance. She would find herself studying many afternoons when it wasn't even raining. She even worked many of the extra finance problems, though Dr. Edens did not assign them in class. Barbara developed a keen respect for her professor, and she often stopped by Dr. Edens' office to discuss various aspects of the course.

One day while Barbara was in Dr. Edens' office she said, "I've been thinking about majoring in finance and possibly becoming a financial analyst for a major bank when I graduate."

"That's an admirable goal, Barbara," replied Dr. Edens. "I hope you realize what might be involved in accomplishing that objective."

"No, not really," she answered, "this is my first course in finance."

"What are your grades so far in college?" asked Dr. Edens.

"I have a blazing 2.2 average so far. It will improve this summer because it looks as if I will make three A's and one B. I'm really not stupid; I just have never found a reason to study that much in the past."

"I am proud of you for what you've accomplished this summer, Barbara," replied Dr. Edens. "But if you're really serious about pursuing a career in finance I'll help you identify what must be accomplished before you will have the opportunity to obtain your goal. Let me list them on a sheet of paper."

1. Improve your grade point average.
2. Take all of the finance and accounting courses that are offered. At State University these courses are recognized as being quite difficult.
3. Develop a good rapport with teachers in this specialty. Many of them have business contacts that could be very beneficial when you're obtaining your first job.

After Dr. Edens had developed the list, he continued his conversation with Barbara by saying, "You took a management course this summer and made an A didn't you? One of the chapters in the course concerned Objectives and Plans. What I would like you to do for me is develop a plan that will help you meet your objectives. Once you have accomplished this task, we will talk some more."

QUESTIONS

1. In order to accomplish the objective Barbara has established, what do you feel should be included in her short-range plans and long-range plans?
2. What are some external factors that could affect Barbara's attaining her goal?

Case Study

Who Establishes the Objectives and Plans?

The organizational chart for Medford Stores, a medium-sized convenience store chain located in the Southeast, is presented as Figure 1. For store managers, duties are well formulated, inasmuch as a strong attempt is made by upper management

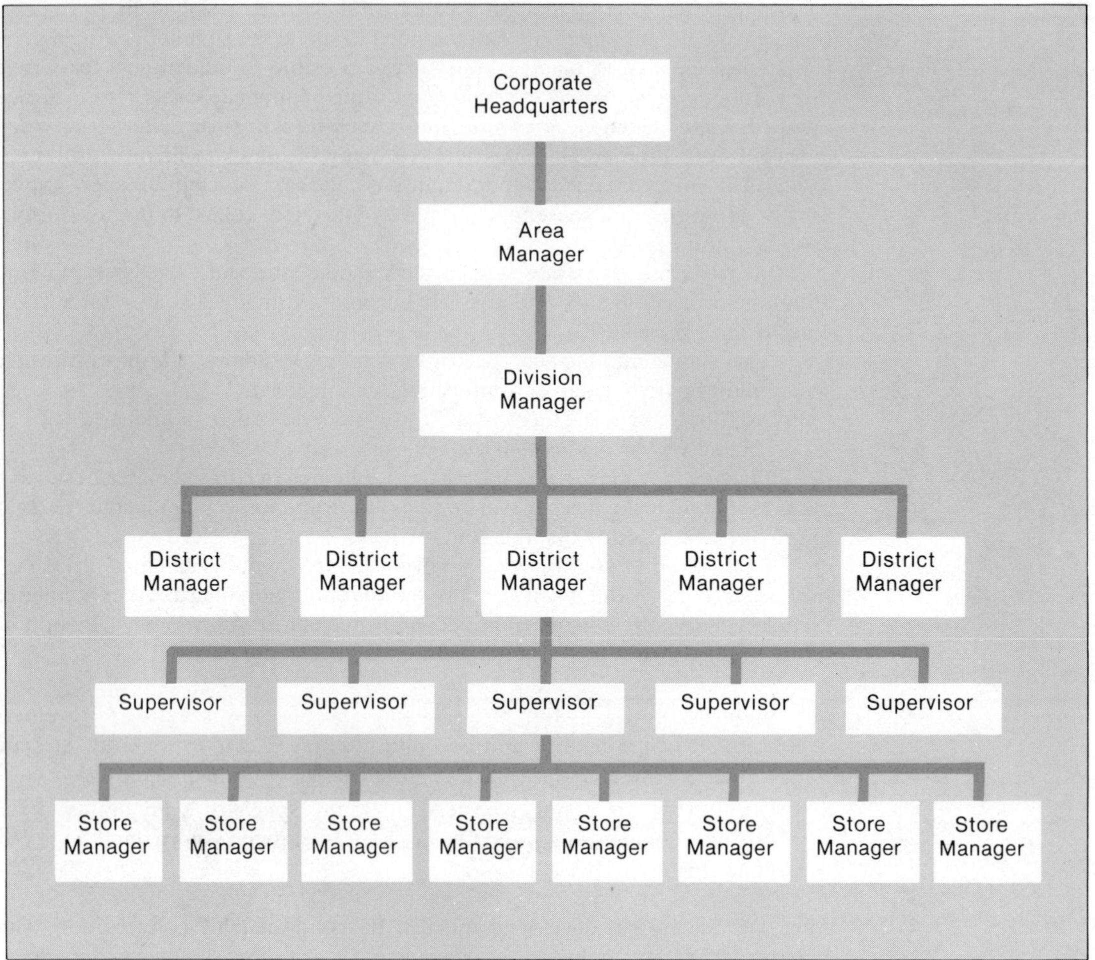

FIGURE 1 *Organizational Chart of Medford Stores*

to standardize operations. Although the manager may have one or two assistants under his or her direct supervision, the "managerial" connotation is often misleading as the manager and assistants normally work different shifts.

Upper management strives to assure uniformity of operation in all areas, including ordering, stocking, customer check-out procedures, and managers' attitudes generally prevailing within a store. Because of the routine nature of work and because of a concerted effort by top management to foster conformity in store managers' duties, there tends to be little discretion on the part of managers regarding day-to-day store operations.

Furthermore, the general lack of freedom in decision making extends itself to supervisory levels of responsibility. Virtually all supervisors are promoted from the ranks of "successful managers" within Medford. As a result, those individuals who conform best to the convenience store environment are promoted. Typically a supervisor has responsibility for eight to ten stores. Normal duties include picking up the previous day's receipts, verifying daily accounting records, monitoring physical conditions of the stores, and making employment recommendations. Most matters not recognized as standard operating procedures are resolved at a higher managerial level.

The authority of district managers is also circumscribed, though to a lesser extent than the supervisor. Typically district managers have responsibility for approximately fifty stores with five supervisors reporting directly to them. Although their district is considered a profit center, their ability to control profits is restricted to routine matters. From a practical standpoint, success or failure of a district manager depends, to a large extent, on the degree of conformity he or she is able to obtain from managers within his or her area of responsibility.

Any decisions that are not covered by standard operating procedures must be made at the division manager level. The division manager is also responsible for establishing objectives and formulating plans. All division managers are promoted from the ranks after successful accomplishment of the duties of a store manager, supervisor, and district manager.

Bob Anderson was recently promoted to division manager after having progressed from store manager to his present position in only ten years. It had been a long struggle, but Bob was pleased to be a division manager finally. Bob is now experiencing some difficulties though. The area manager called Bob in last Wednesday and questioned him about his objectives and plans for the forthcoming year. When Bob said he did not have them and was not really sure what was expected, the area manager became rather upset.

"Bob," the area manager said, "you are expected to do much more creative thinking now than in the past. You can let your subordinates put out the daily fires. Your job is much more encompassing. The very survival of Medford Stores depends on how well your objectives and plans are formulated."

Bob thanked the area manager for his comments and went to the files to find the standard operating procedures for formulating plans for Medford Stores. There were none! Bob's heart sank as he felt totally ill equipped for this endeavor.

QUESTIONS

1. Why does the area manager feel the "very survival" of Medford Stores depends on how well objectives and plans are formulated?
2. Bob's situation is not uncommon in some firms. How could a firm ensure that people such as Bob are equipped to handle the planning function?

References

Allen, David. "Establishing a Financial Objective—A Practical Approach." *Long Range Planning* 12 (December 1979): 11–16.

Allen, L. A. "Managerial Planning: Back to the Basics." *Management Review* 70 (April 1981): 15–20.

Anderson, Carl R., and Paine, Frank T. "Managerial Perceptions and Strategic Behavior." *Academy of Management Journal* 18 (December 1975): 811–823.

Bowman, Edward H. "Risk/Return Paradox for Strategic Management." *Sloan Management Review* 21 (Spring 1980): 17–31.

Camillus, John C., and Grant, John H. "Operational Planning: The Integration of Programming and Budgeting." *Academy of Management Review* 5 (July 1980): 369–379.

Fox, H. W. "Frontiers of Strategic Planning: Intuition or Formal Models." *Management Review* 70 (April 1981): 44–50.

Goldstein, S. G. Mike. "Involving Managers in System-Improvement Planning." *Long Range Planning* 14 (February 1981): 93–99.

Gup, Benton E. "Begin Strategic Planning by Asking Three Questions." *Managerial Planning* 28 (November 1979): 28–31.

Hailden, B. T. "Date and Effective Corporate Planning." *Long Range Planning* 13 (October 1980): 106–111.

Kahalas, Harvey. "Planning Types and Approaches: A Necessary Function." *Managerial Planning* 28 (May–June 1980): 22–27.

Kudla, R. J. "Elements of Effective Corporate Planning." *Long Range Planning* 9 (August 1976): 82–93.

Linsay, W. M., and Rue, L. W. "Impact of the Organization Environment on the Long-Range Planning Process: A Contingency View." *Academy of Management Journal* 23 (September 1980): 385–404.

McCaskey, Michael B. "A Contingency Approach to Planning: Planning with Goals and Planning without Goals." *Academy of Management Journal* 17 (June 1974): 281–291.

Martin, John. "Business Planning: The Gap between Theory and Practice." *Long Range Planning* 12 (December 1979): 2–10.

Michael, Steven R. "Feedforward versus Feedback Controls in Planning." *Managerial Planning* 29 (November–December 1980): 34–38.

Michael, Steven R. "Tailor Made Planning: Making Planning Fit the Firm." *Long Range Planning* 13 (December 1980): 74–79.

Naylon, T. H. "Organizing for Strategic Planning." *Managerial Planning* 28 (July 1979): 3–9.

Pearson, G. J. "Setting Corporate Objectives as a Basis for Action." *Long Range Planning* 12 (August 1979): 13–19.

Pekar, Peter P. "Planning: A Guide to Implementation." *Managerial Planning* 29 (July–August 1980): 3–6.

Ratcliffe, Thomas A., and Logsdon, D. J. "Business Planning Process—A Behavioral Perspective." *Managerial Planning* 28 (March 1980): 32–38.

Simmons, William W. "Future of Planning." *Managerial Planning* 29 (January–February 1981): 2–3.

Snyder, N., and Glueck, W. F. "How Managers Plan the Analysis of Manager's Activities." *Long Range Planning* 18 (February 1980): 70–76.

Stephenson, E. "Assessing Operational Policies." *Omega* 6 (1976): 437–446.

Taylor, Bernard. "Strategies for Planning." *Long Range Planning* (August 1975): 437–446.

Thune, Stanley S., and House, Robert J. "Where Long-Range Planning Pays Off." *Business Horizons* 13 (August 1970): 81–87.

Townsend, Robert. *Up the Organization.* Greenwich, Conn.: Fawcett, 1971.

Vancil, Richard F., and Lorange, Peter. "Strategic Planning in Diversified Companies." *Harvard Business Review* 53 (January–February 1975): 81–90.

Vesper, Volker D. "Strategic Mapping—A Tool for Corporate Planners." *Long Range Planning* 12 (December 1979): 75–92.

Word, E. Peter. "Focussing Innovative Effort through a Convergent Dialogue." *Long Range Planning* 13 (December 1980): 32–41.

KEY TERMS

management by objectives

activity trap

action plans

routine objectives

problem-solving objectives

innovative objectives

personal development objectives

team objectives

LEARNING OBJECTIVES

After completing this chapter you should be able to

1. Describe management by objectives (MBO) and explain the historical development of MBO.
2. Explain the essential elements of the MBO process.
3. State the types of objectives used in MBO programs.
4. Identify the characteristics of MBO objectives for both individual and team objectives.
5. Describe the application of MBO at the Monsanto Company.
6. List and briefly describe the primary benefits and potential problems with MBO programs.

4

Management by Objectives: An Approach to Planning

Joyce Baker, division accounting manager for Virginia Power and Light Company, had just completed a frustrating discussion with her boss, Horace Payne, vice-president and controller of the company. Joyce, describing her meeting with Mr. Payne to Cecyl Thomas, division finance manager, said: "You know, Cecyl, I never have figured out what Mr. Payne expects of me or my division. Each time Payne and I meet, he talks about maintaining high-quality service to our customers and collecting accounts on time. He mentions that we need to establish realistic goals and standards of performance, but he never follows through and explains what he wants us to do. I have never known what Payne expects of me and the accounting division." "Joyce, I understand where you're coming from," Cecyl sympathized. "I have the same problem with Mr. Payne."

Todd Andrews, vice-president for engineering at Scranton Steel, was reviewing a memo from the company president, Lee Johnson, when Preston Pearsol, marketing vice-president, stopped by his office. "Todd, are you ready for a little coffee this morning?" Preston asked. "Yeah, I need a break from this so-called goals memo I've just received from Lee," replied Todd. "I'll never understand Johnson or his so-called participative planning system, as he likes to call it. Here's another memo that dictates the objectives and standards of performance for engineering, without giving me or anyone else in my division a chance for input or discussion. Many of these goals are totally unrealistic and unattainable. I'll never understand why Johnson doesn't involve the managers most familiar with a particular operation before goals and plans are finalized. Isn't that how an MBO system should operate?" "Come on, Todd, haven't you given up trying to change Johnson? Let's get that cup of coffee and continue our discussion."

Joyce Baker's situation illustrates the importance of establishing goals and plans. In this case, goals and standards of performance were not clearly defined. Joyce did not know what was expected of her or the accounting division because her boss, Horace Payne, did not establish and/or communicate goals and performance expectations.

In the second illustration, Todd Andrews was frustrated by the planning and goal-setting system that the company president used, which did not allow for Todd's or any of the engineering division's participation. At Scranton Steel, Lee Johnson believed in establishing goals but did not allow for or encourage the participation of managers and divisions that were most directly affected by the goals. Most people want to know what's expected of them. Particularly, managers and professionals tend to be more committed to goals if they have had an opportunity to participate in establishing them.

Both situations could be improved by an application of a concept referred to as management by objectives (MBO). During the past two decades few other developments in the theory and practice of management have received as much attention and application as MBO. It directs management's attention toward specific targets or "end results" that the organization must attain to be successful. In an MBO system, the efforts of management are goal directed as opposed to being activity centered.

In this chapter the background and development of MBO will first be discussed, followed by a presentation of the MBO process. The steps to follow in developing a practical MBO system will then be presented. This discussion will be supported by an in-depth look at the types and characteristics of objectives as well as the process of establishing objectives. Benefits and limitations of the MBO will also be discussed. Finally, an assessment of the effectiveness of MBO, as well as suggestions for improvements, will be presented.

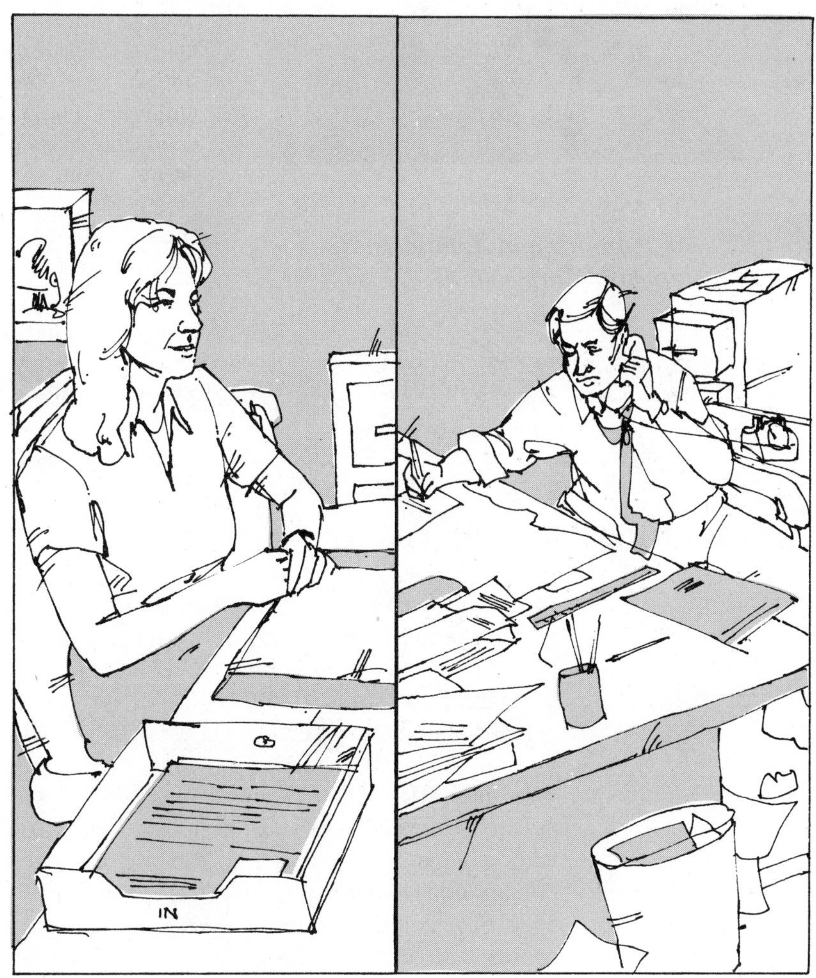

A manager's success is determined by results, not how busy he or she looks.

•CAREER PROFILE•

JERRY O. WILLIAMS
Vice-President, Planning and Administration
Maremont Corporation

MAREMONT Although Jerry O. Williams has a B.S. in electrical engineering and an M.S.E. in operations research, he decided to get out of "pure" engineering functions because of the lack of enough interaction with people. Jerry said, "I found out I enjoyed the functions of organizing, motivating, and planning more than I did working with devices and apparatus." Jerry gives the following reasons for selecting a career in management. He—

- Wanted to be involved in the decision-making process.
- Wanted to have some impact on the process that was charting the company's and his own future.
- Enjoyed working with people and got tremendous satisfaction in motivating and directing a diverse group of people to accomplish a common goal.
- Desired to develop and guide people for larger roles in the corporation.

After being with a large company like General Electric and then going to a smaller company (Stanford Research Institute), Jerry felt he would like

MANAGEMENT BY OBJECTIVES (MBO)

During the past two decades few developments in the theory and practice of management have received as much attention and application as MBO. It directs management's attention toward specific targets or end results that the organization must attain to be successful. In an MBO system, the efforts of management are goal directed as opposed to being activity centered.

As we have discussed in previous chapters, organizations exist to achieve objectives. This is the case whether we are evaluating profit or nonprofit, private or government organizations. Thus, all organizations are concerned with achieving objectives, and the attainment of objectives should be the primary concern of management. As you will recall from Chapter 1, we defined management as the process of planning, organizing, influencing, and controlling to accomplish organizational goals through the coordinated use to be in a medium-sized company where he could have a greater impact on decisions. In order to do this, he went back to General Electric to establish his credentials in strategic planning. Next, he accepted a position with Maremont Corporation to initiate their planning process. Maremont manufactures automobile parts and has approximately 8,000 employees.

Because Jerry has been associated with both engineering- and managerial-related jobs, he can make the following point with regard to earning potential: "A career in management is better than other fields like engineering, which starts with a high salary but levels off much sooner than management." With regard to the importance of education to a manager, Jerry states, "With the proliferation of M.B.A.s, a person needs to have a graduate degree just to participate. This does not guarantee success. However, it does make it possible for a person to participate." When it comes to company loyalty, he also has some interesting observations. He says, "A person should be loyal as long as he is working for a company. However, when it comes to career, do what is best for your career. 'Look out for number one.' Others look out for you only as it affects their careers."

Finally, when Jerry was asked what he believes are the most important qualities for success, he described the following:

- Persevere in achieving goals.
- Enjoy what you are doing and the money will come.
- Develop interpersonal relationships.
- Anticipate the needs of the organization and be able to fill those needs.
- Be dependable—Get the job done on time and correctly.
- Be creative.
- Be a little impatient. Not always satisfied with the status quo. Look for other ways to do things and do them faster.
- Flexibility. Be able to adjust to new techniques, procedures, and policies without getting frustrated.
- Understand the political environment and be able to work within the system.

It's obvious Jerry has followed his own advice as he is now a very successful executive who has much more potential for advancement.

---

of human and material resources. An MBO system causes management to focus its attention on the objectives—the end results. In essence, "MBO is simply common sense in that it is a reflection of the purpose of managing itself."[1]

management by objectives

Effective management practice concentrates on establishing and attaining measurable goals. ***Management by objectives*** *(MBO) provides a systematic and organized approach that allows management to attain maximum results from available resources by focusing on achievable goals.* Above all else, MBO represents an overall philosophy of management; it actually constitutes a way of thinking that concentrates on achieving results. As such, it forces management to predict and plan for the future as opposed to simply responding or reacting on the basis of guesses or hunches. It provides a more systematic and rational approach to management and helps prevent "management by crisis," "fire fighting," or "seat-of-the-pants" methods. MBO emphasizes measurable achievements and results and is designed to lead to improvements in both organizational and individual effectiveness.[2] The approach depends heavily on active participation at all levels of management.

BACKGROUND AND EVALUATION OF MBO

Peter Drucker was first to describe "management by objectives" in 1954 in *The Practice of Management.*[3] According to Drucker, management's primary responsibilities are to balance a number of demands and objectives in all areas where performance and results directly affect the survival, profits, and growth of the business. Drucker stated that specific objectives must be established in the following areas:

- market standing
- innovation
- productivity
- worker performance and attitude
- physical and financial resources
- profitability
- managerial performance and development
- public responsibility

Drucker argued that the first requirement of managing any enterprise is "management by objectives and self-control." As originally described, an MBO system was designed to satisfy three managerial needs.

MBO would provide a basis for more effective planning. Drucker had in mind what might be called the systems approach to planning—that of integrating objectives and plans for every level within the organization. The basic concept of planning consists of *making it happen* as opposed to *just letting things happen.* According to Drucker, MBO is a planning system requiring each manager to be involved in the total planning process by participating in establishing the objectives for his or her own department and for higher levels in the organization.

MBO is designed to improve communications within the firm since managers and employees frequently discuss and reach agreement on performance objectives. In the process, there is frequent review and discussion of the goals and plans of action at all levels within the firm.

Finally, Drucker thought that the implementation of an MBO system would encourage the acceptance of a behavioral or more participative approach to management. By participating in the process of setting objectives, managers and employees develop a better understanding of the broader objectives of the organization and how their goals relate to the total organization.[4]

activity trap

One of the foremost advocates of MBO, George Odiorne, contends that special efforts must be undertaken to avoid the **activity trap.**[5] This trap

exists when managers and employees become so enmeshed in performing assigned functions that they lose sight of the goal or reasons for their performance. As a result, they justify their existence by the energy and sweat expended and avoid questioning whether they have accomplished any result deemed necessary to organizational effectiveness. For example, the fact that John James is frantically shuffling through a mass of paperwork piled on his desk does not mean he is accomplishing his primary objectives. Even though John usually arrives at the office at 7 A.M. and often continues working until 6 or 7 P.M., he is often behind in his work despite his constant appearance of being busy. While John is always *busy,* his efforts are not focused on the most important goals of the business.

Another advocate of MBO, Douglas McGregor, had stressed a slightly different aspect. McGregor, who favored MBO because of its usefulness as a performance appraisal method, thought that the essence of MBO is *management by integration and self-control.* McGregor's philosophy of MBO was based upon what he termed Theory Y. (Now famous, Theory X and Theory Y will be explained in detail in Chapter 10—Motivation.) The basic assumption in Theory Y is that individuals are responsible human beings capable of exercising self-direction and self-control in achieving organizational goals if they are committed to the goals.

In McGregor's approach, individual managers establish their own short-term performance objectives and develop plans to achieve these goals. Although the manager's boss provides assistance in goal setting by creating a climate for effective participation and commitment, the goals are set by the subordinate, not the superior.

STAGES OF DEVELOPMENT OF MBO

In its early years, MBO programs were primarily concerned with the evaluation of the performance of managers. The programs provided a means for reducing the subjectivity in performance appraisal by developing specific objectives and performance standards for each position. An MBO performance appraisal system provided an alternative to traditional performance evaluation, which was often based largely on perceived personality traits of the individual being appraised. It encouraged individuals being rated to participate actively in the process of establishing specific performance goals and in appraising progress toward their accomplishment.

When MBO is used only as an appraisal system, the program will likely receive only mild support from top management. As an appraisal system, responsibility for implementation of the program essentially comes from the personnel department; line management's involvement is usually limited to the completion of the paperwork associated with the program. Performance reviews are conducted annually or semiannually, but they normally involve only subordinates and their bosses.

When MBO is used only as an appraisal system it is possible that less productive employees may be viewed as making greater contributions to the overall success of the firm than other persons who are much more productive. This can occur if management fails to recognize the difference in the levels of difficulty of goal achievement and overall contributions of different employees. For example, with rigid implementation of an MBO appraisal system, Mildred Price, a highly productive employee, may have attained only 60 percent of her targeted results. However, Wayne Miller, another manager in the same department, may have achieved 90 percent of his goals, but the goals were much less demanding and ambitious than the goals of Mildred. Management should recognize the differences in the degree of difficulty in the goals of Mildred and Wayne and reward them accordingly.

MBO as a performance appraisal system has been and continues to be the starting point for many companies. However, if the MBO program does

Most Important Reasons for Success and Effectiveness as a Manager

1. **Insistence on setting personal and corporate objectives with target dates for achieving goals.**
2. **Consistency in measuring progress toward goals.**
3. **Ability to get to the heart of a problem by understanding the subject thoroughly and asking the right questions.**
4. **Insistence on integrity of the company's people and products.**
5. **A strong belief in listening to and evaluating thoroughly the ideas of associates and subordinates.**
6. **The ability to create a team effort.**
7. **Delegation of responsibility with adequate supervision.**
8. **Persistence in pursuing objectives and in problem solving.**

HAROLD F. THAYER, Chairman, President, and Chief Executive Officer, Mallinckrodt, Incorporated

not proceed beyond the performance evaluation stage, overall program effectiveness will be limited. In essence, performance appraisal is part of the system, but only one component. Performance appraisal aspects represent the "end results" of a properly designed MBO system.

During the late 1960s, MBO began to take on a broader perspective; it was incorporated into the organization's planning and control processes. Objectives were related to plans that provided an integrated basis for control through budgets. Results-oriented performance appraisals continued to be an integral part of the MBO program, but there was considerably more top management support than during the earlier phase. In addition, since the

MBO program was closely related to the budgetary process, line management had the primary responsibility for its success. With this approach, there was increased emphasis on the training and development of personnel throughout the organization.

Since the early 1970s, MBO has evolved into a system of management designed to integrate key management processes and functions in a logical and consistent manner. Anthony Raia, a leading advocate of MBO as a system of management, believes that MBO consists of "overall organizational goals and strategic plans; problem-solving and decision-making; performance appraisal, executive compensation, manpower planning, and management training and development."[6] MBO programs have experienced success that may be attributed to these characteristics:

- Direction and thrust come from top management, but managers at all levels are actively involved in the process.
- The increased need for teamwork involves more groups in establishing goals, action planning, and reviewing performance.
- Goal setting is more flexible and covers longer time spans.
- There are more frequent performance reviews.
- There is more emphasis on individual growth and development.[7]

THE MBO PROCESS

Earlier we defined MBO as a systematic and organized approach that allows management to attain maximum results from available resources by focusing on achievable goals. However, this definition of MBO does not provide significant insight into the total process. MBO should be constantly reviewed, modified, and updated. The dynamics of an MBO system are illustrated in Figure 4-1.

Top Management's Philosophy, Support, and Commitment

Any MBO program is doomed from the start without the absolute and enthusiastic support of top management. It is because of the lack of top-level commitment that so many MBO programs fail. To be effective, MBO must be consistent with the philosophy of top management. Obviously, it would be very difficult to implement an effective MBO program if the chief executive lacked trust in the subordinates or was not personally committed to a participative style of management. For example, the chief executive cannot introduce MBO by simply giving an order or a directive. Lower-level managers must be convinced of the merits of the system and desire meaningful participation in the process. MBO relies on the participative approach to manage-

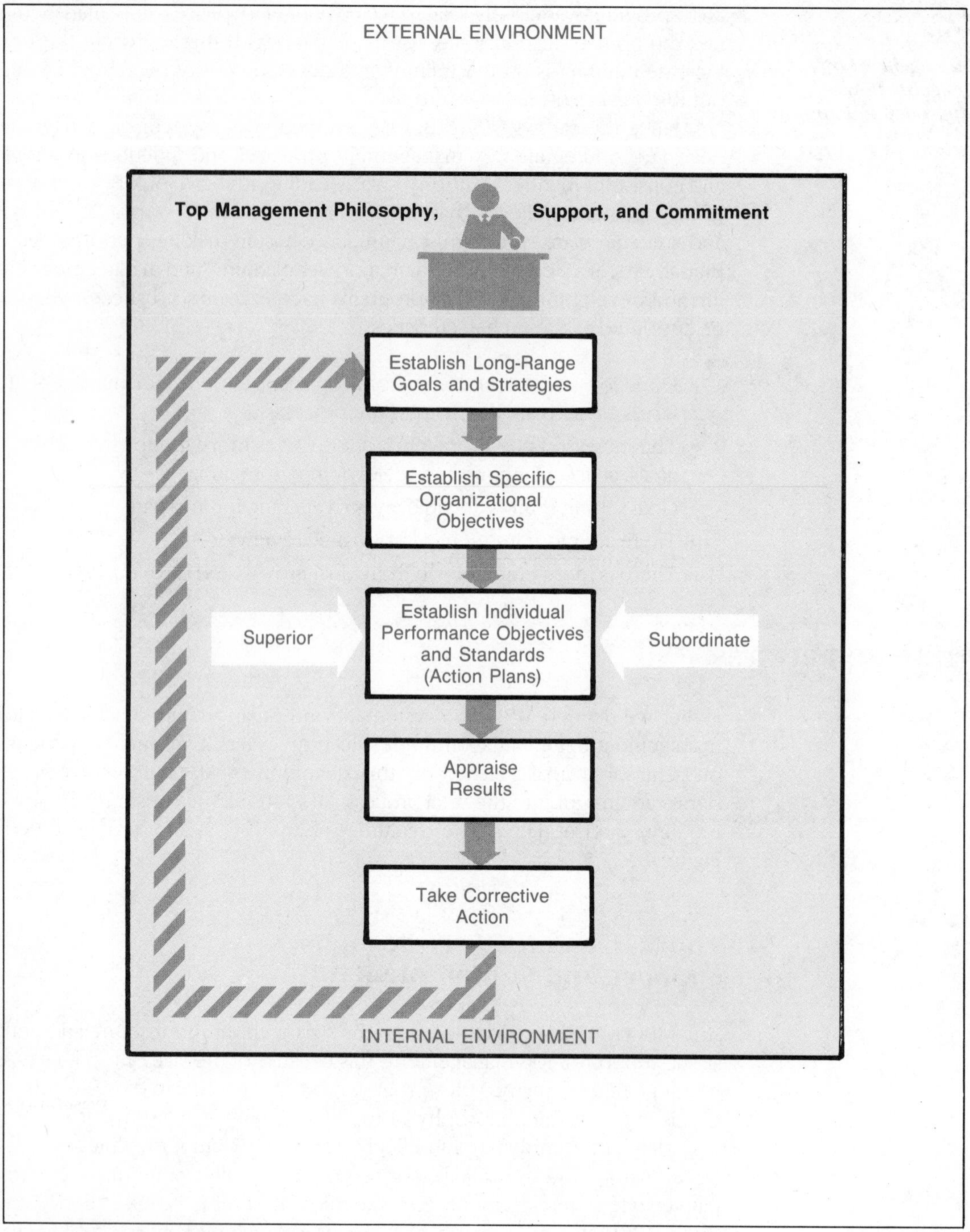

EXTERNAL ENVIRONMENT

Top Management Philosophy, Support, and Commitment

Establish Long-Range Goals and Strategies

Establish Specific Organizational Objectives

Superior

Establish Individual Performance Objectives and Standards (Action Plans)

Subordinate

Appraise Results

Take Corrective Action

INTERNAL ENVIRONMENT

FIGURE 4-1 *The MBO Process*

ment, requiring the active involvement of the managers at all levels in the organization.

Establish Long-range Goals and Strategies

Every successful MBO program must develop long-range goals and the strategies to accomplish these goals. Long-term plans are developed by thoughtful determination of the basic purpose or mission of the organization. Before developing long-range goals, the top management of a firm must attempt to answer such questions as these:

- What is the basic purpose of the organization?
- What business are we in and why?
- What business should we be in?

Long-range planning is essential if management is to identify areas needing improvements.

Long-term goals and strategic planning can be illustrated by a company that has an overall purpose of producing and marketing high-quality color televisions. Several long-term goals and strategies consistent with the overall purpose may be developed. This company may have a goal to increase their rate of return on stockholder investment to 20 percent after taxes and to achieve a share of 15 percent of the total U.S. market for color televisions within seven years. These are long-range goals because they extend beyond one year. The firm's strategic plan—the means to attain the stated goals—might include substantial quality improvements in color televisions. These changes would hopefully create a greater demand and allow the firm to increase the price of its televisions. If the firm was able to control costs and generate greater sales volume, their long-term goals should be attained.

Establish Specific Organizational Objectives

After long-range goals and plans are established, management must be concerned with determining specific objectives to be attained within a given time period. These objectives must be supportive of the overall purpose and key result areas. Usually they are expressed as very specific and quantifiable targets covering such areas as productivity, market, and profitability.

In our example of the color television manufacturer, specific organizational objectives might be represented by the following:

1. Increase sales of television model A1000 to 500,000 units—an increase of 10 percent during the current year.

2. Reduce production costs per TV produced by 5 percent in next twelve months.
3. Increase investment in new product design by 10 percent over last year.
4. Increase profits by 10 percent over last year.

Each of the above would be further subdivided into departmental objectives consistent with attaining the above organizational goals.

Establish Individual Performance Objectives and Standards (Action Plans)

Establishing performance objectives and standards for individuals is known as action planning. The crucial phase of the MBO process requires that challenging but attainable objectives and standards be established through an interaction with superiors and subordinates. **Action plans** require clear delineation of *what* specifically is to be accomplished and *when* it is to be completed. For instance, Terry and his sales manager might have agreed upon the following standards of performance for Terry.

action plans

1. Increase sales of color TVs in the Boston market by 10 percent by June 30.
2. Reduce travel expenses by 5 percent by June 30.

Appraise Results

The next step in the MBO process is to measure and evaluate the actual performance as compared to the goals and standards established. Having specific standards of performance provides management with a basis for such a comparison. When goals are specifically stated and agreed on by both the manager and the subordinate, self-evaluation and control become possible. We will discuss performance appraisal in a later chapter.

Take Corrective Action

Although an MBO system provides the framework for goal setting, managers in the organization must take action to correct areas where results are not being accomplished according to the plans. Such action may take the form of changes in personnel, the organization, or even the goals themselves. Other forms of corrective action may include providing additional training and development of individual managers or employees to enable them to achieve the desired results better. Corrective action should not necessarily have negative connotations. Original objectives can be renegotiated without any penalty or fear of loss of job.

TYPES OF OBJECTIVES

In the paragraphs below we discuss the types of objectives used in MBO programs including routine, problem solving, innovative, and personal development. Examples of each are shown in Table 4-1.

TABLE 4-1. ***Examples of Objectives in an MBO Program in a Manufacturing Company***

Position	Objective	Type of Objective
Production manager	Achieve a 10 percent reduction in late production reports by December 31	Routine
	Reduce product rejects due to inferior quality from 8 percent to 5 percent by December 31	Routine
Finance and accounting manager	Correct problem of low rate of return on the firm's cash by achieving 12 percent annualized rate of return by December 31	Problem solving
	Attend two-week executive development program on improving leadership effectiveness by June 1	Personal development
Manager of engineering, research, and development	Develop and test three new products for entry into the market by June 1	Innovative
	Employ ten recent university engineering graduates—four mechanical engineers, four electrical engineers, and two industrial engineers—by September 1	Routine
Marketing manager	Perform market tests on two products developed by Engineering, Research, and Development by June 30	Routine
	Design and implement a new and more effective advertising program within a budget of $250,000 by August 31	Innovative
Personnel director	Develop and implement program to reduce turnover of engineers and computer programmers from 30 percent to 20 percent by December 31	Innovative
	Complete three courses toward MBA degree by August 31	Personal development

Routine

routine objectives

Routine objectives represent recurring day-to-day activities that are expected to be performed. They represent standards of performance. As indicated in Table 4-1, a routine objective for the production manager would be to reduce product rejects due to inferior quality from 8 percent to 5 percent by December 31. For the marketing manager, a routine objective is to perform market tests on two new products by June 30.

Problem Solving

problem-solving objectives

Problem-solving objectives are concerned with correcting a situation that is creating difficulties for the individual or the firm. Many people believe that the basic management task is that of solving problems. For example, a problem for the manager of finance and accounting is a low rate of return on the firm's cash outputs. To correct this cash-flow problem, a problem-solving objective for the manager of finance and accounting is to achieve a 12 percent annualized rate of return by December 31.

Innovative

innovative objectives

Innovative objectives are concerned with unique or special accomplishments, such as the development of new methods or procedures. MBO goal-setting sessions provide an opportunity for innovative goals to be developed and stated. Designing and implementing a new and more effective advertising program by the marketing manager within a budget of $250,000 by August 31 could well be an innovative objective designed to increase sales of the company's products and overall market share.

Insights to Success

Set high standards for yourself and expect the same of your people.

M. LAMONT BEAN, Chairman, President, and CEO, Pay'n Save Corporation

Personal Development

personal development objectives

Personal development objectives provide the opportunity for each individual to state his or her personal goals and action plans for self-improvement and personal growth and development. Almost all MBO systems include a section on personal growth and development goals. Examples of personal development goals might include a statement such as "completing a two-week executive development program on improving leadership effectiveness by June 1," by the finance and accounting manager. Personal development goals are important because of their potential for helping individuals improve their current skills, preparing them for increased responsibility and career advancement, and improving their current performance.

CHARACTERISTICS OF OBJECTIVES FOR THE INDIVIDUAL

In order for MBO to achieve maximum results, objectives for each individual should be carefully developed. They should be limited in number, highly specific, challenging, and attainable. The number of objectives for each individual should range from four to eight. Having more than eight leads to "spreading oneself too thin," thereby diminishing overall effectiveness. Each objective should be assigned a priority, perhaps ranging from one to three. In this way, should time and resources prove to be more limited than anticipated, the individual has a basis for deciding which objective to pursue.

Perhaps the most emphasized characteristic of good objectives is that they should be stated in specific terms. In most instances, this means quantification and measurability. For example, goals have far less impact when stated in such terms as "improve the effectiveness of the unit," "keep costs to a minimum," or "be alert to market changes." At the performance review, one should be able to look back and definitely answer the question, "Did I do it or not?" For instance, a goal stating that production will be increased by 1,000 units is much clearer than one that merely encourages increased production. Thus, in writing objectives, a special attempt should be made to phrase them in such terms as volume, costs, frequency, ratios, percentages, indexes, degrees, and phases. It is particularly important to place time limits on each objective. In ten of eleven studies that examined the impact of such specific goals on performance, evidence was found supporting the contention that specifically stated goals will increase the level of accomplishment.[8]

Developing challenging and attainable objectives requires a delicate balance of opposing forces. Yet both are essential in motivating the subordinate. Obviously the superior desires that objectives be set at such a level that special efforts on the part of the employee must be made. Some researchers have pointed out that if promotion and salary are related to success in attaining objectives, as they should be, the participatory approach may well be asking the subordinate to construct a "do-it-yourself hangman's kit."[9] For instance, Dean Bishop, a hospital supply sales representative, might indicate to his sales manager that he plans to sell $1 million in surgical instruments and supplies during the next three months. Since no one else in the company had ever accomplished this level of sales in a three-month period and since Dean sold only $1 million in supplies the previous year, it is highly unlikely that he will attain his goal. It is much more likely that Dean has just "hung" himself because his goal is unrealistic and most probably unattainable.

In the initial phases of new MBO programs, one of the more common errors is the establishment of objectives that are unattainable. This is particularly the case if the time period for review is six months to a year. Anything seems possible with that much time. The superior must not allow excessively high goals to be set because this may cause a decline in future expectations and performance of the individual. Specific attention must be given to obstacles that affect accomplishment, particularly the availability of resources necessary for performance. The impact of other personnel on the subordinate's performance must be recognized and discussed.

Research indicates that challenging objectives lead to greater accomplishment only if the subordinate truly accepts the goal as reasonable and only if goal accomplishment actually leads to organizational rewards. Challenging goals with a history of past success will lead to continued success. A series of failures creates a mental set that makes attainment increasingly more difficult. Subordinates with self-assurance do well in relation to challenging goals. The subordinates' assessment of the probability of success should be that they at least have a fifty-fifty chance of achieving the objectives.

CHARACTERISTICS OF TEAM OBJECTIVES

team objectives

The accomplishment of most goals requires that individuals cooperate as a team. There are many factors that can affect the attainment of group or **team objectives.** For instance, it should be apparent that if the sales manager sets a specific objective of selling 50,000 units by March 1, it cannot be done if production does not manufacture that number of units. One of the most recommended approaches to overall goal setting involves team meetings to establish group goals. Team goal setting requires an open and supportive organizational climate. In general, MBO is more effective and achieves more positive results when applied in an organization with an open and supportive climate. In one instance, "a medium-size service company experimented with the team approach and decided to ignore individual objectives altogether, reasoning that too much interlinking support and cooperation are required to blame or reward any individual for the production of any single end result."[10]

If team goal-setting sessions are to be used as a prelude to the more typical individually oriented meeting, some training in group processes most likely is necessary. It is difficult enough for a manager to establish an open and participatory climate with an employee. But it is far more complex and challenging to try the same thing in a group. Programs of training directed toward this end go under the title of *organizational development,* a subject discussed at length in Chapter 13. The following is a suggested sequence in an MBO-team approach: (1) team meetings of top executives to set overall organizational objectives; (2) team meetings at unit level; (3) individual person-to-person goal-setting sessions; (4) individual reviews of accomplishments; (5) team meetings at unit level to review progress and accomplishment; and

(6) review at the top level to determine the degree of overall organizational success.[11] The team goal-setting process improves the chances of success of the MBO program because it improves coordination and communication within the organization.

DETERMINING OBJECTIVES

Objectives may be set (1) by the *superior,* (2) by the *subordinate,* (3) *jointly,* or (4) *jointly* with the aid of a *staff specialist.* When the superior is completely in charge of goal setting, problems often occur. Rather than involving subordinates in the process, they impose a specific, quantitative, and time-bounded goal on employees. This is not MBO but probably should be referred to as RBO (rule by objective). The following conversation between the president of a holding company and the president of one of his subsidiaries illustrates RBO. The subsidiary president had expressed doubt as to whether he could meet the budgetary goal. The holding company president's reply was, "Do I pay you alot of money? Do I argue with you over what you want to spend? Do I bother you? Then don't tell me what the goals should be. . . . My board and my stockholders want me to make my numbers. The way I make my numbers is for you guys to make your numbers. So, *make your numbers!*"[12] The holding company president is practicing RBO.

Most MBO programs require some type of a joint determination of objectives between superiors and subordinates. The particular advantage of having an MBO staff specialist is that it assures that meetings will actually take place, with help and advice being available. The joint process can take a number of variations. Perhaps the closest to RBO would be an initial determination of goals by the superior, followed by a submission to the subordinate asking for reactions. The opposite would be an initial determination by the subordinate, followed by discussion with the superior. In other instances, both come to the meeting with a set of tentative objectives worked out as a basis for discussion.

APPLICATION OF MBO AT THE MONSANTO COMPANY

The Monsanto Company has made an application of MBO since 1974 in an overall system of management that they refer to as the "Management Style." Monsanto's version of MBO is being applied to some 12,000 professional and managerial personnel worldwide. According to William K. Frymoyer, director of organizational and personnel development, "The MBO system has achieved excellent results. It is being applied in every Monsanto division throughout the world except Mexico and Japan. This is the process by which management defines what they want to accomplish and the framework within which they pursue corporate objectives." John W. Hanley, chairman of the board of Monsanto, describes the system as "focused heavily on a positive climate of interpersonal relationships supported by three major components:

- individual results and goal setting
- the Personnel Planning System
- an integrated appraisal and reward system"

In the Monsanto MBO planning process, management devises and proposes broad direction and strategy to corporate management. Once consensus is achieved, the unit is then accountable for implementing the agreed-upon strategy described in its plans. These plans are translated into results and goals for individuals through the Job Results Analysis (JRA)/Goals process.

Monsanto assigns accountability (being answerable for and recognized for assigned accomplishments) to organizational units and individuals by asking, "Who's accountable for what?" The JRA/Goal-setting process is the mechanism by which Monsanto managers assign accountability for results and goals. Under the JRA/Goals system, individual subordinates propose results and goals consistent with the organization's direction. However, it is the manager who assigns accountability. Monsanto's philosophy is that the assignment of accountability for results and goals, as well as gaining commitment to those results and goals, are distinct managerial activities. The first step is relatively easy; the second step—gaining commitment—is the mark of a good manager.

At Monsanto, the purposes of JRA/Goal's analysis are to:

1. Define the results or contributions of each person's job.
2. Provide more effective direction.
3. Promote improved understanding between individuals and their managers as to what accomplishments are important.

JRA is an organized process designed to accomplish goals. The process represents a means for concentrating on the results and goals that are most significant to the company and the individual manager or professional. In order to "capture" the results and goals that are most important, a JRA worksheet is completed. As illustrated in Figure 4-2, the JRA worksheet consists of several categories, which are briefly described below.

1. *Principal Thrust.* This is the first step in setting priorities. Its purpose is to identify the most important direction of the individual's job for the coming year. Goals should relate back to the principal thrust. In determining the principal thrust for the coming year, the key question that Monsanto managers and professionals must ask is, "What is the one area to be highlighted during the year that is of highest value to Monsanto and maximizes future profitability from the job?"

Monsanto — COMPANY CONFIDENTIAL — JOB RESULTS ANALYSIS – GOALS - 19___

PRINCIPAL THRUST

Purpose: to identify the most important item you want to focus on during the year.

LOCATION ______ NAME ______

JRA-DATE Prepared GOALS-DATE Prepared TITLE ______

GENERAL CONDITIONS-PREMISES

Purpose: to establish the climate or environment in which you'll be operating in during the year, and to set results and goals which are realistic, based on that climate.

RESULTS TO BE WORKED TOWARD	MAJOR RESULTS	GOALS	JOINT ACCOUNTABILITY	RANGE: BASIC	RANGE: OUTSTANDING	WEIGHT
* relates to Principal Thrust	(✓)					
Purpose: to indicate those results areas where individual direction contributes significantly to the achievement of the unit direction.	Purpose: to set priorities and direction. Select 3-5 most significant results.	Purpose: to establish the most significant annual targets which if accomplished will contribute to major unit results. (It is recommended the statement include the expected level of performance.)	Purpose: to identify those individuals from whom a significant cooperative effort is required to achieve a major result and goal.	Purpose: to establish basic and outstanding performance levels. BASIC is the minimum level of acceptable performance for the goal's achievement. OUTSTANDING is a truly demanding target which would contribute significantly to the performance of a unit.		Purpose: to establish criticality.
To be signed by supervisor. JRA APPROVED BY ______ DATE ______		To be signed by supervisor. GOALS APPROVED BY ______ DATE ______		Purpose: to insure understanding as to the importance of goals to the entire job. Goals represent ______ % of total performance		

G 3083

FIGURE 4-2 *Job Results Analysis* [*Source: Reprinted by permission of the Monsanto Company.*]

2. *General Conditions/Premises.* The purpose of this section is to establish the climate or environment in which an individual will be operating during the coming year and to set realistic results and goals based on the environment. Statements should be as specific as possible, such as, "The division will grow by 10 percent," rather than "The division will continue to grow." Assumptions that are beyond the control or influence of the individual or business unit are also included.
3. *Results to Be Worked Toward.* This section of the JRA indicates those results areas where individual direction contributes significantly to the achievement of unit direction. Results should be consistent with, and prepared in coordination with, long-range goals and strategic and operating plans.
4. *Major Results.* In this section and direction are established, and the three to five most significant results are identified.
5. *Goals.* The most significant annual targets (goals) are established, which, if accomplished, will contribute to the major unit results. The statement should include the expected level of performance.
6. *Joint Accountability.* The purpose of this section of the JRA is to identify individuals from whom significant cooperation is required to achieve the results and goals. Joint accountability is the commitment by a small group of people to accomplish the same or interdependent goals or results.
7. *Range: Basic and Outstanding.* In this section, basic and outstanding performance levels are established. The purpose is to ensure understanding concerning the important of goals to the overall job. *Basic* refers to the minimum level of acceptable performance for the goal's achievement. *Outstanding* refers to the highest level of goal attainment that would contribute substantially to the performance of the unit. For example, a goal might be to achieve new-customer sales of $1.5 million. The basic level of accomplishment might be $1 million, while outstanding performance would be $2 million.
8. *Weight.* The purpose of this section is to establish priority and criticality of each goal. The following guidelines are recommended:
   a. Allocate 100 points among the goals to reflect the critical accomplishments for the year. No goal gets fewer than 10 points.
   b. Weights should be consistent between manager and subordinates.

Through the use of the JRA/Goals statement, managers and subordinates have a clearer understanding of the priorities and what they must accomplish if the objectives of Monsanto are to be achieved. At a minimum, managers must engage in face-to-face discussion on JRAs and goals with all professionals and managers. While there should be discussion and understanding on each element of the JRA/Goal form, the unit manager has the option of completing the following sections: general conditions, major results checkmarks, joint accountability, weight of goals, and goals represent ______% of total performance.

A tool by which the manager evaluates the contribution of the subordinate and establishes a development plan for improvement and career advancement is referred to as Results Review. As shown in Figure 4-3, the Results Review is an integral part of the management approach at Monsanto and is directly related to the JRA/Goals statement. The Results Review system can be summarized as follows:

- Subordinates have a formal face-to-face Results Review meeting with their manager annually and a discussion at midyear. As needed, additional communications and coaching are recommended.
- At the annual Results Review meeting, at least two subjects will be covered and summarized in writing on the review form:
  1. *Overall performance:* The subordinate will be evaluated on
     —performance on goals
     —performance on fulfilling other results and responsibilities
     —management and development of subordinates (for personnel who manage people)
     —the manager will indicate the individual's overall performance on the continuum marked "performance rating"
  2. *Personal development on the present job:* This includes a discussion and written summary of sections I and II on the reverse side of the form.
- Each subordinate will also have a formal face-to-face discussion on career development and future assignments. This includes a discussion and a written summary of sections III, IV, and V on the form.
- The written form will be reviewed with the manager's superior for agreement and signature and then provided to the subordinate for comment and signature.
- As has been previously stated, "The quality of the verbal and written communications is extremely important." Good verbal communications will ensure understanding and lead to improvement. Good written communications will record that understanding. This is critical because the Results Review is an important factor in reward and recognition.

The application of MBO at Monsanto as an overall management system has proved to be effective. While the *Management Style* at Monsanto has evolved with modifications since its inception in 1974, the overall top management philosophy of and commitment to a participative climate has remained a cornerstone of the corporate style. This is illustrated by the comments of John W. Hanley, chairman and president:

> While our emphasis and components may change, our long-term course will not. We want Monsanto to continue to be a decent place to work. We want our company to be the best. We want to practice good common-sense management. And, finally, as we stated in 1974, we want to create an environment of excellence where (1) you have the opportunity to

Monsanto CONFIDENTIAL *RESULTS REVIEW*

NAME	GRADE	YRS.OF SERV.	YRS. IN JOB
TITLE			

COMPANY/DEPARTMENT	DIVISION	DEPARTMENT	PLANT/LOCATION

PERFORMANCE SUMMARY: Describe, in separate paragraphs, overall performance in accomplishing goals, fulfilling other results and responsibilities, and (for supervisors) managing and developing subordinates.

Not Acceptable [ ] Acceptable [ ] Highest

PERFORMANCE RATING

PROCEDURE

1. Manager and employe independently rough draft the Results Review; discuss conclusions and reconcile differences if possible.
2. Manager discusses the Results Review with immediate superior for agreement and signature; gives typed copy to employe for comment and signature.
3. Manager sends typed copies of Form to personnel representative for distribution.

1. APPRAISED AND DISCUSSED WITH EMPLOYE BY	TITLE	DATE
2. REVIEWED BY	TITLE	DATE
3. EMPLOYE'S SIGNATURE		DATE

G-2735 (REV. 8/80) (OVER)

FIGURE 4-3 *Results Review [Source: Reprinted by permission of the Monsanto Company.]*

PERSONAL DEVELOPMENT – PRESENT POSITION

This section provides an opportunity for a meaningful discussion of ways an employe can add to personal competence and satisfaction on the present job.

I. STRENGTHS AND SIGNIFICANT AREAS FOR IMPROVEMENT – Summarize employe's strengths and areas for improvement, as demonstrated in last 12 months.

II. PERSONAL DEVELOPMENT PLAN – Describe plans that will help development in current position.

CAREER DEVELOPMENT – POSSIBLE FUTURE ASSIGNMENTS

NOTE: This section can be completed during the Results Review or at some other time.

III. CAREER INTERESTS – Describe the type of work the employe would like to do in the next two to five years, including willingness to relocate.

IV. POSSIBLE FUTURE ASSIGNMENTS – Evaluate career interests and recommend possible future assignments, if appropriate, for the next two to five years.

V. CAREER DEVELOPMENT PLAN – Describe plans that will help development for future responsibilities.

RESULTS ACHIEVED ON PREVIOUS YEAR'S DEVELOPMENT PLAN –

FIGURE 4-3 *(continued)*

contribute to the establishment of your personal goals as well as the Corporate direction, and (2) you are encouraged to join your fellow employees in realizing your full potential—helping others to reach theirs—thereby moving Monsanto toward achievement of its full Corporate potential.

BENEFITS OF MBO PROGRAMS

Organizations using MBO have experienced several of the following benefits or advantages:

1. **Results in better overall management and the achievement of higher performance levels.** MBO systems provide an overall results-oriented philosophy of management that requires managers to do detailed planning. Managers also must develop action plans and consider the resources needed and control standards.
2. **Provides an effective overall planning system.** MBO helps the manager avoid management by crisis and "fire fighting."
3. **Forces managers to establish priorities and measurable targets or standards of performance.** MBO programs sharpen the planning process. Rather than just saying "do your best" or "give it your best shot," specific goals tend to force specific planning. Such planning is typically more realistic because the program calls for a scheduled review at a designated future date. Subordinates make sure that they can obtain the resources necessary for goal accomplishment and that obstacles to performance are discussed and removed. MBO forces planning of a logical sequence of activities in advance of the start of action.
4. **Clarifies the specific role, responsibilities, and authority of personnel.** Objectives must be set in key result areas and individuals responsible must be given adequate authority to accomplish them. A production plant superintendent who has a goal of producing 10,000 units a day must be given the authority to organize and direct resources to achieve the desired level of production.
5. **Encourages the participation of individual employees and managers in establishing objectives.** If the process of MBO has been undertaken on a joint and participatory basis, the chances are that increased commitment will be obtained.
6. **MBO facilitates the process of control.** Periodic reviews of performance results are scheduled, and information collected is classified by specific objectives. Subordinates are forced to relate what was accomplished rather than concentrate on descriptions of what they did or how hard they worked. MBO also stimulates improvement in the performance of superiors, who are forced to clarify their own thinking and to communicate this to subordinates.

7. **MBO provides a golden opportunity for career development for managers and employees.** Personal development goals are often part of the set of objectives developed in joint sessions. MBO often demonstrates the areas where employees need additional training. Priority establishment provides realistic guides for effort, as well as enabling the concrete demonstration of goal accomplishment. This, in turn, enables a more realistic and specific annual performance review, which, of course, is crucial in deciding on promotions, pay increases, and other organizational rewards.
8. **Other specific strengths of an MBO system** might include:
   a. Lets individuals know what is expected of them.
   b. Provides a more objective and tangible basis for performance appraisal and salary decisions.
   c. Improves communications within the organization.
   d. Helps identify promotable managers and employees.
   e. Facilitates the enterprise's ability to change.
   f. Increases motivation and commitment of employees.[13]

POTENTIAL PROBLEMS WITH MBO

Although there are numerous benefits attributed to MBO, there are also certain problems that may be encountered, such as the following:

1. MBO programs often lack the support and commitment of top management.
2. Goals are often difficult to establish.
3. The implementation of an MBO system can create a "paper mill" if it is not closely monitored.
4. There is a tendency for goals to concentrate too much on the short run at the expense of long-range planning.
5. Some managers believe that MBO programs may be excessively time-consuming.

MBO: ASSESSING ITS OVERALL EFFECTIVENESS

In a review of 185 studies, Jack N. Kondrasuk found that there are numerous arguments pro and con as to the effectiveness of MBO.[14] Many organizations have adopted MBO on "faith" often as a result of questionable case studies or unsubstantiated testimonies. According to another study, "There is relatively little empirical evidence to demonstrate the impact of MBO on any aspect of organizational or individual behavior, including job performance."[15]

TABLE 4-2. *MBO Effectiveness as Applied in 185 Organizations*

Research Approach	Positive	Mixed	Not Positive	Ratio Positive: Not Positive
Case Studies	123	8	10	12:1
Surveys	9	2	1	9:1
Quasi-experiments	20	3	4	5:1
True experiments	1	2	2	1:2
Totals/average	153	15	17	9:1

Source: From Jack N. Kondrasuk, "Studies in MBO Effectiveness," *Academy of Management Review* 6, no. 3 (1981): 425. Used with permission.

As illustrated in Table 4-2, MBO achieved positive results in 153 organizations, a ratio of 9 to 1, positive to not positive. Case studies and surveys show a much higher level of effectiveness for MBO than do experiments. According to Kondrasuk's analysis, "There are tendencies for MBO to be more effective in the short term (less than two years), in the private sector, and in organizations removed from direct contacts with the customer. We may conclude that MBO can be effective, but questions remain about the circumstances under which it is effective."

However, it is believed that since approximately 50 percent of large organizations use MBO, this is indicative of its acceptance as an effective management concept. Despite complaints by managers and researchers, most surveys and case studies of the application of MBO indicate considerable satisfaction with the concept. A number of conclusions regarding MBO can be drawn from the responses of 279 personnel administrators representing a cross-section of private and public sector organizations.[16]

- MBO has been successful in the majority of organizations.
- Effectiveness of an MBO program is not dependent on the type or size of the organization.
- Extensive ongoing training tends to be a fundamental ingredient for a successful MBO program.
- Increased frequency of managerial reviews leads to a more effective MBO program.
- The overall results of MBO programs have not met the expectations of participating managers. Performance did not improve as much as expected.
- Most studies on MBO have tended to emphasize the positive and underrate the negative consequences.
- The major problems associated with an MBO program include insufficient review and evaluation of goals, lack of support of the philosophy of MBO throughout the organization, inadequate participation of employees in goal setting, difficulty in quantifying goals, and too much paperwork required.

SUGGESTIONS FOR IMPROVING THE EFFECTIVENESS OF MBO

MBO programs can be made more effective if management adheres to the following guidelines:

1. Secure top management support and commitment.
2. Specify the overall objectives of the program and communicate them throughout the organization.
3. Emphasize MBO as an overall philosophy or system of management rather than just a performance appraisal technique.
4. Allocate adequate time and resources to instruct each person in the organization in the nature and philosophy of the system.
5. Recognize that all goals must be realistic and attainable and that they must contribute to the overall purpose of the organization.
6. Be willing to modify the goals as changes in the environment dictate. Continuous review is a must.
7. Be sure to clarify responsibility and authority relationships so that everyone understands what's expected in the MBO system.
8. Insist that goals be written and stated in measurable terms to be attained within a specified period of time.
9. Make the goal-setting process a joint activity between superiors and subordinates.
10. Recognize that MBO will not solve all managerial problems.

Summary

The attainment of organizational objectives is the primary concern of management. An approach that aids in goal achievement is management by objectives (MBO). MBO represents an overall philosophy of management—a way of thinking of an approach to planning—that concentrates on measurable goals, targets, or end results. It provides a systematic and rational approach to management and helps prevent management by crisis. To be effective, MBO depends on active participation at all levels of management.

The application of MBO in organizations has progressed through three stages—from an emphasis on performance appraisal, to one on planning and control, and most recently to an integrated system of management. The MBO process consists of several important steps: attaining top management commitment and involvement; establishing long-range goals and strategic plans; defining specific organization objectives; establishing performance objectives and standards for individuals (action planning); measuring results achieved (appraisal); and taking corrective action to ensure the attainment of the desired results (control). The types of objectives established in MBO programs include routine problem solving, innovative, and personal development. Objectives should be limited in number, stated in specific and measurable terms, and should be challenging, prioritized, and attainable.

MBO offers both benefits and problems for managers. Some of the primary advantages of MBO are that it provides an effective planning system; forces managers to establish priorities and specific standards of performance; clarifies specific roles, responsibilities, and authority of personnel; encourages participation in goal setting; aids in control; assists in career development for managers and employees; provides a more objective basis for performance appraisal as well as promotion and salary decisions; and tends to increase the motivation and commitment of personnel. The major problems that may be encountered in using MBO include lack of support and commitment of top management; difficulty in establishing goals; creation of a "paper mill"; tendency for goals to concentrate too much on the short run; and the possibility of being very time-consuming.

Numerous companies have applied MBO. Monsanto's implementation of MBO began in 1974 and extends to the company's 12,000 professional and managerial personnel worldwide. MBO at Monsanto has been integrated with top management's philosophy and commitment to a participative climate.

Research evidence would indicate that MBO has been effective in most organizations; however, one study concluded that MBO tends to be more effective in the short term, in private-sector firms, and in organizations removed from direct contact with customers. While we may not yet be able to deliver the final judgment on the effectiveness of MBO, it is estimated that about 50 percent of large organizations use MBO. This fact of widespread use is considered indicative of effectiveness.

Review Questions

1. What is management by objectives (MBO)? Define and explain its value to management.
2. Compare and contrast Drucker's view of MBO with that of Douglas McGregor.
3. Briefly describe the three distinct phases of MBO programs. What is the present status with regard to MBO?
4. What are the basic steps in the MBO process? Briefly explain each.
5. What are the four types of objectives that can be established in MBO programs? Explain and provide examples of each type of objective.
6. What are the basic characteristics of objectives and how are objectives determined?
7. Briefly discuss the *benefits* and *problems* with MBO. Which are the most significant and why?
8. Has MBO been effective as a management system?
9. What suggestions for improving the effectiveness of MBO could you offer an organization?

Exercises

1. Apply the management by objectives concepts discussed in this chapter by developing clear-cut personal goals for yourself to cover the next year. Be sure to include specific goal statements and completion times for routine, problem solving, innovative, and personal development. Also include specific action plans to ensure goal accomplishment.
2. Visit a firm in your area that uses MBO and ask several managers within the company their reaction to the program. This would be an excellent class project that could be part of a tour of a local business.

Case Study

MBO at the New York Casualty Insurance Company

The New York Casualty Insurance Company began a management by objectives (MBO) program two years ago. Top management of the firm was convinced that MBO would significantly improve the company's overall effectiveness in planning and would provide a system for more accurate evaluation of personnel. Prior to the implementation of MBO, the company had no formal planning system and had used a performance appraisal system that consisted primarily of evaluating such factors as quantity of work, quality of work, judgment, and adaptability. The performance factors were rated from 1 (very poor, unacceptable performance) to 5 (exceptional performance). All personnel including managerial employees were evaluated using this system. The considerable dissatisfaction with this rating system was a primary reason for New York Casualty's implementing an MBO system. At the beginning of each year, overall company objectives as well as departmental goals are formulated and communicated to management personnel throughout the firm. The following is a description of the company's MBO program being applied in the Accounting Services Department.

Barbara Gordon, the accounting services manager, has four supervisors reporting to her. These supervisors are responsible for accounts payable, accounts receivable, payroll, and customer services. At the beginning of each year, Ms. Gordon discusses the company and departmental objectives with each of her four supervisors.

The payroll section supervisor, Dale Frazier, has been with New York Casualty for nine months. Dale had four years of experience in payroll operations at another company and has a B.B.A. in accounting. He is considered to be a very competent supervisor and has five clerks reporting to him. The department processes the payroll for almost 3,000 employees. Dale and Ms. Gordon had agreed on the following goals for the payroll department during Dale's first year as supervisor.

1. Establishment of a consistent account reconciliation program for the 160 payroll-related accounts in the general ledger by June 1.
2. Establishment of a cross-training program for the payroll clerks by June 1.
3. Creation of written documentation for all of the payroll department procedures by September 1 (in accordance with the company's broader statements on policy and procedure).
4. Reduction of employee turnover to 20 percent during the year.

The following is a summary of activities and events that occurred during the year:

- During the year the company experienced rapid growth, adding an average of 75 employees per month.
- Turnover of clerical personnel in the payroll department began in February.

Within the first four months, payroll lost three experienced employees. These personnel changes required considerable on-the-job training for the "new" employees.

Near the end of the year, Ms. Gordon, the accounting services manager, reviewed the progress of the payroll section with Dale. The results were as follows:

Objective 1 Not accomplished. A consistent reconciliation program has not been implemented.

Objective 2 Not accomplished. A cross-training program has not been devised. Several duties have been reassigned as new employees were hired and some jobs have been slightly redesigned.

Objective 3 Not accomplished. Written documentation has increased, but no substantial progress was made during the year toward developing an overall detailed payroll procedures manual.

Objective 4 Not accomplished.

In the conversation with Dale, Ms. Gordon made the following statement, "Dale, I'm very disappointed with the overall performance of the payroll unit. Why did your unit experience these problems?"

Dale agreed the results were not attained as planned but believes employee turnover greatly affected the payroll unit. "Of the three people I hired," he said, "only one was as effective as those who quit."

QUESTIONS

1. If you were Barbara Gordon, how would you rate the performance of Dale Frazier, the payroll supervisor?
2. Evaluate the MBO program being used by the company. Does it meet the criteria for a successful program as discussed in the chapter?
3. Should Dale be retained?

Case Study

Federation Department Stores' MBO Program

Top management of the Federation Department Stores, Inc., a chain of 120 retail stores, had recently decided to implement a management by objectives program throughout their organization. Sam Brown, the manager of the Kansas City department store, had just completed reviewing his objectives for the company's new MBO program with his district manager, Ray Wilson. Sam was both irritated and confused as a result of his meeting with Mr. Wilson.

Three weeks before Sam had received a letter from Mr. Wilson explaining that top management had decided an MBO program would be used to assist all Federation stores in improving efficiency and increasing their profit contribution. The letter indicated the objectives would be used to measure performance and that salary increases and promotions would now be directly related to performance. The accompanying instructions required store managers to list the objectives they felt were appropriate for their store and then stand by for the district manager's review visit.

Sam had realized that he and the five assistant managers of the Kansas City store had a lot at stake in establishing realistic objectives for the store. After discussing the situation, Sam and the assistant managers selected objectives that they felt would be appropriate for their store. They selected performance levels which were improvements from the past year but which they felt they could exceed. Among others, they selected the following objectives:

- Increase selling efficiency as measured by the ratio of sales salaries to sales by 10 percent.
- Reduce inventory shortage to 2 percent of sales.
- Reduce register shortage to ½ percent of sales.
- Improve customer service to the extent that there are 20 percent fewer complaint letters mailed to the home office.

The district manager had arrived late for the MBO review visit, and there had not been much time for discussion. After scanning the objectives Sam submitted, the district manager explained that profit improvement was really what the home office was interested in. Rather than trying to monitor separate objectives from each store, the home office had decided that a 12 percent profit improvement would be a reasonable objective for Sam's store. This single objective would facilitate the monitoring of performance by the home office and would also reduce the amount of information the store would have to submit. The visit was cut short because the district manager had to attend a home office meeting on the advertising budget to be allocated to individual stores.

QUESTIONS

1. The home office of Federation Department Stores planned to use a single MBO plan to measure the performance of each of its stores. Is this a proper way to use MBO?
2. What mistakes, if any, did the home office make in trying to establish their MBO program? Did the MBO system at Federation meet the criteria for an effective program as discussed in the chapter?
3. Will using profit as the sole measure of performance have the results the home office desires?
4. Did Sam have the right approach to setting goals?
5. What indicators of poor communications were apparent?
6. What alternatives does Sam have now in living with the single profit objective established by the home office?

Notes

1. Harold Koontz, "Making MBO Effective," *California Management Review* 20 (Fall 1977): 5.
2. Anthony P. Raia, *Managing by Objectives* (Glenview, Ill.: Scott, Foresman, 1974), pp. 10–12.
3. Peter F. Drucker, *The Practice of Management* (New York: Harper, 1954).
4. Peter F. Drucker, *Management: Tasks, Responsibilities, Practices* (New York: Harper, 1974).
5. See George S. Odiorne, *Management by Objectives* (Belmont, Calif.: Pitman, 1965), and *Management Decisions* (Englewood Cliffs, N.J.: Prentice-Hall, 1969).
6. Raia, *Managing by Objectives,* pp. 14, 15.
7. Ibid., pp. 14–18.
8. Ibid.
9. Gary P. Latham and Gary A. Yuki, "A Review of Research on the Application of Goal Setting in Organizations," *Academy of Management Journal* 18, no. 4 (December 1975): 829.
10. W. J. Reddin, *Effective Management by Objectives* (New York: McGraw-Hil, 1971), p. 16.
11. Richard E. Byrd and John Cowan, "MBO: A Behavioral Science Approach," *Personnel* 51, no. 2 (March–April 1974): 48.
12. Wendell L. French and Robert W. Hollman, "Management by Objectives: The Team Approach," *California Management Review* 17, no. 3 (Spring 1975): 19.
13. See Koontz, "Making MBO Effective," pp. 5–7.
14. Jack N. Kondrasuk, "Studies in MBO Effectiveness," *Academy of Management Review* 6, no. 3 (1981): 419–430.
15. Ibid.
16. Robert C. Ford, Frank S. McLaughlin, and James Nixdorf, "Ten Questions About MBO," *California Management Review* 23, no. 2 (Winter 1980): 90.

References

Babcock, R., and Sorensen, P. F., Jr. "MBO Checklist: Are Conditions Right for Implementation?" *Management Review* 68 (June 1979): 59–62.

Bologna, J. "Why MBO Programs Don't Meet Their Goals." *Management Review* 69 (December 1980): 32.

Denny, W. A. "Ten Rules for Managing by Objectives." *Business Horizons* 22 (October 1979): 66–68.

Dowst, S. "Classify Your Objectives." *Purchasing,* April 25, 1979, p. 38.

Ford, C. H. "MBO: An Idea Whose Time Has Gone?" *Business Horizons* 22 (December 1979): 48–55.

Ford, R. C. "MBO: Seven Strategies for Success." *SAM Advanced Management Journal* 42 (Winter 1977): 4–13.

———, et al. "Ten Questions about MBO." *California Management Review* 23 (Winter 1980): 48–55.

Haines, W. R. "Corporate Planning and Management by Objectives." *Long Range Planning* 10 (August 1977): 13–20.

Jackson, J. H. "Using Management by Objectives: Case Studies of Four Attempts." *Personnel Administrator* 26 (February 1981): 78–81.

Koontz, H. "Making MBO Effective." *California Management Review* 20 (Fall 1977): 13–15.

Lopata, R. "Key Indicators: Simpler Way to Manage." *Iron Age,* January 26, 1981, pp. 41–44.

Migliore, R. Henry. *MBO: Blue Collar to Top Executives.* Washington, D.C.: Bureau of National Affairs, 1977.

Muczyk, J. P. "Dynamics and Hazards of MBO Application." *Personnel Administrator* 24 (May 1979): 51–61.

Pack, R. J., and Vicars, W. M. "MBO—Today and Tomorrow." *Personnel* 56 (May 1979): 68–77.

Schneier, C. E., and Beatty, R. W. "Combining BARS and MBO: Using an Appraisal System to Diagnose Performance Problems." *Personnel Administrator* 24 (September 1979): 51–60.

Tosi, H., et al. "How Real Are Changes Induced by Management by Objectives?" *Administrative Science Quarterly* (June 1976): 276–306.

Weitzul, J. B. "Pros and Cons of an MBO Program." *Best's Review* 81 (January 1981): 72–73.

Wiehrich, H. "TAMBO: Team Approach to MBO." *University of Michigan Business Review* 31 (May 1979): 12–17.

KEY TERMS

decision making
professional decisions
routine decisions
nonroutine decisions
intuition
scientific approach
hypothesis
professional decision maker
risk
decision maker
problem content
payoff relationships
state of nature
model
physical models
schematic models
mathematical models
management information system
microcomputer
minicomputer
telecommuting

LEARNING OBJECTIVES

After completing this chapter you should be able to

1. Define decision making and distinguish between personal and professional decision making and routine and nonroutine decision making.
2. Describe the basic approaches to decision making.
3. Explain the decision-making process.
4. Identify the primary factors affecting the decision-making process and describe the requirements for decision making.
5. Relate the importance of model building to a manager.
6. Describe a management information system (MIS) and identify some of the computer trends that today's managers are expected to confront.

5

Managerial Decision Making

> Robert Ewing, the president of Marathon Energy Company, an integrated petroleum refiner and distributor, is faced with a critical decision: should production capabilities be expanded? Marathon's sales are beginning to exceed the refining capacities of the two existing refineries. Currently, Mr. Ewing is considering three possible sites: California, Texas, and New Jersey. All sites have different strengths and weaknesses. The problem is further complicated by the fact that there is a possibility of a business turndown, in which the current production facilities would be capable of meeting the demand for Marathon's production.

> Barbara Williams is currently the financial vice-president for Security State Bank. The accounting manager has just retired, and his replacement must be selected. Barbara would like to promote from within, but there are also several qualified applicants from outside the firm. Her alternatives are numerous and complicated. If she hires from within, the best-qualified person may not be selected. On the other hand, if she hires from outside the firm, the current employees may not accept the new manager.

> Billy Brown, a first-line supervisor for Kwik Corporation, is disturbed because Allen Smith, one of his employees, violated a serious company policy today by failing to wear his safety glasses on a dangerous job. The company policy states that any employee who does not follow the stated policy will receive a written reprimand on the first offense and will be suspended for two weeks for the second violation. Allen has already received one reprimand, but he is also one of Billy's best workers and has been with the firm for five years. Billy believes that Allen may quit if he receives the suspension.

Robert, Barbara, and Billy are decision makers. The manner in which they resolve these and other problems will determine their success as managers. In fact, decision making should be viewed as if it were synonymous with managing, thereby suggesting that it accounts for a large portion of a manager's job.

Merely because individuals have a managerial title does not mean that they are managers. There are many individuals with elaborate titles who are not managers in that they are not decision makers. The key to whether a person should be classified as a manager involves determining whether he or she is in a position to decide among various alternatives and also chooses to make the needed decision.

On the other hand, some individuals who are in a position to make decisions cannot be considered managers. If managers have the authority but refuse to make a decision, they should not be classified as managers. One of the most important qualities for success as a manager is to not procrastinate on decisions, hoping problems will go away if ignored. True, a decision to do nothing may, in its broadest sense, imply that a choice has been made. A constant pattern of failure to decide does not give a person the right to be called a manager.

Increasingly, managers are being measured by the results of their decisions. Companies do not want dynamic failures; they want individuals who are equipped properly to make the correct decision. This does not imply that the manager must be right 100 percent of the time; no one is that perfect. It does suggest that successful managers have a higher "batting average" than less successful managers, and there is a growing tendency to evaluate managers primarily on the results of their decisions. For instance, as in the above example, it is not likely Robert, Barbara, or Billy will always be correct in their decisions. If they are to be effective, however, their ratio of success to failure in choosing the best decision must be high.

In this chapter, we define decision making and identify some of the major factors that affect the decision-making process. Next, the steps in the decision-making process are presented, followed by an explanation of the requirements that must be fulfilled if decision making is to take place. Because models are used so extensively in the decision-making process, an explanation of the use of models will also be presented. Finally, a brief discussion of computers and management information systems (MIS) will be provided as they relate to decision making. The intent of the chapter will be for the student to gain an appreciation of the decision-making process as it relates to managers.

DECISION MAKING DEFINED

decision making

Decision making can be described as *the process by which we evaluate alternatives and make a choice among them*. As such, decision making is a universal requirement for all of us. Basically, each individual who is involved in the decision-making process must first search for opportunities to make decisions and identify alternatives. Next, the individual must choose one alternative, and the choice of this alternative is defined as the decision. However, to place decision making in perspective, we need to distinguish between several classifications of decisions such as personal versus professional decisions and routine versus nonroutine decisions.

Personal versus Professional Decision Making

Although a similar thought process exists in both personal and professional decision making, a person should be aware of the differences between the two. Here is a brief overview of personal and professional decision making.

Personal Decisions

A wide variety of decisions are considered personal. Decisions to study, go on a date, watch television, or go to bed early are examples of personal decisions made routinely by college students each day. Personal decisions can ultimately affect an organization. A personal decision to purchase a Ford rather than a Chevrolet actually helps one firm due to the sale and hurts another because of the lost sale.

A portion of a manager's time is spent discussing an employee's personal problems and what can be done about them. The supervisor should recognize that employees who are experiencing difficulties in their personal lives may bring these problems to the job. Thus, a supervisor may be involved to some degree in the personal decisions of his or her employees, whether the supervisor desires to be or not.

Professional Decisions

Virtually every gainfully employed person is required to engage in decision-making activities as part of the work he or she performs. College professors make decisions concerning the nature of the information they will present to their students. Physicians diagnose problems and prescribe treatments. Scientists formulate hypotheses and select experiments for testing them. Managers of baseball teams, football coaches, politicians, plumbers, and clergy—in fact, all who are gainfully employed—are required to make decisions as part of their professional lives. Yet the administrator of a business organization is labeled a manager, whereas many of the other decision makers are not. *Managers are expected to be professional decision makers; their reason for being is to make decisions.*

Why are managers labeled professional decision makers whereas others—the physicians and scientists—are not? The answer is visibility. The manager of an organization operates in an open environment. A managerial decision affects many people (customers, stockholders, employees, the general public). The professional manager sees the results of decisions reflected in the firm's earnings report, the welfare of employees, and the economic health of the community and the country. Decisions made by professional managers may be no more or no less crucial than those of the physicians or scientists,

---

Most Important Reasons for Success and Effectiveness as a Manager

Early involvement in nearly all facets of business with participation in decisions with resulting years of training in management and decision making.

K. B. WATSON, President and CEO, Pioneer Corporation

---

but their decisions affect a greater number of people. Managers' careers cannot be made by only one good decision. Their careers must be marked by a series of decisions that are acceptable. Hence, as Levitt contends, unlike the lawyer, scientist, or physician, "the manager is judged not for what he knows about the work that is done in his field, but by how well he actually does the work."[1] To survive, the manager must be able to make **professional decisions.**

professional decisions

Routine versus Nonroutine Decision Making

As was the situation with Robert, Barbara, and Billy, managers are continually confronted with the need to make a variety of decisions. Professional decisions may range from such major ones as whether to build a new plant or to enter a new business all the way to the rather routine decisions such as deciding which supplier to purchase the bathroom paper towels from. The two major categories of professional decision making are routine and nonroutine. We briefly discuss routine and nonroutine decisions and the conditions under which decisions must be made.

Routine Decisions

routine decisions

Most managers make numerous daily or routine decisions in the performance of their jobs. **Routine decisions** made by managers are governed by the policies, procedures, and rules of the organization, as well as the personal habits of the managers. For example, decisions related to appropriate disciplinary action when an employee has violated company safety rules, such as the decision that Billy Brown must make regarding Allen Smith, may be governed by company policies, procedures, and rules. In terms of personal decisions, deciding where to go to lunch and whom to eat with are examples of routine decisions that may be determined to a great extent by habit of the individual.

Since routine decisions are relatively easy and simple for managers to make, they *free* managers for more challenging and difficult problem solving. Many organizations set forth policies, procedures, and rules that provide a framework for decision making. However, managers are little more than a robot or a clerk if they simply adhere to the "rule book" and do not exercise personal judgment.

Nonroutine Decisions

nonroutine decisions

While routine or programmed decisions may take up a considerable portion of a manager's time, individuals *make or break it* as managers on the basis of the success of their nonroutine decision-making ability. **Nonroutine decisions** *are those that are designed to deal with unique problems or situations.* The decision to expand to foreign markets, build a new production plant, or buy a more advanced computer system are all examples of nonrou-

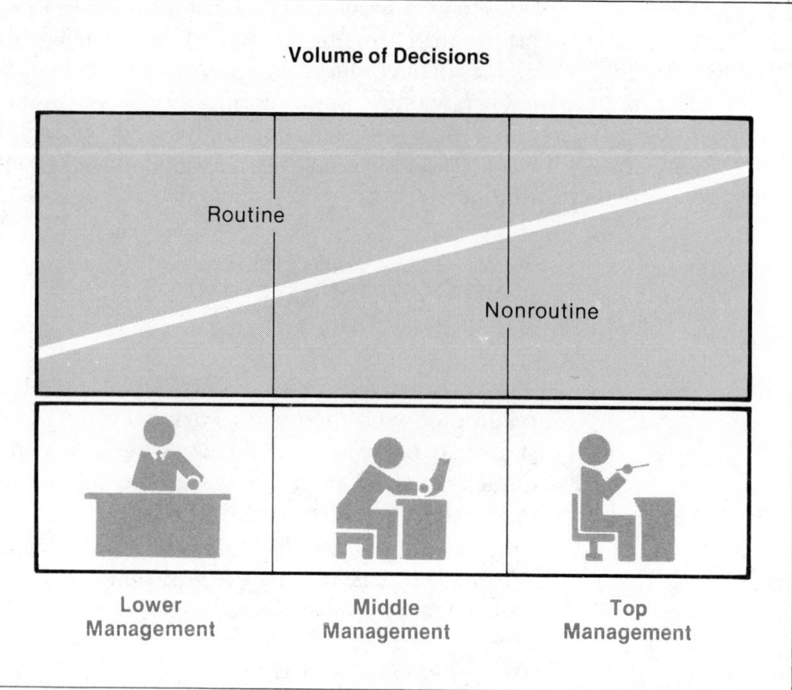

FIGURE 5-1

Managerial Levels and the Amount of Routine versus Nonroutine Decisions

tine or unique decision situations. While these are examples of nonroutine decisions made by upper management, managers at all levels in the organization make nonroutine decisions. For instance, nonroutine decisions made by a first-line supervisor might include firing an employee or changing the layout or work flow procedures in his or her department.

Figure 5-1 illustrates the relationship between three levels of management and the percentage of routine and nonroutine decisions made at these different levels of management. As a manager progresses to higher levels, the number of nonroutine decisions increases. Nonroutine decisions require that managers exercise creativeness, intuition, and good judgment in resolving these types of problems.

APPROACHES TO DECISION MAKING

There are two basic approaches to decision making: intuition and research. Each will next be briefly discussed and broadened to include the professional decision maker.

Intuition

Individuals who rely on intuition make their decisons based on accumulated experience. **Intuition** is acquired through experience and accomplishments

intuition

rather than through a formal decision-making process. Experience tends to be a good teacher as evidenced by the fact that many college recruiters place major emphasis on the business experience a student has gained while in college and extracurricular activities he or she has participated in. They believe the learning process for a particular job may be shortened if a student has been active in other endeavors while in college. But decision makers who rely only on intuition base a judgment on their "feel" for the situation. Alternatives are chosen on the basis of a hunch. If decision makers confront a situation to which they have not been previously exposed, a wrong decision often results. The intuitive approach has several obvious shortcomings such as:

1. Learning from experience is usually random.
2. Although we learn experience, there is no *guarantee* we learn from experience.
3. That which we learn from experience is necessarily circumscribed by the limits of our experience.
4. Conditions change and experiences of the past may not be good indicators of current or future conditions.[2]
5. The question may be asked, "Do you have twenty years of experience or do you have one year of experience twenty times?"

Research and the Scientific Method

scientific approach

The research approach is based on a systematic, formal approach to decision making. It stresses that the scientific method should be used in problem solving. The **scientific approach** can be conveniently divided into four distinct but interrelated phases—observation of events, hypothesis formulation, experimentation, and verification.

Observation of Events

The first step in the scientific method requires that a person has the desire to explore fully the relationships among the elements of a system and a curiosity to know *how* and *why* they produce a particular outcome. The process begins by observing an occurrence and then asking why it happened.

Hypothesis Formulation

hypothesis

The second step in the scientific method requires the creation of an explanation as to the hows and whys of the observed event. A **hypothesis** is a tentative statement of the nature of the relationships that exist. A hypothesis provides an explanation of the cause that brought about the observed effect. For instance, you might hypothesize that a relationship exists between turnover and job satisfaction.

• CAREER PROFILE •

LEE R. FLANDREAU
Vice-President and Chief Operating Officer
International
Signode Corporation

SIGNODE Little did Lee Flandreau realize when he graduated from Miami University of Ohio with a degree in geology that one day he would be responsible for an international division that comprises 40 percent of Signode's overall business and encompasses all of the products Signode sells outside the United States. The International Division includes thirteen foreign subsidiaries and manufacturing operations, along with twenty-two licensees, sixty-three distributors, three joint ventures, a trading company, and an export operation. Signode does industrial material and equipment business in over one hundred countries outside the United States and is the leader in its industry.

One of the critical moments in Flandreau's career was whether to leave the field of geology. He said, "Major oil companies at that time were not hiring geology majors. After a year of working as a surveyor, I decided to enter business as an industrial salesperson. I took a substantial reduction in pay, but the opportunities for long-range growth were greater and more directly related to personal effort. The job I took was as a sales representative for Signode." From that beginning, Lee has moved successfully up the ladder to his present position. Some of the responsibilities Mr. Flandreau

Experimentation

The scientist subjects the hypothesis to one or a series of tests to determine whether the tentatively stated relationship does in fact exist. Tests confirm or support the hypothesis or prove it to be unsound.

Verification

The final step in the scientific method is verification of the findings obtained from the experiment. Sometimes this may take the form of another experiment or a series of experiments. Such is the case when a marketing researcher finds that a sample market is highly receptive to a new market and then verifies these results in additional test cities when the product is actually placed in the home.

has held with Signode include: special sales representative, brick industry; manager, special industry projects; project manager, corporate planning; director of field sales (domestic); president, Signode Canada, Ltd.; and corporate vice-president, international.

When Lee was asked why he chose a career in management, he said, "A career in management offers a wide variety of challenges and rewards and an opportunity to use a blend of skills, ranging from technical to motivational. Any particular outstanding skills or traits that one possesses, whether in organizing, writing, speaking, enthusiasm, or a high energy level, can be utilized in producing successful results in a management position."

Mr. Flandreau believes that management affects the health of an enterprise and through that the lives and careers of many people. The quality of management affects millions daily and long term. He said, "I would only suggest a management career to those who are comfortable with the prospect of this kind of responsibility and with long work hours, strong company loyalty, and with the business of selecting, training, and dealing with people. Technical skills alone are no indication that an individual will enjoy or be successful in management. One of the qualities that we look for in a potential manager is the ability to sort out priorities in a complex situation, determine the steps to be taken to accomplish the objective, and do them well."

For students seeking a career in management, his philosophy is to join an organization of promise in a position available and be the best in the world at that position. The opportunities for advancement are unpredictable, circumstantial, and frequent, but they will take care of themselves. His present objective, for instance, is to be the best international executive in the world.

For those seeking a career in international business, Lee said, "I would suggest that they be flexible in assignments, willing to relocate anywhere in the world, and have an interest in geography. Success in international business requires an interest in the languages, cultures, customs, and laws of various countries, as well as patience and perseverance. Most foreign environments are also less comfortable than ours. American industry as a whole is very poor at exporting its products, and the need for good international managers is great."

The Professional Decision Maker

professional decision maker

The **professional decision maker** must adopt an approach that uses the best features of both the intuitive and the research approaches and goes one step further in that all the information that managers are able to obtain is used to assist in decision making. Intuition is an essential part of good research. This experience provides valuable insight into what may occur if a certain decision is made. The research approach, on the other hand, forces the decision maker to evaluate critically what is known and to recognize what is unknown before jumping to a decision based solely on a feel for the situation or a hunch. Professor Ralph C. Davis's classic statement summarizes the need for a bond between these two approaches in this discussion of the professionally trained executive:

A man who has nothing but background is a theorist. A man who has nothing but practical experience is a business mechanic. A professionally trained executive is one in whom there is an effective integration of these two general types of experiences, combined with adequate intelligence regarding the types of problems with which he must deal.[3]

THE DECISION-MAKING PROCESS

Decision making involves choosing among various courses of action. It is often as simple as deciding whether you will work overtime or as complicated as deciding on the future objectives of the firm. If an organization is to be successful, it must have people who are willing and able to make decisions that will be best for the firm. As such, decision makers are the architects of an organization. They have developed the ability to obtain solutions to problems that occur in their area of responsibility.

A complete representation of the decision-making process can be seen in Figure 5-2. As illustrated, all decisions must be made within the constraints of both the internal and external environment. The internal and external factors surrounding the decision maker may change, based on whether the decision is made by top-, middle-, or lower-level management, but the general process does not. For instance, the president will likely have to consider the views of the stockholders when making a decision to build a new plant. On the other hand, the production supervisor may have company policy restraints that dictate what decision can be made with regard to the reasons an employee can be terminated.

Insights to Success

I have, over the years, helped a great many young people move up the ladder in their careers with airline management. This help is gladly given to those who create the image of being interested in personal growth and, at the same time, are truly interested in handling the business at hand in the most efficient manner.

I generally take one or two people into union contract negotiations with me. The person who grasps the significance or importance of such negotiations (even though at times they are boring, repetitive, and seemingly very wasteful for management time) is the kind of individual to whom I will give other opportunities. The person who takes an interest in the total operation and is aware of significant events and attempts to form and suggest resolutions when appropriate opportunities arise also gets my attention.

M. W. TAYLOR, Vice-President—Maintenance, Continental Airlines

---

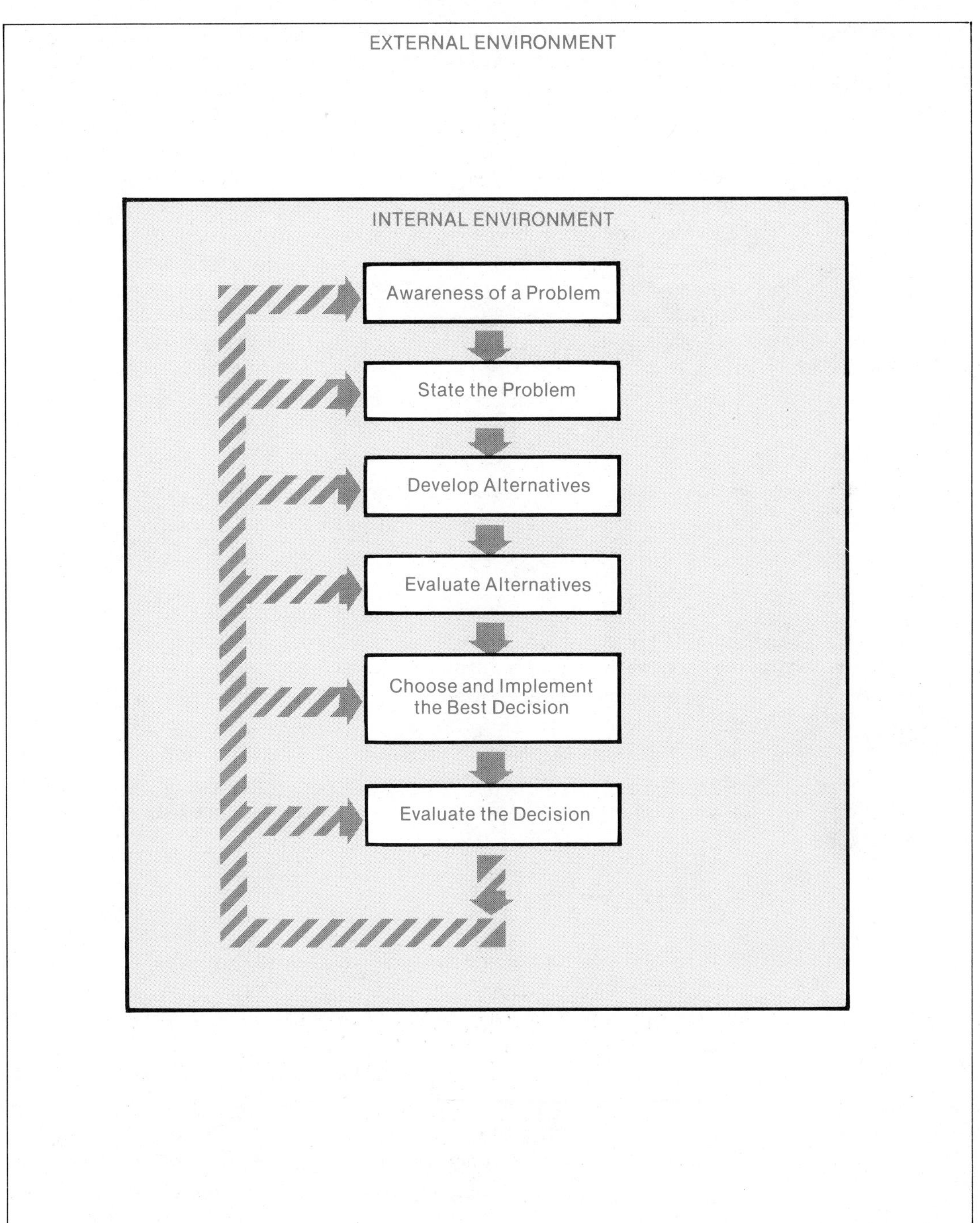

FIGURE 5-2 *The Decision-Making Process*

It should also be noted that the implementation of a decision does not complete the decision-making process. The arrows in the decision-making process model indicate that there is constant reevaluation and feedback to every phase of decision making. The outcome—whether good or bad—provides information through which future decisions are made. As such, decision making is an on-going, dynamic process. For example, if a manager makes the decision to implement a new work procedure and it proves unsatisfactory, a different alternative would likely be chosen. If the new procedure works, a learning process has resulted. Successful managers learn from their mistakes. The less successful managers make the same mistake over and over and wonder why their decisions are consistently wrong. Elements of the decision-making process are discussed next.

Awareness of a Problem

When a person doesn't realize a problem exists, nothing can be done to solve the problem. We have all heard the answer to the question, "Why are you doing it this way?" The answer, "We've always done it that way," causes a person who is truly interested in problem recognition to go into a state of shock. This situation often occurs because we have stopped looking for problems that need solving. As professional managers, a fraction of our time should be spent looking for opportunities to make decisions.

Problems are recognized primarily through the planning and control functions. However, the problem itself may deal with any of the management functions of planning, organizing, influencing, and controlling. The establishment of plans and the development of procedures to monitor their accomplishment makes a person aware that a problem exists.

State the Problem

The second step is to define the problem as clearly and concisely as possible. As Robert J. Sweeney, president of Murphy Oil Corporation, said, "A successful manager must have the ability to weed out the wheat from the chaff before deciding on a course of action." A major point for consideration is that the manager must solve the problem, not the symptoms. Too often managers treat symptoms and do not identify the actual problem. Let us assume, for instance, that a large number of new employees are failing a particular portion of their training (symptom). The problem may be identified as the difficulty of the training material or the lack of ability of the employees, although the real problem was that the trainer could not teach the subject matter in an understandable manner. Until the trainer can identify the real problem, the situation cannot be corrected. Another example of an incorrect problem definition would be to define the problem of a company as not making a sufficient profit. Not making a profit may be a symptom but not the real cause. The causes might include ineffective cost controls, excessive

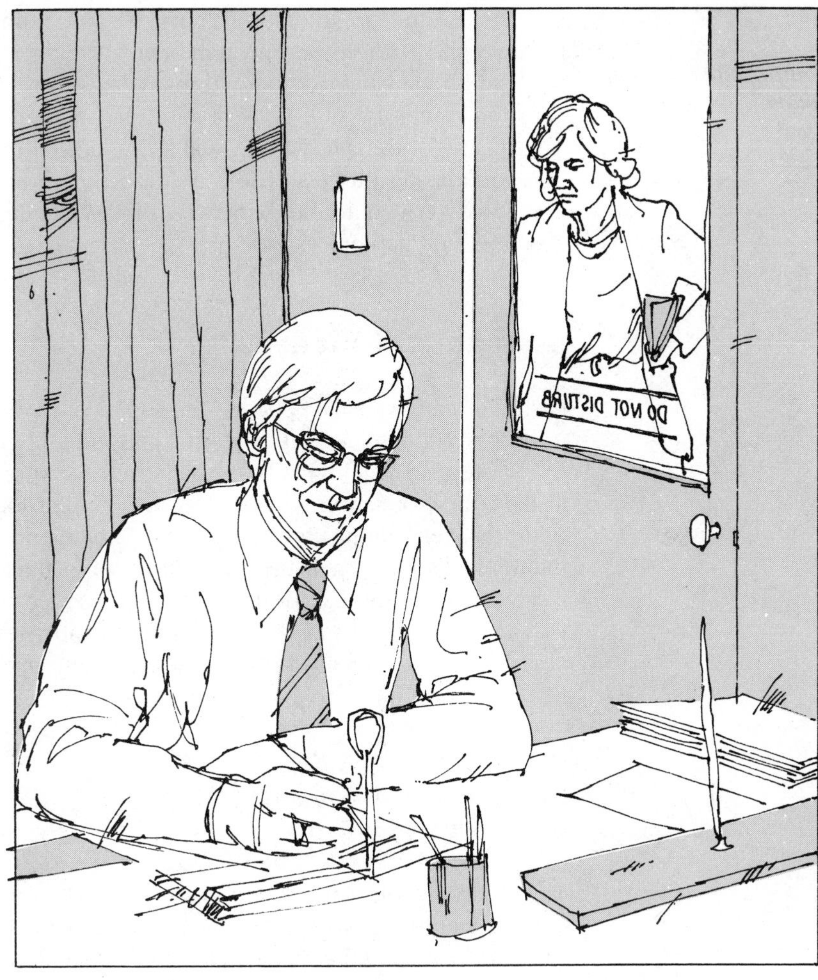

You can't solve the problem until you recognize that a problem exists.

inventory, high turnover of personnel, or a multitude of other factors. Whatever the instance, identification of symptoms rather than causes can hurt the decision-making process and result in inappropriate decisions being made.

Develop Alternatives

The manager next generates alternative courses of action that may be implemented as a solution to the problem. Naturally the number of alternatives generated is limited by the amount of time available for the decision as well as by the importance of the decision itself. Obviously, however, the best decision cannot be made if it is not considered as an alternative course of action. For instance, the company that was not making a profit might consider a number of alternatives such as cost control or incentives to workers to correct the cause of the problem. However, if the correct alternative is not considered, the problem cannot be solved.

The means for generating alternatives are numerous. Managers may get together and *brainstorm*. Through brainstorming, individuals are encouraged to identify as many possible alternatives as they can. When brainstorming is taking place, the task is to obtain a large number of potential solutions. The quality of the alternatives will be judged in the evaluation stage of the decision-making process. There are also numerous quantitative techniques that have proven to be beneficial in developing alternatives. These are described in Chapters 15 and 16.

Evaluate Alternatives

Each alternative that has been developed must be evaluated with respect to how it will interact with external and internal environmental conditions. In this step, answers must be provided for the question, "What will happen if this course of action is taken?" A major point for consideration is that an optimum decision at times cannot be implemented. The external environment may force a manager to make a less than optimum decision. For instance, an airline may desire to expand service out of a particular airport. However, the local public may create so much disturbance and potential ill will over the increased noise that the airline may decide on another, less than optimum alternative.

Choose and Implement the Best Decision

The ability to select the *best* course of action from several possible alternatives separates the successful managers from the less successful ones. The alternative offering the highest promise of attaining the objective, taking into consideration the overall situation, should be selected. This step may sound easy, but for managers it is the toughest part of their job. Fear of making the wrong decision sometimes causes managers to make no decision at all. It is in this stage that weak managers sometimes fail. It is no wonder that relatively high salaries are afforded the managers who have gained a reputation for not only having the internal strength to make decisions but also for making the correct ones the majority of the time. It is easy to be a "Monday morning quarterback" who criticizes the coach for making the wrong decision. However, the coach had to make decisions on the football field, and the coach hopes to make the correct decision more often than the incorrect one.

Directly or indirectly, the decision maker must implement the decision. When individuals other than the decision maker are required to implement the act, the decision maker must make certain that the appropriate steps have been taken. It is here that the decision-making process often falls short. Some managers, because they are action oriented, believe that once the decision has been made, it will automatically be implemented. Good managers monitor the situation to ensure that their decisions are accomplished.

Evaluate the Decision

No decision-making process is complete until the decision has been exposed to the realities of the actual business environment. Evaluation requires an objective assessment of how the decision has solved the problem. It is the process by which managers learn and develop useful experience. Without this step, the decision-making process has no value beyond providing an immediate solution to a problem. It is perhaps for this reason that some firms stress decentralized management in which lower-level managers are provided the opportunity to become more involved in the decision-making process. This process provides the younger managers with decision-making experience. Intuition and judgment increase with more exposure to decision making. Through decentralization an individual does not have to wait until he or she finally is promoted to a high-level position before being given the opportunity to make decisions. It is better to make a wrong decision at a lower level, and learn from this experience, than to make a more crucial decision at a higher level and be wrong.

FACTORS AFFECTING THE DECISION-MAKING PROCESS

There are two primary factors—risk and time—that can have a major impact on the decision-making process.

Risk

risk

The probability that an incorrect decision will have an adverse effect on the organization is referred to as **risk.** It is a factor that all managers consider (consciously or unconsciously) in decision making. For instance, Betty Harris, president of a small book publishing company, is considering paying $100,000 to a well-known author to write a book. If the book sells well, the firm could make $500,000, but if it doesn't, Betty's company will lose the $100,000 plus an additional $75,000 in developmental and promotional cost. Betty decides not to take the risk because the loss of $175,000 could put the company out of business.

On the other hand, Bill Anderson, purchasing manager for General Motors, daily signs contracts for automobile parts that greatly exceed $1 million. The risk in these types of decisions is typically low. Even the loss of $1 million for General Motors would not have a disastrous effect on the firm. As the risk increases, more time and effort are often devoted to the decision-making process.

Time

The amount of time that can be devoted to decision making is often a critical factor that must be considered. A manager would prefer to have sufficient time to evaluate and analyze thoroughly all alternatives prior to making a decision. Most business people are not afforded this luxury; they must make decisions in a time-pressure situation in which there is often not sufficient time to evaluate all alternatives. Suppose, for instance, that a customer of yours offers to purchase a large number of items for a price that is lower than you normally receive. Although the firm will make a profit on this order, the profit is not as large as normally obtained. Today there are no other orders to choose from, but tomorrow there may be. However, the decision must be made today or the buyer will go to another manufacturer. The company is truly under time pressure. It is much easier to make decisions when there is enough time to evaluate all the alternatives, but managers often do not have the extra time to decide.

REQUIREMENTS FOR DECISION MAKING

As previously stated, the most important quality that a business person needs is the ability to make correct decisions. This one quality often separates the successful from the less successful managers. There are, however, certain conditions that must be present before a decision problem can exist. These conditions must be met for all types of decision making. A decision problem must contain the following five conditions: decision maker, problem content, courses of action, payoff relationship, and the state of nature.

Decision Maker

decision maker

While Harry Truman was president of the United States, he always kept a plaque on his desk that stated, "The buck stops here." He was the person responsible, and he made the final decision. The **decision maker** has the responsibility for choosing the course of action that will solve the problem within the area for which he or she is accountable.

The role of decision maker may be assumed by an individual or by a group of individuals depending on how the organization is managed. This takes into consideration the various management styles and the way in which the organization is structured. Basically, however, if there is no decision maker, there is no decision problem. At times, decision makers are not easy to identify. Contrary to some thinking, everyone does not enjoy making decisions even though they are charged with the responsibility.

Problem Content

problem content

The **problem content** includes the environment within which the problem exists, the decision maker's knowledge of that environment, as well as the environment that will exist after a choice is made. Because of the significance of taking into consideration the environment in decision making, a decision that may be considered optimum in one organization may result in complete failure in another. For instance, if a nonunion firm decided that because of reduced sales, 10 percent of the work force must be laid off, the least productive workers would likely be the first to be laid off. On the other hand, a unionized firm facing the same circumstances would adhere to the labor-management agreement and lay off the employees with the least seniority.

Courses of Action

To have a decision problem, the decision maker must have more than one alternative from which to choose. Alternatives may be many or few in number. They may merely represent the option of "doing something" or "doing nothing." A good decision maker, however, attempts to identify and evaluate as many alternatives as possible given the time and resource restrictions.

Payoff Relationships

payoff relationships

The various alternatives must be evaluated in terms of what the objective was in making the decision. The establishment of **payoff relationships** implies the ability to measure the costs or profits of various courses of action and the benefits that may be obtained. When the profits and costs associated with a particular alternative cannot be expressed mathematically, the decision maker suffers severely. For example, decision making is made much easier if it can be stated that a particular decision will result in a savings of $50,000 as opposed to merely expressing an opinion that costs will be lowered.

State of Nature

state of nature

The **state of nature** refers to the various situations that could occur and the probability of this situation happening. For example, you have all heard a weather reporter say, "There is a 20 percent chance of rain." Rain would be one state of nature, and no rain would be the other state. If there was no element of choice, we would all be excellent decision makers. Choice may be required when the precise relationships among alternatives are known and the problem is simply to define what the relationships mean in terms of an objective. Choice may, on the other hand, come about because of uncertainty about the future environment or because precise relationships between alternatives are not known. Any person who has ever played five-card draw poker understands the uncertainty about the future and the imprecise relationships that can exist. The good decision maker, as with the good poker player, studies the situation thoroughly in the hope that his or her decisions will be correct more often than not. Because of the state of doubt, it is most likely a decision maker will never be 100 percent correct.

A DECISION-MAKING PROBLEM

Let us illustrate a decision-making problem through an example of how to choose a part-time job. Suppose you are considering two possible job positions at a local pizza restaurant that has recently opened. One of the positions is for an assistant manager and the salary is based on commission. The alternative is as a pizza cook for which there is an hourly wage of $4.00.

Because the pizza house is relatively new, a trend has not been established as to the sales potential of the business. However, based on the experience within the community, you estimate that there is a 20 percent chance of high sales, 50 percent chance of average sales, and 30 percent probability of low sales. You recognize these states of nature will have a major impact on the amount of money received from the assistant manager's position. As an assistant manager, you estimate the payoff for high sales will be $8.00 an hour, for average sales it will be $6.00 an hour, and if low sales occur you will only receive $1.00 an hour. However, you will receive $4.00 an hour no matter what the sales are if you choose the job as a pizza cook. The payoff relationship between each act and state of nature is provided in Table 5-1. You are now in a position to evaluate the two alternatives.

$$\text{Expected earnings for pizza cook} = .2(4.00) + .5(4.00) + .3(4.00) = \$4.00$$

$$\text{Expected earnings for assistant manager} = .2(8.00) + .5(6.00) + .3(1.00) = \$4.90$$

Thus, if you are willing to accept the alternative that has the higher expected value, you will take the assistant manager position that offers commission (expected value of $4.90 versus $4.00 per hour). However, as with other managers, there may be other facts that must be considered before an actual decision is made. Your financial situation may prevent you from taking the chance of receiving only one dollar per hour if sales are poor. Other alternatives also might have been evaluated. For instance, there may have been other jobs available to consider. However, although there are numerous considerations, the example should provide you with a brief appreciation of the thought process that should go into managerial decision making.

TABLE 5-1. *The Pizza House Job Matrix*

Alternatives	High Sales	Average Sales	Low Sales
Probabilities	.20	.50	.30
Hourly wage	$4.00	$4.00	$4.00
Commission	$8.00	$6.00	$1.00

MODEL BUILDING

model

A procedure quite beneficial to a manager in all phases of the decision-making process is model building. A **model** is defined as *an abstraction of a real world situation.* It is an attempt to portray reality through various means without having to work directly with the real world. For instance, suppose a manager must make a major decision involving many millions of dollars as to where to build a new factory. Once funds have been spent on the plant, the decision is irreversible. Model building permits the decision maker to develop alternatives that can be evaluated prior to making the *real* decision, which commits funds. As such, model building is an extremely useful tool for managers in the decision-making process.

In business, models can be expressed in many ways and can have many meanings. This is true because managers must constantly deal with highly complex business systems that must be simplified to be understood. Model building provides the means for simplifying a difficult situation. For instance, the plant manager might develop a three-dimensional model of the plant planned for construction. Then, as if shifting furniture in a doll house, the manager can move the equipment around to see what effect the shift of the equipment might have on plant operations. If the plant was built and then the movement of the equipment was attempted, the results could prove to be quite costly.

The model builder must first determine the purpose of the model as it relates to depicting a real world situation. The purpose of the model should be consistent with the overall objectives of the firm. Next, it must be decided which parts should be included. This factor alone is a major advantage of model building. If there are certain components that would be included in the real world, but have no effect on the problem under consideration, they can be omitted. As in the above plant equipment example, the electrical hookup may be omitted because most likely its placement can be decided on after the equipment has been installed. Finally, the model builder must define the interrelationships that exist among the parts. Does one piece of equipment produce a part that will be used by another machine? The understanding of these interrelationships is vital in model building.

In a true sense, the model is a tool for extending the manager's understanding of the organization. Models are more widely employed than commonly realized. Many times a manager may not even realize a model is being used. If a manager envisions what would occur if a particular decision is made, model building is actually taking place. The manager has a picture (model) of the relationships that will result if a particular decision is made. Whether they recognize it or not, managers are constantly using models to support their decision-making activities.

One means by which we can examine models is through the language the modeler employs. By language, we mean *the technique chosen to communicate understanding.* Models may use physical, schematic, or mathematical "languages."

Physical Models

physical models

Physical models were among the first to be used in management and are the most familiar. Systems represented by physical models can include people, ships, airplanes, automobiles, houses, dams, shopping centers, factories, retail stores, and so on. **Physical models** generally *look like* the system they represent. Physical models can, however, be more abstract representations. A photograph captures the physical appearance of a person as does a portrait, but in painting the portrait, the artist can deemphasize or exaggerate features to make the subject appear more or less handsome.

Schematic Models

schematic models

Line drawings, flowcharts, graphs, maps, organization charts, and similar items that represent the major features of a particular system are **schematic models.** Schematic models may or may not be related in *scale* to the object being abstracted. Elements of a highway system are represented by road maps, which are two-dimensional scale models. On the other hand, schematics depicting electrical circuitry found on the back of a radio or television set usually are not drawn to scale.

Schematic models have been widely used in management to define components of the organization and to analyze problems. Schematics are used to describe processes and procedures as well as physical components. For example, a computer programmer uses schematic models—the flowchart—to illustrate the steps that must be accomplished in writing a program. Although schematic models are useful to managers in each major business function, production management (now called production and operations management) has, perhaps, utilized them more than any of the others. Production and operations management models are discussed in Chapters 15 and 16.

Mathematical Models

mathematical models

A mathematical equation(s) that defines and represents the relationship among elements of a system is a **mathematical model.** These models portray in quantitative terms the essential elements and interrelationships among elements of the systems they describe. The language used, mathematics, is a powerful one, because it is not so subject to misinterpretation. However, for mathematical models to represent reality, we must know a good deal about reality. In many instances this by itself is a problem. The primary limitation to the application of mathematical models in assisting management is the constraint imposed by our inability to measure the relationships among elements of the environment.

MANAGEMENT INFORMATION SYSTEMS

management information system

Since the advent of high-speed computers, management has been fascinated with the amount and speed with which data can be prepared. Correct and timely information is extremely valuable to a manager in the decision-making process. A means that managers use in obtaining timely, accurate, and useful information with which to make decisions is a **management information system** (MIS). While the computer has made management aware of the importance of a properly designed MIS, the use of an MIS should not depend on a computer; a firm without a computer can also have a very effective management information system.

Historically, a major problem confronting management has been obtaining information that is timely, accurate, and useful. Management has encountered numerous instances in which the information is timely and accurate but not useful in making decisions. Perhaps the type of information received is not relevant to the type of problems facing management. For example, timely and accurate information of how many parking spaces are being used will be of little value to the production manager who is attempting to obtain the weekly quota of producing 1,000 units.

The development of a management information system does not necessarily require the use of a computer; the computer has merely made it possible to obtain the data with the speed that would make the information useful. Thus, a MIS should be designed without considering what computer should be selected. A computer system can be chosen once MIS has been designed.

The procedure that is used in the design of a MIS is relatively simple. The details are what cause the problem. Described below are the general steps that should facilitate the development of a useful MIS.

Study the Present System

A person cannot tell where they want to go until they know where they have been. Possible questions to ask are: (1) What is the present flow of information? (2) How is the information used? and (3) How valuable is this information in terms of decision making? At one stage in his career one of the authors was a team member in charge of developing one of the first state highway information systems. One of the agencies that had to be integrated into the system was the state highway patrol. In conversations with local troop members, it was discovered that one weekly report that caused considerable difficulty in preparation was being sent to headquarters. For each troop (there were thirteen) it took one officer four hours to prepare the report. Once the author went to headquarters to determine how the data were used in the decision-making process and an interesting situation was discovered. Each weekly report was neatly filed by a secretary and the data were never used. However, if the report was not submitted, a letter of reprimand was sent to the unit commander.

Develop a Priority of Information That Managers Need

Once the current system is throughly understood, the next step involves developing a priority of information that managers need. There is certain information a manager must have if proper decisions are to be made; there are also data that are merely *nice* to have but not critical for the manager to perform his or her job. The MIS that is designed must concentrate on providing the high-priority information. Data lower in the priority list will be generated on an "if possible" basis.

Once individual managers have developed their own priority list, the separate lists will be integrated into a priority list for the entire organization. Certain departments may discover that the information that they identified as top priority will be far down the list. The needs of the entire organization must be taken into consideration with this list.

Develop the Information System

A system will now be developed that satisfies the needs of the organization. Reports are prepared that will provide this information. As items lower on the priority list are considered, their benefit to the organization diminishes. At a certain point on the list the costs do not justify the information and these items will not be included.

The MIS that was prepared for one state government is presented in Figure 5-3. As can be seen, there are many types of input data necessary to satisfy the needs of the system. The highway safety information system provides various types of information that is available for both administration and operations. All areas are tied together into a complete information system. Data that come in from one department of the state can provide the information used in another department. If a person has a car wreck and is given a ticket, this information not only is used by law enforcement agencies but also forms a data base to identify high accident locations. When properly designed, the important information an organization needs in the decision-making process is available.

Choose a Computer

Because of the ever-expanding use of computers, it is becoming increasingly important for managers to be "computer literate." This does not mean that managers must be data-processing experts any more than they must be

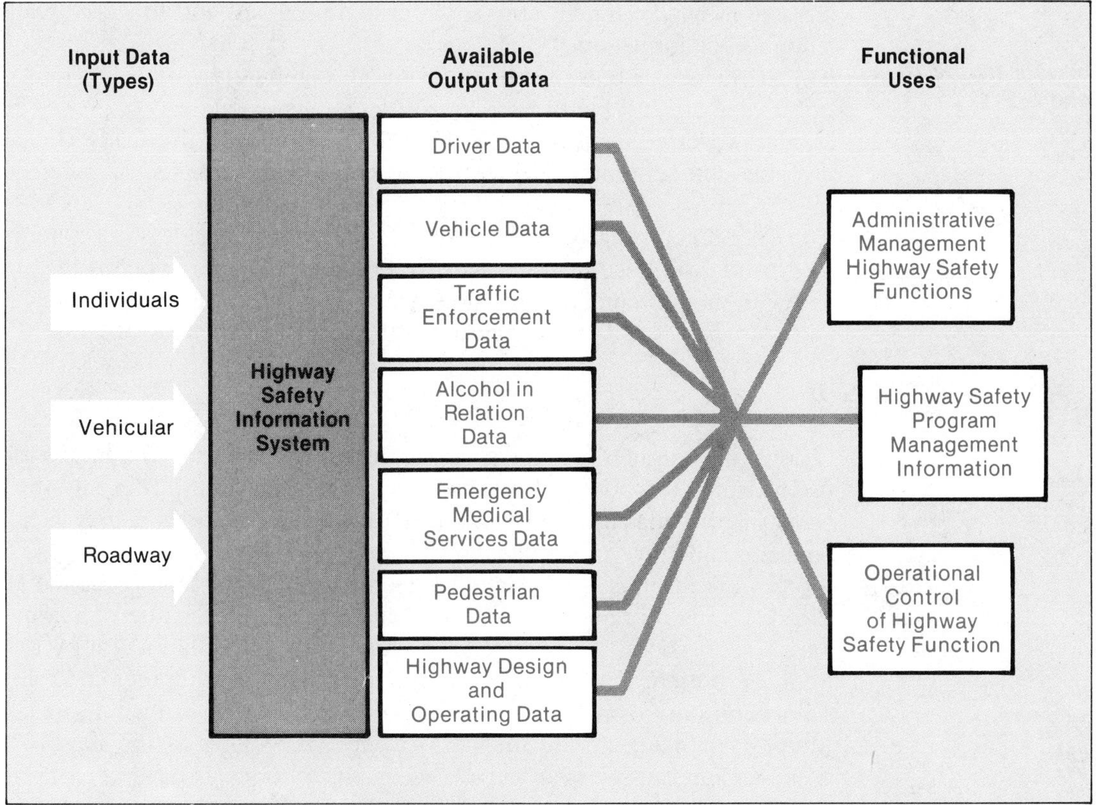

FIGURE 5-3 *Highway Safety Information System*

professional accountants. But just as managers need some accounting knowledge to understand and interpret financial reports, they need to know what computers *can* and *cannot* do. Managers need to know enough to make good decisions regarding the use of computers. Fear of using computers has caused some managers not to use this most valuable tool.

The mistake many firms make is that they purchase or lease a computer and then attempt to design the information system around the computer. If a computer is needed to provide accurate, timely, and useful information, the computer chosen should provide the best capability of processing the data that management needs. This in itself is not an easy task. There are many sizes and capabilities from which to choose. The smallest version of a computer is the **microcomputer.** In recent years, the availability of these computers has permitted many smaller firms to afford their own computer system. Micros are relatively small but quite powerful, with costs ranging from $2,000 to $20,000 depending upon the system's sophistication.[4] Some applications involving micros include accounts payable, accounts receivable, and point-of-sale acquisition.

microcomputer

minicomputer

Minicomputers are larger and more powerful than microcomputers. Costs for minicomputers range from $20,000 to $1 million. Minicomputers are able to handle much more sophisticated programs and to store greater amounts of information.

At the upper end of the spectrum are computers costing millions of dollars that are capable of handling vast amounts of data and of processing several programs virtually at the same time. Because of the many choices available, the computer selected should be based on the specific needs of the firm.

Undoubtedly management information systems in business will continue to expand. As it becomes necessary for business decisions to be made faster and with more accuracy, computers will become increasingly important. As such, MIS becomes a valuable facilitator to the decision-making process.

COMPUTER TRENDS

Changes in computer technology are occurring virtually daily. It is impossible to foresee all the new uses for computers that will occur. The only thing certain is that managers must be alert to these innovations if they are to remain competitive in this rapidly changing world. For instance, the use of robots in the factory environment is increasing at a dramatic pace. We are already seeing robot-assisted assembly lines in the manufacture of automobiles. Sales of robots are expected to be more than 8,000 units a year by 1985 from the present level of 2,000.[5] Some estimates see computer-controlled robots and other sophisticated machines as affecting more than 45 million American workers during the next twenty years. One of the reasons is costs. As you can see from Figure 5-4, as unit labor costs have been rising, computer power has been getting cheaper. Because of the trend, robots are expected to be used extensively in the future.

telecommuting

The computer has begun to change the location of where people actually accomplish their work. Computer hookups from office to home have added a new dimension to the work-at-home routine, called **telecommuting.** Moving the computer terminal into the home has permitted businesses to reach labor markets that might not otherwise be reached. However, managers must be trained to cope with this new working relationship. Some managers find it quite difficult to supervise workers they do not see. Also, workers sometimes find working at home an isolating experience because of the elimination of office politics, gossip, and that most important coffee break with friends.[6]

The office of the future is also expected to change dramatically because of the computer. Specialized work stations are being created for professionals and managers. The benefit of this trend is that it fulfills an urgent need to increase worker productivity, particularly in the office.[7] These work stations should provide executives with quick access to information by merely touching a button.

Sophisticated data communication systems involving computers are affecting the way managers perform their daily tasks. Already in use in some firms is the electronic mail box (EMB). Through EMB, messages are transmitted from worker to worker through the computer. For instance, an execu-

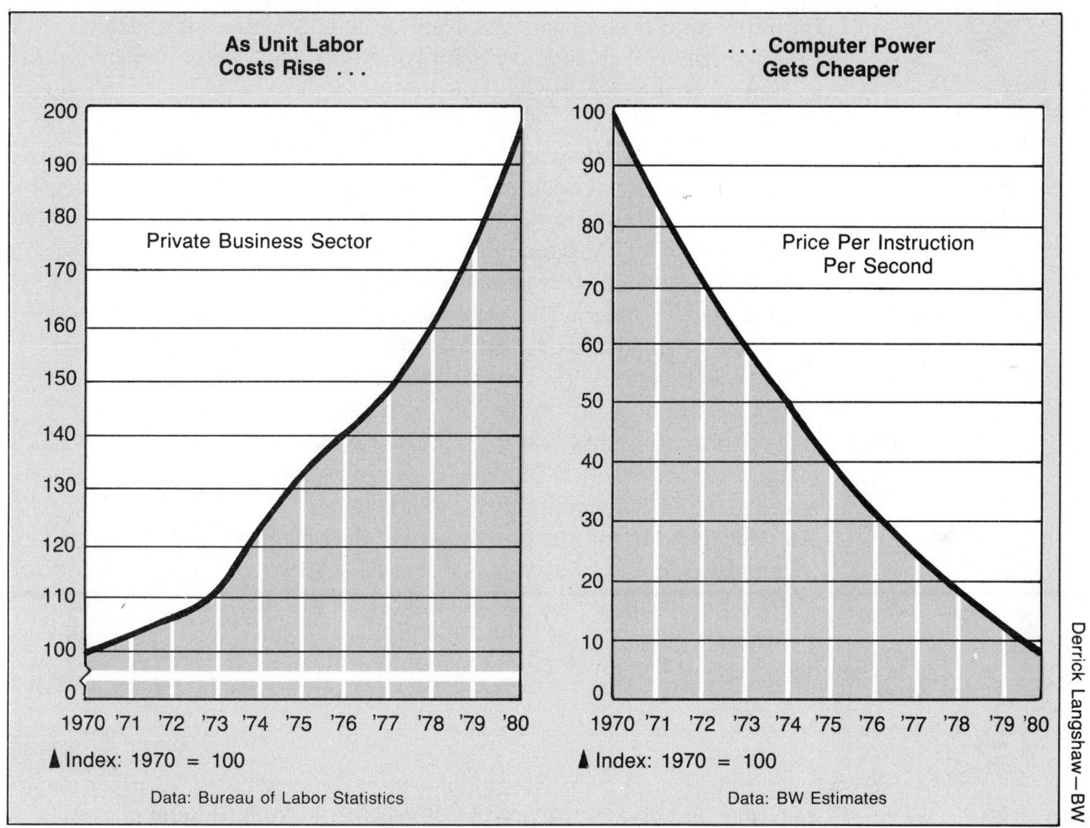

FIGURE 5-4 ***Comparison of Labor Cost and Computer Cost*** [*Source: "The Speedup in Automation." Reprinted from the August 3, 1981, issue of* Business Week *by special permission, © 1981 by McGraw-Hill, Inc., New York, NY 10020. All rights reserved.*]

tive located in California may wish to ask several New York managers a complicated question. The question is entered through a terminal at the California headquarters and is received virtually instantly by the managers in New York. No mail delay is involved, and security is maintained because the message can be scrambled and unscrambled by the computer. The managers in New York can research the question, enter their response in their terminals, and the answer will then be transmitted confidentially back to California. A hard copy can be produced by merely pressing a button.

Summary

A person who has the authority to make decisions, but refuses, should not be classified as a manager. Decision making is the most important responsibility of a manager. The actual decision-making process is simple to state but is often difficult to implement. Once an individual is aware a problem exists, the problem should be clearly stated, and then alternatives to the solution of the problem can be developed. Next, each alternative is evaluated, and the best alternative is chosen to be implemented. The decision-making process continues as the decision is evaluated to determine if the proper decision was made.

Before a decision can be made, certain basic requirements must be achieved. Naturally a decision must be made by a decision maker. Problem content, courses of action, and the payoff relationships must be identified. A most important consideration is identifying the state of nature of selecting a particular decision. It is because of this state of doubt that even the best managers will occasionally make incorrect decisions. However, good managers make correct and effective decisions more often than not.

Model building allows alternatives to be identified, developed, and evaluated. A model is an abstraction of a real world situation. Some of the most common models available for use by managers include physical, schematic, and mathematical models. These models let the manager portray the real world through various means indirectly.

Management information systems (MIS) provide another way to assist the manager in the decision-making process. MIS is a technique that provides management with timely, accurate, and useful information to assist in the decision-making process. The benefits of MIS have been significantly enhanced since the development of high-speed computers.

Review Questions

1. Define and discuss the process of decision making. How important do you feel it is to a manager?
2. Distinguish between personal decisions and professional decisions. Why are managers expected to be professional decision makers?
3. What effect do risk and time have on decision making?
4. Discuss the strengths and weaknesses of the person who makes decisions based on intuition and the person who makes decisions based on research.
5. What are the basic requirements that must be present in decision making?
6. Distinguish among physical models, schematic models, and mathematical models. Give an example of each.
7. Define *management information system*. What steps should be followed in developing a MIS?

Exercises

1. We are all decision makers. In a one-hour period during the day list the top five decisions you made. Were they based primarily on intuition, the scientific approach, or the professional approach? Why?
2. Make a list of the different types of models you observe during a twenty-four hour period.

3. Develop a small decision-making problem in which there are two courses of action and three states of nature. Remember that the probabilities must total one.

Case Study

A Case of the Request for Special Favors

Bill Thompson is the manager of the payroll department of the Wellingham Manufacturing Company. Bill reports to the company comptroller. A major function of the department is processing the company biweekly payroll for the more than 2,000 employees of the company. The work load in payroll is very task and deadline oriented. The work load is even more demanding during holiday periods—such as during Thanksgiving, Christmas, and New Years.

At the beginning of December, Betty Jones, a twenty-year-old clerk, informs Bill Thompson she needs to take a week of vacation between Christmas and New Year's Day in order to "visit her family during the holidays." Since the payroll is processed every other week, it has been customary for the payroll department manager and clerical personnel to schedule vacations during the weeks that the payroll is not processed. Betty, an efficient worker, has been employed since March and became eligible for one week of vacation in October. (An employee is eligible for one week of vacation after six months or two weeks upon the completion of one year.) At the time Betty was employed, specific vacation arrangements were not discussed, only the minimum time for eligibility.

Betty's request for a one-week vacation during the holiday period would make it difficult for the payroll department to meet its deadlines. The department will lose two days during the period because Christmas Eve and Christmas Day are holidays. Thus, Bill is very concerned about getting the payroll processed that week, especially with Betty on vacation.

Bill and Betty discussed work load requirements during the week in question. He told her the department needs her effort that week, particularly since it is a short week. Betty responded by saying, "My husband has made plans for us to go and he says we're going." Bill feels that while Betty is a satisfactory performer, she apparently lacks commitment to the job and company. He is also concerned about the effects on other members of the work group if he approves Betty's vacation request.

QUESTIONS

1. What decision should Bill make regarding Betty Jones' request for vacation? In order to assist Bill, use the decision-making process developed in the chapter.
2. In making the decision, what additional situational factors should be considered other than the fact that she intends to take the vacation against the wishes of the supervisor?

Case Study

A Decision to Move a Bank Teller

Commerce is a small midwestern town in a rural area. Two new farm-related industries recently opened factories in the area and created an increase in the general business activity for Commerce. Due to the increased business, First National Bank of Commerce, the largest of the three banks in town, experienced long waiting lines for the paying and receiving tellers. On the basis of a questionnaire sent to its customers, the bank's executives decided to open a new drive-through facility. The bank purchased a vacant lot across the street and built one drive-through window facility. Room for expansion was possible if the new service proved to be as popular as expected.

Eight tellers were employed by the bank. All were considered good workers and had good relations with the customers. Mrs. Williams, age forty-eight, a widow, was chosen by a bank vice-president to be the teller in the new drive-through facility. She had been with the bank for nine years. The reasons given for her selection were as follows: (1) she can service customers rapidly; (2) she has a responsible attitude toward the work to be accomplished (she helps others when her work is finished and the other tellers seek her advice when they have a problem); and (3) she works well without supervision. An additional teller was employed inside the bank to take Mrs. Williams' place.

The opening day for the new window was hectic, but thanks to Mrs. Williams' organization and work habits, the opening was considered to be a success by the customers and by bank officials. Mrs. Williams complained of a headache, but she attributed it to "opening day jitters." As the following week progressed, Mrs. Williams' headaches increased, and she was becoming despondent. The next week Mrs. Williams was late twice and made some errors on her accounts. The bank president then told the vice-president to reevaluate his choice of Mrs. Williams as the teller for the new drive-through facility.

QUESTIONS

1. What other factors should the vice-president have considered prior to moving Mrs. Williams to the new drive-through facility?
2. What do you believe are the real causes of the difficulties that Mrs. Williams experienced?
3. At what point did the decision-making process break down?

Notes

1. Theodore Levitt, "The Managerial Merry-Go-Round," *Harvard Business Review* 52 (July–August 1974): 120.
2. Items 1–4 adapted from Alvar O. Elbing, *Behavioral Decision in Organizations* (Glenview, Ill.: Scott, Foresman, 1970), p. 14.
3. Ralph C. Davis, *The Fundamentals of Top Management* (New York: Harper, 1951), p. 55.
4. Jay Daniel Conger and Fred R. McFadden, *First Course in Data Processing with BASIC, COBOL, FORTRAN, RPG* (New York: Wiley, 1981), p. 167.
5. "The Speedup in Automation," *Business Week,* August 3, 1981, p. 59.
6. "The Potential for Telecommuting," *Business Week,* January 26, 1981, p. 94.
7. "Will the Boss Go Electronics, Too?" *Business Week,* May 11, 1981, p. 106.

References

Archer, Earnest R. "How to Make a Business Decision: An Analysis of Theory and Practice." *Management Review* 69 (February 1980): 54–61.

Brown, Rex V. "Do Managers Find Decision Theory Useful?" *Harvard Business Review* 51 (May–June 1970): 78–89.

Daniel, D. W. "What Influences a Decision? Some Results from a Highly Controlled Defense Game." *Omega* 8 (November 1980): 409–419.

Roy, Delwin A., and Simpson, Claude A. "Export Attitudes of Business Executives in a Smaller Manufacturing Firm." *Journal of Small Business Management* 19 (April 1981): 16–22.

Grayson, C. Jackson, Jr. "Management Science and Business Practice." *Harvard Business Review* 51 (July–August 1973): 41–48.

Hagarth, Robin M., and Mankridakis, Spyors. "Value of Decision Making in a Complex Environment—An Experimental Approach." *Management Science* 27 (January 1981): 93–107.

Henderson, John C. "Influence of Decision Style on Decision Making Behavior." *Management Science* 26 (April 1980): 371–386.

Hughes, Robard Y. "A Realistic Look at Decision Making." *Supervisory Management* 25, no. 1 (January 1980): 2–8.

Kirby, Peter G. "Quality Decisions Start with Good Questions." *Supervisory Management* 25, no. 8 (August 1980): 2–7.

McKenny, J. L., and Keen, P. G. W. "How Managers' Minds Work." *Harvard Business Review* 52, no. 3 (May–June 1974): 79–90.

Mangrum, Claude T. "Determining the Right Regimen of Managerial Exercises." *Supervisory Management* 26, no. 2 (February 1981): 26–30.

Pitz, Gordon F.; Sachs, Natalie J.; and Heerboth, Joel. "Procedures for Eliciting Choices in the Analysis of Individual Decisions." *Organizational Behavior and Human Performance* 26, no. 3 (December 1980): 396–408.

Simon, Herbert A. *The New Science of Management Decision.* Rev. ed. Englewood Cliffs, N.J.: Prentice-Hall, 1977.

________. "Rational Decision Making in Business Organization." *American Economic Review* 69, no. 4 (September 1979): 493–513.

Vroom, Victor H. "A New Look at Managerial Decision Making." *Organizational Dynamics* 1, no. 4 (Spring 1973): 66–80.

Wright, Peter. "The Harassed Decision Maker: Time Pressures, Distractions and the Use of Evidence." *Journal of Applied Psychology* 59, no. 5 (October 1974): 555–561.

CASE STUDY FOR PARTS I AND II

Airomatic Tool, Inc. (ATCO)

On a cold December morning James Holt got into his 1962 Thunderbird to go to work at Custom Valve Manufacturing Company, a firm that he and his brother, Brad, started six months previously. The only thing different about this particular morning was that the old, reliable T-Bird would not back out of James' garage. The reverse gear band had snapped in the transmission, and James was stranded in his garage. Being mechanically inclined, James proceeded to repair the car himself after calling his office to tell them that he would be late. He changed clothes, grabbed some wrenches, and slipped under the car to make what he thought would be an easy adjustment. After four hours of frustration, James finally emerged from under the T-Bird. He had succeeded in repairing the car, but his hands were sore and battered, and he was muttering to himself—"there must be a better way."

This experience remained in James' mind along with the need for a tool that would have prevented the battering of his knuckles and fingers, as well as his psyche. Stimulated by this experience, in addition to his background in plumbing, carpentry, air-conditioning and heating, and television repair, he began attempting to develop a concept of a power wrench. After a year of research and design, trial and error, he produced a prototype of the first "pneumatic ratchet wrench." After about six months, he and his brother, Brad, had invested considerable time and almost $12,000 of Custom Value's very limited capital in this project. About a year from his experience in his garage trying to repair his car, James and Brad had successfully developed what they thought would be a highly useful power tool.

The Holts now had a new product with seemingly great potential, but no market research had been conducted to estimate the demand for the product. A patent attorney was employed, and a U.S. patent was acquired on the new wrench. Several of the prototypes were loaned to mechanics for the purpose of "testing" the product to see if it would perform what the

This case was prepared by R. Dean Lewis of Sam Houston State University and Robert E. Holmes of Southwest Texas State University as a basis for class discussion rather than to illustrate either effective or ineffective handling of an administrative situation. Presented at a Case Research Association Workshop and distributed by the Intercollegiate Case Clearing House, Soldiers Field, Boston, Mass. 02163.

mechanic needed when repairing an automobile. Without exception, the mechanics indicated that they were very impressed with the pneumatic wrench and greatly encouraged the Holts to produce and market it. Encouraged and excited by the mechanics' reactions, James and Brad Holt decided to form a new company, Airomatic Tool, Inc., which would manufacture the tool. Shortly after forming the new company, the brand name ATCO was adopted and the officers of the firm were James Holt, president; Brad Holt, vice-president; and Danny Jones, secretary-treasurer. All three men were excellent mechanics, and while none were graduate engineers or designers, all three possessed strong technical expertise. Each of the three had only limited management experience and none had any prior background in marketing.

ATCO's first problem was that of acquiring needed developmental capital. Commercial lenders were not willing to risk the needed capital with so little collateral on a new product venture. Finally, the U.S. Small Business Administration through the Security Bank of Cato, Texas, provided a $120,000 loan to ATCO to purchase equipment and build a 5,600 square feet building. A condition of this loan was that ATCO would be moved to Cato, a small town of about 600 located approximately sixty-five miles from Dallas.

The new facilities were developed and ATCO started producing the air-powered ratchets. Sales were initially slow, and working capital was soon exhausted. In December 1970, another Small Business Administration loan through the Security Bank of Cato was granted for the amount of $76,000.

James had continued to be very active in the research and development area. He had developed three additional models of the "air ratchets," an air drill, an impact wrench, swivel hose assemblies, and a twin connector for air hoses. He acquired patent rights to all these products except the twin connector.

With the additional working capital, the corporation started producing all of these products. However, the basic pneumatic ratchet accounted for about 75 percent of sales.

COMPETITION

The attributes of the pneumatic ratchet wrench and the market potential of the product were very apparent and immediately drew attention from domestic and foreign tool manufacturers. Within two years after ATCO had introduced the new tool concept, two large domestic producers and one

Japanese manufacturer had comparable tools on the market. These firms had discovered weaknesses in the patents and engineered around the ATCO products. The exclusive rights to the swivel hose connector was considered one of the greatest losses to the firm since it was becoming a universal accessory used with all pneumatic hose products. ATCO believed these competitive products were outright infringements on its patent rights but did not have the money to get involved in lengthy court battles with these large firms.

The larger competitors had established channels of distribution available for the new products along with huge promotional budgets. They were able to price their products lower than ATCO due to lower operating costs and the acceptance of lower margins. These firms had other successful products to spread costs over and their total volume was much greater than ATCO's, thus permitting lower unit margins. One competitor rapidly moved into private branding of its pneumatic ratchet with several large retailers.

MARKETING

Initially ATCO sales were brisk, and it was difficult for the company to keep pace with demand for the new pneumatic ratchet. By the end of the first year of being on the market, pneumatic tools sales reached 300 units per month. Barely into the second year of operation, the company accepted a contract from a large distributor for 1,000 units per month. ATCO did not have the production capacity to meet this demand, but in an effort to try, the company either dropped or significantly limited its supply to other clients. This, naturally, greatly irritated ATCO's other purchasers who were forced to obtain their wrenches from ATCO's competitors. The contract with the large distributor was dropped the next year, and ATCO was left "holding the bag." This event created considerable misfortune for ATCO, making it difficult for them to continue in business. Since competition had increased significantly, most of ATCO's older clients had shifted their business to other suppliers. Suddenly, ATCO was faced with virtually no market demand and more plant capacity and labor than was needed. After the large distributor cancelled their contract for 1,000 pneumatic ratchets per month, demand for ATCO's products was at fewer than 300 units per month.

ATCO utilized industrial distributors as the primary element of its distribution system. The company had no full-time sales staff of its own, although James Holt attempted to make personal calls on all corporate distributors. James indicated that this was most difficult, and he was not able to consistently accomplish these sales calls. Despite James Holt's personal sales calls, management had very limited feedback from the final users of the wrenches. The Holts did very limited advertising, but ATCO did conduct a direct mail campaign directed at all independent garage owners in Texas. This campaign involved a series of three mail-outs describing ATCO's products. However, the firm received only very limited response to the mail-outs. A survey of competitive products indicated that ATCO's prices were higher than most of the other companies in the industry.

FINANCES

Sales of ATCO had peaked at just over $1 million three years after the firm began operations but had recently declined to about $500,000. After earning a profit after taxes of $76,000 their second year in business, ATCO sustained a net loss of $124,500 in their most recent year.

Pondering the financial results of the past year, James and Brad Holt were wondering if ATCO could survive. And if the firm was to survive, what actions would be necessary?

Questions

1. Identify the problems at ATCO. What were the causes of these problems?
2. Could the problems have been avoided? If so, how?
3. Would the concept of strategic planning, or other elements of planning have helped ATCO management? Discuss.
4. Describe the backgrounds and experiences of the managers at ATCO. Were they capable of adjusting to increasing competition?

PART III

Organizing

KEY TERMS

organization
function
specialization or division of labor
work simplification
functionalization
downward differentiation
span of management
outward differentiation
functional similarity
departmentation

LEARNING OBJECTIVES

After completing this chapter you should be able to

1. Define and describe the organizing process.
2. In organizational terms, describe a function and specialization and identify the benefits and limitations of specialization.
3. Describe and give examples of the process of downward and outward differentiation.
4. Describe functional similarity and identify the factors that determine the extent to which it can be applied.
5. Identify and describe the primary means of departmentation.

6

The Organizing Process

"One small step for man and one giant leap for mankind"—the words of Neil Armstrong in July 1969 as he stepped onto the surface of the moon have become part of American history and represent the realization of our dream to explore space and walk on the moon. Landing on the moon was the culmination of one of the most highly organized and technically complex endeavors ever achieved. Few other programs in the history of humanity illustrate the importance of management and, in particular, the organizing function of management better than the U.S. space program.

NASA has developed the goals of the space program despite the changes in the economic and political climate of the country. Most recent and notable among these accomplishments is the successful flights of the space shuttle, Columbia. Despite the fact that the space shuttle program fell three years behind schedule and more than $1 billion over the initial cost estimate, the success of the United States' space program could not have been attained without a sound application of the organizing process of management. Organizing and coordinating the extremely complex technology, the diverse and highly trained personnel, and the contributions of hundreds of subcontractors and still attaining the goals of the space program was a monumental task. Exploration of space can be only achieved through skillful application of technological advancements and through the effective organization, coordination, and utilization of physical and human resources.

The managerial function of organizing is essentially the same for all types of organizations, whether one is concerned with the U.S. space program or with managing a university, hospital, government organization, or large company like Exxon. Once the objectives and plans of an organization have been developed and stated, management must design an orderly manner of bringing together and coordinating human and physical resources. In this chapter we discuss the concepts, principles, and practices of the organizing function.

ORGANIZATION DEFINED

The term organization is widely used; most of us are quite aware of it each day as we read newspapers, walk about the university campus, watch television programs, or listen to the radio. To some people the word *organization* causes thoughts in terms of large companies such as Sears, General Motors, U.S. Steel, or the social clubs, churches, or service groups in every community. Rarely do we think of the local grocery store, service station, fast food restaurant, or nursery school as an organization. Each of these, however, is an organization.

Organizations, large or small, have at least these three common characteristics:

- They are composed of people.
- They exist to achieve goals.
- Each has some degree of structure that results in a definition and limitation of the behavior of its members.

organization

Thus, an **organization** can be defined as *two or more people working together in a coordinated manner to achieve group results.* Since most of us spend a considerable part of our lives working in organizations, it is important for us to understand fully how organizations function and how organizations can be managed effectively. To be effective, a manager must be capable of organizing *human resources, physical factors,* and *functions*—production, marketing, finance, personnel—in a manner to ensure the achievement of the goals of the firm. This process is crucial to the success of every organization where people work together as a group.

THE PROCESS OF ORGANIZING

The managerial function of organizing is illustrated in Figure 6-1. As you can see, the external environment will also affect the organizing process. For instance, government legislation and public demand for clean water and air may create the need to add personnel to monitor and implement changes needed to conform to the laws and the public's expectations. Managers perform the organizing process by:

- Establishing what is to be accomplished (objectives).
- Determining the type of work that needs to be accomplished (functions).
- Assessing human resources.
- Assessing physical resources requirements.
- Grouping the functions, physical resources, and human resources into an organizational structure (functionalization and departmentation).
- Assigning the obligation to perform a certain job (responsibility) and the right to make decisions or take action to accomplish the job (authority).
- Assigning specific work activities.
- Determining if the job was accomplished (accountability of personnel).

Why should a manager be concerned with the organizing process? The primary purpose of the organizing function is to achieve an effective and efficient blending of the essential ingredients for organizational success: people, physical resources, and structure. This coordination is imperative if the firm is to achieve its goals. Without good organization, chaos may result. When the organizing function is performed effectively, personnel understand the goals of the firm, as well as the role and functions they are expected to fulfill. In addition, all persons have a clearer understanding of their responsibility and to whom they report and are accountable to, as well as how their work relates to the work of others in the organization.

In this chapter we will discuss the upper half of Figure 6-1, which is a model of the organizing process. In Chapter 7, we will discuss the delegation of responsibility and authority and the organization structure in the lower half of the same model (as Figure 7-1).

The organizing function must be closely integrated with the planning function. In fact, the first step in organizing is the establishment of objectives, as noted above and as shown in Figure 6-1. Before a manager can determine what functions or resources are needed, clearly defined objectives are essential. The manager must know what is to be accomplished. Once goals and plans have been established, the organizing process begins.

THE ORGANIZING PROCESS: AN EXAMPLE

The following example of a newly formed company illustrates the organizing process. Gregory Johnson, a systems engineering manager for ten years with IBM, has recently decided to resign his position and form a computer services company, which he has named Computer Systems Incorporated (CSI). Johnson and his two partners, Wes Roach and Milton Bishop, also IBM managers, are making plans to develop a computer services firm specializing in the development, installation, and maintenance of computer software systems for life insurance companies.

The goal for CSI is to provide high-quality, specialized computer services to life insurance companies at a profit. After establishing the *objectives* for the new company, Johnson and his partners *determine* the *functions.* They determined that the type of work that needs to be accomplished includes: systems engineering and design, programming development, and the installation and maintenance of computer systems. Based on the functions that need to be accomplished, *human* and *physical resources* required to accomplish the work are then determined. Johnson, an experienced computer systems manager, realized that CSI will require highly trained systems analysts, computer programmers, and marketing personnel, as well as a clerical support staff if the firm is to achieve its goals. In addition to the personnel required, physical resources such as capital, computer equipment, office space, and office furnishings are essential. Johnson must determine not only the type of personnel needed but also the number of specialists needed for each major function. In addition, he must secure sufficient capital from banks, the other owners, other stockholders, or other sources to begin and continue operations. Johnson will need money to lease office space, purchase or lease equipment, employ and compensate personnel, and pay for supplies.

Johnson realizes that he must now coordinate the *functions* and the *physical* and *human resources* into a workable organization structure. He decides that three departments are needed: (1) systems design and program-

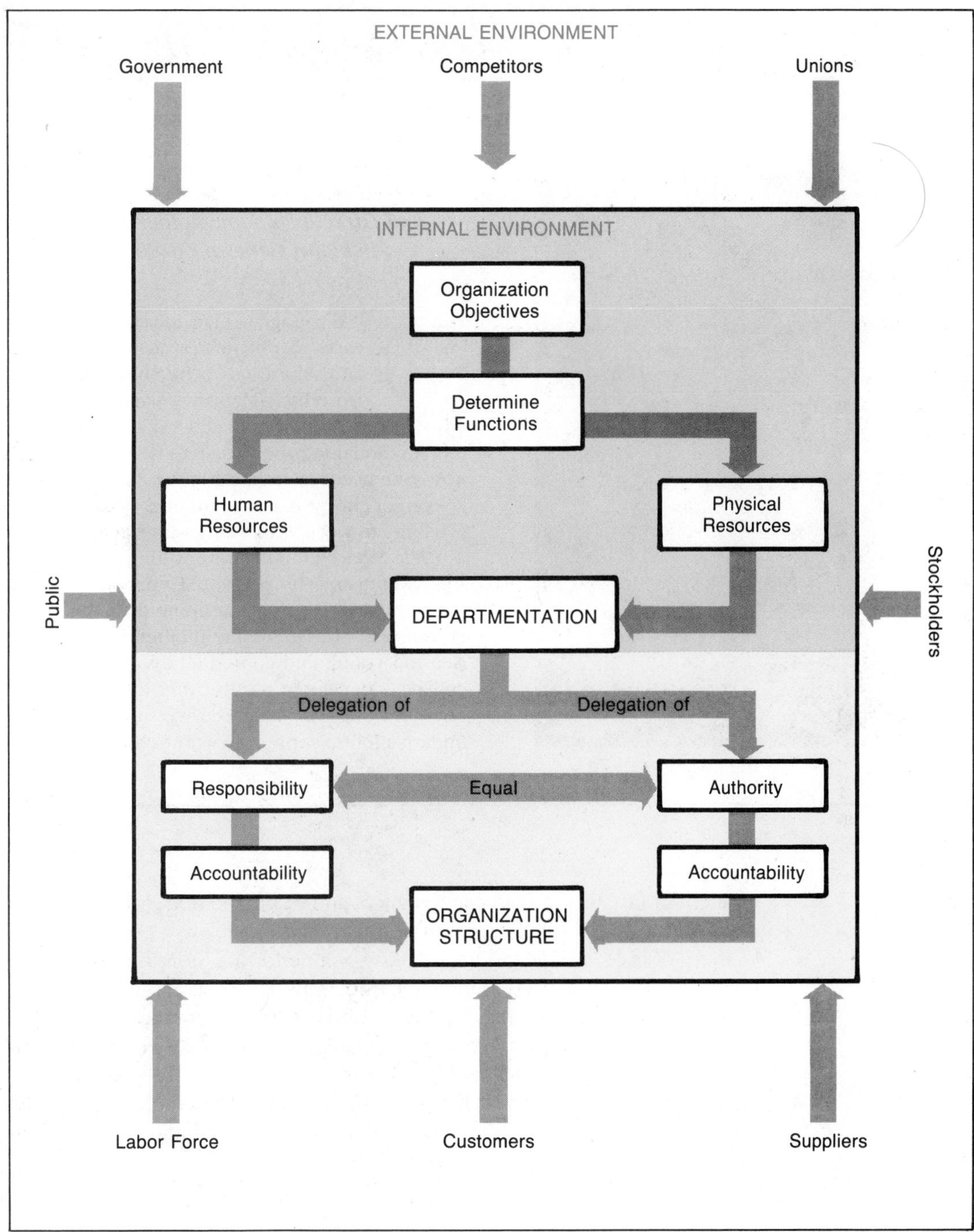

FIGURE 6-1 *The Organizing Process*

•CAREER PROFILE•

DOROTHY H. MOORE

Vice-President, Corporate Secretary, and Director of Stockholder Relations Michigan General Corporation

"A young woman today should begin early to obtain the necessary training and education to be successful," says Dorothy H. Moore. "I want my daughter, who just completed high school, to look past tomorrow and think about a career twenty years from now. She needs to realize that she can be a doctor, lawyer, or choose from any number of careers if she is willing to work with a long-range goal in mind."

Ms. Moore graduated from high school when she was fifteen. This presented a problem because she was more restricted at home than were older classmates. "To escape my mother's rules, I married too young and consequently didn't go on to college," Ms. Moore recalls. After the marriage did not work out, she was faced with the necessity of finding a job to support her four children.

ming, (2) installation and maintenance, and (3) marketing. Johnson understands that in his newly formed company, personnel will perform a wide variety of tasks. But as CSI grows, they will perform a more limited number of specialized functions. Once the functions have been grouped into a coordinated organizational structure, Johnson will assign appropriate levels of responsibility, authority, and accountability to all employees in CSI. Johnson's final phase in performing the organizing function is the assignment of specific work activities. For instance, the marketing manager performs such work activities as calling on potential customers, designing promotion and advertising, and recruiting and training sales personnel.

FUNCTIONS

Once objectives have been established, it is necessary to determine the types of functions or work that must be performed within the organization.

From the beginning of her working days, Dorothy was determined to succeed. At one of the first places she was employed, she handled the secretarial work for two attorneys. When she asked for a raise, she was offered only $15. "At that point, I found another job. I was and still am willing to do any work necessary, but I want to be paid for it."

She worked for a period with a Dallas attorney for whom she felt great respect. When he moved to New York City, she later obtained a secretarial job with Ira G. Corn, Jr., a financial consultant, and Joseph P. Driscoll, an independent oilman. Corn and Driscoll cooperated on several investments and eventually co-founded two large companies, including Michigan General. As her work expanded, Ms. Moore became Mr. Corn's personal secretary and within three years, was being introduced formally as his assistant. "In those early days with the two men," she remembers, "no one ever told me what to do. I looked to see what needed to be done, got things organized, and did it. I took over as acting office manager and if the floor needed mopping I would do that. My advice to anyone is do a good job, look for things to do. Don't wait to be told." She attributes much of her success to her ability to organize personnel and other resources.

When Michigan General was organized in 1968, Ms. Moore helped with the details of putting the various mergers together. In 1973, Ms. Moore became the second woman to be named to Michigan General Corporation's board of directors. In 1978, she was elected a vice-president of the company. Although she has a number of college hours, Dorothy regrets that she never obtained a degree. "A formal education is extremely important because it prepares one for life and it teaches a student to finish what he starts. It opens doors all through life," she points out.

Her tips for success also include a recommendation that an employee be 100 percent loyal to the company. "Make your boss's job easier. Make yourself hard to replace. If you can't be loyal or feel that success and advancement is not possible, the thing to do is look for another job. But always be determined to work hard to attain that long-term goal."

---

function A **function** is a type of work activity that can be identified and distinguished from other work.

On the typical baseball team, several distinct functions must be performed effectively if the team is to win games. Players on the team must perform the basic functions of fielding, throwing, and hitting the baseball. A good team must develop specialists capable of performing each of these activities. For instance, a team needs a pitching staff consisting of starters, long-term relievers, and short-term relievers. The team also has infielders who specialize in playing third base, shortstop, second base, or first base.

As in the baseball example, basic functions or work activities can be defined in any business, government, or educational organization. The major functions of a manufacturer are production, marketing, and finance. For a retailing company, the basic functions are buying and selling of merchandise and extending credit. The major functions in a bank include depositing or receiving a customer's money and making loans to borrowers. In a university, teaching, research, and service are the primary functions that must be per-

General Philosophy about Managing Your Organization

Decentralization! Put an employee in charge of an operation. Give him complete authority and let him go! But you must have some checks to monitor his performance.

HUGH O'NEILL, Chairman, Leaseway Transportation Company

formed. Functions performed by individuals within the organization must be identified, defined, and separated from the work performed by other people.

Specialization

specialization or division of labor

Specialization or **division of labor** has been a major element of the organizing process. It has been essential for the achievement of efficiency in mass-production industries. In fact, most work activities performed in nearly all organizations are of a specialized nature. In many of today's organizations, specialization of labor is often referred to as work simplification. The **work simplification** approach to job design has organized jobs into small, highly specialized components. Organizations have several options as to the degree of specialization associated with each job. For instance, if a company produces small transistor radios, several different approaches might be available, such as:

work simplification

1. Each employee assembles the entire radio (low degree of specialization).
2. Each employee assembles several major components of the radio (perhaps the plastic casing and primary transistor circuit board).
3. Each employee assembles one component of the radio (the case).
4. Each employee performs a few routine operations such as putting the knobs on for tuner and volume control (high degree of specialization).

Advantages of Specialization

Specialization or work simplification offers the following advantages:

- Allows workers to concentrate skills on a narrow range of work, thus increasing work output.
- Permits managers to supervise a larger number of employees.
- Facilitates the selection and training of workers to perform identical activities; jobs can be learned in less time.
- Leads to more efficient utilization of workers because they can develop and practice specialized skills.

- Contributes to better consistency of quality in products or services.
- Facilitates the achievement of complex goals.

A worker who is able to concentrate skill and effort on a small number of tasks can usually achieve a higher level of output. In manufacturing electronic components, output per worker tends to be much higher in situations where employees perform highly specialized work activities. Similarly, high performance results are apparent in many fast food restaurants where employees perform specialized functions, for example, cooking hamburgers or french fries. This is in contrast to the more traditional restaurants where employees may perform a wide variety of jobs.

In addition to higher output, specialization may permit a manager to supervise a larger number of employees. A manager may be able effectively to supervise thirty to fifty workers who are performing the same specialized tasks. If workers are performing a number of diverse tasks, the number of employees that a manager can effectively supervise is fewer.

Generally, a more specialized job can be learned more quickly than a job involving numerous work activities. When training time is reduced, the workers become productive at a faster rate. For instance, the time required to train a worker to cook french fries or prepare milk shakes would be minimal when compared with the time required to learn all the jobs performed in a fast food restaurant.

Work simplification leads to a more efficient utilization of employees because they can develop and practice their specialized skills. A worker can be more efficient and produce more by concentrating on one or a few activities. A typical professional football player is a highly trained specialist. Rarely does one player perform more than a few specialized activities. Most place kickers in professional football specialize only in kicking extra points and field goals. Quarterbacks, linemen, and running backs all specialize in what they do best and try to continue to develop and improve their skills.

Specialization contributes to consistently higher-quality products and services. It has been said that we live in an age of specialization, one in which most people are employed as specialists. Many students who choose to pursue a degree in business administration specialize in accounting, computer science, finance, management, or marketing. Few professions demonstrate the move to specialization more than medicine. As more is learned about each phase of medicine, entire careers emerge concentrating on a specific part of the body or a specific symptom. Forty or fifty years ago most medical doctors treated all ailments of each member of the family. More recently, most physicians specialize, becoming pediatricians, cardiologists, ophthalmologists, internists, gynecologists, gerontologists, proctologists, and so forth. By specializing in a narrow range of the medical profession, a physician is able to offer the best diagnosis and treatment the current research and technology of that field has available.

Finally, specialization facilitates the achievement of complex goals. The successful completion of any complex project usually requires a number of specialists. The United States' successful space program, our example at the beginning of the chapter, would not have been possible without the contribution of thousands of specialists. NASA assembled a team of specialists, each knowledgeable regarding a particular phase of the project. Similarly, the design and construction of airplanes or builders of large projects often require the contributions of many specialists.

Disadvantages of Specialization

Despite the advantages of the specialization of labor, its application may not always be desirable. In some organizations, certain jobs have become oversimplified. Too much specialization in the design of jobs may create boredom and fatigue among the employees. For example, some people find it very difficult to perform a job on an assembly line requiring the tightening of a bolt 10,000 times a day. Typically the highest degree of specialization is found in assembly line work, which sometimes has caused employee turnover, absenteeism, and a deteriorating quality of output. These negative consequences of specialization may cause an increase in operational costs.

Functionalization

functionalization

The process of splitting and differentiating functions as the organization grows is known as **functionalization.** In a newly formed small organization, an owner-manager performs all the major functions of the business, such as providing the necessary financing, procuring materials, designing the product, and making and selling the product. As the volume of business grows, the work required will increase beyond the capacities of one person. At this point, the process of functionalization begins as additional personnel are employed. Downward and outward differentiation are discussed below.

Downward Differentiation

downward differentiation

As a business grows, additional workers will be added to perform certain functions. This process requires two levels of organization to be created: managerial and operative. However, managerial employees perform operative work in addition to directing the operative employee. The manager may retain the sales and finance functions and allocate the production work to the new employee. This is an example of **downward differentiation.**

As the volume of the business continues to grow, additional personnel will be added and more operative functions differentiated and allocated, as illustrated in Figure 6-2. The original person may now serve in the capacity of full-time manager with the additional worker performing the various functions of sales, production, and finance—a two-level organization.

span of management

The process of adding personnel to the second level has its limits because one manager cannot continue to supervise an unlimited number of personnel. This limitation is usually referred to as the **span of management** or span of control. According to the span of management, there is a limit to the number of employees a manager can effectively supervise or control. This

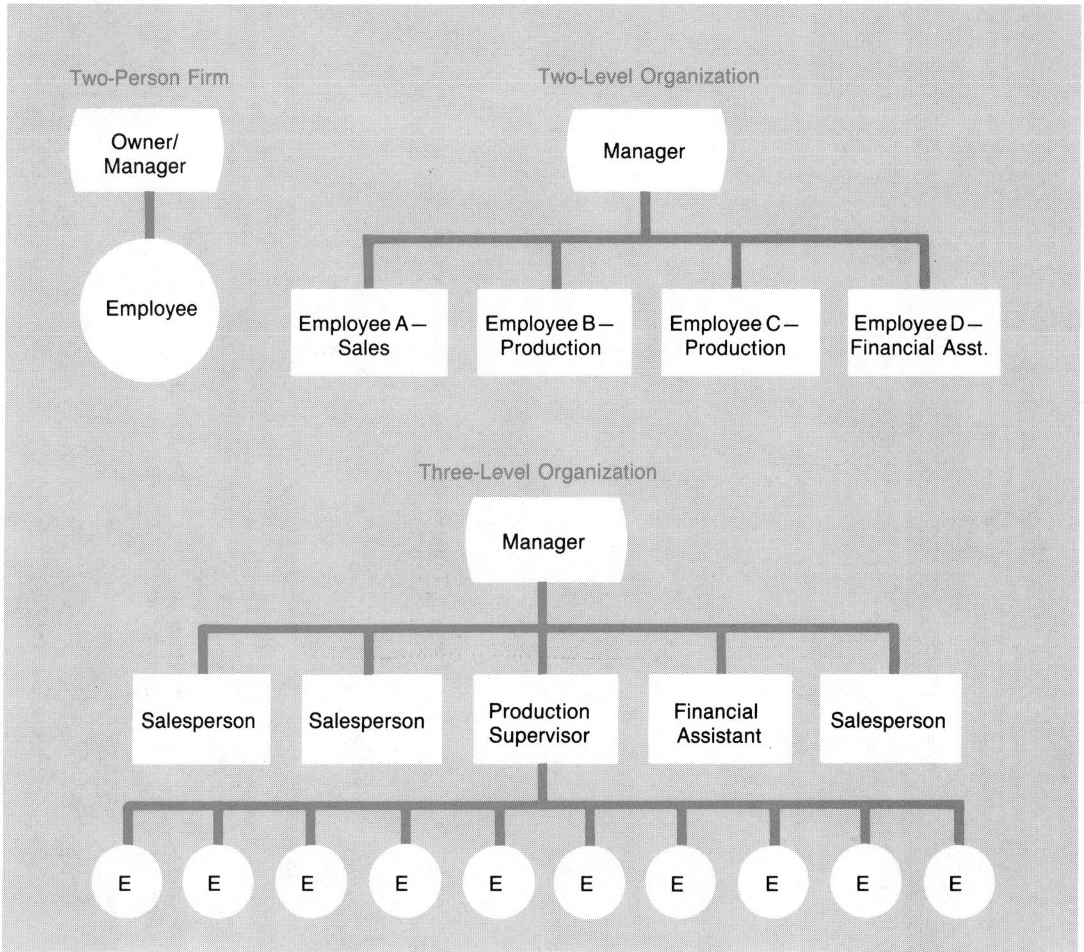

FIGURE 6-2 *Functional Differentiation Downward and Outward*

principle is an organizational generalization based on the theory that managers cannot effectively supervise a large number of people (for example 100), but they obviously can supervise more than one. Somewhere between these two extremes lies an ideal answer. When a manager's span of management is overloaded, one of the employees may be designated a supervisor, and subordinates are placed under this person's direction. The newly appointed supervisor is still responsible to the original manager. This creates three levels in the organization and does not overwork the capacities of one manager. The span of management as a fundamental principle is discussed in greater detail in Chapter 7.

Outward Differentiation

The first direction of organizational growth from the one-person enterprise is usually downward. However, at some point, growth of the firm will cause

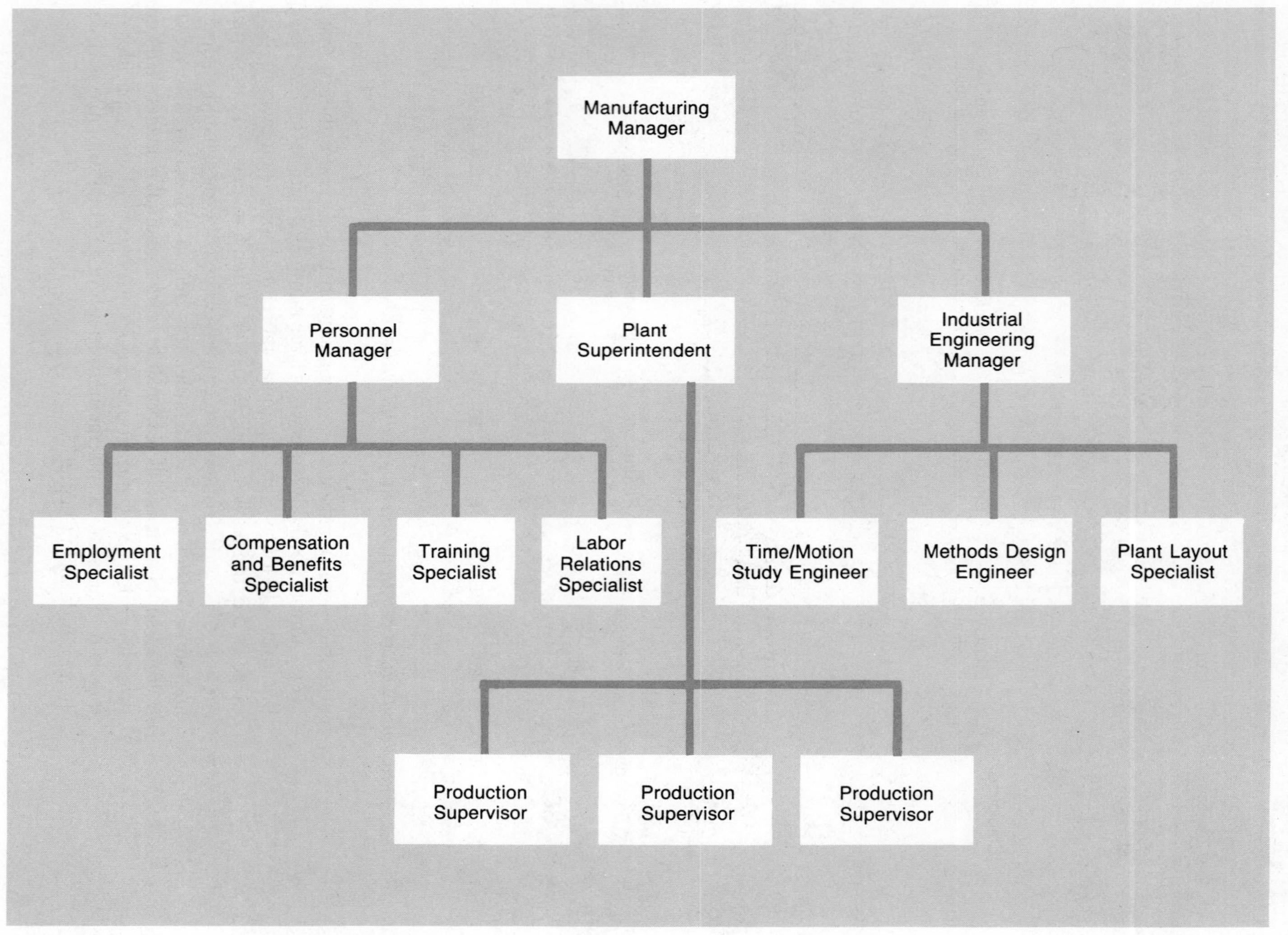

FIGURE 6-3 *Development of Staff Departments*

a splitting out of functions, forming horizontal levels in the organization (**outward differentiation**). Personnel performing these functions will be newly appointed. Ordinarily outward differentiation occurs because the original manager finds that certain functions can be more effectively and economically performed by a specialist. For example, a manager may find sales a weak area because of ineffective or inadequate training programs. Therefore, a sales trainer would be employed to take over that phase of the business so the manager can devote more time to other areas. Outward growth usually occurs at the supervisory levels first in the organization and at lower levels as additional workers are required. As the organization grows, outward differentiation usually results in functions being split off that are the most complex and are least similar to any other functions of the firm.

outward differentiation

If the organization continues to grow, the specialist will find that the volume of work exceeds the time available. The second stage of outward differentiation is likely to be the creation of a department. An additional employee is hired to assist the original specialist. A secondary chain of command has now been formed. It should be noted that growth at this point becomes downward differentiation again. The span of management concept applies to this new unit or department.

As shown in Figure 6-2, outward differentiation usually occurs in several areas of an organization. We previously used the example of a sales trainer. Others benefitting from this type of growth are employment specialists, labor relations specialists, design specialists, and engineering and production specialists. Sometimes it becomes necessary to group several functions together under a single manager to reduce the span of management. This is to ensure coordination and compatibility among the functions. We might combine training, employment, and labor relations together, creating a personnel department as may be seen in Figure 6-3.

The ideal result of the process of downward or outward differentiation is to facilitate the accomplishment of the organization's goals through the use of specialists. The benefits of creating additional specialists in any organization—profit or nonprofit—must not exceed their costs.

Let's suppose that a firm has doubled the size of its sales force without splitting out the training function from the work of the sales manager. Quite possibly, employing a sales training specialist may add greater benefit than cost to the company.

GROUPING FUNCTIONS: PRINCIPLE OF FUNCTIONAL SIMILARITY

Objectives determine the work to be performed. The total work load must be divided among the available personnel. Individual jobs, or units of responsibility, are created by selecting and grouping functions into individual assignments. The basic guide that governs this process is that of **functional similarity.** Work that is similar in content and activities is grouped together fol-

functional similarity

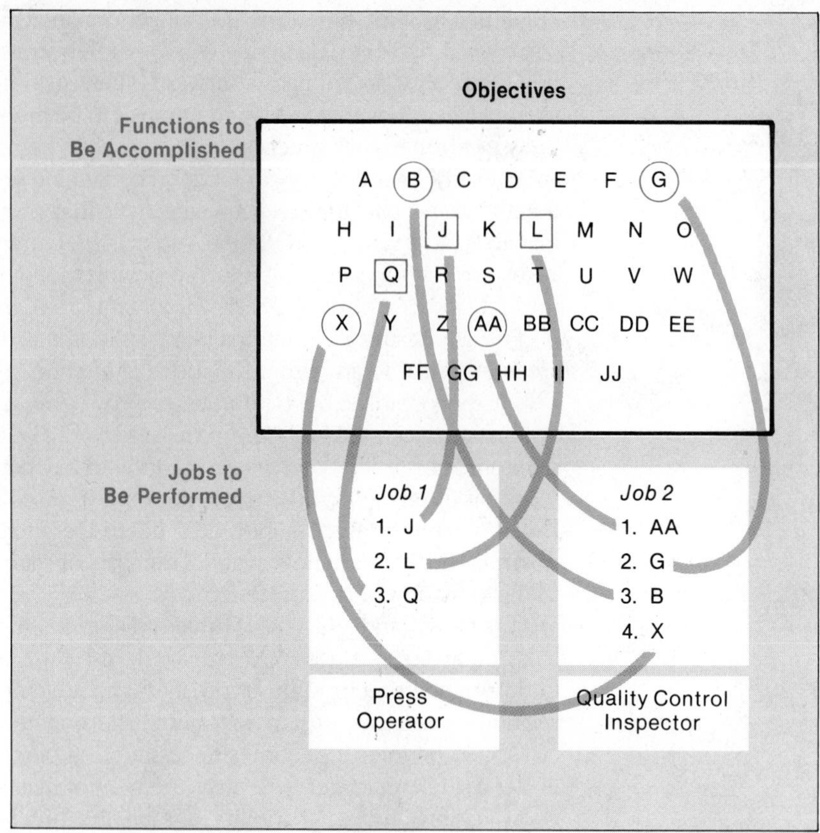

FIGURE 6-4

Illustration of Functional Similarity

lowing the principle of functional similarity. In Figure 6-4, functions J, L, and Q are shown to be sufficiently similar in objectives and content to comprise the work assignments for Job 1, a press operator. Therefore, a person with the skills and abilities necessary to execute this job must be found. Job 2, the quality

Insights to Success

The initial years of a career are important in building a strong understanding of company operations. We encourage individuals to take advantage of the many types of training positions available in the company and to treat each job as equally important to advancement. A generalized initial career, including staff, factory, branch, and overseas accounting, rather than an initial specialized career will provide individuals greater opportunity for advancement.

J. W. ENGLAND, Vice-President and Comptroller, Deere & Company control inspector, consists of functions AA, G, B, and X. The same principles also guide us in the creation of sections, departments, and divisions. Jobs with similar objectives and requirements are grouped to form a section. A person with the background necessary to supervise these functions effectively should be assigned as the manager.

Although functional similarity is desired, the extent to which it can be applied depends on several factors.

Sufficient Volume of Work

There must be a sufficient volume of work to enable some specialization. In the small firm, personnel will have to cope with a wide assortment of jobs. But with increases in volume, the concept can be applied more rigorously. For example, let's compare the operations of a small grocery store versus a large supermarket. In the small store, one person might perform such functions as stocking shelves, working in the produce section, checking, and sacking groceries. In the large supermarket, personnel will tend to specialize in one or only a few of the basic functions. It's common to have individual managers of the produce section, stocking, checking, and sacking functions.

Personnel Qualifications

A second factor that may work against the concept of functional similarity is the qualifications of the personnel who are currently employed. It may be that certain employees have seniority or other restrictive qualifications and cannot be assigned certain tasks. However, the manager attempts to develop a unit of responsibility based on the capabilities of the "typical" person.

Functions Similar to Others in the Organization

A third complicating factor is that the particular function in question is often similar to other functions. For example, the function of inventory control would appear to fit logically with the purchasing function. The purchasing department buys the material and thus has need for records of inventory levels. However, production uses these materials and, in scheduling, must work with these same inventory records. Inventory control could then be placed in either section.

Separation of Functions for Control or Motivation

A fourth complication is the occasional necessity for separating similar functions for purposes of control or motivation. For instance, inspection is a function that is intimately involved in production; inspectors frequently work side by side with production employees. However, the inspector should not be unduly influenced by the production manager's interest in quantity and cost. Thus, inspection, although similar to production, should be separate from production to protect its independence.

Combining Dissimilar Functions

Finally, there are occasions when two dissimilar functions must be combined for purposes of effective action and control. Though purchasing is clearly differentiated from selling in a factory organization, buying and selling are so interdependent in department stores that one person is often made responsible for both. The theory is that "a well-bought dress or hat is half sold."

DEPARTMENTATION

departmentation

The process of grouping related functions or major work activities into manageable units to achieve more effective and efficient overall coordination of organization resources is known as **departmentation.** The primary means for departmentation are by function, product, customer, geographic territory, and project. In most large organizations, several of these bases for departmentation are used.

Departmentation by Function

Departmentation by function is perhaps the most common means of grouping related functions (see Figure 6-5). Departments are formed on the basis of specialized functions such as production, marketing, engineering, finance, and personnel and assist management in making efficient utilization of the resources of the organization. However, departmentation by function may create problems for management in the sense that employees in these spe-

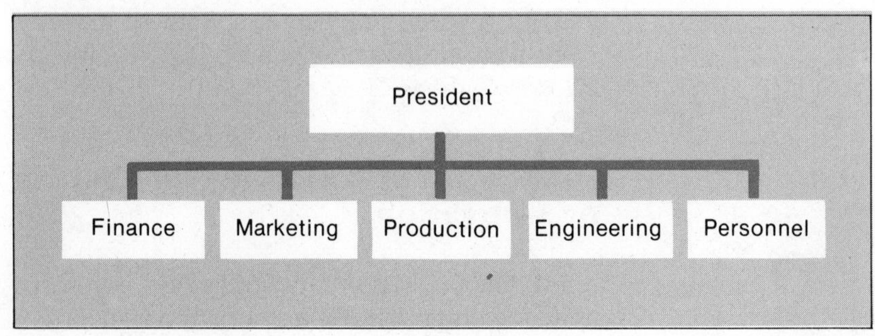

FIGURE 6-5
Departmentation by Function

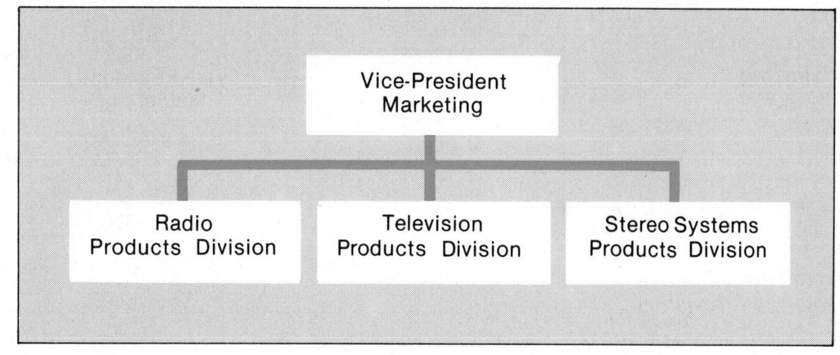

FIGURE 6-6
Departmentation by Product

cialized functions may become more concerned with their own department than with the overall company.

Departmentation by Product

This means of departmentation is concerned with organizing according to the type of product being produced and/or sold by the firm. This means of departmentation enhances the use of specialized knowledge of particular products or services and is often used by rather large, diversified companies. As shown in Figure 6-6, a large electronics firm is organized into three product divisions.

Departmentation by Customer

Departmentation by types of customers is used by organizations that have a special need to provide better service to different types of customers. As illustrated in Figure 6-7, a diversified manufacturing company has an industrial, government, and consumer products division. Large retailers and banks use departmentation along customer lines to provide better service to different customer groups.

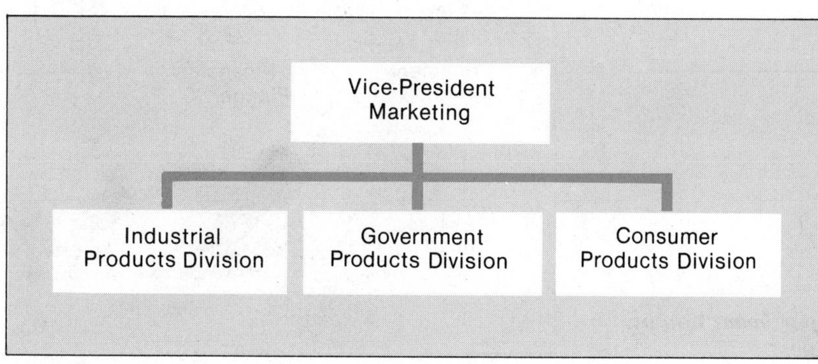

FIGURE 6-7
Departmentation by Customer

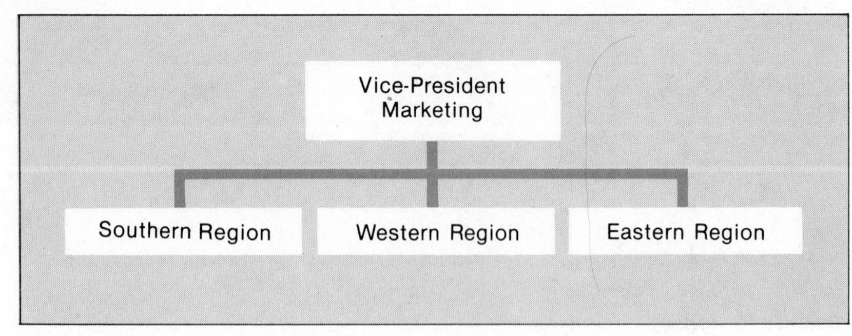

FIGURE 6-8

Departmentation by Geographic Territory

Departmentation by Geographic Territory

Grouping activities according to geographic territory is used by organizations that have physically dispersed and/or independent operations or markets to serve. The marketing function of the company shown in Figure 6-8 is organized into the southern, western, and eastern regional divisions. Geographic departmentation offers the advantages of better service with local or regional personnel, often at less cost.

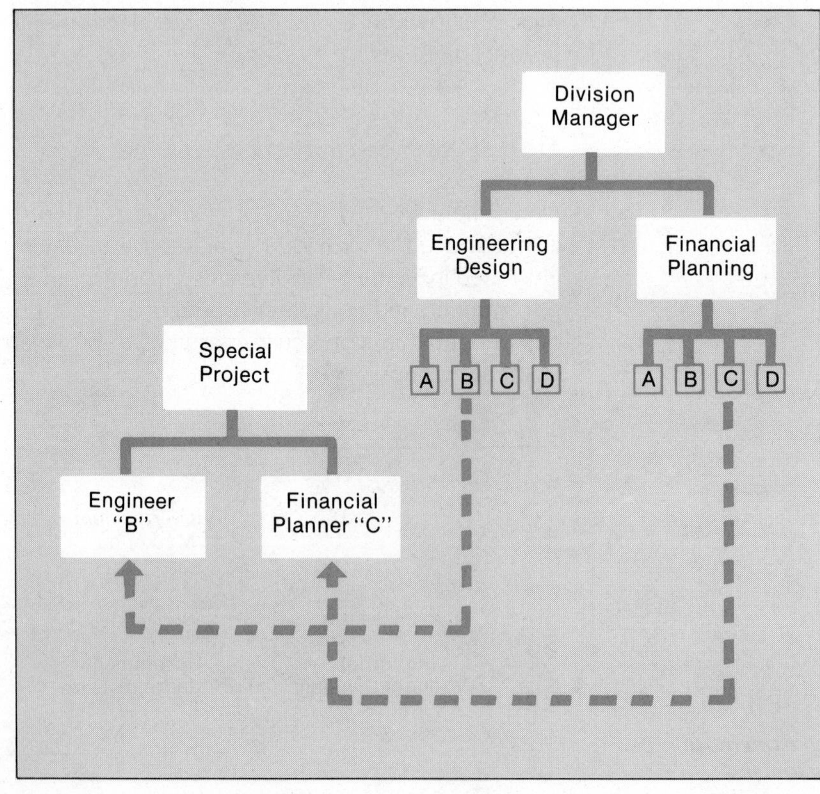

FIGURE 6-9

Departmentation by Project

Departmentation by Project

Departmentation by project is a method of bringing together personnel with various work backgrounds to form a team. Figure 6-9 provides an illustration of departmentation for the special project of developing an aircraft plan. Engineer B and Financial Planner C are to accomplish this special project. The team has been assigned a specific task or objective to be accomplished within a given time period. On completion of the project, Engineer B and Financial Planner C will return to their regular work assignments. Departmentation by project has received considerable usage in recent years by the construction and aerospace industries.

Departmentation: A Combination Approach

Unless the organization is quite small, it is likely that several different bases for departmentation will be used. No one form of departmentation can meet the needs of most firms, particularly in such firms as General Motors, General Electric, or Exxon. An organization chart illustrating various forms of departmentation is shown in Figure 6-10. In this case, the manufacturing company

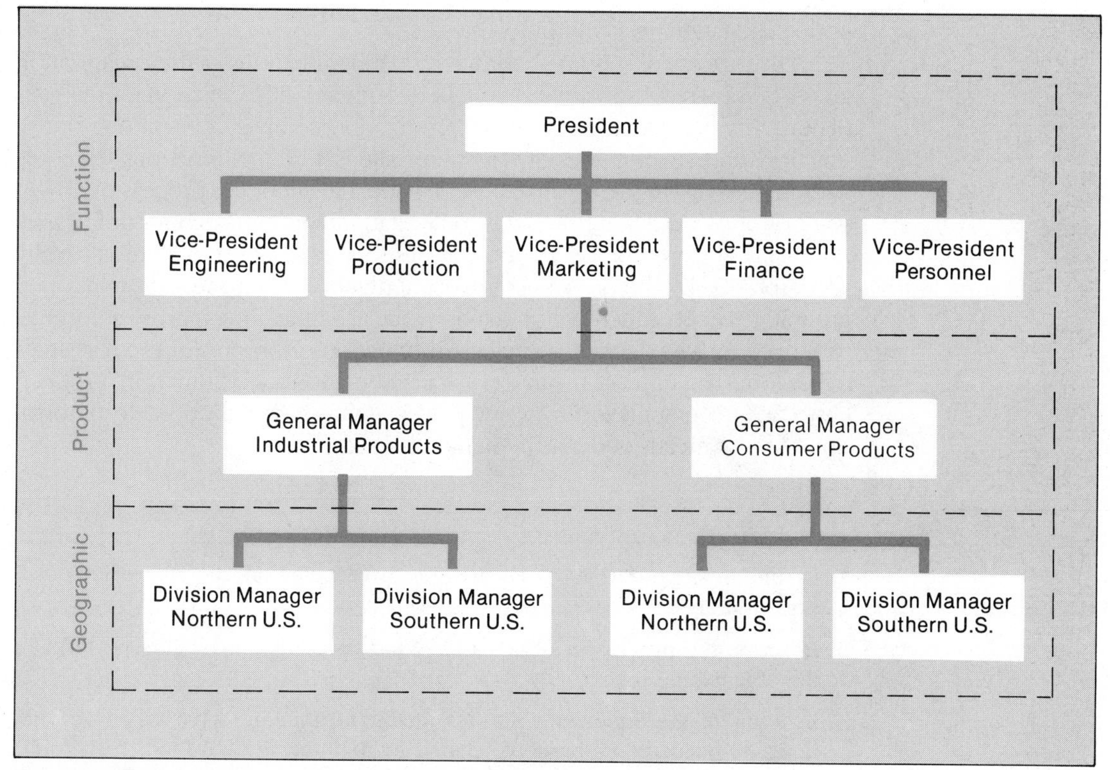

FIGURE 6-10 *Organization Chart Illustrating Departmentation*

is departmentalized by type of functions performed (engineering, production, marketing, and so on), type of products (industrial and consumer), and geographic territory. The precise form of departmentation a firm chooses must be based upon its own needs.

Summary

An organization can be defined as two or more people working together in a coordinated manner to achieve group results. To be effective, a manager must be capable of organizing human resources, physical factors, and functions in a manner that ensures the achievement of the firm's goals. The primary purpose of the organizing function is to achieve an effective and efficient blending of the essential elements of the organization that lead to success.

A function is a type of work activity that can be identified and distinguished from other work. Functions performed by individuals within the organization must be identified, defined, and separated from the work performed by others.

Work simplification or specialization of labor is the traditional approach to work design; jobs are organized into small, highly specialized components. Despite the numerous advantages of specialization, certain jobs have been oversimplified in some organizations and have at times led to work that is boring and fatiguing for employees.

The process of splitting and differentiating functions as the organization grows is known as functionalization. In downward differentiation more levels of authority are added. Outward differentiation involves the splitting out of functions and dividing the work responsibilities, forming horizontal (or equal authority) levels in the organization. The ideal result of the process of downward or outward differentiation is to facilitate the accomplishment of organizational goals through the use of specialists. Specialization of labor is usually accomplished by the process of departmentation. Departmentation involves grouping related functions or major work activities into manageable units to achieve more effective and efficient overall coordination of the resources of the firm. The primary means for departmentation are by function, product, customer, geographic territory, and project. In most organizations, a combination of these means of departmentation is used.

Review Questions

1. Define an organization. What are the three common characteristics of an organization?
2. Describe the process of organizing. What tasks must managers perform in the organizing process?
3. In terms of the organizing process, define a function. What types of functions are needed on a baseball team? a football team? a fast foods restaurant? a small-appliance assembly plant?

4. Define specialization. What are the advantages and disadvantages of specialization?
5. Distinguish by example and definition between downward and outward differentiation.
6. Define the concept of functional similarity. What factors could prevent the use of this concept?
7. What does the term *departmentation* mean? What are the primary means of departmentation?

Exercises

1. Specialization has both advantages and disadvantages. List the specialized education and training required for the following professions. Which profession(s) are possible with your present level of education and training? Which could you achieve?
   a. an electrical draftsman
   b. a neurosurgeon
   c. a machine operator
   d. a college president
   e. a personnel manager
2. Assume that you are production manager for a small firm. The firm currently is experiencing much growth and success with its product line, and sales have tripled in the past year. As a result, you have hired forty new employees over the last six months to keep up production demands. Describe the outward and downward differentiation that you would implement in the company for maximum efficiency as the organization continues to grow.

Case Study

The Organization of Quality Control

Robert Belham is production manager for Memorand, Inc., a small component parts manufacturer. He has been with the firm for fifteen years and has progressed from foreman to his current position. Robert—Bob as his employees call him—is completely dedicated to the company and its future. He has had numerous opportunities to obtain a higher paying and more prestigious position with competing firms but has chosen to remain with Memorand because he likes his job and the employees.

Kathy Wells is in charge of the quality control section with Memorand and reports directly to Bob. She has been with the company for ten years, having started as a departmental secretary for Mr. Belham. Bob has been highly supportive of her getting a college degree and has allowed her to take time off to attend classes at the university. After several years of attending the university, she recently obtained a degree in industrial management with a specialty in quality control. Because of the patience and support that Mr. Belham gave her, Kathy has a strong loyalty to Bob and to Memorand.

A very difficult situation occurred yesterday that has now caused a severe strain to be placed on the relationship between Bob and Kathy. The firm was awarded a very lucrative contract by CBU with the provision that Memorand would produce the parts within one week. If Memorand completes the order on time, it has the potential for obtaining additional contracts from CBU, which would increase overall company sales by at least 10 percent a year. The order comes at the right time because business has been relatively bad for Memorand and there was a good chance that the firm would have to reduce its work force.

As Kathy met with Bob yesterday morning the following conversation took place:

Kathy: "Bob, the quality of the parts we're making for CBU is not as good as those we normally make. I believe we should slow down and inspect all the parts to ensure that we don't send out an inferior product."

Bob: "Are the parts below standard?"

Kathy: "No, but there are a lot of marginal parts being produced. I believe that if we are to improve our chances of obtaining additional orders, we must slow down the production line."

Bob: "If we slow down the production line, we won't make the deadline we promised CBU. If we don't make the deadline, most likely Memorand will not even have a chance to receive follow-up contracts. I expect you to see to it the production schedule is met."

After receiving such a firm demand, Kathy left the office. She felt she was right but didn't know what to do.

QUESTIONS

1. How would you reorganize the relationship of the production department and the quality control section to ensure that the conflict experienced by Kathy and Bob would not occur in the future?
2. If you agree with Kathy, what do you think she should do? Discuss.
3. Do you believe Bob was correct in his assessment of the situation? Discuss.

Case Study

Materials Organization at Newco Manufacturing

Tom Johnson, the newly employed materials manager for the Newco Manufacturing Company, was concerned about the lack of organization in his department. Newco was a small company of 250 employees that manufactured small electrical motors. Mr. Johnson reported to the vice-president of manufacturing, Charles McDowell, and had fifteen people in his department performing such functions as stocking, receiving, inventory control, purchasing, and outside sales.

Because the workflow was not very predictable, the previous materials manager told the department's personnel to do whatever they thought necessary. This would involve working the parts issue windows while mechanics were ordering parts, stocking the parts bins when time permitted, receiving parts when deliveries were made, and shipping orders to customers. Employees answered the phone and handled outside sales as required. Employee complaints had been frequent regarding such matters as inadequate pay, unclear work assignments, and lack of competent leadership.

Tom had received a rather detailed account about the materials operation from his boss, Mr. McDowell. McDowell described the materials department as performing very poorly and attributed this to a lack of overall direction, ineffective organization, and incompetent personnel. McDowell described several of the department's personnel as "dope heads" or "long hairs" who did as little work as possible. The turnover rate had been in excess of 200 percent per year for the past three years. McDowell suggested that Johnson "clean house" by firing most of the employees in the department and start with a fresh crew.

Johnson was obviously shaken by the comments made by Mr. McDowell and the complaints of the personnel in the department and considered finding a new position. However, he chose not to leave the company until he had given the assignment his best efforts for at least a few months.

QUESTIONS

1. Using concepts and principles discussed in this chapter, what actions would you recommend that Mr. Johnson take to improve the materials department?
2. What type organization chart would you recommend Mr. Johnson develop?
3. Should Mr. Johnson "clean house" as suggested by Mr. McDowell?

References

Alexander, E. R. "Design of Alternatives in Organizational Contexts: A Pilot Study." *Administrative Science Quarterly* 24 (September 1979): 382–404.

Bobbitt, H. R., Jr., and Ford, J. D. "Decision-Maker Choice as a Determinant of Organizational Structure." *Academy of Management Review* 5 (January 1980): 13–23.

Cherman, C. "Organizing for Strength." *Personnel Journal* 58 (July 1979): 437–438.

Dalton, D. R.; Todor, W. D.; Spendelini, J.; Fielding, J.; and Porter, L. W. "Organization Structure and Performance: A Critical Review." *Academy of Management Review* 5 (January 1980): 61–64.

Gerwin, D. "Relationships between Structure and Technology at the Organizational and Job Levels." *Journal of Management Studies* 16 (February 1979): 70–79.

Handy, C. "Shape of Organizations to Come." *Personnel Management* 11 (June 1979): 24–27.

________. "Through the Organizational Looking Glass." *Harvard Business Review* 58, no. 1 (January–February 1980): 115–121.

Huber, G. P., et al. "Optimum Organization Design: An Analytic Adoptive Approach." *Academy of Management Review* 4 (October 1979): 567–578.

Naylor, T. H. "Organizing for Strategic Planning." *Managerial Planning* 28 (July 1979): 3–9.

Scanlan, K. "Maintaining Organizational Effectiveness—A Prescription for Good Health." *Personnel Journal* 58, no. 5 (May 1980): 381–386.

Slocum, J. W., Jr., and Hellriegel, D. "Using Organizational Designs to Cope with Change." *Business Horizons* 22 (December 1979): 65–76.

KEY TERMS

- responsibility
- authority
- centralization
- decentralization
- delegation
- accountability
- single accountability
- chain of command
- span of management
- organization structure
- line organization
- line and staff organization
- functional authority
- functional organization
- project organization
- matrix organization

LEARNING OBJECTIVES

After completing this chapter you should be able to

1. Distinguish between authority, responsibility, and accountability.
2. Identify the advantages and disadvantages of centralization and decentralization.
3. Define delegation and describe the reasons for delegation.
4. Explain the basic principles related to authority, responsibility, and accountability.
5. Define span of management and identify the factors affecting the span of management.
6. Identify the basic types of organizational structures and the advantages and disadvantages of each.

7

Authority, Responsibility, and Organizational Structure

David Wolfe was hired three months ago as the marketing manager of the eastern division of Flextron Corporation, a multibillion dollar firm specializing in the manufacturing of oil field equipment. David has already become frustrated in his position with Flextron. Prior to Flextron, he had worked for three years as a regional sales manager for the Northeastern Division of Centron Oil Field Equipment Company, a major competitor of Flextron. Centron has a clearly defined organizational structure and very distinguishable patterns of organizational relationships and lines of communication.

In a recent conversation with his boss, Randall Johnston, vice-president of marketing, David said:

> Randall, I am totally confused about my role in the organization. It may be my imagination, but I feel that the eight district sales managers who are supposed to report to me are instead going directly to you with their problems. I feel that I am responsible for the performance of these eight sales districts, but I'm not clear what is expected of me.

Randall was quick to explain:

> David, I understand and appreciate your concern for wanting to do a good job, but you should understand two things: (1) I've known most of these district sales managers for a number of years and was their boss until two years ago when I became vice-president. And (2) I do not believe in highly formalized or structured relationships. My philosophy is that if a firm employs good managers, they will do a good job regardless of the organization or its structure.

The above example illustrates just how frustrating it can be when organizational relationships are unclear and/or when expectations are ambiguous. In order to function effectively in any organization, managers must have a clear understanding of what's expected and the levels of responsibility and authority they possess. The primary purpose of an organizational structure is to clarify and communicate roles of managers and other personnel within the firm.

As described in Chapter 6, organizing is the process of bringing together functions and human and physical resources for the purpose of achieving the objectives of the firm. We discussed the various types of functions that must be performed and how these functions may be grouped in organizations. This chapter is concerned with developing organizational frameworks or patterns for organizing the functions, personnel, and formal relationships. What concepts/principles should managers understand and apply in performing the organizing function? First, we discuss delegation of responsibility, authority, and accountability. In addition, several principles or guidelines important to a manager's performance of the organizing function are discussed. In the final section of the chapter, we discuss the design and types of organizational structures.

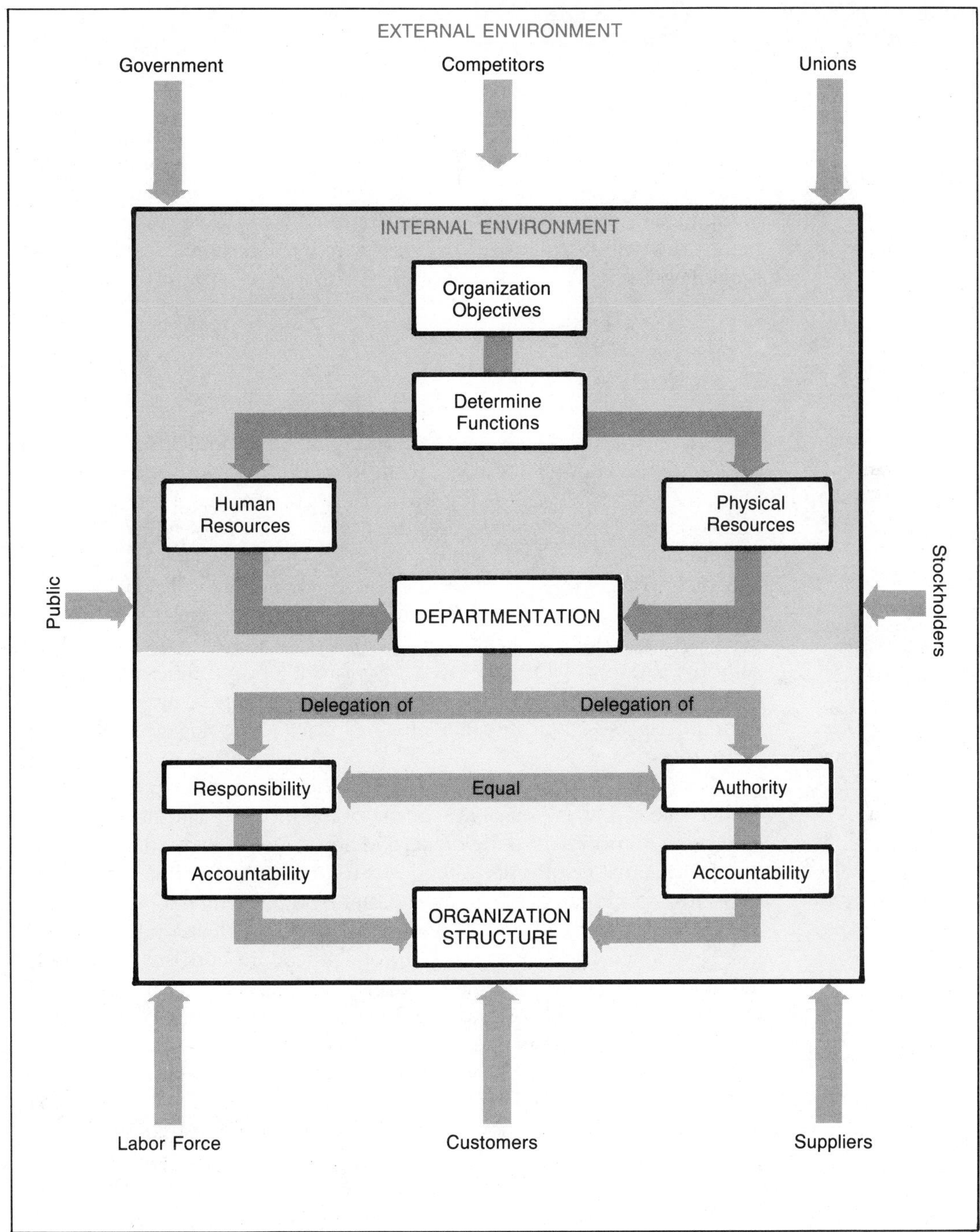

FIGURE 7-1 *The Organizing Process*

CONCEPTS OF DELEGATION, RESPONSIBILITY, AUTHORITY, AND ACCOUNTABILITY

The first portion of the organizing process was described in Chapter 6. The remainder of the organizing process (see lower half of Figure 7-1) will be presented in this chapter. As can be seen in illustration, an interrelationship exists among the concepts of delegation, responsibility, authority, and accountability. We will next discuss the importance of delegation to management. This will be followed by sections on responsibility, authority, and accountability.

Delegation

delegation

The process of making specific work assignments to individuals within the organization and providing them with the right or power to perform those functions is referred to as **delegation.** Delegation is one of the most significant concepts or practices affecting a manager's ability to perform the organizing function. However, delegation creates a risk for the managers for they are ultimately responsible for either the success or the failure of an operation. As a result, some managers have attempted to reduce the risk by avoiding delegation and doing tasks themselves. Yet delegation of responsibility and authority is essential if the manager is to provide opportunities for the development of people. One of the greatest weaknesses and causes of failure of some managers is their unwillingness or inability to delegate responsibility and authority.

Delegation is essential if the work of the organization is to be accomplished effectively and efficiently. Some of the more significant reasons why delegation is important to the organizing process are illustrated in Figure 7-2.

Delegation of authority often leads to quicker action and faster, better decisions. Action can be taken much faster by delegating than if we must go to a higher level of authority in the organization for a decision. For example, if an employee has a question on work procedure and the supervisor is required to go to the next higher level of management for a decision, the employee and supervisor become frustrated and time may be wasted. In general, when routine matters are handled at a level higher than necessary, time is wasted and work output will likely be less than optimum.

Delegation tends to be an important factor in training and developing personnel in the organization. An employee or manager cannot learn to perform a certain function or make decisions unless he or she is given the opportunity. Delegation of responsibility and authority is essential if the firm is concerned about the development of personnel to assume more challenging and demanding jobs in the future. In addition, delegation may lead to a higher level of motivation of the personnel since they feel they are being trusted and that management has confidence in their abilities. Delegation not only builds the confidence of personnel but also tends to improve attitudes and morale.

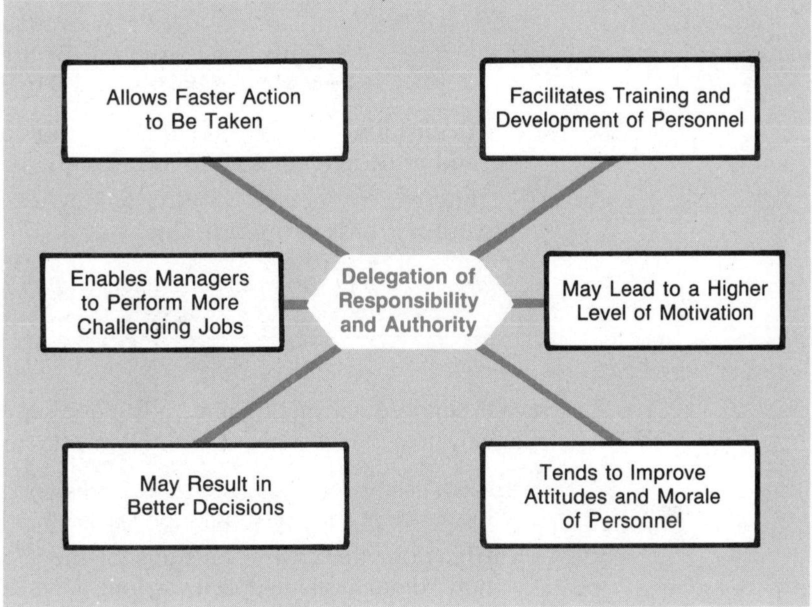

FIGURE 7-2

Reasons for Delegation

Despite these and other reasons for delegating responsibility and authority, certain limitations or potential problems should be considered:

- If improper feedback is provided, the manager may lose control and may not have the time to correct the situation should a problem occur.
- Delegation can fail if the level of responsibility and authority is not clearly defined and understood.
- If the delegatee does not possess the ability, skills, and/or experience to accomplish the jobs or make decisions, delegation can prove disastrous.
- Problems can result if an employee is given a responsibility but insufficient authority to perform the task.

Responsibility

responsibility

Responsibility is an *obligation* to perform work activities. For example, if we say that James Lewis, a manager, is responsible for the data processing center, we mean that he has an obligation to plan, organize, influence, control, and coordinate the work of computer operators and analysts. And that's not all. He also has the obligation for the maintenance of the computer equipment and programs, plus numerous other activities that are essential to the success of the data processing department.

A key consideration every manager must keep in mind is that responsibilities or obligations to perform certain functions must be clearly defined. Nothing is more frustrating to a manager or a worker than not to know the nature, scope, and details of his or her specific job responsibilities. For in-

Qualities Needed for Success as a Manager in Your Organization

- **Dedication, interest, cooperative attitude, concern for people, and pride in team accomplishments.**
- **Energy, enthusiasm, loyalty, willingness to try new methods, and alertness to opportunities.**

M. G. MITCHELL, Chairman and President, Chicago Bridge & Iron Company

stance, suppose that Susan James, a first-line supervisor for a large insurance company, had the following conversation with her boss, Phil Williams.

Susan: Is my unit responsible for processing the new commercial fire insurance policies or should Joe Davis's unit handle them?

Phil: I don't think it really matters too much which unit handles these new commercial fire policies so long as it's done correctly and thoroughly.

Susan: But what am I expected to do?

Phil: I'll get back to you later on this—I'm busy at the moment.

Obviously Phil's comments create ambiguous expectations for Susan. She doesn't know what her specific responsibilities are with regard to the new commercial fire insurance policies and gets no help from Phil toward clarifying her role. Accomplishing the objectives of processing the commercial fire insurance policies may be quite difficult. In order to perform any job adequately, an individual must understand the objectives, functions, and specific responsibilities. As was illustrated in Figure 7-1, objectives, functions, responsibilities, and authority must be closely integrated if there is to be effective organization.

Personnel in the organization are delegated responsibilities or work assignments by their superiors. When a manager delegates a responsibility to a subordinate, a relationship based on an obligation exists between the two. However, managers should remember an important point: *one cannot relieve oneself of any portion of the original responsibility; delegation allows only for someone else to do the work.* Responsibility is, thus, a series of obligations established between two levels in an organization.

Authority

Once responsibility has been assigned, it is then necessary to delegate the authority necessary to accomplish the job. Viewed in terms of management, **authority** *is the right to decide, to direct others to take action,* or to *perform certain duties in achieving organizational goals.*

authority

The concept of authority is often difficult to understand. As defined above, there are at least three key characteristics of authority.

1. Authority is a *right.*
2. Exercising authority involves *making decisions* and taking actions or the performance of duties.
3. Authority is used to *achieve organizational goals.*

Authority is absolutely essential if the manager is to organize and direct the use of resources to attain the goals of the organization.

Division of Authority

Delegation of authority and responsibility cannot and should not be separated. This is made evident in a widely accepted basic principle of management that states that *authority should equal responsibility.* This principle

Some managers act like kings and feel they should make all the decisions.

•CAREER PROFILE•

DR. LEE H. SMITH
President
Travel Host, Inc.

TRAVELHOST Dr. Lee H. Smith is president of Travel Host, Inc., a Dallas-based publishing firm whose major publication reaches 70 million readers annually and has the largest number of unduplicated pages of advertising lineage in the nation, surpassing such industry giants as *Time* and *TV Guide*.

Lee Smith became president of Travel Host in 1981 after serving as president of Southwest Texas State University since 1974. Although he was a practicing engineer for a few years, most of his professional life has been in academe where he has held virtually every academic title from assistant professor to president.

After receiving his bachelor's degree in mathematics from Texas A&M University in 1957, he completed a master's degree in engineering administration from Southern Methodist University and a doctor of philosophy degree in statistics from Texas A&M.

Lee Smith takes great pride in being known as a professional manager, having built the reputation as an innovative manager while serving as president of Southwest Texas State University in San Marcos, Texas.

At the time of his appointment as president of Southwest Texas in 1974, the university was threatened with significant enrollment losses, a deteriorating physical plant, and inadequate funding at almost every level. Today the university is

indicates that delegation of responsibility should carry with it an equal amount of authority. In other words, a manager who is given a job to do (responsibility) should have adequate authority (or rights) to get the job done.

The concept as stated sounds good in theory. Yet one of the most common complaints of first-level supervisors is that they have more responsibility than authority. Authority deals with rights, and these must be made specific in terms of the responsibility delegated. For example, if a supervisor is made responsible for staffing a department, he or she can be delegated any one of the following levels of authority:

- Rights to recruit, screen, and hire all personnel.

among the fastest growing universities in the state, registering a 24 percent enrollment increase during Dr. Smith's tenure. During the 1978 legislative appropriation session, the university received more building repair and rehabilitation funds than any other institution in the state and more than the combined totals for the entire previous history of Southwest Texas. Under Lee's leadership, contract and grant research dollar volume increased five-fold, a $20 million building program was launched, and the campus grew by more than 40 percent through a $12 million land acquisition.

Lee believes that two of the most significant problems that confront any organization are "shortness of the corporate memory" and "ambiguity of expectations." According to Dr. Smith, "shortness of the corporate memory means that people in an organization spend far too much of their time 'reinventing the wheel' and not enough time concentrating on the really important work of the organization." "Ambiguity of expectations refers to the fact that people often lack a clear-cut understanding of their job responsibilities." Smith has developed and implemented a management system designed to alleviate or minimize these difficulties.

"Discipline is the key to organizational management," Lee believes. "The executive management team at Southwest Texas made an explicit commitment in 1974 to the regular practice of discipline. Each time a problem or opportunity was encountered, a decisive and timely product—in the form of a solution or an innovation—would be sought. At the same time, the process for attaining the product was thoroughly documented. Thus, as a product was developed, the data collected, analyses made, decision processes invoked, persons involved, and all other pertinent data were carefully noted. In addition, a mechanism for regularly and automatically updating and improving both the process and the product for use in future situations became an integral part of the documentation."

Lee believes that the most important result of his management system is that the quality and amount of work accomplished by the individual is increased. His system is applicable to any organization, and he has begun putting it to the test at Travel Host.

"The bottom line for any management system is the quality of work produced," Lee explains. "If you can establish principles which expedite the handling of routine matters, people can get on with the truly important and challenging aspects of their work. That's true of a large corporation or a large university. It's an exciting prospect."

- Rights to recruit, screen, and hire subject to prior approval from a higher-level manager.
- No rights to recruit and screen; this function has been delegated to the personnel department, but the supervisor can accept or reject candidates.
- No rights to hire; the supervisor must take whomever the personnel department sends.

In the last instance, the supervisor is responsible for getting a job done but lacks the authority to perform the job adequately by hiring personnel he or she considers best qualified.

Amount of Authority: Centralization versus Decentralization

centralization

decentralization

It is important that management determine the appropriate levels of responsibility and authority to be delegated. If a limited amount of authority is delegated, the organization is usually characterized as being **centralized.** On the other hand, if a significant amount of authority is delegated to lower levels, the enterprise is described as being **decentralized.**

Centralization and decentralization are opposites, with many different degrees in between them. The real question is not whether a company should decentralize but rather how much. In determining the actual amount of decentralization existing in an organization, the nature and location of decision making must be assessed. In a highly centralized structure, individual managers and workers at lower levels in the organization have a rather narrow range of decisions or actions they can initiate. By contrast, the scope of authority to make decisions and take actions is rather broad for lower-level managers and employees in decentralized organizations. For example, in a highly centralized organizational structure, upper management makes all decisions regarding the hiring or firing of personnel, approval of purchasing of equipment, supplies, or other such activities. In a decentralized structure, lower-level management may make these decisions.

Although recent trends seem to favor decentralization, all forms of decentralization cannot be classified as effective and not all centralization classified as ineffective. Decentralization is advocated by many who believe that a greater share in management decision making should be given to lower organizational levels. If virtually all decisions and orders come from one central source, organization members tend to act as robots and unthinking executors of someone else's commands. Decentralization tends to create a climate for more rapid growth and development of personnel, and as has been discussed in earlier chapters, a primary responsibility of managers, on any level, is the development of people.

In addition to the human behavior implications of decentralization and centralization, there are other factors that will affect a manager's decision in this regard. Centralization

1. produces uniformity of policy and action.
2. results in few risks of errors by subordinates who lack either information or skill.
3. utilizes the skills of central and specialized experts.
4. enables closer control of operations.

On the other hand, decentralization

1. tends to make for speedier decisions and actions on the spot without consulting higher levels.
2. results in decisions that are more likely to be adapted to local conditions.
3. results in greater interest and enthusiasm on the part of the subordinate

to whom the authority has been entrusted (these expanded jobs provide excellent training experiences for possible promotion to higher levels).

4. allows top management to utilize their time for more study and consideration of the basic goals, plans, and policies of the enterprise.

Additional factors to be taken into account concerning the degree of centralization are discussed below.

Size and Complexity of the Organization. The larger the enterprise, the more authority the central manager is forced to delegate. If the firm is engaged in many separate businesses, the limitations of expertise will usually lead to decentralization of authority to the heads of these units. Each major product group is likely to have different production problems, varying kinds of customers, and varied marketing channels. If speed and adaptability to change are necessary to success, decentralization is a must.

Dispersion of the Organization. When the difficulties of size are compounded by geographic dispersion, it is evident that a greater degree of decentralization must occur. General Motors Company is a prime example of decentralization because of size and geographic dispersion. However, not every decision or every function must be decentralized. Control of operations may have to be pushed down to lower levels in the organization, while control of financing may still be centralized. Because of the increasing complexity of federal and state legislation affecting employment practices and unionization, centralization of labor relations is often established for purposes of uniformity throughout the company.

Competency of Personnel Available. A major limiting factor in many organizations is the adequacy or inadequacy of present personnel. If the enterprise has grown up under centralized decision making and control, past experience has often equipped subordinate personnel poorly to start making major decisions. They were hired and trained to be followers, not leaders and decision makers. In some convenience store chains this has developed into a major problem. Store managers are promoted to supervisors because they are able to perform basic store functions, not because of their decision-making ability. Supervisors are promoted to general managers not because of their decision-making ability but because they can ensure that lower managers follow standard operating procedures. In such a situation, a person who eventually makes it to the top is not equipped to cope with the large number of decisions to be made that are not based on established practices and procedures, and those who were inclined toward more independent thought and action may well have been driven away from the centralized firm.

Adequacy of Communications System. The size, complexity, and geographic dispersion lead to the delegation of larger amounts of authority for decision making to lower levels in the organization. The manager can seek to avoid decentralization through the development of a communication system that provides for speed, accuracy, and capacity of information needed for top management to exercise centralized control. In effect, although size and geography may preclude being on the spot, one can attempt to control subordinates by detailing standards of performance and process and by ensuring that information flows quickly and accurately to the central authoritative position.

Accountability

accountability

Once a sufficient amount of authority has been delegated to enable the individual to complete the task for which he or she is responsible, the person can then be held accountable for results. **Accountability** is the *final responsibility for results that a manager cannot delegate to someone else.* Managers are accountable not only for their own actions and decisions but also for the actions of their subordinates even though the manager may have delegated a responsibility and an authority to subordinates.

Before a manager can be held accountable for results, certain conditions should be present. First, responsibilities must be thoroughly and clearly understood. An individual who is unaware of what is expected cannot be held accountable. Second, the person must be qualified and capable of fulfilling the obligation. It would be inconceivable to assign the responsibility and authority for performing engineering or accounting functions to individuals having no previous educational background and/or experience in these areas. Finally, sufficient authority to accomplish the task must be delegated. Assigning a manager the total profit responsibility for a department but no authority to hire or fire employees would mean that insufficient authority has been delegated. This manager should not be held accountable for results.

PRINCIPLES RELATED TO AUTHORITY, RESPONSIBILITY, AND ACCOUNTABILITY

Several important principles relate to the concepts of authority, responsibility, and accountability. These principles are briefly discussed below and are summarized in Table 7-1.

Single Accountability

single accountability

Perhaps the most widely known principle of management governing the relationship of accountability is that of **single accountability,** also referred to as unity of command. Each person should answer to only one immediate superior—one boss to each employee. Single accountability enables better coordination and understanding of what is required, and improves discipline. An employee with two or more bosses can receive contradictory orders.

TABLE 7-1. ***Principles of Authority, Responsibility, and Accountability***

Principle	Definition of	Reason for	Possible Causes of Violation	Possible Results of Violation
Single Accountability	A person should report to only *one* boss. ("one boss")	Clarity and understanding, to ensure unity of effort and direction, and to avoid conflicts	Unclear definition of authority	Dissatisfaction or frustration of employees and perhaps lower efficiency
Authority Should Equal Responsibility	The amount of authority and responsibility should be equal. (Responsibility = Authority)	Allows work to be accomplished more efficiently, develops people, and reduces frustration	Fear on the part of some managers that subordinates might "take over"	Waste of energies and dissatisfaction of employees thereby reducing effectiveness
Scalar Chain of Authority (Chain of Command)	There should be a clear definition of authority in the organization. ("to go through channels")	Clarity of relationship avoids confusion and improves decision making and performance	Uncertainty on the part of the employee or a direct effort by the employee to avoid chain of command	Poor performance, confusion and/or dissatisfaction
Span of Management	There is a limit to the number of employees a manager can effectively supervise.	Increased effectiveness in direction and control of a manager	Overloading a manager due to growth in number of personnel	Lack of efficiency and control resulting in poor performance

Though single accountability is a sound concept, it does have certain limitations. Single accountability does not exist in many organizations. As the size of an organization increases, a person may be accountable to more than one boss.

Equal Authority and Responsibility

An important principle of management is that authority should equal responsibility. Following this principle ensures that work will be performed more efficiently and with a minimum amount of frustration on the part of personnel. By not delegating an adequate amount of authority, energies and resources are wasted and employee dissatisfaction often results.

Scalar Chain of Authority (Chain of Command)

The principle of the scalar chain of authority suggests that there should be a clear definition of authority in the organization. This concept is often referred to as the **chain of command.** Following this principle is very important to management because its application clarifies relationships, avoids confusion,

chain of command

and tends to improve decision making, thus leading to more effective performance. When the scalar chain is in effect, a person communicates in the organization by "going through channels."

Span of Management

span of management

The number of employees a manager can effectively supervise is referred to as the **span of management.** The span of management, or span of control as it is sometimes called, is a fundamental principle related to the organizing function. Adherence to it enables the manager to achieve maximum effectiveness in organizing, motivating, and controlling personnel. According to the span of management principle, there is a limit to the number of employees a manager can effectively supervise or control. The precise number or "span" varies according to the situation. The "correct" or optimum span of management for a manager might vary in a different situation and/or time.

Determining the number of potential relationships that a manager might have with a certain number of subordinates was the subject of research by A. V. Graicunas. A management consultant during the 1930s, Graicunas derived a formula to determine the potential interactions or relationships that were possible when a manager had a given number of employees.[1] Graicunas' formula is as follows: $R = n + n(n - 1) + n(2^{n-1} - 1)$, where R represents the number of relationships or interactions and n is the number of subordinates reporting to the manager.

According to the Graicunas's formula, a manager with two employees would have six potential relationships. For example, if Ed Bishop has two subordinates, John and Susan, the following would illustrate the six possible interactions.

Number of Relationships		
2	Ed may meet and talk with John Ed may meet and talk with Susan	*These are direct relationships*
2	Ed may meet and talk with John with Susan present, and vice-versa	*These are group relationships*
2	John may interact with Susan without Ed's being present or Susan may meet with John without Ed's being present	*These are cross-relationships*
6		

TABLE 7-2. *Possible Relationships with Different Number of Employees*

Number of Employees	Potential Number of Relationships
1	1
2	6
3	18
4	44
5	100
6	222
7	490
8	1,080
9	2,376
10	5,210
11	10,342
12	24,708

As Table 7-2 shows, each additional employee whom a manager supervises creates a substantial number of additional relationships.

FACTORS AFFECTING THE SPAN OF MANAGEMENT

In most private and public-sector organizations, spans of management have historically been relatively narrow and restricted, usually ranging from six to fifteen people. Shorter or more restricted spans of management permit closer supervision of personnel but tend to create "tall" organizational structures with a large number of levels, which may cause difficulties in communications. Larger or wider spans result in relatively fewer levels or "flat" organizations and greater freedom for the individual employee.

While managers agree that the span of management is a fundamentally valid concept, the exact number of subordinates that a manager can effectively supervise cannot be determined precisely. There are, however, a number of factors, including the following, that affect the span of management.

- Complexity of the work
- Degree of similarity to other work
- Degree of interdependency with other work
- Stability of the organization and situation

Insights to Success

Don't expect true managerial responsibilities until earned on the job.

FRED DeCHANT, Personnel Executive, Georgia-Pacific Corporation

- Degree of standardization of the work
- Qualifications, skills, expertise, and experience of the manager
- Qualifications, skills, experience, and motivation of the employees
- Type of technology

In general, the more complex the work, the shorter the span of management. The span of control can be longer if the manager is supervising employees performing similar jobs. If jobs are closely interlocked and interdependent, the manager may have greater problems with coordination, creating the need for a rather limited span of management. Similarly, if the organization is operating in an unstable environment, a narrow span may prove to be more effective. On the other hand, the establishment of numerous standards increases predictability and provides the basis for effective control, thereby resulting in a wider effective span. Another key factor affecting the span of management is the qualifications of managers and nonmanagerial personnel. Managers and employees who are highly skilled, experienced, and motivated generally can operate with wider spans of management and with less supervision.

Finally, technology can have a significant impact on the span of management. Joan Woodward, a British researcher who conducted studies in one hundred English manufacturing firms, discovered that the type of technology had a significant impact on the spans of management actually used in business organizations. Woodward classified production technology on the basis of

- unit or small batch processing (for example, made-to-order goods such as custom-tailored clothing)
- mass production (assembly-line operations)
- process production with continuous long runs of a standardized product such as oil, chemicals, or pharmaceuticals

She discovered that spans of management were widest in those firms using mass production technology. The jobs in a mass production situation tend to be more routine and similar to one another, thereby leading to wider effective spans of management.[2]

ORGANIZATIONAL STRUCTURES

organizational structure

After determining the departments needed and the levels of responsibility, authority, and accountability, we are now prepared to answer the question, "What type of **organizational structure** do we need?" This question is asked frequently by managers of both newly formed companies and firms that have been in business for decades.

Although we usually think of the large company when we discuss organizational structures, every firm, large or small, has a structure. It may or may not have an organizational chart. Small businesses may have simple structures that are easily understood. In fact, the organizational structure may be informal and highly changeable in a small, uncomplicated business. By contrast, large, diverse, and complex organizations usually have a highly formalized structure. But that does not mean the structure is so rigid as not to change perhaps even frequently. Determining the most appropriate organizational design or structure is not a simple matter if one considers the frequency of reorganization to be an indication. Newly formed high-technology companies are most likely to restructure or reorganize frequently, but even some of the largest Fortune 500 industrial firms often experience a major reorganization.

The organizational structure provides guidelines essential for effective employee performance and overall organizational success. The structure clarifies and communicates the lines of responsibility and authority within the firm and assists management in coordinating the overall operation.

Although there are many variations of organizational structures used today, we will discuss line, line and staff, functional, project and matrix structures.

Line Organization

line organization

A **line organization** structure shows the direct, vertical relationships between different levels within the firm. A "pure" line organization would consist of personnel performing or managing functions essential to the successful existence of the firm. In a line organization structure, authority would follow the scalar or vertical chain of command. Figure 7-3 is an illustration of a simple three-level line organizational structure for the modern manufacturing company.

Several advantages are quite often associated with the pure line organization structure.

1. A line structure tends to *simplify and clarify* responsibility, *authority,* and *accountability* relationships within the organization. The levels of responsibility and authority of personnel operating within a line orgazation are likely to be precise and understandable.
2. A line structure *promotes fast decision making and allows the organization to change directions more rapidly, since there are few people to consult when problems arise*.
3. Since pure line organizations are small, there are the advantages of *greater feeling of closeness* of management to the employees, and all personnel usually have an opportunity to know what's going on with the firm.

Despite the above advantages, there are also certain disadvantages of the line structure. The major disadvantage of a line organization structure is its increasing lack of effectiveness as the firm grows larger. At some point, speed and flexibility do not offset the lack of specialized knowledge and skills. In

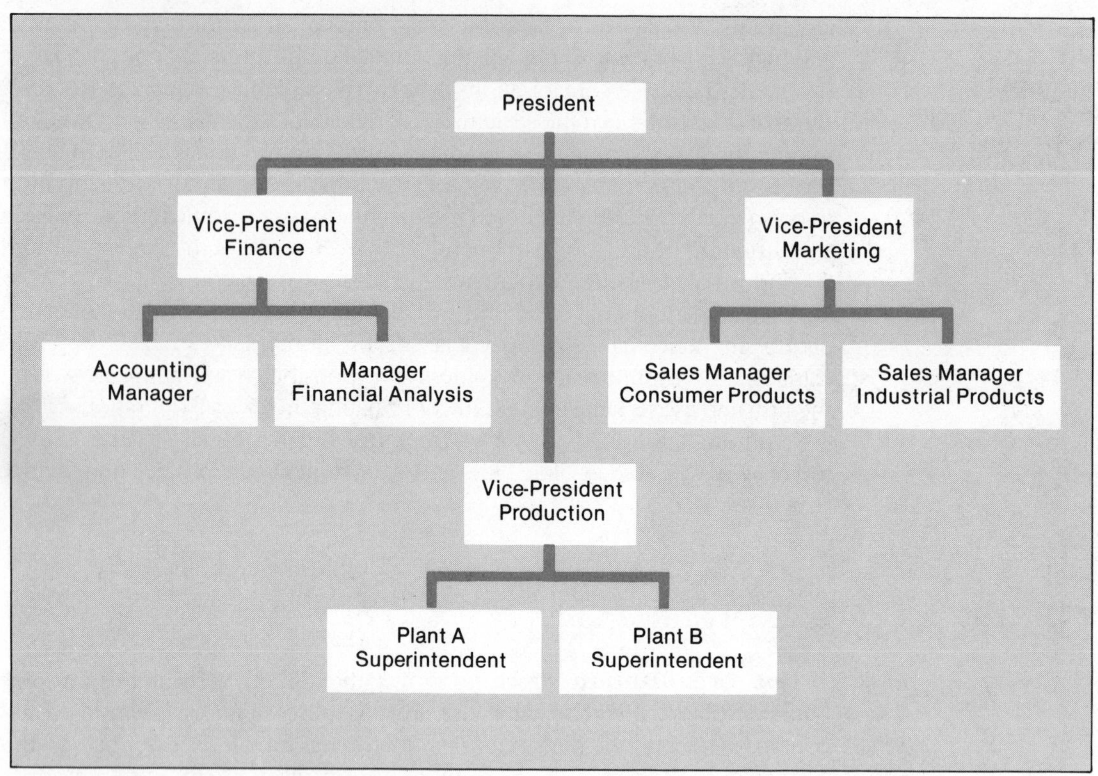

FIGURE 7-3 *A Line Organization Structure*

other words, a line structure may force managers to "wear too many hats" and thereby possibly reduce their effectiveness. In a line organization structure, the firm may have a tendency to become overly dependent on one or a few key people who can perform numerous jobs. If the organization is to remain purely line, one solution is for management to seek help by creating additional levels of organization to share the managerial load. This, however, will result in a lengthening of the chain of command and a consequent loss of some of the values of speed, flexibility, and central control.

Line and Staff Organization

line and staff organization

At some point in the growth of a firm, there will be a need for specialists. When a provision is made for these specialists, one has altered the structure from being a line organization to a **line and staff organization**. The staff function provides advice and support to the organization. Types of staff personnel may be either *general* or *specialized*. A general staff position is usually an assistant with a background very similar to that of the boss. Specialized staffs are the type most frequently encountered. They provide expertise developed by means of concentration on a narrow portion of the firm's activities.

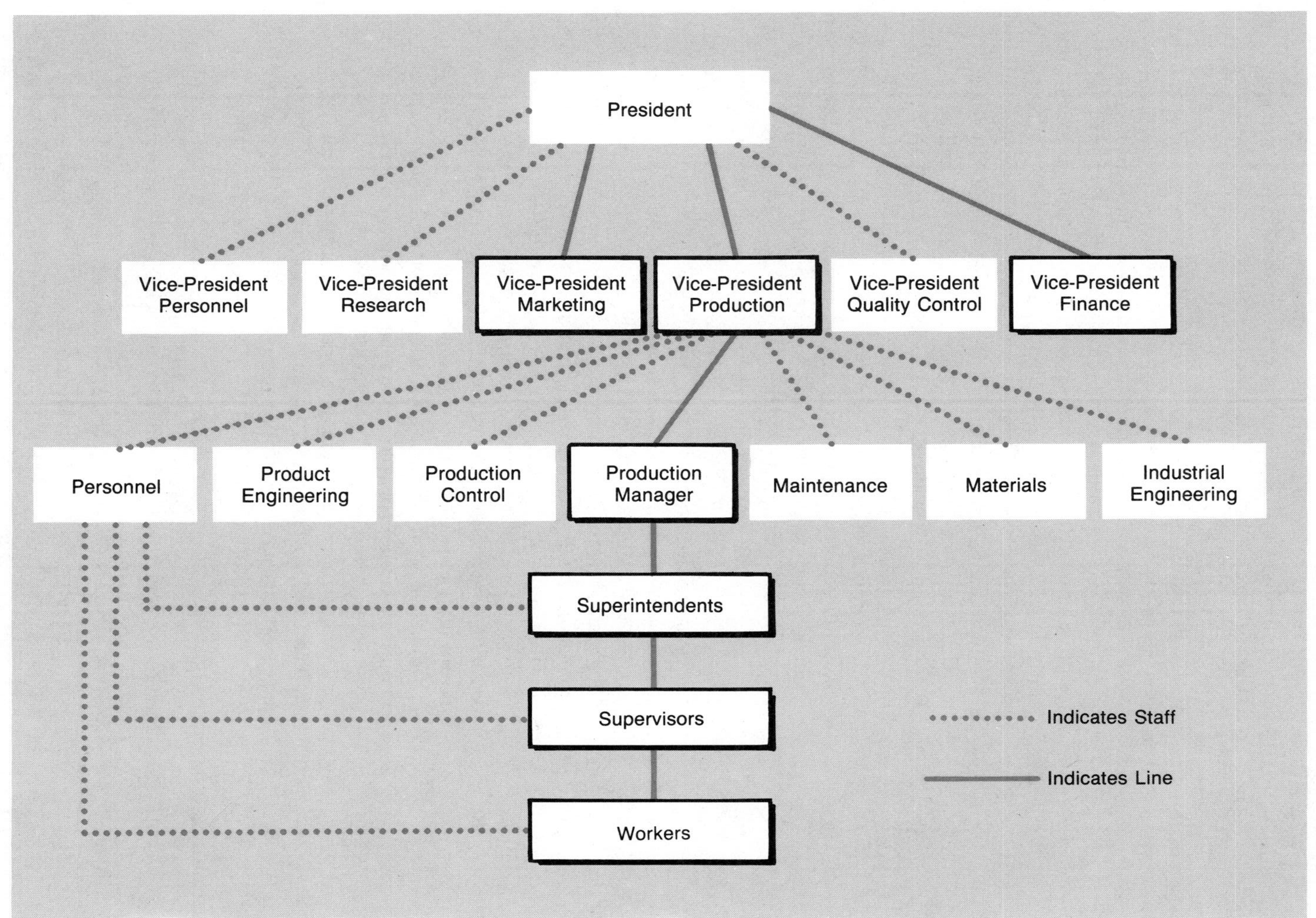

FIGURE 7-4 *Line and Staff Structure of Typical Manufacturing Company*

As shown in the line and staff organization chart in Figure 7-4, staff functions under the president include personnel, research, and quality control. Under the vice-president of production are personnel, product engineering, production control, maintenance, materials, and industrial engineering. These are staff departments that include superintendents, supervisors, and workers. For instance, note the dotted line from personnel to superintendents, supervisors, and workers. While personnel, research, and quality control are staff functions in the firm, there is a direct-line reporting relationship between the vice-presidents of these functions and the president of a typical manufacturing company. Likewise, there is a direct-line reporting relationship between personnel, product engineering, production control, maintenance, materials, and industrial engineering and the vice-president of production.

Three separate types of specialized staffs can be identified: (1) advisory, (2) service, and (3) control. It is possible for one unit to perform all three functions. For example, the personnel manager may advise line managers on the appropriateness of recognizing a particular labor union. The department simultaneously provides a service by procuring and training needed production and sales personnel. A control orientation enters when the personnel manager audits salaries actually paid to ensure conformity to line-approved pay ranges. Some staffs are predominantly one or the other in character; for example, a staff economist advises the establishment of long-range plans, a maintenance staff unit repairs plant and equipment, and a quality control staff unit enforces authorized product standards. It is apparent that the potential for conflicts in coordination between line and staff tends to grow as one moves from advice to service to control. One can possibly ignore advice, but service is needed, and control is often unavoidable.

There are both advantages and disadvantages of a line and staff organization structure. The primary advantage is that it uses the expertise of specialists. The actions of a manager can become more scientific by means of concentrated and skillful analysis of business problems. In addition, the manager's effective span of management can be lengthened—that is, he or she can supervise more people. Some staff personnel operate as an extension of the manager and assist in coordination and control.

Despite the fact that a line and staff structure allows for increased flexibility and specialization, it may create conflicts. When we introduce various specialists into the organization, line managers may feel that they have "lost authority" over certain specialized functions. These managers do not want staff specialists telling them "what to do or how to do it" even though they recognize the specialists' knowledge and expertise. It is important to use staff personnel without destroying single accountability. The *right* of the line manager still remains, though the *ability* to exercise this right may have been considerably weakened. The problem is not so much the type of structure but the individual personnel within the organization. Some staff personnel have difficulty adjusting to the role of being an adviser, especially if line managers are reluctant to accept his or her advice. Staff personnel may resent not having authority, and this may cause a line and staff conflict.

There is a tendency for the specialist to seek to enlarge personal influence by assuming line authority in her or his specialty. This is compounded by a realization that the fundamental purpose of all staff is to produce greater economy and effectiveness of operation. This means that staff must attempt to introduce changes that result in more efficiency. These changes will not always be welcomed with open arms by line personnel. Thus, the introduction of specialized, noncommand personnel into what was once a fairly simple organization structure complicates relationships.

Functional Organization

If a staff specialist is given command or line authority over other personnel in regard to his or her specialty, a functional authority relationship has been created. **Functional authority** is direct line authority over specialized functions or activities. These relationships give rise to what has become known as a **functional organization** structure. In a pure line organization there is limited use of specialists by management. In the line and staff organization, specialization of particular functions characterizes the structure, but the specialists have only advisory authority. However, in the functional structure, specialists are given authority to issue orders in their own name in designated areas of the work. The chain of command of line authority and the notion of single accountability (or having one boss) is broken, creating multiple accountability.

functional authority

functional organization

Even though few, if any, organizations are established on a completely functionalized basis, it is quite common to functionalize the relationship between one or two specialists and the remainder of the organization. If a function is considered to be of crucial importance, it may then be necessary for the specialist to exercise direct rather than advisory authority. The violation of single accountability is undertaken deliberately. The possible losses resulting from confusion and conflicting orders from multiple sources may be more than offset by increased effectiveness in the performance of the specialty.

Good examples of specialties that have been given functional authority in many organizations include quality control, safety, and labor relations (see Figure 7-5). Quality control is a very important function in most manufacturing organizations, and its level of authority and stature within the organization has increased over the years. A staff quality control department would merely advise; if, however, that unit is given the authority or right to issue orders (e.g., to correct defects) in its own name, it can no longer be called staff.

Likewise, safety and labor relations specialists may also exercise functional authority over personnel in other areas throughout the organization, but only in relation to their specific specialties. A safety manager may issue compliance guidelines and give direct interpretations of the Occupational Safety and Health Act (OSHA) throughout the organization. The labor relations specialist often will have complete authority in contract negotiations with the union. In each of the above illustrations—quality control, safety, and labor relations—the traditional chain of command has been split. As long as this splitting process is restricted, coordination and unity of action are not in excessive danger. Many organizations that utilize functional relationships

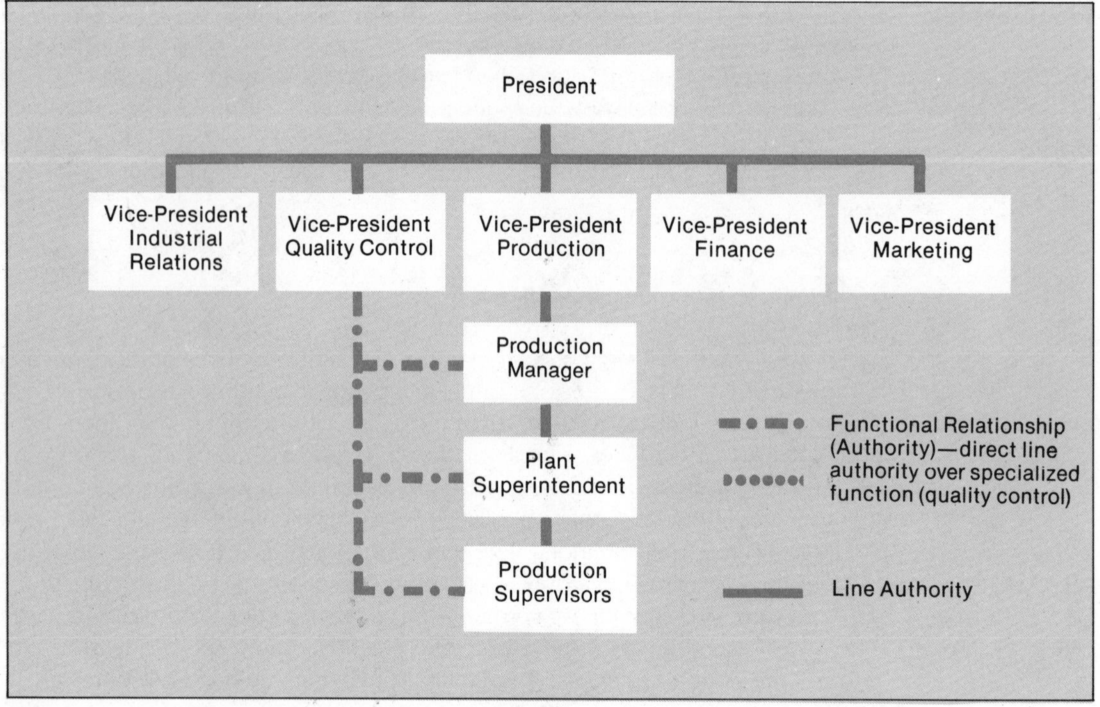

FIGURE 7-5 *Functional Organizational Structure*

attempt to confine its impact to managerial rather than operative levels. Thus, a department supervisor may have to account to more than one boss, but the employees are protected from this possible confusion.

Despite the advantages of a functional organization, the major disadvantages of such structures are: (1) the potential conflicts resulting from the violation of the principle of single accountability and (2) the tendency to keep authority centralized at higher levels in the organization. If the functionalized structure is used extensively, there may be a tendency for the line department supervisor to become little more than a figurehead. The structure can become very complicated when there are corresponding functional specialists on various levels in the organization.

Project and Matrix Organization Structures

The line, line and staff, and functional organization structures have been the traditional approaches to organization. The primary concern of these forms of organizations has been the establishment and distribution of authority to coordinate and control the firm by emphasizing vertical, rather than horizontal, relationships. However, work processes may flow horizontally, diagonally, up, or down, depending on the problem and distribution of talents. Work requirements often result in the need for an organization based on the specific nature of work projects. The organizations that have emerged to cope with this challenge have been referred to as project structures or matrix organizations. The key element in both project and matrix structures is the creation of a structure in which managers and professionals have more than one boss.

project organization

A **project organization** provides a highly effective means by which all of the necessary human talent and physical resources can be focused for a time on a specific project or goal. They are temporary organization structures designed to achieve specific results by using a team of specialists from different functional areas within the organization. The *team* focuses all of its energies and skills on the assigned project. Once the specific project has been completed, the project team is broken up and personnel are reassigned to their regular positions in the organization. Many business organizations and government agencies make use of project teams or task forces to concentrate their efforts on a specific project assignment like the development of a new product or new technology or on the construction of a new plant.

Perhaps the most famous example of the successful use of the project form of organization has been by the National Aeronautic and Space Administration (NASA). The significant space achievements of the United States have been due in part to the project organization structures used by NASA. For each major space goal, a project team was assigned. The terms used to describe our objectives in space exploration, such as the *Gemini Project* and *Apollo Moon Project,* are very familiar project organizations to millions of people.

Project organization structures are probably most valuable when the work is—

1. definable in terms of a specific goal and target date for completion that have been established,
2. somewhat unique and unfamiliar to the existing organization,
3. complex with respect to interdependence of activities and specialized skills necessary to accomplishment,
4. critical in terms of possible gain or loss, and
5. temporary with respect to duration of need.

Figure 7-6 illustrates a highly simplified project organization that is attached to an existing organization. Personnel are assigned to the project from the existing permanent organization and are under the direction and control of the project manager. In simple terms, the project manager specifies what effort is needed and when work will be performed, while the concerned department managers may decide who in their unit is to do the work and how it is to be accomplished. Home base for most personnel is the existing department—engineering, production, purchasing, personnel, or research and development.

The authority over the four project members is shared by both the project manager and the functional managers in the permanent organization.

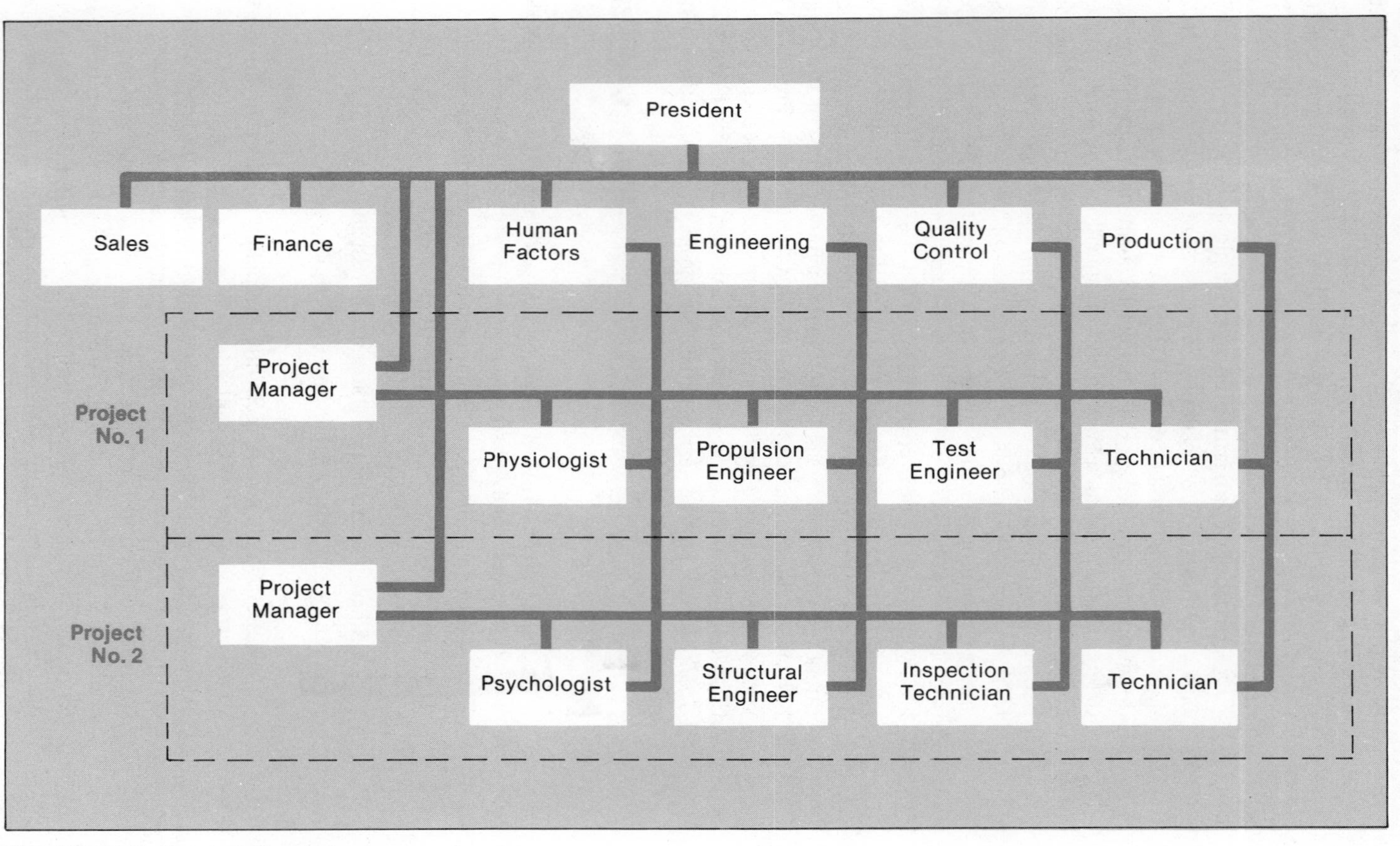

FIGURE 7-6 *Project Structure*

The specialists are temporarily on loan to spend a portion of their time on the project assignment. However, it is apparent that authority is one of the crucial questions of the project structure. A deliberate conflict has been established between the project manager and managers within the permanent organization. The authority relationships are overlapping, presumably in the interest of ensuring that all problems will be covered.

Project managers and department heads are often forced into using means other than formal authority to accomplish results. Informal relationships become more important than formal prescriptions of authority. In the event of conflict and dispute, discussion and consensus are required rather than the forcing of compliance by threat or punishment. Full and free communication, regardless of formal rank, is required among those working on the project. More attention is allocated to roles and competencies in relation to the project than to formal levels of authority.

matrix organization

Project structures are temporary attachments to existing organizations. When the concept is introduced in a more permanent form, it is usually referred to as a **matrix organization**. A matrix structure is often used when it is essential for the firm to be highly responsive to a rapidly changing external environment. For example, an electronics firm operating in a highly competitive market with rapidly changing technology might find that the matrix structure facilitates quick response by the company to its environment. Matrix organization structures have been used successfully in such industries as banking, chemicals, computers, and electronics.

In matrix organizations there are functional managers and product managers. Functional managers are in charge of specialized resources such as production, quality control, inventories, scheduling, and selling. Product managers are in charge of one or more products and are authorized to prepare product strategies and call upon the various functional managers for the necessary resources. When a firm moves to a matrix structure, functional managers must realize that they will lose some of their authority and will have to take some direction from the product managers, who have the budgets to purchase internal resources.

Despite limitations, the effectiveness of the project and matrix management concepts demonstrates that people can work for two or more managers and that managers can effectively influence those over whom they have no clear authority. There is the possibility of conflict and frustration, but the opportunity for prompt, efficient accomplishment is great.

Summary

Determining the appropriate levels of responsibility and authority is essential to sound organization. Derived from functions, responsibility is an obligation to perform certain work activities. It is crucial to the success of a firm that responsibilities be clearly defined. Once responsibilities have been assigned to personnel, it is then necessary to delegate enough authority to get the job done. Authority is the right to decide, to direct others to take action, or to perform certain duties in achieving organizational goals. A basic principle of management is that authority should equal responsibility. The process of making specific work assignments to individuals within the organization and giving them the authority to perform these functions is known as delegation. It is an important concept if work is to be accomplished and people in the organization are to develop expertise. Once authority has been delegated, an individual can then be held accountable for results. Accountability is the final responsibility for results that a manager cannot delegate to someone else.

Depending on the extent of the delegation of authority, an organization is said to be either centralized or decentalized. In a centralized organization, decisions are made primarily by upper management, whereas in a decentralized structure, lower levels in the organization play a more active role in decision making. There are four important principles of authority, responsibility, and accountability that must be considered in the delegation process. They are:

- *Single accountability.* A person should have only one boss.
- *Authority should equal responsibility.*
- *Scalar chain of authority.* Clear definition of authority (through channels).
- *Span of management.* A limit to the number of people a manager can effectively supervise.

The means for organizing the functions, resources, and the formal relationships is the organization structure. Four basic types of organizational structures are the line, line and staff, functional, and project. A line structure is the simplest and most basic form of organization. The line and staff structure allows for increased flexibility and specialization with the introduction of staff specialists who serve as advisers. However, it creates more conflicts over authority. In the functional organization, the staff specialists are given authority to issue orders in designated areas of work. Finally, project and matrix organization structures provide a highly effective means by which all of the necessary human talent and physical resources are allocated for a time to a specific project.

Review Questions

1. Define and illustrate the following:
   a. responsibility
   b. authority
   c. accountability
2. What is meant by centralization and decentralization?
3. What are the advantages and disadvantages of centralization and decentralization?
4. Briefly describe the primary factors to be considered in determining the degree of centralization that is appropriate for an organization.

5. What is meant by delegation? Identify at least four reasons for delegating and four limitations of delegation that managers should consider.
6. Identify and briefly define four significant principles of management governing authority, responsibility, and accountability relationships. What are some possible causes for and results of the violation of these principles?
7. What are the advantages and disadvantages of wide and short spans of management? What factors affect the span of management?
8. Identify four basic types of organizational structures. Draw a simple chart to illustrate each.
9. Briefly discuss the appropriateness of each type of organization identified in number 8.
10. Under what circumstances are project and matrix organization structures most appropriate?

Exercises

1. Analyze the organization charts of a local retail store (e.g. Sears), a bank, a manufacturing company, and your college or university. How are these firms organized and what are the basic means of departmentation used? What changes, if any, would you suggest for the managers of these organizations? Draw new charts if necessary.
2. Go to the library and review two current journal articles describing corporate reorganizations. At the next class meeting report to the class one example of a company that has been reorganized. In your three minute presentation briefly describe the company as well as the reasons for and advantages of the reorganization.

Case Study

Managing Growth at Grumbles Department Stores

It was seven o'clock sharp when O. C. Grumbles unlocked his office door. He had been arriving at this same office at this precise hour six days a week for the past nineteen years—the time when he took over as president of the Grumbles Department Store chain from his late father who had turned a family-operated dry goods business into a three-store operation. Under O. C. Grumbles's leadership, the business had grown into a fifteen-store operation in ten middle-sized cities in a two-state region. O. C. Grumbles was considered a shrewd businessman and a farsighted planner by his peers and business associates, even though he was rigid and paternalistic toward his employees.

The Grumbles Department Store chain was more than a successful business enterprise. During his nineteen years as chief executive, O. C. Grumbles had pioneered the development and implementation of modern management systems including management by objectives, as well as extensive planning, policy, and procedure systems. The organization and its president were reputed as being

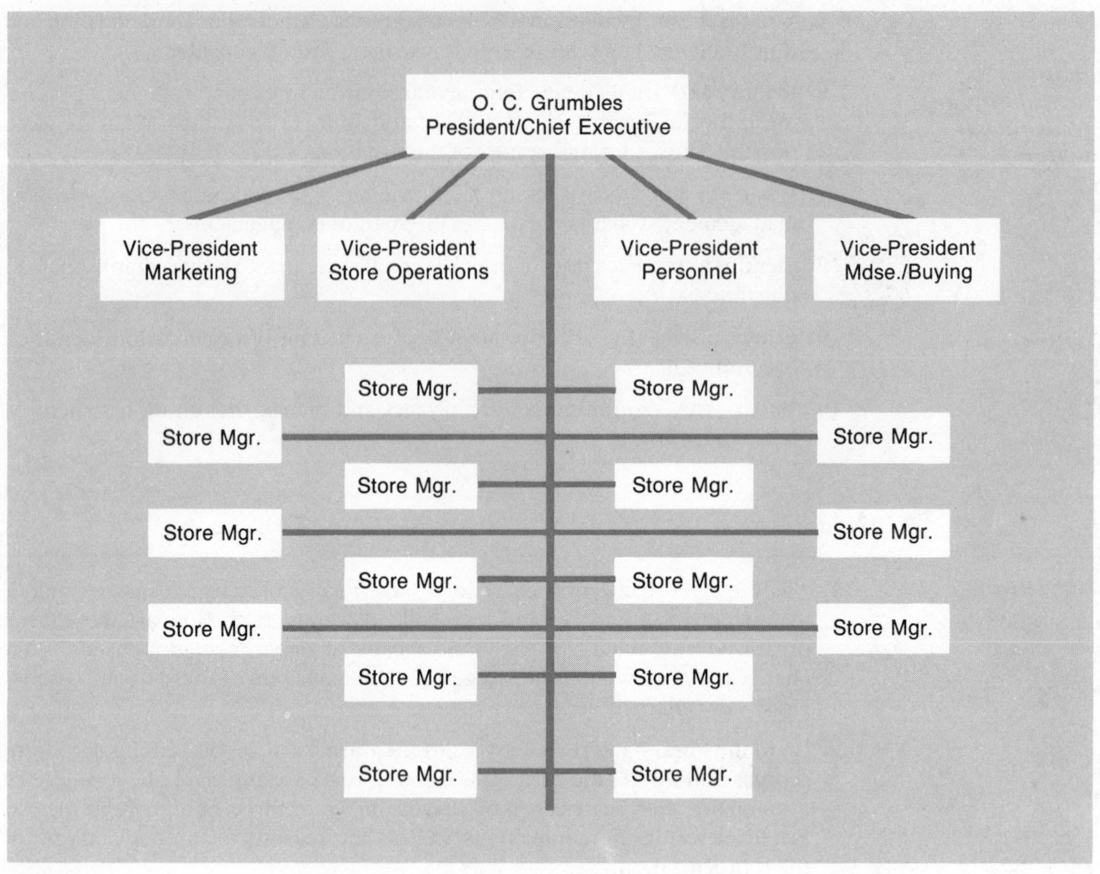

FIGURE 1

an effective and efficient machine. Figure 1 depicts the organizational structure for the Grumbles Department Store chain.

O. C. Grumbles obviously knows how to operate a department store successfully. Few others have known the success he enjoys in a highly competitive field. Each store in the organization is assured of knowing how to handle each step of the operation because O. C. Grumbles has overseen the writing and frequent review of a series of "operating procedures," which give step-by-step methods for each phase of the operation. These "OPs," as O. C. refers to them, are discussed and updated at the monthly managers' meetings. All fifteen store managers, the four vice-presidents, and Mr. Grumbles attend these meetings. It is typical that four of the five hours in meetings are spent on reviewing, discussing, and updating the OPs. The remaining time is spent discussing merchandise, buying, scheduling company-wide sales, planning store expansions, and selecting and training personnel.

In a recent conversation with Diane Williams, vice-president of merchandising, Mr. Grumbles stated that he was disappointed with the overall sales volume and growth rate of the fifteen-store operations. "Diane, I can't understand why Grumbles hasn't achieved faster growth in sales lately. Also, I am finding it more and more difficult for us to add new stores. I have always believed that I could effectively manage a chain of twenty-five or thirty stores with the OP

System we use. I'm having difficulty staying on top of things in the fifteen existing stores! Maybe I'm just getting too old to manage this business with our present organization structure. What do you think?"

QUESTIONS

1. Assume that you are Diane Williams. What would be your response to Mr. Grumbles?
2. If there are problems, what might be the cause?
3. Evaluate the strengths and weaknesses of the present organization structure of Grumbles Department Store chain.
4. Could you suggest any changes in the organizational chart and reporting relationships?

Case Study

"Who Has the Authority?"

Doughboy Snack Foods is a large bakery with approximately 500 employees located in Atlanta, Georgia. The company is six years old, unionized, and features a wide line of products, including various cakes, snack foods, and an extensive array of commercial and household bread items. Doughboy ships its products all over the Southeast. The bread distribution department is the smallest section of the company consisting of one department head, one supervisor, one assistant supervisor, two leadmen, and eight full-time employees.

Jim Davis is the first-shift supervisor and has been with Doughboy since it opened. Before coming to the company, he owned and operated a cabinet shop. He is a no-nonsense, autocratic manager. Jim usually makes all of the decisions and gives them to his assistant, Sam Smith, the second-shift supervisor, who has been with Doughboy for five years. Before Jim leaves each day, he writes down all that needs to be done and leaves Sam in charge. Jim was responsible for Sam's getting the job at Doughboy, for they had worked together in the past when Sam was an employee in Jim's cabinet shop. Furthermore, Jim was responsible for Sam's promotions to leadman and assistant, for Jim's recommendations to his superiors were the reason the positions were approved and Sam was given the job.

The employees in the bread distribution section are the highest paid in the company. Most of them are happy with the company and look forward to a long employment. However, one employee of this section is currently experiencing some problems. Murphy Bowen is the second-shift leadman, but until two months ago he was the third-shift leadman, a position he held for over three years. Murphy accepted the job on the new shift because Jim had assured him he could have Saturdays and Sundays off. However, from the first day on the new job, Murphy has been assigned weekend duty because he is the most experienced employee on the shift to assume weekend supervision of new employees. Murphy spoke with Sam, his shift supervisor, and asked for weekends off. Sam explained the need for the present schedule and gave Murphy the impression that if wanted to continue with the company, the present schedule was his only choice. Company policy dictated that after an employee accepted a job it was up to the management to establish working hours. Also, nothing in the union contract stated that an employee's schedule couldn't be changed after he accepted a specific job.

But Murphy can't help feeling betrayed by the undesirable schedule and angered at Sam for not giving him the hours he had expected when he joined this shift.

To complicate further Murphy's position in this situation, he happened to see Jim one afternoon as he was returning home with some furniture in the back of his truck. Murphy stopped the truck and explained to Jim that he was moving the furniture to his home and asked if it would be all right not to work that evening. Jim consented to let him off, and Murphy figured that since company policy stated that he had to give at least two hours' notice of personal business, he would have an excused absence. As Murphy came into the office the next day, he noticed that Sam was not in the office, Murphy knew that Sam was responsible for the attendance records for his shift, so he checked the records while waiting for Sam to return. He was surprised by the notation of "unexcused" by his name for the previous evening and angered because he felt he had followed company policy in requesting an excused absence two hours before shift time.

Due to these problems, Murphy, who had always been a hard-working employee, began to feel Doughboy was not treating him fairly. He developed a sullen attitude and began to be inefficient in his work. As a matter of fact, the next shift had begun to suffer due to the lack of productivity of Murphy's group.

QUESTIONS

1. What problems relating to authority and responsibility relationships exist in this case?
2. What do you believe should be done to keep this type of problem from recurring?

Notes

1. A. V. Graicunas, "Relationships of Organizations," *Papers on the Science of Administration,* ed. L. Gulick and L. Urwick (New York: Columbia University Press, 1947).
2. Joan Woodward, *Industrial Organization: Theory and Practice* (London: Oxford University Press, 1965), pp. 52–62.

References

Arnold, John D. "The Why, When, and How of Changing Organizational Structures." *Management Review,* (March 1981): 17–20.

Gibson, James L.; Ivancevich, John M.; and Donnelley, James H., Jr., *Organizations: Behavior Structure and Processes.* Dallas: Business Publications, 1981.

Haynes, M. E. "Delegation: There's More to It Than Letting Someone Else Do It." *Supervisory Management* 25 (January 1980): 9–15.

Karasek, R. A., Jr. "Job Demands, Job Decision Latitude for Job Redesign." *Administrative Science Quarterly* 24 (June 1979): 285–308.

Logges, J. G. "Role of Delegation in Improving Productivity." *Personnel Journal* 58 (November 1979): 776–779.

Ouchi, W. G. "Relationship between Organizational Structure and Organizational Control. *Administrative Science Quarterly* 22 (March 1977): 206–216.

Peters, T. J. "Beyond the Marix Organization." *Business Horizons* 22 (October 1979): 15–27.

Potter, B. A. "Speaking with Authority: How to Give Directions." *Supervisory Management* 25 (March 1980): 2–11.

Rousseau, D. M. "Assessment of Technology in Organizations: Closed versus Open Systems Approaches." *Academy of Management Review* 4 (October 1979): 531–542.

Waterman, H., Jr.: Peters, J.; and Phillips, R. "Structure Is Not Organization." *Business Horizons* 23, no. 3 (June 1980): 14–26.

KEY TERMS

group
norms
role
contact chart
cohesiveness
synergism
grapevine
status
status symbol
power
politics

LEARNING OBJECTIVES

After completing this chapter you should be able to

1. Explain how group goals, norms, roles, leadership style, and structure differ in both the formal and informal organization.
2. Describe the importance of cohesiveness, size, and synergism in the informal organization.
3. Identify the benefits and costs of the informal organization.
4. Explain the concept of status, status sources, and status symbols.
5. Relate the importance of understanding power and politics.

8

The Informal Organization

> Jim Brown, the general manager of Ampex Manufacturers, is frustrated. One of his supervisors, Bob Evans, is constantly being asked to supply advice to many people in the organization. On numerous occasions he has seen Bob with the vice-president of production and the vice-president of finance. Not only do people from upper management seek Bob's attention, but also many lower-level employees from several different departments apparently desire Bob's advice and opinions. Jim thinks to himself, "Whatever happened to the chain of command?"
>
> Alice Garcia, the production supervisor for United Wholeselling Company, has just been told by Barbara Adams, one of her new employees, that she will quit on Friday. The reason Barbara gave for leaving was, "I just don't fit in around here. The other workers don't seem to like me and I cannot find anyone to talk to."
>
> Tommy John, a supervisor for Grey Productions, told Bill Stephens, the new machine operator, that extra money above his hourly wage could be earned if he worked faster. Because Bill really wanted to buy a new car, he began by *busting quota* every day. At first Bill was taking home 30 percent more money each week than the average employee. After only one month, however, Bill's production had dropped to the average level in the department. Whereas, at first, Bill did not seem interested in socializing with the other employees, Bill is now seen going to coffee and lunch with the other workers and laughing and joking with them. The supervisor thinks to himself, "The old informal group pressure got to a good worker again."

Jim, Alice, and Tommy have learned from experience that the informal organization can have a significant impact on the work environment. Inserting the human element into an organization reduces the clear, logically designed official structure desired so much by some managers. These managers are proud of the formal organizational structure that has been developed. As may be seen in Figure 8-1, it is very logical and orderly. Everyone knows exactly who they report to and the tasks they are expected to do. Some managers believe they can sit back in their executive suites and the company will "run itself" because of the beautiful structure that has been developed.

When the human factor is inserted, this beautiful creation is often altered. In fact, the manner in which a company is organized and the way the employees interact to accomplish the task may be completely different. In jest, but a somewhat realistic illustration, the manner in which the informal group operates within the formal organization might be as shown in Figure 8-2. As may be seen, the president of the firm is *out to lunch* although he has the official *right* of command. Apparently most of the actual decisions in the firm are made by one person and everyone is attempting to get a share of his

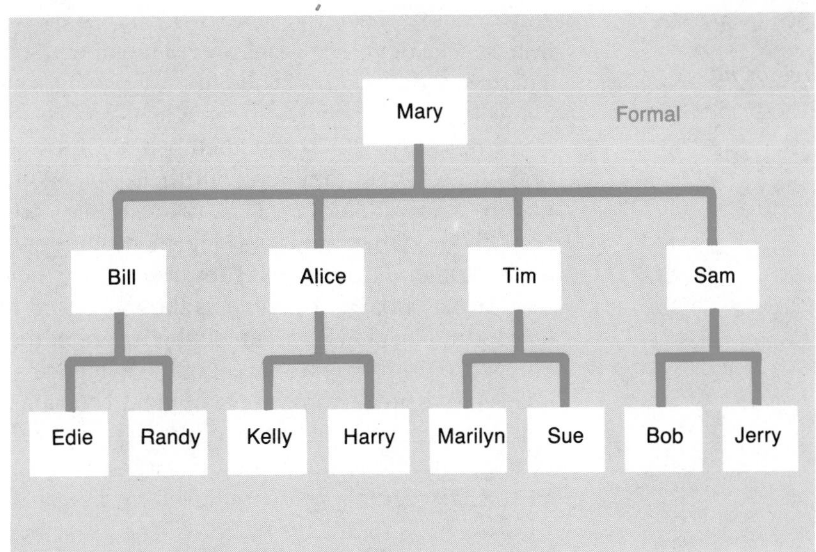

FIGURE 8-1
The Formal Organization

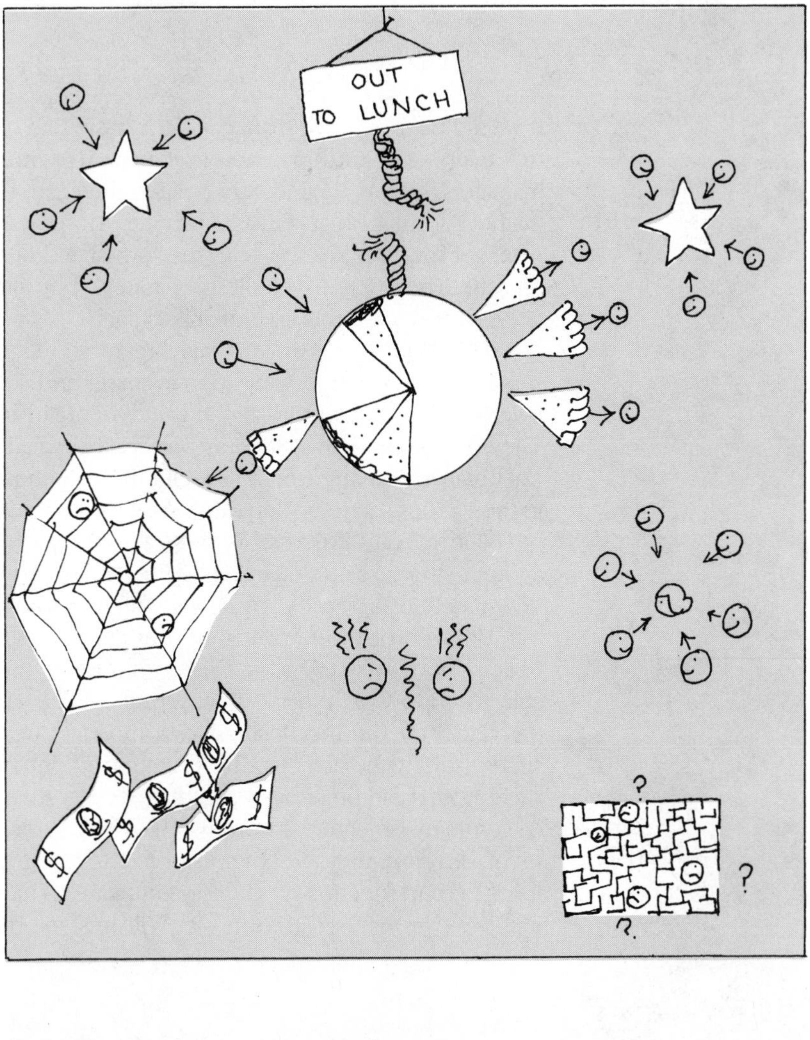

FIGURE 8-2
The Informal Organization

consideration. There are also two *rising stars* who are receiving attention from several devoted organizational members. Some of the employees are in a maze and don't know where they are going while others are covered with cobwebs and are doing nothing. A fight appears to have broken out between two employees, while other members are more attracted to a member of the opposite sex than they are with their jobs. As may be seen, organizational members often do not conform to the formal structure that has been officially prescribed. Rather, they develop friendships and relationships with individuals in other departments. They also choose their own informal leaders that may or may not be the same as those selected by the formal organization.

In this chapter we examine the nature of the informal organization and attempt to gain an appreciation of the influence—both positive and negative—it can have on the formal organization. The ultimate objective of the chapter will be to gain an appreciation of the factors a manager should consider when dealing with the informal group. Status, power, and politics will also be discussed as topics that relate to the informal organization.

THE FORMAL VERSUS THE INFORMAL ORGANIZATION

It would be foolish for managers to assume that they could identify and control every relationship among all persons within the organization. Some managers, however, sincerely believe they can, but the independent nature of the informal organization frustrates those attempts. For this reason, the manager must appreciate both the formal and informal relationships that are present. They may be studied separately, but ultimately they must be integrated into a total organizational package.

The manager of the formal organization establishes what employees should do through organizational charts and job descriptions. Traditional managers tend to emphasize the values of organizational and personal loyalty. They often can tolerate incompetence more readily than disloyalty. The official organization attempts to specify the way things should be accomplished in the various sections, departments, and divisions of the firm.

The official structure is only a portion of the story. There emerges another structure consisting of informal relationships, created not by officially designated managers but by any and all organizational members.

Because of the impact that the informal organization may have on an organization, increasing numbers of firms are training their managers to be able to cope with the informal group. Gerritt Starke, director of corporate personnel for Kemper Insurance Company, says, "We teach our managers/supervisors to be alert to the formation of 'informal work groups' and that such groups can be either a positive or a negative influence on a department or company objective." Corning Glass Works also has an extensive management development program devoted to both understanding how the informal group functions and designing ways to have the informal group work in a positive manner. At Sherwin-Williams, effort is directed toward making

Qualities Needed for Success with Your Organization

In my view, people relationships— i.e., mutual trust and respect with appropriate humility—are probably the single most important factor in relations internally, or with suppliers, customers, shareholders, or internationally with business or government. Adequate relations among people require constant effort to ensure success of the venture.

H. H. LYON, Vice-President, Administration, The Dow Chemical Company

the formal and informal work group one and the same. This means that each work group is managed by a team leader who is both technically and interpersonally competent. Supervisors and employees are trained in effective team skills, which they use in day-to-day problem solving.

We next develop some concepts that pertain to both the formal and informal organizations, although the discussion concentrates upon the informal organization. (Remember that the formal organization is developed quite well in the form of job descriptions and organizational charts.)

Group Goals

group

A **group** exists when two or more people join together to accomplish a desired goal. Workers in sections, departments, and divisions have formal goals directed toward accomplishment of the mission of the organization.

The informal organization also has goals. Although managers often do not like to recognize their existence, it is important that we do. The goals of the informal organization can sometimes mean the difference between the success or failure of organizational goals. If the goals of the informal work group are in agreement with the organization, productivity may improve. On the other hand, if they are contrary to each other, the firm may confront barriers to success. The goals of the informal organization will affect the type of members the group will attract, the type of work that is accomplished within the group, and the standards (norms) that are acceptable to the group members.

Norms

norms

The formal organization has its performance standards, and the informal organization has its **norms**, a standard of behavior that is expected from group members. Those who violate the group norms are helped to see the errors of their ways. Informal pressures to conform to group norms are often more powerful than the official sanctions used by managers to enforce

• CAREER PROFILE •

WILLIAM H. SEAY
Chairman of the Board
Southwestern Life Insurance Company

Upon graduation from high school, William H. Seay went to work in the bookkeeping department of the Westinghouse Corporation in Dallas, Texas. It did not take Mr. Seay long to realize that he needed further education. In 1937 he enrolled at the University of Texas in Austin and graduated with a degree in business administration. Then came World War II. He spent four years in the army infantry, attained the rank of captain, and returned to Dallas when hostilities ended. In 1948 he became a partner in an investment banking firm. From this financial background, he joined Universal Life and Accident Insurance Company of Dallas as vice-president in 1957. His leadership abilities were quickly recognized, and in 1960 he was named executive vice-president. A year later he became president.

Universal was acquired by Southwestern Life Insurance Company in September 1968. Seay was

conformance to organizational standards. A worker who is a high producer (very acceptable to the formal organization) may be sanctioned by the informal organization until his or her production falls back in line with the informal group's norms. In the example at the beginning of the chapter, Bill Stephens was influenced to conform to the group norm of expected output. Group norms are unwritten rules that new members, if they are to remain members, gradually learn. Norms are frequently established concerning how hard one should work, whether one should be friendly, the degree to which one should cooperate with management, and whether one should be innovative.

Role

The concept of role is broader than that of its counterpart in the formal organization—the job. A **role** consists of the total pattern of expected be-

role

named executive vice-president of SwL and elected to the board of directors. A few months later, in January 1969, he was elected president and chief executive officer, becoming the seventh president to serve in the company's then sixty-nine-year history

In late 1972 shareowners authorized the formation of a new holding company, Southwestern Life Corporation. Seay was elected chairman of the board and president, also retaining his title of chairman of the board and chief executive officer of the corporation's life insurance components.

Southwestern Life prospered under Seay's pilotage. In 1974 it was selected in a survey of financial analysts from around the country as one of the five best-managed companies in the Southwest. The arrival of 1980 brought a major change in ownership. SwL became a wholly owned Tenneco, Inc., company in one of the largest stock acquisitions in life insurance annals. Seay's leadership and direction were retained, providing a smooth transition for the company into a new era of strength and opportunity. At the end of 1981, SwL had assets of nearly $2 billion and insurance in force of more than $9 billion, ranking in the top 2 percent of the 2,000 life insurance companies in the nation.

Seay strives to provide direction and motivation for his staff. Mr. Seay said, "Those are the elements essential to top performance. I take pride in the excellent talents of the people around me and of the many who have achieved personal success and happiness with me." Seay also said, "A chief executive doesn't need technical expertise in every specific area himself but must have a working knowledge of all aspects of his business, calling on and depending on his staff for the expertise." The main point Seay stresses when talking about a company's success is loyalty of its people. "Loyalty to an organization," Seay said, "is a cooperative sort of thing, which invariably spells out better results."

For a young person pursuing a career in management, Seay stated, "Set goals, both long and short term." Also, just as education is essential to a successful business career, Seay views an unqualified sense of loyalty, integrity, and honesty as equally essential.

havior. In the formal organization it includes, but goes beyond, the official content of the job description. If a person is officially designated a supervisor, pressure may be exerted to dress, talk, and act similar to other managers in the organization. If managers in a particular firm typically dress formally, the manager who fails to wear the proper "uniform" is not fulfilling the expected role.

Individuals who are members of an informal group also are presented with an expected role to act out. Whether the informal group is supportive of management has a major impact on the roles of the group members. If the group decides they should not support a decision made by top management, the pattern of their behavior (role) may reflect indifference or slowing down on the job. Failure to conform to the expected role may result in a member's being cast out of the informal group.

A person may have many roles that he or she must constantly play. For instance, when working toward a doctorate, one of the authors was a student, a teacher, a consultant, and a military officer in the reserves. For each of these activities, there was a different role, and failure to change roles immediately at the proper time often resulted in difficulties. Being a military officer on the weekend with considerable authority, followed on Monday morning by playing the humble role of a doctoral student, was sometimes not easy. Students who go back to school part-time while working as a supervisor in a firm often encounter the same difficulties.

Leadership

In the formal organization, leaders (managers) are placed in their position of authority by top management. By filling a particular supervisory position, the individual is designated the leader. An entirely different procedure is at work in selecting a leader for the informal organization. The informal group leader *emerges* from the group. There is no formal election; the process of identifying a leader merely occurs. Typically, the person who adheres closest to the norms of the group is the leader. There is no formal title attached to this individual. This person is the one who is looked to for guidance in achieving the group's goal. Should the leader begin to deviate from group norms, another leader who is closer to the group norm will emerge to take his or her place.

Structure

Although not capable of being placed into a formal organizational chart, the informal organization has its own structure. As with the formal structure, informal groups may also have different levels in the chain of command. It may even be charted by management, but the members themselves have not drawn up a formal structure. Gerritt Starke, director of corporate personnel for Kemper Insurance Company, states, "We should recognize that 'informal work groups' exist at all levels of the organization. A formal organization chart can be very misleading in terms of who has 'real' authority and influence."

The dynamic nature of the informal structure constantly changes. As different members enter into and exit from the group, the structure is modified. The structure is heavily based on the communication patterns that develop among group members. If many people attempt to gain the advice of one individual, this individual is often the informal leader, and the structure develops around this individual. Just as formal organizations have vice-presidents, the informal group may have an equivalent counterpart. The structure evolves rather than being formally laid out, but often it is more effective than the formal organizational structure.

contact chart

One means by which the organizational structure of the informal work group may be studied is through the use of a **contact chart**. These charts are developed to identify the connections that an individual has with other members of the organization. As may be seen from the contact chart in Figure 8-3, all contacts do not follow the formal organizational chart. In various

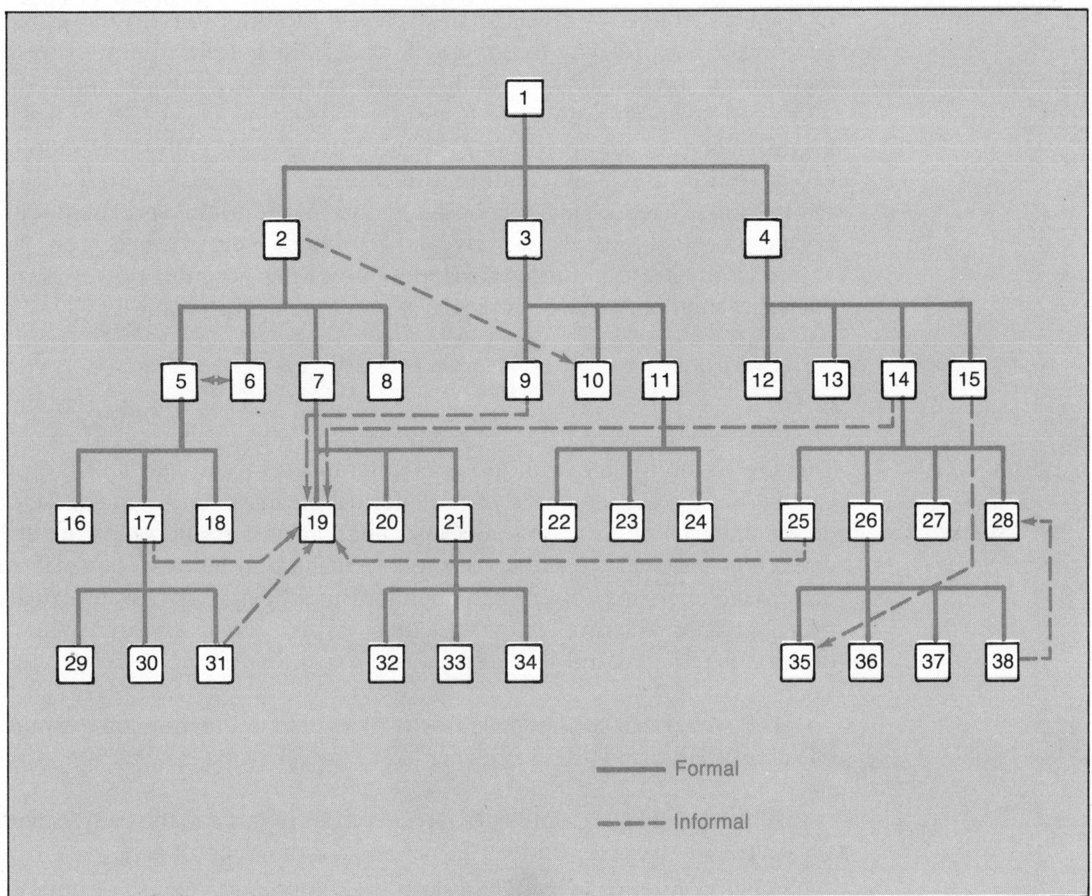

FIGURE 8-3 *A Contact Chart*

instances, certain levels of management are bypassed; others show cross-contact from one chain of command to another. Based on the number of workers contacting the employee, individual 19 appears to be very popular. The difficulty with a contact chart is that it does not show the reasons for these relationships. Also it is possible that these contacts could work either for or against the organization. Individual 19 could be assisting other employees accomplish their tasks. On the other hand, this individual could be *talking down* the organization and promoting disharmony among company employees. In any event, once managers have identified the major contact points, they are in a position either to encourage or discourage the individual within the work group.

Cohesiveness

cohesiveness

The degree of attraction that the group has for each of its members is referred to as **cohesiveness**. It has importance to both the formal and informal organization. It is identified by such attitudes as loyalty to the group, a feeling of responsibility for group effort, defending against outside attack, friendliness, and congeniality. Cohesive informal work groups are powerful instruments that can work for or against the formal organization. For instance, a highly cohesive group whose goals are in agreement with organizational objectives can use this strength to assist the firm in increasing productivity. On the other hand, a highly cohesive group that is not in agreement with organizational objectives can have an extremely negative effect on the accomplishment of the firm's goals. Because of this potential power, some managers attempt to reduce cohesion in order to maintain control.

Size

The size of the formal work group is determined by the needs of the organization; however, the size of the informal organization is a major factor determining its effectiveness. Because interpersonal relationships are the essence of informal organizations, the informal group tends to be small so that its members may interact frequently. But when groups get too small, difficulties arise. The dyad, or two-person group, is a perfect example. When a decision is required and there isn't a consensus, one group member must lose.

There has been considerable research devoted to determining the most effective group size. This research has led to the following conclusions:

- When quality of a complex group decision is important, the use of seven to twelve members under a formal leader is most appropriate.
- When consensus in a conflict situation is important, the use of three to five members with no formal leader will ensure that each member's view will be discussed.
- When both quality and consensus are important, five to seven members seems most appropriate.[1]

There tends to be greater group conflict in even-sized groups, and there is more conflict in groups of two and four members than there is in those of six members. In seating arrangements, members who sit across from each other tend to engage in more frequent and often argumentative communication. If consensus is the goal, members with high conflict potential should be seated alongside each other.

Thus, when dealing with the subject of effective informal organization, we are primarily concerned with small groups. Obviously, many organizations consist of thousands of members. The initial approach to organization must therefore be formal in nature, resulting in the design of official units, jobs, and formal relationships of authority, responsibility, and accountability. Within this formal organization, a limitless number of small, informal work groups will be spontaneously established and, hopefully, will be aligned with overall organizational objectives.

Synergism

synergism

Synergism creates the possibility that when two or more people work together, they can do more than what would have been possible by working separately. It also implies the possibility of accomplishing tasks that could not have been done by two people working alone.[2] The concept of synergism has implications for both the formal and informal organization. Managers need to recognize that greater effort may be achieved when two workers are placed together. However, through the synergistic effect, the informal organization achieves a much more powerful meaning. People in groups have much more influence than each individual has alone.

BENEFITS AND COSTS OF THE INFORMAL ORGANIZATION

Management often has mixed emotions about the informal work group. On the one hand, the work group is capable of contributing to greater organizational effectiveness. On the other, the informal organization is not without its drawbacks; there are certain costs involved. However, if management is properly trained to understand and work with the informal groups, the benefits should exceed the costs. As may be seen in Figure 8-4, the benefits outweigh the costs. However, as with the seesaw, if management is not careful, the losses may exceed the benefits. Both the benefits and costs resulting from the informal work groups will be discussed next.

Benefits of the Informal Organization

It is fortunate that management cannot destroy the informal organization because it is capable of providing significant benefits to an organization's effectiveness. These potential values of the informal work group are discussed below.

Assists in Accomplishing Work

For a manager to be effective, his or her subordinates must be permitted a certain degree of flexibility in accomplishing the assigned tasks. Advance approval of every move is detrimental to achieving success. If people in an organization acted only when they were told to act, followed standard instructions to the letter at all times, and contacted others only when duly authorized, a business would have to cease operations. However, the traditionalist tends to rely more heavily on formal decisions based on a scientific study of business problems.

There are also occasions when the formal command is wrong or inadequate for the situation. If the atmosphere is heavily traditional, subordi-

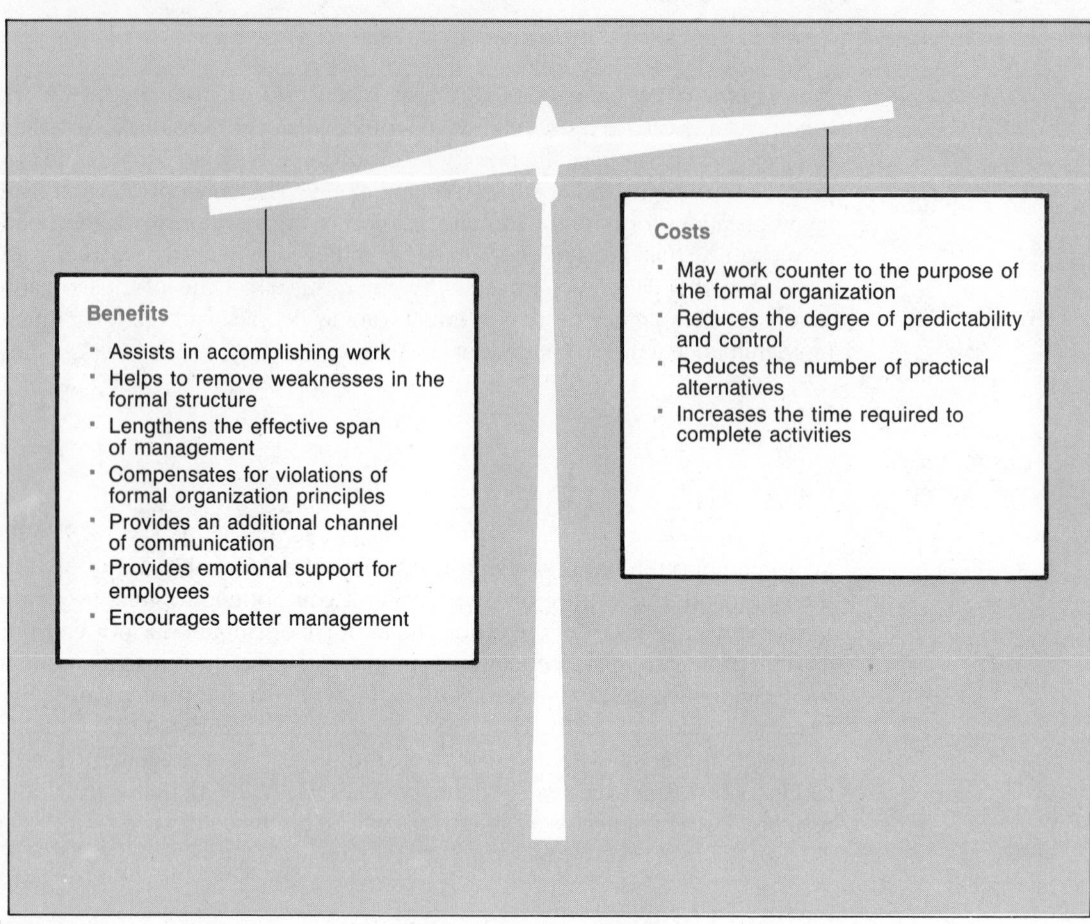

Benefits
Assists in accomplishing work
Helps to remove weaknesses in the formal structure
Lengthens the effective span of management
Compensates for violations of formal organization principles
Provides an additional channel of communication
Provides emotional support for employees
Encourages better management
Costs
May work counter to the purpose of the formal organization
Reduces the degree of predictability and control
Reduces the number of practical alternatives
Increases the time required to complete activities

FIGURE 8-4 *Benefits and Costs of the Informal Work Group*

nates may exhibit *malicious obedience* by executing a command faithfully despite personal knowledge that their action will ultimately result in failure. Many managers have discovered that a subordinate can "Yes, sir" them all day, follow every directive to the letter, and yet will fail miserably. If more faith is placed in informal relationships, subordinates may voluntarily adapt the formal order to the requirements of the actual situation. When loosely structured, groups are often able to achieve organizational objectives more effectively in an informal manner.

Helps to Remove Weaknesses in the Formal Structure

The formal organization often has a number of gaps that the informal group can fill. For example, let's consider a person who is promoted to a position that exceeds his or her current capabilities. This is not an unusual occurrence in the armed services, for instance, where a young officer is appointed unit commander. Without the advice and assistance of an experienced sergeant, young officers might not survive their first assignment. In fact, most likely there are many officers who have been unsuccessful in the military because they have failed to recognize the power of the informal organization. The formal orders and regulations say that he or she is the commander, with certain responsibilities and authorities. By admitting one's temporary weaknesses, help may be obtained from other officers and enlisted personnel. In effect, deficiencies in the formal structure have been removed by sharing decision making with others. In time, the informal group may resemble the formal organization more closely.

Lengthens the Effective Span of Management

As we indicated in Chapter 7 the number of people a manager can effectively supervise is referred to as the span of management. As individuals and small groups learn to interact more effectively and are permitted to do so by their supervisors, the manager should be able to devote less time to each individual worker. This could well contribute to a broadening of a manager's effective span of management.

Compensates for Violations of Formal Organization Principles

The development of informal relationships also influences the effectiveness of certain traditional principles of formal organizations. For example, it has been pointed out that even though authority should equal responsibility, the principle is often violated. As a result, the employee tries to develop informal contacts with personnel over whom he or she has no formal authority. Favors are traded and friendships formed. One quickly learns that the formal prescription of authority often is not a sufficient base for operation. Yet this still does not negate the desirability of having responsibility equal authority.

Provides an Additional Channel of Communication

grapevine

The informal means by which information is transmitted in an organization is referred to as the **grapevine.** To some traditional managers, the grapevine constitutes an obstacle to be destroyed. They seek to channel and control most, if not all, communications through the official chain of command. However, the grapevine can add to organizational effectiveness if the manager will use it. The grapevine is fast and usually accurate in the information it transmits.

The use of the grapevine does not decrease the importance of the official channel of communication and command. Although it can spread much information in a short period, it cannot provide the authority that is necessary for much of the action that will take place.

Insights to Success

Seek involvement in areas outside your specialty field in order to obtain breadth of experience. Try to secure a more responsible and challenging assignment every two to four years.

G. ROBERT BAER, Group Vice-President, Ball Corporation

Provides Emotional Support for Employees

Alice Garcia, the production supervisor for United Wholesaling Company, has just found out how important emotional support can be in keeping workers employed. In fact, over one-half of all voluntary resignations in many organizations occur within the first six months of employment. This is often due to poor induction procedures, when little help is provided the new employee in joining and being accepted within the group. Friendships, or at least speaking acquaintances, are highly essential to a satisfactory working environment for most people. In one hospital where the termination rate among janitorial personnel was high, the formation of cleanup teams reduced turnover considerably. Such personnel felt isolated and uncomfortable when working alone among physicians, nurses, and patients.

Encourages Better Management

Awareness of the nature and impact of the informal organization often leads to better management decisions. The acceptance of the fact that formal relationships will not enable full accomplishment of organizational tasks stimulates management to seek other means of motivation. If most of the work is done informally, the manager will seek to improve his or her knowledge of the nature of the people in general and his or her subordinates in particular. Managers should realize that organizational performance can be affected by the workers who grant or withhold cooperation and enthusiasm. Means other than formal authority must be sought to develop attitudes that support effective performance.

Costs of the Informal Organization

The informal organization is not without its drawbacks. Here are some possible costs of informal work groups.

May Work Counter to the Purposes of the Formal Organization

It is apparent to most managers that individuals and groups can and sometimes do work contrary to the formal goals of an enterprise. If the goals of the informal group could always be the same as those of the organization, few would object to the encouragement of its formation. However, there are results such as work restriction, pressuring other workers to exhibit disinterest in company requirements, disloyalty, insubordination, and unauthorized actions that work at cross-purposes with other functions in the organization.

Reduces the Degree of Predictability and Control

Jim Brown, mentioned at the start of the chapter, is frustrated because his degree of predictability has been removed. One of his supervisors, Bob Evans, has much more influence in the firm than he should have based on his formal position. A basic purpose of an organization is to ensure predictability and control of individual behavior so that the individual will work effectively toward organizational goals. This depends, however, on people interpreting and executing the formal guidelines. If we recognize and accept the possibility of a good outcome from permitted flexibility, we also must accept the risks that accompany this lesser degree of control. The human element can and does add much to an organization's effectiveness; it also can and does add much to the degree of uncertainty.

Reduces the Number of Practical Alternatives

The American Soldier, a four-volume study of the United States Army during World War II, concluded that the natural unit of personal commitment was the informal group, not the total formal organization.[3] The soldiers reported that one of the major reasons for moving forward in combat was to avoid letting the other fellow down. The solidarity developed in the informal group greatly strengthened the motivation of individual members.

The significance of this finding creates problems in the interchangeability of personnel. If natural groups are broken up by moving individual members in and out of them, the degree of motivation and cooperation is reduced. This may well mean that management should think in terms of moving groups around, rather than individuals. If management wishes to capitalize on the considerable values issuing from the development of primary work groups, it must lose some flexibility in decision making.

Increases the Time Required to Complete Activities

If the cooperative efforts of the informal work groups can be aligned with the objectives of the firm, management has the best of both worlds. The collective power generated can be quite phenomenal. Informal work group activities such as gossiping, betting pools, long coffee breaks, and general horseplay are time consuming and may be detrimental to efficient operations. These are acts that will tax the patience of the rigid, rational manager. Yet if an effective work group is to be established, some of these activities will have to be permitted and should even be encouraged. The manager must realize that, despite concern for goal accomplishment, he or she must allow the group time and opportunity to maintain itself in good working order. People can usually sustain action for a longer period of time under an informal atmosphere than they can when the situation is highly rigid, controlled, and formal.

STATUS, POWER, AND POLITICS

Status, power, and politics are involved in both the formal and informal organization. However, the informal relationships associated with status, power, and politics go well beyond the formal prescription in an organization. The following discussion of these concepts concentrates on the manner in which status, power, and politics primarily affect factors associated with the informal work group.

Status

status

A person's rank or position in a group is called **status.** It is an important relationship that has considerable effect on the morale and efficiency of any organization. Status is an inevitable component of human relationships in all aspects of life, business and nonbusiness. In this section, we examine the sources of status in business organizations, the symbols that denote status levels, and the functions of a status system.

Status Sources

The sources of status, or social rank, can be of both an informal and a formal nature. Examples of these sources are as follows:

Formal Organizational Sources	*Personal Sources*
Occupation or job	Education
Organizational level	Age
	Seniority
	Race
	Religion
	Parentage
	Sex
	Competence
	Associates

It is apparent that certain occupations are accorded more prestige than others. For example, white-collar jobs are usually more highly esteemed than blue-collar jobs. Within particular companies, management has discovered, often with great surprise, the following status differentials: long-distance telephone operators had higher social rank than operators handling local calls; cooks who worked on white meat had higher status than those who worked on dark; and cafeteria personnel who handled fish dishes had less prestige than those who served beef. As can be seen, the status of one's occupation depends on the rank accorded it by one's peers, and not by management alone. The job assigned to a person and the level of organization in which it is placed are significant sources of status; in general, the higher the organizational level, the higher the level of prestige.

Finally, there is status that comes from one's associates. This is social rank that comes from friendship, kinship, or social organizations. Membership in a certain fraternity or club and graduation from certain schools are examples of status being assigned to a person on the basis of the status accorded the larger group. Membership in these groups is often based on possession of some of the other personal sources of status.

Status Symbols

status symbol

A visible, external sign of one's social position is referred to as a **status symbol.** A stranger can enter an organization and, if aware of status hierarchies, is able to obtain a social fix quickly by reading the various symbols. However, one must recognize that status symbols often vary from firm to firm. For example, one would usually expect that higher-status positions are accompanied by more elaborate office furnishings. In one organization, however, the high-status positions were given antique roll-top desks, whereas the lower jobs were equipped with new, shiny, modern furniture. Symbols sometimes change with the times. Some typical status symbols in business are the following:

- Job titles
- Pay
- Bonus/stock plans
- Size and location of desk or office
- Location of parking space or reserved parking
- Type of company car assigned
- Secretaries
- Privacy
- Use of executive clubs
- Cocktail party invitations
- Furnishings, including rugs, pictures, tables, and similar items
- Privileges, including freedom to move about, not punching the time clock, and freedom to set own working hours and to regulate coffee break
- Ceremonies of induction
- Number of windows in office

Within the company, however, many of the symbols are within the control of management and constitute the basis for many conflicts. Executives have gotten down on their hands and knees to measure and compare

TABLE 8-1. *Status Symbols*

Visible Appurtenances	Top Dogs	V.I.P.'s	Brass	No. 2s	Eager Beavers	Hoi Polloi
Brief cases	None—they ask the questions	Use backs of envelopes	Someone goes along to carry theirs	Carry their own—empty	Daily—carry their own—filled with work	Too poor to own one
Desks, office	Custom made (to order)	Executive style (to order)	Type A, "Director"	Type B, "Manager"	Castoffs from No, 2s	Yellow Oak—or castoff from Eager Beavers
Tables, office	Coffee tables	End tables or decorative wall tables	Matching tables, type A	Matching tables, type B	Plain work table	None—lucky to have own desk
Carpeting	Nylon—1-inch pile	Nylon—1-inch pile	Wool-twist (with pad)	Wool-twist (without pad)	Used wool pieces—sewed	Asphalt tile
Plant stands	Several—kept filled with strange exotic plants		Two—repotted whenever they take a trip	One medium-sized—repotted annually during vacation	Small—repotted when plant dies	May have one in the department or bring their own from home
Vacuum water bottles	Silver	Silver	Chromium	Plain painted	Coke machine	Water fountains
Library	Private collection	Autographed or complimentary books and reports	Selected references	Impressive titles on covers	Books everywhere	Dictionary
Shoe shine service	Every morning at 10:00	Every morning at 10:15	Every day at 9:00 or 11:00	Every other day	Once a week	Shine their own
Parking space	Private—in front of office	In plant garage	In company garage—if enough seniority	In company properties—somewhere	On the parking lot	Anwhere they can find a space—if they can afford a car

Reprinted by permission of the publisher, from Morris S. Viteles, "What Raises a Man's Morale," *Personnel* (January 1954), p. 305.

the sizes of offices. Windows are counted, steps from the president's office are paced off, secretaries who can take fast dictation are sought (even though the supervisor may never give dictation), parking space is fought for, and company cars are wangled. A humorous, fictional example of status symbols by organizational level is presented in Table 8-1. Some reflection on this table leads one to believe that there is more truth than fiction here.

Some managements have sought to abolish the whole problem of awarding status symbols by attempting to equalize all privileges, offices, and furnishings. For instance, NCR has eliminated the executive dining rooms and uses open-landscaped offices. In some universities the department head position is rotated among the department members, thereby reducing the status attached to the position. Windowless buildings have been constructed, office sizes are completely standardized, and only one type of company car is available. However, as long as there are differences in status, some type of symbol will be worked out by the group.

Status Functions

Status produces several desirable values such as the following:

- **Assisting in meeting the needs of the individual.** Most people wish to be accorded some degree of respect by others. They want to have their abilities and accomplishments recognized, and status symbols constitute tangible evidence of this respect.
- **Facilitating the process of communication.** We receive many messages daily from people we do not know personally. The status title of the person or position helps us to evaluate the worth of the message. For example, if a medical doctor tells you something about your backache, the information will likely have more meaning than if the service station attendant diagnosed the problem.
- **Serving as a motivational device for management.** Management has discovered that employees will strive for prestige and prestige symbols as well as for money. Therefore, nonfinancial incentives can be worked into a more comprehensive incentive system. A job title change is often as satisfying as more money. A change to a job of lesser pay but more prestige is often a change a particular person will find satisfying, providing that the pay is still sufficient. Thus, status as a motivating tool has its greatest use in situations where monetary requirements have been met to a reasonable degree. If management is aware of status systems and the symbols it can control, more comprehensive and coordinated incentives can be developed.

Power

power

The ability of one person to influence the behavior of another person is referred to as **power.** Like status, power is neither completely informal nor formal in nature. The concept of power goes well beyond the capacities provided by the formal organization. Therefore, it is included in this section of the text.

Power is an emotionally laden term, particularly in cultures that emphasize individuality and equality. To label a manager as a *power seeker* is to cast doubt on that manager's motives and actions. Some of these negative views issue from older analyses that have suggested that power is evil, that it corrupts people, that it is largely comprised of naked force, and that the amount is limited in supply. Certainly, the modern business corporation constitutes a major concentration of economic power that has materially improved the standard of living of millions of people. When such concentrations lead to abuse, control rather than its elimination would appear to be the more desirable course of action. Power can be a highly effective instrument for the good of the people.

Sources of Power

The sources of power are many and varied and are not restricted to the legitimate ones provided by management. These sources are presented in the following paragraphs.

Formal Authority as a Result of Position. Significant power results from a person being placed in a formal position of authority. It results from a person occupying a certain position in the organizational structure and being granted legitimate authority.

Informal Authority. Some managers assume that power and authority are identical concepts. Undeniably, formal authority arising from one's position is a very important source of power, but it is not the only source. Power is the broader concept.

In many situations, informal authority is an important source of influence or power in the organization. This concept serves to emphasize the influence that subordinates have with their superiors. An order is received from a superior, and the subordinate can choose among several alternative actions:

- Refuse to obey, thus not delegating informal authority over himself or herself.
- Reluctantly accept the order and execute it on a minimal basis.
- Accept and execute the order with a neutral or indifferent attitude.
- Accept and execute the order with enthusiasm, intelligence, and ingenuity.

The amount of informal authority granted an individual is materially greater in the last alternative. In the Vietnam War, the power of the informal group became significant as entire units refused as a group to follow the formal orders given by officers. Thus, a manager must realize that subordinates can give or withhold their cooperation, which, in effect, means giving or withholding power.

Rewards and Punishments. Rewards and punishments as sources of power are also partly determined by the authority structure of the organization. However, the informal group can also either reward a person through acceptance and liking of a coworker or punish by rejection and the "silent treatment."

Expertise or Knowledge. Even though an individual has limited formal authority, expertise in a particular area will give that person considerable influence or power. Expertise power is often a difficult problem for management to confront. For instance, if a computer programmer becomes so familiar with a system that even his or her supervisor could not adequately supervise the person, problems can result. The supervisor may feel that he or she cannot even reprimand the programmer for fear of losing the expertise the worker possesses.

Another major problem is involved in line and staff relationships—the line has the power that issues from authority, whereas the staff has the power that issues from knowledge. The formal right to manage a firm remains, but the capacity to manage it has been diluted and spread among a number of experts. The person possessing knowledge and expertise has power regardless of the formal authority relationships within the organization.

Identification with Individuals Who Are Respected. The particular personality and characteristics of an individual will also affect the degree to which other persons wish to identify and be associated with that person. If one is liked and respected, we are more likely to be influenced by that person. If he or she is associated with persons occupying high and visible power positions, we are more inclined to pay greater attention. If a person has access to many sources of power, the concept of *exaggerated response* is often encountered. One president of a large enterprise inquired about the hiring procedures currently in effect. After a three-week delay, he received a comprehensive and detailed report covering all facets of hiring, with an emphasis on the current status of minority group members. At this point, it was discovered that a friend of his had a son who wanted a summer job, but because the young man had already found a position elsewhere, the president was no longer interested.

Power versus Formal Authority

After reviewing the various sources of power, you can see that the concept of power extends far beyond that provided by formal authority. We might view the concept of power in terms of the following simple formula:

$$\text{Power} = \text{Formal Authority} \pm \text{Informal Influence}$$

A manager's power is heavily dependent upon the informal influence that an individual can exert. The knowledge that the computer programmer is able to use greatly increases power. Also, notice that there is a plus or minus sign regarding the impact of informal influences. A person can actually lower his or her power level below the formal authority level because of the poor use of informal influence. Even though placed in a formal position, a manager may be limited in accomplishing a job because of a limited amount of power.[4]

Significance of Power to the Manager

Research has shown that a good manager must have a concern for acquiring and using power. In a number of studies, it was found that over 70 percent of managers have a higher need for power than does the general population.[5] And the better managers have a stronger need for power than a need to be liked by others. This need for power is not a desire to be dictatorial, nor is it necessarily a drive for personal enhancement. Rather, it is a concern for influencing others on behalf of the organization. It is a need for socialized power rather than for personal power. When managers feel a greater need to be liked than a need to influence others, they tend to be less effective in many organizations.

The control of situational factors, both in and out of the organization, is of significant concern to the modern manager. It has been noted that when organizations grow so large and complex that no one individual has the capacity to manage all of the interdependencies, a dominant managing group will develop. This coalition is sometimes formalized into a presidential or executive office. It will exist, however, whether or not it is actually recorded on a chart. If the president of the firm heavily depends on the vice-president of finance to develop the crucial programs, that vice-president is likely to be a member of the dominant coalition and have actual power in excess of that suggested by the official chart. Within the organization, smaller and sometimes more temporary coalitions are formed so that a task involving significant interdependencies can be executed. The formation, use, and dissolution of such coalitions are sometimes called *politics.*

Politics

In everyday conversations with the general public, the politician would most likely receive low marks of approval. Political scandals have regularly hit the front page of the daily newspaper. Even though the politician's image is low, politics and politicians are with us in all forms of organized society, and not just the politicians who are in government. Political action can and does provide positive values in promoting cooperation among individuals and groups with differing interests and objectives.

politics

Politics can be described as a "network of interaction by which power is acquired, transferred, and exercised upon others.[6] Let's think about this definition in order to gain a thorough appreciation of what it means. The politician is working with and through many people. As such, politics transcend the traditional organizational structure boundaries. In the process of these interactions the medium of exchange is power. Just as the dollar is used as the medium of exchange in our economic system, power provides virtually the same function in politics. The shrewd politician acquires power and transfers it to another person when it can *purchase* something of value. Politicians use this medium of exchange in the network that they establish to exert pressure on others in order to gain their desired end result. Just like the accountant, the politician has a balance sheet. When power is transferred, something is received in return. To the politician, a favor given now is power to be extracted in the future. Thus, we are all politicians to a certain extent; some are better at it than others.

Role of Politics in Business Organizations

If all actions could be foreseen and prescribed for with accuracy, perhaps there would be little need for politics. This would also assume that all conflicts could be resolved in some rational manner acceptable to all. Inasmuch as neither of these two circumstances is likely, the individual will be asked to adjust and accommodate to varying conditions and pressures. Perhaps *adjustments* and *accommodations* are more understandable terms for this political process. Though going exclusively by the rule book could under certain circumstances be construed as one form of politicking, accommodation usually requires additional interactions to be forthcoming. It sometimes involves a bending of the rules, an exchange of favors, and offers of reward for the cooperation. It often comes as a shock to some students of management to discover that merely doing the job as expected will not extract the expected rewards.

To make the implications of politics more concrete, let us review the following example. An engineer heading up the industrial engineering department has developed a new procedure for processing work in the production department. According to the formal rules of the game, he or she would elect to follow the first suggestion listed below. The others listed are not *formally* required and can be construed as various forms of adjustment and accommodation.

1. The engineer submits the recommendation for approval by the line executive. The supporting data are provided and persuasive arguments are presented. This failing, the engineer appeals to a common line superior, who will decide the case and issue an order accordingly.
2. The engineer attempts to get to know the line executive on a personal basis. This involves casual conversation, inquiries about respective backgrounds, and the like.
3. The engineer attempts to simulate a friendship that is not felt.
4. The engineer arranges to go to lunch with the line executive in the company dining room to promote her or his views on a casual basis.

5. The engineer invites the line executive to lunch away from the company premises at the former's own expense.
6. The engineer offers to exchange favors that are possible within the regular operating rules and policies; for example, he or she agrees to do an immediate restudy of a particular job rate that has been resulting in serious difficulties between the line executive and the union.
7. The engineer agrees to favors involving a slight bending of the procedures and policies; for example, agreeing to delay introduction of a new method and rate, even though fully developed and ready to go, at the request of the line executive.
8. The engineer agrees to a favor involving a more serious bending of the procedures and policies; for example, "discovering" that the particular job rate mentioned in item 6 is too tight, when it is not, and loosening it up for the benefit of the line executive.
9. The engineer agrees to cover for the line executive; for example, the line executive wishes to use the industrial engineering department as an excuse for failing to meet schedules because of presumed work interferences.
10. The engineer, with the assistance of understanding accountants, agrees to a transfer of industrial engineering budget funds to the line executive's department.

There are doubtless other possible actions that might be undertaken to persuade the line executive to cooperate. The available alternatives depend on the extent of power possessed by the two parties.

In instances where one has control over items or services that can be adapted to personal as well as organizational use, the power is even greater. There have been cases where personal furniture has been constructed on company time with company materials, as well as instances where personal cars have been repaired in company motor pools.

The degree of politicking is limited not only by the formal organization restrictions but also by one's personal code of ethics and conscience. The fact that at times politics may be unethical should not preclude a discussion of the subject. That such actions as the above do exist in various business organizations is undeniable. Few businesses are run completely and rigidly by the book, and such politicking cannot be condemned per se. Some accommodations are constructive, whereas others are perhaps destructive of both organized activity and individual morals.

Values of Political Action

It is apparent that some degree of politics is a fact of organized life regardless of the caliber of people involved or the degree of formalization of organization rules and regulations. No doubt some political maneuvering can make a net contribution toward organization effectiveness. Where there is head-on conflict and where interdependencies make some degree of cooperation essential, concessions worked out between the parties often involve some bending or reinterpretation of the rules. On many occasions, the various conflicting interests are all highly legitimate and rest on solid ground. Some type of informal accommodation, compromise, or exchange is essential for a degree of reconciliation that permits the basic work of the organization to continue. One is usually safe, personally, if one sticks to the rule book and the letter of the law. Unfortunately, one also becomes known as a pathological bureaucrat who is more interested in being right, according to the rules, than in accomplishing the objectives as revealed by the situation. On the other hand, organizations could evolve into complete chaos if everyone acted as a power politician above the law and the formal organization. It is clear that neither extreme is the answer.

Summary

The manager of the formal organization establishes what employees should do through organizational charts and job descriptions. However, the official structure is only a portion of the story. There emerges another structure consisting of informal relationships, created not by officially designated managers but by any and all organizational members.

A group exists when two or more people join together to accomplish a desired goal. Both the formal and informal organization have goals, although managers often do not like to recognize the existence of the informal organization. The formal organization has its performance standards, and the informal organization has its norms that are standards of behavior expected from group members. The concept of role is broader than that of its counterpart in the formal organization—the job. A role consists of the total pattern of expected behavior. An entirely different procedure is at work in selecting a leader for the informal organization. The informal group leader emerges from the group. The informal organization also has its structure. The dynamic nature of the informal structure constantly changes.

The degree of attraction that the group has for each of its members is referred to as cohesiveness. The size of the informal organization is a major factor determining its effectiveness. Because interpersonal relationships are the essence of the informal organization, the informal group tends to be small so that its members may interact frequently. Synergism creates the possibility that when two or more people work together, they can do more than what would have been possible by working separately. Although some managers attempt to reduce the influence of the informal organization, it continues to exist and brings with it both benefits and costs to the organization.

Status, power, and politics are concepts that all managers constantly observe. A person's rank or position in a group is referred to as status. Status symbols are visible signs of a person's social position and have several important values of status. It assists in meeting the needs of an individual, aids in the communication process, and serves as a motivational device for management.

Power, on the other hand, refers to the ability of one person to influence the behavior of another person. As with status, it is neither completely formal nor informal. The primary sources of power are: formal authority; informal authority; the ability to provide rewards and punishment; expertise; and identification with individuals who are respected. Power is important to managers because it permits them to benefit others on behalf of the organization.

Politics in an organization provides positive values in promoting cooperation among individuals and groups with differing interests and objectives. Politics is a means by which power can be acquired, transferred, and exerted on others. Through politics, adjustments and accommodations are made to varying conditions and pressures. Some degree of political actions will occur in any organization regardless of the caliber of people involved or the degree of formalization or organization rules and regulations.

Review Questions

1. Describe how group goals, norms, roles, leadership styles, and structure differ in both the formal and informal organization.
2. What effect does cohesiveness, size, and synergism have upon the informal organization?
3. In your own words, describe the values and losses that may be attributed to the informal work group.
4. What is the purpose of a contact chart?
5. Define: *status; power; politics.*
6. What are the three functions of status?
7. In your own words describe the various sources of power. What is the significance of the understanding of power to a manager?
8. What is the role of politics in today's business organization?

Exercises

1. Develop a contact chart for an organization of which you are a member. Interpret the results.
2. Identify three groups of which you are a member. What are the various status symbols associated with the organization?
3. Collect five articles from your daily newspaper that relate to the use of power. Describe how power was used to obtain results or why it failed to achieve results.

Case Study

The Young Accountant Becomes an Informal Leader

Upon graduation, Dave Maddala went to work as an accountant for Bradford, Inc., a manufacturer specializing in producing oil field parts. Dave brought with him an excellent record from his four years in college. Not only was Dave an excellent student, he was also extremely involved in all forms of campus activities. As both a junior and a senior, he was president of his class. People felt comfortable around Dave, and his opinions were well respected by the students and faculty.

Donald Dean, the department head, took great pride in having hired Dave. He bragged to his superiors about how he was able to attract Dave to Bradford. As expected, when Dave began with Bradford, he started with the same intensity that earned him the respect in college. Dave learned the job quickly and within a very short period of time was identifying and initiating changes that could improve operations. Dave followed the chain of command and cleared each modification with Mr. Dean. This pleased Mr. Dean, for he was able to take the credit for the changes with his superiors.

In the department there were ten other accountants who reported to Mr. Dean. However, as the employees came to recognize Dave's expertise, they began to go to him with their particular problems. Dave's personality was the type that made it easy for others to talk to him. Even though Dave was junior in age, the members regarded him as a true professional. As time went on, employees would even go to Dave with their personal problems.

A strange situation ultimately developed. Although not in the formal structure, another layer in the organization had developed. If an employee had a problem he or she would first go to Dave. If Dave could not solve it, he would go to Mr. Dean. Upward communication tended to go entirely through Dave.

Although Mr. Dean did not have the reputation of being extremely "swift," it did not take him long to see what had evolved. Although the department had gained in efficiency since Dave had joined the firm, Mr. Dean did not like the loss of power that he envisioned was occurring. He even felt that his career was in jeopardy. Dean reasoned that the only way to eliminate this "bad" situation was to ensure that Dave was either transferred or terminated.

Dean immediately began his harassment campaign. He would reprimand Dave in front of his peers. Anything that Dave recommended would be immediately disapproved. It did not take long for the other employees to recognize that if they associated with Dave they were in trouble. Various instances of harassment were noticed for those who even spoke to Dave. Ultimately, Donald's strategy worked; Dave quit. But an unanticipated situation also occurred. Six of his best accountants also resigned and the department was thrown into complete confusion.

QUESTIONS

1. Why had Dave Maddala become the informal leader?
2. To what extent was Dave a "threat" to his supervisor, Donald Dean? How important are the issues of status, power, and politics?
3. How can a strong informal group affect the operations of a department such as accounting?

Case Study

The Power of the Informal Group

Doris Prier had recently been hired as production planning manager for Surefire Airlines. Immediately after reporting to her new job, Doris recognized that there were difficulties with the time control section. This section consisted of sixteen clerks and a supervisor who reported to her.

The basic function of the time control section was to maintain records on all rotatable parts used on a fleet of eighty-five passenger aircrafts. Records reflected the date a part was installed or removed and total aircraft flying time. To maintain identification, serial numbers were recorded for each controlled part. The FAA required strict control of life-limited parts. Parts that had operated beyond their approved limit had to be removed and overhauled.

The problem that Doris noticed was that there were numerous instances of inaccurate records. The records were in violation of FAA regulations and poor record keeping resulted in excessive overhaul costs. When Doris studied the situation she observed that the employees had formed an extremely strong informal work group. The members would accept or reject new employees into the work group based on factors completely unrelated to the job. Some outsiders observed that if a new employee's bowling score was not above 175, he or she had little chance for success within the group. The group members bowled three times a week and had a great time together. Those who did not like to bowl and socialize frequently were ignored and made to feel uncomfortable to the point where they would quit. This resulted in an annual turnover rate of approximately 200 percent. Doris realized that this problem had to be solved immediately or major problems could result for Surefire Airlines.

QUESTIONS

1. How did the informal work group affect the operations of the production planning department?
2. What action(s) should Doris Prier take in coping with the informal group?

Notes

1. L. L. Cummings, George P. Huber, and Eugene Arendt, "Effects of Size and Spatial Arrangements in Group Decision Making," *Academy of Management Journal* 17 (September 1974): 473.
2. Arthur D. Sharplin, Northeast Louisiana University, unpublished working paper (December 1981).
3. Samuel A. Stouffer et al., *The American Soldier* (Princeton: Princeton University Press, 1949), 2: 1974.
4. Derived from working papers developed by Robert M. Noe, III, East Texas State University (April 1981).
5. David C. McClelland and David H. Burnham, "Power Is the Great Motivator," *Harvard Business Review* 54 (March-April 1976): 102.
6. John M. Pfiffner and Frank P. Sherwood, *Administrative Organization* (Englewood Cliffs, N.J.: Prentice-Hall, 1960), p. 311.

References

Allen, R. W., et al. "Organizational Politics: Tactics and Characteristics of Its Actors." *California Management Review* 22 (Fall 1979): 77–83.

Briscoe, Dennis R. "Organizational Design: Dealing with the Human Constraint." *California Management Review* 23 (Fall 1980): 71–80.

Franklin, J. E. "Down the Organization: Influence Processes across Levels of Hierarchy." *Administrative Science Quarterly* 20 (June 1975): 153–164.

Hall, R. H., et al. "Patterns of Interorganizational Relationships." *Administrative Science Quarterly* 22 (September 1977): 457–474.

Herker, C., and Aldrich, H. "Boundary Spanning Roles and Organization Structure." *Academy of Management Review* 2 (April 1977): 217–230.

Hodge, John "Getting Along with the Informal Leader." *Supervisory Management* 25 (October 1980): 41–43.

Lincoln, J. R., and Miller, J. "Work and Friendship Ties in Organizations: A Comparative Analysis of Relational Networks." *Administrative Science Quarterly* 24 (June 1979): 181–199.

Lucas, H. C., Jr. "MIS Affects Balance of Power." *Management Accounting* 61 (October 1979): 61–68.

McKenna, R. F. "Blending the Formal with the Informal System." *Journal of System Management* 26 (June 1975): 38–41.

March, James G., and Feldman, Martha S. "Information in Organizations as Signal and Symbol." *Administrative Science Quarterly* 26 (June 1981): 171–186.

Mayes, B. T., and Allen, R. W. "Toward a Definition of Organizational Politics." *Academy of Management Review* 2 (October 1977): 672–678.

Miles, R. H., and Perreault, W. D., Jr. "Organizational Role Conflict: Its Antecedents and Consequences." *Organizational Behavior and Human Performances* 17 (October 1976): 19–44.

Miller, J. "Isolation in Organizations: Alienation from Authority, Control, and Expressive Relations." *Administrative Science Quarterly* 20 (June 1975): 260–271.

Moschis, G. P. "Social Comparison and Informal Group Influence." *Journal of Marketing Research* 13 (August 1976): 237–244.

Quick, J. C. "Dyadic Goal Setting and Role Stress: A Field Study." *Academy of Management Journal* 22 (June 1979): 241–252.

Quinn, R. E. "Coping with Cupid: The Formation, Impact, and Management of Romantic Relationships in Organizations." *Administrative Science Quarterly* 22 (March 1980): 57–71.

Roos, L. L., Jr., and Hall, R. I. "Influence Diagrams and Organizational Power." *Administrative Science Quarterly* 25 (March 1980): 57–71.

Schmidt, S. M., and Kochal, T. A. "Interorganizational Relationships: Patterns and Motivations." *Administrative Science Quarterly* 22 (June 1977): 230–234.

Schriensheim, C. A. "Similarity of Individually Directed and Group Directed Leader Behavior Description." *Academy of Management Journal* 22 (June 1979): 345–355.

KEY TERMS

personnel planning
recruitment
selection
training and development
organizational development
performance appraisal
compensation
health
safety
staffing process
job analysis
job description
job specification
work load analysis
work force analysis
employment requisition
screening interview
employment application
testing
validity
reliability
interview
patterned interview
stress interview
orientation
assessment center

LEARNING OBJECTIVES

After completing this chapter you should be able to

1. Identify and briefly describe the basic human-resources-related functions that must be accomplished if the firm's employment needs are to be accomplished.
2. State the predominant laws that affect the staffing process.
3. Describe what is involved in human resources planning and recruitment.
4. Explain each phase of the selection process.
5. State some special considerations involved in selecting managerial personnel and identify some techniques for identifying managerial talent.

9

Staffing the Organization

Lynn Johnston, the personnel manager for National Insurance Company, was faced with a difficult problem of trying to recruit programmers and systems analysts. The data processing center employed a total of forty-five people, including ten programmers and four systems analysts. During the past six months, seven programmers and three systems analysts have quit for better positions. The people who have departed National were experienced and competent in their positions. A major reason given for leaving the company was a better salary and greater advancement opportunity. Because of the shortage of experienced programmers and analysts, the replacements hired by the company possess little prior experience. This situation has caused the data processing center to run behind schedule continuously.

Harry Miller, vice-president of finance at Sure Oil Corporation, had to make a difficult decision about who would be the new accounting manager. Harry was faced with a dilemma—should he promote Dale Barks to the position or should he hire someone from outside the firm? Dale, twenty-nine, joined Sure six years ago after completing a B.B.A. in accounting. His initial position was as a junior accountant, and he was promoted to a supervisory position two years ago. He's a competent accountant and has performed well as a supervisor. However, Harry is concerned that Dale may not be experienced or mature enough to handle such a responsible position as accounting manager. Harry thinks to himself, "The accounting manager has seven supervisors reporting to him, and after all, there is a lot of difference in supervising accountants and clerical personnel as opposed to a group of managers." Harry also believes that Sure may need some "new blood" in their managerial ranks so he is considering hiring a person from the outside the firm to fill the position.

In the above situations, Lynn and Harry are each concerned with various phases of the staffing function. The situations illustrate some of the types of challenges that confront managers responsible for making staffing decisions.

The success of a firm depends, to a great extent, on its effectiveness in selecting quality personnel. It does little good to have high market potential for a product or service if capable personnel are not present to direct the effort to achieve the market potential. The need for sound selection and development practices is crucial for all types of organizations—banks, retail stores, manufacturing plants, hospitals, universities, or professional football teams.

MANAGEMENT OF HUMAN RESOURCES

Managers must work with the firm's human resources if organizational goals are to be accomplished. The firm must attract, select, train, motivate, and retain qualified people. Employees must also be permitted to satisfy personal needs. There are six basic human-resources-related functions that must be accomplished if the firm's employment needs are to be accomplished. These are staffing, training and development, compensation, health and safety, employee and labor relations, and personnel research.[1]

Staffing: Personnel Planning, Recruitment, and Selection

personnel planning
recruitment
selection

An organization should determine in advance how many workers and what kinds of skills are needed to accomplish the firm's objectives. This analysis of future personnel requirements is referred to as **personnel planning**. **Recruitment** involves encouraging individuals with the needed skills to make application for employment with the firm. **Selection** is the process of identifying those recruited individuals who will best be able to assist the firm in achieving organizational goals. These three tasks must be carefully coordinated if the firm is to satisfy its work-force requirements.

Training and Development

training and development
organizational development

Training and development (T&D) programs are designed to assist individuals, groups, and the entire organization to become more effective. Training is needed because people, jobs, and organizations are always changing. T&D should begin at the time individuals join the firm and continue throughout their careers. Large-scale T&D programs are referred to as **organizational development** (OD). The purpose of OD is to alter the environment within the firm to assist people in performing more productively.[2]

Insights to Success

I do not believe there is, nor do I believe there should be, a clearly delineated track for promotion. When there is, it seems that the person who gets himself on that track and heads upward gets the feeling he has it made. This is followed by a noticeable reduction in productivity and personal growth.

M. W. TAYLOR, Vice-President—Maintenance, Continental Airlines

---

performance appraisal

A management technique that is closely associated with T&D is performance appraisal. Through **performance appraisal,** employees are evaluated to determine how well they are performing their assigned tasks. Any deficiencies identified can often be overcome through effective training and development programs.

• CAREER PROFILE •

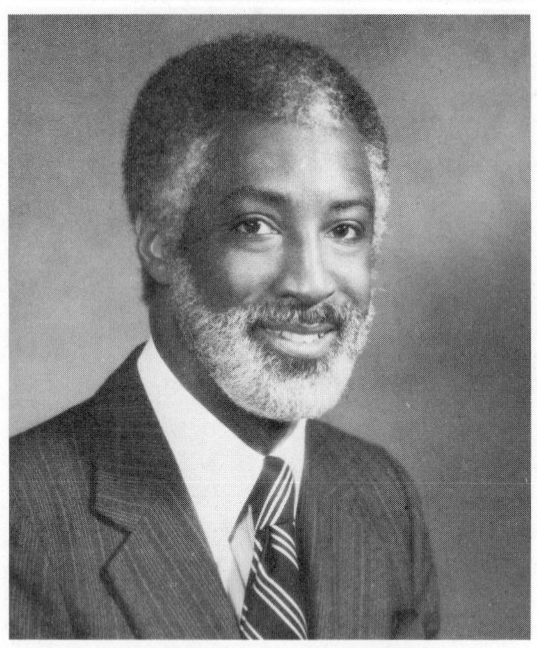

J. ALVIN WAKEFIELD
Vice-President and Partner, Korn/Ferry International

In 1981, J. Alvin Wakefield joined Korn/Ferry International, the world's largest executive recruiting and consulting firm, as a vice-president and partner. At that time he had already achieved considerable success with four major corporations. Just previously, Mr. Wakefield was employed at Avon Products, Inc., where he progressed from manager—employee relations in 1973 to vice-president—personnel—Worldwide in 1977.

"Leaving corporate life was a difficult decision," Mr. Wakefield said, "but I had lost a bit of the corporate inspiration and challenge and wanted to do something that was less staff-oriented and more line-oriented. Joining Korn/Ferry offered me a chance to utilize some of the skills that I had built up in sixteen years of corporate life. It provided me with a new sense of professional direction. There was a possibility of more freedom, both physically and intellectually, and a different kind of compensation more directly tied to my achievements."

Wakefield believes that the management of people is one of the most exciting career endeavors that a person can choose in today's rapidly changing business environment. When asked what

Compensation

The question of what constitutes a fair day's pay has been a major concern of decades. Employees must be provided with adequate and equitable rewards for their contributions to organizational goals. **Compensation** includes all rewards individuals receive as a result of their employment. As such, it is more than monetary income. The reward may be one or a combination of the following:

compensation

- Pay: The money that a person receives for performing jobs. It is the cash that you can jingle in your pockets.
- Benefits: Additional financial rewards other than base pay such as paid holidays, medical insurance, and retirement programs.

words of advice he would give to those who desire to progress into management he said, "Your technical qualifications should be taken as a given. However, the most important ingredient for success as a manager is the ability to work with and through people. No true manager works in a void. As you progress upward in management, your need for people skills and the ability to motivate and counsel people has greater importance. Every day now I see people who are technically well qualified but who have poor human relations skills. The ability to work effectively with your peers, subordinates, and superiors is vitally important."

When asked if there have been critical decisions he has had to make, Mr. Wakefield replied, "When I was with Avon, I was offered the opportunity to remain in personnel or to broaden my experience in a line assignment responsibility. I accepted the line assignment. This gave me an additional experience which was extremely broadening and exciting. Although I enjoyed personnel, I do not believe I would have become an officer at Avon or a partner with Korn/Ferry if I didn't have that other experience in my background. Also it seems that I have been very fortunate, in moving through Mobil, Celanese, Singer, and Avon, for all my moves into the right positions have occurred at exactly the right time."

Mr. Wakefield attended C. A. Johnson High School in Columbia, South Carolina. He received a B.A. in English Literature in 1960 from New York University and completed coursework for his M.B.A. at Pace University Graduate School. Mr. Wakefield is a former chairperson of the Council of Concerned Black Executives and present Board member. In addition he is a member of The Advisory Committee of The National Urban League's Black Executive Exchange Program and Board of Directors of the New York Urban League and the Yorkville Emergency Alliance. He is a member of the National Association of Professional and Corporate Recruiters, 100 Black Men, and is listed among *Who's Who in Black America.*

Mr. Wakefield believes that a major portion of his job consists of making things happen through people. He says, "The key for success in any business is the proper utilization of a company's human resources." As a black who is involved in the field of personnel management, Mr. Wakefield feels that he is making a major contribution to the management of a corporation's most important asset—its people.

- Nonfinancial: Nonmonetary rewards that an employee may receive, such as enjoyment of the work performed and a pleasant working environment.

Health and Safety

health
safety

Health refers to the employees' freedom from illness and is concerned with general physical and mental well-being. **Safety** involves protecting employees from injuries due to work-related accidents. These topics are important to management because employees who enjoy good health and work in a safe environment are more likely to be efficient. For this reason, forward-thinking managers have long advanced safety and health programs.

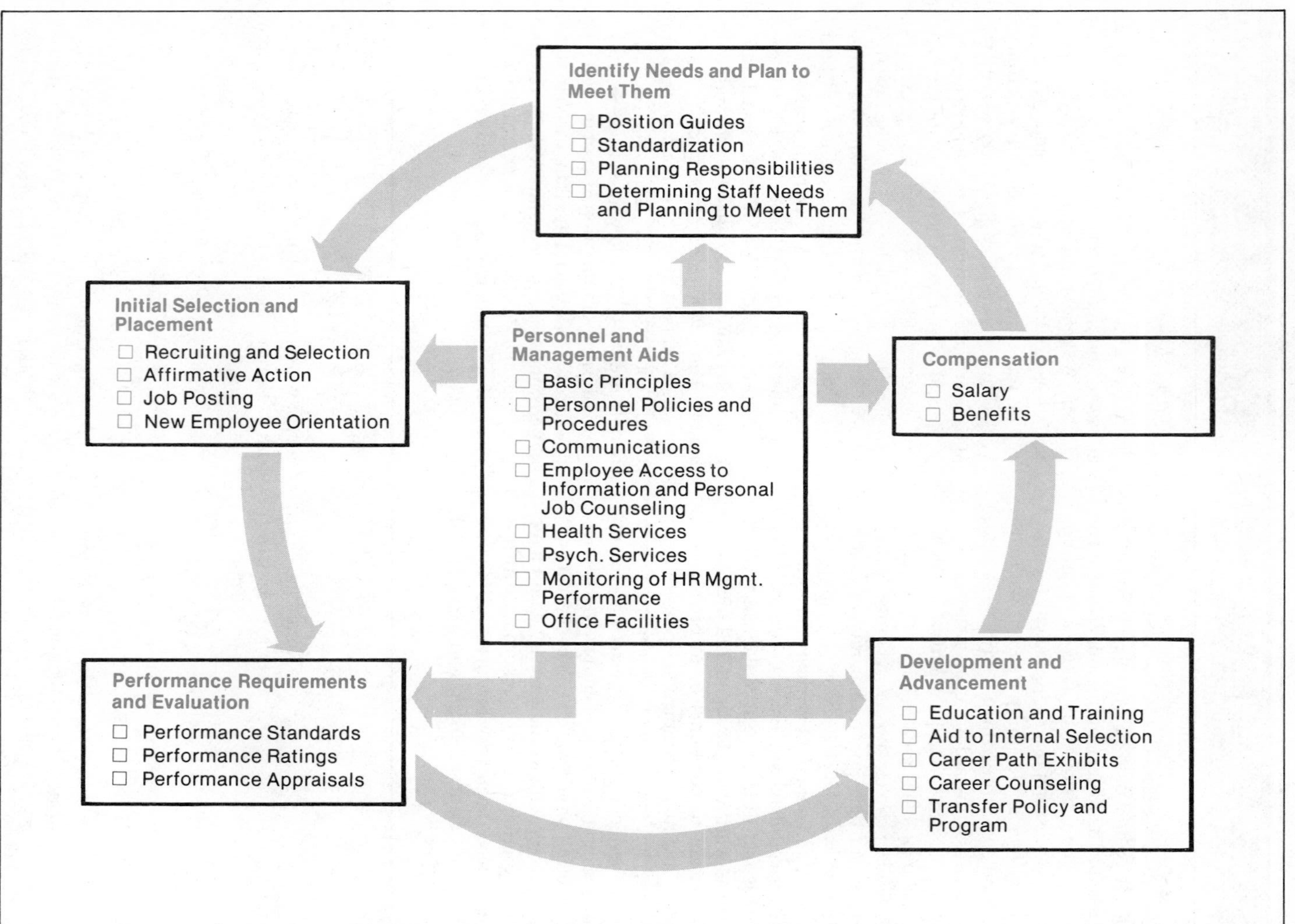

FIGURE 9-1 *Kemper Human Resource System [Used with the permission of Kemper Insurance Companies.]*

Today, because of federal legislation, all organizations have become concerned with their employees' safety and health.

Employee and Labor Relations

Over 20 million employees currently belong to labor unions and employee associations. Business firms are required by law to recognize unions and bargain with them in good faith, and this relationship has become an accepted way of life for many employers.

The vast majority of workers in the United States are not union members. In 1982, approximately 20 percent of the work force was unionized. However, nonunion organizations are often knowledgeable about the union goals and activities. These firms typically strive to satisfy the needs of their employees in every reasonable manner. They attempt to make it clear that a union is not necessary for individuals to achieve their personal goals.

Personnel Research

The personnel manager's research laboratory is the work environment. Research needs permeate every human resources management function. For instance, research may be conducted to determine the type of workers who will prove to be most successful in the firm. Or it may be directed toward determining the causes of certain work-related accidents. Personnel research is expected to be increasingly important to all forms of organizations in the future.

A HUMAN RESOURCES SYSTEM

In recent years, many organizations have developed comprehensive human resources systems such as the Kemper Insurance Company approach illustrated in Figure 9-1. At Kemper, the goal is "to have fully effective personnel at all levels of the organization to meet present and future need." Kemper's Human Resource System includes six major elements and a total of twenty-six components. All twenty-six of the components are integrated into a coordinated management system.

A detailed study of each component in the Kemper Human Resource System is beyond the purpose of this chapter. However, it is important that managers and future managers recognize the scope of a total personnel system in today's complex business organization. Prior to discussing the essential elements of staffing—personnel planning, recruitment, and selection of a firm's work force—managers should have an awareness of the major laws affecting personnel and human resources management.

LEGAL ASPECTS OF STAFFING

The predominant external factor that managers must carefully consider in performing the staffing function is the multitude of government legislation concerning human resources management. Every manager involved in selecting new employees must comply with federal, state, and local laws in staffing the organization. The impact of recent federal laws is illustrated by the following comments of W. L. McMahon, vice-president of Corning Glass:

> Recruitment of personnel in today's organization requires careful consideration of federal laws. This has greatly increased the complexity of selecting qualified personnel at all levels in the company. We must comply with several equal employment opportunity laws often without a clear understanding of how to comply. Compliance is further complicated by the fact that guidelines may have been issued from different sources. The guidelines are often presented in different formats and may provide information that is inconsistent or difficult to implement.

Some of the most important federal laws are described below. While our discussion will focus on the laws affecting staffing since 1960, some federal legislation affecting the staffing process prior to 1960 is presented in Table 9-1.

Equal Pay Act of 1963—Amended 1972

The Equal Pay Act prohibits wage discrimination on the basis of sex where the jobs require equal skills, effort, and responsibility and are performed under similar working conditions. The act is applicable only to employers who are engaged in commerce or in the production of goods for commerce. The act is enforced by the Equal Employment Opportunity Commission (EEOC).

Initially the law applied only to nonsupervisory employees covered by overtime provisions of the Fair Labor Standards Act of 1938. However, in 1972, the act was extended to include executive, administrative, professional, and outside sales force categories, as well as employees in most state and local government, hospitals, and schools. In recent years, thousands of women have received millions of dollars in back pay awards because of violations of the law.

Civil Rights Act of 1964—Amended 1972

Title VII of the Civil Rights Act of 1964 as amended by the Equal Employment Opportunity Act of 1972 has had a significant impact on personnel selection. This legislation prohibits discrimination on the basis of race, color, religion, sex, or national origin in selection, promotion, and other areas of employment. The 1972 act extended coverage to state and municipal employees and to employees in educational institutions and reduced the number of employ-

TABLE 9-1. *Selected Federal Legislation Affecting Personnel prior to 1960*

Legislation	Major Provisions
Railway Labor Act of 1926	Provided procedures for collective bargaining and for settling disputes between labor and management within the railroad industry.
Davis-Bacon Act of 1931	Required federal construction contractors to pay the prevailing wage for a particular geographical area.
Anti-Injunction Act of 1932 (Norris-La Guardia Act)	Severely restricted the use of injunctions in labor disputes and made the "yellow dog" contract legally unenforceable.
National Labor Relations Act of 1935 (Wagner Act)	Guaranteed employees the rights to self-organization and to bargain collectively with their employers, and specifically prohibited five unfair labor practices by management.
Social Security Act of 1935	Established a federal tax to be placed on payrolls and provided for unemployment and retirement benefits.
Walsh-Healey Act of 1936	Required firms doing business with the federal government to pay wages at least equivalent to the prevailing wages in the area where the firm is located. Overtime payments are required after eight hours in one day or forty hours in one week.
Fair Labor Standards Act of 1938	Established minimum wages, overtime pay, and child-labor standards.
Labor-Management Relations Act of 1947 (Taft-Hartley Act)	A major amendment to the Wagner Act. Gave employees the right to refrain from union activity. Denied supervisors protection of the law in obtaining union recognition. Enumerated six unfair labor practices by unions. Outlawed the closed shop and authorized state right-to-work laws.
Labor Management Reporting and Disclosure Act of 1959 (Landrum-Griffin Act)	A major labor reform act aimed at regulating the internal affairs of unions (including their relationships with their members) and regulating certain managerial activities. Also contained important amendments to the Taft-Hartley Act.

Source: R. Wayne Mondy and Robert M. Noe, III, *Personnel: The Management of Human Resources* (Boston: Allyn and Bacon, 1981), p. 34.

ees necessary to bring an organization under its jurisdiction from twenty-five to fifteen. The act is enforced by the EEOC, which has the power to seek compliance with the law and to investigate alleged employment discrimination. The EEOC sometimes requires employers to develop and implement affirmative action programs designed to increase the number of minority and female employees.

The federal courts have had the primary responsibility for interpreting and enforcing the act. Court decisions have significantly affected the person-

Insights to Success

Establish goals. Realize that sheer ability without dedication is a serious deficiency. Corporations don't prosper without dedicated people.

JAMES A. SILBAUGH, Vice-President, Geo. A. Hormel & Co.

nel selection policies and practices. Several court decisions have clarified and strengthened a strict interpretation of the Civil Rights Act.

In *Phillips* v. *Martin Marietta* (1971), the court ruled that the company had discriminated against a woman who was denied a job because she had young children. In a highly significant case, *Griggs et al.* v. *Duke Power Company* (1971), the U.S. Supreme Court ruled that preemployment requirements, including tests, must be job related.

Age Discrimination in Employment Act of 1967 as Amended in 1978

This law protects individuals between the ages of forty and seventy years of age from discrimination in employment—selection, retention, promotion, compensation, and other conditions of employment. The Age Discrimination Act is enforced by the EEOC.

Occupational Safety and Health Act of 1970

Few federal laws have been as controversial or received as much widespread publicity as the Occupational Safety and Health Act (OSHA) of 1970. The act, enforced by the Occupational Safety and Health Administration, was designed to assure American workers of safe and healthy working conditions by requiring employers to comply with safety and health standards. OSHA has taken such a broad view of interpreting and applying safety and health standards that virtually all organizations must comply with the act.

Vocational Rehabilitation Act of 1973

This act covers government contractors or subcontractors or organizations that receive federal grants in excess of $2,500. The Office of Federal Contract Compliance Program administers the act. If the contract or subcontract exceeds $50,000, or if the contractor has fifty or more employees, an affirmative action program must be prepared. The contractor must indicate what reasonable accommodations are being made in hiring and promoting handicapped persons.

This act is expected to have even more impact in the future. The definition of what constitutes "handicapped" has not been thoroughly tested by the courts. In some courts, epilepsy and alcoholism have been considered handicaps.

Federal Privacy Act of 1974

The Federal Privacy Act of 1974 is designed to protect the privacy of individuals by restricting access to files containing personal information. Although the act applies primarily to governmental agencies, it has gained the attention of human resources managers because of the potential for future laws with broader coverage.

Employee Retirement Income Security Act of 1974

One of the most complex laws affecting employee benefit programs is the Employee Retirement Income Security Act (ERISA) of 1974. ERISA was designed to protect the interests of participants in employee benefit plans and their beneficiaries by establishing standards of conduct, responsibility, and obligations for fiduciaries of employee benefit plans. The purpose of ERISA was to "protect employees," not to force employers to create employee benefit plans. The law establishes standards in the areas of participation, vesting of benefits, and funding for existing and new retirement and pension plans. ERISA provides for appropriate remedies, sanctions, and access to the federal courts if provisions of the law are violated.

Pregnancy Discrimination Act of 1978

The Pregnancy Discrimination Act was an amendment to the 1964 Civil Rights Act. The act prohibits discrimination in employment based on pregnancy, childbirth, or complications arising from either. Essentially the act entitles a woman who cannot continue work because of pregnancy to the same rights as her male counterpart who has, for example, a back problem that keeps him off the job. One broad effect of the act is that firms must now equalize their health insurance programs.

EEOC Guidelines—Sexual Harassment

It is anticipated that in the 1980s the most fervently pursued discrimination guidelines by the EEOC will relate to sexual harassment. Managers of profit and nonprofit organizations, in performing all human resources functions including staffing, should be particularly alert to the issue of sexual harassment. In November 1980, EEOC defined sexual harassment as "unwelcome sexual advances, request for sexual favors, and other verbal or physical conduct of a sexual nature that occur under any of the following situations:

- When submission to sexual advance is a condition of keeping or getting a job, whether expressed in explicit terms or not.
- When a supervisor or boss makes a personnel decision based on an employee's submission to or rejection of sexual advances.
- When sexual conduct unreasonably interferes with a person's work performance or creates an intimidating, hostile, or offensive environment."[3]

One of the major implications of the guidelines is that they "make the employer responsible for misbehavior by supervisory personnel, their assistants, coworkers, or outside personnel."[4]

THE STAFFING PROCESS

staffing process

The **staffing process** involves planning for future personnel requirements, recruiting individuals, and selecting from those recruited individuals employees who fulfill the needs of the firm. Figure 9-2 illustrates the basic elements of the staffing. The following discussion concentrates upon human resources planning, recruitment, and personnel selection.

Human Resources Planning

Plans provide the means whereby the objectives of the organization may be achieved. Thus, human resources planning is necessary to assure that the organization will have the right numbers and kinds of people available when and where they are needed to perform useful work. Human resources planning, when performed properly, can do the following:

- Enable management to anticipate shortages and surpluses of labor, allowing the development of plans for avoiding or correcting problems before they become serious.
- Permit forecasts of recruitment needs in terms of both the numbers and types of skills sought.

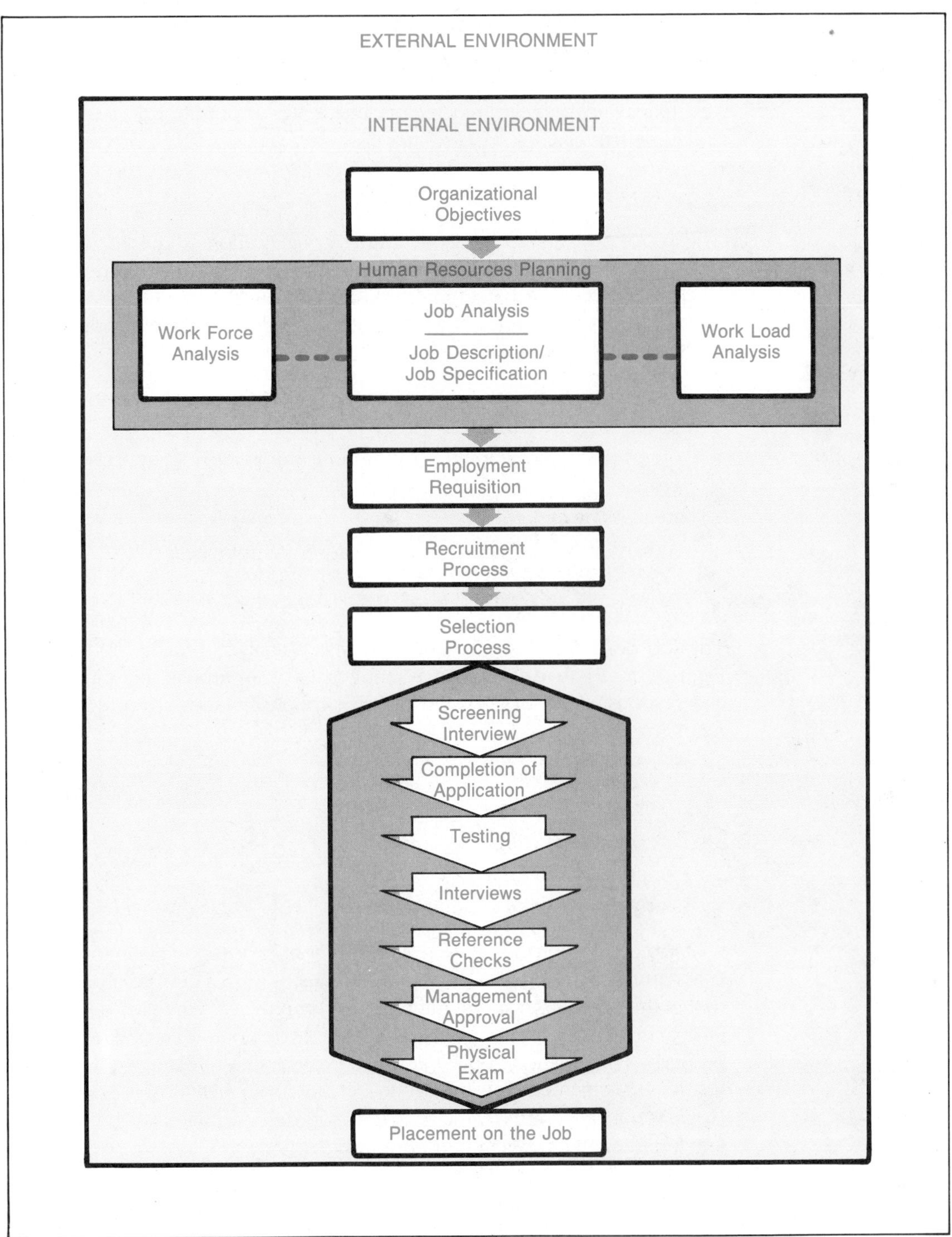
EXTERNAL ENVIRONMENT
INTERNAL ENVIRONMENT
Organizational Objectives
Human Resources Planning
Work Force Analysis
Job Analysis
Job Description/ Job Specification
Work Load Analysis
Employment Requisition
Recruitment Process
Selection Process
Screening Interview
Completion of Application
Testing
Interviews
Reference Checks
Management Approval
Physical Exam
Placement on the Job

FIGURE 9-2 *The Staffing Process*

- Help in the analysis of sources of supply of labor in order to focus recruitment efforts on the most likely supply sources.
- Provide for identification of replacements or "backup" for present key managers from either inside or outside the organization.
- Integrate personnel plans with financial plans and forecasts.[5]

Job Analysis

job analysis

The process of determining the human qualifications required to perform each job is referred to as **job analysis.** It requires identifying the responsibilities and operations of a job, leading to the development of a job description and job specification. Several methods may be used in conducting job analysis including the following:

- Observations of and interviews with present employees performing the jobs
- Questionnaires completed by present employees or supervisors of the work
- Analysis by experts
- A diary of activities performed by present employees.

Job Description

job description

The job description is a product of the job analysis process. As shown in Figure 9-3, a **job description** summarizes the purpose, principal duties, and responsibilities of a job. A job description includes statements on the following items:

1. duties to be performed
2. supervision given and received
3. relationships with other jobs
4. equipment and materials needed
5. physical working conditions

Job descriptions facilitate the recruitment process by clarifying the specific nature of objectives and responsibilities of jobs. They are also a helpful tool in the orientation and training of new employees. While job descriptions exist in many large firms, managers sometimes do not understand or use them properly. For instance, some managers believe that having job descriptions restricts management's flexibility and creativity in staffing the organization. However, to be useful to the manager, job descriptions must be translated into a statement of human requirements.

Job Specifications

job specification

The statement of the minimum acceptable human qualities necessary to perform the job is the **job specification.** The job specification pinpoints such characteristics required for the job as

1. education
2. experience
3. personality
4. physical abilities

Because of the legislation passed since 1960, with regard to discrimination concerning race, color, national origin, religion, sex, age, and handicaps, organizations need to be able to show that the characteristic is job related. The job specification is the standard to which the applicant is compared in each step of the recruitment procedure.

Work Load Analysis

Not only must we know the type of person required for a job but also the number of people necessary to meet organizational needs. Determining the number of personnel needed by an organization requires a prediction of future work loads.

work load analysis

Work load analysis involves estimating the type and volume of work that needs to be performed if the organization is to achieve its objective. It requires that forecasts of work to be accomplished be prepared. These forecasts are then translated into person-hour requirements. Work programs are often stated in terms of units produced, products assembled, boxes packed, customer calls, vouchers processed, and so forth. These are then converted into the number of person-hours by means of time study of the units or by utilizing average past work experience. For example, we may conclude that a specified number of products to be produced will require 1,000 person-hours of work during a forty-hour work week. Thus, by dividing the 1,000 person-hours required by the forty hours in the work week would indicate a need for twenty-five workers.

Work Force Analysis

work force analysis

After determining the number of workers required, a work force analysis is needed. **Work force analysis** consists of identifying the skills of current personnel to determine if work loads can be accomplished by these employees. If the work cannot be performed by the present work force, individuals will have to be recruited from outside the firm. In some organizations a computerized personnel data bank (Human Resources Information System) assists in providing this information. The following is typical of the information included:

- **Personal history**—age, sex, marital status, and similar information
- **Skills**—education, job experience, training, and so forth
- **Special qualifications**—membership in professional organizations, special achievements
- **Salary and job history**—present salary, past salary, dates of raises, and various positions held

JOB TITLE: Manager, Fleet Equipment Fabrication

BASIC FUNCTION:

This position is accountable for the effective management of the Fleet Equipment Fabrication Department. This department produces the service equipment required by the company's field activities.

DIMENSIONS:

Sales: The mill door cost of the equipment produced per year is $4.5 MM

Personnel: Two exempt and one-hundred non-exempt

Payroll: $0.8 MM

NATURE AND SCOPE:

This position, along with the Plant Manager, Manager of Quality Control, Manager of Production Control, Manager of Manufacturing Engineering, Manager of Materials and Building Engineer reports to the Vice-President of Manufacturing.

The Fleet Equipment Fabrication Department is responsible for the manufacture of all of the service equipment used by the company in support of its field operations and for the manufacture of similar equipment sold to customers. This department procures all of its own operating supplies including raw material, paint, welding supplies, nuts, bolts, etc., and maintains its own inventory of finished goods.

The incumbent is responsible for insuring that orders placed upon his department are met in accordance with acceptable delivery and quality. Because the work centers are involved in fabrication and the products utilized for this operation are purchased parts, the incumbent's job is complicated by uncontrollable facets such as delivery, quality and diversity of these required items. He must continually attempt to achieve a work center job schedule to insure sufficient work for all areas and small backlogs.

The incumbent's job is further challenged by the evolution and substitution of equipment fabricated. This constitutes a low volume, highly diversified conglomerate of components to be ordered, stocked and assembled—where work load is determined by component availability rather than a firm schedule.

The position of Manager, Fleet Equipment Fabrication acts with relatively complete freedom within the broad policy structure as established by the Vice-President of Manufacturing and has the following people reporting directly to him:

Project Coordinator (1):

Assists the Manager and acts for him in his absence. General functions include insuring continuity of work flow through the various production processes.

Coordinating all projects. Working out material substitutions with vendors to insure that the new product fits application. Assists the shop foreman where required.

FIGURE 9-3

Job Description: Manager, Fleet Equipment Fabrication

Materials Supervisor (1):

Insure through stock monitoring and updating, that sufficient stockage is maintained. Is also accountable for issuing and accounting for usage.

Shop Foreman (1):

Directs all personnel activities within the fabrication area. These duties are monitoring and distributing CCU work loads that will satisfy delivery needs (date and quantity), rescheduling project requirements that vary from program, in process and final inspection and counseling.

Recommends new fabrication tools and directs maintenance for specific field problems.

Fleet Secretary (1):

This position provides administrative and secretarial assistance to all positions shown above.

Contacts made by the Manager, Fleet Equipment Fabrication will include all of the various departments within the company, many of the component suppliers who supply Fleet inventory as well as machinery and equipment suppliers and others.

Those internal contacts are: **Engineering** to clarify designs and/or offer suggestions regarding same. **Data Processing** to update, alter or initiate programs. **Sales** to receive assistance on priority, order clarification and substitutions. **Payroll** to resolve any problems involved. **Purchasing** to expedite, change specifications and quantity problems. **Production Control** coordinating plant furnished equipment. **O.C.G.** scheduling.

Skills required in this position will include proficiency in mechanical engineering with strong background in administration preferred and with some knowledge of company field activities.

PRINCIPAL ACCOUNTABILITIES:

1. Selects and staffs his department.
2. Devises operational organization and staffs same.
3. Originates policy and procedures for his department within corporate guidelines.
4. Appraises performance and makes salary adjustments.
5. Supervises the technical personnel development program.
6. Develops budgetary requirements of personnel and facility needs for one to five years.
7. Monitors operating statement for expense guidance.
8. Personally guides jobs requiring special handling because of technical and/or time requirements.
9. Forecasts future need of departments including facilities, personnel and equipment.

- **Company data**—benefit plan, retirement information, and seniority
- **Capacity of individual**—test scores, health
- **Special preferences of the individual**—geographic location, work assignments

Employment Requisition

employment requisition

In most large organizations, an **employment requisition** is issued whenever a job becomes available. The requisition is the product of an analysis of a company's personnel requirements and must be closely coordinated with the job specification. In firms where job specifications are detailed, employment requisitions are usually brief, typically including such information as the job title, starting date, pay scale, and a brief summary of principal duties.

Recruitment

The process of searching for prospective employees and stimulating them to apply for available jobs is referred to as *recruitment.* Personnel recruitment can range from locating individuals within the firm who are qualified to a very sophisticated and extensive search for a new president.

Personnel can be recruited using internal and/or external sources of qualified applicants. There are advantages and disadvantages of both internal and external sources of applicants. Internal recruitment or promotion from within is an important source of personnel for positions above the entry level. Promotion from within has several advantages; it

1. increases morale of employees;
2. improves the quality of selection since an organization usually has a more complete evaluation of the strengths and weaknesses of internal applicants as opposed to those from outside the firm;
3. motivates present employees to prepare for more responsible positions;
4. attracts a better quality of external applicants if chances for promotion from within are good;
5. assists the organization to utilize personnel more fully.

According to William F. Comiskey, a partner with Arthur Young & Company, a large public accounting firm,

> A policy of promotion from within is essential if the firm is to attract and retain competent and progressive personnel. Most people want an opportunity for promotion to more responsible jobs; and if this opportunity is not present, they will look elsewhere.

Despite the advantages of internal recruiting, there are several disadvantages to be considered. Two of these are the following:

1. There may be an inadequate supply of qualified applicants.
2. Internal sources may lead to inbreeding of ideas—current employees may lack new ideas on how to do a job more effectively.

External sources of applicants permit an organization to overcome many of the disadvantages of recruiting internally. Such recruitment is also needed merely to maintain a constant labor force created because workers retire, leave the firm, or die. At this time we need to make a distinction between sources and methods of recruitment. *Sources of recruitment* refers to where the potential employees are located. Possible sources of recruitment include high schools and vocational schools, community colleges, colleges and universities, the competition and other firms, and unsolicited applicants.

Methods of recruitment are the means by which job applicants may be encouraged to seek employment with the firm. Some methods are advertising, employment agencies, recruiters, and employee referrals. Essentially, the firm must first determine where potential employees may be found and then use the appropriate methods to encourage them to make application. Only when a firm has applicants for a job can the selection process begin.

THE SELECTION PROCESS

The ultimate objective of recruitment is to select individuals who are most capable of meeting the requirements of the job. This is primarily a matter of comparing applicants' skills, knowledge, and education to the requirements of the job description-job specification. The selection process is shown in Figure 9-4.

Screening Interview

screening interview

Screening interviews are typically used to eliminate the obviously unqualified applicants for reasons such as excessive salary requirements, inadequate education, inability to speak coherently, lack of job-related experience, or other reasons. An applicant who appears to qualify for a position is asked to complete the employment application.

Employment Application

employment application

Almost all organizations use an **employment application** form in selecting new employees. The application collects objective biographical information about an applicant such as education, work experience, special skills, general

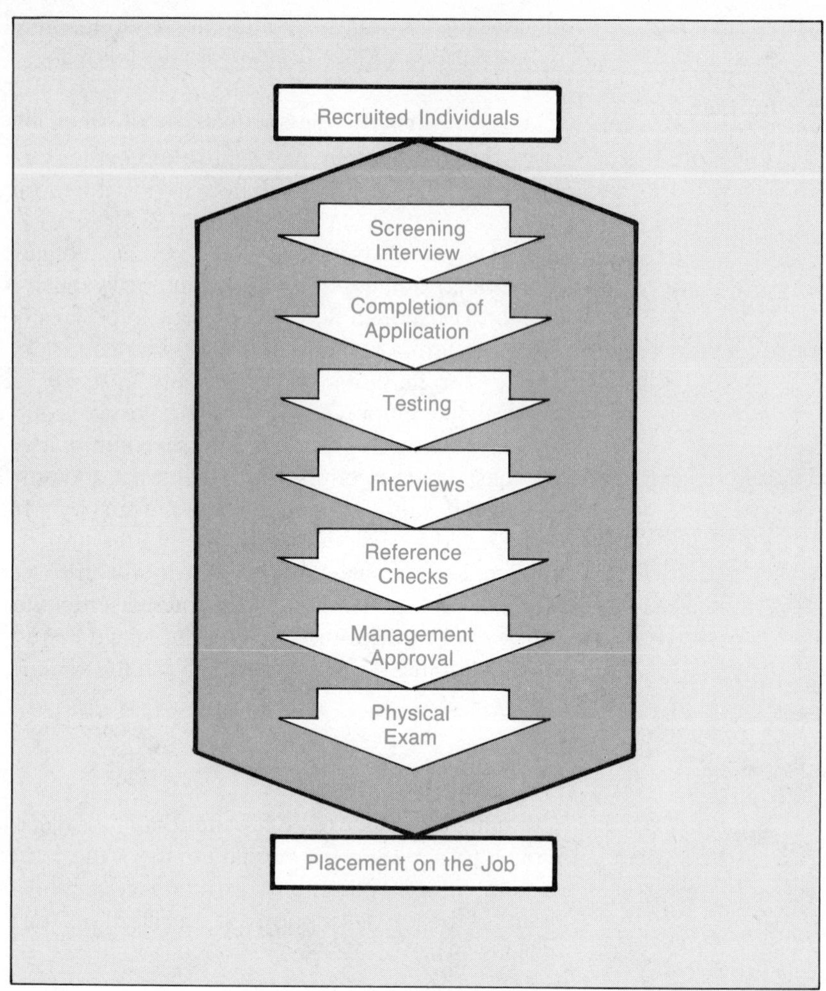

FIGURE 9-4
The Selection Process

background, marital status, and references (see Figure 9-5 for an example of an employment application). Information obtained from the employment application significantly assists managers in selecting quality personnel. Some organizations design and use a weighted application blank by determining relationships between biographical facts and job success. For example, one bank discovered that newly hired secretaries are least likely to quit the job if they are over thirty-five years of age, married, not college graduates, and have more than three years of experience.[6] Biographical analyses can also be used to predict the quality of job performance. It is important to remember that information requested on an employment application should not lead to discrimination against applicants. Questions referring to an applicant's age, sex, race, religion, national origin, or family status may violate Title VII of the Civil Rights Act of 1964.

OTIS

OTIS ENGINEERING CORPORATION
Gen. Offices: Belt Line Rd. at Webb Chapel
P. O. Box 34380, Dallas, Texas 75234

EMPLOYMENT APPLICATION OEC-268-J

FOR OFFICE USE ONLY	REFERRED BY			EMPLOYEE NUMBER	JOB CLASSIFICATION			DEPT/G. L. CODE
	RATE OF PAY	OCCUPATION CODE	LABOR GRADE	EMPLOYMENT DATE	EEO	SEX	BREAK CODES: AM / LUNCH / PM	

NAME: LAST / FIRST / MIDDLE — DATE

STREET ADDRESS — CITY, STATE — ZIP CODE — PHONE NUMBER

POSITION YOU ARE APPLYING FOR: — HAVE YOU EVER PREVIOUSLY WORKED FOR OTIS ENGINEERING CORPORATION OR OTIS PRESSURE CONTROL? ☐ YES ☐ NO — DATE TERMINATED

PERSONAL RECORD

SOCIAL SECURITY NUMBER — DO YOU HAVE ANY OUTSIDE BUSINESS INTERESTS? ☐ YES ☐ NO — IF YES, EXPLAIN

ARE YOU A U.S. CITIZEN? ☐ YES ☐ NO — HAVE YOU ANY PHYSICAL LIMITATIONS? ☐ YES ☐ NO — IF YES, EXPLAIN

DATE OF LAST COMPLETE PHYSICAL EXAMINATION — HAVE YOU EVER BEEN INJURED ON THE JOB? ☐ YES ☐ NO — IF YES, EXPLAIN

DRIVER'S LICENSE TYPE & NO. — TYPE VEHICLES YOU HAVE OPERATED — HAVE YOU HAD ANY TRAFFIC ACCIDENTS WITHIN THE LAST 3 YRS? ☐ YES ☐ NO — IF YES, EXPLAIN

HAVE YOU HAD ANY TRAFFIC VIOLATIONS WITHIN THE PAST YEAR? ☐ YES ☐ NO — HOW MANY? — HAVE YOU EVER HAD YOUR DRIVERS LICENSE SUSPENDED OR REVOKED? ☐ YES ☐ NO — IF YES, EXPLAIN

HAVE YOU EVER BEEN CONVICTED OF A CRIMINAL ACT? ☐ YES ☐ NO — IF YES, EXPLAIN — HAVE YOU BEEN CONVICTED OF A D.W.I. WITHIN THE PAST 3 YEARS? ☐ YES ☐ NO

A CONVICTION RECORD WILL NOT NECESSARILY BE A BAR TO EMPLOYMENT. FACTORS SUCH AS AGE AND TIME OF OFFENSE, SERIOUSNESS AND NATURE OF THE VIOLATION AND REHABILITATION WILL BE TAKEN INTO ACCOUNT.

EDUCATION RECORD

SCHOOL LEVEL	NAME AND LOCATION	DATES ATTENDED FROM	TO	COURSE OF STUDY GENERAL MAJOR	DIPLOMA OR DEGREE
GRADE					
HIGH					
COLLEGE/ UNIVERSITY					
TRADE					
OTHER					

SPECIAL SKILLS

LIST ALL SKILLS, TALENTS, AND/OR ANY MACHINES OR SPECIAL EQUIPMENT YOU HAVE OPERATED.

WHAT ARE YOUR HOBBIES?

PERSONAL REFERENCES

GIVE THE NAMES AND ADDRESSES OF THREE PERSONS WHO CAN BE CONTACTED FOR PERSONAL REFERENCES

NAME	ADDRESS	OCCUPATION	RELATIONSHIP	PHONE NUMBER

EMPLOYMENT RECORD

LIST MOST RECENT EMPLOYMENT FIRST		DATES EMPLOYED	DESCRIPTION OF JOB REASON FOR LEAVING
COMPANY	PHONE	FROM (MO YR) TO (MO YR)	DESCRIBE JOB
ADDRESS			
CITY, STATE	ZIP CODE		
SUPERVISOR		SALARY $	LEFT BECAUSE
COMPANY	PHONE	FROM (MO YR) TO (MO YR)	DESCRIBE JOB
ADDRESS			
CITY, STATE	ZIP CODE		
SUPERVISOR		SALARY $	LEFT BECAUSE
COMPANY	PHONE	FROM (MO YR) TO (MO YR)	DESCRIBE JOB
ADDRESS			
CITY, STATE	ZIP CODE		
SUPERVISOR		SALARY $	LEFT BECAUSE
COMPANY	PHONE	FROM (MO YR) TO (MO YR)	DESCRIBE JOB
ADDRESS			
CITY, STATE	ZIP CODE		
SUPERVISOR		SALARY $	LEFT BECAUSE
COMPANY	PHONE	FROM (MO YR) TO (MO YR)	DESCRIBE JOB
ADDRESS			
CITY, STATE	ZIP CODE		
SUPERVISOR		SALARY $	LEFT BECAUSE
COMPANY	PHONE	FROM (MO YR) TO (MO YR)	DESCRIBE JOB
ADDRESS			
CITY, STATE	ZIP CODE		
SUPERVISOR		SALARY $	LEFT BECAUSE

MILITARY RECORD

HAVE YOU EVER SERVED IN THE ARMED SERVICES? ☐ YES ☐ NO — BRANCH OF SERVICE — DRAFT OR RESERVE STATUS

LENGTH OF TIME IN SERVICE FROM — TO — IF IN THE RESERVE, WHAT BRANCH OR UNIT?

PERSON TO NOTIFY IN CASE OF EMERGENCY — NAME — RELATIONSHIP — ADDRESS — PHONE NUMBER

The statements made in this application are true and correct to the best of my knowledge. The Otis Engineering Corporation has my permission to verify any statement or reference, and all Companies or persons supplying information about my character, work habits or skills are hereby fully released from any liability for damages arising from giving this Company such information. I understand that any false statement on this application can be grounds for immediate dismissal.

In processing your application for employment we may make inquiry for a consumer employment report. Such a report may include information concerning character, general reputation, personal characteristics or mode of living. If you want further information concerning the scope of the report, please contact us.

APPLICANT'S SIGNATURE — DATE APPLICATION COMPLETED

APPLICANTS — DO NOT WRITE BELOW THIS LINE

INTERVIEWED BY — DATE — TEST RESULTS

INTERVIEWER'S COMMENTS

DISPOSITION OF APPLICATION

HIRING SUPERVISOR'S COMMENTS

FIGURE 9-5 *Employment Application—Otis Engineering Corporation* [*Reprinted with the permission of Otis Engineering Corporation.*]

Testing

testing Traditionally, **testing** has been an integral component in the selection process. Tests have been used to screen applicants in terms of skills, abilities, aptitudes, interest, personality, and attitudes that cannot be objectively judged in other ways. Tests to determine specific skills such as typing or shorthand are in wide use. However, in recent years many organizations have significantly curtailed or eliminated their psychological and intelligence pre-employment testing programs. This has occurred because some tests have been found to be instruments of discrimination against minorities.

Testing is used in screening recruits in some organizations in which one would normally not expect tests to be administered. For example, the Dallas Cowboys and several other National Football League clubs give prospective players an intelligence test prior to the NFL players' draft. The Cowboys have found the test they use to be a predicator of a player's ability to learn the Cowboys' system and to be successful in the league.

However, if all organizations, large and small, are considered, it is apparent that most are *not* using intelligence and psychological testing. In order to meet legal requirements, tests must possess validity and reliability.

validity Test **validity** is concerned with the relationship between the score on the test and performance on the job. A test is *valid* if the score on the test is a predicator of job success. Does the test measure what we want to measure? Validity is highly specific in nature. A test may be valid for one objective and invalid for another. For instance, the Otis Test of Mental Ability may be highly valid for measuring abstract intelligence. It certainly will be far less valid in predicting the success of a supervisor.

reliability **Reliability** is concerned with the degree of consistency of test results. If a test possesses high reliability, a person tested a second or third time with the same test, under the same conditions, will obtain approximately the same score.

An organization choosing to use testing in the employment process should be careful to avoid potential discriminatory aspects of tests and use tests only as an aid in the process, not as the determining factor.

Interviewing

interview The **interview** is the most widely used and probably the most important method of assessing the qualifications of job applicants. In general there are several objectives to be achieved in interviewing job applicants such as these:

1. assessing potential for advancement
2. determining the ability to get along with others
3. assessing personality
4. determining if the person will fit into the organization.

patterned interview

There are two basic types of interviews: direct (patterned) and unstructured (nondirect). In recent years there has been increased interest in the use of a directed or patterned interview. In **patterned interviews**, the interviewer follows a predetermined series of questions in interviewing applicants. The interviewer asks questions and records the applicant's responses. The use of a patterned or structured interview usually yields more complete, consistent, and reliable information about an applicant. Also, its use permits the comparison of several applicants and tends to minimize interviewer bias and prejudices.

Unstructured or nondirected interviews have no predetermined interviewing strategy or list of questions. Broad, rather open-ended types of questions such as "Tell me about yourself" are part of the unstructured interview. The unstructured interview may be useful in assessing characteristics of an individual such as ability to communicate, personal values, personality, and other factors.

Other types of interviewing techniques have also been used for special purposes. One of these techniques, the group interview, has been frequently used in the selection of managerial trainees. Group interviews are used where a small group of five or six applicants is observed and evaluated in small group discussions by two or more company managers or interviewers. The panel interview is a situation in which an applicant is interviewed by several people at the same time.

stress interview

The **stress interview** is another approach that is sometimes used in the selection of managers and potential managers. The stress interview attempts to make the applicant defensive by putting pressure on the person in order to observe his or her reactions to stress and tension.

One of the authors, in an early stage of his career, was exposed to a stress interview when he applied for a sales position. The initial interview for the job had gone well, so a second interview was scheduled with the firm's sales manager. On meeting the sales manager, the author was bluntly told he was not qualified for the position. At that point, the author had no idea a stress interview was in progress. The author was put on the defensive, but being a rather confident person, maintained he was the best-qualified person for the job. At the end of the two-hour stress interview, the author was offered the job. Not until several months later was it discovered that a stress interview had been conducted and that the job would not have been offered to the author if he had not responded to the stress with confidence.

Regardless of the type of method used, the interview is the most important element in the selection of new personnel. Since most managers must rely on interviewing when selecting new employees, and evaluating candidates for promotion, following sound practices, is essential. The following guidelines have been found to be helpful in conducting effective interviews:

1. **Plan for the interview**—review job specification and description as well as the applications of candidates.
2. **Create a good climate for interview**—try to establish a friendly, open rapport with the applicant.

3. **Allow sufficient time for an uninterrupted interview.**
4. **Conduct a goal-oriented interview**—seek the information needed to assist in the employment decision.
5. **Avoid certain types of questions**—try not to ask "leading" questions or questions that may imply discrimination.
6. **Seek answers to all questions and check for inconsistencies.**
7. **Record the results of the interview immediately upon completion.**[7]

Over the years, the interview, much like testing, has received considerable criticism concerning its ability to predict success on the job. In interviewing an applicant for employment, many factors influence the decision of the interviewer. For example, the interviewer may allow a first impression of an applicant to influence unduly the outcome of the interview. In a large insurance company, the personnel manager was a great believer in the importance of initial impressions in evaluating applicants for jobs. He placed considerable emphasis on his initial reactions to an applicant's handshake, speed of walking, and eye contact. For male applicants, the personnel manager was careful to observe whether the applicant could pass the "firm handshake," "fast walk," and "eye contact" tests. The manager strongly believed that if the applicant had a "firm handshake" and maintained good eye contact when meeting others as well as the ability to keep up with the personnel manager's walking pace, the applicant was both confident and aggressive. Many managers rely on similar, but sometimes questionable, practices in selecting personnel.

Interviews can be instruments of discrimination, and for this reason, they have received close scrutiny by the EEOC in recent years. Charges of possible discrimination have led to an increase in the use of the patterned interview since it has significantly higher reliability and validity than other methods of interviewing.

An effective means of assessing the success of an organization's interviewing process is to compare performance of employees with the evaluation of these same employees when they were interviewed for the job. In other words, how effective or valid is the interview in predicting job success?

Background and Reference Checks

Once an applicant successfully clears the interviewing "hurdles," the practice of many organizations is to conduct background and reference checks. The purpose of checking a person's background and references is to verify the information provided by the applicant in the interview and on the employment application.

In recent years, thorough and reliable reference checks have often been difficult to obtain because of the Privacy Act of 1974. It is quite likely the reference check will "become a process of verifying that the prospective employee was at a certain place doing a certain job for a specified period of time at a verified compensation level."[8] Under the law, the former employer may be required to obtain a release from the ex-employee to provide information to prospective employers about his or her quality of performance.

Management Approval

In most large organizations, many of the above functions are performed by a personnel department. However, the personnel department does not usually make the final decision as to which person is selected for a particular position. Under most circumstances, the manager or supervisor who will be the immediate superior of the new employee will make the final hiring decision. The selection decision is usually made after interviewing the applicants and reviewing the recommendations of the personnel department. The immediate supervisor knows the needs of his or her unit or department and is in the best position to evaluate the qualifications and characteristics of prospective employees. The supervisor or manager should be able to identify factors in the applicant's background or work experience that would be helpful to the new employee in fitting into the work unit.

Physical Exams

After a prospective employee has successfully completed the other phases in the selection process, most organizations require a physical exam. The physical exam has at least these three basic goals:

1. To determine if the applicant can meet the physical demands of the job.
2. To provide a record to protect the organization against claims for previously incurred injuries.
3. To prevent communicable diseases from entering the firm.

Placement on the Job: Orientation

orientation

Once individuals have been selected for a particular position, they must receive an orientation to the organization. **Orientation** is the process of introducing the new employee to the organization. Every new employee goes through an orientation period regardless of whether the firm has a formal orientation program. New recruits must "learn the ropes" or "rules of the game" if they are to succeed. Much of the new employee orientation takes place on an informal basis—during coffee breaks, at lunch, or during work—by interactions with employees often referred to as "old-timers." However, most organizations have formal orientation programs designed to acquaint new personnel with the areas as shown in Figure 9-6.

1. History and nature of the business
2. Goals of the company
3. Basic products/services provided by the firm
4. Organizational structure
5. Policies, procedures, and rules covering such areas as:
   a. Work schedules
   b. Salaries and payment periods
   c. Physical facilities
   d. Attendance and absenteeism
   e. Working conditions and safety standards
   f. Lunch and coffee breaks
   g. Discipline and grievance
   h. Parking
6. Company benefits
   a. Insurance programs
   b. Pension and/or profit sharing plans
   c. Recreational programs—bowling, tennis, golf, etc.
   d. Vacations and holidays
7. Opportunities
   a. Advancement, promotion
   b. Suggestion systems
8. Specific departmental responsibilities
   a. Department functions
   b. Job duties/responsibilities/authority
   c. Introduction to other employees in work group

FIGURE 9-6

Orientation Outline

SPECIAL CONSIDERATIONS IN SELECTING MANAGERIAL PERSONNEL

In recruiting and selecting nonmanagerial personnel, it is usually possible to use more objective factors in identifying potentially successful employees. However, more subjective judgment is often involved in selecting managerial personnel. In selecting managers, concern is typically focused on an evaluation of skills, abilities, attitudes, and characteristics, many of which are intangible. Some of these include:

- Planning skills
- Communication ability
- Decision-making skills
- Organizing ability
- Motivation and leadership skills
- Conceptual skills

- Adaptability to change
- Qualities such as self-confidence, aggressiveness, and empathy

The recruitment and development of quality managerial personnel is essential to the continuing success of every organization. Because of this, organizations must be concerned with determining needs for managerial personnel and identifying persons with managerial potential.

Determining Executive Needs

Decisions concerning the number of executives required by an organization involve a comparison of (1) predicted future needs and (2) present inventory of talent. Determining needs for managerial personnel requires an "inventory" of personnel currently available within the organization. *Inventory* is a term often used in relation to the counting of tangible objects such as raw materials, goods in process, and finished products. In the inventory of managerial and executive talent, however, the items are generally intangible. The inventory is not simply a counting of heads; it includes a cataloging of present and potential abilities and attitudes. It is an assessment not only of skills, experience, and abilities but also personal motivation. It sometimes happens that a person who appears to be properly prepared for a promotion indicates a desire to transfer, to change occupational area, or to remain on the present job.

In making up the inventory, a decision must be made as to the personnel to be included. Certainly, present lower- and middle-management personnel will be included. In some companies all salaried personnel compensated on a monthly or semimonthly basis are included. Each first-level supervisor may be asked to submit recommendations of those deemed to have the potential for advancement. For each individual included, detailed information must be gathered to supplement and update existing data, such as education, experience, performance ratings, health, psychological test results, recreational interests, hobbies, and civic groups. Such data can be computerized in order that (1) assessment as to current adequacy of talent reservoirs can be made, and (2) searches can be made to fill particular vacancies arising. Figure 9-7 illustrates the Xerox Corporation's approach to such an inventory. The Xeorx system provides management with personal history and performance data on present personnel who may be qualified to fill anticipated vacancies resulting from retirements, resignations, termination, promotions, or expansion.

Many companies maintain backup organizational charts to show listings of available talent for each key managerial position in the organization. For example, Associated Dry Goods, Inc., a large retailing firm with over 51,000 employees and sales of $1.5 billion, utilizes such a backup chart. This company has an organizational chart that includes the names of at least two individuals as replacements for each key position. The chart also includes an assessment of eligibility for promotion and is targeted for certain key positions.

NAME	EEO INFORMATION	EMPLOYEE NO.	Previous Reviews YR	RATING
Mary R. Wells		3514	5/74	4
TITLE Branch Manager I	PLEASE CIRCLE 1 2 3 4 (5)	MONTHLY MIDPOINT 4186	12/74	3
ORGANIZATION LOCATION San Francisco, Western Region	M (F)	MOS. IN POSITION 20	6/75	4

PERFORMANCE APPRAISAL

1	2	3	4	5
			X	
Unsatisfactory Performance	Meets Minimum Performance	Normal, Reasonable Expected Level of Performance	Consistently Exceeds Expected Level of Performance	Exceptional Performance

Provide Summary Comments

Mary always meets or exceeds job targets. She is an aggressive, highly results-oriented manager who works well under heavy job demands. She motivates her people well and promotes strong team spirit; however, she must allow her people greater participation in the decision-making process. In this way, they will be provided with an optimum of development related experience. Mary does not try to solve problems with a status quo approach. Her approaches to problems are creative. She assimilates new concepts readily and acts decisively. She is flexible and cooperative and requires little direct supervision to accomplish even the most complex tasks.

APPRAISAL OF PROMOTABILITY – CHECK ONE

A	B	C	D	E	F	G
X						
Immediately Eligible for Promotion	Eligible in 12 Months after Further Development	Eligible in 24 Months after Further Development	Recommend Transfer for Further Development	Not Eligible in 24 Months, Should Continue to Develop in Present Job	Recommend Less Responsibility	Too Soon to Appraise

Suggested Positions Use exact Titles and Organization — Title	When Ready: Current Now	Current 1 year	Current 2 years	Previous HRP Now	Previous HRP 1 year	Previous HRP 2 years
1 Manager, Branch Operations, Region	X				X	
2 Regional Sales Manager, Region			X			
3						

My signature indicates I have held a Career Guidance Sesseion and discussed Career Objectives with my subordinate.

DATE PREPARED	PREPARED BY	REVIEWED BY
6/1/76	Charles F. White	John W. Gunther

I have reviewed my HRP and discussed the contents with my manager. My signature means that I have been advised of my performance and appraisal of promotability, it does not necessarily imply that I agree with the HRP's contents.

EMPLOYEE SIGNATURE	DATE
Mary R. Wells	6/30/76

EMPLOYEE NAME Mary R. Wells

DATA FOR KEYPUNCHING

EMPLOYEE NUMBER 1–4	AOP 5	JOB CODE 1 6–12	YRS 13	PREV HRP 14	JOB CODE 2 15–21	YRS 22	PREV HRP 23	JOB CODE 3 24–30	YRS 31	PREV HRP 32
3 5 1 4	B	H 0 0 2 5 1 5	0	1	H 0 0 4 0 2 4	2				

(Columns 5–32: DEVELOPMENTAL OR PROMOTIONAL POSITIONS & WHEN READY)

NAME	HIRE DATE	DATE PREPARED
Mary R. Wells	9/1/66	6/1/76

Career Objectives

Manager Branch Operations in two years.

Vice President and Region General Manager in five years.

Check one ☐ Not interested in promotional move at this time but would like to develop within current job ☒ Would like additional responsibility ☐ Would like to change career path

Education

Washington University 9/53-9/57, St. Louis, Mo. — Business Admin Economics — B.A.

St. Louis University 6/57-12/59, St. Louis, Mo. — Masters Business Admin — MBA

Xerox Courses: Field Management Action Workshop, FED

Other Data

Graduated with honors from Washington University

Speak German fluently

Pre-Xerox Experience

12/59 - 2/63 Sales Rep., Brunswick Corp. St. Louis, Mo.
Directed sales of Hospital equipment to dealers.

2/63 - 9/66 Sales Manager, Brunswick Corp. St. Louis, Mo.
Directed Medical sales team.

Xerox Experience

9/66 - 3/69 Territory Rep. Xerox St. Louis, Mo.
3/69 - 3/70 Financial Planning Analyst Xerox Rochester
Provide support to sales planning through close liaison with finance on sales force size and impact. Create data base for sales analysis system.
3/70 - 3/72 Market Manager Xerox Rochester
Direct responsibility for development of marketing plans and approach to the automotive industry. Potential market 4 million dollars. Increase 10% realized in first six months of program.
5/72 - 9/74 Branch Manager II Xerox Denver, Co.
9/74 - Pres. Branch Manager I Xerox San Fran., Cal.

- IF ADDITIONAL SPACE IS REQUIRED, USE EXTRA SHEET AND CHECK HERE ☐
- WOULD YOU RELOCATE: ☒ YES ☐ NO

NOTE: Your Manager will provide you with a complete copy of your HRP after it has been validated.
Form 56598 (3/76) Printed in U.S.A.

FIGURE 9-7 *Human Resources Information System [Used with permission of Xerox, Inc.]*

Techniques for Identifying Managerial Talent

Identifying individuals with potential executive talent has become an increasingly important activity in large organizations. In general, the activity has taken these two directions:

1. Determining the significant personal characteristics or behaviors that seem to predict managerial success.
2. Establishing managerial talent assessment centers

Personal Characteristics

Over the years, there has been considerable interest in determining the personal characteristics related to managerial success. Major companies such as AT&T, Sears, General Electric, Standard Oil, and many others have engaged in research within their firms to identify a series of traits or characteristics necessary for success. The studies related measures of job performance such as productivity, salary level, and quality of work of successful managers with personal characteristics and attitudes of these managers. Some of the characteristics of managers included in these studies were grades in college, level of self-confidence, organized and orderly thought, personal values of a practical and economic nature, intelligence, nonverbal reasoning, and general attitudes. Research at AT&T found a significant relationship between grades in college and salary level achieved. In a study of 10,000 managers in the Bell System, it was found that 51 percent of those in the top 10 percent of their college class were located in the top third of the salary levels in the company. For the most part, studies of personal characteristics of managers have not yielded accurate predictions of managerial success.

Assessment Center

In an effort to improve managerial selection, a second technique for identifying talent has become popular in recent years. This approach is the

assessment center

assessment center designed to provide for the systematic evaluation of the potential of individuals for future management positions. In the typical assessment center, a series of activities is designed to test the potential manager's skills, abilities, attitudes, and judgment. Figure 9-8 illustrates a three-day assessment center that uses a number of different bases on which to evaluate executive candidates. The assessment center approach was introduced to American business in the mid-1950s by the American Telephone and Telegraph Company and has grown in popularity since. More than 200 large companies now utilize assessment centers.

A survey of thirty-three companies reveals that the three most widely used assessment techniques are in-basket exercises (thirty-one firms), business games (thirty firms), and leaderless group discussion (thirty-one firms).[9] An in-basket consists of a set of notes, messages, telephone calls, letters, and reports that the candidate is expected to handle within a period of one or

Day 1	Orientation of dozen candidates
	Break-up into groups of four to play a *Management Game* (observe and assess organizing ability, financial acumen, quickness of thinking efficiency under stress, adaptability, leadership)
	Psychological Testing (measure and assess verbal and numerical abilities, reasoning, interests, and attitudes) and/or **Depth Interviews** (assess motivation)
	Leaderless Group Discussion (observe and assess aggressiveness, persuasiveness, expository skill, energy, flexibility, self-confidence)
Day 2	**In-Basket Exercise** (observe and assess decision making under stress, organizing ability, memory and ability to interrelate events, preparation for decision making, ability to delegate, concern for others)
	Role-playing of Employment or Performance Appraisal Interview (observe and assess sensitivity to others, ability to probe for information, insight, empathy)
	Group Roles in preparation of a budget (observe and assess collaboration abilities, financial knowledge, expository skill, leadership, drive)
Day 3	**Individual Case Analyses** (observe expository skill, awareness of problems, background information possessed for problems, typically involving marketing, personnel, accounting, operations, and financial elements)
	Obtainment of **Peer Ratings** from all candidates.
	Staff assessors meet to discuss and rate all candidates
Weeks later	Manager with assessor experience meets with each candidate to discuss assessment with counseling concerning career guides and areas to develop

FIGURE 9-8

Typical Assessment Center Schedule

two hours. The candidate's decisions can be rated by assessors with respect to such abilities as willingness to take action and organizing of interrelated events.

A business game is a competitive simulation where teams are required to make decisions concerning production, marketing, purchasing, and finance in competition with each other. The leaderless group discussion assesses participant activities in taking the lead in discussion, influencing others, mediating arguments, speaking effectively, and summarizing and classifying issues. In addition, various other exercises are often designed to fit the firm's particular situation. For example, J. C. Penney utilizes the "Irate Customer Phone Call," made by an assessor, in order to rate the candidate's ability to control emotions, demonstrate tact, and satisfy the complaint.[10] Psychological tests and depth interviewing are frequently used techniques but generally show lower levels of accuracy in predicting future success. Personality tests, in particular, appear to be the weakest predictor.

In determining the predictive accuracy of the assessment center approach, the initial study at AT&T was most impressive. Assessor ratings were not communicated to company management for a period of eight years in order not to contaminate the results. In a sample of fifty-five candidates who achieved the middle-management ranks during that period, the center correctly predicted 78 percent of them.[11] Of seventy-three persons who did not progress beyond the first level of management, 95 percent were correctly predicted by the assessment staff. As a result, this company has maintained its centers, processing an average of 10,000 candidates a year. Reviewing ratings and actual progress of 5,943 personnel over a ten-year period demonstrated a high validity of assessment center predictions.[12]

Summary

People are the most important asset of any organization. Most firms today realize that acquiring and developing quality human resources is essential if the organization is to survive and grow. This statement provides an excellent summary of the significance of staffing to every organization. In most large firms, a human resources or personnel department is responsible for administering the organization's staffing function. However, every manager, regardless of function, must understand and participate in the staffing process.

The six basic human-resources-related functions are staffing, training and development, compensation, health and safety, employee and labor relations, and personnel research. Staffing primarily involves personnel planning, recruitment, and selection. Training and development programs are designed to assist individuals, groups, and the entire organization to become more effective. Compensation includes all rewards individuals receive as a result of their employment. Health and safety programs are designed to enable workers to have a safe and healthy work environment. Employee and labor relations involves dealing with the union or developing an environment where employees believe the union is unnecessary. Personnel research is directed toward gaining a better understanding of human relations problems.

Every manager involved with human resources management is affected by government legislation. Some of the most important legislation passed during the last twenty years includes: Equal Pay Act of 1963, as amended in 1972; Civil Rights Act of 1964, as amended in 1972; Age Discrimination in Employment Act of 1967, as amended in 1978; Occupational Safety and Health Act of 1970; Vocational Rehabilitation Act of 1973; Federal Privacy Act of 1974; Employee Retirement Income Security Act of 1974; and the Pregnancy Discrimination Act of 1978.

The staffing process involves planning for future personnel requirements, recruiting individuals, and selecting from those recruited individuals employees who fulfill the needs of the firm. The process of determining the human qualifications required to perform the job is called job analysis. A job description summarizes the purpose, principal duties, and responsibilities of the job. The statement of the minimum acceptable human qualities necessary to perform the job is the job specification. Work load analysis involves estimating the type and volume of work that needs to be performed if the organization is to achieve its objectives. Work force analysis consists of identifying the skills of current personnel to determine if work loads can be accomplished by these employees.

In most large organizations, an employee requisition is issued whenever a job becomes available. Recruitment may then begin. The ultimate objective of recruitment is to select individuals who are most capable of meeting the requirements of the job. Selection from among those recruited applicants is the next step. The steps in the selection process are: (1) screening interview, (2) completion of application, (3) testing, (4) interviews, (5) reference checks, (6) management approval, (7) physical exam. Once individuals have been selected, they need to receive an orientation to the organization.

Review Questions

1. Describe and discuss the different phases in the staffing process.
2. Distinguish between a job description and job specification.
3. What are the major federal laws that affect the staffing process?
4. Describe the advantages and disadvantages of promotion from within.
5. What are the general objectives that need to be achieved in interviewing job applicants?
6. What steps are involved in the personnel selection process?
7. What is the purpose of an assessment center? Discuss.

Exercises

1. Assume you are a personnel director for the following type of firms and have a vacancy that requires the skills identified below. What phase(s) of the personnel selection process do you believe would require special attention?
   a. Faculty member for a major university that stresses research
   b. A general laborer for a construction firm
   c. A skilled welder for work on an assembly line
   d. A senior secretary who is required to take dictation and type 70 words per minute
   e. A first-level production supervisor
2. Consult the personnel wanted section of a major Sunday newspaper. Evaluate the positions that are available for the following career fields. Can you detect a general pattern of job requirements that are needed for an applicant?
   a. Personnel manager
   b. Computer specialist
   c. Car salesperson
   d. Production supervisor

Case Study

A Case of Alleged Discrimination

John Williams, a black clerical employee, has been with the Della Corporation for over fifteen years. During his tenure he has held various positions, all within the same department. He has advanced to the position of senior clerk, a semi-supervisory position concerned with work direction but not hiring, firing, or promoting authority. He has attained this position not as much through outstanding work as through longevity in the department. Over the years he has developed a very abrasive personality. This normally is demonstrated by such things as never greeting the other employees in the morning, never doing any of the "dirty work," and acting as if answering questions is a real imposition on him.

This insensitive type of personality has had an adverse effect on the working effectiveness of the section as evidenced by an above-average turnover rate of the clerical staff and has reduced accuracy and efficiency of the work performed in the department. When terminated employees are questioned on their exit interviews, statements such as "Don't like John" or "Can't stand to work in that department" are common. On several occasions John's supervisor has discussed these comments with him. John tends to pass these off as merely racially discriminatory remarks.

John's supervisor does not know how to react in this situation because it is based on such intangible evidence. None of his actions by themselves warrant termination. The personnel director has cautioned the supervisor that she must be careful of disciplinary action because of the discrimination implications. John has no room for advancement into another position in the department because of educational requirements and cannot change departments easily because his entire work experience has been in one area.

QUESTIONS

1. What should John's supervisor do?
2. How much consideration should be given to John's longevity and minority status?
3. How difficult would it be to terminate John in view of the laws discussed in this chapter?

Case Study

Absenteeism of a Long-Service Employee

Quality Business Forms, Inc. has a policy stating that employee absenteeism should not exceed four days during a ninety-day work period without medical verification. If an employee does not have medical reasons for excessive absences, he or she may be subject to disciplinary action.

Ed Thompson has been employed by Quality for over twenty-one years. In the past three years he has had an abnormal number of absences, which his supervisor chose to ignore due to Ed's long tenure with the company. When Ed's supervisor was transferred and another individual in the department, Alice Randall, assumed the supervisory position, she immediately advised Ed that his absenteeism was excessive and that it would have to cease or disciplinary action would be taken. Ed claimed that he was injured five years previously on his job and that his absences were a result of that injury. A review of Ed's health records was undertaken; no such injury had ever been reported.

Ed's attendance improved during the first six months under Randall's supervision but began to deteriorate during the latter part of the year. Ed, warned again about the absenteeism, came back with his previous excuse. At this point, Randall contacted the personnel manager for assistance in dealing with Ed. She was told that further disciplinary steps should be taken along with a complete physical evaluation by the corporate medical doctor. The physical exam was given immediately and no physical abnormalities were found.

This information was given to Ed verbally by the doctor, but Ed did not accept the findings. He was then counseled by the personnel manager, his supervisor, and his department manager. Ed listened very intently to what was being said and took notes. Ed was told that the next step in the disciplinary procedure would be dismissal if his absenteeism continued. He said he understood and that he would work when he felt good and would not work when he did not feel good.

Thirty days later Ed and his supervisor were called in to the personnel office at 7:00 in the morning and Ed was terminated. It was a shock to Ed that he had actually been fired, since it was necessary for the president of the company to approve the termination of employees with a long service record. A discrimination charge was filed but was dropped after no grounds could be established. A Workmen's Compensation claim came in but could not be substantiated. The last item was an unemployment claim that was to be levied against the corporation, but on an appeal it too was found in favor of the corporation.

QUESTIONS

1. Do you agree with the standards developed by the firm with regard to absenteeism?
2. What responsibilities rest with an employer in regards to when a long-term employee should be terminated?
3. How much documentation is really needed to be fair?

Notes

1. The following section is based on the discussion in the book by R. Wayne Mondy and Robert M. Noe, III, *Personnel: The Management of Human Resources* (Boston: Allyn and Bacon, 1981), pp. 8–11.
2. Lester A. Digman, "Let's Keep the OD People Honest," *Personnel* 56 (January–February 1979): 23.
3. Eliza G. C. Collins and Timothy Blodgett, "Sexual Harassment: Some See It—Some Won't," *Harvard Business Review* 59, no. 2 (March–April 1981): 79.
4. Ibid.
5. Lewis E. Albright, "Staffing Policies and Strategies," *ASPA Handbook of Personnel and Industrial Relations,* ed. Dale Yoder and Herbert Heneman (Washington, D.C.: Bureau of National Affairs, 1974), 1: 4–21.
6. Stanley R. Novack, "Developing an Effective Application Blank," *Personnel Journal* 49 (May 1970): 421.
7. C. Harold Stone and Floyd L. Ruch, "Selection, Interviewing, and Testing," in *ASPA Handbook of Personnel and Industrial Relations,* Dale Yoder and Herbert

G. Heneman, eds. (Washington, D.C.: Bureau of National Affairs, 1979), pp. 152–154.

8. Lawrence A. Wanger, "Employee Reference Request Revisited," *Personnel Administrator* 20 (November 1975): 62.
9. Joseph M. Bender, "What Is 'Typical' of Assessment Centers?" *Personnel* 50 (July–August 1973): 51.
10. William C. Byham, "Assessment Centers for Spotting Future Managers," *Harvard Business Review* 48 (July–August 1970): 158.
11. Douglas W. Bray and Donald L. Grant, "The Assessment Center in the Measurement of Potential for Business Management," *Psychological Monographs,* vol. 80, no. 17 (1966), p. 24.
12. James R. Huck, "Assessment Centers: A Review of the External and Internal Validities," *Personnel Psychology* 26 (Summer 1973): 198.

References

Breaugh, J. A. "Relationship between Recruiting Sources and Employee Performance, Absenteeism, and Work Attitudes." *Academy of Management Journal* 24 (March 1981): 142–147.

Bucalo, J. "Personnel Directors: What You Should Know before Recommending MBO." *Personnel Journal* 56 (April 1977): 176–178.

Byham, William C. "Assessment Centers for Spotting Future Managers." *Harvard Business Review* 40 (July–August 1970): 158.

Collins, E. G. C., and Blodgett, F. B. "Sexual Harassment: Some See It—Some Won't." *Harvard Business Review* 59 (March–April 1980): 77–94.

Davies, G. S. "Consistent Recruitment in a Graded Manpower System." *Management Science* 22 (July 1976): 1215–1220.

Dhanens, T. P. "Implications of the New EEOC Guidelines." *Personnel* 56 (September 1979): 32–39.

Heflich, D. L. "Matching People and Jobs: Value Systems and Employee Selection." *Personnel Administration* 26 (January 1981): 77–85.

Henderson, J. A. "What the Chief Executive Expects of the Personnel Function." *Personnel Administration* 22 (May 1977): 40–45.

Higgins, James M. "A Manager's Guide to the Equal Employment Opportunity Laws." *Personnel Journal* 55 (August 1976): 406–412.

Hoffman, W. H., and Wyatt, L. L. "Human Resources Planning." *Personnel Administration* 22 (January 1977): 19–23.

Hollingsworth, A. T., and Preston, P. "Corporate Planning: A Challenge for Personnel Executives." *Personnel Journal* 55 (August 1976): 386–389.

Malinowski, F. A. "Job Selection Using Task Analysis." *Personnel Journal* 60 (April 1981): 288–291.

Marr, R., and Schneider, J. "Self-Assessment Test for the 1978 Uniform Guidelines on Employee Selection Procedures." *Personnel Administration* 26 (May 1981): 103–108.

CASE STUDY FOR PART III

Personnel at Odds: Organizational Problems at First Federal Savings and Loan

Raymond Thompson, president of First Federal Savings and Loan Association of Portland, described a recent incident that occurred at a staff meeting requested by one segment of his office staff. This meeting represented the culmination of an ongoing problem, which threatened the tranquility of his normally smoothly running organization. The comments of the association president and of the principals are described in the following paragraphs.

THE COMPANY

First Federal Savings and Loan Association of Portland was established in 1934. It got its start as a result of the Federal Home Loan Bank Act of 1933. This act was passed with the idea of assisting home owners in getting long-term loans, which had not been readily obtainable through existing financial institutions. First Federal Savings and Loan of Portland was one of the first 200 such institutions in the country chartered under the Federal Home Loan Bank Act.

Mr. R. S. Thompson, who was active in management until 1972, founded the association. Mr. Thompson had prior experience with a commercial bank and also had run a building and loan association for about a year. First Federal moved into a new building in 1975 and in the month prior to the writing of this case had assets of $21.7 million. This represented a doubling in size since the 1975 move to the new building.

This case was prepared by Ed D. Roach of Southwest Texas State University and Robert H. Solomon of Stephen F. Austin State University as a basis for class discussion rather than to illustrate either effective or ineffective handling of an administrative situation. Presented at a Case Research Association Workshop.

MAIN CHARACTERS (see Figure 1)

Raymond Thompson. President of the association is Raymond Thompson, son of the late R. S. Thompson. Raymond Thompson has seventeen years of experience in the savings and loan business. He was working for a Seattle newspaper as a sportswriter when his father asked him to join the association. He entered the business in 1960 and according to his account: "I learned

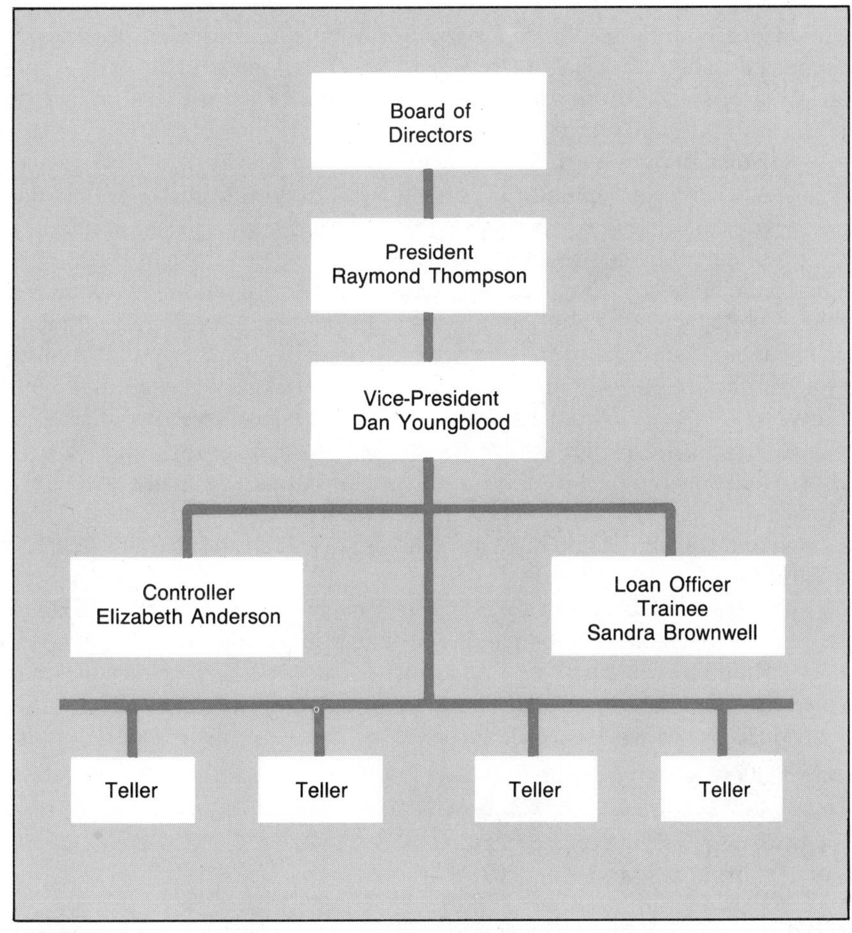

FIGURE 1 *Organizational Structure of First Federal Savings and Loan Association*

through doing. All these things connected with management and running the association I've learned with his [the father's] help."

Dan Youngblood. Vice-President and secretary of the association is Dan Youngblood. Youngblood joined First Federal in 1976. He holds a B.B.A. degree in marketing. Prior to joining First Federal he spent several years in the real estate business in Portland.

Elizabeth Anderson. Elizabeth Anderson came to the association in 1971. She previously had worked ten years with a local commercial bank. Anderson is the equivalent of office manager. She handles accounting for the association and, according to Mr. Thompson, is really the chief controller. The tellers work under the supervision of Anderson. Anderson has a high-school education. She has expressed to several women in the office the ambition of some day becoming a vice-president of the association and of ultimately being named to the board of directors.

Sandra Brownwell. Mrs. Brownwell joined First Federal Savings and Loan Association in September 1976. She was hired initially to do general office work in the home loan area of the association. It was the intention of the president and vice-president, however, to move her along as fast as possible to the point of having her close loans. Brownwell's working hours were 8:30–4:00, which were the same hours as the president and vice-president of the association. This contrasted with the hours worked in the teller area, which were from 8:30 until they finished, which was normally around 5:00. Brownwell replaced a woman who was dismissed because she was unable to move beyond the clerical work to the desired loan-closing duties. When Brownwell was hired, she said that she was told that she might ultimately work into a loan officer's position if she was able to perform in her loan-closing duties satisfactorily. Brownwell holds bachelor's and master's degrees in business-related areas.

Tellers. Marilyn Simon, Carolyn Jones, Linda Coleman, and Lynn Daniel work in the teller area. Simon handles insurance and taxes primarily. According to Thompson, she has "no title as such." Carolyn Jones, Linda Coleman, and Lynn Daniel perform teller work and general office work. All of these individuals have high school educations or the equivalent and report to Anderson.

THE PRESIDENT'S DESCRIPTION OF THE PROBLEM

Some of the women in the teller area, headed by Mrs. Anderson, asked for a meeting as I recall. I knew that there had been some friction between Mrs.

Anderson and Mrs. Brownwell, but I had no idea that it was to be brought out in the meeting that morning. These women requested the previous afternoon that I call a staff meeting the next morning before the office opened.

However, I was not aware of the agenda for the meeting. We had previously told our staff that they could ask for meetings when they wanted to talk about problems within the organization. Of course, everybody was free to bring up things—some problems that exist—and that's what was done in this case.

The tenor of that meeting was unfriendly; reflecting on it I would assume that one clique had decided that they would make an effort to just force management's hand. It didn't work out that way. The problems discussed were extremely superficial. I think it actually reflected immaturity on the part of one of our people. I'd say that the points raised that morning were perhaps really symptoms of underlying causes.

I was aware of them a long time ago. From the very start I was aware that there was a feeling of friction there which I had hoped would work out because I would say the Sandra Brownwell did far more than she needed to in order to try and resolve the situation.

None of the issues raised were major in nature—nothing that we normally wouldn't be able to resolve by simply talking about them; and if they had been raised in a calmer voice without any idea of indictment, I think that they would have been perfectly justified. There were little things that could be taken care of and were justified in being raised. They were not as serious as these women pretended them to be, however.

Most of the complaints were directed at Sandra. There were some, of course, which were directed at me and at Dan, but for the most part they were upset at Sandra. The woman whom Sandra replaced did pretty routine or petty things like answering the telephone. Though I have heard that some of the people in the teller area considered Sandra's loan-closing duties clerical as well, I think the resentment was there from the very start, and I don't know how to tie it to anything except that it perhaps just may be a threat to one of the women.

I suppose that they would like to see, as perhaps anyone would, a new person coming in to start at the very bottom and work up. Here was a new person coming in and taking a job and, rightly or wrongly, they assumed that she was assuming things that she had no right to assume. And perhaps they concluded also that she was doing things that someone of more advanced status should do and also the salary problem is always with us. Sandra was making more than a normal starter in that area would make, and there was resentment there. As raises were given, there continued to be resentment.

Truthfully, I don't know whether the outcome of the meeting was positive or not. But at least it got it out in the open, and I think and hope that it did blow over to a great extent. After a few shed tears I thinks things did settle down. Of course, I'm sure there's always going to be that undercurrent of resentment or whatever you want to call it. But at least on the surface we seem to be operating fairly well, and perhaps my belief that sometimes doing nothing is better than taking some positive step one way or another is the best way to handle the situation. I'm hoping that in this case doing nothing was really the best way to deal with the problem.

SANDRA BROWNWELL'S ACCOUNT OF THE PROBLEM

I was hired at First Federal to replace Mrs. Doyle, who was dismissed. She had started out performing secretarial-type duties with the hope that she would eventually be able to prepare closing papers and to assist Dan Youngblood, particularly with the closings. So when I was hired, it was with the expectation that I would move into the loan-closing duties. They also mentioned a loan officer's position if I worked out well in loan-closing duties. But initially I performed as secretary, receptionist, etc. I also was given some routine filing, which Marilyn Simon had been performing until I came.

She indicated that she had too much other work to do—which probably was true. I don't know exactly how the filing duties got assigned to my desk. I just know that when I started, there was a stack of files on my desk.

I was not overly pleased with my starting salary of $800 per month. I felt it was too low for what they wanted, but I was told that if I worked out that I could expect a $200 raise per month in six months.

I was first interviewed by Dan Youngblood, vice-president of First Federal. The following day I was interviewed by Mr. Thompson for approximately thirty minutes. He really didn't indicate what my duties would be. He didn't go into this much. Dan Youngblood had talked more about the job duties. Mr. Thompson approached the subject of telling about the fringe benefits of First Federal, such as their retirement plan, the insurance program, and the Christmas bonus. Who I would report to was never discussed, but in effect I was working with Dan and Mr. Thompson. Most of my contact was with Dan—almost 90 percent of it.

As I started working there, it turned out that Mr. Thompson was a little more reserved about giving me any duties. He was reluctant at first to let me do closing papers for him even after I was already doing closing papers and closing the loans for Dan. However, when he did get to the point that he would let me work up his papers, very shortly after that he turned almost 100 percent of the closings over to me. I started closing loans approximately two months after starting the job.

However, they never removed the clerical and filing duties from my job. As a matter of fact, we almost reached a crisis in December. Mr. Thompson was off for two weeks because typically there is very little happening in the savings and loan business at this time of year. This particular December, however, turned out to be the busiest month First Federal had ever had up to that point. I was to close approximately thirty loans in the month. I did not have time to file. I had to take all of the closing papers home with me at night and do several sets. In the morning I would hurry to the office and type them before the people got there. I had no assistance whatsoever.

Dan Youngblood was there, but he was handling loan application interviews and that sort of thing. I was handling all of the closes. I mentioned at one time that I needed help as the papers really started piling up on my desk. But when I did ask for help it caused a problem in the other part of the office because evidently I was in a department by myself—in fact, the only person in the department. (See Case Figure 2 for the office layout of First Federal Savings and Loan Association)

It caused a problem in that when I asked for help on the filing of the title policies, Mr. Thompson, who was by then back from his vacation, had gone directly to one of the women in Elizabeth Anderson's department. He did not go through Elizabeth. I think that was the problem. She resented him going to the person and asking her to help file some of those things.

Elizabeth Anderson was offended that someone else would be helping me because that person worked for her. She really did get up-tight about having to help me. One afternoon she and one other person who worked for her picked up the title policies off my desk and filed them all afternoon. The two of them together voiced their opposition to having to help me, not to me directly but where I could hear it. It was as if she was just trying to make a point.

I had no one to work with or to assist me in any way. It got to the point that I was responsible for all the closings, but I never got rid of any of the initial duties I had been assigned except the answering of the telephone. At first, I answered the telephone for the entire association. I was answering the telephones when I was doing the loan closings, and I would have to be sure and tell them when I was going in the other office to close loans or they wouldn't pick up the telephone. They would never pick up the phone as

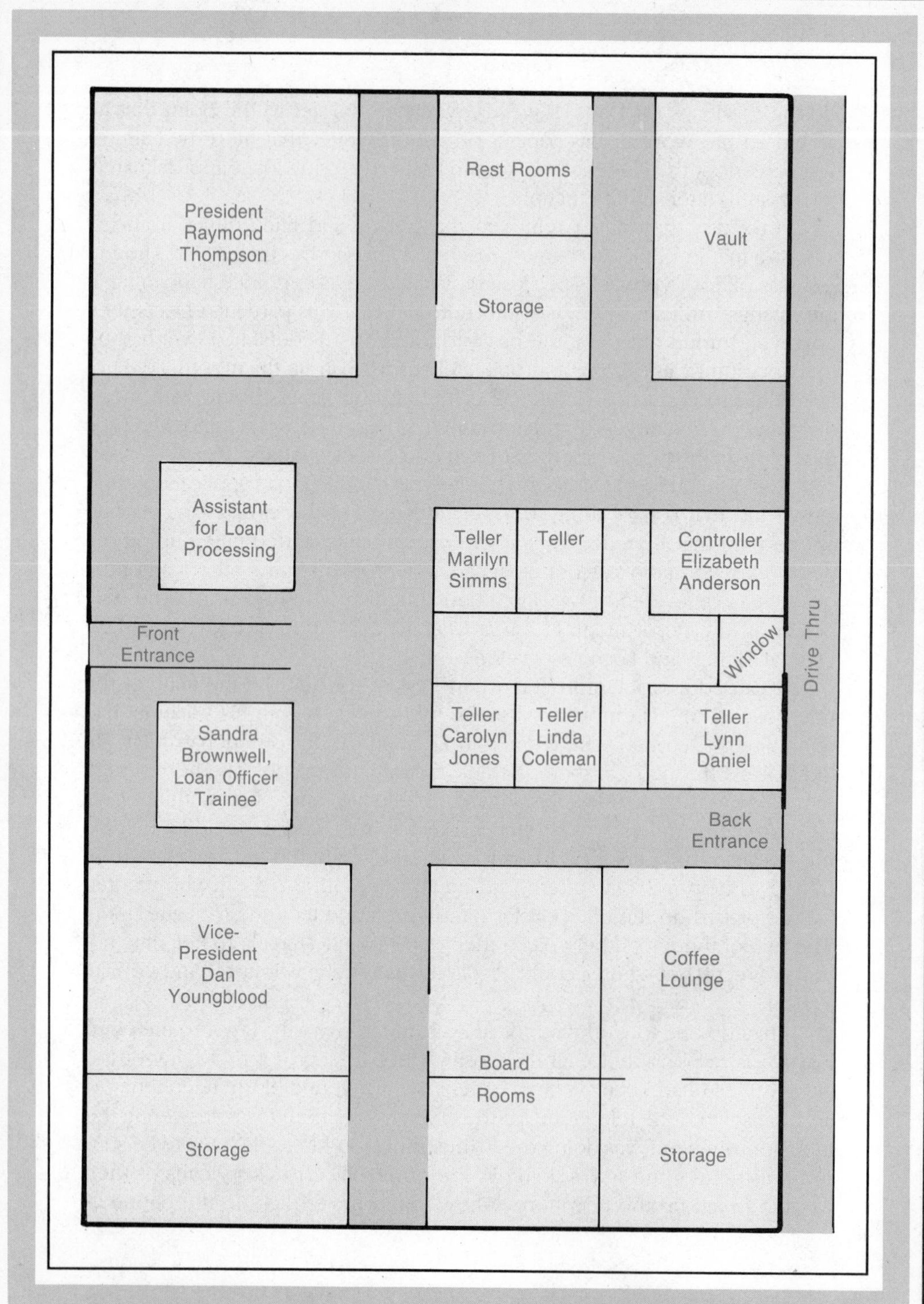

President
Raymond
Thompson
Rest Rooms
Storage
Vault
Assistant
for Loan
Processing
Teller
Marilyn
Simms
Teller
Controller
Elizabeth
Anderson
Front
Entrance
Window
Drive Thru
Sandra
Brownwell,
Loan Officer
Trainee
Teller
Carolyn
Jones
Teller
Linda
Coleman
Teller
Lynn
Daniel
Back
Entrance
Vice-
President
Dan
Youngblood
Coffee
Lounge
Board
Rooms
Storage
Storage

long as I was out there. If I had to go to the ladies' room of if I had to go to the attorney's office, I had to make a point of going over and telling them that I was leaving because they would just let it ring for twenty times before they would pick it up. They thought that was my job.

I first noticed there was a problem that day I asked for some help. I felt like I was in another association. There was one association with the four or five women out front, and I was totally separated. They were friendly enough to me, but they didn't want anything to do with loan closings in any way. Never could I ask for help. Even if I were snowed under with heavy closing schedules, I could not get any help typing the closing papers.

Elizabeth Anderson was the office manager. She supervised the tellers. They would take care of the mortgage payments; they would take care of the CD's and the savings. I'm not really familiar with that. I only worked in the teller position a few times when they got really rushed and they had no one else. I would go to the window and try to make the transaction, but I knew very little about it.

The only area where I interacted with Elizabeth Anderson's office was at the end of a loan closing. After I closed the loan and was sure that all the transactions had been covered and that everything was right, I would take a balance sheet out to her and tell her, "I need these checks." Or what I would do (which turned out to be a major error) would be to walk into the box where the tellers were and ask, "Are any of you free to write checks?" Much to my surprise, that offended Elizabeth because she was the office manager, and she wanted me to come to her and give her the balance sheet and tell her what needed to be done; then she would get up out of her chair and go tell somebody to do it. I did not know until much later that it bothered her for me to ask someone directly to write the checks. I was simply trying to get any of the four people who were authorized to write checks to write them.

In addition to being office manager, Elizabeth was also controller. That is, she was supposedly the office manager; but in face she was office manager in name only. She really made no major decisions. They made them and told her how it was and she resented that—and rightfully so. I think she wanted to have full authority over hiring the people who worked for her.

By "they" I mean Mr. Thompson and Mr. Youngblood. They would hire the people who worked in her area. They would ask her opinion after they interviewed people and let her talk to some of them they were inter-

FIGURE 2 *Office Layout of First Federal Savings and Loan Association* ested in. She would give them her opinion, but they did not necessarily hire whoever she suggested. They hired whoever they felt would be the best qualified—which caused problems again. Also, they determined raises for people in Elizabeth's area. Again, they would discuss it with her after they had made their decisions—which she didn't like either.

On occasion she voiced these feelings to me. At one time when I was given a raise, a person in her office was given a raise also. She did not know about it until after the board meeting, and she resented the fact that they didn't ask her about it. They just told her, "We've given her a $25 raise."

Strangely enough, I always found Elizabeth to be warm to me—at least to my face. She could be very kind and helpful. But I learned that if there were ever any problems, she would go to Mr. Thompson afterward and be very critical of the way I handled the problem. She would never talk to me about it to my face. I learned about this from Dan Youngblood. He told me if there was a problem and discussed it with me. Occasionally Mr. Thompson would talk to me about it.

Mr. Thompson would indicate to me that the people up front, that is, in the teller area, really did not realize all that was involved in closing a loan. They acted as if it was just a clerical position. But Mr. Thompson himself never really talked in specific terms about what the position was that I did hold.

So, except as Dan and Mr. Thompson occasionally would indicate to me, I did not have any real evidence that Elizabeth resented me. As a matter of fact it was very much of a surprise to me that she resented me because she did such a good job of covering it up. I will always think that she basically liked me, but she resented the fact that she did not think they appreciated her position and that for years she had worked for too little pay.

In the weeks prior to this blow-up, we got along well for the most part. As to the staff meeting which laid everything out in the open, I really didn't have any idea as to the agenda for the meeting which was requested. I had been especially busy at that time, and I was just told that there would be a staff meeting the next morning. I didn't even know who requested the meeting.

But, as it turned out, the women in the teller's area were the ones who wanted the meeting. It had always been understood that if there was a problem which we needed to discuss that we could call a meeting. The tellers told Mr. Thompson that they would like to have a meeting, and he then informed the rest of the association.

It's my recollection that Mr. Thompson started the meeting that morning by indicating that the tellers had wanted to have a meeting to discuss something. From what I can remember Elizabeth Anderson said very little. It seems to me that Linda Coleman had a list of complaints.

These complaints were never voiced directly against me; the truth of the matter is on a lot of the things, Mr. Thompson was the most guilty party. It was just the way things had been handled for one reason or the other. As a matter of fact, there weren't three of the complaints that were anything other than little silly picky things, like the way I answered the telephone. Once I answered the phone when Linda Coleman was out of the office, and one of the people up front answered it at the same time. The party asked to speak to me. I said, "This is Sandra Brownwell." It offended the person in the other office because she said that I should have hung up and let her buzz me to tell me I was wanted on the telephone. She said that I was rude. Everything as I can remember was just about that picky.

I believe the real resentment was that I was the only one out of the five women in the office who had even the first day of college. Also, they saw that I was ahead of each of them salary-wise and fast approaching Elizabeth. I feel that they definitely resented that I was likely to move into a loan officer's position. For some reason this bothered them—that is, that I would be part of the management of the organization. To show the extent of this resentment, Elizabeth once questioned Mr. Thompson about a person he was considering. She asked, "Are we not going to hire anybody but people with college degrees or college professors for husbands?" I think both of these charges really were slams back at me. They did not want to hire anyone who had a college background regardless of the qualifications because they felt threatened.

Our office opened at 8:30 and as I recall the meeting was still going on then. I remember that we had to close the office door because a customer came in and Elizabeth was hurling accusations at me about all the things that I had not done. For example, I had not always come straight to her when checks needed to be written but instead had sometimes directly asked one of her people to write the checks.

As I said, Linda Coleman had a list. She had apparently given considerable thought to the meeting. In fact, I had the feeling they had huddled together and planned all that they were going to bring up that morning. Elizabeth was careful to try and stay in the background and let Linda handle most of the charges—in effect, to run interference for her. Only when I would put someone down because their accusations were so petty would Elizabeth come in and try to help bail them out. She wanted to stay in the background, but she was obviously in favor of the items they brought up that morning.

I had the feeling that Elizabeth and the women who worked for her not only constituted a formal organization but a sort of an informal group as well. They were always kind enough to me, but never was I a part of their group. This did not bother me because I did not really want to be a part of their clique. In fact, I had very little in common with them. I had most of my contact with Mr. Thompson and Dan Youngblood.

After the meeting I had a talk with both Dan and Mr. Thompson and indicated to them that I didn't quite understand what had happened. They both felt like it was an obvious confrontation and that it was poorly handled by those requesting the meeting.

I also met later with Elizabeth Anderson to discuss some of the points brought up in the meeting. However, before we met she had a couple of meetings later that same day with Mr. Thompson. I didn't really know too much about what happened, but Dan did mention the fact that Elizabeth told Mr. Thompson that either I was going to go or she was going to go—that she just couldn't work with me. Mr. Thompson told her that it wasn't going to be handled that way. I think that they backed her up a little bit from her rigid position.

I actually think she tried to get me fired. When I had a meeting with her a couple of days later I told her that I really didn't understand all that had happened. I expressed my concern about her going directly to Mr. Thompson about problems rather than coming to me and talking them out. She told me that she thought it was her job to go to Mr. Thompson with these situations. She was rather depressed in our meeting and indicated that they had not been very supportive of her in the conversations held after the staff meeting. She said they "talked to me worse than a dog."

Assuming that I stay with First Federal, I still believe that I will work into a loan officer's position. They told me that if the association continued to grow they would need another loan officer.

Questions

1. What are the major problems at First Federal Savings and Loan of Portland?
2. What are the primary causes of the problems at First Federal and how did Mr. Thompson, Mrs. Brownwell, and Mrs. Anderson contribute to the situation?

3. Explain the organizational structure at First Federal. How clear were the responsibilities and authority of the personnel at First Federal?
4. How have the role perceptions of Sandra Brownwell and Elizabeth Anderson contributed to the situation described in the case?
5. Chart the informal organization at First Federal. What is the role of the informal organization at the savings and loan? What functions does the informal organization appear to be fulfilling? Which are positive and which are negative?
6. Describe how status, power, and politics have influenced the people in this organization
7. How did the lack of clearly defined and carefully communicated personnel policies affect management at First Federal Savings and Loan?

PART

IV

Influencing

KEY TERMS

motivation
motives
Theory X
Theory Y
hierarchy of needs
E-R-G theory
hygiene factors
motivators
need for achievement
need for power
need for affiliation
expectancy
valence
reinforcement theory
organizational behavior modification (OBM)
reinforcers
equity
self-fulfilling prophecies
job design
job enrichment
job enlargement
quality circles
Theory Z
Seven S Model

LEARNING OBJECTIVES

After completing this chapter you should be able to

1. Define motivation and explain some basic philosophies of human nature.
2. Distinguish between the motivation theories of Abraham Maslow and Clayton Alderfer.
3. Explain the motivation theory of Frederick Herzberg.
4. Describe the work of David McClelland as it relates to motivation.
5. Explain how expectancy theory, organizational behavior modification, and the self-fulfilling prophecy might be applied in business.
6. Explain job design and its relationship to job enrichment and job enlargement.

10

Motivation

> Bill Brown, a machine operator for New York Manufacturing Company, thought he had a great idea for increasing production. Bill was modifying the machine setup when his supervisor, John Weems, walked by and said, "Hey, Bill what's going on? What are you doing?" Bill said, "Guess what, John. I have figured out how to increase production by . . . ." At this point, John interrupted Bill by saying, "That's not your job. You're not supposed to modify the machines around here—your job is to do the work. If I catch you doing that again, we're going to have some real trouble. You do it my way or you're fired."

This type of motivation may have worked at the turn of the century, but today many employees would tell their supervisor to "take this job and shove it." Today's "new breed" of employees does not respond to "traditional" values that might have motivated them twenty or thirty years ago. Employees in today's organizations are better educated, more highly skilled, and work with more advanced technology. They have significantly higher expectations, which creates difficult challenges for managers.

In general, our society has achieved a higher quality of life, and people expect the improvements resulting from this higher living standard will continue. In addition, there have been rather significant changes in the makeup of the labor force. In 1982, 43 percent of the labor force was female compared to 30 percent in 1960. Along with the increased size and complexity of today's organizations, the proportion of manual workers relative to the number of professional and technical workers in the total labor force has declined. These changes provide a significant challenge to managers to provide a climate in which employees will contribute toward the accomplishment of organizational goals.

In view of these major developments, the manager must ask, "How do I create a climate that will motivate my employees to perform more effectively and efficiently?" This question reflects one of the most challenging aspects of a manager's job. The topic of motivation is one of the most important and frequently discussed subjects in management. In this chapter, the objective of our discussion is to provide managerial insight into the following concepts:

- The process of motivation
- Philosophies of human nature
- Theories of motivation
- Approaches and techniques available to enhance motivation

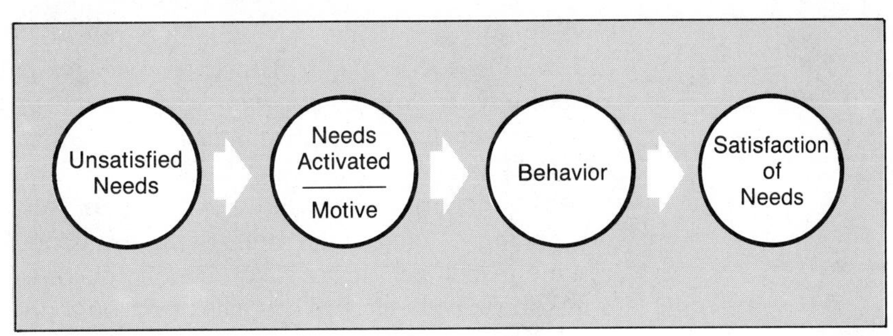

FIGURE 10-1

The Motivation Process

MOTIVATION DEFINED

Motivating a worker today is considerably more complex than the simple application of the "carrot and the stick" approach used by many managers of yesterday. *motivation* **Motivation** is the process of influencing or stimulating a person to take action by creating a work environment whereby the goals of the organization and the needs of people are satisfied. In an organization, personnel are said to be motivated if they perform their jobs efficiently and effectively.

In Figure 10-1, a basic but simple model of motivation is illustrated. Everyone has certain needs. A person cannot be motivated until a need is activated (this need activation is referred to as a motive). *motives* **Motives** explain why people engage in certain behavior and are the drives or impulses within an individual that cause the behavior.

An aroused need (motive) will cause some type of behavior to take place. Such behavior is directed toward a particular goal or want that the person has learned will satisfy the need. For example, a person who feels hunger has a need for food. This results in action designed ultimately to obtain food. In our complex society, this typically entails searching for and obtaining a job so that money can be secured. The successful accomplishment of this goal or want results in food being obtained and, thus, the satisfaction of the need. Or a person may feel a need to associate with other people. This leads to actions of searching out other individuals and associating and interacting with them in the hope of obtaining the goal of friendship.

The simple explanation of motivation does not represent the true complexity of the process. Any single act by a particular person may well be reflecting a number of different needs. Striving for a promotion may be caused by a need for material possessions or a need for recognition. The same act by another person may be due to different needs. One person may seek friendships to satisfy his or her need for association with other people, whereas another individual may wish to use friendships for advancing a career. One person seeks recognition through hard work; another seeks it by being the fastest driver on the highway. The same need can be expressed in a number of different ways.

Management has traditionally relied on the use of rewards such as increased pay, job security, and good working conditions, or punishments such as dismissal, demotions, or withholding rewards to motivate employees to achieve high performance. However, management in today's environment cannot rely on the *manipulation* of pay, benefits, or working conditions to motivate personnel to perform effectively. Motivation is a much more complicated process.

The modern manager must be sufficiently aware of basic human needs and attempt to understand much of the behavior observed. Managers cannot assume that all people are alike. The one major commonality is that there is a reason for all behavior. The manager would do well not to condemn any act as being idiotic, pointless, or senseless. In the eyes of the individual, the behavior makes sense. The manager must seek to understand the forces that energize the behavior. It is the responsibility of the manager to develop an effective work environment or climate that will make use of the enormous energy that is within every person. In essence, then, a manager's major task in "motivating" personnel is to create and develop a climate or environment in which they will want to be productive, contributing members of the organization.

PHILOSOPHIES OF HUMAN NATURE

In order to learn how to create an environment conducive to a high level of employee motivation, it is essential that managers develop a more complete understanding of the philosophies of human nature.

The assumptions that managers have regarding other people are a major factor in determining the climate for motivation. For instance, John Weems, the supervisor mentioned at the beginning of the chapter, may believe that employees are not capable of being creative. When Bill had an idea that he thought would increase production output, John quickly disregarded and reprimanded Bill for his suggestions. A manager's positive or negative view of human nature has a major influence on the process of motivation.

Words of Advice

Work in a basic unit such as manufacturing or technical department for two to three years. Move into sales, then marketing (MBA helpful). Take on as much responsibility as possible. Make presentations. Move into a position when you can run (or have major influence on) a segment of the business. Set goals and work hard to meet them.

JAMES A. MACK, President and General Manager, Chemicals Division, Sherwin-Williams Company

---

McGregor's Theory X and Theory Y

Douglas McGregor stressed the importance of understanding the relationships between motivation and philosophies of human nature.[1] In observing the practices and approaches of traditional managers, McGregor believed that managers usually attempt to motivate employees by one of two basic approaches. He referred to these approaches as Theory X and Theory Y.

Theory X

Theory X, or the traditional view of management, suggests that managers are required to coerce, control, or threaten employees in order to motivate them. In contrast, McGregor proposed an alternative philosophy of human nature, which he referred to as **Theory Y**. Following Theory Y, a manager basically believes people are capable of being responsible and mature. Thus, employees do not require coercion or excessive control by the manager in order to perform effectively. McGregor's basic belief was that Theory Y is a more realistic assessment of people.

Theory Y

Table 10-1 illustrates the different assumptions of these two philosophies of human nature. The Theory Y assumptions represent the manager's high degree of faith in the capacity and potential of people. If one accepts the Theory Y philosophy of human nature, managerial practices such as the following will be seriously considered: (1) abandonment of time clocks, (2) flexible working hours on an individual basis, (3) job enrichment, (4) management by objectives, and (5) participative decision making. All are based on the beliefs that abilities are widespread in the population and each person is trusted to behave in a responsible manner. Thus, management would create an environment that will permit workers to be motivated to fully utilize their potential. However, one should not conclude that McGregor advocated Theory Y as the panacea for all managerial problems. The Theory

TABLE 10-1. *A Comparison of McGregor's Theory X and Theory Y Assumptions about Human Nature*

Theory X	Theory Y
The average person inherently dislikes work and will avoid it if possible.	The expenditure of physical and mental effort in work is as natural as play or rest.
Because of the dislike of work, most people must be coerced, controlled, directed, and threatened with punishment to get them to perform effectively.	People will exercise self-direction and self-control in the service of objectives to which they are committed.
The average person lacks ambition, avoids responsibility, and seeks security and economic rewards above all else.	Commitment to objectives is a function of the rewards associated with achievement.
Most people lack creative ability and are resistant to change.	The average person learns, under proper conditions, not only to accept but to seek responsibility.
Since most people are self-centered, they are not concerned with the goals of the organization.	The capacity to exercise a relatively high degree of imagination, ingenuity, and creativity in the solution of organizational problems is widely, not narrowly, distributed in the population.

Source: Based on Douglas McGregor. *The Human Side of Enterprise* (New York: McGraw-Hill, 1960).

•CAREER PROFILE•

DORIS C. ETELSON
Vice-President—Service Standards
Howard Johnson's

Doris C. Etelson has been in the restaurant business since she started working at her family's restaurant as a girl—"from pot-sink up." Her success as a manager is even more significant when one considers that Doris wears two hats—a family person and a successful business executive. The Etelsons were married in 1950, and for the first years of their marriage, Mrs. Etelson owned and operated a cafeteria in an industrial plant. She stopped working between 1958 and 1961 to care for her two young daughters.

In 1961, she joined Howard Johnson as a food supervisor for seven restaurants. Doris became head supervisor for twenty-five restaurants in 1965 and in 1968 became area manager. She was named staff assistant to a divisional manager in 1970 and advanced to director of administration in 1972. While working upward in Howard Johnson's, Doris was also obtaining her college degree in economics from the State University of New York in 1974 and is currently working toward her M.B.A. In 1977, she was named to her present position as vice-president—service standards. Her current job entails finding ways of upgrading the quality of customer service at Howard Johnson's and the development of new concepts. The job carries a profit and loss responsibility.

Progression into top management has not been an easy one, but from the beginning, Doris has had a clear-cut goal of going "as far as I could in management and to take it step by step." Her husband owns a successful air-freight company in Newark, New Jersey, and she works in Boston. In order to maintain two successful careers, every weekend Mrs. Etelson drives or hops on a plane to visit Mr. Etelson. Twice a week, her husband takes a plane to Boston. Two days a week, they are apart. They have been able to keep this schedule because their children are in their twenties and are no longer at home and because Mr. Etelson has encouraged his wife's career. Her husband, she says, is a "totally emancipated man. He's my best supporter in pursuing career goals."

For Mrs. Etelson, the most important aspect of any job is the "ability and willingness to make a tremendous effort. I'm constantly preparing for the next job, willing to do more than necessary. I have a policy of total involvement in whatever I'm doing. I definitely aspire to move to the very top of my potential." Doris Etelson is a person of tomorrow. "Looking ahead means making changes. Change is never easy, but the only alternative is standing still." The career pattern of the Etelsons is one that may increase significantly in the future as more and more women aspire to fulfill their full potential.

Y philosophy is not utopia, but McGregor argued that it did provide a basis for improved management and organizational performance.

Argyris's Maturity Theory

The research of Chris Argyris has also aided managers in developing a more complete understanding of human behavior. Argyris emphasized the importance of the process of maturity. He suggests that there is a basic difference between the demands of the mature personality and the demands of the typical organization. Argyris concluded that if plans, policies, and methods/procedures are prescribed in detail, an employee will need to be submissive and passive, which suggests a *Theory X* type of organization. The demand is for the subordinate to concentrate on the orders as given and not question or attempt to understand these orders in a broader perspective. In brief, such a detailed prescription may ask individuals to work in an environment where:

1. they are provided minimal control over their workaday world.
2. they are expected to be passive, dependent, and subordinate.
3. they are expected to have a short time perspective.
4. they are induced to perfect and value the frequent use of a few shallow abilities.
5. they are expected to produce under conditions leading to psychological failure.[2]

When the mature employee encounters the conditions described above, three reactions are possible:

1. **Escape.** An employee may escape by quitting the job, being absent from work, or attempting to climb to higher levels in the firm where the structure is less rigid.
2. **Fight.** A person can "fight the system" by exerting pressure on the organization by means of informal groups or through formally organized labor unions.
3. **Adapt.** The most typical reaction by employees is one of adaptation by developing an attitude of apathy or indifference. The employee "plays the game," and pay becomes the compensation for the penalty of working.

According to Argyris, adaptation is the least representative of good mental health.

Managers cannot assume that all employees are mature as defined by Argyris or Theory Y types as defined by McGregor. These assumptions may be valid when managers are dealing with highly educated professional, technical, and managerial employees, but security may mean more to the industrial worker than to the highly educated professional. The industrial worker may value the freedom of thought permitted by the highly structured and repetitive tasks that may be boring to others.

It could be argued that a highly structured environment requires employees to act in an immature manner. In fact, managers have conditioned employees to prefer that type of behavior. Many people can and have adjusted to tightly regimented work situations that Argyris contends would demand immature behavior. One need only observe workers on an assembly line to recognize this conclusion. The resulting condition or adaptation is one of indifference and apathy, which may be a successful, acceptable adaptation. However, only a fraction of the jobs in American business are of the highly structured, totally controlled type. To the degree that an open job market operates effectively, there will be some matching of varying human needs and organizational demands.

The philosophical theories of human nature discussed above provide the basis for a manager's approach to motivation and leadership. As such, the theories of both McGregor and Argyris should be kept in mind as we discuss the various concepts of human motivation in this chapter and as we discuss leadership styles in Chapter 11.

MOTIVATION THEORIES

There are nearly as many theories of motivation as there are psychologists who develop them. Because of the vast amount of difference associated with the theories, the acceptance of one may actually mean that another theory will be rejected. None of the theories provides a universally accepted approach that explains all human behavior. Human beings are far too complex. However, a basic understanding of these theories can be useful to managers as they attempt to motivate people in their organizations. Our purpose in presenting different theories of human motivation is not to identify one as being superior. Rather, it is to develop a thought process that will ultimately lead managers to their own concept of motivation.

Maslow's Hierarchy of Needs

Many psychologists believe that there are certain patterns or configurations of human needs, although there obviously are individual differences. A common approach to establishing this need pattern is that of developing a universal need hierarchy. Abraham Maslow has proposed one widely accepted pattern, which is illustrated in Figure 10-2. Examples of how an organization might help to satisfy these basic needs are also presented. Maslow states that individuals are motivated to satisfy certain unsatisfied needs. His theory of human motivation is based on the following assumptions:

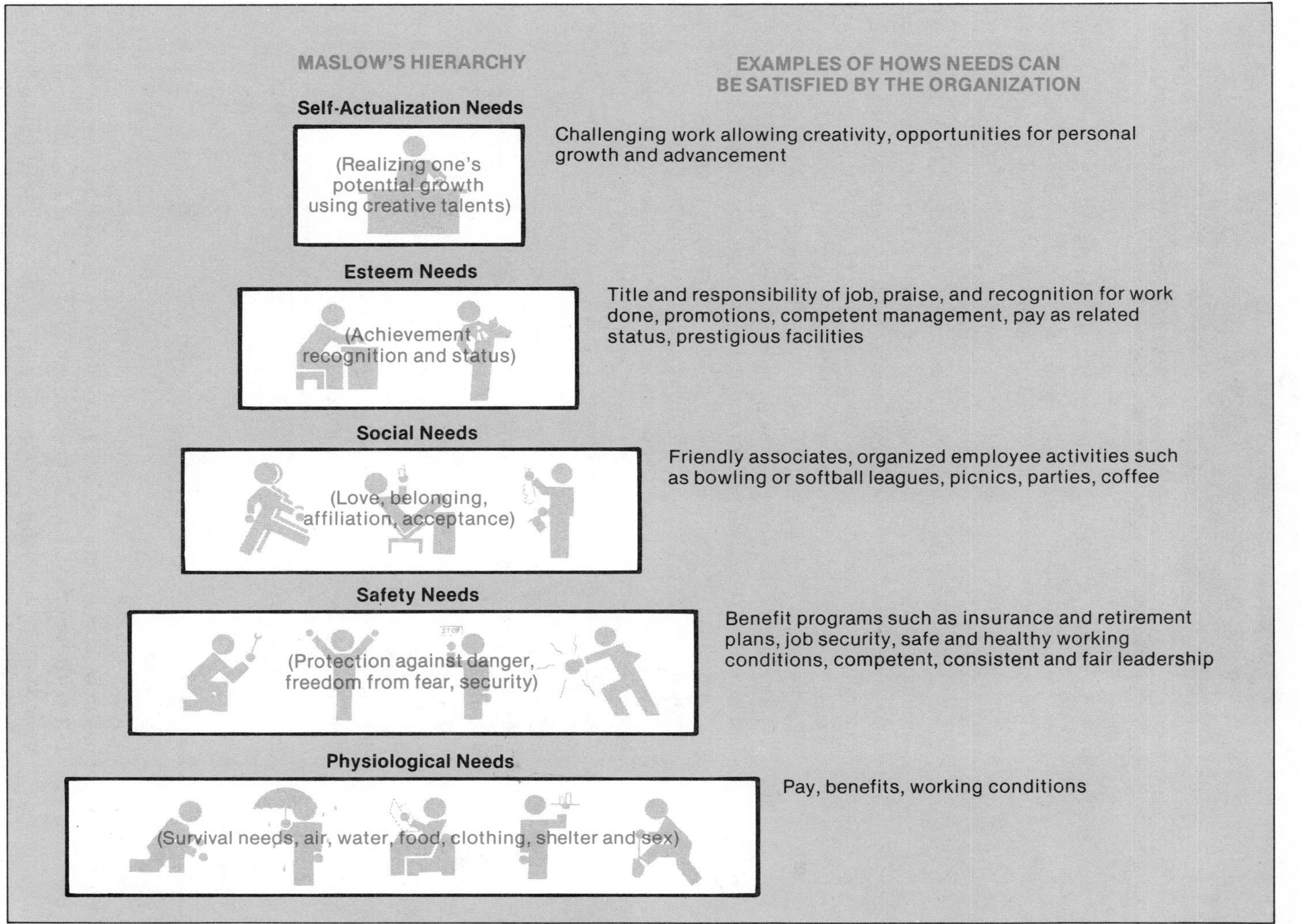

FIGURE 10-2 *Maslow's Need Hierarchy and How Needs Are Satisfied by the Organization* [*Data (for diagram) based on Hierarchy of Needs in "A Theory of Human Motivation" in* Motivation and Personality, *2nd Edition, by Abraham H. Maslow. Copyright © 1970 by Abraham H. Maslow. By permission of Harper & Row, Publishers, Inc.*]

- Needs that are not satisfied motivate or influence behavior. Satisfied needs do not motivate behavior.
- Needs are arranged according to a hierarchy of importance.
- An individual's needs at any level on the hierarchy emerge only when the lower-level needs are reasonably well satisfied.[3]

hierarchy of needs

According to Maslow's **hierarchy of needs** theory, an individual's needs are arranged in a hierarchy from the lower-level physiological needs to the higher-level needs for self-actualization. The physiological needs are the highest priority because until they are reasonably satisfied, other higher-level needs will not emerge to motivate behavior.

A person is never completely satisfied on any need level, but a sufficient amount of gratification of lower-priority needs must be met if the individual is to seek to satisfy upper-level needs. Maslow suggests a hypothetical example for an average person who is 85 percent satisfied in physiological needs, 70 percent in safety needs, 50 percent in love needs, 40 percent in the self-esteem category, and 10 percent in self-actualization needs.

The use of the universal needs hierarchy by a manager in motivating employees is based on the concept that reasonably well-satisfied needs do not motivate. Therefore, if an individual's lower-level needs are fairly well satisfied, management cannot use these needs to motivate behavior.

While Maslow's theory of human needs is widely known and adopted by many practicing managers, some research studies have contradicted it. These studies suggest that there are only two or three distinct categories of needs, not five as Maslow proposed. In addition, some critics question the *order* of the hierarchy of needs. It is argued that while considerable importance is placed on physiological needs if they have not been satisfied, a person does not move up the hierarchy in an orderly or predictable manner once the physiological needs are satisfied. A clear-cut pattern of the progression of needs that require satisfaction has not emerged. According to Maslow, a need that has been relatively well satisfied ceases to motivate. This may well be the case for the physiological, security, and social needs. But such a conclusion may not be warranted if we are talking about the upper-level needs of esteem and self-actualization, achievement, recognition, or acceptance of responsibility.

Alderfer's E-R-G Theory

E-R-G theory

Clayton Alderfer has developed a more modern version of Maslow's needs hierarchy, which he referred to as the existence-relatedness-growth, or **E-R-G theory.**[4] Alderfer's theory is an attempt to make Maslow's theory more consistent with knowledge of human needs. Table 10-2 illustrates the relationship between Alderfer's and Maslow's theories of human needs. Alderfer's classification condensed Maslow's categorization into three categories of needs:

TABLE 10-2. *Alderfer's and Maslow's Theories: A Comparison*

Needs theories	Level 1	Level 2	Level 3
Maslow's hierarchy of needs theory	Physiological needs	Social needs, security needs	Self-fulfillment needs, esteem needs
Alderfer's E-R-G theory	Existence needs	Relatedness needs	Growth needs

- **Existence Needs.** Types of physical or material needs
- **Relatedness Needs.** Relationships with other people
- **Growth Needs.** All forms of creative efforts to achieve or gain recognition to satisfy needs for esteem and attain high degree of personal fulfillment.

In contrast to the satisfaction of existence and relatedness needs, the importance of growth needs may increase as an individual achieves satisfaction of these needs. According to the E-R-G theory, each level becomes increasingly abstract and more difficult to satisfy. While some individuals follow a logical progression in satisfying needs from level 1 through 3, some people experience frustration. A person who is unable to satisfy growth needs reverts back one level and concentrates on the more concrete relatedness or existence needs.

Richard McKnight, an assembly-line worker, has a job that fails to satisfy his need for recognition or personal satisfaction. Frustrated by this, Richard concentrates on improving his personal relationships and friendships with other employees and gaining additional pay and job security.

Herzberg's Motivation-Hygiene Theory

One of the most widely known and controversial theories of motivation is that of Frederick Herzberg.[5] His motivation-hygiene theory grew out of research directed toward determining what factors lead to satisfaction on the job. The usual approach is one of examining a number of factors, such as the work itself, pay, working conditions, supervision, status, and security.

The Herzberg theory proposes that there are in reality two significantly different classes of factors and thus two different continuums. One class, referred to as hygiene factors, makes up a continuum ranging from dissatisfaction to no dissatisfaction. As illustrated in Figure 10-3, **hygiene factors** relate to the environment and are external to the job. Herzberg indicates that these factors do not serve to promote job satisfaction; rather, their absence or deficiency can create dissatisfaction. Hygiene factors "maintain" an employee; they do not make a person healthy but rather prevent unhealthiness. An organization that meets the hygiene needs of its employees will eliminate dissatisfaction but will not motivate employees to work harder.

hygiene factors

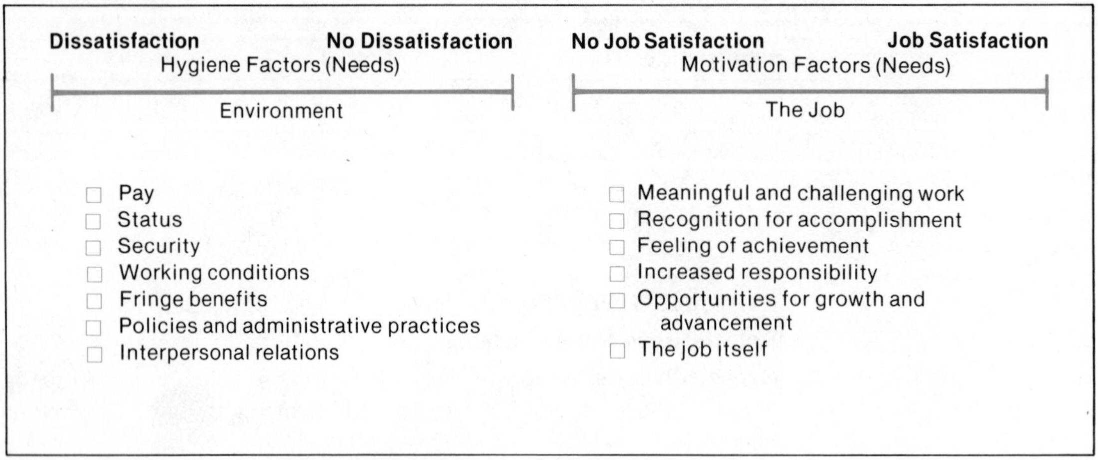

Dissatisfaction	No Dissatisfaction	No Job Satisfaction	Job Satisfaction
Hygiene Factors (Needs)		Motivation Factors (Needs)	
Environment		The Job	

Hygiene factors:
- ☐ Pay
- ☐ Status
- ☐ Security
- ☐ Working conditions
- ☐ Fringe benefits
- ☐ Policies and administrative practices
- ☐ Interpersonal relations

Motivation factors:
- ☐ Meaningful and challenging work
- ☐ Recognition for accomplishment
- ☐ Feeling of achievement
- ☐ Increased responsibility
- ☐ Opportunities for growth and advancement
- ☐ The job itself

FIGURE 10-3 *Motivation and Hygiene Factors*

motivators

The second class of factors or needs, referred to as **motivators,** makes up a continuum leading from "not motivated" to "highly motivated." As illustrated in Figure 10-3, the work itself, recognition, achievement, possibility of growth, and advancement are motivation needs. These are concerned with the work itself rather than its surrounding physical, administrative, or social environment. They are internal to the job, and if the worker is to be truly motivated, the job is the major source of that motivation.

Herzberg's theory seems to suggest a clear delineation between motivators and hygiene in terms of absolute categories—pay is categorized as a hygiene factor for each individual. Pay may be a dissatisfier to some individuals and a satisfier to others. Thus, it can be argued that hygiene and motivation factors should not be considered as absolute categories.

Specific criticisms of Herzberg's theory include the following:

1. The research methodology using the critical incident technique of asking people to reflect back on experiences may cause people to recall only the most recent experiences. Also, analysis of the responses derived from this approach is highly subjective.
2. The theory is most applicable to knowledge workers—managers, engineers, accountants, and other professional-level personnel. Thus, it is not possible to say that the findings apply equally to other occupational groups. Most studies have shown that when the employees are professional or managerial-level employees, the theory is applicable. However, studies of lower-level or manual workers are less supportive of the theory.
3. The theory focuses too much attention on "satisfaction" or "dissatisfaction" rather than on the performance level of the individual. Satisfaction may or may not be directly related to job performance.

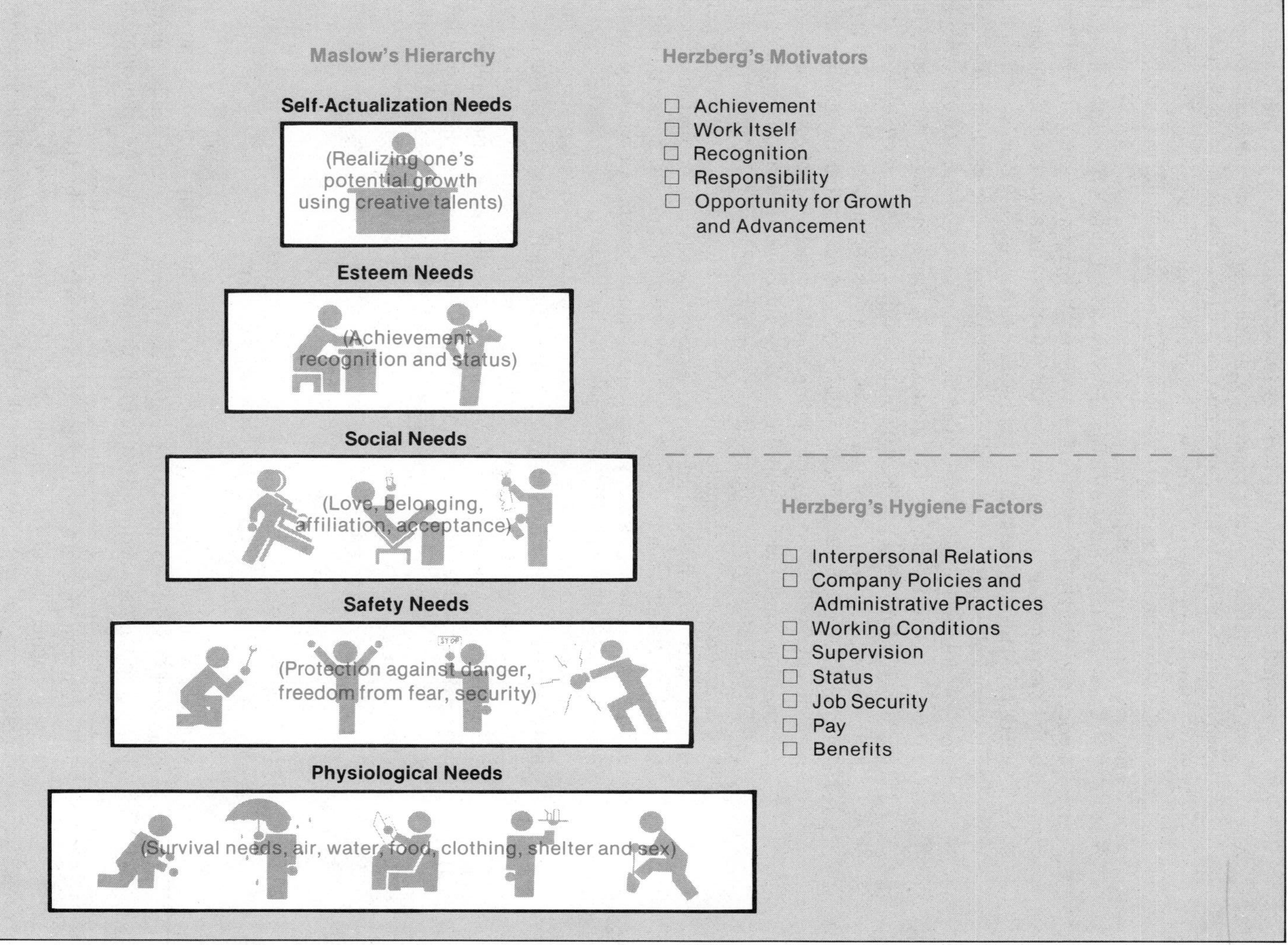
Maslow's Hierarchy
Self-Actualization Needs
(Realizing one's potential growth using creative talents)
Esteem Needs
(Achievement recognition and status)
Social Needs
(Love, belonging, affiliation, acceptance)
Safety Needs
(Protection against danger, freedom from fear, security)
STOP
Physiological Needs
(Survival needs, air, water, food, clothing, shelter and sex)
Herzberg's Motivators
Achievement
Work Itself
Recognition
Responsibility
Opportunity for Growth and Advancement
Herzberg's Hygiene Factors
Interpersonal Relations
Company Policies and Administrative Practices
Working Conditions
Supervision
Status
Job Security
Pay
Benefits

FIGURE 10-4 *Maslow and Herzberg Related*

Despite these criticisms, Herzberg's two-factor theory has made a significant contribution toward improving a manager's basic understanding of motivation. As a result, managers must be aware of the potentially successful application of the theory as our work force becomes increasingly better educated and develops higher expectations of management and as organizational life becomes more complex.

There is a fairly close relationship between Maslow's hierarchy of needs theory and Herzberg's motivation-hygiene theory (see Figure 10-4). Herzberg's *motivators* are most closely related to the esteem and self-actualization needs on Maslow's hierarchy. The hygiene factors closely correspond to the physiological, safety, and social needs. Herzberg's basic contention is that most organizations give inadequate attention to the *motivation factors* in the work environment. Most of the efforts of managers are concentrated on meeting the low-level needs, which are satisfied by the *hygiene factors.* But just because the hygiene or maintenance needs are satisfied—by good pay, benefits, or working conditions—this does not mean that the individual's performance will be positively influenced. To achieve effectiveness, the organization must satisfy both the hygiene and the motivation needs of its employees. Most organizations have given considerable attention to the hygiene needs but inadequate attention to the motivation needs of its personnel. This is understandable since hygiene needs can be met in a more tangible or specific manner than can the motivational needs. It may be easier to provide employees with improved pay, fringe benefits, or working conditions than a job that is more responsible or challenging.

Advocates of Herzberg's two-factor theory of motivation suggest that management can assist employees in meeting their motivational needs by providing employees with more challenging and responsible jobs. According to Herzberg, increasing the level of autonomy, skill variety, task significance, and feedback will lead to a better job performance and more satisfied employees. This is known as *job enrichment,* which will be discussed later in the chapter.

McClelland's Manifest Needs Theory

Whereas Maslow's theory stresses a universal hierarchy of needs, the research of David McClelland emphasizes that there are certain needs that are learned and socially acquired as the individual interacts with the environment. McClelland's manifest needs theory is concerned with how individual needs and environmental factors combine to form three basic human motives: the need for achievement (*n Ach*), the need for power (*n Pow*), and the need for affiliation (*n Aff*). As previously discussed, motives explain behavior. McClelland conducted numerous studies attempting to define and measure basic human motives.

Need for Achievement

need for achievement A person with a high **need for achievement** tends to be characterized as an individual who

- wants to take personal responsibility for finding solutions to problems.
- is goal oriented.
- seeks a challenge—and establishes moderate, realistic, and attainable goals that involve risk but are not impossible to attain.
- desires concrete feedback on performance.
- has a high level of energy and is willing to work hard.

People exhibiting a high *n Ach* have found the above pattern of behavior personally rewarding. McClelland's research has shown that a high *n Ach* is probably a strong or dominant need in only 10 percent of the U.S. population. Persons high in the need for achievement tend to gravitate toward entrepreneurial and sales positions. In these occupations, individuals are better able to "manage" themselves and satisfy the basic drive for achievement.

Need for Power

need for power A high **need for power** means that an individual seeks to influence or control others. Such an individual tends to be characterized by the following types of behavior:

- Is concerned with acquiring, exercising, or retaining power or influence over others.
- Likes to compete with others in situations that allow him or her to be dominant.
- Enjoys confrontations with others.

McClelland says that there are two basic aspects of power: positive and negative. Positive use of power is essential if a manager is to accomplish results through the efforts of others. The negative "face" of power is when an individual seeks power for his or her own personal benefit, which may prove detrimental to the organization.[6]

Need for Affiliation

need for affiliation The **need for affiliation** is related to the desire for affection and establishing friendly relationships. A person with a high need for affiliation tends to be characterized as one who—

- seeks to establish and maintain friendships and close emotional relationships with others.
- wants to be liked by others.

- enjoys parties, social activities, and "bull" sessions.
- seeks a sense of belonging by joining groups or organizations.

To varying degrees, each of us possesses these three motives. However, one of the needs will tend to be more characteristic of the individual than the other two.[7] People in a given culture may have the same needs, but the relative strength of those needs differs. Each of the three motives evokes a different type of feeling of satisfaction. For example, the achievement motive tends to evoke a sense of accomplishment, whereas a manager may have a feeling of being in control or influencing others when the power motive is prevalent. According to this theory, the probability that an individual will perform a job effectively and efficiently depends on a combination of:

- The strength of the motive or need relative to other needs
- The possibility of success in performing the task
- The strength value of the incentive or reward for performance

The most effective mixture of these three motives depends on the situation. In studies of over 500 managers, it was concluded that the most effective managers have a high need for power, a moderate need for achievement, and a low need for affiliation. These managers tended to use their power in a participative manner for the good of the organization. Managers had a moderate need for achievement, but it was not strong enough to interfere with the management process. After all, management is getting things done through the efforts of others and not shoving them aside so that you can do the task yourself.

Outstanding sales personnel tend to be high in the need for achievement and moderately high in the need for power. Entrepreneurs who develop ideas and promote specific enterprises tend to be high in achievement motivation. They delight in personally solving problems and getting immediate feedback on the degree of success. Entrepreneurs sometimes are unable to make the transition to top-level management positions. Their need for personal achievement gets in the way of the requirements for effectively influencing the organization's employees.

Vroom's Expectancy Theory of Motivation

It is essential for managers to develop an understanding of human needs and the variety of organizational means available to satisfy the needs of employees. However, the *needs* approach to motivation as developed by Maslow, Alderfer, and Herzberg does not adequately account for differences in individual employees or explain why people behave in certain ways in accomplishing goals. Victor Vroom developed an approach to motivation known as *expectancy theory* **expectancy theory** that attempts to explain behavior in terms of an individual's goals, choices, and the expectations of achieving these goals.[8] It assumes people can determine which outcomes they prefer and make realistic estimates of the chances of obtaining them.

The key concepts of the expectancy theory are that motivation depends on:

expectancy

- An individual's **expectancy** (his or her perception of the chances or probability) that a particular outcome will occur as a result of certain behavior
- How much value an individual places on a specific outcome is known as **valence**

valence

These factors—expectancy and valence—determine motivation. Both must be present before a high level of motivation can occur. In other words, a high expectancy or a high valence alone will not ensure motivation. For example, if an employee had a low expectancy (perceived little chance) of receiving a pay increase but placed a high value on money, the employee would not be highly motivated to work hard to obtain the increase.

All employees in an organization do not share the same goals or values regarding pay, job security, promotions, benefits, or working conditions. For instance, Susan Johnson, a supervisor in the systems and programming division, places a high value on receiving a promotion to a more challenging and responsible position. Susan perceives that excellent performance in her current supervisory position is essential to achieving her desired promotion. Susan's manager recognizes the value that Susan places on a promotion. Therefore, the manager attempts to let Susan know that there is a high probability of being promoted if she performs effectively in her current position. Thus, Susan will seek to perform in a superior manner in order to achieve the promotion. Another employee, Bill Thomas, an office supervisor, values stability and job security and is not interested in a promotion because he does not want more responsibility. Thus, Bill will not be motivated by an opportunity for a promotion.

A key factor in the expectancy model is what the employee perceives as important or of value, not what the manager believes the employee should seek or value. Thus, employees are motivated by what they perceive or expect in terms of rewards as a result of a given behavior. A manager's ability to motivate employees depends on a thorough knowledge of each individual employee as to background, goals, experiences, and other attributes. The manager needs to identify what sparks motivation in the employee.

A major contribution of the expectancy theory is that it explains how the goals of employees influence their behavior on the job. The employees' behavior depends on their assessment of the probability that the behavior will actually lead to the attainment of the goal.

In summary, the manager who wishes to use the expectancy model of motivation should devote attention to the following:

1. Ensuring that employees have sufficient training to do the task assigned.
2. Removing organizational obstacles to proper performance.
3. Instilling employees' confidence concerning capacity to perform.
4. Selecting organizational rewards that will meet specific employee needs.
5. Communicating clearly the relationship between rewards and performance.
6. Administering the reward system in a consistent and equitable fashion so that employees will perceive a relationship between performance and the rewards they receive.

Skinner's Reinforcement Theory: Behavior Modification

Although most managers over the years have used informal versions of the expectancy model, the concept is carried to its fullest with reinforcement theories or under programs labeled organizational behavior modification. Reinforcement theory is based primarily on the research of B. F. Skinner and has been increasingly applied in business situations. According to Skinner, employees can be motivated by reinforcing desired behavior.

reinforcement theory

Reinforcement theory is concerned with the ways in which behavior is learned as the result of either positive or negative consequences. People tend to repeat behaviors that they have learned will produce pleasant outcomes. Behavior that is reinforced will be repeated, and behavior that is not reinforced will not be repeated. If Ted Wilson desires additional pay, and he learns that by working harder his pay increases, he is likely to continue this action. On the other hand, if Ted discovers that pay increases may be obtained by playing politics, he may engage in this practice.

Skinner contends that people's behavior can be controlled and shaped by rewarding (reinforcing) desired behavior while ignoring undesirable actions. Over time, the reinforced behavior will tend to be repeated, whereas the unrewarded behavior will tend to be extinguished and will disappear. Punishment of undesired behavior is to be avoided since it may contribute to feelings of restraint and actions of rebellion. Thus, over a period of years, the conditioner can control human behavior without the person becoming aware of being controlled. In his book, *Beyond Freedom and Dignity,* Skinner says that people can be controlled and shaped while at the same time feeling free.[9]

Skinner's theory of shaping behavior is useful to managers, but one should not assume that human behavior is simple to understand and/or modify. Obtaining immediate feedback of results on an enriched job is a form of instant reward related to behavior on the job. The primary technique suggested by Skinner is organizational behavior modification.

organizational behavior modification (OBM)

Organizational behavior modification (OBM) rests on two fundamental concepts: (1) people act in ways they find most personally rewarding, and (2) people's behavior can be shaped and determined by controlling the

Most Important Reasons for Success and Effectiveness as a Manager

Managers succeed if they understand and can motivate people. Managers who understand leadership will be successful. Add the characteristics of loyalty and willingness to give the job all the time it requires. Very few clock-watchers ever make it to the top.

CHARLES W. MERRITT, President, Commercial Metals Company

reinforcers

rewards. In OBM, rewards are termed **reinforcers** because the goal is to stimulate continuation of the rewarded behavior. Which reinforcers actually work in motivating people is determined by a manager's trial and error and experience. What is successful with one employee may not work with another because their needs and wants differ. Praise is used most frequently because it is most readily available. However, it becomes less effective whenever it becomes predictable or is continuously applied. Money is also used, as are public or private letters of commendation, time off, and increased status.

In OBM, punishment is rejected as a reinforcer because it suppresses the undesired behavior while at the same time stimulating anger, hostility, aggression, and rebellion. And at times, it is difficult to identify the punishment. In one instance, placing prisoners in solitary confinement on bread and water turned out to be a high-status symbol and led to repetition of offenses. When the bread and water was changed to baby food, the status symbol disappeared, leading to a significant reduction in the number of undesirable acts. When undesired behavior is not rewarded, it tends to disappear over time.

In reinforcing desired behavior in a positive fashion, it is important to allocate the rewards soon after the behavior occurs so that the person perceives a clear and immediate linkage. Fast and accurate feedback of information to the performer in itself constitutes a reinforcer.

Organizational behavior modification has been used successfully in a number of organizations to improve performance. In one firm, positive reinforcement was used to reduce absenteeism.[10] Each day an employee came to work on time, he or she received a playing card. At the end of the week, the highest poker hand received $20. Over a three-month period, the absenteeism rate of the experimental group decreased 18 percent, whereas that of a control group actually increased. In their use of OBM, Michigan Bell Telephone identified specific desired behaviors such as the following: (1) service promptness in answering calls, (2) shortness of time taken to give information, (3) use of proper references in handling the call, and (4) attendance.[11] Praise and recognition were the dominant reinforcers. The results were an improvement in attendance by 50 percent and above standard productivity and efficiency levels.

The Emery Air Freight OBM program is one of the biggest success stories to date.[12] It used the simple reinforcers of information feedback and praise to condition employee behavior. In responding to customer questions about service and schedules within a standard ninety-minute period, performance moved from 30 percent of the standard to 90 percent within a few days. Employees were provided with feedback charts through which they could monitor their own performance. Employees who did not achieve the desired results were reminded of the goal and then praised for their honesty. This 90 percent achievement remained stable for over three years. As a result of the application of OBM, estimated savings to Emery Air Freight were placed at $650,000 per year.

If the manager desires to use OBM, the following actions are necessary:

- Identifying the desired performance in specific terms, for example, improving attendance rates or answering questions within one hour.
- Identifying the rewards that will reinforce the desired behavior, for example, praise, money, time off.
- Making the reward a direct consequence of the behavior.
- Selecting the optimum reinforcement schedule.

Despite the successes achieved by behavior modification, it has been criticized as being a manipulative and autocratic approach to the management of people. People are conditioned to change their behavior in the direction required by management and the organization. Some critics argue that OBM is not consistent with the theories of such behavioral scientists as Maslow, Argyris, or McGregor. The assumption underlying these theories is that people are motivated by their own internal needs and are capable of a degree of self-control. On the other hand, OBM assumes that the causes of human behavior are in the environment and therefore external to the individual.

APPROACHES AND TECHNIQUES AVAILABLE TO ENHANCE MOTIVATION

In addition to the above theories of motivation, there are several approaches and techniques that the practicing manager should consider.

The Role of Money as a Motivator

One of the oldest and longest standing rewards or reinforcers of behavior is money. As you will recall, Fredrick Taylor was identified in Chapter 1 as the father of scientific management. He was among the first to introduce individual incentive wage plans into American industry. Managers are hopeful that money can be utilized for two basic purposes: (1) to attract and retain qualified personnel in the organization and (2) to motivate these personnel to higher levels of performance. In the hierarchy of human needs presented earlier in this chapter, money can serve to satisfy the basic physiological and security needs. Money also can become a status symbol, thus contributing to esteem needs. Without contending that it is the only or most important reward, we can state that money plays a significant role in motivating people.

Herzberg's motivation-hygiene theory tends to place money in the hygiene category. Herzberg's research indicates that salary has more potency as a job dissatisfier than as a job satisfier. This view argues that monetary systems can only produce peace and harmony at best (satisfy the employee's hygiene needs) but have little potential for motivating higher levels of performance. The conclusions of Herzberg's theory have been challenged on the basis that many organizations have not established clear reward systems that directly link pay and performance. It can be argued that if an organization establishes a direct relationship between pay and performance, then money may actually serve as a motivator.

If money is to motivate behavior, employees must both desire it and believe that it will be forthcoming if they behave in the manner prescribed. Determining the degree of importance of money to employees requires knowledge of each individual's current need level. If employees have a need for higher pay and expect to receive it if they perform more effectively, then pay can motivate performance.

Employee Performance and Equity

equity

Equity involves an individual comparing his or her performance and the rewards received with the performance and rewards others receive for doing similar work. Managers must deal with employees who continually compare the pay and rewards they are receiving with the rewards other employees receive. The degree of perceived equity is important to each employee. When an employee receives compensation from the organization, perceptions of equity are affected by two factors: (1) comparison of the compensation received to such factors as one's input of effort, education, training, and endurance of adverse working conditions and (2) the comparison of the perceived equity of pay and rewards received compared to other people. For example, even though the employee values money and expects that it will be paid if he or she performs, comparisons will be made to the rewards received by others. Thus, if the employee likes money and believes that an $800 raise will be forthcoming when performing well, motivational force decreases if he or she perceives that other employees are receiving $1,000 for the same performance level.

Motivation: The Self-Fulfilling Prophecy

A manager's expectations have a significant influence on employee motivation and performance. According to J. Sterling Livingston,

- a manager's expectations of employees and the way he or she treats them largely determine their performance and career progress.
- a unique characteristic of superior managers is their ability to create high performance expectations that subordinates fulfill
- less effective managers fail to develop similar expectations, and, as a consequence, the productivity of their subordinates suffers.
- subordinates, more often than not, appear to do what they believe they are expected to do.[13]

self-fulfilling prophecies

High performance expectations tend to be **self-fulfilling prophecies**. A manager communicates expectations through both verbal and nonverbal means. The manager's facial expressions, eye contact, body posture, or tone of voice can indicate high approval and high expectations or just the reverse.

Numerous studies support the notion of the self-fulfilling prophecy. In one such study, eighteen elementary school teachers were informed that about 20 percent of their student were "intellectual bloomers." The teachers were told that these youngsters would achieve remarkable progress during the school year. In actuality, the 20 percent sample of students was chosen at random and did not differ in intelligence or abilities from the remainder of the students in the classes. The only variable was the teacher's expectations of the group of "intellectual bloomers." The students actually achieved significantly greater progress during the school year. Thus, the teacher's expectations of the students became a self-fulfilling prophecy.

Similar results have been achieved by managers. More often than not, if managers have high expectations of their employees, the employees' performance will meet those expectations. For example, the high expectations of the manager of a large computer center at a major university substantially changed the life and work of a janitor. The manager believed that George Johnson, a janitor with limited formal education, had the potential to become a computer operator. The computer center manager had high expectations and believed that George could learn the new job. After several months of training, George Johnson did become a successful computer operator and ultimately progressed to the point of providing training to others. This illustrates how the expectations of one person (in this case the manager of the computer center) can have a significant impact on the actions of another.

Many businesses have not developed effective managers rapidly enough to meet the needs of their organization. As a consequence, organizations are not developing their most valuable resource—talented young men and women. In fact, the self-fulfilling prophecy seems to have the greatest potential impact on younger employees and managers. By failing to create high expectations and provide for the training and development of their personnel, firms are experiencing high costs due to excessive employee turnover. Also, managers who fail to communicate high expectations may significantly damage the attitudes and career aspirations of younger personnel.

Managers in every organization who are interested in high productivity must meet the challenge of encouraging the development of managers who will treat their employees in ways that contribute to high performance and career development and personal satisfaction. Effective managers who have high expectations of subordinates tend to build the employees' self-confidence and develop their performance capabilities. By contrast, ineffective managers tend to create a climate of negative or low expectations of subordinates. And as a result, the employee's level of motivation and performance will be lower, and their self-esteem or self-image as well as their careers may be severely damaged.[14]

JOB DESIGN

Is it possible to enhance employee motivation, improve job satisfaction, and maximize production all at the same time? This question poses a significant challenge for managers. Increasingly, America's more highly educated work force has expectations for a job that not only provides for their basic needs but also allows them to achieve satisfaction of such needs as achievement, growth, recognition, and self-fulfillment. Another important challenge is to increase the productivity of the American worker by finding ways to "unlock the potential that exists in the overwhelming majority of our workforce."[15]

During the past decade there has been a decline in the productivity growth rate in the United States compared to most other industrialized nations. In addition, there has been a "subtle but substantial decrease in job satisfaction among factory workers, clerical personnel and millions of other people who in the final analysis do the productive work in our complex organization."[16]

On the other hand, J. Richard Hackman and Greg R. Oldham contend that it is possible to achieve an improvement of the quality or work life and also to increase or maximize worker productivity.[17] They challenge several traditionally held assumptions such as:

- the basic nature of work is fixed and cannot be changed,
- technology and work processes determine job design, and
- all management can do is properly select and train personnel.

job design

Work or job design has been identified as an approach that can assist in increasing productivity. We define **job design** as the process of altering the nature and structure of jobs for the purpose of increasing productivity. Job design is concerned with the specific tasks to be performed, the methods used in performing the task, and how the job relates to other work in the organization. In their book, *Work Redesign*, Hackman and Oldham assert that if managers wish to create a climate for a high level of motivation, reliable feedback on performance must be provided; there must be a sense that the worker is accountable for specific results and a feeling that the job has meaning beyond pay.[18] Workers get more satisfaction from completing a "whole and identifiable piece of work" than from producing indistinguishable pieces. Because of this, job design becomes an important concept in creating a motivational climate for today's work force.

Technology constraints on job design include the type of equipment and tools as well as the particular work layout and methods used in producing the product or services. Technology may make job redesign difficult and perhaps expensive though not impossible. For example, adapting or redesigning the assembly-line production of automobiles or electronic components may not be technically or economically feasible.[19]

Economic factors affect job design. The question must be asked, "Are sufficient resources available to the organization should the firm wish to redesign some or all of its jobs?" While we may suggest ways to redesign jobs to improve output and the level of worker satisfaction, the cost may be prohibitive. A manager must continually balance the benefits of job design with the costs.

Job design is also affected by government requirements or regulations. Management may wish to design a job in a way that might increase worker performance but be in violation of labor laws or environmental or safety standards. Some proponents of work redesign have even urged the federal government to legislate changes in work design.

If a company has a union, job design can be affected by the philosophy, policies, and strategies of the union. Typically, the contract between the company and the union specifies and defines the types of jobs and the duties and responsibilities of workers. Unions have traditionally been opposed to many work redesign experiments. They perceive them to be attempts by management to "squeeze more work out of the worker" without any increase in wages. Also, unions may view job redesign as a threat to their power and position with the workers.

Important considerations for job design are the abilities, attitudes, and motivation of personnel within the organization. Obviously, the design of particular jobs depends on the ability or training of present or potential employees. It would be ridiculous to design a job that would be considerably more complex than the ability level of employees available for the positions. The ability and willingness of employees to be trained can limit job redesign.

Finally, management philosophy, objectives, and strategies may determine the degree of job redesign possible. Top management must be committed to the concept of job redesign. Job redesign may allow employees to gain greater authority to determine how their jobs are performed and how the worker is managed. Thus, managers who identify with Theory X assumptions would likely have difficulty with job redesign.

Job Enrichment

job enrichment

In the past two decades there has been considerable interest in and application of job enrichment in a wide variety of organizations. Strongly advocated by Frederick Herzberg, **job enrichment** refers to basic changes in the content and level of responsibility of a job so as to provide for the satisfaction of the *motivation* needs of personnel. The individual is provided with an opportunity to derive a feeling of greater achievement, recognition, responsibility, and personal growth in performing the job. Although job enrichment programs have not always achieved positive results, such programs have demonstrated improvements in job performance and in the level of satisfaction of personnel in many organizations.

AT&T, Polaroid, Texas Instruments, Monsanto, Weyerhaeuser, General Motors, Corning Glass, and many other firms have achieved excellent results after implementing job enrichment programs. In most instances productivity and job satisfaction increased, accompanied by reduction in employee turnover and absenteeism.[20]

According to Herzberg, there are a number of principles applicable for implementing job enrichment:

1. **Increasing job demands.** Changing the job in such a way as to increase the level of difficulty and responsibility of the job.
2. **Increasing a worker's accountability.** Allowing more individual control and authority over the work, while retaining accountability of the manager.
3. **Providing work scheduling freedom.** Within limits, allowing individual workers to schedule their own work.
4. **Providing feedback.** Making timely periodic reports on performance to employees (directly to the worker rather than to the supervisor).
5. **Providing new learning experiences.** Work situations should encourage opportunities for new experiences and personal growth of the individual.[21]

Job Enlargement

job enlargement

Many people have attempted to differentiate between job enrichment and job enlargment. **Job enlargement** is said to provide a horizontal expansion of duties. For example, instead of knowing how to operate only one machine, a person is taught to operate two or even three. But no additional responsibility is provided. On the other hand, job enrichment entails providing a person with additional responsibilities. There may be other tasks to perform, but responsibility is given with the tasks. For instance, the worker may be given the responsibility of scheduling the three machines. Increased responsibility means providing the worker with increased freedom to do the job—make decisions and exercise more self-control over the work.

QUALITY CIRCLES

quality circles

Another technique that has been shown to be effective in enhancing motivation and achieving improved quality and productivity in several hundred U.S. companies is a concept known as quality circles.[22] In most firms, **quality**

circles (QCs) consist of periodic meetings of small groups of employees who get together to brainstorm ways to improve the quality and quantity of work.[23]

At Xerox's Reprographics Technology Group, QCs have been established that involve horizontal councils of people on the same level from different departments and vertical work-study groups from different levels within a department. This prevents the QC from considering improvements in only one department, therefore requiring the consideration of problems and universal solutions for the company as a whole. General Motors has implemented various forms of QCs in over ninety of its plants worldwide. One particularly successful QC in a Dayton, Ohio, plant implemented a process developed in Britain known as the sociotechnical system—a method of integrating workers' ideas for improving jobs with technical requirements set by engineers. This allowed the laborers who carried out the detailed plans of the engineers to add their own suggestions for time- or motion-saving techniques (or human considerations) to the process. At Shackley Corporation's plant in Norman, Oklahoma, employees working in teams have achieved the same volume of production at approximately 40 percent of the previous labor costs. One QC at a Westinghouse plant is responsible for a $22,000 cost savings to the company because the workers devised the scheme that one employee reports to work fifteen minutes ahead of the shift in order to activate wire-bonding machines, thus preventing the remaining employees on the shift from being idle until the equipment could be readied.[24]

At an Iowa plant of Butler Manufacturing Company, work teams were allowed to set their own production goals. The man-hours required per building unit have been reduced by 30 to 35 percent during the first two years as compared with production in two older plants of the company. Many current business-related periodicals tell numerous success stories when employees are encouraged to work together to improve the quality and quantity of the company. Quality circles encourage the worker's energy and creativity to solve the company's—and the workers'—problems.

MANAGEMENT LESSONS FROM THE JAPANESE

William Ouchi, in his book *Theory Z: How American Business Can Meet the Japanese Challenge,* and Richard Pascale and Anthony Athos's *The Art of Japanese Management,* describe management practices in a number of progressive American companies that are similar to what successful Japanese firms have been utilizing for years.[25] Ouchi identifies Hewlett-Packard, IBM, Procter and Gamble, and Eastman Kodak as Theory Z organizations. **Theory Z** type companies show a strong relationship between the company and its employees and demonstrate unusual responsibility toward their employees; the employees in turn show great loyalty toward the company. Type Z companies tend to practice a system of lifetime employment and avoid layoffs. The companies usually enjoy low employee turnover, low absenteeism, and

Theory Z

high employee morale. The workers are more involved in their jobs with the company, a factor that leads to increased productivity and performance. Theory Z companies tend to develop their own traditions, ideals, and culture and foster somewhat of a "family environment." This "family" or culture within the organization tends to bond its members—employees and managers—thereby facilitating decision making and communications within the company. All of this has much in common with Japanese patterns and practices. Companies in the United States have not necessarily imitated Japanese practices but have developed their own management style through the recognition of the types of employees who make up today's U.S. work force.

Seven S Model

Pascale and Athos's book, *The Art of Japanese Management: Applications for American Executives,* identifies many of the same companies mentioned in the Ouchi book (Eastman Kodak, IBM, Hewlett-Packard) as practitioners of the Theory Z style of management. However, it also includes Delta Airlines, Boeing, and 3M as companies with management styles similar to Japanese firms. Pascale and Athos present what they refer to as a "**Seven S Model.**" This model attempts to identify what makes enterprises succeed or fail. The seven S's are described below.

Strategy	Plan or course of action leading to the use of resources to achieve goals
Structure	Manner in which the firm is organized—type of departmentation and responsibility and authority of managers
Systems	Policies, procedures, and methods that managers use in making decisions, implementing change, or communicating with others in the organization
Staff	"Demographic" characteristics of personnel within the firm
Skills	Distinctive capabilities of key personnel
Style	Patterns of behavior of key managers in achieving the organization's goals; cultural style of the organization
Superordinate goals	The overall purpose of the organization—guiding values and principles that integrate individual and organizational purposes[26]

The first three elements, strategy, structure, and systems, are known as the "hard S's" or the more traditional elements that a company relies on for effective management. The other four factors, or "soft S's," are often not adequately addressed by firms. Pascale and Athos argue that the more successful and progressive companies address all seven S's and give particular attention to the four soft S's. They place significant emphasis on what they refer to as "superordinate goals" and explain as the "glue" that holds the other six S's—strategy, structure, systems, style, staff, and skills—together.

Well-managed companies, such as those described in Ouchi's *Theory Z* and Pascale and Athos's *The Art of Japanese Management,* usually have superordinate goals expressed in terms of the firm's responsibility to its employees, to its customers, and to the surrounding community. Thus, superordinate goals assist the firm in becoming more internally unified and self-sustaining over a period of time. For instance, at IBM, the goal of never sacrificing customer service, or Delta Airlines' dedication to quality service—which they consider to be a direct result of the motivated and friendly work force—are examples of superordinate goals at work for successful businesses. Delta's approach, which includes open door access for its more than 36,000 employees, has enabled the airline to maintain a highly motivated work force and remain nonunion in an industry plagued by labor-management difficulties. Delta's philosophy is "the Delta family feeling" and identifies a culture that has become institutionalized within the company over the years and makes this company's internal relationships different from those of other airlines. Outstanding companies are usually very advanced in their grasp of strategy, structure, and systems, but unlike less successful firms, which rely primarily upon these three S's, the best managed companies usually have great sophistication in the four soft S's as well. The most effective firms link their purposes and ways of realizing them to human values as well as to economic measures such as profit and efficiency.[27]

MOTIVATION: IMPLICATIONS FOR MANAGEMENT PRACTICE

From our discussion of the theories of motivation, several implications for managers can be derived. Management should recognize many factors that affect job performance. These factors include: (1) skills and abilities of personnel, (2) levels of education and training of employees, (3) existing technology, and (4) available equipment and tools to perform the job. A manager may not be able to "motivate" an employee to better job performance if the employee does not possess the education, skills, training, and equipment to perform the job effectively. If any of these factors is inadequate, performance may be adversely affected. Employees may possess the necessary skills and be highly motivated to perform a certain job effectively, but their overall performance level may be quite low because they may not know how to do the job. This is a problem that is sometimes overlooked by managers who believe that an employee is simply *not motivated* when in fact the employee does not understand what he or she is required to do or lacks the proper training or equipment to perform efficiently and effectively. It does little good, and may cause considerable harm, if managers persist in *driving* employees in an effort to motivate them when motivation is not the problem.

- Managers must keep in mind that effective motivation is not so much something that a manager "does" to an employee. A manager's primary responsibility is the "creation of the climate" where personnel will want to be productive and creative in their work.

- Managers should recognize and try to develop a better understanding of human behavior if they are to create a climate that encourages greater employee performance and satisfaction.
- Human needs that are reasonably well satisfied do not motivate behavior. The lower-level needs on Maslow's hierarchy (physiological, safety, and social) are fairly well satisfied for many U.S. employees and therefore have little significant influence in motivating behavior. Thus, management should devote more of its attention toward providing a climate for the satisfaction of the upper-level needs of esteem and self-actualization.
- Personnel have been underutilized and *overmanaged.* Organizations should try to provide more responsible and challenging jobs that allow a greater degree of individual self-control.
- Many managers have adopted the Theory X assumptions regarding the expected behavior of their subordinates. These managers have created a climate of distrust and one that encourages immature actions on the part of the employees. These conditions do not lead to more effective performance or a higher level of employee satisfaction.

Summary

Motivation is one of the most important and frequently discussed subjects in management. Today's employees are better educated, more highly skilled, and often do not respond to traditional values that may have motivated them twenty or thirty years ago. Motivation is the process of influencing or stimulating a person to take action by creating a work environment whereby the goals of the organization and the needs of the people are satisfied. In an organization, personnel are said to be motivated if they perform their jobs effectively and efficiently. Management has traditionally relied on the use of rewards such as increased pay, job security, good working conditions, or punishment such as dismissal, demotions, or withholding rewards to "motivate" employees. But today, management cannot rely on the manipulation of pay, benefits, or working conditions to motivate personnel to perform effectively. Motivation is a much more complicated process.

Managers must attempt to understand human nature and a person's basic needs if they are to create a climate for motivation. McGregor's Theory X and Theory Y and Argyris's maturity theory have aided managers in developing a better understanding of human behavior. The theories of Maslow, Herzberg, McClelland, Vroom, Skinner, and Alderfer are very helpful to managers as they attempt to gain a more complete appreciation of our basic needs and the reasons for human behavior.

Maslow's hierarchy of needs is a widely accepted theory, which supports the idea that people are motivated by unsatisfied needs. According to Maslow, a person's needs are arranged in priority from the basic physiological to the complex self-actualization needs. The key point for managers to accept is that needs that are fairly well satisfied do not motivate behavior. Alderfer's E-R-G theory classifies needs into three levels in order of progression—existence, relatedness, and growth. Each level of need becomes increasingly difficult to satisfy. Herzberg's motivation-hygiene theory classifies human needs into two categories—hygiene factors and motivators. The hygiene factors correspond to the lower-level needs on Maslow's hierarchy, while the motivators represent upper-level needs. Herzberg contends that despite the fact that most managers and organizations concentrate on satisfying the hygiene needs, this action does not motivate employees. He feels firms should direct more attention to the motivators and to enriched or more challenging jobs, but at the same time firms should not forget to be concerned about the hygiene needs. McClelland's theory stresses that there are certain needs that are learned. He argues that each person's need for achievement, power, and affiliation affects his or her behavior in the work environment.

The needs approach to motivation as developed by Maslow, Alderfer, and Herzberg does not adequately explain individual differences in the way people behave in accomplishing goals. Victor Vroom's expectancy theory of motivation attempts to explain behavior in terms of an individual's goals, choices, and the expectations of achieving the goals. Employees are motivated by what they expect in terms of rewards as a result of their behavior. B. F. Skinner contends that behavior can be controlled and shaped by reinforcing desired behavior. The primary approach suggested by Skinner is organizational behavior modification (OBM), which has been successfully applied in a number of organizations. Under this approach, people act in the way they find most rewarding and by controlling rewards, people's behavior can be directed and/or modified.

In addition to the major theories of motivation, managers should also develop an understanding of the role of money as a motivator and the importance of equity between an individual's performance and the pay he or she receives. Managers should also be aware that their expectations have a significant influence on employee motivation and performance.

Work design is the process of altering the nature and structure of jobs for the purpose of increasing productivity. Job design is concerned with the specific tasks to be performed, the methods used in performing the tasks, and how the job relates to the others in the organization. Some of the factors affecting work design include: technology, economy, government, union personnel, and management philosophy.

Job enrichment refers to basic changes in the content and level of responsibility of a job in an attempt to provide for the satisfaction of the needs of personnel. Job enlargement is merely a horizontal expansion of duties and no additional responsibilities are provided.

Another technique that has been shown to be effective in enhancing motivation and achieving improved quality and productivity in several hundred U.S. companies is a concept known as quality circles. In most firms, quality circles consist of periodic meetings of small groups who get together to brainstorm ways to improve the quality and quantity of work.

Ouchi identifies Hewlett-Packard, IBM, Procter and Gamble, and Eastman Kodak as Theory Z organizations. A fundamental characteristic of Theory Z type companies is the strong relationship between the company and its employees, who in turn demonstrate great loyalty toward the company. Type Z companies tend to practice a system of lifetime employment, low turnover, low absenteeism, and high employee morale.

Review Questions

1. How would you define motivation?
2. Compare and contrast McGregor's Theory X and Theory Y. What are some examples of managerial practices that are consistent with a Theory Y philosophy of human nature?
3. What is Argyris's maturation theory? How does it apply to motivation?
4. Relate Herzberg's theory of motivation to the theory developed by Maslow and Alderfer.
5. Describe McClelland's theory of human motives. How does it relate to motivation, and what are the basic characteristics of individuals described by the theory?
6. What is expectancy theory, and how can managers use it in the motivation process? Provide examples.
7. Briefly describe organizational behavior modification. How can it be used in motivating people? Give illustrations.
8. What is the role of money as a motivator? How important is the issue of equity of pay in terms of motivation? Explain.
9. What is meant by job enrichment, and how does it differ from job enlargement? How would you apply job enrichment? Give an example.
10. What is the notion of the "self-fulfilling prophecy?" How is it related to management and motivation?
11. What are quality circles and how successful have they been in improving the quality and quantity of work?
12. What characterizes "Theory Z" type companies?

Exercises

1. Interview three managers—for example, a bank president, a college dean, and a local retailer. Ask these managers to describe their approach to creating a climate for motivating personnel within their organization. Compare their comments with the concepts on motivation presented in this chapter.
2. Using Maslow's hierarchy of needs as a guide, describe how *your* various needs have been satisfied on any job(s) you have held. Were any of your needs not met? Why or why not? How could they have been satisfied?

Case Study

A Philosophy of Motivation

Trent Pratter is the advertising manager for a major tire manufacturer. There are eight advertising specialists who report directly to Trent. Within Trent's department there is a wide diversity of talent and experience. It is obvious to most outsiders that some of the specialists are far superior to others in their advertising talents.

Wayne Sanders is one of the specialists who is recognized for his superior talents. He is able to develop and implement a campaign from start to finish. His creativity is second to none. Billy Miller, on the other hand, does a minimum amount of work—just enough to get by. He does what is required but virtually nothing extra. If he is assigned a project, he typically complains that he is working too hard. He always appears to be busy but rarely gets much accomplished.

Trent openly recognizes that Billy does not produce as much as the other employees but believes that he can make Billy more productive. Therefore, rather than reward people like Wayne, he concentrates his attention and special privileges on individuals like Billy. If there is a seminar for professional development, Billy is typically chosen to attend. Billy is afforded time off whenever he wants it. Wayne works a minimum of sixty hours a week but never receives any recognition for his work. In fact, it would appear to an outsider that Trent rewards inefficiency and condemns effectiveness. All his efforts are directed toward helping the "underdog."

Over a period of years there has been a tendency for the best qualified advertising specialists to leave the company and the less capable to remain. This trend was continued the other day as Wayne turned in his resignation. Trent is confused and requests your assistance in resolving the problem.

QUESTIONS

1. What caused Wayne Sanders to terminate his employment?
2. How would the situation approach to motivation be helpful to Trent in analyzing the problem?
3. What advice would you give to Trent regarding his approach to motivation?

Case Study

Motivating a Dissatisfied Manager

Alice Ross had been a district sales manager with Finn Productions for ten years. She was recognized by her peers and supervisors as a person who ran a good department. However, everyone realized that Alice was extremely ambitious and was seeking a higher-level management position. When one of her sales representatives did a good job in a particular quarter, Alice would attempt to take the credit. However, if a problem arose, it was not Alice's fault.

When the marketing manager retired, Alice applied for the position. The company decided to do a thorough search because of the responsibility and importance associated with the position. When the search was concluded, the decision was made to go "outside" for a person to fill the position. The consensus of top management was that Alice, although a good district sales manager, might have difficulties in working with her new peer group. They felt that she might alienate the other managers if she tried to take credit for their work.

Alice was heartbroken. She had wanted that particular job for a long time and had dedicated all of her energies toward obtaining it. She became very despondent and her work deteriorated. The department functioned in spite of her, not because of her. Decisions were made slowly if at all, and she began to be late with her sales reports. Although her sales staff continued to be productive, Alice could not take the credit.

When the new marketing manager took over, one of the first major problems that he confronted was how to motivate Alice to her former level of performance. He recognized that Alice had been with the company for a long time, but something had to be done. Alice was receiving an excellent salary for doing virtually nothing.

QUESTIONS

1. As the new marketing manager, what approach would you use to motivate Alice?
2. Do you believe that Alice can be motivated to become a productive member of the organization once again? Why or why not? Discuss.

Notes

1. Douglas McGregor, *The Human Side of Enterprise* (New York: McGraw-Hill, 1960).
2. Chris Argyris, *Personality and Organization* (New York: Harper, 1957).
3. Abraham Maslow, *Motivation and Personality* (New York: Harper, 1954).
4. Clayton P. Alderfer, "A Critique of Salancik and Pfeffer's Examination of Need-Satisfaction Theories," *Administration Science Quarterly* 22 (December 1977): 658–672.
5. Frederick Herzberg, *Work and the Nature of Man* (Cleveland: World, 1966).
6. D. C. McClelland and David H. Burnham, "Power Is the Great Motivator," *Harvard Business Review* 54 (March–April 1976): 103.
7. David R. Hampton, Charles E. Summer, and Ross A. Webber, *Organizational Behavior and the Practice of Management* (Glenview, Ill.: Scott, Foresman, 1978), pp. 11–15.
8. Victor Vroom, *Work and Motivation* (New York: Wiley, 1964).
9. B. F. Skinner, *Beyond Freedom and Dignity* (New York: Knopf, 1971).
10. Ed Pedalino and Victor U. Gamboa, "Behavior Modification and Absenteeism," *Journal of Applied Psychology* 59 (December 1974): 694–698.
11. W. Clay Hamner and Ellen P. Hamner, "Behavior Modification on the Bottom Line," *Organizational Dynamics* 4 (Spring 1976): 12.
12. "At Emery Air Freight: Positive Reinforcement Boosts Performance," *Organizational Dynamics* 1 (Autumn 1973): 41–50.
13. J. Sterling Livingston, "Pygmalion in Management," *Harvard Business Review* (July–August 1969).
14. John L. Single, "The Power of Expectations: Productivity and the Self-Fulfilling Prophecy," *Management World* (November 1980): 19, 37–38.

15. Robert H. Guest, "Review of Work Redesign," "From the Manager's Bookshelf," *Harvard Business Review* (January–February 1981): 46–47, 52.
16. Ibid., p. 46.
17. Ibid.
18. J. Richard Hackman and Greg R. Oldham, *Work Redesign* (Reading, Mass.: Addison-Wesley, 1980).
19. John F. Runcie, "By Days I Make the Cars," "Quality of Work Life," *Harvard Business Review* (May–June 1980): 106–115.
20. See "Case Studies in the Humanization of Work," in *Work in America. Report of Special Task Force to the Secretary of Health, Education and Welfare* (Cambridge, Mass: M.I.T. Press, 1973), Appendix, pp. 188–200.
21. Frederick Herzberg, "One More Time: How Do You Motivate Employees?" *Harvard Business Review* 46 (January–February 1968): 53–62. See also Frederick Herzberg, "Motivation and Innovation: Who Are Workers Serving?" *California Management Review* 22, no. 2 (Winter 1979).
22. "Will the Slide Kill Quality Circles," *Business Week,* January 11, 1982, pp. 108–109.
23. "The New Industrial Revolution," *Business Week,* May 11, 1981, pp. 85–98.
24. "The Workers Know Best," *Time,* January 28, 1980, p. 65.
25. William Ouchi, *Theory Z: How American Business Can Meet the Japanese Challenge* (Reading, Mass.: Addison-Wesley, 1981); Richard Pascale and Anthony Athos, *The Art of Japanese Management: Applications for American Executives* (New York: Simon and Schuster, 1981).
26. Pascale and Athos, *Art,* p. 81.
27. Ibid., p. 178.

References

Armstrong, J. "How to Motivate." *Management Today* 12 (February 1977): 60–63.

Berry, L. E. "Motivation Management." *Journal of Systems Management* 30 (April 1979): 30–32.

Cook, C. W. "Guidelines for Managing Motivation." *Business Horizons* 23 (April 1980): 61–69.

Gallagher, W. E., Jr., and Einhorn, H. J. "Motivation Theory and Job Design." *Journal of Business* 49 (July 1976): 358–373.

Gayle, J. B. and Searle, F. R. "Maslow, Motivation, and the Manager." *Management World* 9 (September 1980): 18–20.

Giblin, E. J. "Motivating Employees: A Closer Look." *Personnel Journal* 55 (April 1976): 68–71.

Hackman, J. R. "Is Job Enrichment Just a Fad?" *Harvard Business Review* 53 (September 1975): 129–138.

Hatuany, N., and Puick, V. "Japanese Management Practices and Productivity." *Organizational Dynamics* 9 (Spring 1981): 4–21.

Klimoski, R. J., and Hayes, N. J. "Leader Behavior and Subordinate Motivation." *Personnel Psychology* 33 (Autumn 1980): 543–555.

McClelland, D. C., and Burnham, D. H. "Power Is the Great Motivator." *Harvard Business Review* 54 (March 1976): 100–110.

Miller, William B. "Motivation Techniques: Does One Work Best?" *Management Review* (February 1981): 47–52.

Neider, L. L. "Experimental Field Investigation Utilizing an Expectancy Theory View of Participation." *Organizational Behavior and Human Performance* 26 (December 1980): 425–442.

Odiorne, G. S. "Uneasy Look at Motivation Theory." *Training and Development Journal* 34 (June 1980): 106–112.

Ouchi, William G. "Organizational Paragrams: A Commentary on Japanese Management and Theory Z Organizations." *Organizational Dynamics* 9 (Spring 1981): 36–42.

______. "Theory Z Corporations." *Industry Week,* May 4, 1981, pp. 49–51.

Peters, Thomas J. "Putting Excellence into Management." *Business Week,* July 21, 1980, pp. 196–205.

Pinder, C. C. "Concerning the Application of Human Motivation Theories in Organizational Settings." *Academy of Management Review* 2 (July 1977): 384–397.

Quick, J. C. "Dyadic Goal Setting within Organizations: Rolemaking and Motivational Considerations." *Academy of Management Review* 4 (July 1979): 377–380.

Rehder, R. R. "What American and Japanese Managers Are Learning About Each Other." *Business Horizons* 24 (March–April 1981): 63–70.

Rosenthal, Robert. "The Pygmalion Effect Lives." *Psychology Today* (September 1973): 56–60.

Runcie, John F., " 'By Days I Make the Cars.' " *Harvard Business Review* (May–June 1980): 106–115.

Schmitt, N., and Son, L. "Evaluation of Valence Models of Motivation to Pursue Various Post High School Alternatives." *Organizational Behavior and Human Performance* 27 (February 1981): 135–150.

Speigel, D. "How Not to Motivate." *Supervisory Management* 22 (November 1977): 41–45.

Trautman, L. J., et al. "Managing People: Choosing the Right Motivator." *Mortgage Banker* 40 (August 1980): 34–37.

KEY TERMS

leadership
formal power
reward power
coercive power
expert power
referent power
trait approach
Likert's systems of management
managerial grid
Ohio State leadership studies
initiating structure
consideration
path-goal theory
leadership continuum
Fiedler's contingency leadership model
leader-member relations
task structure
position power of the leader
Hersey and Blanchard's situational leadership theory
task behavior
relationship behavior
task-relevant maturity

LEARNING OBJECTIVES

After completing this chapter you should be able to

1. Describe leadership and define the types of power a leader may possess.
2. Explain the trait approach to the study of leadership.
3. Identify and describe the major leadership theories which advocate a universal leadership style.
4. State and describe the major behavioral leadership theories.
5. Identify and explain the major situational leadership theories and describe the integrated approach to leadership.

11

Leadership

Martha Garrett, president of Sanford Electronics, was worried as she made a presentation to the key officers in her firm. The decisions she had made to enter a new market would affect the overall direction of Sanford's. She needed the total support of the top management of Sanford's if the changes were to be successfully implemented. At the end of her presentation, Martha could sense that the mood of the group was positive. Comments such as "We're behind you Martha," and "Good show, my people will be with you," were heard around the table. Martha breathed a sigh of relief, for without their support pursuing the new market would not be appropriate.

Carlos Martinez, district manager for Northwest Telephone Company, was asked by one of his supervisors, Betty Jones, the difference between leadership and management. Carlos thought for a moment and replied, "Well, Betty, if I announced to all the employees that we were going to close the office this afternoon and have a party, and if everyone followed me to the party, I guess you could say that I was a good leader. However, the telephone company would say I wasn't a good manager for their objective is to 'keep the phones ringing.' Therefore, a good manager must be a good leader, but a good leader is not necessarily a good manager."

The questions then must be asked, "What does it take to be an effective manager?" and "What is the most effective leadership style?" These questions have perplexed and challenged managers for generations. Literally thousands of research studies concerning leadership have been conducted to provide greater insight into these questions. However, such studies of leaders and the leadership process have not yielded any set of traits or qualities that are consistently related to effective leadership. The basic conclusion that can be drawn from these studies is that there is *no one* most effective leadership style. What we do know is that effective leadership is absolutely essential to the survival and overall growth of every organization.

As we noted at the beginning of Chapter 1, 50 percent of all new businesses fail within the first two years. Despite high salaries and excellent opportunities in large corporations, there continues to be a shortage of competent managers who are effective leaders. The lack of capable leadership is not just confined to business organizations but has also been felt in government, churches, education, and all other types of organizations. The problem is not a lack of people who want to be leaders or managers but rather a scarcity of skilled people who are capable of performing effectively in leadership positions. The primary challenge of leadership or management is to guide an organization toward the accomplishment of its objectives. The leader achieves this by influencing and encouraging employees of the organization to attain the highest level of performance possible within the limitation of available resources, skills, and technology.

Many large businesses and even countries have made successful turnarounds as a result of a change in leadership. Even though we don't have all the answers, a more complete knowledge of the skills, attitudes, and values that are related to effective leadership would greatly improve our ability to select, train, and develop more effective managers. This is precisely the purpose of this chapter. We will first define leadership and then discuss the more significant theories of leadership. Finally, an integrative approach to leadership will be presented that should prove beneficial to individuals as they develop their leadership styles.

LEADERSHIP DEFINED

leadership

Leadership is the process of influencing others toward the accomplishment of goals. **Leadership** is any attempt at influencing the behavior of others for goals or purposes that may or may not coincide with the objectives of the organization. Carlos Martinez might have been a good leader by closing the telephone company and having the employees follow him to the party. But he would not be a good manager because the goals of the company were not being achieved. In this chapter our discussion will be primarily concerned with managers as leaders. By definition, a good manager is a good leader, but a good leader may not necessarily be an effective manager.

As the result of a consulting assignment with a mobile home manufacturer, one of the authors observed a production manager exerting effective leadership but ineffective management. A team of consultants had prepared a feasibility study for the president of a newly formed mobile home manufacturer. The study recommended that the new plant produce a relatively low-priced mobile home because the firm was in a low-income geographic area. However, the company hired a production manager with an excellent reputation who had several years of experience with a manufacturer of higher-priced, higher-quality mobile homes. Against the advice of the consultants and without the knowledge of the board of directors, the production manager decided to direct his production supervisors and workers to produce a higher-priced mobile home. The results proved to be disastrous for the newly established company.

The sales staff was not able to sell these high-priced units, causing the firm to invest over $350,000 of its working capital in an inventory of mobile homes that could not be sold. This was a major factor contributing to the firm's bankruptcy within nine months of its beginning business. In this illustration, the production manager exercised effective leadership because he significantly influenced the behavior of his workers. However, he was an ineffective manager because he had the employees pursuing goals that were not in the best interest of the company.

Thus a company can actually go bankrupt, even though leadership has been effectively influencing the behavior of others to accomplish goals, if

•CAREER PROFILE•

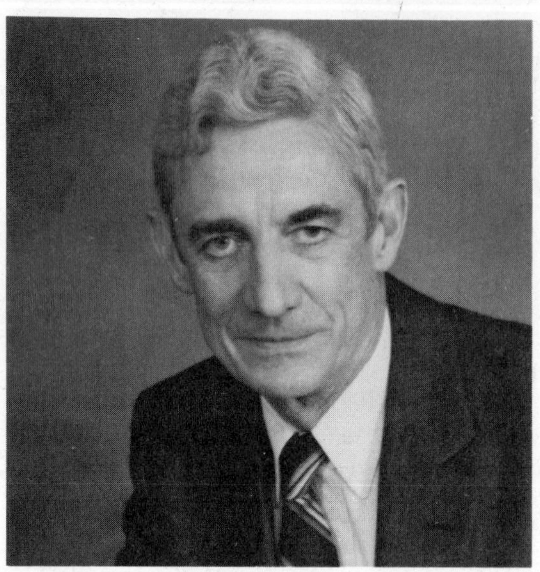

ROBERT J. SWEENEY
President and CEO, Murphy Oil Corporation

MURPHY OIL CORPORATION

When Robert Sweeney graduated from college at the age of twenty, he did not realize that one day he would be president of a company with over 4,400 employees and annual sales of $2.57 billion. However, his success did not happen overnight. On his way to the top, Mr. Sweeney served as a reservoir engineer, chief reservoir engineer, chief engineer, assistant manager of production and exploration, president of Murphy Eastern Oil Company, and in 1972 became president and chief operating officer.

When questioned regarding any critical events in his life, Mr. Sweeney said that a change of employment decision was one. "The decision to leave Arkansas Natural Companies and join Murphy Oil in 1952 was a major one," he said. "As I recall, the Arkansas Natural Companies were subject to a consent decree negotiated by Cities Service, the majority stockholder, and the Justice Department. Under the terms of the consent decree, the utility businesses were to be divested and the oil and pipeline businesses merged into Cities Service. Be-

these goals are inappropriate for the company. Also, it should be noted that a person can have the title of manager but have very little influence over the behavior and actions of others. On the other hand, an individual might not carry the title of manager but be an important informal leader excising considerable influence over the behavior of others in the work group.

Leaders are able to influence others because they possess power. We discussed the various types of power in Chapter 8. However, we will briefly

Insights to Success

A leader must *lead*, not drive. People are unpredictable, different from one another, often irascible, frequently petty, sometimes vain, but always magnificent if they are properly motivated

ZOLTAN MERSZEI, Chairman, Dow Chemical Company

cause of this situation I think it fair to say that the Arkansas Natural Companies had been forced into a holding pattern pending implementation of the consent decree. In any event, I knew I was dissatisfied with the trend of things, but coming to Murphy was a soul-searching decision. I wanted to work for a large corporation, and Murphy at the time was a family-owned enterprise with assets perhaps around $50 million and thirty-five or forty employees. I also knew that it was difficult to move from a small company to a larger one. In general, companies tend to promote from within or hire outside people from larger companies, not smaller companies. To the extent this was true, my chances of ever regaining employment with a large company appeared minimal if I accepted the Murphy offer. After talking with Mr. Murphy, however, I was convinced that he fully intended to build a large company. I simply placed my bets on his ability and took the job."

Being too young nearly caused him some problems. Sweeney commented, "Because I graduated from college at a relatively early age (twenty) and was lucky in the sense of having a knack of being in the right place at the right time, I usually found myself to be quite young for the position I held at any given time. Further, my bosses were always relatively young; therefore I could never see any clear-cut path of progression during most of my career with Murphy. In the end, though, I always decided against alternative employment because I was happy with my work; I was comfortable with the high ethical standards of the Murphy enterprise; and, in fact, history had proved me wrong over and over again as regards my being 'boxed in.' In short the good things associated with working for the Murphy enterprise always outweighed the increased income that might be realized through a change."

Finally, Mr. Sweeney said, "I will never know, of course, whether I made the proper decision at any of these critical moments, but I do know that I am reasonably pleased with the way it turned out and have no desire to turn back the clock and run the 'gauntlet' again."

review these below. Power can be in one or any combination of the following forms:

formal power

- **Formal power.** Derived from authority or legitimate position in the firm.

reward power

- **Reward power.** Based on the leader's ability to administer and control rewards (such as pay, promotions, and praise) to others for complying with the leader's directives

coercive power

- **Coercive power.** Based on the leader's ability to administer and control punishments (such as the power to fire, demote, or reprimand) to others for not following the leader's requests.

expert power

- **Expert power.** Based on the special knowledge, expertise, skill, or experience possessed by the leader. For example, employees may view Frank Wilson, an engineer, as a "real pro" in the engineering department. While Frank is not the manager of the department, other engineers and managers may go to him for technical assistance with structural design problems.

referent power

- **Referent power.** Based on the leader's possession of personal characteristics that make them "attractive" to other people. Some individuals are said to possess "charisma," one form of referent power. Another form of referent power can be derived from one's association with another powerful leader. For instance, Bob Haldeman and John Ehrlichman possessed referent power as aides to former President Nixon because many people believed they were acting with the approval of the president.

THE TRAIT APPROACH TO LEADERSHIP

The leader has always occupied a strong and central role in traditional management theory. Most of the early research on leadership attempted to (1) compare the traits of people who became leaders with those who remain

Who is the leader?

TABLE 11-1. *Ghiselli's Managerial Traits*

Traits	Importance Value[a]
Supervisory ability (A)	100
Occupational achievement (M)	76
Intelligence (A)	64
Self-actualization (M)	63
Self-assurance (P)	62
Decisiveness (P)	61
Lack of need for security (M)	54
Working-class affinity (P)	47
Initiative (A)	34
Lack of need for high financial reward (M)	20
Need for power (M)	10
Maturity (P)	5
Masculinity-femininity (P)	0

Source: James F. Gavin, "A Test of Ghiselli's Theory of Managerial Traits," *Journal of Business Research* (February 1976): 46. Reprinted by permission.

Note: A = ability trait; P = personality trait; M = motivational trait.

[a]100 = very important; 0 = plays no part in managerial talent

as followers and (2) identify characteristics and traits possessed by effective leaders. Research studies comparing the traits of leaders and nonleaders have found that leaders tend to be somewhat taller, more outgoing, more self-confident, and more intelligent than nonleaders. But a specific combination of traits has not been found that would differentiate the leader or potential leader from the follower. As portrayed in the illustration on the previous page, it is difficult to identify the leader from an initial impression.

There has been considerable research to compare the traits of effective and ineffective leaders. Traits such as aggressiveness, ambition, decisiveness, dominance, initiative, intelligence, physical characteristics (looks, height, and weight), self-assurance, and other personality factors were studied to determine if they were related to effective leadership. The major question was: "Could such traits differentiate effective from ineffective leaders?" Perhaps the underlying assumption to personal trait research has been that leaders are born, not made. Although research has demonstrated that this is not the case, some people still believe there are certain inborn traits that make a person a good leader. Research has not shown that certain traits can distinguish effective from ineffective leaders.

trait approach

However, the **trait approach** to the study of leadership is not dead. Edwin Ghiselli has continued to conduct research in an effort to identify personality and motivational traits related to effective leadership.[1] Ghiselli identified thirteen trait factors. Subsequent research studies of these trait factors have ranked these in order of significance as illustrated in Table 11-1. The six most significant traits are defined below.

1. **Supervisory ability.** The performance of the basic functions of management, including planning, organizing, influencing, and controlling the work of others.

2. **Need for occupational achievement.** The seeking of responsibility and the desire for success.
3. **Intelligence.** Creative and verbal ability, including judgment, reasoning, and thinking capacity.
4. **Decisiveness.** Ability to make decisions and solve problems capably and competently.
5. **Self-assurance.** The extent to which the individual views himself or herself as capable of coping with problems.
6. **Initiative.** Ability to act independently and develop courses of action not readily apparent to other people. Self-starter—able to find new or innovative ways of doing things.

In spite of the contributions of Ghiselli, the trait approach to the study of leadership has left many unanswered questions concerning what is required for effective leadership. Perhaps one of the major problems with the trait approach is defining who is effective. Does the mere fact that a person has a powerful position make the individual a leader? Former President Carter had position power, but many questioned his effectiveness as a leader because of his lack of success in resolving foreign and domestic problems. For instance, Carter's ineffectiveness in handling the Iranian hostage crisis and in controlling inflation made many people question his leadership ability. As a rebuttal, people overwhelmingly elected Ronald Reagan as the new leader.

BEHAVIORAL THEORIES OF LEADERSHIP

Dissatisfaction with the trait approach caused most researchers to focus attention on the actual behavior and actions as opposed to traits or characteristics of leaders. During the 1950s and 1960s leadership was approached from the standpoint of identifying the types of behavior or styles that are available to leaders. Theories developed by Rensis Likert and Robert Blake and Jane Mouton advocate a universal style that is best for all leaders. Three other behavioral theories of leadership—Ohio State, path-goal, and Tannenbaum and Schmidt—suggest that a variety of factors determines the appropriate leadership behavior of managers.

Likert's Systems of Management

Likert's systems of management

Rensis Likert, former director of the Institute for Social Research at the University of Michigan, developed a universal theory of leadership. Likert's theory consists of a continuum of styles ranging from autocratic to participative. **Likert's** four basic **systems of management** are as follows: System I, Exploitative Autocratic; System II, Benevolent Autocratic; System III, Consultative; and System IV, Participative Team. Only the last style—System IV—was deemed best in the long run for all situations.[2]

System I—Exploitative Autocratic

Managers make all decisions. They decide what is to be done,who will do it, and how and when it is to be accomplished. Failure to complete work as assigned results in threats or punishment. Under this system, management exhibits little confidence or trust in employees. A typical managerial response with this system is, "You do it my way or you're fired." According to Likert there is a low level of trust and confidence between management and employees.

System II—Benevolent Autocratic

Managers still make the decisions, but employees have some degree of freedom and flexibility in performing their jobs so long as they conform to specific procedures. Under this system, managers take a very paternalistic attitude—"I'll take care of you if you perform well." With System II, there is a fairly low level of trust between management and the employees, which causes employees to use caution when dealing with management.

System III—Consultative

Managers consult with employees prior to establishing the goals and making decisions about the work. Employees have a considerable degree of freedom in making their own decisions as to how to accomplish the work. A manager using System III might say to an employee, "Charlie, I'd like your opinion on this before I make the decision." Management tends to rely on rewards as opposed to punishments to motivate employees. Also, the level of trust between the employees and management is fairly high. This creates a climate in which employees feel relatively free to discuss openly work-related matters with management.

System IV—Participative Team

This is Likert's recommended system or style of management. The emphasis of System IV is on a group participative role with full involvement of the employees in the process of establishing goals and making job-related decisions. Employees feel free to discuss matters with their manager, who displays supportive rather than condescending or threatening behavior. It is contended that an entire organization should be designed along System IV lines, with work being performed by a series of overlapping groups. The leader provides a link between the group and other units at higher levels in the organization. This concept is often referred to as the linking-pin theory. Decision making is widespread throughout the enterprise, with the power of knowledge usually taking precedence over the power of authority.

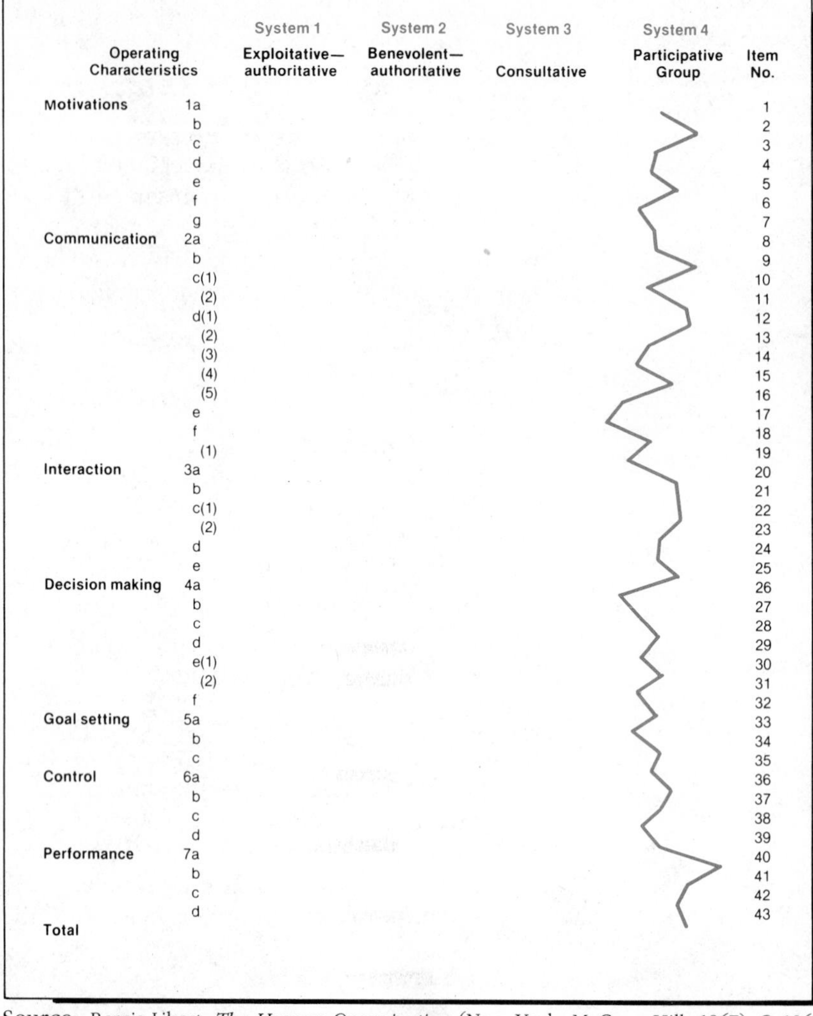

FIGURE 11-1

Likert Chart—Management Systems

Source: Rensis Likert. *The Human Organization* (New York: McGraw-Hill, 1967). © 1967 by McGraw-Hill Book Company. Used with permission.

Note: Management system used by the most productive plant (Plant L) of a well-managed company, as seen by middle- and upper-level managers.

Measurement of the type of style in the Likert framework is usually accomplished by having the employees assess the organizational climate and management system on a Likert scale. A profile showing the management system existing within an organization is developed through this survey of opinion (Figure 11-1). For example, when the question, "Extent to which superiors are willing to share information with subordinates?" is asked, the employee can answer on the continuum from "provide minimum information" all the way to "seeks to give subordinates all relevant information and all information they want" (see question 3C2 in Figure 11-2). It has been

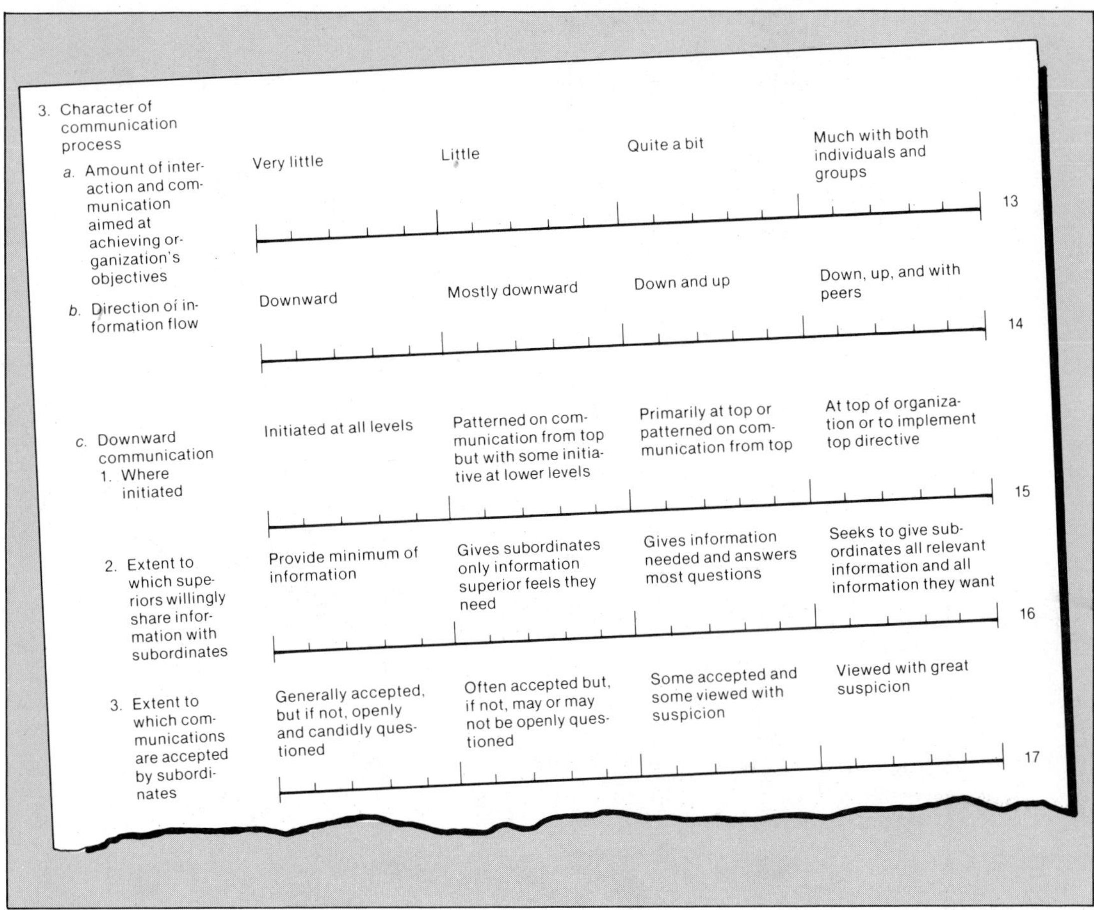

FIGURE 11-2 ***Sample of Questions on Likert Scale Relating to Communications Within the Organization*** [***Source:*** *Rensis Likert,* The Human Organization *(New York: McGraw-Hill, 1967). © 1967 by McGraw-Hill Book Company. Used with permission.*]

found that the positions on these scales can be significantly altered through organizational and management development programs, which will be discussed in Chapter 13.

Blake and Mouton's Managerial Grid

managerial grid

Perhaps the most widely known of all leadership theories is the **managerial grid** developed by Robert R. Blake and Jane S. Mouton.[3] The managerial grid is illustrated in Figure 11-3. The two dimensions of the 9 × 9 grid are labeled "concern for people" and "concern for production." A score of 1 indicates low concern and a score of 9 shows a high concern. The grid depicts five major leadership styles representing the degree of concern for "people" and "production."

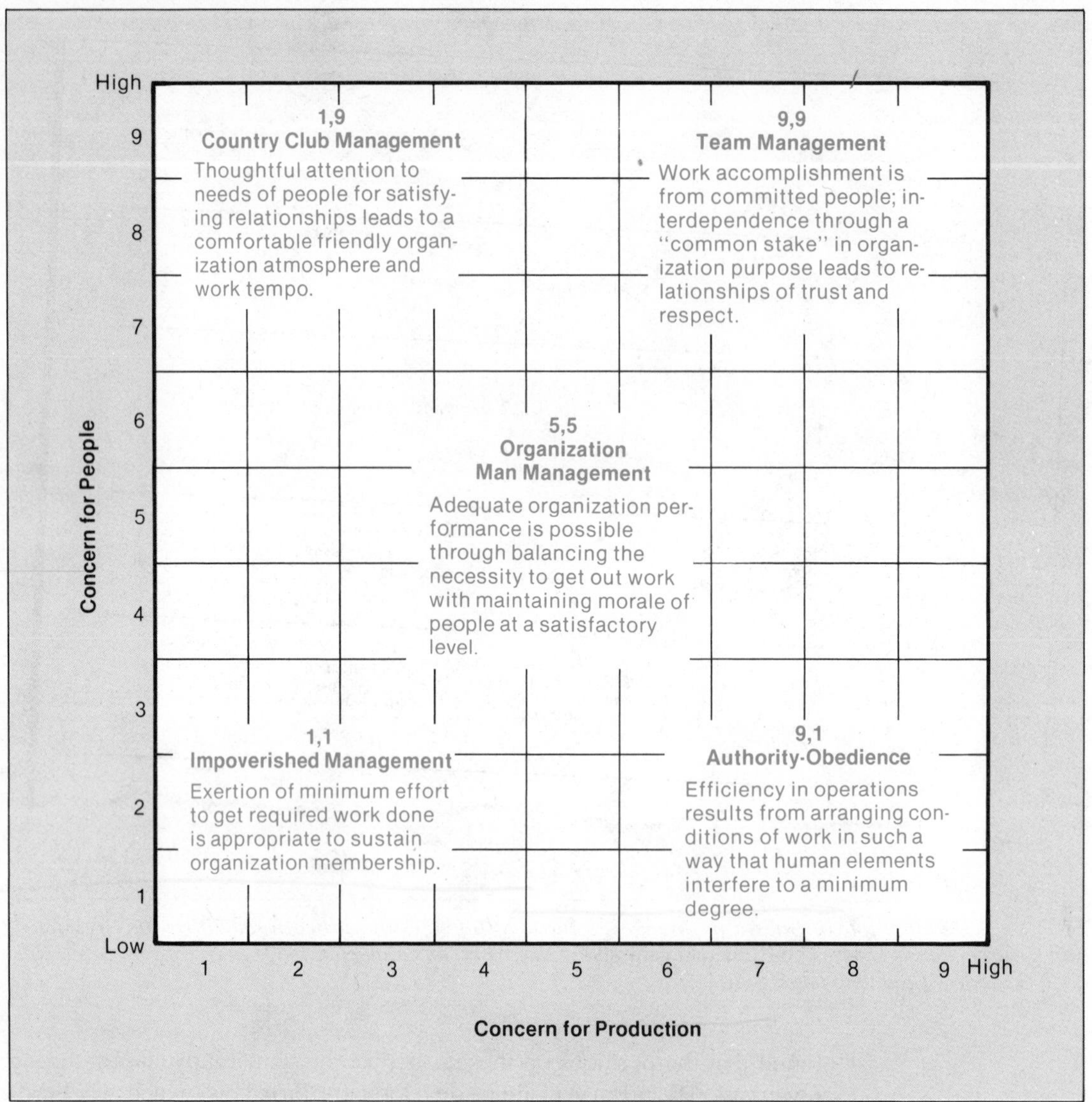

FIGURE 11-3 *Blake and Mouton's Managerial Grid®* [*Source:* The New Managerial Grid, *by Robert R. Blake and Jane Nrygley Mouton. Houston: Gulf Publishing Company, Copyright © 1978, page 11. Reproduced by permission.*]

- 1,1 **Impoverished Management**—The manager has little concern for either people or production.
- 9,1 **Authority-Obedience**—The manager stresses operating efficiently through controls in situations where human elements cannot interfere.
- 1,9 **Country Club Management**—The manager is thoughtful, comfortable, and friendly, and has little concern for output.

- 5,5 **Organization Man Management**—The manager attempts to balance and trade off concern for work in exchange for a satisfactory level of morale—a compromiser.
- 9,9 **Team Management**—The manager seeks high output through committed people, achieved through mutual trust, respect, and a realization of interdependence.[4]

According to Blake and Mouton, the first four styles listed are not the most effective leadership styles. They strongly suggest that only the 9,9 position of maximum concern for both output and people is the most effective. They argue that using the 9,9 team approach will result in improved performance, lower employee turnover and absenteeism, and greater employee satisfaction. The use of job enrichment and subordinate participation in managerial decision making contributes to this 9,9 situation where both the organization and its members are accorded maximum and equal concern. The managerial grid concept has been introduced to many managers throughout the world since its development in the early 1960s and has influenced the management philosophies and practices of many of them. Blake and Mouton have conducted grid training seminars around the world.

Ohio State Leadership Studies

Ohio State leadership studies

Beginning in 1945, researchers in the Bureau of Business Research at Ohio State University made a series of in-depth studies of the behavior of leaders in a wide variety of organizations. The key concern of the **Ohio State leadership studies** was the leader's behavior in directing the efforts of others toward group goals. After a considerable number of studies had been completed, two important dimensions of leader behavior were identified:

initiating structure

1. **Initiating Structure**—the extent to which leaders establish goals and structure their roles and the roles of subordinates toward the attainment of the goals.

consideration

2. **Consideration**—the extent to which leaders have relationships with subordinates characterized by mutual trust, respect, and consideration of employees' ideas and feelings.

Initiating structure and consideration were identified as separate and distinct dimensions of leadership behavior. As illustrated in Figure 11-4, there are four basic leadership styles representing different combinations of leadership behavior. A manager can be high in both consideration and initiating structure, low in both, or high in one and low in the other. Although there are two important elements of leadership behavior, the *one* most effective combination that meets the needs of all situations was not suggested by the Ohio State model. Rather, the combination or appropriate level of initiating structure and consideration was determined by the demands of the situation.

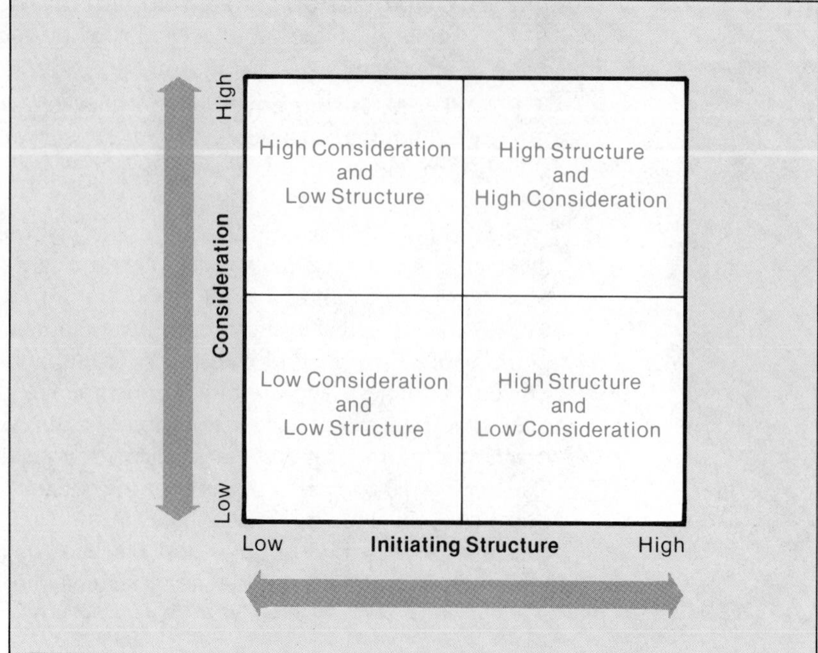

FIGURE 11-4

Ohio State Leadership Model

Among the many situational variables that must be related to leadership behavior are the following:

- expectations of the led
- degree of task structuring imposed by technology
- pressures of schedules and time
- degrees of interpersonal contact possible between leader and the led
- degree of influence of the leader outside of the group
- congruency of style with that of one's superior

The following observations can be made with regard to the type of leadership styles proposed in the Ohio State model:

- If a group expects and wants authoritarian leadership behavior, it is more likely to be satisfied with that type of leadership.
- If group members have less authoritarian expectations, a leader who strongly emphasizes initiating structure will be resented.
- If the work situation is highly structured by technology and the pressures of time, the supervisor who is high in consideration is more likely to meet with success as measured by absenteeism, turnover, and grievances.
- If task structuring precludes individual and group self-actualization, it will be useless to look for motivation from this source.

- When subordinates have little contact with their supervisor, they tend to prefer a more autocratic style.
- If employees must work and interact continuously, they usually want the superior to be high in consideration.

Path-Goal Theory of Leadership

path-goal theory

Robert House, extending the Ohio State studies, developed what he termed the **path-goal theory** of leadership.[5] This approach to leadership is also closely related to the expectancy theory of motivation discussed in Chapter 10. House concluded that managers can facilitate job performance by showing employees how their performance directly affects their receiving desired rewards. In other words, a manager's behavior causes or contributes to employee satisfaction and acceptance of the manager if it increases goal attainment by employees. According to the path-goal approach, effective job performance results if the manager clearly defines the job, provides training for the employee, assists the employee in performing the job effectively, and rewards the employee for effective performance.

Four distinct leadership behaviors are associated with the path-goal approach.

- **Directive**—The manager tells the subordinate what to do and when to do it (no employee participation in decision making).
- **Supportive**—The manager is friendly with and shows interest in employees.
- **Participative**—The manager seeks suggestions and involves employees in decision making.
- **Achievement oriented**—The manager establishes challenging goals and demonstrates confidence in employees in achieving these goals.

Following the path-goal theory, a manager may use all four of the behaviors in different situations. For instance, a manager may use directive behavior when supervising an inexperienced employee and supportive behavior when supervising a well-trained, experienced worker who is aware of the goals to be attained. The primary focus of the path-goal approach is on how managers can increase employee motivation and job satisfaction by clarifying performance goals and the path to achieve the goals.[6]

Tannenbaum and Schmidt's Leadership Continuum

Robert Tannenbaum and Warren H. Schmidt described a series of factors that they thought influenced a manager's selection of the most appropriate leadership style. Their approach advocated a continuum of leadership behavior sup-

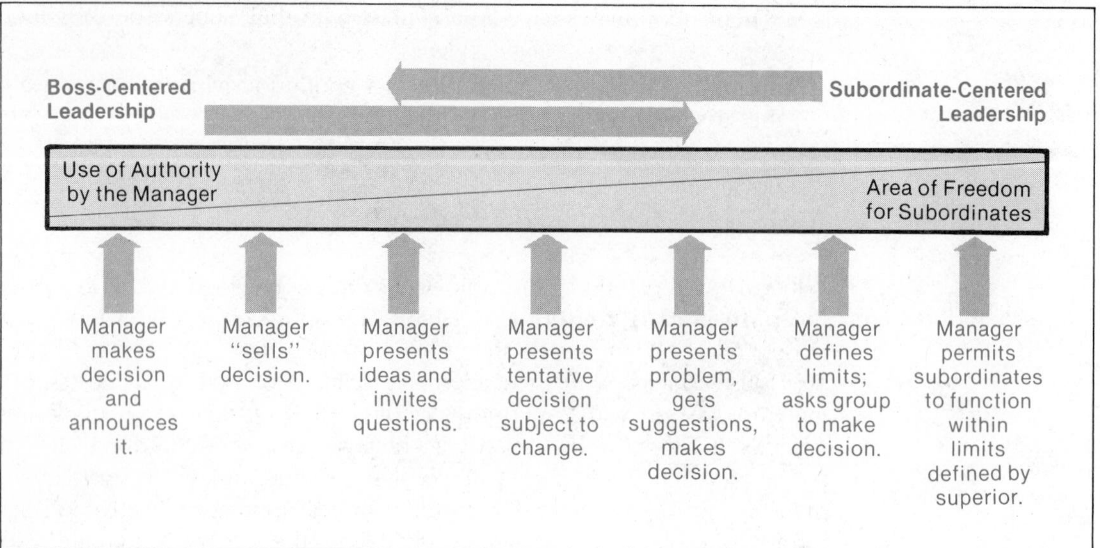

FIGURE 11-5 *Continuum of Leadership Behavior.* [*Source: Reprinted by permission of the* Harvard Business Review. *Exhibit from "How to Choose a Leadership Pattern" by Robert Tannenbaum and Warren H. Schmidt (May/June 1973). Copyright © 1973 by the President and Fellows of Harvard College. All rights reserved.*]

porting the notion that choosing an effective leadership style depends on the demands of the situation. As illustrated in Figure 11-5, leadership behavior ranges from "Boss-Centered" to "Subordinate-Centered," which is similar in concept to the other dimensions of leadership behavior discussed. Tannenbaum and Schmidt emphasized that a manager should gvie careful consideration to the following factors before selecting a leadership style:

- **Characteristics of the manager**—background, education, experience, values, knowledge, goals, and expectations
- **Characteristics of the employees**—background, education, experience, knowledge, goals, values, and expectations
- **Requirements of the situation**—size, complexity, goals, structure, and climate of the organization, as well as the impact of technology, time pressure, and nature of the work

leadership continuum

According to the Tannenbaum and Schmidt **leadership continuum,** a manager may engage in a more participative leadership style when subordinates

- Seek independence and freedom of action
- Understand and are committed to the goals of the organization
- Are well educated and experienced in performing the jobs
- Seek responsibility for decision making
- Expect a participative style of leadership

If the above conditions do not exist, managers may need to adopt a more autocratic or "boss-centered" leadership style. Thus, in essence, managers must be able to diagnose the situations confronting them and then attempt to choose a leadership style that will improve their chances for effectiveness. The most effective leaders are neither "task centered" nor "people centered," but rather they are flexible enough to select a leadership style that fits their needs as well as the needs of their subordinates and the situation.

SITUATIONAL LEADERSHIP STYLES

The current trend in the study of leadership has been toward a situational approach. In this section, we discuss two situational theories of leadership. Increased knowledge and understanding of these theories can be of significant benefit to managers and those who aspire to managerial positions.

1. Fred Fiedler's Contingency Leadership Model
2. Hersey and Blanchard's Situational Leadership Model

Fiedler's Contingency Leadership Model

Fiedler's contingency leadership model

The contingency theory developed by Fred E. Fiedler has received considerable recognition as a situational approach to leadership.[7] **Fiedler's contingency leadership model** suggests that there is no one most effective style that is appropriate to every situation. He says that there are a number of styles that may be effective depending on the situation. The framework is made up of eight significantly different situations and two basic types of leadership orientations. Three major elements seem to determine whether a given situation is favorable to a leader. These are:

leader-member relations

- **leader-member relations**—the degree to which the leader feels accepted by subordinates. The atmosphere may be friendly or unfriendly, relaxed or tense, and threatening or supportive.

task structure

- **task structure**—clearly defined goals, decisions, and solutions to problems.

position power of the leader

- **position power of the leader**—the degree of influence over rewards and punishments, as well as by his or her official authority.

The concept of leader-member relations is similar to the consideration or relationship behavior concepts, while task structure and position power are closely related to initiating structure or task behavior as discussed previously. By mixing these three elements, eight situations can be identified in Table 11-2.

TABLE 11-2. *Framework of Fiedler's Contingency Leadership Model*

Situation	Degree of Favorableness of Situation to Leader	Leader-Member Relations	Task Structure	Position Power of Leader
1	Favorable	Good	Structured	High
2	Favorable	Good	Structured	Low
3	Favorable	Good	Unstructured	High
4	Moderately Favorable	Good	Unstructured	Low
5	Moderately Favorable	Poor	Structured	High
6	Moderately Favorable	Poor	Structured	Low
7	Moderately Favorable	Poor	Unstructured	High
8	Unfavorable	Poor	Unstructured	Low

Source: Edwin B. Flippo and Gary M. Munsinger, *Management,* 4th ed. (Boston: Allyn and Bacon, 1978), p. 381.

These eight situations vary in accordance with the degree of favorableness of a situation to a leader—which is the leader's influence and control over the group. A leader has maximum influence in situation 1 and very little in situation 8. Research evidence indicates that a task-oriented, controlling leader will be most effective when the situations are either very favorable or easy (1, 2, and 3) or very difficult (see Table 11-2).[8] The more permissive, considerate leader performs more effectively in the intermediate situations, which are moderately favorable to the leader (4, 5, 6, and 7). Another way to illustrate Fiedler's framework is seen in Figure 11-6. The task-oriented style of leader is more effective in situations 1, 2, 3, and 8 while the relationship-oriented style is more effective in situations 4, 5, 6, and 7. As demonstrated

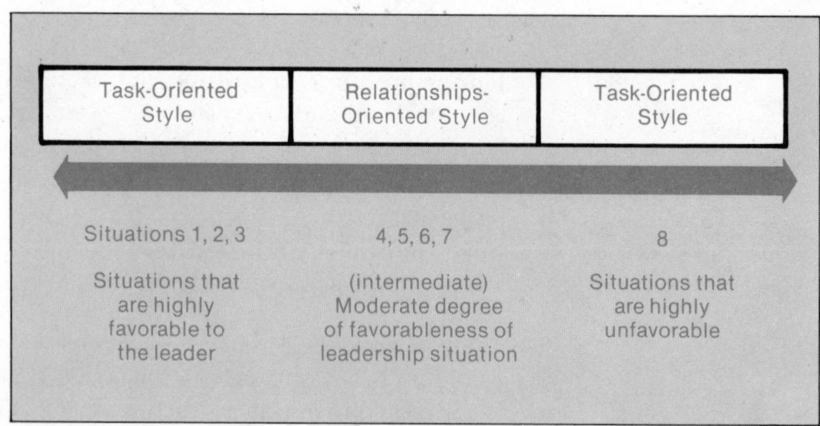

FIGURE 11-6

Appropriateness of Leadership Styles to Situation

Source: Adapted from Edwin B. Flippo and Gary M. Munsinger, *Management,* 4th ed. (Boston: Allyn and Bacon, 1978), p. 381.

by Fiedler's theory, the most effective leadership style is contingent on many situational factors.

Hersey and Blanchard's Situational Leadership Theory

Hersey and Blanchard's situational leadership theory

Paul Hersey and Kenneth Blanchard have developed a situational leadership theory that has attracted considerable attention on the part of managers.[9] **Hersey and Blanchard's situational leadership theory** is based on the notion that the most effective leadership style varies according to the level of maturity of the followers and demands of the situation. Their model uses two dimensions of leadership behavior—task and relationship. These are similar to the classifications used in the leadership models developed by Ohio State and the managerial grid. Hersey and Blanchard argue that an effective leader is one who can diagnose the demands of the situation and the level of maturity of the followers and use a leadership style that is appropriate. Their theory is based on a relationship between these factors:

task behavior

relationship behavior

task-relevant maturity

1. The amount of **task behavior** the leader exhibits—(providing direction and emphasis on getting the job done)
2. The amount of **relationship behavior** the leader provides (consideration of people, level of emotional support for people)
3. The level of **task-relevant maturity** followers exhibit toward the specific goal, task or function that the leader wants accomplished.

The key concept of their leadership theory is the level of task-relevant maturity of the followers. Maturity is not defined as age or psychological stability. The maturity level of the followers is defined as:

- *A desire for achievement*—(level of achievement motivation) based on the need to set high but attainable goals
- *The willingness and ability to accept responsibility*
- *Education and/or experience and skills* relevant to the particular task

A leader should consider the level of maturity of his or her followers only in relation to the work or job to be performed. Certainly employees are "mature" on some tasks when they have the experience and skills as well as the desire to achieve and are capable of assuming responsibility. For example, Dianne Crawford, an accountant, may be very "mature" in the manner in which she prepares accurate quarterly IRS tax reports, but Dianne may not exhibit the same level of maturity when preparing written audits of the company's operations. Dianne needs very little direction or task-related behavior from her manager in preparing the tax reports but may require considerably closer supervision and direction over the preparation and writing of audits. Dianne may not have the skills and/or motivation to prepare audits, but with proper training, direction, and encouragement from her manager can assume greater responsibility in this area.

Qualities Needed for Success as a Manager in Your Organization

- **Finding the fine line between a workaholic and an 8:00 to 5:00'er that lets you make sure you keep your perspective with regard to other responsibilities, i.e., family, community, church, self. Time should be an ally, not an enemy.**
- **Putting people where they can perform profitably for the company and themselves.**
- **A "can do" attitude.**
- **Understanding the difference between leadership and dictatorship.**

BERL M. SPRINGER, President, Southwestern Public Service Company

---

Hersey and Blanchard argue that leadership style and effectiveness can be measured, and they have designed an instrument for this purpose—the Leader Effectiveness & Adaptability Description (LEAD). The LEAD provides feedback on leadership style and the effectiveness of the individual completing the instrument.[10]

As illustrated in Figure 11-7, the appropriate leadership style used by a manager varies according to the maturity level (represented by M1 through M4) of the followers. There are four distinct leadership styles that are appropriate given different levels of maturity. As the task-relevant maturity level of followers increases, the manager should reduce task behavior and increase relationship behavior. These are illustrated by the classifications of the styles as:

S1—Telling	High task Low relationship
S2—Selling	High task High relationship
S3—Participating	High relationship Low task
S4—Delegating	Low relationship Low task

With the S1 (Telling) high-task, low-relationship leadership style, the leader uses one-way communication, defines the goals and roles of employ-

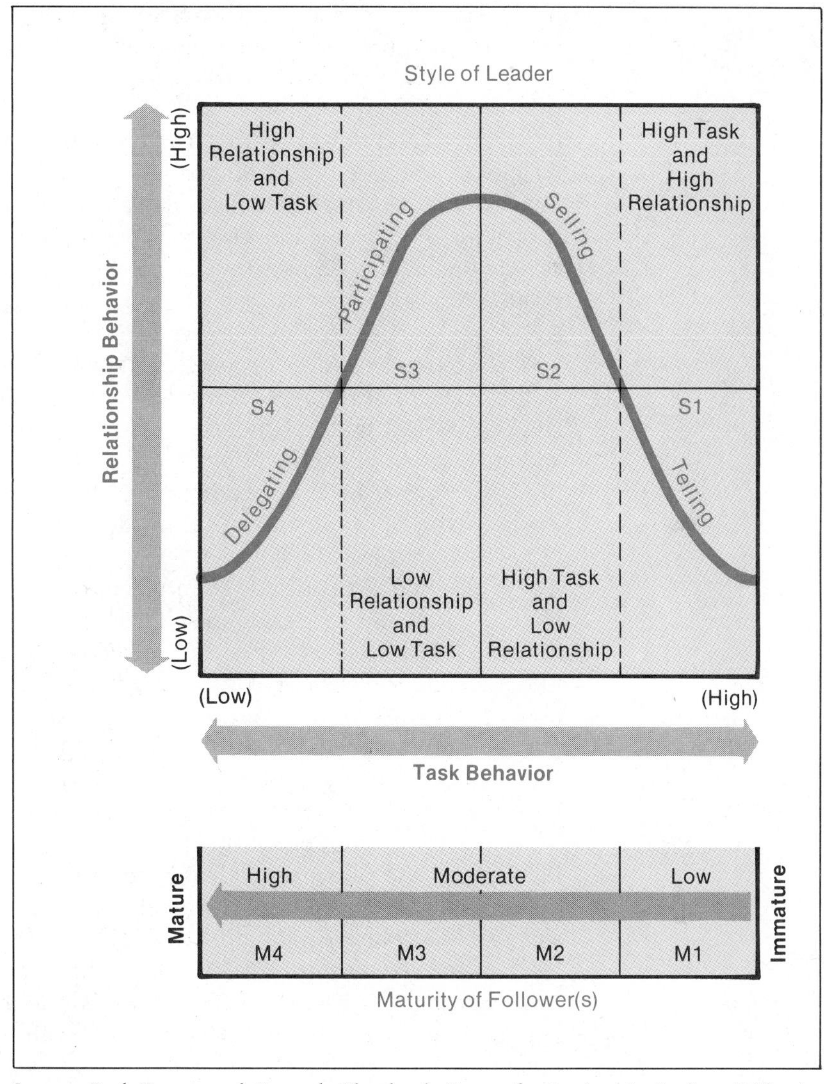

FIGURE 11-7
Situational Leadership

Source: Paul Hersey and Kenneth Blanchard. Center for Leadership Studies. California American University, 1977. Used with permission.

ees, and tells them what, how, when, and where to do the work. This style is very appropriate when dealing with subordinates who lack task-relevant maturity. For example, in supervising a group of relatively new, inexperienced employees, a high level of task-directed behavior and low-relationship behavior may be an appropriate leadership approach. Inexperienced employees need to be told what to do and how to accomplish their jobs.

As employees learn their jobs, the manager begins to use an S2 leadership style. There still is a need for a high level of task behavior since the employees do not yet have the experience or skills to assume more responsibility, but the manager provides a higher level of emotional support—

high-relationship behavior. The manager encourages the employees and demonstrates greater trust and confidence in them.

As we move toward the S3 leadership style, the employee begins to exhibit an increase in task-relevant maturity. As employees become more experienced and skilled, as well as more achievement motivated and more willing to assume responsibility, the leader should reduce the amount of task behavior but continue the high level of emotional support and consideration. A continuation of a high level of relationship behavior is the manager's way of reinforcing the employees' responsible performance. Thus, S3—high-relationship and low-task behavior—becomes the appropriate leadership style.

The S4 leadership style represents the highest level of follower maturity. In this stage, the employees possess a very high level of task maturity. They are very skilled and experienced, possess high achievement motivation, and are capable of exercising self-control. Thus, the leadership style that is most appropriate for this situation is S4—low relationship and low task. At this point the employees no longer need or expect a high level of supportive or task behavior from their leader.

We should not conclude from this discussion that it is simple to determine the appropriate leadership style. The ability to diagnose the maturity level of the followers, as well as the specific needs of the situation, is complex. The leader must have insight into the abilities, needs, demands, and expectations of followers and be aware that these can and do change over time. Also, managers must recognize that they must adapt or change their style of leadership whenever there is a change in the level of maturity of followers for whatever reason—change in jobs, personal or family problems, or change in complexity of present job due perhaps to new technology. For example, Bill Woodall, the sales manager, has been using an S4 leadership style in supervising John Chriswell, a normally highly productive sales representative. But suppose that John's pending divorce has recently been adversely affecting his performance. In this situation, Bill might increase both the level of task and relationship behavior in order to provide John with the direction, support, and confidence he may need to cope with his problems and improve his performance.

In summary, Hersey and Blanchard's theory provides a useful and understandable framework for situational leadership. In essence, their model suggests that there is *no one* best leadership style that meets the needs of all situations. Rather, a manager's leadership style must be adaptable and flexible enough to meet the changing needs of employees and situations. The effective manager is one who can change styles as employees develop and change or as required by the situation.

AN INTEGRATED APPROACH TO LEADERSHIP

The notion that there is one "best" leadership style has been criticized as being unrealistic and overly simplistic. Is it logical to assume that the *same* leadership style would be equally effective in managing such diverse groups as auto assemblers, research scientists, clerk-typists, college professors, lawyers, or construction workers? We think not! From our previous discussion of the situational leadership theories, it should be apparent that there is no one best style of leadership that is equally effective for all circumstances. The most effective leadership style is one that meets the needs of the particular situation at hand. This requires a careful consideration of forces in the leader, the followers, and the specific situation.

The development of an integrated approach to effective leadership requires that we consider several important situational factors. As shown in Figure 11-8, forces in the leader, the followers, and the situation all interrelate to determine the most effective leadership style. Although the situational factors are presented in a different format, the importance of giving careful

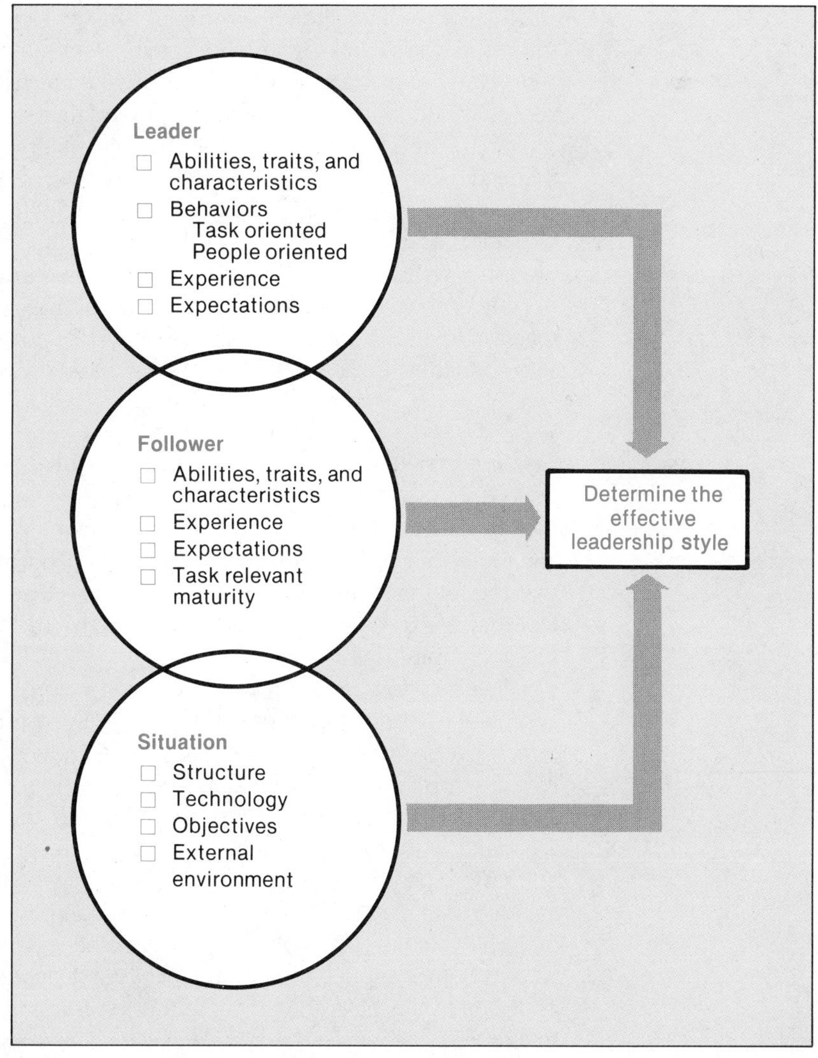

FIGURE 11-8

An Integrated Approach to Leadership

consideration to these factors remains. The *management approach* is associated with the leader. The followers represent the *personnel.* The situation includes the *structure,* the *technology, objectives,* and the *external environment.* Each of these elements will be discussed as it is a determinant of effective leadership style.

Leader

All of us have different combinations of abilities, personalities, experiences, and expectations. Because of these factors each of us develops different patterns of accomplishing tasks. If it has been discovered that a certain behavioral pattern has worked successfully in the past, this approach will likely continue in the future. A person who has found that being an autocratic manager will get the job done will likely continue this pattern unless events occur that show this style is no longer appropriate. The same situation may evolve for a person who has developed participative patterns. A participative style may also continue to be used unless it is proved that it is no longer effective.

With the integrated approach to leadership, managers must recognize the leadership style they are currently using. Then an evaluation is made as to what managerial approach will be most effective based on a careful consideration of the nature of the followers and the situation. The leader adapts his or her style to meet the needs of the followers and the situation. This does not mean that the manager's basic beliefs change. However, it does mean that for the time a manager is in a particular leadership role, his or her leadership style must be adapted to the followers and the situation.

Followers

Like the leader, followers have different abilities, personalities, experiences, and expectations. With the integrated approach to leadership it is recognized that the followers may not necessarily obey a leader's order. If the followers feel that it is in their best interest to abide by the wishes of the leader, they will accomplish the task.

Thus, followers are a major factor for consideration in the integrated approach to leadership. If the followers are inexperienced, lack the necessary education or skills, and do not seek more individual responsibility for their job, the most effective leadership style will tend to be more directive or autocratic, emphasizing task accomplishment. On the other hand, if personnel are highly educated, experienced, and seek responsibility for decision making, a more participative style of leadership may be most appropriate. At times a manager may need to emphasize task accomplishment strongly and a statement like "let's get the job done" may be necessary to accomplish the work. At other times a much more participative style suggested by a comment such as "I need your help and advice if this job is going to be done" will provide the most effective leadership. Managers must take into consideration the needs, goals, capabilities, and experiences of the followers if their effectiveness is to be achieved.

Situation

The four factors of structure, technology, objectives, and the external environment comprise the situation (check back to Figure 11-8). Each must be considered if leaders are to determine their most effective style.

The organizational structure and the environment in which the manager operates affect the leadership style. In a highly structured environment, a more autocratic style may be most appropriate.

Technology is another major factor that affects the selection of the most appropriate leadership style. Technology has an impact on the design of work, which may in turn determine the most appropriate leadership style.

As the objectives of the firm change, a change in leadership style may be necessary. For example, if a firm determines that it should be an innovative organization, personnel changes may require a modification of leadership styles. The personnel who are hired to make the transition to an innovative firm may not accept the autocratic style of its predecessor. As the level of professional and technical capabilities increases, the style of leadership may lean toward a more relationship-oriented leadership style. On the other hand, if the firm's goal is survival, the leadership style may again move toward a greater emphasis on task accomplishment.

The external environment has considerable influence on determining the most effective leadership style. Obviously economic, political, social, and cultural forces must be considered. For example, during periods of economic crunches or slowdowns, which cause a decline in sales for a company, some managers tend to become more direct and cost-conscious and place greater emphasis on the efficiency of task accomplishment. The interaction of all the situational variables must be a consideration by managers who wish to use the most effective leadership style.

During the past two decades, there has been a significant increase in the educational level of the people entering the work force. There have also been changes in social and cultural values, which, in effect, are demanding that leaders be able to adapt to the situation. These trends support the conclusion that there is no one best style of leadership that will meet the needs of all followers or the demands of every situation.

Summary

Effective leadership is essential to the survival and growth of every organization. Leadership is the process of motivating and directing others toward the accomplishment of goals. But what is required to be an effective manager and what is the most effective leadership style? These questions have been of concern to managers for generations and have been the subject of thousands of research studies. Despite volumes of leadership research, no simple list of traits or characteristics has been identified that is consistently related to effective leadership. In fact, the basic conclusion of these studies is that there is no one most effective leadership style.

Three basic theories of leadership were discussed in this chapter—trait, behavioral, and situational. The early studies of leadership attempted to identify the traits and characteristics of effective leaders. Traits relating to physical characteristics, personality, or intelligence were studied to determine if they were related to effective leadership. For the most part, research has not shown that traits alone can distinguish effective from ineffective leaders. Despite these findings, the trait approach to the study of leadership has continued. Edwin Ghiselli has identified six traits/characteristics that his extensive research indicates are related to effective leadership. These include supervisory ability, need for occupational achievement, intelligence, decisiveness, self-assurance, and initiative.

Dissatisfaction with the trait approach to the study of leadership caused the research emphasis to concentrate on the behavior and actions of leaders. The behavioral theories identified two basic dimensions of leadership behavior. Although these two behaviors have been referred to by several different names, they are the leader's behavior and concern for (1) the accomplishment of tasks (task behavior) and (2) the relationship with people (relationship behavior). One of the most widely known leadership theories is the managerial grid. The two dimensions of leadership behavior identified in the 9 × 9 managerial grid is "concern for people" and "concern for production." Five basic styles of leadership on the grid were do nothing (1,1), task centered (9,1), country club (1,9), organization man (5,5), and team builder (9,9). Blake and Mouton, the developers of the grid theory, suggest that the 9,9 style of leadership is the most effective and achieves the best results in terms of performance.

In recent years, considerable attention has been given to the situational approach to the study of leadership. The basic conclusion of this approach is that the most effective leaders are neither task centered nor people centered. Rather effective leaders must be flexible enough to adopt a leadership style that fits their needs as well as the needs of their subordinates and the situation.

The theories of Fred Fiedler and Paul Hersey and Kenneth Blanchard suggest there is no one most effective style of leadership that is appropriate to every situation. In Fiedler's theory, the degree of favorableness or unfavorableness of the leader-member relations, task structure, and position power of the leader determine the style of leadership that is most effective. Finally, Hersey and Blanchard's theory is based on the notion that the most effective leadership style varies according to the level of maturity of the followers and the demands of the situation. Their theory offers four basic styles or combinations of task and relationship behavior of the leader. If the leader is dealing with "highly mature followers" the appropriate leadership style might be low emphasis on both relationships and task behavior.

Perhaps the most realistic approach to leadership is an integrated one that carefully considers the forces in the leader, the followers, and the situation. To be truly effective in achieving goals, the leader must recognize that no one approach will be equally effective for all circumstances.

Review Questions

1. What is meant by the term *leadership*? Why is it an important subject?
2. What is the distinction between management and leadership? Is it possible to be a good leader but an ineffective manager?
3. In the chapter, what caused the bankruptcy of the mobile home company?
4. Briefly describe and contrast the types of power a leader may possess to influence the behavior of others.
5. What is the trait approach to the study of leadership? To what extent are certain traits related to effective leadership?
6. List several significant traits identified by the research of Edwin Ghiselli as being important for effective leadership.
7. What are the four basic styles or systems of management identified by Rensis Likert? Explain each.
8. Describe the five leadership styles presented in the Managerial Grid. Which style is recommended as most effective by Blake and Mouton?
9. What were the Ohio State leadership studies? What basic dimensions of leadership behavior were identified? What were some of the factors that determined the most effective style of leadership?
10. What basic conclusion can be derived from the Tannenbaum and Schmidt leadership continuum? What factors should be considered before choosing a given style of leadership?
11. What is the basic contention of Fiedler's theory of leadership? In what situations are task-centered leaders most effective? People-centered leaders?
12. Briefly explain Hersey and Blanchard's situational leadership theory. What is the key concept of their theory?
13. Describe what is meant by an integrated approach to leadership.

Exercises

1. Assume you have just been promoted to the position of office manager in charge of twelve clerical personnel—eight typists and four general clerks. The previous manager was removed from the position because the office staff was not able to complete their work on schedule. In addition, the office experienced excessive turnover of employees, and several of the employees had expressed concern about poor quality of work and attitudes of the clerical staff. Under the previous manager, the employees showed little interest in their jobs and generally viewed the office manager as a "soft touch."

a. What style of leadership would you utilize as you assume the position of office manager?

b. Explain, in terms of situational leadership theory presented in this chapter, how your leadership style would change should output improve and employee turnover decrease.

2. Go to the library and make a copy of the article "So You Want To Know Your Leadership Style?" by Paul Hersey and Kenneth Blanchard, *Training and Development Journal* (February 1974): 22–32. Complete the Leader Adaptability and Style (LASI) instrument contained in the article. Then read the article. What is your leadership style as per the LASI? Discuss in class.

Case Study

Choosing an Appropriate Leadership Style

Allen Russell was chosen six months ago to be manager of the research and development department for Western Engineering. The senior vice-president who made the decision reasoned that the R&D department could use the expertise of a person who was experienced in production problems. Allen had been a line foreman and had an excellent reputation for getting the job done. He was well organized and was credited with being able to solve problems prior to their reaching upper-level management. The primary emphasis of the research and development department was to conduct practical research for the purpose of developing marketable products. Thus, top management believed Allen would do well in this assignment because of his knowledge of production operations.

When Allen arrived at his new job he could not believe how "unorganized" the researchers were. They might come to work at 10:00 and leave at 3:00 (Allen did not realize that many of them worked late at night). The employees were all dedicated researchers and considered themselves professionals. They did not feel that a task had to be lined out in detail for the job to be done.

Allen believed that these conditions were not conducive to maximum productivity. He had been taught on the production line that efficiency is a direct result of the organization and structure of tasks. If it works in one situation, it should work in another.

The first decision that Allen made was to install a time clock. He reasoned that if the department members were to be productive, they must be at their desks during certain hours of the day. The researchers in Allen's department expressed disbelief of this decision. Before Allen became supervisor, most of the researchers were working an average of twelve hours a day. Although they might not be at the office between eight and five, they were recognized as being very productive. Many of the researchers actually liked to work Saturday morning because the activity level of the plant was lower and they could concentrate better. Without realizing it, Allen was actually telling the departmental members to reduce their work time by one-third.

When Allen arrived at work at 8:00 on Monday he was pleased to see that all of the researchers clocked in at the proper time. They remained at their desk the entire day and left promptly at 5:00. He reasoned that everything was going to be great. The employees had accepted him as their superior. This euphoria did not last for long. People throughout the company began calling him to ask why their particular project was not finished. When he checked with the persons who were responsible for the project, he found out that they had been working on it but had not had time to complete it. In virtually every instance this was the case.

Allen came to the conclusion that the researchers were "goofing off," and he issued numerous letters of reprimand. Meanwhile, several key employees resigned to take other positions. The situation continued to deteriorate until there was virtually no useful work being conducted in the department. When the vice-president finally asked Allen what was causing this inefficiency, he responded, "They were all a bunch of super-egos but I can get them in shape." The vice-president is not so sure that this is the problem and asks for your advice.

QUESTIONS

1. What assumptions did management make with regard to making Allen Russell the research and development department manager?
2. How would you describe the leadership style of Allen? How appropriate was this style to the management of the research and development department?
3. What style of leadership would likely be most effective in managing a group of researchers?
4. Assume that you are the vice-president of Western (Allen's boss). What action would you take to improve the situation?

Case Study

Failure to Take a Promotion

Nancy Rodgers had been employed with Stockton, Inc. as an accountant since she graduated from college five years ago. She enjoyed her work and the close association she had made with the other accountants and staff within the office. During this time Nancy gained a reputation for being highly efficient and for being able to react quickly to a crisis. When she was evaluated by her supervisor each year, Nancy consistently received the highest rating in the department. She had no idea that these excellent evaluations might ultimately return to haunt her.

When the departmental supervisor was promoted to the position of controller, Nancy was a prime contender for the supervisory position. Everyone liked Nancy, and her superiority on the job was recognized by all. It did not take long for management to make the decision that Nancy was the one to become the new department head. The promotion would mean a substantial increase in salary and respectability within the firm.

The only problem was that Nancy did not want the promotion. She enjoyed the work she was doing and had absolutely no aspiration to obtain a managerial position. The new controller was shocked to find out that Nancy rejected the offer. He felt that it was a "slap in his face" and took a personal offense that the person he recommended would refuse the offer. When a new supervisor was selected from outside the firm, the bad feelings that the controller had regarding Nancy were communicated to the new supervisor. The controller's attitude was not directed toward Nancy's work (her efficiency was a well-known fact). The tone of his comments related to "company loyalty," "dedication," and "faithfulness." This attitude ultimately filtered down to the employees in Nancy's department. Many of her "friends" were not as close to Nancy as they once were.

The few friends who remained were not accepted by the other members of the work group. When the time for Nancy's annual evaluation arrived, it was not nearly as good as it had been in the past.

Nancy became extremely depressed by the loss of respect and friendships within the department. This was reflected in her work as she began making numerous errors. Also, ideas that she presented to her peers and the department manager were frequently rejected. Her drop in efficiency caused her to receive several reprimands by the manager. After the third reprimand Nancy was told she was terminated. She was given two weeks pay but was asked to leave the company immediately.

QUESTIONS

1. What caused this situation to develop?
2. In view of the circumstances, do you feel it would have been in Nancy's best interest to accept the promotion?
3. What mistake(s) did the new controller make regarding Nancy? Discuss.
4. What approach to leadership would have been appropriate in this situation? In other words, how should the company and especially the controller have reacted to Nancy's not wanting to become the department supervisor?

Notes

1. Edwin Ghiselli, *Explorations in Managerial Talent* (Pacific Palisades, Calif.: Goodyear, 1971).
2. Rensis Likert, *The Human Organization* (New York: McGraw-Hill, 1967).
3. Used with permission of Robert R. Blake and Jane S. Mouton, *The New Managerial Grid* (Houston: Gulf Publishing, 1978), p. 11.
4. Ibid.
5. Robert House, "A Path-Goal Theory of Leadership Effectiveness," *Administrative Science Quarterly* 16 (September 1971): 321–338.
6. Alan C. Filley, Robert House, and Steven Kerr, *Managerial Process and Organizational Behavior* (Glenview, Ill.: Scott, Foresman, 1976), pp. 256–260.
7. Fred E. Fiedler, *A Theory of Leadership Effectiveness* (New York: McGraw-Hill, 1967).
8. William J. Reddin, *Managerial Effectiveness* (New York: McGraw-Hill, 1970).
9. Paul Hersey and Kenneth Blanchard, *Management of Organizational Behavior: Utilizing Human Resources,* 3d ed. (Englewood Cliffs, N.J.: Prentice-Hall, 1977), pp. 94–95.
10. See Paul Hersey and Kenneth Blanchard, "So You Want to Know Your Leadership Style?" *Training and Development Journal* (February 1974): 22–32. This article contains the Leader Adaptability and Style Inventory (LASI), an instrument that can be used to examine your leadership behavior, style adaptability, and effectiveness. Since this article, the LASI has become the Leader Effectiveness and Adaptability Description (LEAD). Information, LEAD inventories and training materials may be obtained from the Center for Leadership Studies, 17253 Caminito Canasto, Rancho Bernardo, San Diego, CA 92127.

References

Burke, W. W. "Leadership: Is There One Best Approach?" *Management Review* 69 (November, 1980): 54–56.

Butler, Mark C., and Jones, Allan P. "Perceived Leader Behavior, Individual Characteristics, and Injury Occurrence in Hazardous Work Environments." *Journal of Applied Psychology* 64, no. 3 (June 1979): 299–304.

Carbone, T. C. "Theory X and Theory Y Revisited." *Mangerial Planning* 29 (May–June 1981): 24–27.

Fiedler, F. E. "Job Engineering for Effective Leadership: A New Approach." *Management Review* 66 (September 1977): 29–31.

———, and Mahar, Linda. "The Effectiveness of Contingency Model Training: A Review of the Validation of Leader Match." *Personnel Psychology* 32, no. 1 (Spring 1979): 45–62.

Fox, W. M. "Limits to the Use of Consultative-Participative Management." *California Management Review* 20 (Winter 1977): 17–22.

Green, S. G., and Nebeker, D. M. "Effects of Situational Factors and Leadership Style on Leader Behavior." *Organizational Behavior and Human Performance* 19 (August 1977): 368–377.

Greene, Charles N. "Questions of Causation in the Path-Goal Theory of Leadership." *Academy of Management Journal* 22, no. 1 (March 1979): 22–41.

Griffin, R. W. "Relationships among Individual, Task Design and Leader Behavior Variables." *Academy of Management Journal* 23 (December 1980): 665–683.

Himes, G. K. "Management Leadership Styles." *Supervision* 42 (November 1980): 9–11.

Katz, R. "Influence of Group Conflict on Leadership Effectiveness." *Organizational Behavior and Human Performance* 20 (December 1977): 265–286.

Klimoski, R. J., and Hayes, N. J. "Leadership Behavior and Subordinate Motivation." *Personnel Psychology* 33 (Autumn 1980): 543–545.

Leister, A., et al. "Validation of Contingency Model Leadership Training: Leader Match." *Academy of Management Journal* 20 (September 1977): 464–470.

Likert, R. "Management Styles and the Human Component." *Management Review* 66 (October 1977): 23–28.

Miner, Frederick C., Jr. "A Comparative Analysis of Three Diverse Group Decision Making Approaches." *Academy of Management Journal* 22, no. 1 (March 1979): 81–93.

Peters, Thomas J. "Leadership: Sad Facts and Silver Linings." *Harvard Business Review* 57, no. 6 (November–December 1979): 164–172.

Schriesheim, C. A., and Schriesheim, J. F. "Test of the Path-Goal Theory of Leadership and Some Suggested Direction for Future Research." *Personnel Psychology* 33 (Summer 1980): 368–370.

Sinetar, M. "Developing Leadership Potential." *Personnel Journal* 60 (March 1981): 193–196.

Zeleznik, A. "Managers and Leaders: Are They Different?" *Harvard Business Review* 55 (May 1977): 67–68.

Zierden, William E. "Leading Through the Follower's Point of View." *Organizational Dynamics* 8, no. 4 (Spring 1980): 27–46.

KEY TERMS

- communication
- source (sender)
- receiver
- barriers to communication
- timing
- communication overload
- filtering
- perception set
- empathy
- listening
- body language
- transactional analysis
- Parent
- Child
- Adult
- conflict management
- arbitration
- mediator

LEARNING OBJECTIVES

After completing this chapter you should be able to

1. Describe the basic components of the communication process and state what should be communicated to workers.
2. Explain the basic forms of organizational channels of communication.
3. Identify the barriers that can cause breakdowns in communication.
4. Describe the facilitators that are available to improve communication.
5. Explain conflict management and identify various means of dealing with conflict.

12

Communication

Pat Steen, the production foreman for Abbot Electronics, had just been told by his supervisor that production output had to be increased if the company was to meet the deadline on a large contract. He called his workers together and said, "We are under a big push to get the contract completed. I will make it worth your while if output increases."

Outwardly the workers told Pat that they would try to meet his request. Inwardly, the majority were thinking, "Pat has made these promises before and has never come through. I just don't trust him anymore. I am not going to work harder just to make him look good and receive no reward. His word is just no good."

Alice Stevens, office manager for Apex Supply, was experiencing problems. Her car wouldn't start this morning, she had been reprimanded by her boss for sending an incorrect report forward, and she couldn't sleep well the night before. Just at that moment Phyllis Rule came to Alice to discuss a problem with regard to how to fill out the new report. After describing the problem in detail to Alice, Phyllis asked, "What do you think I should do?"

"Perhaps all my car needs is a new battery," was Alice's reply as she started off into the room. At that point, Phyllis left the office. Alice just wasn't listening to her problem.

The situations of Pat and Alice provide illustrations of breakdowns in communication. Breakdowns in communication occur frequently in all organizations where people work together to accomplish results. Unless these barriers are removed, the work cannot be accomplished effectively.

Perhaps the worst criticism that managers can receive from their peers, superiors, and subordinates is that they cannot communicate effectively. This was further stressed by Marvin F. Gade, executive vice-president for Kimberly-Clark Corporation, when he said, "Unless an individual is capable of clear and timely communication with deputies, peers and principals he or she is near totally ineffective." In a previous chapter management was defined as the accomplishment of objectives through the efforts of other people. In order for an employee to achieve the goals of the manager, he or she must know what the supervisor desires to be accomplished. When the goals of the manager do not match what has actually been completed, a breakdown in communication is often found to be the source of the difficulty. A statement by a frustrated manager such as "You did what you thought I meant very effectively. Unfortunately, that was not what I wanted you to do," reveals that communication did not take place.

communication

Communication will be defined as the achievement of meaning and understanding between people through verbal and nonverbal means in order to affect behavior and achieve desired end results. In an organization, communication has two primary purposes. First, it provides the means by which the objectives of the firm may be accomplished. The manner in which plans are to be implemented and actions coordinated to achieve a particular goal must be communicated to the individuals who must accomplish the task. In fact, it has been estimated that managers spend a large portion of their time communicating—approximately 75 percent. Second, communication provides the means by which members of the firm may be stimulated to accomplish organizational plans willingly and enthusiastically.

The inability to communicate effectively can severely hamper a manager in the accomplishment of his or her duties. In fact, a person can actually cease to be effective as a manager unless communication skills can be improved. At times we see a manager performing tasks that a subordinate should be doing. The supervisor may say that he or she is doing the job because the worker is not capable of completing the assigned job. Often this is not the case; the manager may feel incapable of communicating his or her desires effectively. Rather than stand a chance of this occurring, the manager decides to do the work of the subordinate. In these instances, the failure to communicate has caused the efficiency of the unit to deteriorate because both the subordinates and the manager are not accomplishing the work for which they were hired.

The one redeeming feature of communication is that it is a learned quality. A person who truly desires to improve his or her ability to communicate can improve by giving proper attention to the task. The basic purpose of this chapter entails understanding the communication process. Concentration will first be placed on items that can cause a breakdown in communication. Next, factors that can assist or facilitate the communication process will be presented. Finally, means by which conflict can be managed will be discussed.

THE COMMUNICATION PROCESS

Communication must always take place between two or more people. Shouting for help on a desert island is not communication; similarly, if the professor lectures and no one listens or understands, there is no communication. The basic elements of the communication process may be seen in Figure 12-1. Each step in the sequence is critical to the ultimate success of the process.

source (sender)

The **source (sender)** is the person who has an idea or message to communicate to another person or persons. A problem that often affects the communication process is that each of us has different backgrounds, experiences, and goals. Senders must encode their messages or ideas into a set of symbols that the receiver will understand. Words on a written page are symbols to you as a reader. The sound of a car's horn on a busy freeway may have meaning that danger is approaching. When communication is attempted, messages are transmitted through such means as speaking, writing, acting, and drawing.

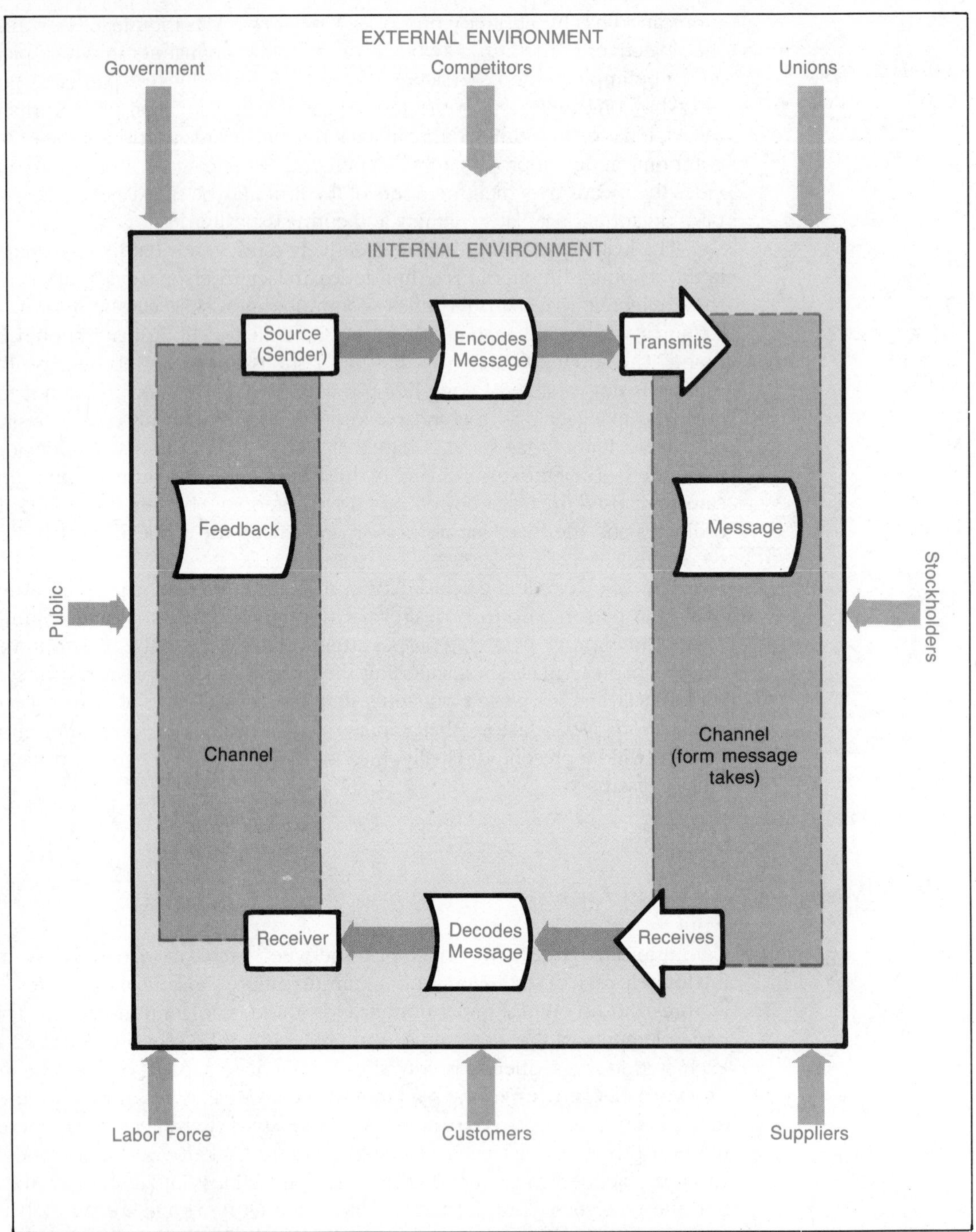

FIGURE 12-1 *The Communication Process* [*Source: Adapted from H. Joseph Reitz,* Behavior in Organizations *(Homewood, Ill.: Irwin, 1977), p. 342. Copyright © 1977 by Richard D. Irwin, Inc. Used with permission.*]

There are a number of channels that may be used to transmit the message. The spoken word can use such methods as face-to-face, telephone, radio, and television. Books, articles, and letters can serve as the channel for the spoken word. The senses of sight, sound, touch, smell, and taste assist in communication. Communication can often take place without a word being spoken.

receiver

The **receiver** of the message must decode it by converting the symbols into meaning. We must remember that the receiver also has diverse backgrounds, experiences, and aspirations that may be significantly different from those of the sender. Understanding is the key to decoding. Communication effectiveness is determined to the extent that the receiver's decoding matches the sender's encoding. Based on the meaning of the message, the receiver will act in response to the communication. This action can be to ignore the message, perform some task, store the information for future use, or something else. Feedback is provided in order that the sender will know if the message was accurately received and the proper action occurred.

WHAT SHOULD BE COMMUNICATED?

In the past, managers have tended to communicate not much more than the orders necessary to achieve results. Today, communication takes on a much larger scope. As W. D. Johnson, vice-president of personnel for Baxter-Travenol Labs, Inc., stated,"Every day it becomes dramatically apparent that communication with employees is a critical requirement of good management." Behavioral scientists have demonstrated the motivational qualities of information. Research has also underscored the need for subordinates to be heard and understood by their supervisors.

Determining what specific topics are to be communicated is often very difficult. The manager who believes that everything is suitable for transmission will not only clog the channels with insignificant trivia but may harm operations by releasing information that should be retained. The National Association of Manufacturers has suggested that the following should be communicated:

1. Information about the company—its operations, products, and prospects.
2. Information about company policies and practices related to personnel and their jobs, such as vacations, seniority, and pay systems.
3. Information about specific situations that arise in the company, such as a change in management or a change in plant layout.
4. Information about the general economic system in which a company and its employees operate.

Within these broad areas, many specific details must be considered. For example, management should inform its employees of the company's prod-

•CAREER PROFILE•

MR. W. L. (BUD) McMAHON
Vice President of Salaried Personnel
Corning Glass Works

CORNING As vice-president of salaried personnel for Corning Glass Works, Mr. W. L. (Bud) McMahon is responsible for approximately 9,000 salaried employees located throughout the world. Twenty years in various personnel assignments provided the experience to progress to this position of responsibility within Corning Glass Works.

Bud received his B.S. from St. Bonaventure University and his M.S. from the University of Pittsburgh. After a few years as the company's industrial hygienist, he was assigned to help initiate the Management Development Department. From there he was appointed to the Research and Engineering Division as a personnel manager and later promoted to manager of manpower development of the corporate staff. He was appointed vice-president in 1971.

In response to a question on critical decisions he has made, he quickly identified the time in 1975 when Corning was confronted with the need to follow a retrenchment strategy. Because of the general economic conditions, management found it necessary to terminate a high percentage of the firm's managerial, technical, and professional employees. These decisions were especially difficult because Corning is a "close" company. Bud says, "This was an extremely traumatic experience, but Corning provided very generous assistance in placing the employees who were separated. The company received national recognition and praise for its innovative out-placement program for employees who were terminated. I hope I never have to experience this type of thing again."

Mr. McMahon feels that "a successful corporation devotes as much—or more—time to managing its people as it does its money and technology." Bud believes,

> Providing that the basic incentives are competitive, clarity of corporate and individual business objectives becomes essential in order to establish authority and responsibility in the decision-making process. Achieving this end in a multibusiness, worldwide corporation is a difficult, but essential, task if the goal is to delegate more complete responsibility to all levels of management.

Bud believes that the key to success is the ability to make the informal system work for you.

ucts, believing that their understanding will inspire interest, loyalty, and cooperation. But on the other hand, disclosure of future product plans may jeopardize the company's future in a highly competitive industry. In matters more closely related to the employee's interests, such as seniority and pay, the tendency is toward providing all information that could possibly be desired.

The two best guides for determining what information to provide relate to answering the following questions:

- What must personnel know in order to relate effectively to others and to the organization as a whole?
- What do employees want to know before cooperation will be given willingly and with enthusiasm?

The typical employee wants to know such things as—

- His or her standing in relation to the official, formal authority structure.
- His or her standing in relation to the informal organization with respect to individual status, power, acceptance, and so forth.
- Events that have bearing upon future economic security.
- Operational information that will enable him or her to develop pride in the job.

Insights to Success

1. **Be mentally prepared to work on "off shifts" (4 P.M. to 12 midnight or midnight to 8 A.M.) in early part of career.**
2. **Realize that those in management usually work longer hours than those in service departments.**
3. **The ability to communicate both orally and in writing is essential.**

JOHN F. LIVINGSTON, Vice-President—Manufacturing, Graniteville Company

ORGANIZATIONAL CHANNELS OF COMMUNICATION

An important component of communication processes is the channel through which the signals flow between sender and receiver. If only superiors and subordinates are considered, these channels are of two types: downward and upward.

Downward Channels

The traditional manager is likely to emphasize the importance of the downward channels of communication. Managers are aware of the necessity for conveying upper management's orders and viewpoints to subordinates. It is believed that the logic of these orders will stimulate desired action. Some of the various channels available to carry the information downward are provided in Table 12-1.

There are doubtless many other channels that are used every day by management in attempting to communicate with subordinates. Middle- and low-level managers are usually contacted personally by written memos, policy manuals, and authorized schedules. External means, such as radio, television, and the press, can be used to communicate with employees as well as the general public.

TABLE 12-1. *Downward Channels of Communication*

The chain of command	Orders and information can be given face-to-face or in written fashion and transmitted from one level to another. This is the most frequently used channel and is appropriate on either an individual or a group basis.
Posters and bulletin boards	Many employees refuse to read such boards, and thus this channel is useful only as a supplementary device.
Company periodicals	A great deal of information about the company, its products, and policies can be disseminated in this manner. To attract readership, a certain percentage of space must be devoted to personal items about employees, and thus the periodical plays a part in developing the social life of the organization.
Letters and pay inserts	This is a form of direct mail contact and is ordinarily used when the president of the organization wishes to present something of special interest. Letters are usually directed to the employee's home address. The use of pay inserts ensures exposure to every employee.
Employee handbooks and pamphlets	Handbooks are frequently used during the hiring and orientation process as an introduction to the organization. Too often, however, they are unread even when the firm demands a signed statement that the employee is acquainted with their contents. When special systems are being introduced, such as a pension plan or a job evaluation system, concise, highly illustrated pamphlets are often prepared to facilitate understanding and stimulate acceptance.
Information racks	In a relatively small number of organizations, racks containing free paperback literature of all types are provided. Mixed in with books on hobbies and sports are pamphlets on the profit system, the company, management techniques, and the like.

TABLE 12-1 *(continued)*

Loudspeaker system	The loudspeaker system is used not only for paging purposes, but also to make announcements while they are "hot." Such systems can also be misused, as in the case where the president of a company sent his greetings from his cool vacation place in the mountains to the hot, sweaty workers on the production floor.
Grapevine	Though the grapevine is an informal means of communication, it has been suggested that management should "feed, water, and cultivate" its growth by providing factual information to combat rumors.
Annual reports	A review of typical annual reports would indicate that they are increasingly being written for the benefit of the employee and the union as well as for the stockholder. It is a channel that appears to be designed for one group, the owners, to which others "tap in," hoping to obtain information not intended for them.
The labor union	The union can be very helpful in communicating certain philosophies to company employees. The union voice, added to the management voice, can be highly persuasive.

Upward Channels

Advocates of participative management have emphasized the establishment of upward channels of communication from subordinate to supervisor. This is necessary not only to determine if subordinates have understood the information that was sent downward but also to meet the needs of people. An upward flow of information is also necessary if management is to coordinate the various activities of the organization. As may be seen in Table 12-2, there are many channels from which to choose for the upward flow of information.

TABLE 12-2. *Upward Channels of Communication*

The chain of command	Theoretically, the flow of communications is two-way between superior and subordinate. The superior should have an open-door attitude as well as some of the skills of a counselor. If one has more courage, group meetings can be held in which expression of gripes and attitudes is encouraged.
The grievance procedure	A systematic grievance procedure is one of the most fundamental devices for upward communication. The subordinate knows that there is a mechanism for appeal beyond the authority of the immediate supervisor. If this grievance procedure is backed up by the presence of a labor union, one is even more encouraged to voice true feelings.

TABLE 12-2 *(continued)*

The complaint system	In addition to grievance procedures, some firms encourage all types of upward communication by establishing means of preserving the identity of the complainant. "Gripe boxes" may be established, into which an employee can place a written complaint or rumor, which management will investigate. In one firm, a blackboard was divided into halves, one side being for employee complaints or rumors, the other for management's replies. An answer of some sort was guaranteed within a twenty-four hour period.
Counseling	Though all supervisors have a counseling obligation, the authority barrier makes true communication difficult. For this reason, special staff counselors may be provided to allow employees to discuss matters with them in privacy and confidence.
Morale questionnaires	This channel also preserves the identity of the employee when answering specific questions about the firm and its management.
An open-door policy	An open-door attitude on the part of each supervisor toward immediate subordinates is to be highly commended. With regard to higher management it is seldom used, because the employee is usually reluctant to bypass his or her immediate supervisor.
Exit interview	If the employee leaves the organization, there is one last chance in the exit interview to discover feelings and views about the firm in general and reasons for quitting in particular. Follow-up questionnaires are also used at times, because employees are reluctant to give full and truthful information at the time of departure.
Grapevine	Though management may be reluctant to feed and cultivate the grapevine, it should always listen to it. The grapevine is a spontaneous and natural phenomenon that serves as a means of emotional release and provides management with significant clues concerning the attitudes and feelings of organization members. If the grapevine should ever become silent, that is the time to worry. Management should remember that although the grapevine is usually quite accurate, "it is nearly always uncharitable."[a]
Labor union	A prime purpose of the labor union is to convey to management the feelings and demands of employees. Collective bargaining sessions constitute a legal channel of communication for any aspect of employer-employee relations.
Special meetings	Special employee meetings to discuss particular company policies or procedures are sometimes scheduled by management to obtain employee feedback. The keystone of teamwork in the Pitney Bowes Company is monthly meetings in all departments involving all employees. In addition, a central employee council of 13 employee representatives

TABLE 12-2 *(continued)*

	meets with top executives on a monthly basis. Employees on this main council are elected for two-year terms and devote full time to investigating company problems and improving communication processes.
The ombudsman	Though little used in this country, it has been suggested that corporate justice in nonunionized firms requires a special person to act as the president's eyes and ears. In essence, the ombudsman acts as a complaint officer to whom employees may go when they feel they have exhausted the typical avenues of receiving an acceptable hearing. An ombudsman has only the rights of acceptance or rejection of complaints, investigation, and recommendation of action to the top organizational official. Most complaints center around salary, performance appraisal, layoff, and fringe benefits. In many instances, low-level managers make voluntary adjustments precluding specific recommendations from the ombudsman. Though the position has existed for about 150 years, only recently have some American business firms adopted the concept. Xerox Corporation inaugurated the position in 1972 and reports that 40 percent of the final decisions clearly favored the employee, 30 percent were against the employee, and 30 percent represented some type of compromise.[b]

[a] Quotation is from J. Hargreaves, "Six Keys to Good Communication," *International Management* 31 (December 1976): 54–56.

[b] Information on Xerox Corporation from "Where Ombudsmen Work Out," *Business Week*, May 3, 1976, pp. 114–116.

BARRIERS TO COMMUNICATION

Effective communication means that the receiver correctly interprets the message of the sender. Often this is not the case due to various breakdowns that can occur in communication. If a manager tells an employee to "produce a few more parts," and the employee makes two but the manager wanted two hundred, a breakdown in communication certainly took place. If a manager is to develop his or her communication ability, the manner in which communication breakdowns can occur must be fully understood.

barriers to communication

As seen in Figure 12-2, successful management decisions must pass through the bottleneck or **barriers to communication** if organizational goals are to be achieved. If the barriers are excessive, communication may be reduced to the point where the firm's objectives cannot be achieved. Barriers may be classified as technical, language, or psychological. Knowledge of these possible communication breakdowns places managers in a position to improve their communication ability.

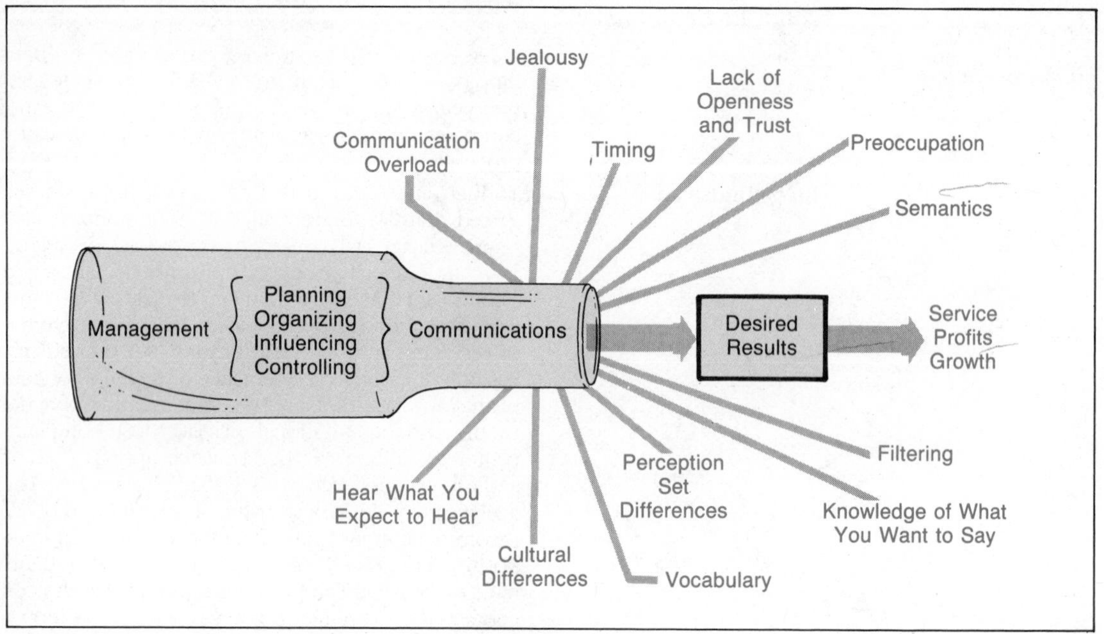

FIGURE 12-2 *Successful Management Decisions Must Pass Through the "Bottleneck" or Barriers to Communications Prior to Achieving Desired Results*

Technical

Environmental barriers to communication are referred to as technical breakdowns. Some of these include timing, communication overload, and cultural differences.

Timing

timing

Determining when a message should be communicated is referred to as **timing**. It is often quite important for a manager to determine the most appropriate time to transmit a message. For instance, a manager who must

---

Most Important Reason for Success and Effectiveness as a Manager

The ability to develop business plans and strategies and then communicate them to the people who can share in and build on these concepts.

L. W. LEHR, Chairman and CEO, 3M Company

---

reprimand a worker for excessive tardiness would likely want to speak with the worker as soon after the event occurred as possible. The worker would likely have forgotten the event if, say, six months passed before the reprimand was received.

Communication Overload

communication overload

With the many channels and media available as well as the changed philosophy toward a greater sharing of information, it is little wonder that communication overload often occurs. **Communication overload** occurs when the sender attempts to present too much information to the receiver at one time. A person can absorb only so many facts and figures at a particular time. When excessive information is provided, a major breakdown in communication can occur. As a professor, one of the authors experienced communication overload in a classroom. While teaching a statistics class that met one day a week for four hours, excessive overload was encountered. For the first hour, students were eager to take notes. Progressing toward the fourth hour, few students could tell another person what had been said by the instructor. Communication overload had definitely occurred. Some students have discovered that their grades suffer when they attempt to take all of their classes in the morning on Monday, Wednesday, and Friday. By the end of the last class many of the students have no idea what the teacher has said and their grades suffer.

Cultural Differences

Cultural differences can also cause a breakdown in communication. In the United States, time is a highly valuable commodity, and a deadline suggests urgency. In the Middle East, the giving of a deadline to another conveys meanings of rudeness and is likely to be ignored. If a client is kept waiting in the outer office for thirty minutes in the United States, it may mean that a person has low status. In Latin America, a thirty-minute wait means nothing. If a contract offer has not been acted on in this country over a period of several months or a year, the conclusion is that the party has lost interest. In Japan, long delays mean no slackening of interest, and delay is often a highly effective negotiation tactic when used on impatient Americans.

Americans conduct most business at an interpersonal interval of from five to eight feet, and a distance of one to three feet suggests more personal or intimate undertakings. The normal business distance in Latin America is closer to the personal distance of the United States. Thus, we observe the highly interesting communication difficulties of a back-pedaling American as his or her Latin American counterpart presses ever closer. Regarding status symbols, an American manager's office that is spacious, well furnished, and located on the top floor conveys meanings of high prestige. In the Middle East, size and decor of office mean little or nothing, and in France, the manager is likely to be located in the midst of subordinates in order to control them.

Language

Barriers to communication can occur because of language problems resulting from vocabulary and different meanings being applied to the same word (semantics).

Vocabulary

A manager must understand the type of audience being addressed. Obviously, statisticians, skilled mechanics, and ditch diggers have different vocabulary sets. Words that the staff engineers might fully understand have little meaning to ditch diggers, or vice-versa. Breakdowns in communication often occur when the sender does not tailor the message to match the knowledge base of the receiver.

All of us have a common level of vocabulary (see Figure 12-3 for an illustration). If we speak using level 4 words, both the statistician and the ditch digger will understand. As we progress above this base level more and more people will not be able to comprehend the message. If the statistician uses words above the scale of 6, communication with the skilled mechanic is lost. It will cease at level 4 with the ditch digger. Naturally, there will be times when higher-level words must be used to communicate a technical concept, but if managers can concentrate their messages in the common vocabulary base, they should experience a much better chance of being understood.

Two systems for measurement of reading ease are the fog index developed by the late Robert Gunning and the Flesch system developed by Rudolph Flesch. The purpose of the fog index is to determine the reading level of a manuscript. A fog index of 10 would mean that tenth graders can

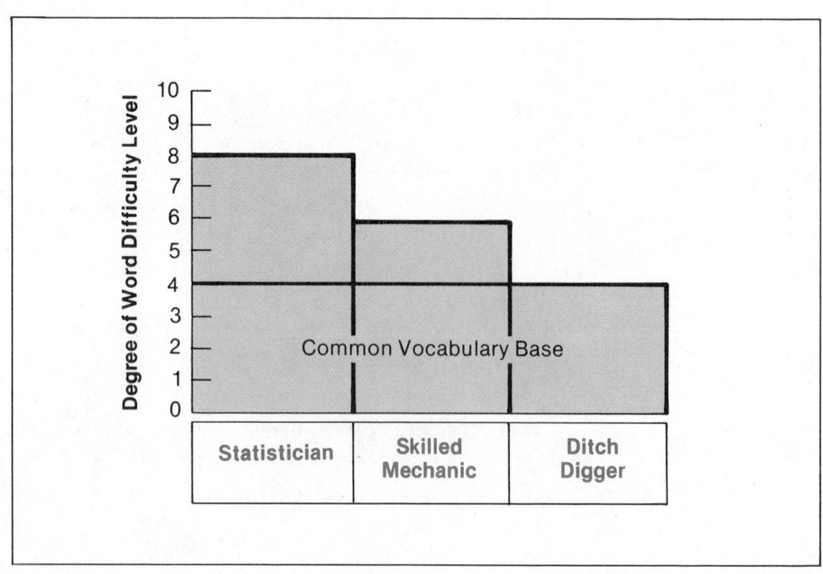

FIGURE 12-3
Common Vocabulary Base

understand what you write.[1] The Flesch system helps you determine whether your writing is interesting to read. The means by which both systems are used may be seen in Figure 12-4.

The objective of both of these systems is to reduce the amount of pompous jargon and inflated prose. Of course, there is more to communication than can be revealed by counting syllables and sentence lengths. Each communicator must have a clear and coherent grasp of the idea one hopes to transmit. The Flesch and Gunning indexes merely aid the writer in keeping the audience in mind.

Is your writing hard to understand? Do eyeballs glaze after a glance at your prose? Experts have devised measurements of reading ease, and you can rate your own performance.

One of the simplest and most consistent tests is the "fog index" developed by the late Robert Gunning. Here's how it works: Choose at random a medium-length paragraph of your own writing. A paragraph of about 120 words is ideal, says Douglas Mueller, president of the Gunning-Mueller Clear Writing Institute in Santa Barbara, Calif. Dates and other number combinations are single words. Count the number of words in your sample, then the number of sentences. Divide the word total by the sentence total to obtain the average number of words per sentence.

Step two is slightly more complex. Skim your sample and note each word of three or more syllables. Don't count words that are made by combining common short words, such as butterfly. And don't count verbs that acquire their extra syllable from tense endings—es or ed. Don't count words that begin with capital letters—place names, for example. And exclude the first word of any sentence. "I don't know why, but it works," says Mueller. "If you start a sentence with a polysyllable, it lowers the fog index. Magazines such as *The New Yorker* do it constantly."

Saying it simply. Once you have your polysyllable count, add it to the word average and multiply the total by 0.4. The product will be a number corresponding to a reading comprehension grade level. A nine means that a ninth-grader can understand what you write. If you score 17 or more, then your prose is so densely wrapped in fog that only a graduate student will be able to grope through it. The Gettysburg Address has a fog index of 10. Most news magazines manage 11 (*Business Week* averages 10). The article that you are now reading scores eight.

If you want to know whether your prose is interesting to read, Rudolph Flesch, one of the most eminent of reading and writing specialists, has devised a human-interest score. Using a sample of 100 words, count the personal words, which Flesch defines as pronouns—I, you, he, she, them, but not it or a plural pronoun referring to a thing. Count all words with gender, such as father or sister, actress, businessman, and proper names. And count collective nouns such as people and folks.

Attracting the reader. Next, count up your sample's personal sentences: any sentence containing speech, set off by quotation marks or by references such as "she said"; sentences addressed directly to the reader as a question, a command, a suggestion; a sentence cast as an exclamation; any incomplete sentence of a conversational nature (Flesch's examples: "Doesn't know a word of English. Handsome though." Those are two incomplete but comprehensible sentences.).

Once you have done all this, the arithmetic is a little complicated. Multiply the number of personal words in your 100-word sample by 3.635. Multiply the number of personal sentences by .314, and add the two products. The total is your human interest score, which runs from dull at 5, through interesting at 30, to dramatic at 80. What you have been reading, by the way, scores about 21: mildly interesting.

FIGURE 12-4 *Measure Your "Fog Index"* [*Source: Reprinted from the July 6, 1981, issue of* Business Week *by special permission,*]

Semantics

When a sender sends words to which a receiver attaches different meaning than those intended by the sender, a semantic—or meaning of words—communication breakdown has occurred. A major difficulty with the American language is that multiple meanings may be attached to a word, for instance, the word *charge.* A manager may place an employee *in charge* of a section. The company *charges* for their services. A person gets a *charge* out of a humorous story. When two individuals attach different meanings to a word, a breakdown in communication can occur.

The use of jargon can also create a barrier to communication. Virtually every industry develops certain jargon that is used in everyday business. The statistician, computer programmer, typist, or ditch digger likely develops expressions peculiar to his or her specific profession. When speaking to an individual not associated with the trade jargon, a breakdown in communication may occur. It is likely for this reason that many firms provide new personnel with a list and definition of terms associated with the particular industry.

Psychological

Although technical factors and semantic differences are credited with causing breakdowns in communication, psychological barriers tend to be the major reasons for miscommunication and communication breakdowns. These include various forms of distortion and problems involving interpersonal relationships.

Knowledge of What You Want to Say

The old expression, "The mouth was in gear before the mind was operating" provides one form of breakdown in communication. Directives, orders, and even comments that are not well thought out can develop an image that the sender does not know what they actually want. A manager who asks for one thing and expects another has had a breakdown in communication.

Filtering

filtering

An attempt to alter and color information to present a more favorable image to the manager is referred to as **filtering.** Managers often discover that information that has been provided them by subordinates has been filtered. As subordinates contribute information to superiors, they know that it will be used for at least two purposes: (1) to aid management in controlling and directing the firm (and therefore the worker) and (2) to evaluate the worth of their performance. Managers at all levels are tempted to filter information as it progresses up the chain of command. Even the president may filter information before it goes to the board of directors.

Because the data have been filtered, an incorrect impression of the true situation may occur. There have been many managerial attempts to reduce both the number and thickness of the authority filters that clog organization communication channels. It should be apparent that decentralization reduces the number of managerial levels from eight to four, with a consequent speeding up of the communication process. Such reorganizations are drastic and require considerable efforts in the area of retraining and establishing realistic control standards.

A consultant can serve as a means of reducing communication filters. In one company, there was a steady decrease in productivity for no reason that could be identified by management. The consultant systematically interviewed all employees over a six-month period. The results of these many interviews indicated strong feelings on the part of many employees that work standards were too high, that older employees resented the high wage scales of the new employees, and that temporary transfers to new jobs to avoid layoff were widely resented. In each case, management had felt that it had communicated effectively its intent to the employees.

Lack of Trust and Openness

Openness and trust on the part of managers and employees must exist if orderly changes in the organization are to occur. When employees feel that openness and trust do not exist, barriers to communication are present. Pat Steen, the production foreman for Abbot Electronics (mentioned at the start of the chapter), is not likely to obtain increased productivity because his workers don't trust him. Remember what they said: "Pat has made these promises before and has never come through. I just don't trust him. I'm not going to work harder just to make him look good and receive no reward. His word is just no good."

As was illustrated in Figure 12-1, the sender needs feedback to know whether communication has occurred. If employees perceive the manager as being open and receptive to their ideas, communication is encouraged. On the other hand, should managers give the impression that feedback is not desired and that their statements should never be questioned, communication tends to be stifled.

One of the major factors in the success of Japanese businesses is that managers trust not only their workers but also their peers and superiors. As a result, there evolves a simpler organizational structure. For instance, Ford Motor Company has eleven layers of management between the factory worker and the chairman, while Toyota Motor Company has only six. These many layers cause high overhead and much red tape. Japanese firms assume that personnel at all levels are trustworthy, and they do not have to employ high-paid executives to review the work of other highly paid executives.[2]

Jealousy

It is perhaps a difficult lesson for a manager to learn, but everyone, especially peers and subordinates, may not be pleased to see you perform successfully. Competency and effective performance may actually be viewed as a threat to the security of peers and subordinates. Individuals may attempt to diminish the accomplishments of another person because they are jealous. If the jealous person is able to gain the attention of the supervisor, there is a possibility that when you attempt to communicate, a "less receptive ear" may be present. Because of jealousy, the effectiveness of the communication may be reduced.

Preoccupation

Some people are so preoccupied with themselves they may listen in such a way that they hear little or none of the message. Preoccupation may cause a person to respond in a certain rather predictable manner even though it is an inappropriate response. A New York columnist tells the story of attending a party at a well-known socialite's home. The socialite was famous for being so preoccupied with making a favorable impression on her guests that she did not listen to what the guests said. The columnist decided to play a trick on the socialite, so he deliberately came late to one of her parties. As he entered, he gave this explanation of being late: "I'm sorry to be late, but I killed my wife this evening and had a difficult time stuffing her body into the trunk of my car." The charming hostess beamed and said, "Well, darling, the important thing is that you have arrived; now the party can really begin."

We Hear What We Expect to Hear

Like preoccupation, most of us are often conditioned in the communication process to hear what we expect to hear, not what is actually said. Because of past experiences we have developed a concept of what will be said. At times we hear what we want to hear. An employee who has been reprimanded quite a few times by a certain supervisor may even interpret a compliment by the manager as a negative statement.

Perception Set Differences

perception set

Another major barrier to communication is **perception set** differences between individuals attempting to communicate with each other. Differences in past experiences, educational background, emotions, values, and beliefs—to name just a few—affect each person's perception of a message or of words. The word *management,* for example, may be defined by two individuals as planning, organizing, influencing, and controlling the activities of others. If one person's parents have been managers and the second's parents have been labor union organizers, it is apparent that the word *management* will evoke drastically different meanings. It is difficult enough if words are representative of tangible objects such as *chair, pencil,* or *hat.* But one can imagine the difficulties in using such terms as *liberal, conservative, philosophy, group dynamics,* and *communication.*

FACILITATORS TO COMMUNICATION

Once it is recognized that breakdowns in communication can occur, a manager is then in a position to work toward improving communication ability.

As previously mentioned, the major factor that should be remembered is that communication is learned. If persons truly desire to improve their communication ability, there are means available to assist in this undertaking. Empathy, listening, reading skill improvement, observation, word choice, body language, actions, and transactional analysis will be discussed as facilitators to communication in the following sections.

Empathy

empathy

You have likely heard the expression, "I see where you are coming from." When statements such as that are made, empathy is being expressed. **Empathy** is the ability to identify with the various feelings and thoughts of another person. It does not mean that you necessarily agree with the other person, but while you are with the individual, you can appreciate why that

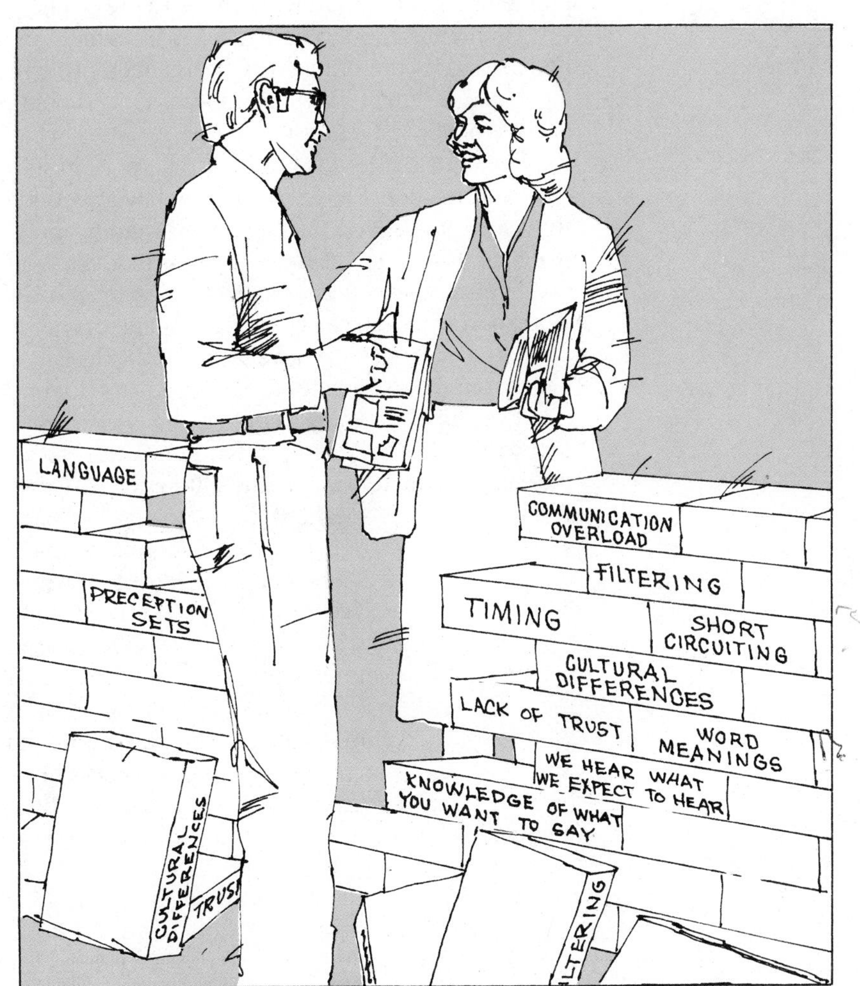

Barriers to communication can be reduced if individuals desire to improve their communication ability.

person speaks and acts as he or she does. If a person is bitter, you are able to relate to this bitterness; if he or she is scared, you understand this fear.

Taken in its broadest meaning, an empathetic person is communicating. It is for this reason that managers should take the time to understand as much as possible about the people whom they must work with daily. With this information, the manager is in a much better position to understand why people act as they do. The manager may not agree with the individual, but if the time is taken to understand the reason for certain action, problems may more easily be resolved.

Listening

One of the most effective tools a manager has at his or her disposal to facilitate communication is the ability to listen. A person who is constantly talking is not listening or learning. **Listening** assists a manager in discovering problems and determining solutions to problems.

listening

Communication cannot take place unless messages are received and understood by the other party. It has been observed that the average speaking speed is 120 words per minute. One is able to listen more than four times as rapidly. The question therefore arises, what does the listener do with the free time that results from this difference in speeds?

At least three types of listening have been identified: marginal, evaluative, and projective. The speed of listening provides the opportunity for marginal listening, a dangerous type that can lead to misunderstanding of and even insult to the speaker. For instance, most of us have experienced a situation where we have been speaking to a person but we know that their mind is a million miles away. The individual may occasionally hear some words, but the majority of the message was not understood.

Evaluative listening requires the second party to allocate full attention to the speaker. The excess time is devoted to evaluating and judging the nature of the remarks heard. Often, we are forming rebuttal remarks while the sender is still speaking, thus moving into a type of marginal listening. As soon as the sender says something that is not accepted, communication ceases and the receiver begins to develop a response in his or her own mind. Thoughts such as "this person does not know what he is talking about. I was in Vietnam and I know the way it was" can significantly reduce, or even eliminate, the communication process. Instead of one idea being transmitted and held by two people, we often end up with two ideas, neither of which is really communicated to the other. If the listener allocated too much time to disapproving or approving of what is heard, it is doubtful whether he or she has the time to understand fully. This is particularly true when the remarks are loaded with emotion or concern over the security and status of the receiver.

Active or nonevaluative listening holds the greatest potential for effective communication. Listeners fully utilize their time by attempting to project themselves into the position of the speaker and understand what is being said from the speaker's viewpoint. We should first listen without evaluation. After feeling that we understand what has been said, we can then evaluate what has been said. Rogers suggested a rule to be followed to ensure some degree of projective listening: "Each person can speak for himself only *after* he has related the ideas and feelings of the previous speaker accurately and to that speaker's satisfaction."[3] There is no need to agree with the statements, but there is a need to understand them as the speaker intended. Only in this way is it possible to frame a reply that will actually respond to the speaker's remarks. Effective listening is empathic listening. It requires an ability to listen for feeling as well as for words. The person attempts to place himself or herself in the "shoes of the other person."

Improved Reading Skills

Reading skills have received great attention in our society. The amount of written material a manager must cover has increased significantly, and some attempt should first be made to consolidate and reduce it. However, the ability to read rapidly and with understanding is an essential communication skill, particularly in larger organizations. It has been found that reading speeds can be doubled and tripled with little or no loss in comprehension.

Observation

As in the case of listening, there are too few attempts to increase skill in observation outside of training for law enforcement. Most of us have heard reports where there were many witnesses to a traffic accident. When the police arrived and questioned the witnesses, there were many different versions to what actually occurred. "The blue car went through the stop light," said one witness. "No, that is not correct," said another. "The light was green." Most people miss a great deal by not carefully observing important elements in the environment. It was mentioned earlier that some managers are very adept at assessing the general atmosphere of an organization by merely strolling through its work places. Observation of furnishings, housekeeping, dress of personnel, and activities can convey much information. Using our powers of observation to supplement listening and reading will add immeasurably to our understanding of what is actually transpiring.

Word Choice

As mentioned previously, there is a certain threshold of words that virtually everyone can understand. If a manager desires to communicate effectively, he or she must make certain that the choice of the words transmitted by the sender is in the vocabulary set of the receiver. Generally simple or common words provide the best means through which communication is accomplished.

Body Language

Most subordinates do not have to be told when their boss is displeased with them. A frown or arms crossed and not smiling may communicate this message clearly. **Body language** is defined as a nonverbal method of communication in which physical actions such as motions, gestures, and facial expressions convey thoughts and emotions.

body language

Appreciation of the importance of understanding of body language in the communication process is also quite important for a manager. All people—managers, superiors, and subordinates—give off unintentional signals that can provide significant insight into the exact meaning that a person is attempting to communicate. The manager particularly must be constantly aware of the signals that he or she is presenting. Employees grasp at these small symbols to determine what the "boss" means. A frown, even though the words were positive in nature, may be taken wrong. A sarcastic smile when "you did a good job" was mentioned will not likely be interpreted to mean that the worker actually did a good job. A blank stare may mean to the employee that the manager is not interested.

A manager must also be aware of the signals that a subordinate may be giving off. Sweaty hands or nail biting in the presence of the supervisor may mean that the worker feels ill at ease. Managers need to recognize these signs and be prepared to adjust their action.

Actions

The manager must also recognize that one communicates by what one does or does not do. If a person comes to work one day and finds her or his desk moved from a location in a private office to one in an open area, communication of a sort has taken place. If no verbal explanation accompanies the action, people will interpret it their own way; the missing symbol or signal will be supplied by the observer. And despite any verbal statement to the contrary, such a move will likely be interpreted as a demotion for the person.

In one company, management had introduced a change in procedure for a small crew of employees. The new method was timed and piece rates were established. None of the personnel produced more than half of the standard amount and were therefore on a time-wage basis rather than piece rates. They all filed grievances protesting the unfairness of the standard. Management tried everything it could think of to correct the problem, from all-day time studies to providing each employee with a private instructor in the new method. A check on similar jobs in other companies revealed that the standard was in line. Thus, management concluded that a concerted work restriction was involved.

The next move was one of communication by *action*. An engineer was sent to the production department, and he proceeded to measure various angles and spaces on the floor. He volunteered no information to the group. Finally, one man's curiosity got the best of him and he asked the engineer what he was doing. The engineer indicated that management wanted to see if there was sufficient room to locate certain machinery that could do the work of this crew. He continued about his business of measuring. The next day, all work crew members were producing amounts well above the established standard.

Transactional Analysis

transactional analysis

With **transactional analysis** (TA) there are three ego states that are constantly present and at work within each individual: the Parent, the Adult, and the Child.[4] The manner in which individual ego states interact can have a significant effect upon interpersonal relations and an organization's effectiveness.

Parent

Parent

The **Parent** ego state may take on the characteristic of being either the Nurturing or the Negative Parent. When the Nuturing Parent dominates, the person gives praise and recognition, comfort in time of distress, and reassurance in time of need. Statements such as "you have done a good job" or "I am certain the problem will work out all right" might be associated with the Nurturing Parent. On the other hand, the Negative Parent is overcontrolling, suffocating, critical, and oppressive. Comments such as "women should be seen and not heard" or "be careful, you can hurt yourself with the knife" might be associated with the Negative Parent. When the Negative Parent dominates, the person tends to lecture, believes that his or her moral standard is best for everyone, and often will not accept other ideas.

Child

Child

The **Child** may take on the characteristics of either the Natural Child, the Little Professor, or the Adaptive Child. The Natural Child is spontaneous, impulsive, untrained, expressive, self-centered, affectionate, and curious. The Little Professor tends to be intuitive, manipulative, and creative. The Adaptive Child tends to react in a way determined by parental figures.

Adult

Adult

A person who tends to evaluate the situation and attempts to make decisions based on information and facts is in the **Adult** ego state. No emotions are involved, and the individual tends to function like a computer, with all decisions based on logic.

The interaction of ego states can have a significant impact upon behavior in organizations. The manager must recognize that a person will not always be in the Adult state and make decisions based entirely on logic. In fact, the greatest amount of creativity is associated with the Child. Also, the manager will be able to recognize when communication is impossible. For instance, the manager who is in the Adult state may attempt to speak to the Adult of the employee. The Child state of the employee returns the conversation to the Parent of the manager. The following conversation is given to illustrate such a communication problem.

Manager: This task needs to be completed today.

Employee: Why are you always pushing me to work harder?

Communication has broken down because the employee is not addressing the problem that the manager was attempting to communicate.

Managers should also be aware of the ego state that they themselves are speaking from. If the state is properly interpreted, managers will recognize and possibly change their actions. Should you recognize that you are in one state and an employeee is in a state that precludes effective communication, it may be best to postpone discussion. For instance, if the manager is in the Child state and the employee is in the Adult state, communication may be postponed. The employee who is in the Adult state is serious about his work at this time and may misinterpret joking remarks.

Applying TA concepts on a broad basis may prove valuable in producing desired organizational change. As individuals in a firm learn to analyze their own social interactions, better communication and greater organizational effectiveness can occur.

MANAGEMENT OF CONFLICT

conflict management

Some people view conflict management strategies as providing a means for improving communication within the organization. In its broadest interpretation, **conflict management** is a facilitator to communication because it has the ability to resolve disagreements between individuals within the organization that could have an adverse effect on attaining organizational goals. When this definition is applied, it is clear that all conflict is not bad. In fact, a certain amount of conflict is healthy.

An organization is comprised of individuals who have been brought together to accomplish objectives. Unless it is a very unusual company, these employees have different backgrounds, experiences, aspirations, and personalities. These differences alone can create a situation of potential conflict and a breakdown in communication. Even the most happily married, perfectly matched couple may have occasional disagreements.

A firm brings together even more diversity of ideas and sets the stage for potentially greater conflict. When individuals are brought together in a highly structured environment, a potential for major disagreements exists. It may be nothing more than a difference in opinion of how to accomplish the same goal or as critical as a disagreement as to what the goals are. At times, conflict occurs because of unclear authority in that a person does not have a clearly defined role within the firm. Also, roles may overlap, which has the potential to create considerable conflict among employees. Unless a person believes in a utopian world, conflict will occur in any organization.

There may be an optimum level of conflict that should be developed and maintained for the good of the organization. Too little conflict may lead to mediocrity, apathy, and at times, destruction. The Penn Central Railroad went quietly into bankruptcy when its board of directors offered no challenging questions to management. If former President Nixon had not surrounded himself with "yes men," the events of Watergate might not have occurred. Certainly, the conflict surrounding the civil rights movement led to social decisions more in keeping with the long-run interests of the United States.

Interpersonal Conflict Management

The techniques of dealing with conflict between two or more individuals are numerous. They range from the use of force by a superior over a subordinate to the problem solving approach. Possible ways of dealing with interpersonal conflict management are discussed below.

Force

When force is used in the resolution of conflict, official authority may compel one party to accept a solution. The old expression, "He may not be right but he's still the boss," applies in this instance. The party for which the decision was directed may not agree with the results, but if he or she is to stay within the organization, the directive must be accepted.

Withdrawal

A solution that some individuals use in resolving conflict is to withdraw or avoid the person with whom the conflict exists. Conflict is reduced, but the reason that originated the conflict remains. It would be the same as seeing a person you do not want to speak to approaching you on the street, and you walk around the block to keep from having to speak to the individual.

Smoothing

When smoothing is used, a manager attempts to provide a semblance of peaceful cooperation by presenting an image that "we're one big happy family." With this approach, problems are rarely permitted to come to the surface, but the potential for conflict remains.

Compromise

Neither party gets all it wants when compromise is used. This is the most typical way of dealing with labor management conflict. For example, management may offer to increase wages by 8 percent, while the union may be seeking a 12 percent pay hike. A compromise figure of a 10 percent pay increase may result in a reasonable settlement of the conflict.

Mediation and Arbitration

Both arbitration and mediation call for outside neutral parties to enter the situation to assist in resolving the conflict. *arbitration* **Arbitration** is used considerably in union-management grievance conflicts. The arbitrator is given the authority to act as a judge in making a decision. The decision rendered is usually final in that both union and management agreed in advance to this condition. A *mediator* **mediator**, on the other hand, can only suggest, recommend, and attempt to keep the two parties talking in the hope of reaching a solution. The United States could be considered a mediator in the Arab-Israeli conflict.

Superordinate Goals

At times, a goal may be encountered that supersedes the conflict of two opposing factions. If the firm is in danger of going out of business, both union and management have been known to put aside minor conflict and work toward the common goal of survival. There have been instances where union members have taken a decrease in pay and benefits in order to assist in the survival of the firm. For example, union members and management at Chrysler and General Motors and other firms have cooperatively worked together to ensure the survival of their firms. Chrysler and General Motors, responding to major financial crises, have experienced significant reductions and changes in their management ranks as well as reductions in the work force, wages, and benefits.

Problem Solving

Another approach to conflict management is problem solving. As usually practiced, problem solving is characterized by an open and trusting exchange of views and facts. A person realizes that conflict is caused by relationships among people and is not within the person. With the problem-solving approach, an individual can disagree with your ideas and still remain your friend. It is a healthy approach in which rarely is one person completely right and the other person completely wrong. Granting a concession is not a sign of weakness and a person does not feel that he or she has to win every battle to maintain his or her self-respect.

With the problem-solving approach, a person recognizes that a certain amount of conflict is healthy. For instance, if a difference of opinion exists between two individuals and they openly discuss their difficulties, a superior solution often results. With problem solving, a person is encouraged to bring difficulties into the open without fear of reprisal. When this occurs, a situation that initially appeared to be a major problem may evolve into only a minor instance, which is easily resolved.

Structural Conflict Management

Conflict can also be managed by changing procedures, organizational structure, physical layout, or expanding resources. These methods for resolving conflict are discussed next.

Procedural Changes

There are times when conflict can occur because a procedure is illogically sequenced. When a credit manager and a sales manager were both about to be fired because of an irreconcilable personality conflict, it was discovered that the processing of credit applications too late in the procedure was the cause of the difficulty. The credit manager was forced to cancel too many deals already made. When the credit check was placed earlier in the procedure, most of the conflict disappeared. In another instance, the personnel director and the production manager were in continuous disagreement. At times the conflict actually came to blows. Then it was discovered that the production manager was not being permitted to review the applicants at an early stage of the hiring sequence and provide input regarding an applicant. When the procedure was changed, many of the difficulties were resolved.

Organizational Changes

The organization can be changed to either promote or reduce conflict. There are times when a department becomes too complacent, and although there is little conflict, very little is accomplished. To reduce undesired conflict within an organization, transfers of incompatible personnel can be made. Often this procedure is quite acceptable, but a manager must be careful that the workers are transferred for the proper reason. To transfer a worker who is incompetent merely because you as a manager are afraid to deal with the individual does an injustice to the overall goals of the organization. Some managers begin to suspect why an employee who is to be transferred to their department arrives there with "too glowing" recommendations. The question is asked, "If he is that good, why don't you keep him?" But if transfers are handled on a professional basis, both the company and the employee benefit.

When the conflict is between two units of the organization, special liaison personnel can be assigned. A traditional problem exists between production and marketing. Production personnel have been taught to cut costs, and the technique to accomplish this goal is to produce as few variations of a product as possible. Marketing personnel want products of different colors, styles, and shapes. A person who understands and appreciates the problems of both departments can greatly assist in resolving conflict.

Physical Layout Changes

Changes in the design of the physical work places have been used effectively to reduce or eliminate conflict. Office space can be designed to either force interaction or to make it difficult. Personnel can use desks as barriers and buffers. Some offices have dividers to separate workers. However, if a manager desires to stimulate a problem-solving atmosphere, a more open office arrangement may be permitted. When known antagonists are seated in conference directly across from each other, the amount of conflict increases. When they are seated side by side, the conflict tends to decrease.

A detrimental conflict involving physical layout existed between two groups of workers in a truck assembly plant. Working at different phases on the assembly line, the two groups came into conflict because both had to obtain parts from the same shelving unit. Each group would deliberately rearrange the other group's supply of parts, which sometimes resulted in fights. The conflict was resolved by moving the shelving unit between the two groups so as to set up a barrier between each work group. Thus, each group had its own supply area or "territory." As a result of this change, mistakes were reduced by 50 percent within two days.[5]

Expand Resources

A source of conflict caused by incompatibility of goals can be reduced if resources can be expanded. Thus, in a growing organization everything looks rosy. When hard times come, the contest begins for one's share of the smaller pie. As enrollment goes down in some colleges and universities, the battle begins to emerge. Should everyone get a graduate assistant, should the senior faculty members get one, or should the most productive but perhaps junior member get the assistant? The same question must be asked when summer teaching assignments are made. Under these conditions, skills in conflict management of the highest order are demanded. Whatever the situation, the effective use of conflict management will have a major impact upon organizational effectiveness.

Summary

Communication is defined as the achievement of meaning and understanding between people through verbal and nonverbal means in order to affect behavior and achieve desired end results. The source (sender) is the person who has an idea or message to communicate to another person or persons. When communication is attempted, messages are transmitted through such means as speaking, writing, acting, and drawing. A number of channels may be used to transmit the message. The receiver of the message must decode it by converting the symbols into meaning. Communication effectiveness is determined to the extent that the receiver's decoding matches the sender's encoding.

There are numerous channels of communication through which a manager transmits information. Downward channels provide means through which management's orders and viewpoints are transmitted to subordinates.

Upward channels provide means through which subordinates can communicate with their superiors.

Effective communication is often not achieved because of various breakdowns that can affect the communication process. Barriers may cause communication to be reduced to the point that the firm's objectives cannot be achieved. Barriers may be classified as technical, language, or psychological. Technical barriers include improper timing, communication overload, and cultural differences. Language barriers result when different meanings are applied to the same word. Psychological barriers include various forms of distortion and problems involving interpersonal relationships.

Although there are many barriers to communication, there are means available to eliminate or reduce these breakdowns. The use of empathy and the development of good listening skills can facilitate the communication process. In addition, reading and observation skills as well as making better choices of words can aid the manager in better communication with employees. Studying transactional analysis and developing the ability to read body language have been used to improve a manager's ability to communicate.

Management of conflict is important within an organization because there are so many different backgrounds, experiences, aspirations, and personalities among employees. In its broadest interpretation, conflict management can be used to overcome communication problems by resolving disagreements between individuals within the organization. Conflict management may be classified as interpersonal or structural. Interpersonal conflict management deals with conflict between two or more individuals. Structural conflict management is concerned with changing the structures and processes that can have an effect on behavior.

Review Questions

1. Define communication. Describe the basic communication process.
2. Distinguish by definition between downward and upward communication. What are examples of both types of channels of communication?
3. What is meant by the phrase "barriers to communication"? Distinguish among technical, language, and psychological barriers.
4. List the topics that have been identified as facilitators to communication. Briefly define each.
5. Explain how empathy may be used to assist a person become a better listener.
6. What is transactional analysis? How can it be used as a facilitator?
7. Describe how conflict management can be used as a facilitator to communication.

Exercises

1. Over a twenty-four-hour period, identify factors and situations that created barriers to communication. Attempt to secure at least one example of each

of the barriers to communication identified in the text. What facilitators of communication could have been used to reduce these barriers to effective communication?

2. Visit a business of your choice. Attempt to identify the various means of both downward and upward communication.
3. This is an exercise regarding observation skills. With one of your classmates, go to the window and observe what is occurring on the outside for ten seconds. Each of you will now write down what you saw. After completing the list, compare your list with your partner's list. Compare the differences.

Case Study

The Promise

Philip Jackson was a graduate from a large midwestern university and had an excellent reputation for preparing business graduates to take responsible jobs in industry. Philip was in the top 10 percent of his graduating class and was extremely active in social activities on campus. On graduating, Philip had many job opportunities. He took the time to study the firms and the type of positions that were available. He ultimately decided to take a position with Bedford International, a large conglomerate.

Philip and twenty other recent college graduates were hired as management trainees. All of the management trainees were to start as first-line supervisors. There were not formalized training sessions, just on-the-job training. But, after one year, the individual trainees were all promised advancement to higher-level positions.

Philip was considered to possess excellent management potential. During the quarterly progress reviews, he was told that his performance was exceptional in all areas. His employees showed less turnover, lower absenteeism, and higher performance than other similar groups.

Due to the large number of trainees hired, and the low turnover rate of managers at Bedford, few openings for the next managerial positions were available. Philip felt that recognition was nearly impossible. At the end of one year, no new positions were available, yet many promises had been made regarding his advancement opportunities. At the end of eighteen months, there were still no new positions available.

A few weeks later, Philip was approached by a professional recruiter and after several interviews, he received an offer from another company. The offer Philip received included a 20 percent increase in salary and an increase in managerial responsibilities. Philip felt obligated to talk to his supervisor prior to accepting any offers. In his conversation with the supervisor, Philip reminded his supervisor of the promises that had been made but not fulfilled.

QUESTIONS

1. What do you believe Philip should do with regard to the job offer?
2. How do you believe Philip's supervisor should answer the questions that Philip asked?
3. What problems in communication are evident from this case?

Case Study

Laurie Atkins, Management Trainee

Laurie Atkins, a recent graduate of Michigan State University, had just joined Bellingham Electric Company as a management trainee. Bellingham was one of the largest manufacturers of electric light bulbs, transformers, and generators in the United States with headquarters in Detroit. Laurie had first made contact with the company through the placement office of Michigan State. Bellingham had achieved excellent results over a period of many years in recruiting management trainees through college placement offices. In a typical year, the company would hire 200 management trainees from their college recruiting efforts.

The company had a well-established management training program, lasting one year, during which time the trainee was assigned to a branch location to learn various phases of company operations. The program, designed to prepare individuals for branch management, included training in the following areas: shipping and receiving, inventory control, purchasing, personnel, production, order service, and outside sales. In addition to this on-the-job experience, the trainee was returned to Detroit four times during the year for one week of classroom-type instruction and to compare notes and review individual progress with members of upper management.

Laurie was assigned to a branch operation in Indianapolis, Indiana, and was under direct supervision of Mr. Clayton Thomas, the branch manager. Mr. Thomas, fifty-five, had been with Bellingham for thirty-five years, having joined the company at the end of World War II. He had not attended college, but had worked his way up and believed this way of making it into management provided better training than the company's one-year rotation program. Laurie was assigned to perform various jobs in the branch but not according to the planned program. Laurie was asked to fill in as needed, and she became very concerned about not receiving the type of training required to prepare her for her first management position.

During her second trip to headquarters for a one-week training session, Laurie discussed her problem with the coordinator of management training and development, John Wilson. Mr. Wilson assured Laurie that he would look into the matter.

On her return to the branch, Laurie was reprimanded by Mr. Thomas for discussing the problem with Mr. Wilson. The conversation proceeded as follows:

Mr. Thomas: "Laurie, why did you discuss your problems with John Wilson? You work for me, at least as long as you are at this branch."

Laurie: "I don't know—I guess I was just frustrated with the training I've received."

Mr. Thomas: "You're just like a lot of young college graduates. You think your degree should entitle you to special treatment. Well, I'm sorry, but in my book it doesn't mean a thing."

Laurie: "What should I do now?"

Mr. Thomas: "Go back to work and don't cause any more trouble."

QUESTIONS

1. What action do you think Laurie Atkins should take?

2. **To what extent should Mr. Wilson have discussed Laurie's problem with the local branch manager, Mr. Thomas?**
3. **What evidence is there of a breakdown in communication between the branch office and the intentions of headquarters? Discuss.**

Notes

1. Robert Gunning, "How to Improve Your Writing," *Factory Management and Maintenance* 110 (June 1952): 134.
2. "Trust: The New Ingredient in Management," *Business Week,* July 6, 1981, p. 104.
3. Carl R. Rogers and F. J. Roethlisberger, "Barriers and Gateways to Communication," *Harvard Business Review* 30 (July–August 1952): 48.
4. For an expanded coverage of transactional analysis, see Thomas A. Harris, *I'm O.K. – You're O.K.* (New York: Harper, 1969).
5. H. Kenneth Bobele and Peter J. Buchanan, "Building a More Productive Environment," *Management World* 8 (January 1979): 8.

References

Allen, T. H. "Communication Networks: The Hidden Organizational Chart." *Personnel Administrator* 21 (September 1976): 31–35.

Davis, Keith. "Cut Those Rumors Down to Size." *Supervisory Management* 20 (June 1975): 2–6.

Deutsch, A. R. "Does Your Company Practice Affirmative Action in Its Communication?" *Harvard Businesss Review* 54 (November–December 1976): 16.

Donath, Bob. "Corporate Communications." *Industrial Marketing* 65 (July 1980): 52–53.

Ewing, David W., and Banks, Pamela M. "Listening and Responding to Employees' Concerns." *Harvard Business Review* 58 (January–February 1980): 101–114.

Foltz, Roy G. "Internal Communications, Give Them Facts." *Public Relations Journal* 36 (October 1980): 35.

Gildea, Joyce A., and Emanuel, Myron. "Internal Communications: The Impact on Productivity." *Public Relations Journal* 36 (February 1980): 8–12.

Hargreaves, J. "Six Keys to Good Communications." *International Management* 31 (December 1976): 54–56.

Huseman, R. C. "Managing Change Through Communication." *Personnel Journal* 57 (January 1978): 20–25.

Kikoski, John F. "Communication: Understanding It, Improving It." *Personnel Journal* 59 (February 1980): 126.

Laing, G. J. "Communication and Its Constraints on the Structure of Organizations." *Omega* 8 (1980): 287–301.

Leavitt, Harold J. *Managerial Psychology.* 2d ed. Chicago: University of Chicago Press, 1964.

Levine, Edward. "Let's Talk: Breaking Down Barriers to Effective Communication." *Supervisory Management* 25 (August 1980): 3–12.

Lewis, Carl B. "How to Make Internal Communications Work." *Public Relations Journal* 36 (February 1980): 14–17.

McMaster, J. B. "Getting the Word to the Top." *Management Review* 68 (February 1979): 62–65.

Miles, James M. "How to Establish a Good Industrial Relations Climate." *Management Review* 67 (August 1980): 42–44.

Muchinsky, P. M. "Organizational Communication: Relationships to Organizational Climate and Job Satisfaction." *Academy of Management Journal* 20 (December 1977): 592–607.

Roberts, Karlene H., and O'Reilly, Charles A. III. "Failures in Upward Communication in Organizations: Three Possible Culprits." *Academy of Management Journal* 17 (June 1974): 205–215.

Schlachtmeyer, Albert, and Halperin, F. "Criteria-Based Planning for Employee Communication." *Personnel Administrator* 24 (August 1979): 77–81.

Schuler, Randall S. "Effective Use of Communication to Minimize Employee Stress." *Personnel Administrator* 24 (June 1979): 40–44.

Tavernier, Gerard. "Improving Managerial Productivity: The Key Ingredient Is One-on-One Communication." *Management Review* 70 (February 1981): 13–16.

KEY TERMS

organizational climate
participative climate
organizational development
survey feedback
team building
sensitivity training
change agent
management development programs
stress
executive burnout

LEARNING OBJECTIVES

After completing this chapter you should be able to

1. Explain the concept of organizational climate and describe the factors that determine it.
2. Describe a participative climate and identify the values and limitations of participation.
3. Identify and describe the change sequence and relate sources of resistance to change and the approaches that can be used in reducing resistance to change.
4. Describe the organizational development techniques that are available to implement change.
5. Explain the causes of stress management and executive burnout.

13

Organizational Climate, Change, and Development

Bill Alexander was an accounting manager for First National Bank. He had been with First National for five years but hated his job. Only this morning he said to his wife, "Honey, my boss is driving me crazy. He doesn't trust anyone. I virtually have to get permission to go to the restroom. The money is good, but I don't know how long I can stand staying there."

Betty Smith loves her job as a welder with South Construction company. She has been with South three years, and it has been one of the most enjoyable experiences of her life. It is difficult work, but she loves it. Only yesterday, she said to her friend, "People are great at South Construction. Whenever I have a problem, my boss takes time to listen. I believe he is really concerned with my well-being."

Different climates created by Bill's and Betty's managers exist in the First National Bank and South Construction Company. Bill Alexander very likely will leave his job because of his boss's attitude at the bank. Although the work is difficult at South Construction, Betty Smith loves her job. Her supervisor has apparently created a very supportive climate. Just as individuals have different personalities, you will see that an organization also has its own distinct climate or personality. In fact, two firms in the same type of business may have completely different climates.

This chapter first defines organizational climate and then identifies factors that determine a firm's climate. Various types of climates are then identified and described. The change sequence is presented next. Sources of resistance to change and approaches in reducing resistance to change follow. Organizational development techniques for implementing change from an organizational viewpoint are then described. We end the chapter with a discussion of stress management and executive burnout. The intent of the chapter is to prepare a person to recognize the importance of the organizational climate to a firm and how managers may change the firm to the best possible environment to achieve maximum results.

ORGANIZATIONAL CLIMATE DEFINED

organizational climate

The psychological environment of the firm is described as the **organizational climate.** It is similar in concept to meteorological climate. Just as the weather consists of such variables as temperature, humidity, and precipitation, organizational climate is composed of such factors as friendliness, supportiveness, risk taking, and the like. For instance, the weather of the southwestern United States may be described as warm and pleasant, the

Most Important Reasons for Success and Effectiveness as a Manager

No executive can be more effective than the team of people working for him; and nowhere is this more apparent than in a people-oriented business like broadcasting. Much of the success and effectiveness I've achieved can be traced to finding talented managers, encouraging them to function as a team, and creating an organizational climate in which they can operate smoothly, creatively, and happily.

ELTON H. RULE, President, American Broadcasting Companies, Incorporated

employees may characterize their organization as being open and supportive. This perception is gradually formed over a period of time as the person performs an assigned activity under the general guidance of a superior and a set of organizational guides. The climate existing within a firm has an impact on the employees' degree of satisfaction with the job, as well as on the level and quality of their performance. The assessment of how good or bad the organization's climate is is in the eyes of the employee. One person may perceive the same environment as bad, and another may perceive the environment as good. An employee may actually leave an organization in hope of finding a better climate.

FACTORS THAT DETERMINE ORGANIZATIONAL CLIMATE

The previous three chapters concentrated on the topics of motivation, leadership, and communication. These topics were presented prior to a discussion of organizational climate because of the impact they can have on a firm's psychological environment. We will now identify typical factors that affect organizational climate such as work groups, organization characteristics, supervision, and administration.[1] These factors may be seen in Figure 13-1. As you can see, it would be difficult to discuss these topics without a good understanding of the concepts of motivation, leadership, and communication.

The nature of the immediate work group will affect one's perception of the quality of climate. The factor commitment refers to whether or not this group is just going through the motions associated with a job. If such a state does exist, it would be difficult for a particular individual to derive high levels of output and satisfaction. The factor of hindrance is concerned with the degree to which a great deal of busywork of doubtful value is given to the group. Morale and friendliness within the group are factors with which most readers are familiar.

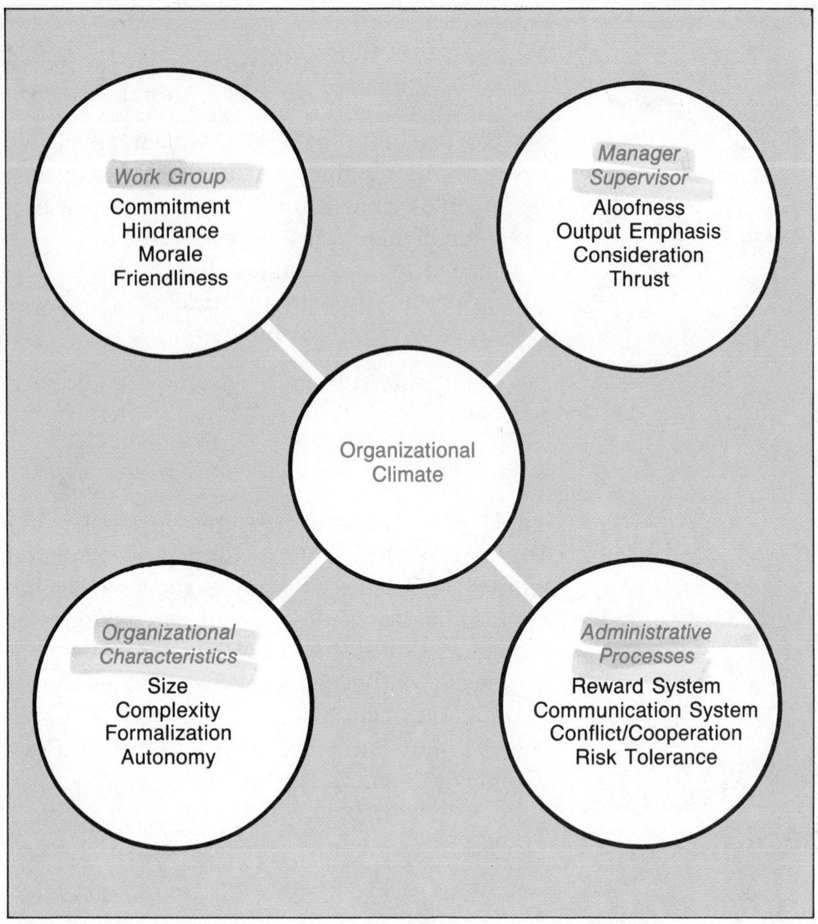

FIGURE 13-1

Factors That Determine Organizational Climate

The leadership style of the immediate supervisor will have a considerable effect on the climate of the group, and vice-versa. If the manager is aloof and distant in dealing with subordinates, this will have an impact. If the supervisor is always pushing for output, this alters the environment. Thrust refers to supervisory behavior characterized by personally working hard and setting an example. Consideration is a leadership characteristic.

Organizational characteristics may also affect the type of organizational climate. Organizations vary on such attributes as size and complexity. Large organizations tend toward higher degrees of specialization and greater impersonalization. Labor unions often find that large firms are easier to organize than the smaller ones because the smaller firms tend to be closer and have more informal relationships between employees and management. Complex organizations tend to employ a greater number of professionals and specialists, which alters the general approach to solving problems. Organizations also vary in the degree to which they write things down and attempt to program behavior through rules, procedures, and regulations. They can also be distinguished on the basis of the degree of decentralization of decision-making authority, which affects the degrees of autonomy and freedom of personnel within the organization.

Organizational climate can be affected by administrative processes. Firms that can develop a direct link between performance and rewards tend to create climates conducive to achievement. Communication systems that are open and free-flowing tend to promote participation and creative atmospheres. The general attitudes that exist toward the handling of risk and the tolerance of conflict will, in turn, have considerable impact on the type of teamwork effected. They also affect the amount of organizational innovation and creativity.

From these sixteen factors organization members will develop a subjective impression of "what kind of place this is to work for." This general impression will have some impact on performance, satisfaction, creativity, and commitment to the organization.

TYPES OF CLIMATES

At times an organization must alter its entire personality or climate in order to survive. What are the types of organizational climates that a firm may wish to emulate, and why should one particular climate prove superior to another? The one advocated by most behavioralists, such as Rensis Likert and Robert Blake, is the open and/or **participative climate,** characterized by such attributes as these:

participative climate

- trust in subordinates
- openness in communications
- considerate and supportive leadership
- group problem solving
- worker autonomy
- information sharing
- establishment of high output goals

Some behavioralists contend this is the *only* viable climate for *all* situations.

The opposite of the open and supportive climate would be a *closed and threatening* one. It, too, would be characterized by high output goals. But such goals are more likely to be declared and imposed on the organization by autocratic and threatening leaders. There is greater rigidity in this climate, which results from strict adherence to the formal chain of command, shorter spans of management, and stricter individual accountability. The emphasis is on the individual rather than teamwork. Employee reactions are often characterized by *going through the motions* and doing as one is told.

Despite criticism by behavioralists, a more participative philosophy may not work on all occasions. In one instance involving the packaging of the product of low-priced china, low productivity of the work group was

•CAREER PROFILE•

BOONE POWELL

Chairman of the Executive Committee
Baylor University Medical Center

When the term *manager* is mentioned, a person likely thinks of presidents of major firms. But an administrator of a major medical center has many of the same problems and responsibilities of a corporate president; the organizational environment is merely different. Boone Powell, currently chairman of the executive committee of Baylor University Medical Center in Dallas, Texas, is one of those men. From the time he was named administrator and chief executive officer in 1948, Boone Powell has had to function as a business manager. The reputation that the Medical Center has gained throughout the world supports the contention that he is a highly effective manager.

He received the Distinguished Service Award of the American Hospital Association in 1977, becoming the only Texan ever to receive this significant honor. The award proclamation read that "he has the methods of a businessman and the efficient mind of an administrator, but he also has a profound appreciation of the value of education and the application of the advantages of science."

A conversation with Powell will quickly assure a person that he is, in the truest sense of the word, a manager. He provides these comments to individuals interested in pursuing a career in management:

- *Planning* is essential to the survival of any enterprise in our society today.
- Recognize the importance of *involving people* in the planning and decision-making process—those who have a vested interest and those who have something significant to contribute. Involvement leads to commitment by those who participate to see that implementation of plans and decisions is achieved.
- Involvement also becomes an effective means of *communication.*
- Involvement at all levels—trustees, medical staff, department heads, and employees—fosters a spirit of cooperation and rapport, which results in better working relationships among these groups.
- Recognize that the intricacies of a medical center operation require the understanding and support of many groups of people.
- Recognize the human element in the ultimate success of any institution.
- Be alert to the constant and rapid changes in medical science and evaluate new developments to determine those that should be incorporated into the diagnostic and therapeutic service structure of the Medical Center.

caused by excessive and unnecessary interaction between employees during working hours. Management found that the threat of termination did not prevent the unproductive talking because these low-skilled and low-paid employees were eligible for government subsidy programs. In this situation space allocated to the china packaging process was redesigned by building cubicles for each worker. These cubicles, constructed of sound-proofing material, virtually eliminated the unproductive conversation between workers. As a result, productivity increased substantially and employee turnover was reduced. The total cost was $3,200, which was recovered during the first three weeks.[2]

THE PARTICIPATIVE CLIMATE

As has been indicated previously, the prevailing managerial approach in most organizations has been one characterized as being highly structured. Consequently, most of the attempts to alter organizational climates have been directed toward creating a more open and participative climate. The theme of participation developed by individuals such as McGregor, Herzberg, and Maslow relates primarily to self-actualization, motivator factors, consultative and democratic leadership, job enrichment, and management by objectives.

Values of Participation

The possible values of involving more people in the decision-making process within a firm relate primarily to productivity and morale. Increased productivity can result from the stimulation of ideas and from the encouragement of greater effort and cooperation. If employees are psychologically involved, they will often respond to shared problems with innovative suggestions and unusual efforts.

Open and participative climates are often used to improve the levels of morale and satisfaction. Specific values in this area include:

- Increased acceptability of management's ideas
- Increased cooperation with members of management and staff
- Reduced turnover
- Reduced absenteeism
- Reduced complaints and grievances
- Greater acceptance of changes
- Improved attitudes toward the job and the organization

In general, the development of greater employee participation appears to have a direct and immediate effect on employee morale. Employees take a greater interest in the job and the organization. They tend to accept, and sometimes initiate, changes not only because of their understanding of the necessity for change but also because their fear of insecurity has been reduced by knowing more about the change. Thus, even though a credibility gap may exist for practicing managers in the area of productivity, most experience and research indicate a positive relationship between employee participation and measures of morale, turnover, and absenteeism. However, there has been little evidence presented that would suggest a positive relationship exists between job satisfaction and productivity. If productivity is not harmed by participation, it would appear that these supplementary values would make a program worthwhile. If productivity is actually decreased, then serious decisions will have to made concerning management's philosophy of organizational and human values.

Qualities Needed for Success as a Manager in Your Organization

- **A willingness to accept change**
- **A skill in motivation of people**
- **Technical ability**
- **An attitude that pushes one to go that extra mile**
- **Being in the right place at the *right time***

HENRY C. GOODRICH, Chairman & CEO, Southern Natural Resources, Inc.

Limitations of Participation

Despite the values of a participative approach to management, there are some limitations. There are certain prerequisites to and limitations on greater employee participation in decision making. The requirements for greater participation in decision making are (1) sufficient time; (2) adequate ability and interest on the part of the participants; and (3) restrictions generated by the present structure and system.

If immediate decisions are required, time cannot be spared for group participation. The manager decides what to do and issues the order accordingly. Should management decide to switch from a practice of autocracy to one of increased participation, some time for adjustment on the part of both parties will be required. Participation calls for some measure of ability to govern oneself instead of leaning on others. In addition, it requires time for the subordinate to learn to handle this new-found freedom and time for the supervisor to learn to trust the subordinate.

Whether greater involvement in decision making can be developed largely depends on the ability and interest of the participants, both subordinates and managers. This is not an easy concept to implement. Obviously, if

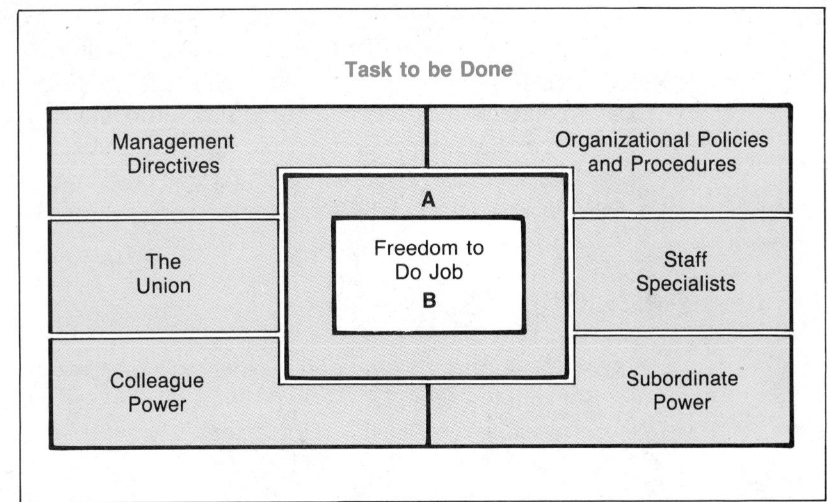

FIGURE 13-2

Limits to Participative Freedom

Source: Edwin B. Flippo and Gary M. Munsinger, *Management,* 5th ed. (Boston: Allyn and Bacon, 1982), p. 360.

the subordinate has neither knowledge of nor interest in a subject, there is little need to consult. As organizations and technology become increasingly complex and as management becomes more professionalized, it is likely that employee participation will become more characterized by cooperation seeking or information gathering. It should also be noted that not all employees are equally desirous of participation. Managers must face the fact that some workers, hopefully just a few, do not seek more responsibility and greater involvement in their job.

Finally, as indicated in Figure 13-2, the area of job freedom left to the individual may be quite restricted, but can be expanded. An individual's task is governed by management directives, organizational policies and procedures, the union contract, relations with the union steward, staff specialists, and the degree to which one can obtain the cooperation of subordinates. The greater the area in the Freedom To Do Job section, the greater the degree of participative freedom that is available. In the illustration, *A* would have more freedom to accomplish the job than *B*.

TO CHANGE OR NOT TO CHANGE

Perhaps the most important question to ask regarding the subject of change is, "Is this change necessary?" There are some who unwisely believe that changes should be made merely for the sake of change. Managers who make a change merely to satisfy a personal desire may create a disruptive effect on their section. When one of the authors was working as a consultant for a manufacturing firm, he inadvertently noticed a note on the desk of a new vice-president who had been brought in from the outside to attempt to improve the performance of a division that was doing poorly. The note said,

"Do not make any major changes for three months." The new executive obviously wanted to be aware of the total situation before changes were made. If he began to make changes immediately, inappropriate changes could be made and an entire division could be further damaged. Organizations and people desire some degree of stability in order to accomplish their assigned tasks. But there are times when changes are necessary and failure to deal effectively with them can have a disastrous effect.

THE CHANGE SEQUENCE

The sequence of events needed to bring about change in an organization may be seen in Figure 13-3. As may be seen, management must first recognize that there is a need for change. Then the specific change method(s) must be chosen. The actual change process cannot begin until these stages are completed.

Recognition of the Need for Change

Managers must train themselves to constantly seek improvement activities (areas for change). This is not always easy because of the tendency to lapse into a condition of euphoria; if it was successful in the past, it will continue to be successful in the future. People who have been successful under an old system often resist; the old way was the vehicle that was used to bring them to power. If the system is modified, some may feel that their power will be reduced. There are three basic conditions—curiosity and discontent, open-mindedness and respect for oneself—a manager must develop in order to recognize that change is needed and have the courage to implement the change.[3]

Curiosity and Discontent

The two terms provide perhaps a strange combination with regard to establishing a condition to recognize that a change is desired. A person should have sufficient curiosity to ask searching questions regarding why a task is being performed in a certain manner; it is vital in recognizing where change is needed. Discontent, on the other hand, has the implication that a person should fight the system. He or she is not satisfied merely to let things go along in their old and established pattern and concede that the old way is the best way. Through curiosity and discontent, managers place themselves in a position to recognize when a change may be needed.

Open-Mindedness

Managers who believe that their way is always the best will recognize that a change is needed only if they personally make the discovery. Subordinates' opinions are not considered. A manager who is open-minded recognizes and

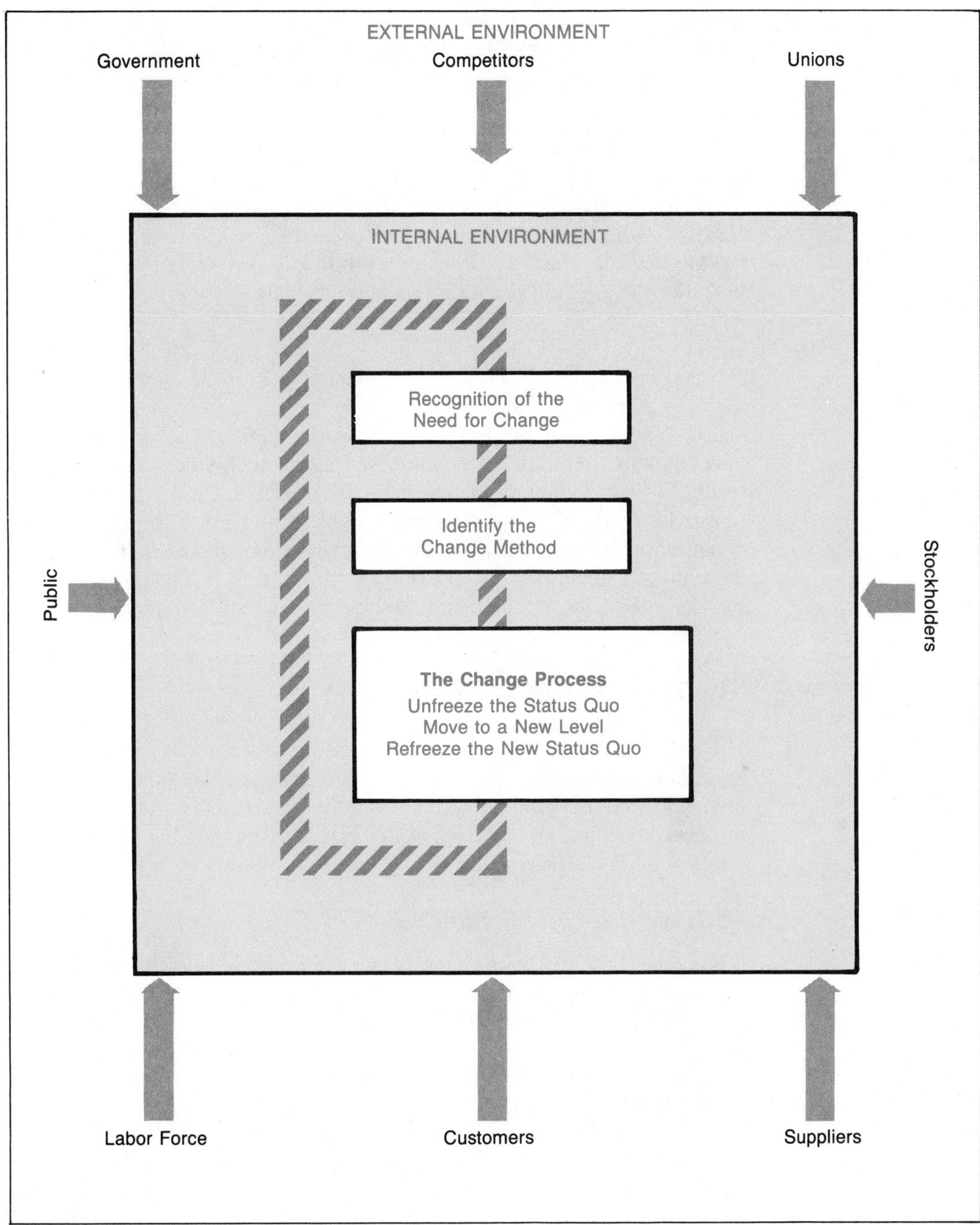

FIGURE 13-3 *The Change Sequence*

permits subordinates to make suggestions. They believe that there are many times when "two heads are better than one" and that useful ideas can evolve from lower-level personnel if they are provided the opportunity.

Respect for Oneself

It is often easier to "travel in the well-worn ruts of the past" rather than make a decision to change a procedure that will likely produce some resistance. Managers who have respect for themselves do not fear to attempt a modification that may draw initial resistance but will eventually result in a better operation. These individuals believe in their ability.

Identifying the Change Method

Management has at its disposal numerous organizational or management development methods or techniques. Specific techniques include survey feedback, team building, management by objectives, job enrichment, and sensitivity training. The technique chosen should meet the needs of the organization in reacting to the external environment and the identification of the type of climate that will provide for the greatest productivity in the organization. Specific techniques are discussed later in the chapter.

The Process of Change

The steps involved in the change process are easier to describe than they are to implement. Simply stated, the change process as outlined by Lewin, involves three fundamental stages: (1) unfreeze the status quo, (2) move to the new level, and (3) refreeze at the new level, which becomes the new status quo.[4] Each stage of the change process will next be briefly discussed.

Unfreezing the Status Quo

If individuals are to change their present attitudes, current beliefs must be altered or unfrozen. Resistance to change must be eliminated or reduced if a change is to be effective. Once resistance to change has been reduced, the manager is in a position to implement the desired change. Sources of resistance to change and approaches to reduce resistance to change are discussed later in the chapter.

Unfreezing in the change process generates self-doubt and provides a means of remedying the situation. Employees must be made to feel that ineffectiveness is undesirable but it can be remedied. If organization members are to be receptive to change, they must feel that they can change.

Moving to a New Level (Changing)

The initiation of a change can come from an order, a recommendation, or a self-directed impetus. A manager with authority can command that a change be made and enforce its implementation by threats, punishments, and close supervision. If this path of implementing change is taken, the manager will likely find that the change must be constantly monitored. Change is more permanent and substantial if a person truly wants and feels a need to change.

The most effective approach to initiate change is for a two-way relationship to exist between the person who is attempting to implement the change and the person(s) who will be changed. Rather than a one-way flow of commands or recommendations, the person implementing the change should make suggestions, and the changees should be encouraged to contribute and participate. Those initiating the change should be responsive to suggestion, either by reformulating the change or by providing explanations as to why the suggestions cannot be incorporated.

Refreezing the New Status Quo

If a person changes to a new set of work habits for a week and then reverts to former practices, the change has not been effective. Too often changes that are introduced do not stick. If the change is to be permanent, changees must be convinced that it is in their own and the organization's best interest. One of the best ways to accomplish this is to collect objective evidence of the success of the change. A manager who sees production increase because of a change in leadership style has obtained excellent evidence of the success of the change. People should have feelings of competence and pleasure in using the new behavior. But the change will be completely accepted only if the reward system of the organization is geared to the new form of behavior. If a university states that all their faculty must begin to publish articles and there is no reward attached to publishing, it is likely that few faculty members could be motivated to make this change. An employee's job may be substantially enriched in terms of content and self-supervision, but if the change is not accomplished by properly enriched pay and status symbols, dissatisfaction is likely to result. People tend to repeat behavior that they find rewarding.

SOURCES OF RESISTANCE TO CHANGE

A change may involve some loss to the person who is affected by it. Attachments to old and familiar habits, places, and people must be given up. In major and unexpected changes, there is often daze, shock, recoil, and turmoil.[5] Some of the many sources of resistance to change are looked at next.

Insecurity

Once people have operated in a particular environment for a long time, they begin to feel comfortable. A change of environment often brings about uncertainty; one does not know exactly what to expect. The feeling of insecurity surrounded virtually all of us as the transition was made from high school to college. The same sense of insecurity continues as the move is made from undergraduate to graduate work or when individuals move from one job to another or to a new city. It is perhaps because of this feeling of insecurity that some people seemingly become perpetual students.

Possible Social Loss

A change has the potential to bring about social losses. As was discussed in Chapter 8, the informal work group may be extremely powerful. If change causes individuals in the group to be transferred, the power of the group is likely diminished. A change may cause established status symbols to be destroyed or an individual of lower status may even be awarded a high-status symbol.

The impact that a change can have on the social environment was vividly illustrated when one of the authors was doing a consulting job for a regional medical center. The hospital had been a small, local 100-bed hospital, but because industry was moving rapidly into the area, the board of directors had decided to expand the hospital to 300 beds. In one department all personnel reported directly to the department head, and a close rapport had developed among the members. On a rotating shift, staff members would have to work the evening and night shift, but they still maintained close contact with the other department members.

Because of the great increase in work load the work force was expanded, and a decision was made to have three shifts with a shift supervisor for each shift. The department head now had only three people reporting directly to him, and it was believed that the work could be performed much more efficiently. But the social loss was drastic. Subordinates no longer had a close relationship with the department head; some, because they were on a different shift, rarely saw the department head. This created a tremendous social loss to several long-term employees and resulted in over 50 percent of the personnel quitting in six months.

Economic Losses

Technology may be introduced that can produce the same amount of output with fewer personnel. While most companies make an honest attempt to transfer or retain employees who have been affected by the change, the fear remains. When the computer was first introduced, the number of clerical personnel needed was often drastically reduced. The computer firms attempted to lessen this fear by claiming that the number of jobs had actually increased through the use of the computer. This did not help the employee

Regardless of the benefit of a change, employees often resist even minor ones.

who was capable only of accomplishing the clerical work. To this individual it was a major economic loss.

Inconvenience

Even if there were no social or economic loss associated with a change, any change represents a new way of doing things. As such, new procedures and techniques may have to be learned. This means that physical and mental energy must be expended (for some people this is not an enjoyable task). When a new phone system was installed at a university, there initially were many complaints. The new system meant that time and effort had to be expended. It took approximately one year for the system to be accepted by a majority of the university personnel.

Resentment of Control

Taken as a whole, Americans are very independent. When employees are told that a change must take place, they are made to realize that they do not have control over their destiny. Even though the change may be for the better, a certain amount of resentment may develop. For instance, a major government agency decided to implement a management by objectives (MBO) system. While management pointed out the many benefits of the new MBO system, many employees resented the new approach to planning and goal setting because they perceived it as a threat to their way of life in the organization.

Unanticipated Repercussions

Because the organization is a system, a change in one part is likely to have unforeseen repercussions in another portion. For example, a newly enriched job is likely to demand a change in supervisory behavior. The supervisor may resist this change in his or her behavior even though he or she initially supported the concept of job enrichment.

Union Opposition

Labor union representatives are at times inclined to oppose on principle any change suggested by management. Employees are often more comfortable with a fighting union than they are with one inclined to cooperate with management on changes designed to promote organizational interest. However, there are indications to suggest that the old adversarial relationship is being replaced by a more cooperative attitude between companies and the unions. Sometimes joint collaboration is occurring with regard to improving productivity and enhancing the quality of work life. Recent surveys have indicated that many rank and file workers want something more from their jobs and their unions than just wages, benefits, and job security.[6]

APPROACHES IN REDUCING RESISTANCE TO CHANGE

One of the authors, while working as a personnel administrator for a large insurance company, observed that an anticipated change in computers brought about considerable employee resistance. Management of the company had announced that a new computer system with greatly increased capacity would be installed in about six months. The new computer would cause substantial changes in many of the clerical jobs being performed by office personnel. Uncertain as to what to expect from the change in computer systems, numerous employees began expressing fear and concern about the impact of the change.

Before management took any action, the employees caused a rather severe slowdown in work flow in the office. Customer and agent complaints rose substantially during the six-week period after the announced change. Management took action to correct the situation by holding a series of small group meetings to explain the new computer system and how it would affect each job and each work group. While there would be several major changes in job functions affecting some individuals and work groups, management made a commitment to all employees that no one would be dismissed as a result of the installation of the new computer. The company would provide retraining programs to increase the affected employees' skills, thereby improving their adaptability to the new system.

Make Only Necessary Changes

Changes should be made only when the situation demands, not because of a whim on the part of a manager. A manager who gains a reputation for making change for the sake of making change will discover that the support for any change, whether beneficial or not, will receive only minimum acceptance.

Attempt to Maintain Useful Customs and Informal Relationships

As was mentioned in Chapter 8, the informal work group has real value from the standpoint of interpersonal understanding and cooperation. When possible, changes should be made to coincide with the culture of the personnel within the organization. When safety shoes were first introduced, few would wear them willingly because of their appearance. When they were redesigned to resemble dress shoes, resistance faded. The granting of fictional rank to civilian consultants who are to work with military personnel makes their integration into ongoing operations more understandable and acceptable. A staff expert who wants a change introduced may find it advisable to have the announcement made by a line executive with some sharing of the credit. Changes that go against established customs and informal norms will likely experience resistance and a minimum chance of acceptance.

Build Trust

If a manager has obtained a reputation for providing reliable and timely information to employees in the past, the explanation as to why a change is to be made will likely be more believable. The change may still be resisted, but if the manager is trusted by the employees, problems will be minimized. On the other hand, managers who have gained a reputation for providing incomplete or inaccurate information will often find it difficult for employees to believe that the change is "good" for them.

Provide Information in Advance

Whenever possible, the manager should provide the reasons for the change, its nature, planned timing, and the possible impact upon the organization and its personnel. Withholding information that could seriously affect the lives and futures of particular individuals, such as keeping secret the planned closure of a plant in order to preserve the work-force level until the last possible moment, should be avoided if possible. The firm that gains a reputation for such actions will have a difficult time making future changes. There are occasions when competitive survival requires that information be closely held until shortly before introduction. In these cases, the information should be provided on an *as required* basis.

Encourage Participation

When possible, subordinate participation should be encouraged in establishing the change. A person who is involved in implementing change procedures will likely be more supportive of the change. It will be recalled from Chapter 10 that Theory Y assumes that abilities are widespread in the population. Thus, many valuable ideas may be gained by permitting employees a degree of participation in implementing the change. A company that has gained a reputation for participative management is Xerox Corporation. David T. Kearns, president, said to his employees, "I pledge to you that management of this company at all levels will listen to you and put your ideas to work."[7]

Guarantee against Loss

To promote acceptance of technological changes, some organizations guarantee no layoffs as a result of such changes. In cases of a change in methods and output standard, employees are often guaranteed retention of their present level of earnings during the learning period.

Provide Counseling

At times some form of nonthreatening discussion and counseling may not only prevent rebellion but have some chance of stimulating voluntary adaptation. Nondirective counseling has been used effectively in many change situations. The approach rests on a fundamental belief that people have the ability to solve their problems with the aid of a sympathetic listener. The role of a counselor is one of understanding rather than of passing judgment. This requires a somewhat permissive, friendly atmosphere, with actions and statements that exhibit continuing interest but not judgment. In most instances, managers with authority are unable to establish this type of atmosphere. Successful nondirective counseling must usually be undertaken by staff psychologists. What the manager can do is to permit some subordinate ventilation of feelings, particularly those of frustration and anger. Just talking about the "good old days" will assist in the transition process. Discovering that others have similar feelings and doubts will often make the transition less painful; "misery loves company."

Allow for Negotiation

Resistance to change can be reduced by the process of negotiation. Negotiation is the primary method used by labor unions to effect modification of proposed managerial changes. For example, in return for accepting many changes in work rules, a West Coast employer at one time provided a $29 million benefit fund to aid longshoremen through early retirement and a type of annual wage guarantee.

ORGANIZATIONAL DEVELOPMENT

One Monday morning, employees of a midwestern railroad company arrived at their office at the usual time. They tried the door and were surprised to find it locked. A notice was attached to the corridor wall, which read that effective immediately that office of the company had been eliminated. The rooms were empty and all equipment had been moved to a more central office 600 miles away. No one was laid off, but if an employee wished to retain employment, he or she would have to be on the train the next afternoon headed for the consolidated central office. Should an employee wish to resign, personal effects on his or her desk would be mailed back. Over the preceding weekend, moving vans had cleared the local office of all equipment and had transported it to the new office.

The change may be technically justified, assuming that the railroad is in serious financial difficulties. The manner of introducing the change is, however, subject to criticism. The company's approach was to make the change an accomplished fact, utilizing the power of the "new" status quo. Rapidity of execution was, they felt, the only answer to resistance that could never be overcome anyway.

organizational development

We will describe several change efforts that involve the entire organization and are referred to as **organizational development** (OD). The organizational development movement has been strongly advocated by Chris Argyris and Warren Bennis. OD is a planned and calculated attempt to change the organization, typically to a more behavioral environment. Its education and training strategies are designed to develop a more open, real, and compatible environment regardless of existing differences in personalities, culture, or technologies.[8]

Survey Feedback

survey feedback

The systematic collection and measurement of subordinate attitudes by anonymous questionnaires is referred to as **survey feedback.** Three basic steps are involved in the process. First, data are collected from members of the organization by a consultant. Surveys are typically either the objective multiple-choice type (see Figure 13-4) or a scaled answer to suggest agreement or disagreement to a particular question (see Figure 13-5). Normally, anonymously answered questionnaires are used. If we are to obtain truthful information concerning attitudes, the employee must feel comfortable, secure, and confident in responding.

In the second step, the results of the study are presented to concerned organizational units. In the final step, the data are analyzed and decisions are made. Some means by which the data may be compared and analyzed include:

- Scores for the entire organization now and in the past
- Scores for each department now and in the past
- Scores by organizational level
- Scores by seniority
- Relative scores on each question
- Scores for each question for each category of personnel cited above

Why did you decide to do what you are now doing?

a. Desire to aid or assist others
b. Influenced by another person or situation
c. Always wanted to be in this vocation
d. Lack of opportunity or interest in other vocational fields
e. Opportunities provided by this vocation
f. Personal satisfaction from doing this work

What do you like least about your job?

a. Nothing
b. Pay
c. Supervisor relations
d. Problems with fellow workers
e. Facilities
f. Paper work and reports

FIGURE 13-4

Examples of Multiple-Choice Response to Survey Questions

Source: R. Wayne Mondy and Robert M. Noe, III, *Personnel: The Management of Human Resources* (Boston: Allyn and Bacon, Inc., 1981), p. 493.

Considering all aspects of your job, evaluate your compensation with regard to your contributions to the needs of the organization. Circle the number that best describes how you feel.

Pay too Low		Pay Low		Pay Average		Pay Above Average		Pay Too High	
1	2	3	4	5	6	7	8	9	10

What are your feelings about overtime work requirements? Circle the number that best indicates how you feel.

Unnecessary			Necessary on Occasion				Necessary		
1	2	3	4	5	6	7	8	9	10

FIGURE 13-5 ***Examples of Scaled Responses to Survey Questions*** [*Source: R. Wayne Mondy and Robert M. Noe, III,* Personnel: The Management of Human Resources *(Boston: Allyn and Bacon, 1981), p. 493.*]

The decisions are directed at improving relationships in the organization. This is accomplished by revealing problem areas and dealing with them through straightforward discussions.

Team Building

team building

One of the major techniques in the arsenal of the organizational development consultant is **team building,** a conscious effort to develop effective work groups throughout the organization.[9] The focus of team building is the development of effective management teams. These work groups focus on solving actual problems in building efficient management teams. The team-building process begins when the team leader defines a problem that requires organizational change. Next, the group analyzes the problem to determine the underlying causes of the problems. These factors may be related to such areas as communication, role clarifications, leadership styles, organizational structure, and interpersonal frictions. The next step involves proposing alternative solutions and then selecting the most appropriate one. Through this process, the participants are likely to be committed to the solution. Interpersonal support and trust develops. The overall improvement in the interpersonal support and trust of group members enhances the implementation of the change.[10]

Sensitivity Training

sensitivity training

An OD technique that involves the use of leadership discussion groups is referred to as **sensitivity training** (also called T-group training and laboratory training.) The general goal of sensitivity training is to develop awareness of and sensitivity to oneself and others. More specifically, the goals of sensitivity training include the following:

- Increased openness with others
- Greater concern for needs of others
- Increased tolerance for individual differences
- Less ethnic prejudice
- Awareness and understanding of group processes
- Enhanced listening skills
- Greater appreciation of the complexities of behaving competently
- Establishment of more realistic personal standards of behavior

Sensitivity training is not widely used in business today as an OD technique.[11] It has been labeled "psychotherapy" rather than proper business training. Leaders of T-groups have been criticized as having an insufficient background in psychology. It has been suggested that individual defense mechanisms that have been built up to preserve the personality over a period of years may be destroyed with little help being provided in replacing them with more satisfactory behavioral patterns. It is contended that one cannot exist without ego defense mechanisms.

Also, in business organizations, managers frequently must make unpleasant decisions that work to the detriment of particular individuals and groups. Excessive empathy and sympathy will not necessarily lead to a reversal of the decision and may exact an excessively high emotional cost for the decision maker. Many business organizations have internal environments characterized by competition and autocratic leadership. The power structure may not be compatible with openness and trust. In some instances, an effective manager must practice diplomacy by telling only part of the truth, or perhaps even telling different stories to two different persons or groups. Truth is not always most conducive to effective interpersonal and group relations. Sensitivity training would also tend to ignore organizational values that are derived from aggressiveness, initiative, and the charismatic appeals of a particular leader.

Management by Objectives

In Chapter 4, we described management by objectives as a systematic approach that facilitates achievement of results by directing efforts toward attainable goals. MBO is a philosophy of management that encourages managers to plan for the future. Because MBO emphasizes participative management approaches, it has been called a philosophy of management. Within this broader context, MBO becomes an important method of organizational development. The participation of individuals in setting goals and the emphasis on self-control promote not only individual development but also development for the entire organization.

Job Enrichment

The deliberate restructuring of a job to make it more challenging, meaningful, and interesting is referred to as job enrichment. As we suggested in Chapter 10, the individual is provided with an opportunity to derive greater achievement, recognition, responsibility, and personal growth in performing the job.

The Grid Approach to OD

One of the best known predesigned OD programs is the managerial grid by Robert Blake and Jane Mouton. As we discussed in Chapter 11, Blake and Mouton suggest that the most effective leadership style is that which stresses maximum concern for both output and people. The managerial grid provides a systematic approach for analyzing managerial styles and assisting the organization in moving to the best style.

CHANGE AGENTS

change agent

The person who is responsible for assuring that the planned change in OD is properly implemented is referred to as a **change agent.** This individual(s) may be either an external or an internal consultant(s). Change agents have knowledge in the OD techniques previously described and use this knowledge to assist organizational change.

When an organization first attempts to change, outside consultants are often used. This is likely because the outside expert may bring more objectivity to a situation and be better able to obtain acceptance by and trust from organizational members. With time, internal consultants may move into the role of a change agent.

MANAGEMENT DEVELOPMENT

management development programs

Organizational development techniques are designed to change the entire organization. However, **management development programs** (MDP) are specifically tailored to enhance the development of management.[12] Managers learn more effective approaches to managing people and other resources. With MDP, specific areas that have been identified as possible organization weaknesses are included in the program. Some of these areas might relate to leadership style, motivation approaches, or communication effectiveness.

The training programs may be administrated by either in-house or external personnel. An illustration of a management development program that was utilized by a major independent telephone company is provided in Figure 13-6. The intent of MDP is not only to learn new methods and techniques but to develop an inquisitive thought process. Too often personnel within

I. Management Development Program Title:
"Improving Group Effectiveness and Team Building"

II. Objectives:
(1) To identify the reasons for group formation
(2) To understand the types of groups and their attributes
(3) To discover the implications of research on group dynamics
(4) To acquire an understanding as to forces in intra- and intergroup processes
(5) To learn the characteristics of teamwork and ways to achieve it
(6) To provide experience in analyzing and diagnosing work group dimensions
(7) To acquire an appreciation for various team-building techniques

III. Description and Evaluation:
The course is designed to provide greater understanding of, and ability to work with and through, groups. Special emphasis is given to understanding the various need levels of groups and what can be done to appeal more effectively to those levels. Actual practice in team-building techniques is given, as well as experience in analyzing work groups. Evaluation is made of the major contingencies affecting groups. Observing group behavior through various media is a portion of the course content.

IV. Size of Class:
The class should have a maximum enrollment of 20 participants so as to allow the group process to be seen in action in the group itself, yet small enough to allow for active participation.

V. Assignment of Instructor:
The instructor allocates an equal amount of time to lecture and active class discussion with approximately one-third of the time devoted to various media presentations and group involvement. The course is designed for a two- or three-day session.

VI. Enrollment Requirements:
Middle- and upper-level managerial experience desired

FIGURE 13-6
Course Content for a Management Development Program

a firm become so accustomed to performing the same task day after day that they forget how to think. A properly designed management development program places a person in a frame of mind to analyze problems and is often used to provide the foundation for a change to occur.

STRESS MANAGEMENT

stress

A by-product of some change is the stress that can develop in workers. **Stress** is defined as the nonspecific response of the body to any demands made upon it. Over a period of time or under intense conditions, stress can take its toll on the wear and tear of one's body. A vast array of ailments ranging from lower back pains to headaches to coronary problems and cancer are considered to be by-products of stress. If stress is strong enough and permitted to last long enough, it can damage both mental and physical health. Unmanaged coping with stress can create anxiety, depression, paranoia, and other mental difficulties for the individual. The cost and pain of stress are enormous. Stress-related absenteeism, illness, and premature death have been estimated to cost American industry between $20 and $50 billion each year.[13]

Fortunately, managers are now beginning to realize that effective stress management is important to them, to their employees, and to the organization. Job-related stress can be as disruptive, and as costly, to the corporation as any accident that occurs to an employee. In fact, many employee accidents are considered to be stress related.

It is important for managers to recognize employee behavior patterns that may suggest stress overload. Some of these patterns are:

- Working late more than usual or the opposite, increased tardiness or absenteeism
- Difficulty in making decisions
- Increases in the number of careless mistakes
- Missing deadlines or forgetting appointments
- Problems interacting and getting along with others
- Focusing on mistakes and personal failure[14]

Naturally, all behavioral change is not stress related, but astute managers can be made alert to changes in employee patterns. A normally productive worker becomes sloppy and productivity decreases. Or a normally friendly worker becomes irritable and short-tempered.

There is that old saying that goes like this: "An ounce of prevention is worth a pound of cure." It is certainly that way in stress management. Firms can do much to reduce stressful conditions. For instance, if management finally recognizes that the organizational climate produces considerable stress, efforts can be made to change the climate. Perhaps the climate would move toward a more open and less threatening one where workers can do their jobs without fear. Another means of reducing stress might be to redesign jobs or change the work-flow schedule. Stressful conditions might be eliminated through this procedure. Also, the physical environment might be changed. Perhaps the noise level is excessive. Ear plugs might be furnished or the noise level reduced.

One rapidly growing area of stress reduction is the development of company physical fitness programs for their employees. Xerox Corporation has eight in-house physical fitness laboratories at locations across the United States. A program is designed for each individual to help them feel and look better. It also helps them build their self-concept. The Xerox Executive Fitness Program emphasizes four areas: (1) cardiovascular fitness, (2) flexibility, (3) relaxation by means of biofeedback, and (4) weight conditioning. Similar programs are expected to increase dramatically in the future. Firms are beginning to see how stress-related problems affect the profitability of the organization.[15]

EXECUTIVE BURNOUT

executive burnout

Although closely related to stress, executive burnout is somewhat different. **Executive burnout** has been defined as "someone in a state of fatigue or frustration brought about by devotion to a cause, way of life, or relationship that failed to produce the expected reward."[16] Burnout is said to affect approximately 10 percent of managers and executives.[17] A major problem associated with burnout is that it is extremely contagious. Executives who become burnout victims are likely to become cynical, negativistic, and pessimistic. They are literally ready to explode. An entire work group can be quickly turned into a collection of burnouts.[18] Therefore, it is extremely important for burnout symptoms to be recognized. One burnout victim can affect many people.

Some of the symptoms of burnout include: (1) chronic fatigue; (2) anger at those making demands; (3) self-criticism for putting up with the demands; (4) cynicism, negativism, and irritability; (5) a sense of being beseiged; and (6) a hair-trigger display of emotions.[19] Other symptoms might include recurring health problems, such as ulcers, back pain, and frequent headaches. The burnout victim is often unable to maintain an even keel emotionally. Unwarranted hostility may occur in completely inappropriate situations.

Burnout often occurs among talented, achievement-oriented workers. Many of these people are business executives. Perhaps they have set their standards too high and then refuse to admit that they cannot be achieved. Sometimes the organization itself designs situations that are capable of causing burnout. Giving a manager a job to do and then making it virtually impossible to accomplish provides an example. Burnout is the "consequence of a work situation in which the person gets the feeling he's butting his head against the wall day after day, year after year."[20]

The problem can be corrected. Some firms are arranging full-time counselors on staff to help employees who are experiencing burnout. Seminars are being given to help managers to help their workers overcome the problem. Some firms are granting disability leaves until the worker recovers.

Firms can also take measures to *prevent* burnout among their employees. For example, workers should not be permitted to work too much overtime, even on critical problems. It is often the best person who is always called upon in times of crisis. These are the very people who are likely to burn out. Another method might be to rotate employees who are working on stressful jobs. Moving people to a new project may help. Some firms are starting physical exercise programs and counseling programs. Breaks in the business routines are helpful.[21] The job at hand should not overshadow all other aspects of living.

Summary

The psychological environment of the firm is described as the organizational climate. The climate existing within a firm has an impact on the employees' degree of satisfaction with the job, as well as on the level and quality of their performance. Typical factors that affect organizational climate are provided under the headings of work group, organizational characteristics, supervisor, and administrative processes. The climate advocated by most behavioralists is the open and/or participative climate, which is characterized by such attributes as trust in subordinates, openness in communication, considerate and supportive leadership, group problem solving, worker autonomy, information sharing, and the establishment of high output goals.

The sequence of events that are needed to bring about change in an organization begins with management's recognizing a need for change. Next, the change method to be used is identified. The change process consists of unfreezing the status quo, moving to a new level, and freezing the new status quo.

A change may involve some loss to the person who is affected by it and thus generate resistance. Some of the possible sources of resistance to change include: insecurity, possible social loss, economic losses, inconvenience, resentment of control, unanticipated repercussions, and union opposition. Approaches that may be used to reduce resistance to change include: make only necessary changes, attempt to maintain useful customs and informal relationships, build trust, provide information in advance, encourage participation, guarantee against loss, provide counseling, and allow for negotiation.

Change efforts that involve the entire organization are referred to as organizational development (OD). OD is a planned and calculated attempt to change the organization, typically to a more behavioral environment. Some of the OD techniques available include survey feedback, team building, sensitivity training, management by objectives, job enrichment, and the grid approach. The person who is responsible for ensuring that the planned change in OD is properly implemented is referred to as a change agent.

Whereas organizational development techniques are designed to change the entire organization, management development programs are specifically tailored to benefit managers. Some of the areas for development might include leadership style, motivation approaches, and communication effectiveness.

Stress management and executive burnout are of increasing concern to modern managers. Stress is the nonspecific response of the body to any demands made upon it. A person experiencing executive burnout is someone in a state of fatigue or frustration brought about by devotion to a cause, way of life, or relationship that failed to produce the desired reward. There are numerous ways to identify and treat both stress and executive burnout.

Exercises

1. **Identify the major changes that have occurred in your life during the past year. How did you react to these changes?**
2. **Visit three businesses. Attempt to assess the type of climate that exists in each of the firms.**

3. Assume that you are the president of a college or a university and you would like to make the following changes:
   a. Students must be professionally attired at all times.
   b. Faculty members must be at their office by 8:00.
   c. All single students must live in the dormitory.

   Assuming that all of the above-mentioned changes are made for a logical reason, what type of resistance to these changes could you expect? How could you possibly overcome some of the resistance to these changes?

Review Questions

1. Define *organizational climate*. What are the factors that interact to determine the type of organizational climate that exists in a firm?
2. Identify the values and limitations of a participative climate.
3. What is the primary reason for making a change in business? Relate the situational factors in making a decision to change.
4. List and describe the change sequence discussed in the text.
5. What are the sources of resistance to change as described in the text?
6. Describe the approaches that may be used in reducing resistance to change.
7. Define each of the following terms:
   a. Organizational development
   b. Team building
   c. Sensitivity training
8. Define and distinguish between stress and burnout.

Case Study

A Change in Environment

Until one year ago Wayne, Don, and Robert had been supervisors with a small chain of thirty-nine grocery stores. Each supervisor had responsibility for thirteen stores and reported directly to the company president. All three supervisors worked well together, and there was a constant exchange of information, which was quite useful in coordinating the activities of the stores. Each supervisor had specific strengths that were useful in helping the others. Wayne coordinated the deployment of the part-time help at all thirty-nine stores. Don monitored the inventories, and Robert interviewed prospective new employees prior to sending them to Wayne and Don for review. It was a complete team effort directed toward getting the job done.

One year later a completely different environment existed at the chain. The president, wishing to relieve himself of many daily details, decided to promote Robert to vice-president. Another supervisor, Phillip, was hired for Robert's position. Robert had a completely different idea of how the activities of the supervisors should be conducted. Under Robert's leadership each supervisor was now responsible for the activities at only his stores. If a problem occurred, the supervisor was to discuss it with Robert, and he would provide the solution. When either Wayne, Don, or Phillip attempted to solve problems on their own, they were reprimanded by Robert. After a few "chewing outs" Wayne, Don, and Phillip decided not to fight the system and did as Robert wanted; they rarely saw each other any more. If Don had a problem at his stores that caused him to work all night that was not any concern of Wayne or Phillip.

The only problem with the new system was that efficiency dropped drastically. For instance, Wayne was a good coordinator of part-time help. He had the type of personality that could talk a person into coming to work at 5:00 on Saturday when the individual had a date at 6:00. Wayne's stores remained well staffed with part-time help, but the others suffered. Many times the part-time help did not show up and either Don or Phillip had to act as the replacement if the store manager could not be convinced to work overtime. On the other hand, Wayne's inventory control suffered because Don was best qualified in this area.

Robert accused the three supervisors of working against him and threatened them with dismissal if operations did not get better. Wayne, Don, and Phillip felt that they could not be productive in this environment and found other positions. When the president discovered what had occurred, Robert was fired. It took the president six months to get the operations back to the level of efficiency that it had achieved previously.

QUESTIONS

1. What different organizational environment was created as a result of promoting Robert to vice-president?
2. How do you feel that this situation could have been avoided? Discuss the possibility of the use of the participative approach in this instance.

Case Study

Rumors at Duncan Electric

Donna Garcia is a supervisor for Duncan Electric Corporation, a manufacturer of high-quality electrical parts. Donna had been with the firm for five years and had a reputation for having one of the best teams in the plant. Donna had picked the majority of these employees and was proud of the reputation they had achieved. But a problem was now brewing that had the potential of destroying her department.

For weeks, rumors of a substantial reduction in personnel at Duncan Electric have been circulating. Donna has not received any confirmation from the corporate office regarding the reduction. The rumors, all claiming to be from reliable sources, range from minor reductions to a large-scale reduction in personnel. Every day someone claims to have the inside story, and every day the story changes. Donna, who has a reputation for leveling with her people, successfully discounted the rumors for awhile. But as the doubts began to grow, work output began to suffer. Her employees were now spending time trying to verify the latest rumor. Speculation increased to the point where the best-qualified employees were starting to shop around.

The action by these employees does not make sense unless there is to be a very large-scale layoff. Donna was convinced that a minor layoff was the worst that could possibly happen and she was demoralized to see things falling apart for no good reason.

On Friday, Bob Phillips and Henry Barham, two of the most skilled employees in the department, told Donna that they had taken a job with a competitor. This situation was what she had feared most; the most qualified workers would leave and the least qualified workers would remain. Instead of having one of the best departments at Duncan Electric, she may now have the worst.

QUESTIONS

1. To what extent have the rumors of the anticipated change in the work force damaged the morale of the employees?
2. What should management do to reduce the fear of the anticipated change?
3. What should Donna do in a situation like this?

Notes

1. Many of the factors were taken from the Organizational Climate Description Questionnaire generated by Halpin and Croft as described in Andrew W. Halpin, *Theory and Research in Administration* (New York: Macmillan, 1966), Chap. 4. Another widely used measure is that of Litwin and Stringer found in G. Litwin and R. Stringer, *Motivation and Organizational Climate* (Cambridge: Harvard University Press, 1968).
2. H. Kenneth Bobele and Peter J. Buchanan, "Building a More Productive Environment," *Management World* 1 (January 1979): 8.
3. Addison C. Bennet, "The Manager's Responsibility for Work Improvement," in *Improving the Effectiveness of Hospital Management* (New York: Preston, 1972), pp. 161–162.
4. Kurt Lewin, *Field Theory and Social Science* (New York: Harper, 1964), chaps. 9, 10.
5. Ralph G. Huschowitz, "The Human Aspects of Managing Transition," *Personnel* 51 (May–June 1974): 13.
6. "The New Industrial Relations," *Business Week,* May 11, 1981, p. 98.
7. Ibid.
8. Portions of the following discussion were adapted from R. Wayne Mondy and Robert M. Noe, III, *Personnel: The Management of Human Resources* (Boston: Allyn and Bacon, 1981), pp. 204–217.
9. Edgar F. Huse, *Organization Development and Change* (St. Paul, Minn.: West, 1975), p. 230.
10. Michael A. Hitt, R. Dennis Middlemist, and Robert Q. Mathis, *Effective Management* (St. Paul, Minn.: West, 1979), pp. 462–464.
11. For a detailed review of one hundred research studies on sensitivity training, see P. B. Smith, "Control Studies on the Outcome of Sensitivity Training," *Psychological Bulletin* (July 1975): 597–622.
12. Jon English and Anthony R. Marchione, "Nine Steps in Management Development," *Business Horizons* 6 (June 1977): 88–94.
13. Oliver L. Niehouse and Karen B. Massoni, "Stress—An Inevitable Part of Change," *Advanced Management Journal* 44 (Spring 1979): 17.

14. John M. Ivancevich and Michael T. Matteson, *Stress and Work: A Managerial Perspective* (Glenview, Ill.: Scott, Foresman, 1980), p. 208.
15. Mondy and Noe, *Personnel,* pp. 371–372.
16. Herbert J. Freudenberger, *Burnout: The High Cost of High Achievement* (Garden City, N.Y.: Anchor Press, Doubleday, 1980), p. 13.
17. Beverly Norman, "Career Burnout," *Black Enterprises* 11 (July 1981): 46.
18. Cary Cherniss, "Job Burnout: Growing Worry for Workers, Bosses," *U.S. News and World Report* 88 (February 27, 1980), p. 72.
19. Harry Levinson, "When Executives Burn Out," *Harvard Business Review* 59 (May–June 1981): 76.
20. Freudenberger, *Burnout,* pp. 17–18.
21. Levinson, "When Executives Burn Out," pp. 78–81.

References

Allen R. F., and Silverzweig, S. "Changing Community and Organizational Cultures." *Training and Development Journal* 31 (July 1977): 28–34.

Baird, John E., Jr. "Supervisory and Managerial Training through Communication by Objectives." *Personnel Administrator* 26 (July 1981): 28–32.

Baysinger, Rebecca T., and Woodman, Richard W. "The Use of Management by Objectives in Management Training Programs." *Personnel Administrator* 26 (February 1981): 83–86.

Bensahel, J. G. "How to Overcome Resistance to Change." *International Management* 32 (September 1977): 66–67.

Biggart, N. W. "Creative-Destructive Process of Organizational Change: The Case of the Post Office." *Administrative Science Quarterly* 22 (September 1977): 410–426.

Carlson, H. C. "Organizational Research and Organizational Change." *Personnel* 54 (July 1977): 11–22.

Davis, L. E. "Individuals and the Organization." *California Management Review* 22 (Spring 1980): 5–14.

Gordon, G. G., and Goldberg, B. E. "Is There a Climate for Success?" *Management Review* 66 (May 1977): 37–44.

Greiner, Larry E. "Evolution and Revolution as Organizations Grow." *Harvard Business Review* 50 (July 1971): 37–46.

Hellriegel, Don, and Slocum, John W., Jr. "Organizational Climate: Measures, Research, and Contingencies." *Academy of Management Journal* 17 (June 1974): 255–280.

Howe, R. J. et al. "Introducing Innovation Through Organizational Development." *Management Review* 67 (February 1978): 52–56.

Huse, E. F. *Organization Development and Change.* (St. Paul, Minn.: West, 1980).

Jennings, Eugene E. "How to Develop Your Management Talent Internally." *Personnel Administrator* 26 (July 1981): 20–23.

Kelly, Joe, and Khozan, Kamiran. "Participative Management: Can It Work?" *Business Horizons* (August 1980): 74–79.

Margerison, Charles, and New, Colin. "Management Development by Intercompany Consortiums." *Personnel Management* 12 (November 1980): 42–45.

Miles, James M. "How to Establish a Good Industrial Relations Climate." *Management Review* 67 (August 1980): 42–44.

Miller, Danny, and Friesen, Peter H. "Momentum and Revaluations in Organizational Adaptation." *Academy of Management Journal* 23 (December 1980): 591–614.

Mintzberg, Henry. "Organizational Design: Fashion or Fit?" *Harvard Business Review* 59 (January–February 1981): 103–116.

Monat, Jonathan S. "A Perspective on the Evaluation of Training and Development Programs." *Personnel Administrator* 26 (July 1981): 47–52.

Olivas, Louis. "Using Assessment Centers for Individual and Organizational Development." *Personnel* 57 (May–June 1980): 63–67.

Oriorne, George S. "The Change Registers." *Personnel Administrator* 26 (January 1981): 57–63.

Peters, James W., and Mabry, Edward A. "The Personnel Officer as Internal Consultant." *Personnel Administrator* 26 (April 1981): 29–32.

Scott, Walter B. "Participative Management at Motorola—The Results." *Management Review* 70 (July 1981): 26–28.

CASE STUDY FOR PART IV

The Organizational Climate at Lincoln Electric

Lincoln Electric Company is the world's largest manufacturer of welding machines and electrodes with 2,600 employees in two U.S. factories near Cleveland, Ohio, and approximately 600 in three factories located in other countries. Lincoln's market share is more than 40 percent of the U.S. market for arc-welding equipment and supplies.

A HISTORICAL SKETCH

In 1895, after being "frozen out" of the depression-ravaged Elliott-Lincoln company, John C. Lincoln obtained his second patent and began to manufacture an improved motor. He began business with $200 he had earned redesigning a motor for young Herbert Henry Dow, who later founded The Dow Chemical Company.

In 1906, Lincoln incorporated and moved from a one-room, fourth-floor factory to a new three-story building erected in east Cleveland. He expanded his work force to 30 and sales grew to over $50,000 a year. John Lincoln preferred being an engineer and inventor rather than a manager, though, and it was left to another Lincoln to manage the company through its years of success.

In 1907, after a bout with typhoid fever forced him from Ohio State in his senior year, James F. Lincoln, John's younger brother, joined the fledgling company. In 1914, with the company still small and determined to improve its financial condition, he became the active head of the firm, with the titles of general manager and vice-president. John Lincoln remained president of the company for some years, but he became more involved in other business ventures and in his work as an inventor.

One of James Lincoln's early actions as head of the firm was to ask the employees to elect representatives to a committee to advise him on company

This case was prepared by Arthur D. Sharplin of Northeast Louisiana University as a basis for class discussion rather than to illustrate either effective or ineffective handling of an administrative situation.

operations. The advisory board has met with the chief executive officer twice monthly since that time. The first year the advisory board was in existence, working hours were reduced from fifty-five per week—then standard—to fifty hours a week. In 1915, the company gave each employee a paid-up life insurance policy. In 1918, an employee bonus plan was attempted but was not continued, although the idea was to resurface and become the backbone of the Lincoln Management System.

The Lincoln Electric Employees' Association was formed in 1919 to provide health benefits and social activities. This organization continues today and has assumed several additional functions over the years. By 1923, a piecework pay system was in effect, employees got two-week paid vacations each year, and wages were adjusted for changes in the Consumer Price Index. Approximately 30 percent of Lincoln's stock was set aside for key employees in 1914 when James F. Lincoln became general manager, and a stock purchase plan for all employees was begun in 1925.

The board of directors voted to start a suggestion system in 1929. The program is still in effect, but cash awards, a part of the early program, were discontinued several years ago. Now, suggestions are rewarded by additional performance appraisal "points," which affect year-end bonuses. The legendary Lincoln bonus plan was proposed by the advisory board and accepted on a trial basis by James Lincoln in 1934. The first annual bonus amounted to about 25 percent of wages. There has been a bonus every year since then. The bonus plan has been a cornerstone of the Lincoln Management System and recent bonuses have approximated annual wages.

James F. Lincoln died in 1965 and there was some concern, even among employees, that the Lincoln system would fall into disarray, that profits would decline, and that year-end bonuses might be discontinued. Quite the contrary, seventeen years after Lincoln's death, the company appears stronger than ever. Each year since 1965 has seen higher profits and bonuses. Employee morale and productivity remain high; employee turnover is almost nonexistent except for retirements, and Lincoln's market share is stable.

COMPANY PHILOSOPHY

James F. Lincoln was the son of a Congregational minister, and Christian principles were at the center of his business philosophy. While Christian principles have served as important guidelines for business operations, there is no indication that the company has attempted to evangelize its employees or customers—or the general public for that matter. The current board chairman, Mr. Irrgang, and the President, Mr. Willis, do not even mention the Christian gospel in their recent speeches and interviews. The company motto, "The actual is limited, the possible is immense," is prominently displayed, but there is no display of religious slogans and there is no company chapel.

Attitude toward the Customer

James Lincoln saw the customer's needs as the raison d'être for every company. "When any company has achieved success so that it is attractive as an investment," he wrote, "all money usually needed for expansion is supplied by the customer in retained earnings. It is obvious that the customer's interests, not the stockholder's, should come first" (Lincoln, 1961, p. 119). In 1947 he said, "Care should be taken . . . not to rivet attention on profit. Between 'How much do I get?' and 'How do I make this better, cheaper, more useful?' the difference is fundamental and decisive." Lincoln's goal, often stated, is "to build a better and better product at a lower and lower price." It is obvious, James Lincoln said, "that the customer's interests should be the first goal of industry." (1961, p. 117)

Attitude toward Stockholders

Stockholders are given last priority at Lincoln. This is a continuation of James Lincoln's philosophy: "The last group to be considered is the stockholders who own stock because they think it will be more profitable than investing money in any other way" (1961, p. 38). Concerning division of the largess produced by incentive management, Lincoln writes, "The absentee stockholders also will get his share, even if undeserved, out of the greatly increased profit that the efficiency produces."

Attitude toward Unionism

There has never been a serious effort to organize Lincoln employees. While James Lincoln criticized the labor movement for "selfishly attempting to better its position at the expense of the people it must serve" (1961, p. 18), he still had kind words for union members. He excused abuses of union power as "the natural reactions of human beings to the abuses to which management has subjected them" (1961, p. 76). Lincoln's idea of the correct relationship between workers and managers is shown by this comment: "Labor and management are properly not warring camps; they are parts of one organization in which they must and should cooperate fully and happily" (1961, p. 72).

Beliefs and Assumptions about Employees

If fulfilling customer needs is the desired goal of business, then employee performance and productivity are the means by which this goal can best be achieved. It is the Lincoln attitude toward employees, reflected in the following quotations (all taken from Lincoln, 1961):

> The greatest fear of the worker, which is the same as the greatest fear of the industrialist in operating a company, is lack of income . . . The industrial manager is very conscious of his company's need of uninterrupted income. He is completely oblivious, evidently, of the fact that the worker has the same need (p. 36).
>
> He is just as eager as any manager is to be part of a team that is properly organized and working for the advancement of our economy . . . He has no desire to make profits for those who do not hold up their end in production, as is true of absentee stockholders and inactive people in the company (p. 75).
>
> If money is to be used as an incentive, the program must provide that what is paid to the worker is what he has earned. The earnings of each must be in accordance with accomplishment (p. 98).
>
> Status is of great importance in all human relationships. The greatest incentive that money has, usually, is that it is a symbol of success . . . The resulting status is the real incentive . . . Money alone can be an incentive to the miser only (p. 92).
>
> There must be complete honesty and understanding between the hourly worker and management if high efficiency is to be obtained (p. 39).

George E. Willis, president, dispels the impression that Lincoln management is "soft" management. "We care about one another around here, but we are quite autocratic. When managers tell workers to do something, they expect it to be done."

ORGANIZATIONAL STRUCTURE

Lincoln has never had a formal organization chart. The objective of this policy is to insure maximum flexibility. An open door policy is practiced throughout the company and personnel are encouraged to take problems to the person most capable of resolving them. Perhaps because of the quality and enthusiasm of the Lincoln work force, routine supervision is almost nonexistent. A typical production foreman, for example, supervises as many as 100 workers, a span-of-control which does not allow more than infrequent worker-supervisor interaction. Position titles and traditional flows of authority do imply something of an organization structure, however. For example, the vice-president, sales, and the vice-president, electrode division, report to the president, as do various staff assistants such as the personnel director and the director of purchasing. From such implied relationships, it has been determined that production workers have two or, at most, three levels of supervision between themselves and the president.

PERSONNEL POLICIES

Recruitment and Selection

Every job opening at Lincoln is advertised internally on company bulletin boards, and any employee can apply for any job so advertised. External hiring is done only for entry level positions. Selection for these jobs is done on the basis of personal interviews—there is no aptitude or psychological testing. In 1979, out of about 3500 applicants interviewed by the personnel department fewer than 300 were hired. Final selection is made by the supervisor who has the job opening.

Job Security and Compensation

After one year, employees are guaranteed thirty hours per week and promised that they will not be discharged except for misconduct.There has been no layoff at Lincoln since 1949.

Insofar as possible, base wage rates are translated into piece rates. Practically all production workers and many others—for example, some fork truck drivers—are paid by piece rate. Once established, piece rates are never changed unless a substantive change in the way a job is done results from a source other than the worker doing the job. In December of each year, a portion of annual profits is distributed to employees as bonuses. Incentive bonuses since 1934 have averaged about the same as annual wages and somewhat more than after-tax profits. For example, the average bonus for 1981 was about $17,600.

Training and Education

Production workers are given a short period of on-the-job training and then placed on a piecework pay system. Lincoln does not pay for offsite education. The idea behind this latter policy is that everyone cannot take advantage of such a program and it is unfair to expend company funds for an advantage to which there is unequal access. Sales personnel are given on-the-job training in the plant followed by a period of work and training at one of the regional sales offices.

Fringe Benefits and Executive Perquisites

A medical plan and a company-paid retirement program have been in effect for many years. A plant cafeteria, operated on a break-even basis, serves meals at about 60 percent of usual costs. An employee association, to which the company does not contribute, provides disability insurance and organizes social and athletic activities. An employee stock ownership program, instituted in about 1925, and regular stock purchases have resulted in employee ownership of about 50 percent of Lincoln's stock.

As to executive perquisites, there are none—crowded, austere offices, no executive washrooms or lunchrooms, and no reserved parking spaces. Even the company president pays for his own meals and eats in the cafeteria.

FINANCIAL MANAGEMENT

James F. Lincoln felt strongly that financing for company growth should come within the company—through initial cash investment by the founders, through retention of earnings, and through stock purchases by those who work in the firm. The company uses a minimum of debt in its capital structure. There is no borrowing at all, with the debt being limited to current payables. Even the new $20,000,000 plant in Mentor, Ohio was financed totally from earnings.

The unusual pricing policy at Lincoln is succinctly stated by President Willis: ". . . at all times price on the basis of cost and at all times keep pressure on our costs." This policy resulted in Lincoln's price for the most popular welding electrode then in use going from 16 cents a pound in 1929 to 4.7 cents in 1938. More recently the SA-200 welder, Lincoln's largest selling portable machine, decreased in price from 1958 through 1965. According to Dr. C. Jackson Grayson of the American Productivity Center in Houston, Texas,

Lincoln's prices in general have increased only one-fifth as fast as the Consumer Price Index since 1934. This has resulted in a welding products market in which Lincoln is the undisputed price leader for the products it manufactures. Not even the major Japanese manufacturers, such as Nippon Steel for welding electrodes and Osaka Transformer for welding machines, have been able to penetrate this market.

WORKER PERFORMANCE AND ATTITUDES

Exceptional worker performance at Lincoln is a matter of record. The typical Lincoln employee earns about twice as much as other factory workers in the Cleveland area. Yet the labor cost per sales dollar at Lincoln, currently 23.5 cents, is well below industry averages.

Annual sales per Lincoln production employee is approximately $157,000. An observer at the factory quickly sees why this figure is so high. Each worker is proceeding busily and thoughtfully about his task. There is no idle chatter. Most workers take no coffee breaks. Many operate several machines and make a substantial component unaided. The supervisors, some with as many as 100 subordinates, are busy with planning and recordkeeping duties with hardly a glance at the people they supervise. The manufacturing procedures appear efficient—no unnecessary steps, no wasted motions, no wasted materials. Finished components move smoothly to subsequent work on hand.

Worker turnover at Lincoln is practically nonexistent except for retirements and departures by new employees.

In an effort to gain greater insight into company practices and the attitudes and perceptions of employees, a series of interviews were conducted. The following are excerpts from interviews with employees at Lincoln by the casewriter.

- **Ed Sanderson, a twenty-three-year-old high school graduate who had been with Lincoln for four years as a machine operator.**

  Q. Roughly, what were your earnings last year including your bonus?

  A. $37,000.

  Q. What have you done with the money since you have been here?

  A. Well, we've lived pretty well and we've bought a condominium.

Q. Have you paid for the condo?

A. No, but I could!

Q. Are you paid on a piece-rate basis?

A. My gang is. There are nine of us who make the bare electrodes and the whole gang gets paid on how many electrodes we make.

Q. Why do you think Lincoln employees produce more than workers in other plants?

A. That's the way the company is set up. The more you put out the more you are going to make.

Q. Do you think it's the piece rate and bonus together?

A. I don't think people would work here if they didn't know that they would be rewarded at the end of the year.

Q. Do you think Lincoln employees will ever join a union?

A. No! We don't have a union shop and I don't think I could work in a union shop.

- **Betty Stewart, a fifty-two-year-old high school graduate with Lincoln for thirteen years and who was working as a cost accounting clerk.**

Q. What jobs have you held here besides the one you have now?

A. I worked in payroll for a while and then came into cost accounting.

Q. How much did you earn last year?

A. Roughly $20,000, but I was off several weeks because of back surgery.

Q. You weren't paid while you were off for back surgery?

A. No.

Q. Did the Employees' Association help out?

A. Yes. The company doesn't furnish that, though. We pay $6 a month into the Employees' Association. I think my check from them was $105.00 a week.

Q. How did you get your job at Lincoln?

A. I was bored silly where I was working and I had heard that Lincoln kept their people busy. So I applied and got the job.

- **Roger Lewis, twenty-three-year-old Purdue graduate in mechanical engineering, who had been in the Lincoln sales program for fifteen months.**

Q. How did you get your job at Lincoln?

A. I saw that Lincoln was interviewing on campus at Purdue and I went by. I later came to Cleveland for a plant tour and was offered a job.

Q. Do you think Lincoln salesmen work harder than those in other companies?

A. Yes. I don't think there are many salesmen for other companies who are putting in fifty- to sixty-hour weeks. Everybody here works harder. You can go out in the plant or you can go upstairs and there's nobody sitting around.

Q. Why do you think Lincoln employees have such high productivity?

A. Piecework has a lot to do with it. Lincoln is smaller than many plants, too; you can stand in one place and see the materials come in one side and the product go out the other. You feel a part of the company. The chance to get ahead is important, too. They have a strict policy of promoting from within; you know you have a chance. I think in a lot of other places you may not get as fair a shake as you do here. The sales offices are on a smaller scale, too. I like that. I tell someone that we have two people in the Baltimore office and they say, "You've got to be kidding." It's smaller and more personal. Pay is the most important thing. I have heard that this is the highest paying factory in the world.

- **Joe Trahan, fifty-eight-year-old high school graduate, had been with Lincoln thirty-nine years and was employed as a working supervisor in the tool room.**

Q. Roughly, what was your pay last year and how much was your bonus?

A. Around $55,000; salary, bonus, stock dividends. My bonus was about $23,000.

Q. What do you think of the executives at Lincoln?

A. They're really top notch.

Q. Why do you think you produce more than people in similar jobs?

A. We are on the incentive system. Everything we do we try to improve to make a better product with a minimum of outlay. We try to improve the bonus.

Q. Tell me something about Mr. James Lincoln, who died in 1965.

A. You are talking about Jimmy, Sr. He always strolled through the shop in his shirt sleeves. Big Fellow. Always looked distiguished. Grey hair. Friendly sort of guy. I was a member of the advisory board one year. He was there each time.

Questions

1. Describe Lincoln Electric's management philosophy, especially with regards to the motivation and leadership of the firm's work force.
2. The typical Lincoln employee earns about twice as much as other factory workers, yet labor costs are well below industry averages. Why? How can this be explained?
3. What are the major factors contributing to the high employee productivity at Lincoln Electric? Discuss.
4. What can other companies learn from Lincoln Electric's experience? Why haven't other firms applied the Lincoln philosophy and approach?
5. Would you want to work for Lincoln Electric? Explain your response.

REFERENCES

Lincoln, James F. *Incentive Management.* Cleveland, Ohio: Lincoln Electric Company, 1951.

Lincoln, James F. *A New Approach to Industrial Economics.* New York: Devin-Adair Company, 1961.

PART V

Controlling

KEY TERMS

control
control process
standards
quantity control
quality standard
time standards
budgetary standards
initial controls
overseeing controls
comparison controls
strategic control points
budget
financial budget
operating budget
cash budget
capital budget
planning-programming budgeting system
zero base budgeting
disciplinary action
progressive discipline

LEARNING OBJECTIVES

After completing this chapter you should be able to

1. Define controls and describe the control process.
2. Explain the specific types of controls that are available to management.
3. Describe and identify the characteristics of strategic control points.
4. Relate the reasons for negative reactions to controls and describe ways of overcoming negative reactions to controls.
5. Explain budgets and identify the benefits and limitations of budgets.
6. Distinguish between planning-programming budgeting system (PPBS) and zero base budgeting (ZBB).
7. Explain the importance of disciplinary action and describe what is meant by the concept of progressive discipline.

14

Management and Control

Joan Lynwood, the keypunch supervisor for Multifact Productions, has recently observed that the number of keypunch errors in her department has exceeded the 3 percent standard during the past week.

Robert Seay, a department head for State University, has just been advised that he has exceeded his annual travel budget by $500.

Alyson Sanders, a nursing supervisor for McGovern Regional Medical Center, has noticed that her employees have exceeded the number of overtime hours allocated to the department by fifty hours.

In the above situations, controls had been established that enabled managers to recognize that potential problems existed and to correct the deviation. Joan may have discovered that one of her keypunch operators was making excessive errors due to a lack of training. Robert can explain his difficulty because he has had to do extensive recruiting to fill two new faculty positions. Alyson realizes that she must cut back on the number of overtime hours because they are not actually needed.

As in the above instances, a properly designed control system alerts managers of the existence of potential problems and permits them to take corrective actions when necessary. The control function, therefore, is a valuable part of the management process. Controlling is concerned with ensuring that results are achieved according to plan. Stated another way, controls provide the manager with the means of finding out if the tasks are performed properly. One might think that if the functions of planning, organizing, and influencing are completed satisfactorily, there would be little need for the control function. This could not be further from the truth. Events often occur that have not been anticipated. Controls provide management with the capability of recognizing a deviation from a plan. Then a manager is in a position to make the necessary corrections that will bring the situation back into agreement with the plan.

This chapter first concentrates on the nature of controls and the control process. Next, the various types of controls that are available to the manager are discussed. Procedures for establishing strategic control points are then provided, followed by a discussion of how controls differ at various levels of management. Reasons for negative reactions to controls are followed by a description of how they may be overcome. The budgeting process is then described. Finally, disciplinary action as a means of control is discussed. The overall objective of the chapter is to provide you with a clear understanding of the need for adequate controls within the firm.

THE NATURE OF CONTROL

control **Control** is the proces of comparing actual performance with established standards for the purpose of taking action to correct deviations. For instance, Joan Lynwood, the keypunch supervisor, knew that if the number of defects was above the 3 percent standard, a potential control problem existed. Thus, effective control requires comparing actual performance with preestablished goals. If results differ from established standards, corrective action may need to be taken.

Effective control depends on sound planning by management. As we discussed in Chapter 3, objectives and plans provide the basis for the control process. The purpose of the control function is to ensure that the objectives of the organization are achieved. As such, the planning and control functions are highly dependent on each other. Plans must be properly prepared and in agreement with the objectives of the firm. Controls ensure that actions taken by management to implement plans are appropriate.

Before standards can be established, objectives and plans must be developed. These objectives serve as the desired end results. Plans are created to specify the manner in which objectives are to be accomplished. Appropriate policies and methods and procedures are created to state, in greater detail, the manner in which the goals will be achieved.

Standards are very important in the control process. They provide the link between the planning and the controlling process (see Figure 14-1). The controlling process may begin once standards, created to determine if the various aspects of the plan have been achieved, have been established. Next, actual performance is measured, and this performance is compared to standards. If deviations exist, corrective action may be taken. A feedback loop from corrective action to objectives exists so that objectives may be modified if needed.

THE PROCESS OF CONTROL

control process The **control process** involves three critical areas: establishment of standards, comparison of performance to standard, and taking corrective action. A discussion of each phase follows.

Establishment of Standards

standards There can be no control process without standards. **Standards** specify the type of performance results that are desired. As such, they must be tied closely to organizational objectives. For instance, a clothing manufacturer may have a goal of achieving 10 percent of the market share for men's suits. If the forecasted sales for the industry is $500 million, then the objective of the company is to achieve sales of $50 million. This $50 million then becomes

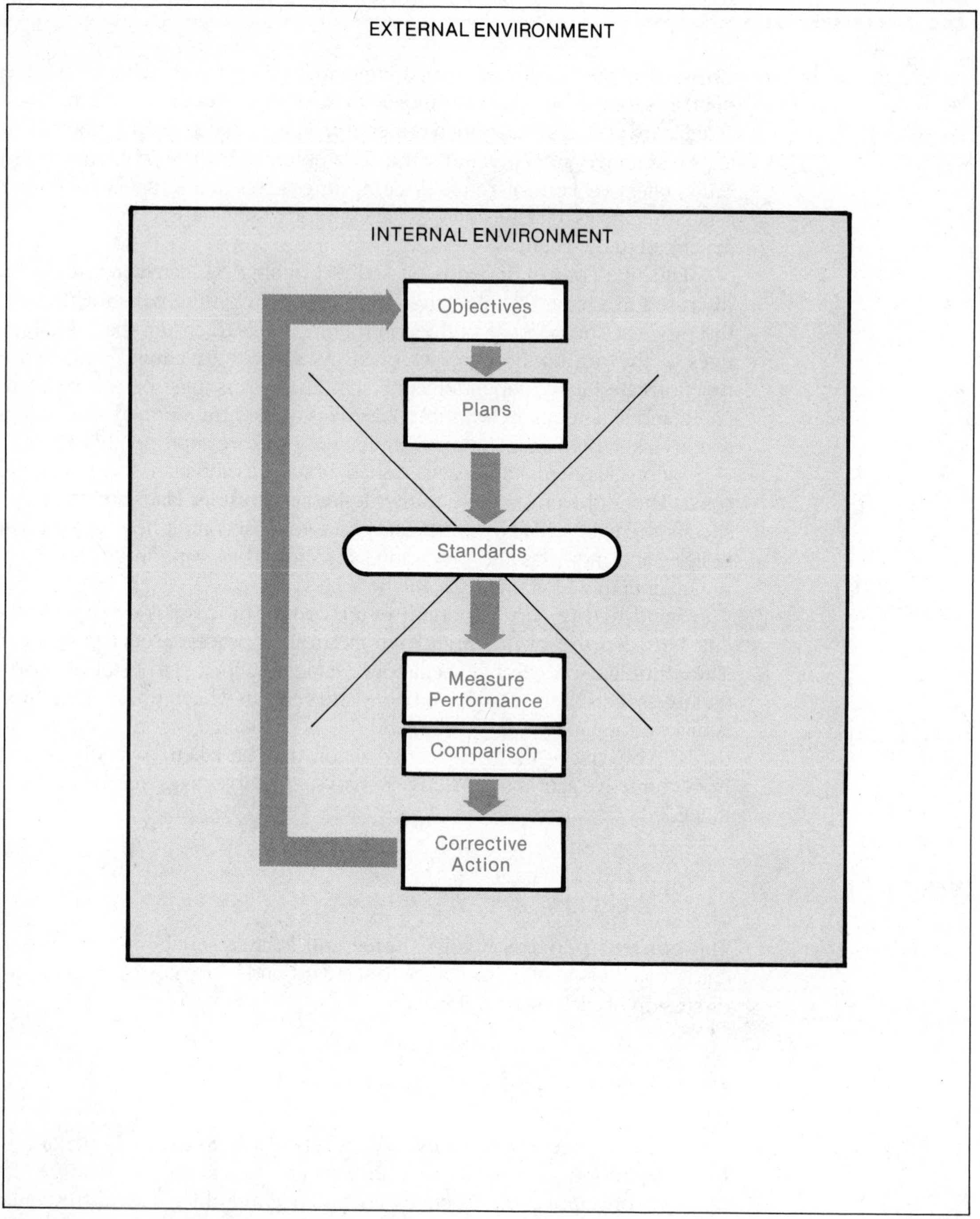

FIGURE 14-1 *The Planning and Control Process*

Insights to Success

After people in an organization reach a certain level of productivity, I feel that extraordinary incentives must be used to move them up one more notch, such as good "down and up" communication, perhaps part ownership in the company, achievement recognition, etc.

JOHN W. DIXON, President and Chairman, E-Systems, Incorporated

a standard by which to measure performance, but if it is not divided into controllable units, a control system may be difficult to implement.

Specific standards for the different sales managers might be allocated as follows: Northern District, $15 million; Southern District, $10 million; Eastern District, $12 million; and Western District, $13 million. Progressing still further in establishing standards, each district manager will likely assign a sales quota to the sales representatives. For instance, Joe Drake, a sales representative for the state of Missouri, might be given a sales quota (standard) of $500,000. Through this process of progressive controls, the company will be in a position to realize where difficulties may exist in accomplishing their objectives.

Actual Performance Compared to Standards

quantity control
quality standard
time standards
budgetary standards

It does little good to have standards unless actual performance is compared to these standards. In an organization, the most important means by which performance can be compared to standards relate to: (1) quantity, (2) quality, (3) time, and (4) budget (cost.). With **quantity control,** the standard has been established in terms of volume or numbers. The **quality standard** for a product relates to degrees of conformity to such factors as form, composition, and color. **Time standards** entail monitoring the time that is required to complete a project. **Budgetary standards** are concerned with the comparison of actual to planned expenditures. While the importance of each one is likely to depend on the goals of the firm, all types are typically being used to varying degrees in business and other types of organizations. It is likely that a combination of these four types will be in use at any one time within an organization.

Corrective Action

If no significant deviations are discovered, the manager only needs to continue to monitor the activity. Corrective action is needed either to correct

•CAREER PROFILE•

MRS. OLIVE ANN BEECH
Chairman Emeritus of the Board
Beech Aircraft Corporation

Climbing the ladder from secretary and bookkeeper to president and then chairman of the board is only a dream for many people. Most people would not be capable of adapting to the many different situations that Mrs. Beech has confronted. However, it has been a reality for Mrs. Olive Ann Beech, who is now chairman of Beech Aircraft Corporation. Mrs. Beech is today one of the most outstanding individuals in business in the world.

In 1924, the young and aspiring Olive Ann Mellor tied her future to the young but rapidly developing aviation industry. When she joined the Travel Air Manufacturing Company of Wichita, Kansas, she was the only female among its twelve employees. One of the twelve employees was pioneer aviator Walter H. Beech, who later became president and general manager of the company.

deviations from planned performance or alter the plan to allow for obstacles that cannot be removed. The goal is to restore effective, coordinated action.

There are two general types of corrective action—immediate and basic. The type most frequently recognized is the immediate; something must be done now to correct the situation and get back on track. For example, a particular project is a week behind schedule and, if not corrected, will seriously affect other projects. The first problem is not to worry about who caused the difficulty but rather to get the project back on schedule. Depending on the authority of the manager, the following corrective actions may be ordered: (1) overtime hours may be authorized; (2) additional workers and equipment may be assigned; (3) a full-time director may be assigned to personally push the project through; (4) an extra effort may be asked from all employees; or (5) if all these fail, the schedule may have to be readjusted, thereby requiring changes all along the line.

With an opportunity to learn the airplane manufacturing business from the ground up, and showing an unusual business and financial perceptiveness, she advanced rapidly, becoming office manager and secretary to the president. By 1929, Travel Air Manufacturing Company was the world's largest producer of commercial aircraft.

She and Walter Beech were married in 1930 and became residents of New York City where Mr. Beech headed up the Curtiss-Wright Airplane Company, after selling his interests in Travel Air. Two years later they returned to Wichita to co-found Beech Aircraft Company. Mrs. Beech was secretary-treasurer and the financial guiding hand of the company.

From this unheralded beginning, with a handful of employees and a couple of lean years, the company created two new airplanes. These planes brought wide recognition and served as the backbone of the company for many years. They ultimately led to the establishment of the Beech Aircraft Corporation—now recognized as a major designer and producer of high-performance private, commercial and military airplanes.

The company's directors elected Mrs. Beech president and chairman of the board in 1950, following the death of Walter Beech. Under her guidance, Beech Aircraft continued to progress, expanding into diversified, aviation-related fields and growing steadily in the production of business and corporate aircraft. In the middle 1950s, she led the corporation to the establishment of a research and development division to become a pioneer in the science of super-cold—cryogenics. From this activity have come vital systems and assemblies for the successful Gemini, Apollo, Skylab, and Apollo-Soyuz Test Project and the space shuttle program.

Mrs. Beech relinquished the role of president in 1968 to a veteran executive of the company, retaining the position of chairman of the board, and chief executive officer. In 1981 she was elected chairman emeritus.

Widely acclaimed as a philanthropist, patron of the arts, and strong supporter of youth, Mrs. Beech also has earned the highest respect from her peers in aviation and business through awards, recognition, and appointments to high-ranking positions locally and throughout the state and nation.

After the degree of stress has lessened through any of the above measures, attention can then be devoted to the second type of corrective action. Just how and why did events stray from their planned course? What can be done to prevent a recurrence of this type of difficulty? Many managers fail at this phase. Too often they find themselves "putting out daily fires," and they never discover the actual cause of the problem. For instance, managers may find themselves constantly having to interview and hire new people to replace those who are leaving the firm. A manager may be working twelve hours a day attempting to locate new employees. But the high turnover problem is not solved merely by employing new workers. Managers must take some type of corrective action after they have determined what has actually caused the high turnover. A supervisor may be extremely difficult to work with, or the pay scale may not be competitive for the area. Whatever the problem, it must be identified and corrected or the high turnover problem is likely to continue. The dull work of basic corrective action must be done for the sake of future economical and effective operations.

As illustrated by the project that was not on schedule, the manager may discover various fundamental causes for the difficulty. The schedule may not have been met because of a continuing difficulty in one department. Or it may be discovered that not only was this particular project in trouble, but most of the other projects in this company are behind schedule. In the first example, investigation may reveal that poor equipment in the one department is the major source of trouble. Thus, basic corrective actions would involve new or improved equipment or new or improved management. The project that initially experienced the difficulty will not likely be helped by this action; however, future projects should be improved.

If most of the projects in a firm are usually behind schedule, an even more serious type of basic corrective action may be demanded. There may be a drastic overhaul of general control procedures. There might even be a reorganization of the entire company.

SPECIFIC TYPES OF CONTROL

The control function can be divided into three basic types: initial, overseeing, and comparison controls. *Initial controls* take place as resources enter the organization. *Overseeing controls* are used during the process when the products and services are being produced. *Comparison controls* are used after the final product or service has been produced. Each type of control will next be briefly discussed along with specific means available to accomplish the control process.

Initial Controls

initial controls

The manager uses **initial controls** primarily as a preventive measure. With initial controls, an attempt is made to monitor the resources—material, human, and capital—that come into the organization for the purpose of ensuring that they can be used effectively to achieve organizational objectives. An effort is made to control the resources that enter the organization. Specific types of initial controls will be described next.

Material Controls

The material resources an organization requires must meet specified quality standards and be available when needed by the firm. If Ethan Allen purchased lower-quality wood with which to manufacture furniture, their image for producing high-quality furniture could not be maintained. In order to assist in ensuring material control, statistical sampling is often used (to be discussed in greater detail in Chapter 16). With statistical sampling, a portion of the items received into the firm are studied in an attempt to estimate the quality of the entire lot. For instance, a certain percentage of lumber (say 5 percent) might be studied to estimate the quality of all lumber received. The quality and reliability of material can be detemined with acceptable accuracy without having to expend the time and resources to inspect each item.

Personnel Selection Controls

If a firm is to maintain its present level of operations, there must continue to be an infusion of new workers into the company. This constant search for new employees is necessary because of such factors as deaths, retirements, loss of employees to other organizations, and any growth that the firm is experiencing. In order to obtain new people who are capable of sustaining the organization, certain controls must be established regarding the selection of individuals employed by the firm. Skill requirements of each job must be determined, and new employees should meet or exceed these skills before being employed.

Capital Controls

The firm must have sufficient capital available to achieve its objectives. Equipment must be obtained and financed. However, when funds are expended on capital goods, we are exchanging today's dollars in the anticipation of future profits. A firm wants to purchase capital equipment that will produce the greatest cost savings or profit for the company. This is no easy matter when we are looking into the future. However, there are numerous techniques available to assess capital expenditure alternatives. One of the most useful approaches takes into consideration the time value of money (a dollar received today is more valuable than a dollar received ten years into the future). The procedure for using net present value and the benefits of the technique will be described in Chapter 15.

Overseeing Controls

overseeing controls

Overseeing controls are used to monitor the actual creation of products or services. This type of control is accomplished largely by observation and by conference between supervisor and subordinate. Overseeing controls occur as the actual work activities are being performed. A large portion of the operating manager's time is devoted to this function.

The greatest opportunity for the discovery and correction of undesired deviations takes place while the work is being performed. If an entire lot of fifty units is completed by a worker, and inspection reveals that all fifty are too small, there is little that can be done about it. If, during the operation, someone had personally checked the work, much material and labor would have been saved. The amount of overseeing necessary depends on such factors as skill and attitude of the worker, the skill of the manager, and the discipline of the work place.

The greatest opportunity for the discovery and correction of undesired deviations takes place while the work is being performed.

Comparison Controls

Comparison is the function of determining the degree of agreement between performance results and performance standards and can take place on or away from the point of operation. It can be applied to the cumulative performance results of departments or of the entire organization. The objective of **comparison controls** is to determine whether deviations from plans have taken place and, if necessary, to bring the deviations to the attention of the responsible managers.

comparison controls

There are several differences between the overseeing and comparison phases of control. Both involve relating what is going on to what should be going on. Overseeing occurs while the work is in progress. Comparison comes later and relies on information received after a step in the project is completed or on the results of the entire project.

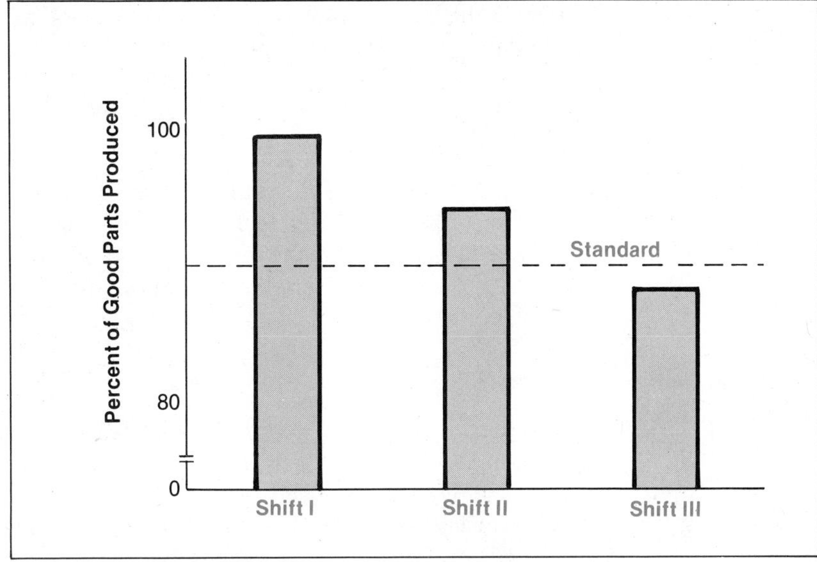

FIGURE 14-2

Monthly Quality Comparison Report, by Shifts

A second difference between the two functions occurs as a result of the contrast in timing. Overseeing has to be accomplished by the immediate supervisor. Comparison, however, can be done not only by the supervisor but also by higher line managers or various staff officials. Because it relies on reporting, it can be separated physically from the point of operation.

Finally, overseeing requires face-to-face contacts and personal observation as the method of obtaining information. The manager must evaluate work in both qualitative and quantitative terms and must be adept in human relation skills. Comparison, however, is usually concerned with only a quantitative and statistical evaluation of actions that have reached some state of completion. A monthly production report comparison of the quality of all parts for three shifts is provided in Figure 14-2. As can be seen, Shifts I and II are above the 90 percent standard, while Shift III is slightly below standard. Though observation can be used to gain such information, it more frequently involves written reports, charts, graphs, and similar forms of communication. Specific types of comparison controls will be described next.

Evaluation of Employee Performance

Given a particular task to be accomplished, we would all likely perform at different levels of efficiency. One manager may be quite proficient in planning techniques and another in communication skills. But if we are to improve, we must know our deficiencies and determine what can be done to overcome these obstacles. An effective employee performance system is a means of control whereby individuals learn of their strengths and weaknesses and are told what should be done to overcome deficiencies. Employee performance evaluation systems that give each worker the same ratings do not benefit the individual who is a superior performer nor do they assist the substandard worker who desires to improve.

Quotas

Much of comparison control relates to quotas that have been established for individuals, units, departments, or divisions. Sales quotas specify the amount of sales an individual, district, or region is expected to meet. Production quotas specify the amount of an item that needs to be produced. Control of quotas at every level is important if the organization is to achieve its objectives.

Quality Control

The purpose of quality control is to ensure that a certain level of excellence is attained. As greater levels of quality are built into a product, costs increase significantly. It is, therefore, quite important to identify in the planning stage what quality level is desired to meet company objectives.

For example, there are significant differences in the quality of watches, and of course, the higher the quality, the greater the cost. An individual who purchases a high-quality watch may desire a timepiece that may deviate only a few seconds during an entire year. On the other hand, a student may purchase a watch of lesser quality because he or she does not see the importance of being a few minutes early or late for class, feeling perhaps that the instructor will tell the same joke again at the first of the class.

Network Controls

A means by which the progress of a particular project may be monitored is referred to as network controls. With network controls, critical areas of a project can be identified and carefully monitored to assure a successful completion time. Two of the best-known means of network controls are PERT and CPM, which will be described in Chapter 16.

Controls Through Financial Analysis

The financial statement provides valuable information with regard to whether a company, department, or unit is effectively utilizing its financial resources. Intelligent interpretation of financial data provides an excellent means through which management can control its financial welfare. In order to analyze the financial position, a firm would likely begin with ratio analysis. Financial ratio analysis provides management with a basis for comparing current to past performance. In addition, financial ratios can be compared not only to past trends within the company but also to other divisions within the company and to other firms in the industry. If the ratios are not in line with what is considered acceptable, the manager is in a position to make corrections. There are four basic types of ratios:

- **Liquidity ratios** measure a firm's ability to meet its current obligations.
- **Leverage ratios** measure whether a firm has effectively used outside financing.
- **Activity ratios** measure how efficiently the firm is utilizing its resources.
- **Profitability ratios** measure the overall operating efficiency and profitability of the firm.

Names of ratios, the formula for their calculation, and the meaning and definition of the ratios may be seen in Table 14-1.

TABLE 14-1. *Summary of Financial Ratio Analysis*

Category of Ratio	Name of Ratio	Formula for Calculation	Meaning and Definition of Ratio
Liquidity	Current ratio	current assets / current liabilities	Measures ability to meet debts when due—short-term liquidity
	Quick ratio	current assets-inventory / current liabilities	Measures ability to meet debts when due—very short-term liquidity
Leverage	Debt to total assets	total debt / total assets	Measures percentage of total funds that have been provided by creditors (debt = total assets − equity)
	Times interest earned	profit before tax + interest charges / interest charges	Measures the extent to which interest charges are covered by gross income
Profitability	Return on sales (net profit margin)	net income / sales revenue	Measures percent of profit earned on each dollar of sales
	Return on total assets	net income (AT) / total assets	Measures the return on total investment of a firm
	Return on equity	net income (AT) / stockholder equity	Measures rate of return on stockholders' investment
	Earnings per share	net income (AT) / number of common shares outstanding	Measures profit earned for each share of common stock
Activity	Total asset turnover	revenues / total assets	Measures effectiveness of assets in generating revenues
	Collection period	receivables / revenues per day	Measures amount of credit extended to customers
	Inventory turnover	sales / inventory	Measures number of times inventory is used to generate sales

ESTABLISHING STRATEGIC CONTROL POINTS

Management is concerned with monitoring a system comprised of resources, processes, activities, and outputs. The problem often encountered is the determination of the phases of the system that should be monitored. However, this is not always easy. Theoretically, every resource, processing activity, and output should be measured, reported, and compared to some predetermined standard. This can be extremely costly and time-consuming as all activities are not equally important. A manager must determine what to measure and when to measure an activity. These critical areas will be referred to as **strategic control points.** These are areas that must be monitored if the organization's objectives are to be achieved.

strategic control points

Strategic control points have a number of basic characteristics. First, it is a point established to regulate key operations or events. If a difficulty occurs at a strategic control point, the entire operation may grind to a halt. For instance, if the word processing center manager for Prudential Insurance Company does not have control of the type and quality of equipment purchased, inaccurate and untimely information may be sent to policyholders. The problem created by poor-quality equipment may have a detrimental impact on the sales of the company even though the word processing personnel and sales force are of exceptional quality.

Qualities Needed for Success as a Manager in Your Organization

- Willingness to make a decision
- Ability to weed out the wheat from the chaff before deciding on a course of action
- Desire to apply the above talents to the job

ROBERT J. SWEENEY, President, Murphy Oil Corporation

A second major characteristic of a strategic control point is that it must be set up so that problems can be identified before serious damage occurs. If the control point is properly located, action can be taken to stop or alter a defective process before major harm is done. It does little good to discover after the fact that a million defective parts have been produced. The control point should be located so deviations can be quickly identified and corrections made.

In the early days of one of the authors' careers, he had the opportunity of observing how the improper selection of strategic control points virtually caused a major tire manufacturer to be forced to cease operation. In the manufacture of a tire, four basic phases were required (see Figure 14-3). The

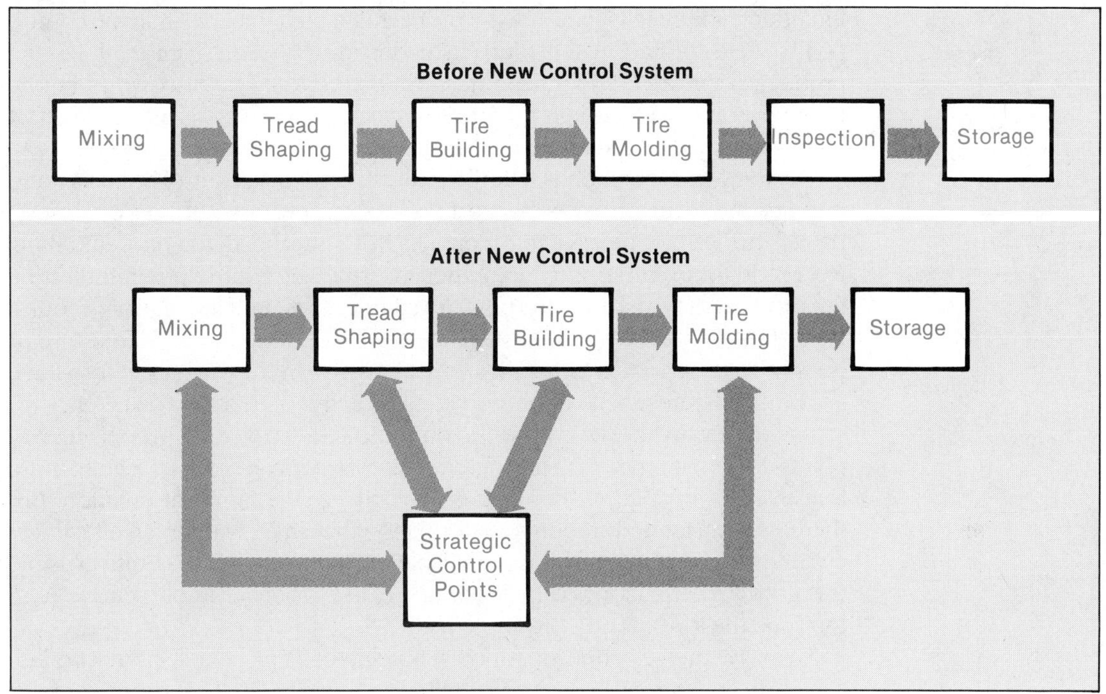

FIGURE 14-3 *Example of Placement of Strategic Control Points*

mixing department must obtain the proper blend of rubber for the type of tire that is being produced. The tread is then shaped with specific attention being given to length, width, and thickness. The next phase, building, entails placing the various components such as the tread, steel belting, and white walls together. In the molding department, the tires are heated and shaped into final form.

A major problem occurred that forced the tire company to reevaluate their entire control procedure. The old system of control consisted only of inspecting tires after they had been molded. Because there was already a large investment in a tire at this stage, a tire would have to have a major defect before it would be rejected. Recognition of the deficiency in the control process occurred when the tire manufacturing firm received an order for several million dollars from a company that purchased tires and sold them at retail outlets under a different brand name. The retail chain, after careful inspection of the tires, rejected the order and demanded that the entire batch be redone. The tire manufacturing firm nearly went out of business because of this decision. Due to the large investment that was tied up in rejected inventory, the firm had to go heavily into debt to remake the order.

It was after this experience that major changes were made in the control process. A separate quality control department, reporting directly to the president, was established. Quality control inspectors were hired and given authority to stop operations, even over the advice of the production superintendent, if they felt it was needed to maintain high quality. Strategic control points were located in the four major departments (see Figure 14-3.). If a problem occurred in the mixing department, it would be discovered before the tire progressed through the other stages. Because of this intensive effort to improve quality, the firm was able to survive and prosper.

A third consideration is that the choice of strategic control points should indicate the level of performance for a broad spectrum of key events. At times, this comprehensiveness conflicts with the need for proper timing. Net profit, for example, is a comprehensive strategic control point, indicating the progress of the entire enterprise. Yet if one waits until the regular accounting period to obtain this figure, one loses control of the immediate future. It does little good to recognize that you are now bankrupt; you need to have accounting figures ahead of time so that corrective action may be taken.

Economy is the fourth consideration in the choice of proper control points. With computer and management information systems available, there is a strong temptation to demand every conceivable bit of information. But there is only a limited amount of information that an executive can effectively use. If every bit of information is available to the executive, it is quite possible that critical information will be lost in the masses of data. Simply stated, "You can't see the forest for the trees."

Finally, the selection of various strategic control points should be balanced. If only credit losses are watched and controlled, for example, sales may suffer because of an overly stringent policy in accepting credit risks. If sales are emphasized out of proportion, then credit losses will mount. There is a tendency to place tight control over tangible functions, such as production and sales, while maintaining limited control over the intangible functions such as personnel development and other staff services. This often leads to a state of imbalance where production line executives are held to exact standards, and staff executives are seemingly given blank checks.

CONTROL AND LEVELS OF MANAGEMENT

Managers, unless they are the top officers in the firm, link two levels of organization. As may be seen in Figure 14-4, each management level plans for, organizes, and influences the lower level. Lower levels of management of course require more specific planning, organizing, and influencing. The higher-level manager issues orders to a lower-level supervisor to accomplish tasks generally planned by top management. As tasks are accomplished, results are provided both the immediate supervisor and other levels of management. This enables immediate supervisors to control within the limits of their specific plan. The immediate supervisor must then provide the information to higher management to ensure that higher-level plans are being fulfilled. This information enables each level of management to determine if the actions of the lower levels are conforming to general plans and objectives and if corrective measures need to be taken.

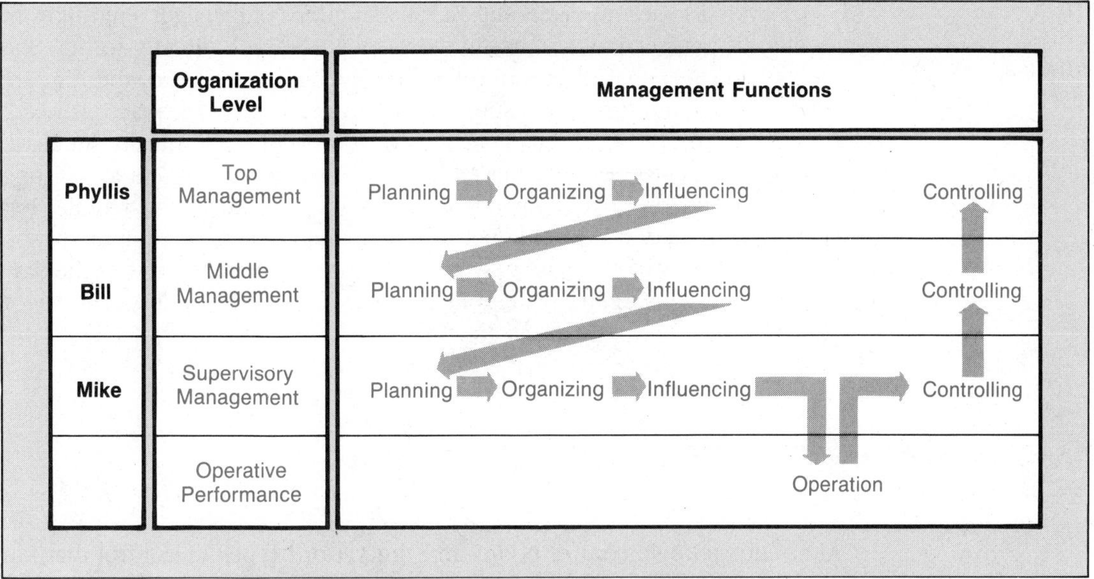

FIGURE 14-4 *Organization Levels and Linking Management Functions [Source: Adapted from Edwin B. Flippo and Gary M. Munsinger,* Management, *5th ed. (Boston: Allyn and Bacon, 1982), p. 384.]*

Let us now progress through an illustration of the types of controls a person would confront as he or she moved from a supervisory management position to a top management position. Mike Miller is a shift foreman for a firm that manufactures aluminum window and door frames. Each Monday, Mike is provided a weekly schedule of items that must be produced each day for that week. With this schedule, Mike plans, organizes, and directs the activities that must be accomplished this week. He knows the standards that have been established for each piece of equipment and monitors each of his employees to ensure that the correct number of frames are being manufactured. If an employee is deficient in any task, Mike must take immediate corrective action to ensure that the daily and weekly schedules are achieved. Each day, Mike sends a report of activities to the general manager, Bill Alexander.

Bill Alexander supervises the activities of ten shift foremen within a division. He must plan, organize, and influence their efforts. As such, he works in a much longer time frame and views his task as coordinating the work of the foremen. He studies the reports of each of the foremen and determines if they need help to solve particular problems. If a foreman is consistently below standard, Bill will analyze the situation to determine what action must be taken. Rarely will any decision be made entirely on one day's performance of one of the shifts, but the general overall trend is studied. Bill submits a weekly performance report of his sections to Phyllis Towne, the vice-president of operations.

Phyllis also accomplishes the various functions of management but from a different perspective. She has five divisions reporting directly to her. She views control as that of ensuring that the overall objectives of the firm are achieved. She attempts to ensure that a consistent level of quality is maintained, but she must also consider the cost of reaching the quality standard. Her plans tend to be longer in nature, and she views controls as assisting her in solving problems that the divisions may be unable to handle. For instance, if quality is declining because of an aging piece of equipment, she has the authority to purchase new machinery. She is concerned with the day-to-day operations of the plants but is not as involved as Bill Alexander or Mike Miller.

REASONS FOR NEGATIVE REACTIONS TO CONTROLS

Although strategic control points and the various types of control that we have discussed are important in effective management, controls are often viewed in a negative way by employees being "controlled." When the term *controls* is mentioned, it makes some of us realize that other people have the power to regulate our activities. There is a natural resistance to controls because a certain amount of individual freedom has been taken away. Some controls are necessary if an organization is to accomplish its objectives in the most efficient manner. Employees may not like to be controlled, but they will likely accept the fact that some controls are necessary if the organization is to function successfully. It is when controls are established that are inappropriate, unattainable, unpredictable, uncontrolled, or contradictory that major negative resistance is encountered.[1]

Inappropriate Controls

Controls that do not conform to the needs of the situation are referred to as inappropriate controls. In many instances, workers recognize before management where controls need to be placed if efficiency is to be increased. Inappropriate controls can inhibit the accomplishment of the goals of a department or unit within the organization. For instance, in one firm, because of an immediate need for more highly trained machine operators, the control system was changed from a measurement of skill level to one that measured numbers of machine operators who were "trained." Many more workers completed the training program, but there was considerable grumbling among the production foremen bcause the skill level of the machine operators had actually declined. True, more people were available to run the machines, but performance had dropped to the point that the quality level could not be maintained. The controls that had been established were inappropriate to meet the needs of the situation.

Unattainable Standards

Employees realize when a standard is unrealistic. When unattainable controls are established, it may actually cause some employees to work below their capabilities. For instance, suppose that you are a machine operator and had been producing effectively at a standard of twenty units an hour. If management arbitrarily increased the standard to forty units, you may feel that the standard is unattainable. Productivity may actually be lowered below the original twenty units.

Unpredictable Standards

When the control system is unpredictable and constantly changed, much frustration and resentment of the control process can result. For instance, if a production manager is told that he or she should strive to achieve maximum output and once this high output level has been achieved, told that quality is more important, resentment to the control process can result. The production manager could not predict what standard he or she was to be evaluated on.

No Control over the Situation

A frustrating encounter that can occur to anyone is to be reprimanded for something you cannot control. Suppose, for instance, that a manager is told that she will be evaluated regarding the profit and loss of her department, but she does not have the authority to hire and fire employees. Frustration becomes extremely high in instances such as this and can work to the detriment of the entire control system.

Contradictory Standards

At times, various controls may be established that do not complement each other. It may appear to the manager that if one standard is achieved, it would be impossible to accomplish the other. For instance, it might appear to some managers that high quality and maximum output are contradictory in nature. To a marketing manager, a control system that stresses both increased sales and reducing the advertising expenditure rate may appear contradictory.

OVERCOMING NEGATIVE REACTIONS TO CONTROLS

Although there are numerous reasons why people may resist controls, there are also means that a manager can use to assist in reducing negative reactions. While some of the reasons discussed below may appear obvious, the ineffectiveness of some control systems makes it clear that they are not observed at times. Some of the basic means through which negative reactions to controls may be overcome are discussed.

Justifiable

If employees believe that there is a need for a particular control system, compliance is much easier to obtain. For instance, the firm may have to increase the quality of their product in order to obtain future contracts. These contracts will mean not only profit for the firm but job stability for the employees. A control system will have higher acceptability if the reason for the control appears justifiable to those who must comply.

Understandable

Employees who know exactly what is expected of them with regard to a control system tend to exhibit less resistance. For instance, a statement by a manager that quality should increase does not clearly convey what is expected. A requirement that the number of defects should decrease by 10 percent is precise and understandable. It is when workers do not understand what is expected of them that frustration and resentment can occur.

Realistic

A realistic control system is one that permits the organization to achieve its goals and is also obtainable by the employees who work within the control system. For example, at times it may appear that controls are established merely to harass the worker. Excessive standards that are higher than needed to accomplish the purpose of the organization are not only expensive but may well be resisted by company employees.

Timely

For a control system to be effective, information regarding deviations needs to be communicated to employees as quickly as practical. It does little good to tell workers that their performance was below standard three weeks ago. If a problem is to be corrected, it must receive immediate attention.

Accurate

Nothing could be worse than to have a control system that provides inaccurate information. If information feedback has proved incorrect in the past, it may be difficult to convince individuals that their effort is below standards. If workers consistently find errors made by supervisors, belief in their ideas may be questioned. An employee who receives a low performance evaluation may have reason to suspect the evaluation is inaccurate even if it is not.

THE BUDGETING PROCESS

budget

Though there are many devices that mangers can use in controlling costs or expenditures, the most widely known and used is the budget. A **budget** is merely a formal statement of financial resources—planned expenditures of money for employment, time, space, or equipment. Budgetary control is concerned with the comparison of actual to planned expenditures. Most areas of operations in a business enterprise—marketing, production, materials, labor, manufacturing expense, capital expenditures, and cash—can be reduced to expenditures in the budget.

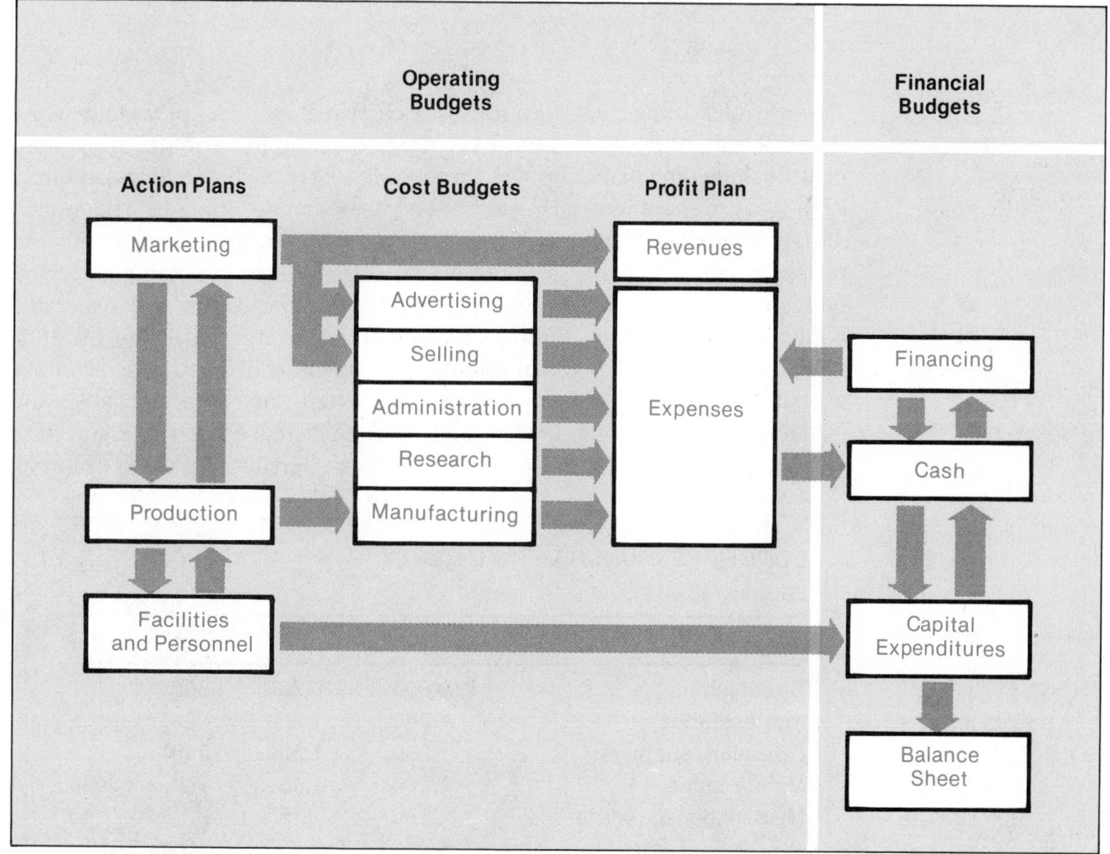

FIGURE 14-5 *Types of Budgets* [*Source: Gordon Shillinglaw; Managerial Cost Accounting. 4th ed. (Homewood, Ill.; Irwin, 1977), p. 137. Copyright © 1977 by Richard D. Irwin, Inc.*]

Types of Budgets

financial budget
operating budget

Budgets are important documents used by managers in planning and controlling operations. There are basically two broad categories of budgets: **financial budget** and **operating budget**. An overview of the components of these two types of budgets is provided in Figure 14-5.

- *Operating budgets* indicate the revenues and expenses the business expects from producing goods and services during a given year. As illustrated in Figure 14-5, these budgets consist of action plans, cost budgets, and a profit plan.
- *Financial budgets* indicate the amount of capital the organization will need and where it will obtain the capital. Two financial budgets are usually developed. These are the **cash budget** and the **capital budget**. The cash budget summarizes planned cash receipts and disbursements while the capital budget indicates planned capital acquisition, usually for the purpose of purchasing additional facilities or equipment.

cash budget
capital budget

An Illustration of Budgetary Control

The use of a budget as a control device is relatively simple. Figure 14-6 shows the monthly budget for a keypunch department. The major expense items include direct labor (wages for the unit's keypunch operators), indirect labor (the department manager's salary), operating supplies (keypunch cards), maintenance expenses (repair of machines), and miscellaneous expense. As shown in Figure 14-6, actual expenditures are compared with budgeted or planned expenditures. In this department, actual exceeded budgeted expenditures for direct labor and operating supplies by $800 and $250, respectively. Actual spending for maintenance and miscellaneous was under the budgeted amount by $440. Budgetary control enables the manager to identify significant deviations in actual versus budgeted or planned expenses and to take corrective action when necessary. For example,

FIGURE 14-6
Department Operating Budget

BUDGET KEYPUNCH DEPARTMENT
January 131

Item	*Budget*	*Actual*	*Over*	*Under*
Direct labor	$10,000	$10,800	$800	
Indirect labor	1,800	1,800		
Operating supplies	1,250	1,500	$250	
Maintenance	1,800	1,400		$400
Misc. expense (telephone)	190	150		40
Total	$15,040	$15,650	Over $610	

the $800 over budgeted expenses for the wages of keypunch operators may have been caused by the necessity to pay overtime wages. This may have resulted from ineffective work scheduling or the sudden appearance of a rush job. This situation, if it occurred in several successive periods, may cause the manager to take actions such as requesting additional personnel or improving the scheduling of work to correct the problem. In any event, budgeting control is a very useful tool of managers at virtually every level of an organization.

Benefits of the Budgeting Process

The fact that virtually every type of organization—profit or nonprofit—operates within the framework of budgets attests to their benefits. Budgeting is very significant as a part of both the planning and controlling process. Budgets are widely used by managers to plan, monitor, and control various activities and operations at every level of an organization. There are several important advantages for preparing and using budgets. Some of the benefits of the budgeting process are:

1. *Provides standards against which actual performance can be measured.* Budgets are a quantified plan that allows management to measure and control performance more objectively. If, for instance, a department knows that the budgeted expenditure for supplies is $1000 per month, the manager is then in a position to monitor and control the expenses for supplies.
2. *Provides managers with additional insight into actual organizational goals.* Monetary allocation of funds as opposed to merely lip-service more often than not is the true test of a firm's dedication to a particular goal. For instance, suppose that two firms of relatively equal size had a stated policy of hiring minority personnel. Firm A allocates $100,000 and Firm B provides $10,000. A manager from Firm A likely realizes that a much stronger commitment to minority hiring is expressed by Firm A as opposed to Firm B.
3. *Tends to be a positive influence on the motivation of personnel.* People typically like to know what is expected of them, and budgets clarify specific performance standards.
4. *Causes managers to divert some of their attention from current to future operations.* To some extent, a budget forces managers to anticipate and forecast changes in the external environment. For example, an increase in transportation costs created by higher-priced petroleum might force the firm to seek an alternative transportation or distribution system.
5. *Improves top management's ability to coordinate the overall operation of the organization.* Budgets are blueprints of the company's plans for the coming year and greatly aid top management in coordinating the operations/activities of each division or department.

6. *Enables management to recognize and/or anticipate problems in time to take the necessary corrective action.* For example, if production costs are substantially ahead of the budgeted amount, management will be alerted to make changes that may realign actual costs with the budget.
7. *Facilitates communications throughout the organization.* The budget significantly improves management's ability to communicate the objectives, plans, and standards of performance, which is important to the organization. Budgets are especially helpful to lower-level managers by letting them know how their operations relate to other units or departments within the organization. Also, budgets tend to pinpoint managers' responsibility and improve their understanding of the goals of the organization. This process usually results in increased morale and commitment on the part of managers.
8. *Helps managers recognize when change is needed.* The budgeting process requires managers to review carefully and critically the company's operations to determine if the firm's resources are being allocated to the *right* activities and programs. The budgeting process causes management to focus on such questions as: What products appear to have the greatest demand? What markets appear to offer the best potential? What business are we in? Which business(es) should we be in?[2]

Limitations of the Budgeting Process

Although there are numerous benefits that can be attributed to the use of budgets, potential problems may also arise. If the budgetary process is to achieve its maximum effectiveness, these difficulties must be recognized and an attempt made to reduce the potential damaging side-effects associated with the use of budgets. Some of the major problems are:

- The attitude by some, that all funds allocated in a budget must be spent, may actually work against the intent of the budgetary process. Some managers have learned from experience that if they do not spend the funds that have been budgeted, their budget will be reduced the following year. Managers have found that they can actually hurt their department because of their conscientious cost-effectiveness approach. A manager who operates in this type of environment may make an extraordinary effort to spend extra funds for reasons that may be marginal at best.
- A budget may be so restrictive that supervisors are permitted little discretion in managing their resources. The actual amount that can be spent for each item may be specified, and funds cannot be transferred from one account to another. This has sometimes resulted in some unusual situations. There may be funds for typewriter paper but no money available for typewriter ribbons.

- Budgets may be used to evaluate the performance of a manager as opposed to evaluating the actual results that the individual has accomplished. If this philosophy is prevalent within the firm, a poor manager may be recognized as superior because he or she met the budget, but a good manager may be reprimanded for failure to follow the exact budgetary guidelines. With this corporate philosophy, the amount of risk a manager will be willing to take may be severely reduced. Managers may spend a majority of their time ensuring that they are in compliance with the budget when their time might be best spent in developing new or innovative ideas.

Specific Budgeting Systems: PPBS and ZBB

planning-programming budgeting system
zero base budgeting

In recent years, two specific budgeting systems have received considerable attention. These two approaches are the **planning-programming budgeting system** (PPBS) and **zero base budgeting** (ZBB). Although PPBS and ZBB have been used infrequently in business organizations, the techniques have been applied by numerous federal, state, and local governments.[3]

Planning-Programming Budgeting System

PPBS was designed to aid management in identifying and eliminating costly programs that were duplicates of other programs and to provide a means for the careful analysis of the benefits and costs of each program or activity. The essential elements of PPBS include the following:

1. Careful analysis and specification of basic objectives in each major program area. A vital starting point for PPBS is to answer such questions as "What is our basic purpose or mission?" and "What, specifically, are we trying to accomplish?"
2. Analyze the output of each program in terms of the specific objectives. In other words, how effectively are we achieving our goals?
3. Measure and analyze the total costs of the program over several years. For example, in budgeting for additional plants, you would need to consider not only the initial costs of construction but also costs of operating and maintaining the facilities in future years.
4. Determine which alternatives are the most effective in achieving the basic objectives at the least cost.
5. Implement PPBS in an organized and systematic manner so that over time most budgetary decisions are subject to rigorous analysis.

PPBS was first applied by the Defense Department in the preparation of the 1962 budget and was used by all other federal government agencies beginning in 1966. However by 1971, the system was abandoned by the federal government, although it has continued to be used by the Defense Department and some public and private institutions of higher education. PPBS was not accepted by most departments and agencies of the government nor did it have the support of the U.S. Congress. The system was implemented under presidential edict with an inadequate amount of time to explain the advantages of PPBS, much less the techniques involved in using it.

Zero Base Budgeting

ZBB, originally developed by Texas Instruments, received widespread recognition when Jimmy Carter implemented the system when he was governor of Georgia. In 1977, President Carter required that ZBB be used in preparing budgets in the executive branch of the federal government. ZBB requires management to take a fresh look at all programs and activities each year rather than merely building on last year's budget. In other words, last year's budget allocations are not considered as a basis for this year's budget. Each program, or "decision packages" as they are called, must be justified on the basis of a cost-benefit analysis. There are three main features of zero base budgeting:

1. The activities of individual departments are divided into *decision packages.* Each decision package provides information so that management can compare costs and benefits of the program or activity.
2. Each decision package is evaluated and ranked in the order of decreasing importance to the organization. Priorities are established for all programs and activities. Each of these is evaluated by top management to arrive at a final ranking.
3. Resources are allocated according to the final rankings of the programs by top management. As a rule, decisions to allocate resources for high-priority items will be made rather quickly, whereas greater analysis or scrutiny will be given lower-priority programs or activities.[5]

ZBB is not a panacea for solving all problems associated with the budgeting process. Organizations may experience problems in implementing ZBB. Most managers are reluctant to admit that all of their activities are not of the highest priority or to submit their programs to close scrutiny. However, it does establish a system whereby an organization's resources are allocated to the higher-priority programs. Under this system, programs of lower priority are reduced or eliminated. Thus, the benefits of zero base budgeting appear to outweigh the costs.[6]

DISCIPLINARY ACTION

John Phillip, a machine operator for Terry Manufacturing, was not wearing his safety glasses when his supervisor came to his work area. The glasses are required by a company directive to be work by all personnel when working in that particular location of the plant.

Jodi Haun, an accounts receivable specialist for Southeast Utilities, has arrived one hour late for work four times this week, and it is only Thursday. She has never called in to explain the reason for being late.

Betty Garcia, an airline hostess for Tree Top Airline, has been advised that the public relations office has received a large number of passenger complaints regarding her attitude and performance on the plane.

In the above three instances, a potential for disciplinary action exists. However, because the details of each circumstance are not known, a person cannot readily determine if disciplinary action is actually required. But if a control system does not exist to identify problems when they occur, potential problems will go unrecognized. The purpose of establishing controls is to determine if deviations have taken place regarding a particular standard. It follows that a natural by-product of controls is disciplinary action. We will define **disciplinary action** as the process of invoking a penalty against an employee who fails to adhere to standards (that is, policies, procedures, or rules). Many of the problems a manager faces relate to disciplinary actions. Approximately half of all grievance cases appealed to an impartial arbitrator by labor unions involve disciplinary action, and management's decisions are overturned in approximately half of these cases. It is evident from the above statistics that managers are not applying disciplinary action in a manner that is generally acceptable.

disciplinary action

The disciplinary action process may be seen in Figure 14-7. The process begins with gaining a clear understanding of organizational objectives. Standards should be created to facilitate accomplishment of these objectives, and they should be clearly communicated to affected employees. Performance is then observed and compared to standard. No difficulty exists if performance is in line with standards. However, disciplinary action *may* be needed when performance deviation exists. Once disciplinary action has been taken, it serves to reinforce the importance of the standard to other employees.

At all times, efforts must be made to make the penalty appropriate to the violation or accumulated violations. This process is known as **progressive discipline** and the sequence may be seen in Figure 14-8.

progressive discipline

As you can see, once improper behavior is determined, a series of questions are asked. As you progress down the list of questions, discipline gets progressively more severe. Also notice that the mere fact that a violation occurred does not mean that disciplinary action must be taken. The manager may use his or her discretion and decide that no action should be taken. On the other hand, fighting on the job may result in automatic suspension.

Managers have identified guides to assist in handling disciplinary cases. Some of these are listed here:

- The manager should exhibit the attitude of assuming that all employees desire to conform to reasonable organizational requirements. One should not appear to invite trouble.

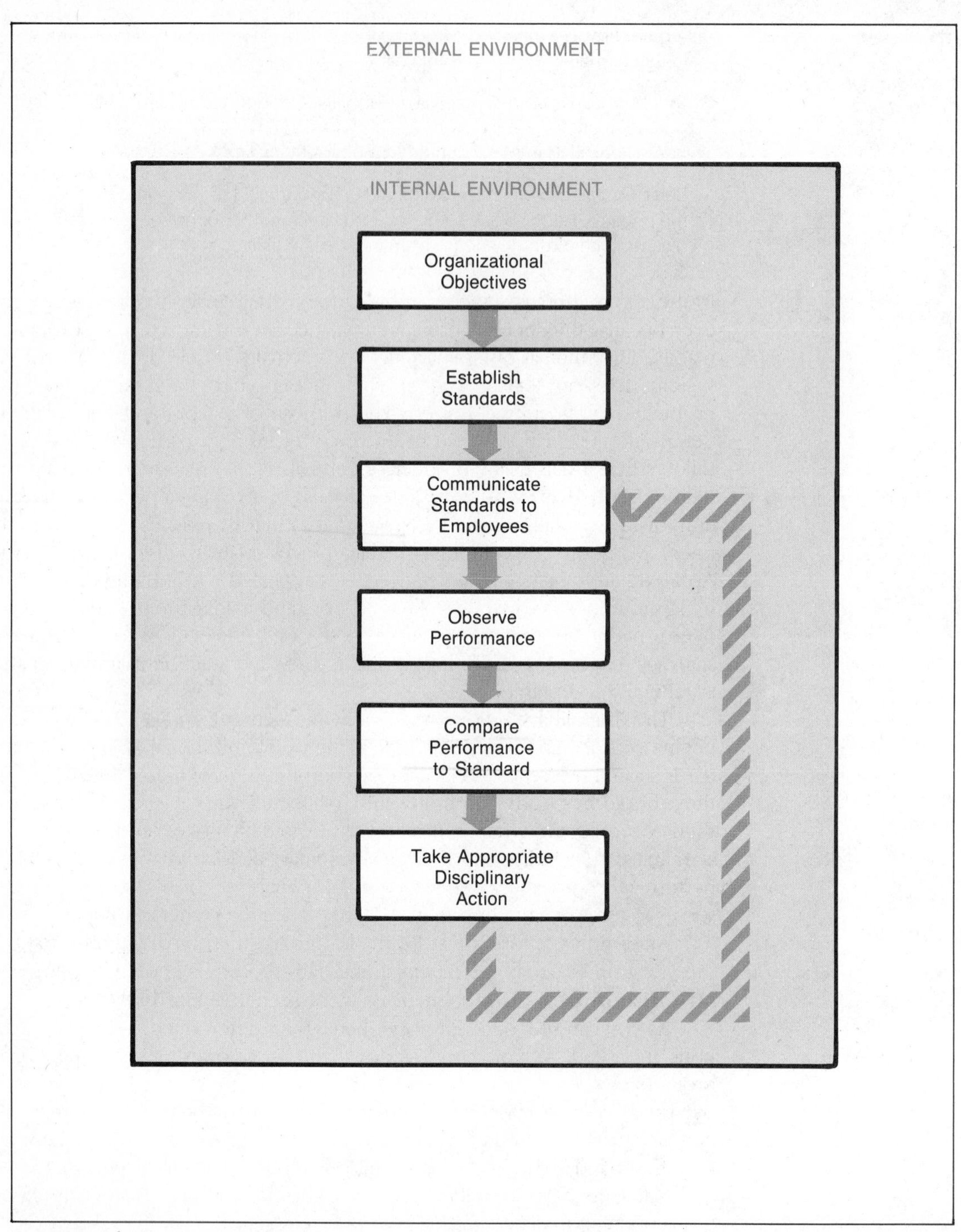

FIGURE 14-7 *The Disciplinary Action Process [Source: Adapted from R. Wayne Mondy and Robert M. Noe, III,* Personnel: The Management of Human Resources *(Boston: Allyn and Bacon, 1981), p. 436.*]

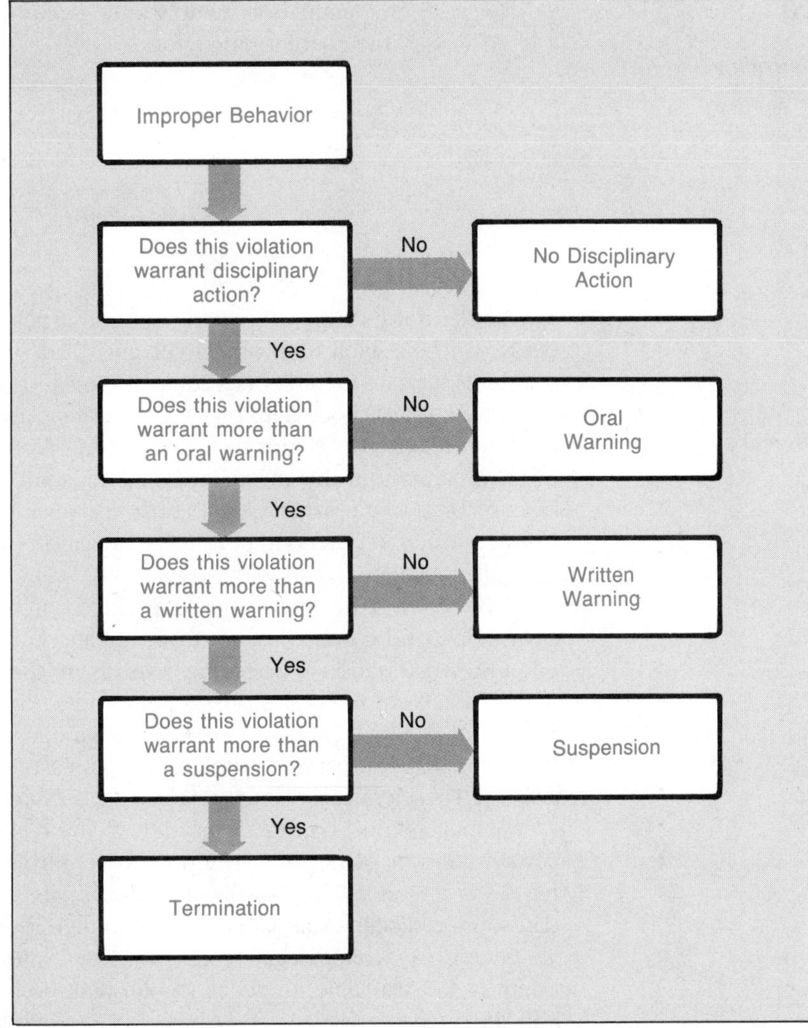

FIGURE 14-8
Progressive Discipline

Source: Adapted from R. Wayne Mondy and Robert M. Noe, III. *Personnel: The Management of Human Resources* (Boston: Allyn and Bacon, 1981), p. 439.

- The act, rather than the person, should be condemned.
- Although the act may be the basis for penalty, a model of future desired behavior should be communicated.
- Reasonable promptness is important so that the employee can connect the penalty to the violation.
- A managerial listening role is highly essential to (a) effect greater understanding of the reasons for the act and (b) prevent hasty decisions that may lead to unjustified penalties.
- Negative disciplinary action should be administered in private so that the employee can save face among colleagues.

- Definite, but tactful, follow-up should occur to determine the degree of success of the conditioning effort.
- Consistency and flexibility, though apparently contradictory, are both desirable elements of a superior's style of disciplining.

Summary

Control is the process of comparing actual performances with established standards for the purpose of taking corrective action. However, before standards can be established, objectives and plans must be developed. Thus, standards serve as the link between planning and control.

The control process involves three critical areas: establishment of standards, comparison of performance to standards, and taking corrective action. In an organization, the most important means by which performance can be compared to standards relate to quantity, quality, time, and budget (costs). Corrective action is needed to remove deviations from planned performance or to alter the plan to allow for obstacles that cannot be removed.

The control function can be divided into three basic types: initial, overseeing, and comparison controls. Initial controls take place as resources enter the organization. Overseeing controls are used during the process when the products and services are being produced. Comparison controls are used after the final product or service has been produced. However, at all times a manager must determine what to measure and when to measure an activity. These critical areas are referred to as strategic control points.

Managers must constantly be alert to the realization that there will be a certain amount of negative reactions to controls. Some of these negative reactions are caused as a result of inappropriate controls, unattainable standards, unpredictable standards, and contradictory standards. However, there are means by which negative reactions to controls may be overcome. If controls are justifiable, understandable, realistic, timely, and accurate, they will likely receive the least resistance.

Perhaps the most widely known and applied device that managers use in controlling cost and expenditures is the budget. A budget is a formal statement of financial resources; it is a planned expenditure of money for personnel, time, space, or equipment. Although numerous benefits may be associated with the budgeting process, it also has limitations. A budget will not solve all of a manager's monetary problems.

In recent years, two specific budgeting systems have received considerable attention. The Planning-Programming-Budgeting System (PPBS) was designed to aid management in identifying and eliminating costly programs that were duplicates of other programs and to provide a means for the careful analysis of the benefits and costs of each program or activity. Zero Base Budgeting (ZBB) requires management to take a fresh look at all programs and activities each year rather than merely building on last year's budget.

A natural by-product of controls is disciplinary action, the process of invoking a penalty against an employee who fails to adhere to standards (that is, policies, procedures, and rules). At all times, efforts must be made to make the penalty appropriate to the violation or accumulated violations. This process is known as progressive discipline. Although there are difficulties that arise through the use of disciplinary action, there are guides in handling disciplinary cases.

Review Questions

1. Define control as a process for assisting a manager to accomplish his or her objectives.
2. Explain in your own words why the functions of planning and controlling are so closely related.
3. What are the steps that are involved in the control process?
4. What are the four means by which actual performance may be compared to standards? Briefly discuss each.
5. Why are budgets so important to managers? Discuss.
6. Distinguish initial controls, overseeing controls, and comparison controls. When would each type be used?
7. What factors should a manager consider in establishing strategic control points?
8. What effect does the level of management have on the process of control?
9. What are some guidelines that a manager should follow when disciplinary action must be used?

Exercises

1. Develop objective(s), plans, and standards for obtaining an A in this course. What type of control measures must be developed for you to accomplish this goal?
2. Think of the following types of businesses and managers. What types of controls do you believe they must have to ensure that they accomplish their objectives?
   a. A small convenience store
   b. A college or university
   c. A firm that manufactures a high-quality hand calculator
   d. An insurance agency
   e. An automobile repair shop

Case Study

A Problem of Inventory Control

As supervisor of ten stores in a convenience store chain, Martha Young is responsible for their general operation. Each of these small stores has a day manager and two assistant managers who work the evening and midnight shifts. These "managers" are not really managers because they have no subordinates reporting directly to them. The day manager is typically the senior person and has chosen the day shift. (A person might want to visit a convenience store to gain a better appreciation of the work environment.)

Mark McCall is the day manager of one of the stores that Martha supervises. Mark has been at the store for three months and sales have been increasing steadily. Mark maintains his store in good order, and the first two monthly inventory checks have been satisfactory. But as Martha reads the inventory report for this month, she becomes quite disturbed. Inventory is $1,000 short for the previous month (anything over $200 is considered out of the ordinary).

Martha realizes that this report is extremely serious. Other managers have been terminated for inventory shortages of this amount. She likes Mark but something must be done to keep this situation from occurring in the future. Martha sits down and reviews the situation regarding the store. The following points come to mind:

- The store is located close to a school. When Mark took control of the store, school was not in session. There might be some shoplifting occurring.
- One of the assistant managers has been with the store for only one month. There is a possibility that there could be internal theft.
- The other assistant manager broke up with his girlfriend last month. There is a possibility that he has not been paying close attention to his job.

QUESTIONS

1. What type of controls, if any, should Martha instigate?
2. If the inventory is short next month, what do you think Martha should do?

Case Study

Differing Philosophies

Collins and Bradford (C&B) is a manufacturing company with sales of approximately $250 million. C&B employs twelve college-trained accountants at its headquarters. These positions are divided among financial accounting, cost accounting, accounts payable, and auditing. Tom Brown came to work at C&B in the financial accounting department. He had a B.B.A. from a major university and two years of previous work experience in accounting. He caught on quickly, did a good job, and was well liked by his supervisor and fellow employees. After eleven months, a position became available in the cost accounting department that offered Tom a higher salary and an opportunity to develop professionally in another area.

After three months in the cost accounting department it became apparent to Tom that he and his supervisor, Ed Blake, simply could not work together. Tom disagreed with Ed's training techniques and Ed's philosophy on how certain problems should be handled. It also became evident that they had a severe personality conflict. After a full month of deliberation on what to do, Tom decided to go to John Collins, Ed's supervisor, and ask for a transfer. He explained that he wanted to remain at C&B but that neither he nor the cost department was benefiting from his being in his present position.

Ed and John had been friends and working associates for years, and John's initial reaction was to blame Tom for the bad situation. He surveyed the other accounting positions and did not see any openings coming up in the near future. John felt that he had three alternatives—to create an additional accounting position in another department and transfer Tom, to work with Ed and Tom to reconcile the problems, or to terminate Tom.

QUESTIONS

1. What might have caused the conflict between Tom and Ed? How can this type of conflict be controlled so as not to affect adversely a firm's operations?
2. What action should John take? Is he limited to the three alternatives mentioned at the end of the case?
3. If you were Tom Brown, what would you do?

Notes

1. Robert N. Anthony and Regina E. Herzlinger, *Management Control in Non-Profit Organizations* (Homewood, Ill.: Irwin, 1975), pp. 222–226.
2. Ibid.
3. Anthony and Herzlinger, *Management Control.*
4. See ibid., pp. 223, 224, and James A. F. Stoner, *Management* (Englewood Cliffs, N.J.: Prentice-Hall, 1978), pp. 600–677.
5. See Stoner, *Management,* pp. 608–609.
6. Gordon Shillinglaw, *Managerial Cost Accounting: Analysis and Control,* 4th ed. (Homewood, Ill.: Irwin, 1977), pp. 142–143.

References

Buffa, Elwood S. *Modern Production-Operations Management,* 6th ed. New York: Wiley, 1980.

Camillus, John C. "Six Approaches to Preventive Management Control." *Financial Executive* 48 (December 1980): 28–31.

Chase, Richard B., and Aquilano, Nicholas J. *Production and Operations Management: A Life Cycle Approach.* Homewood, Ill.: Irwin, 1981.

Dalton, Dan R., and Todor, William D. "Win, Lose, Draw: The Grievance Process in Practice." *Personnel Administrator* 26 (March 1981): 25–29.

DeWelt, R. L. "Control: Key to Making Financial Strategy Work." *Management Review* 66 (March 1977): 18–25.

Flamholtz, Eric. "Organizational Control Systems as a Managerial Tool." *California Management Review* 22 (Winter 1979): 50–59.

Gannon, John S. "How to Handle Discipline within the New National Labor Relations Board Requirements." *Personnel Administrator* 26 (March 1981): 43–47.

Gitman, Lawrence J. *Principles of Managerial Finance,* 2d ed. New York: Harper, 1979.

Hayhurst, B. "Proposal for a Corporate Control System." *Management International Review* 16 (1976): 93–103.

Horovitz, J. H. "Strategic Control: A New Task for Top Management." *Long Range Planning* 12 (June 1979): 2–7.

Lissy, William E. "Necessity of Proof to Support Disciplinary Action." *Supervision* 40 (June 1978): 13.

Machin, John L., and Wilson, Lyn S. "Closing the Gap between Planning and Control." *Long Range Planning* 12 (April 1979): 16–32.

Mondy, R. Wayne, and Noe, Robert M., III. *Personnel: The Management of Human Resources.* Boston: Allyn and Bacon, 1981.

Nelson, E. G., and Machin, J. L. "Management Control: Systems Thinking Applied to Development of a Framework for Empirical Studies." *Journal Of Management Studies* (October 1976): 274–287.

Ouchi, W. G. "Relationship between Organizational Structure and Organizational Control." *Administrative Science Quarterly* 22, no. 1 (March 1981): 95–113.

Pingpank, Jeffery C., and Mooney, Thomas B. "Wrongful Discharge: A New Danger for Employers." *Personnel Administrator* 26 (March 1981): 31–35.

Schroeder, Roger G. *Operations Management: Decision Making in the Operations Function.* New York: McGraw-Hill, 1981.

Solomon, Ezra, and Pringle, John J. *An Introduction to Financial Management.* Santa Monica, Calif.: Goodyear, 1980.

Swann, James P., Jr. "Formal Grievance Procedures in Non-Union Plants." *Personnel Administrator* 26 (August 1981): 66–70.

CASE STUDY FOR PART V

Hiwasse Homes, Inc.

For several years, Mr. Roger Thomas had been interested in the growth and development of the mobile home industry. Thomas was impressed by the operation of a successful mobile home manufacturing plant located in the area. Thomas had been engaged in the hardware and lumber business for several years in Hiwasse, Arkansas, population 425, located in the extreme corner of northwestern Arkansas. The hardware and lumber company was a very successful operation, and Thomas had earned the reputation as a capable businessman.

However, Thomas was seeking new business opportunities and believed that the bright prospects for the mobile home industry would continue, since mobile homes had become a primary housing alternative for low-income families and families interested in weekend or vacation homes. Because of the economic and demographic characteristics of Arkansas and the surrounding states, as well as the absence of any major mobile home producers, Thomas was reasonably certain that the mobile home manufacturing business provided an exceptional business opportunity. Since Thomas had no prior experience in the mobile home business, and in an effort to gain more information concerning the feasibility of establishing a mobile home manufacturing plant, he contacted a former professor at a nearby university to discuss his plans. He asked the professor if, as a class project, a graduate class could conduct a feasibility study of his proposed entry into the mobile home business. The professor liked the idea and made arrangements for the study to be conducted by a team of eight graduate business administration students.

CONCLUSIONS OF THE STUDY

The consultants recommended northwestern Arkansas as a very favorable region for the establishment of a mobile home manufacturing plant. This conclusion was based on three primary factors.

This case was written by Robert E. Holmes of Southwest Texas State University and R. Dean Lewis of Sam Houston State University. Reprinted with permission.

The Market

The present and future market for mobile homes will be expanding considerably from all indications. National mobile home demand is expected to reach 650,000 units within five years, a 10 percent annual growth rate. Potential demand in the four-state region of Arkansas, Oklahoma, Missouri, and Kansas is predicted to increase by 60 percent during the next five years. The region does appear vulnerable to additional firms entering the regional area at this time.

Nature and Extent of Competition

Competition in the mobile home industry is essentially based on product quality, price, and service by dealers. There are thirty-eight mobile home plants in the four-state region, and three additional ones are scheduled for construction during the current year. The market is a seller's market in this region and is expected to remain as such for several more years. It is estimated that demand for mobile homes will exceed the supply of mobile homes by approximately 4,000 units next year in the four-state region.

While the market for mobile homes is expected to increase substantially during the next several years, in order to be financially successful, a prospective firm must develop and implement sound production, personnel, and finance plans. Specifically, the successful entry and operation of a new mobile home manufacturing plant depends upon:

- an efficient plant layout and process flow designed to minimize production delays and idle time while maintaining product quality;
- producing a low to moderate priced unit to meet market demand in the regional market;
- selection and retention of key personnel; and
- the determination of and procurement of adequate financing.

RECOMMENDATIONS

The following recommendations were made by the consultants:

- Construction of a mobile home plant in northwest Arkansas.
- A plant with an output of four units a day, reached by the beginning of the sixth month of operation.

a. A plant size necessary to accommodate the recommended production (325 ft. by 100 ft.).
b. The recommended plant layout combined with the suggested process flow designed to provide maximum efficiency.

- The plant should produce and market an inexpensive 12 ft. by 60 ft. mobile home that is currently the largest selling line. The plant should have the flexibility to produce other size units including modular homes.
- The personnel required for the manufacturing facility consists of fifty production workers, two office/clerical people and four managers.
- The capital required to establish the proposed plant is $320,000, which includes $75,000 for working capital and initial operational contingencies.

In their closing comments in the study, the consultants noted that, while it was relatively easy to enter the mobile home business, failure rates have been substantial. The consultants stated that the probabilities of success seem to be primarily dependent upon: financial strength (particularly during the first several months of operation and especially during recessionary periods), managerial expertise and ability (especially in selecting key personnel), production and technical expertise, and the ability to establish an effective dealer network.

SUBSEQUENT MOVES

After reviewing the conclusions and recommendations of the feasibility study, Mr. Thomas and a group of investors were very encouraged about prospects for the mobile home plant. Mr. Thomas and several investors were able to arrange the necessary financing, and construction of the plant began on December 1. Hiwasse was organized with a financial structure consisting of $61,250 of capital supplied by selling 12,500 shares of common stock at $4.90 per share, and loans from the Small Business Administration and a local bank totalling $300,000. The plant was to be located in Gravett, Arkansas, a town with a population of 600.

The top management of Hiwasse consisted of:

- An eight-member board of directors consisted of several prominent local community leaders including an M.D., lawyer, banker, and leading retailer. Mr. Thomas controlled 51 percent of Hiwasse's stock and was chairman of the board and chief executive officer. Hiwasse's general manager was also on the board.

- Mr. Roger Thomas, chairman of the board and president, held a bachelor's and master's degree in business administration and had more than ten years of successful experience in the hardware and lumber business.
- Mr. Dick Johnson, the thirty-nine-year-old general manager, was a high school graduate, had eight years' experience as a production superintendent at a large mobile home company noted for producing high quality/high priced units. His overall responsibilities will include planning, directing, and controlling production operations. In addition, he is to coordinate production plans with the sales manager.
- Mr. Bill Melton, sales manager, was thirty-six years old and a college graduate with a major in marketing. He was Dick Johnson's brother-in-law and had previous experience as a mobile home sales representative with the same company as Johnson had been with prior to joining Hiwasse.
- Mr. Graham Richards, purchasing manager, was twenty-eight years old and an industrial management graduate of Kansas State. Although he had no experience in the manufacture of mobile homes, he had been a production supervisor in a nearby garments manufacturing plant.

Stockholders, the board, top management at Hiwasse, as well as many people in the small town of Gravett, were encouraged and excited about the prospects for a successful manufacturing plant. The company would provide needed jobs and be an asset to the community. The major goals of Hiwasse, according to Mr. Thomas were:

- profit—achieve return on stockholder investment of 25 percent per year after the first year of operation
- provide needed jobs for area residents and thus increased economic prosperity
- produce an inexpensive mobile home, but of higher quality than those of competitors within the price range.

One week prior to the start of production operations, Mr. Thomas sent a letter to each stockholder. The following are excerpts from this letter.

> The building is nearing completion and most of the equipment has been installed. Most of the hand tools and portable power tools have been received including the bulk of the stapling and nailing equipment. . . .
>
> To date, materials have been ordered for the first ten units; the specialty items, or items that are fabricated, have been ordered for the second ten units. Many of the materials have been received with more to be received soon. Production is scheduled to start next week with approximately fifteen new production employees beginning work at that time. The first unit should be finished within five days of the starting of production. Workers will be added as needed each week for the first six or eight weeks. . . .
>
> At the present time we have two sales representatives on the road starting to establish our dealer network. To date, the response from the dealers has been approximately 75 percent favorable. We anticipate no problems in marketing the first twenty units scheduled for production. We have firm orders for five units now.

Despite top management's optimism, the company began experiencing serious difficulties by the end of the first month of operation. The following is a summary of several board of directors' meetings held during the first few months after Hiwasse began production operations on December 1 relating to some of their problems.

January 19 Board Meeting

Mr. Thomas, the president, and the general manager, Mr. Dick Johnson, presented a summary of activities during the building of the plant and initial production operations. It was reported that the company has a cash flow problem due primarily to a lack of sales. There have been only two firm sales of mobile homes, although the company has several pending orders. Finished goods inventory currently is $92,500 (twenty unsold mobile homes).

The company is currently experiencing some production and management problems that should be resolved within the next two weeks. Prior to adjourning, the board set a goal of $55,000 worth of mobile home sales during the next two weeks.

February 2 Board Meeting

Mr. Thomas reported that ten mobile home units at $5,100 each had been sold to a dealer in Tulsa with a promised delivery date of March 1. To date,

Hiwasse only received money from the sale of two mobile homes totalling $10,500. Several deliveries have been made for which money has not yet been received. The company's sales, production and internal problems were again discussed at length. President Thomas stated that he thought that part of the company's difficulties were due to errors in judgment by General Manager Johnson and, in Thomas's opinion, inadequate performance by Johnson and the sales force. Thomas stated that Johnson had decided that Hiwasse should produce a higher quality/higher priced mobile home. After considerable discussion, no definite decisions were reached by the board.

February 15 Board Meeting

President Thomas reported that it was necessary to temporarily lay off twenty production employees at the end of the week. As cash flow improves, these workers will be recalled. The company has a signed order from a dealer in Joplin, Missouri, for ten units at $7,150 each. However, Hiwasse had to sign a repurchase agreement for any units remaining unsold after ninety days, and for any units sold they have to pay the dealer a rebate of $200 per unit plus a 5 percent discount on net cost.

The company currently has a finished goods inventory of mobile homes of $150,000–$170,000. The company's sales, production, and internal conflicts were again discussed at length. President Thomas asked that the board void Dick Johnson's employment contract and that he himself, at least until the company's financial position is more favorable, assume the duties of general manager in addition to his duties as president. The board declined to act on Mr. Thomas's request.

March 10 Special Board Meeting

All board members except Mr. Thomas signed the following statement, which was being placed in the board minutes.

> We, the undersigned shareholders and directors of Hiwasse Homes, Inc., wish to place the following comments and observations on the record of the minutes of the special meeting of March 10.
>
> We are of the opinion that the decision of Roger Thomas to terminate contractual relations with the "management team" (specifically Dick Johnson and Bill Melton) is not well founded. These people were personally selected by Mr. Thomas and were represented to us by Mr. Thomas as being the best qualified people available in the field for manage-

ment of the corporation. We do not agree that they are not competent in this capacity and that they have failed to perform satisfactorily at this time.

We are further of the opinion that the board of directors has not been kept fully informed at regular meetings as to the performance or lack of performance of the executive and supervisory personnel. Nor have we been supplied with a regular, comprehensive presentation of the financial condition of the firm. We have not been appraised of the creation and current status of liabilities in the form of loans and accounts payable, which we feel are policy matters subject to the approval and review by the board of directors as a whole. We recognize that Roger Thomas, by virtue of the capital structure of the corporation, probably has the ability, at a regularly constituted annual meeting, to establish a board of directors, the majority of whom would be of his (Thomas's) own choosing. Therefore, in the event of the realignment of the board of directors as outlined above, we feel that the success or failure of the corporation will rest squarely upon Mr. Thomas rather than upon the undersigned who feel that they have not been permitted to function as a board of directors would ordinarily do.

We are most hopeful that the policies of Mr. Thomas, and consequently the direction the corporation takes, will be successful, both for the sake of those investors who placed their faith in Mr. Thomas and for the economic benefit of the community as a whole. We do not wish to harass or deter the progress of the firm and are hopeful of the problems being resolved by Mr. Thomas and extend to him our sincere wish for his success in this effort.

In other action for consideration by the board, Mr. Thomas reported that there were several firms that might be interested in purchasing a portion or possibly all of the stock of Hiwasse Homes. The board authorized Thomas to pursue any such possibilities immediately.

The board authorized Mr. Thomas to fire Mr. Bill Melton for failure to adequately perform as sales manager. Mr. Dick Johnson offered to resign from the company and requested that he be granted one week's paid vacation. A board member moved that Hiwasse regretfully accept Johnson's resignation and grant him fifteen days of paid vacation. The motion was approved unanimously with Johnson's resignation effective on March 25.

HIWASSE DISCONTINUES OPERATIONS

It was a typical hot August day in northwestern Arkansas as Mr. Thomas made final preparations for closing Hiwasse Homes. Hiwasse Homes was bankrupt after only nine months of operation. Mr. Thomas, the founder and president of Hiwasse, was very disappointed to see his dreams and two years of planning and hard work end in the failure of the business.

From mid-March to the final closing of the plant on August 1, Hiwasse continued to experience financial and operational problems. After the departure of Johnson, Mr. Thomas assumed almost total responsibility for plant operations. The plant continued to produce mobile homes with an average output of one per day but experienced considerable difficulty selling its finished products. During the first six months of operation, Hiwasse sustained a net loss of over $81,000.

Questions

1. If you were Mr. Thomas and had just reviewed the conclusions and recommendations of the feasibility study, would you have entered the mobile home manufacturing business?
2. What were Mr. Thomas's basic objectives in starting Hiwasse Homes? Did he have standards of performance for his new business?
3. What types of initial controls did Mr. Thomas use in beginning Hiwasse? Specifically, comment on controls in the areas of material, personnel selection, and capital.
4. Despite considerable planning and a detailed feasibility study, Hiwasse Homes failed just a few months after it began operations. Why? What were the primary reasons for the failure of Hiwasse?

PART VI

Production and Operations Management

KEY TERMS

product layout
process layout
flow process chart
operations chart
worker machine charts
stopwatch method
work sampling
break-even analysis
fixed costs
variable costs
discounted cash flow
make/buy planning decision
purchase/lease decision
linear programming
objective function
constraint functions
demand forecasting
trend
cyclical
seasonal
random
moving averages
exponential smoothing
regression analysis
time series analysis

LEARNING OBJECTIVES

After completing this chapter you should be able to

1. Identify and describe some of the traditional production management techniques.
2. Explain some of the basic financial approaches to planning.
3. Describe linear programming and state some of the uses of linear programming.
4. Explain forecasting and describe some of the forecasting techniques.

15

Traditional Production Management and Planning Techniques

Brian Jones, vice-president of production for Marlboro Corporation, is faced with a critical decision. He must make a choice between two machines that will be used to increase production efficiency at Marlboro. One piece of equipment costs $200,000 and is capable of providing a savings of $50,000 a year over the next seven years. The other machine costs $150,000 but will generate a savings of $60,000 over the next four years. Brian thinks to himself—"Gee, I wish I knew more about evaluating financial alternatives."

Barry Williams, the production manager for Ampex Corporation, a small furniture manufacturing company, is in the process of making a difficult decison. The firm plans to manufacture a new line of tables and chairs. Barry has determined that he can make a profit of five dollars on each chair and seven dollars per table. However, there are only sixty hours available in the machine shop to work on either tables or chairs, and there are only forty-eight hours available in the paint shop. He knows that it takes four hours to machine a chair and two hours to machine a table and two hours to paint a chair and four hours to paint a table. Barry wants to maximize profits for the firm but doesn't know how many tables and chairs to make.

Lisa Thompson, the director of planning for Finn Manufacturing, was sitting in her office when Molly Holmes, the marketing director, came rushing into her office. Molly said, "We need to double production of our Super X product. Sales doubled this month." Lisa said, "That's great, Molly, but something seems wrong. Sales have never increased more than 10 percent over the last six years. Let's do a little research before a decision is made to double production."

Brian, Barry, and Lisa could all benefit from the use of production and operations management and planning techniques. They provide managers with a wide variety of principles and procedures related to production economies, quality control, inventory control, work measurement, scheduling, cost control, and others. Procedures that assist in more effectively accomplishing the purpose for which the firm was created are included. In this and the following chapter, specific approaches useful to a manager are developed. They are described from the standpoint of how they are being used in business today. A major portion of the explanation is devoted to gaining an appreciation of what techniques are available, what the manager needs to know in order to use them, and how they have been used to solve actual business problems.

Only a few years ago, production and operations management was taught exclusively as it related to the factory environment. Production was assumed to be completely factory oriented. The techniques assisted in the production process for plants or factories. For instance, production management techniques might be utilized to optimize the procedures for manufacturing automobiles. Today, production and operations management takes on a much broader application in that any organization, including hospitals, schools, and government agencies, may conceivably benefit through the use of the techniques. Most of the quantitative techniques now apply to both factory and service industries, and the term has also been expanded to include production and operations management.

BASIC CONCEPTS OF TRADITIONAL PRODUCTION MANAGEMENT

There are several concepts that at one time were used primarily in the manufacturing environment. Although today they have been used in other than factory settings, the following tools and concepts have been identified as traditionally production and will be discussed separately.

Site Selection

Every firm has different reasons for choosing a particular site for locating a new facility. There are many factors to consider, however, if a firm is to achieve long-run benefits from proper site selection. Factors such as the supply of skilled labor, union activities, living conditions, and, of course, actual costs are some items that warrant consideration. For many reasons, a site that may be completely satisfactory for one company may be totally unacceptable for another.

In order to evaluate objectively different site opportunities, a firm must identify factors they feel are important in choosing a particular location and those items they feel would possibly be detrimental to long-run success. For instance, it may be extremely important for the area surrounding the site to have skilled workers and an ample supply of natural resources. Next, these factors are ranked according to their relative importance. Each site that is considered is then compared to these factors and scored. The site with the highest score is likely to be the best in terms of the company objectives.

Plant Layout

The type of plant layout that will prove to be optimum for the manufacture of a particular product deserves special consideration. Generally, layouts may be identified as being process or product. The selection of one over another depends on the type of product to be manufactured, the type of equipment to be used in the process, and the amount of the particular product to be produced.

product layout

Product layout generally refers to assembly lines. A large amount of a single product can be produced at a relatively low cost per unit when product layouts are used. Equipment is sequenced to permit a product to go from start to finish through the use of automated equipment and assembly lines. The manufacture of automobiles in the United States provides an excellent example of a product layout.

process layout

On the other hand, when **process layouts** are used, pieces of equipment that perform virtually the same function are grouped together. For instance, all drills would be placed in one area and presses placed in another area. It is likely that additional workers and handling time will be required for a process layout. When smaller quantities of a product are to be manufactured (normally referred to as batch processing), most likely the process layout will prove to be superior.

The selection of one layout over another involves analyzing the cost effectiveness of moving the product from an unfinished to a finished stage. The layout that maximizes employee effectiveness and minimizes handling cost is likely to be advantageous.

Work Methods

There are certain tasks that an individual can do better than a machine and others that machines can handle better. For instance, people do a better job in areas that require exercising judgment and developing concepts. On the other hand, machines have proved to be superior in areas where repetitive and routine tasks are to be performed.

Numerous techniques are used to maximize the efficiency associated with a particular process. The flow process chart, operations chart, and worker-machine chart have proved to be beneficial for this purpose.

Flow Process Charts

flow process chart

The symbols that are used in a **flow process chart** to depict the flow of a job are:

○ Operation

⇨ Transportation

□ Inspection

D Delay

▽ Storage

Each task to be accomplished is identified along with the time it will take. A manager then is able to study the sequence of tasks to determine if there is

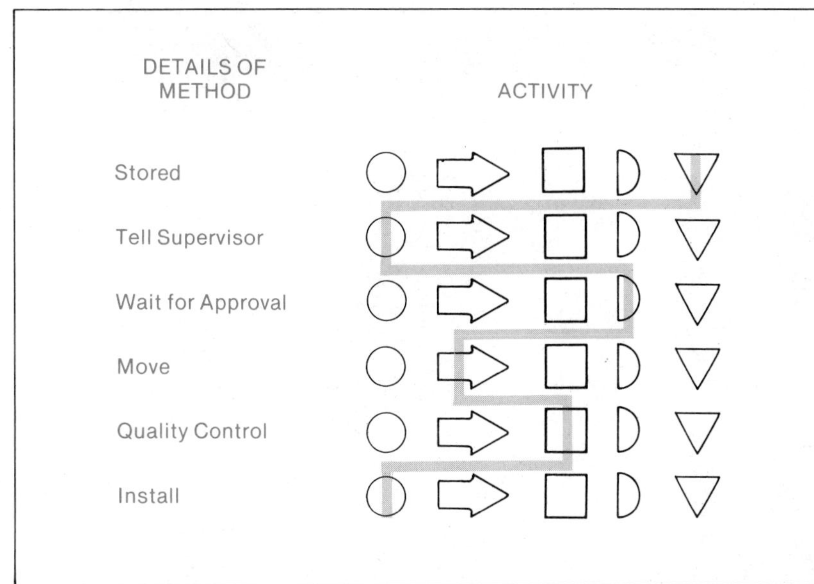

FIGURE 15-1
Flow Process Chart

a better way to accomplish the job. A simple flow process chart is presented in Figure 15-1.

Operations Charts

operations chart

In a production operation, the movement of the right and left hand is analyzed through the use of an **operations chart.** Its use is essentially appropriate when the time from start to finish of an operation (cycle time) is fairly short. A major benefit of an operations chart is that it permits a manager to view a task to see if it is being completed in an optimum manner.

Worker Machine Charts

worker machine charts

These charts are beneficial when both a worker and a machine are used to perform a particular task. Through studying **worker machine charts** a manager is able to determine if there is excessive idle time associated with either the worker or the machine. If the worker is idle, he or she may be assigned an additional machine to control. On the other hand, if the machine is expensive and needs to be kept operating a majority of the time, it may be worth the cost of an additional worker to help operate the machine even though the idle time of the worker goes up.

Principles of Motion Economy

The principles of motion economy presented in Table 15-1 are useful in improving efficiency and reducing fatigue. They relate to principles concerning the use of the human body, arrangement of the work place, and design

•CAREER PROFILE•

MR. GENE BARHAM

Director of Manufacturing, Plastics Division
Monsanto Chemical Company

Monsanto A college degree in chemical engineering but a desire to pursue a career in management has produced an interesting career progression path for Gene Barham, currently director of manufacturing, plastics division, of Monsanto Company. When Gene graduated from college in 1959, he had already made up his mind that he wanted ultimately to be in management. "I've always wanted to run my own show," said Gene, "and recently as a general manager with Fisher Controls, I experienced success on a small scale. This was the closest thing there is to running your own business within a major corporation. There is relative independence —as long as you do well. Now I have moved to a major part of Monsanto, and I am trying to create a 'profit team movement' to make the plastics division more profitable."

Gene began his career in the technical end of the chemical business in the agricultural product plant in Luling, Louisiana, with Monsanto, Inc. His managerial skills were soon recognized, and in 1967 he was promoted to manufacturing superintendent and transferred to Muscatine, Iowa. Next, he was plant manager at Bridgeview in Chicago for two years; he then served for three years as a plant manager at Lingonier, Indiana. Gene saw another portion of the business world in 1975 when he was made marketing manager of blownware products for the Monsanto Commercial Products Company. This experience in marketing provided the necessary ingredient to progress to general manager, Fisher Controls Company, a division of Monsanto Company, in 1977. In 1980, Gene returned to Monsanto to apply management skills to reduce manufacturing costs in the Plastics Division.

Gene believes that the ability to communicate and get people to work toward common objectives is the real key to getting results. A major responsibility of a manager is to provide a clear set of directions for everyone to work toward. Gene is very committed to developing people and depends heavily on others in the organization. He says, "People who work with me have a lot of freedom to accomplish results, as well as opportunities for cross training. It is good for them and for the company."

TABLE 15-1. *Principles of Motion Economy*

Use of the Human Body	Arrangement of the Work Place	Design of Tools and Equipment
1. The two hands should begin as well as complete their motions at the same time. 2. The two hands should not be idle at the same time except during rest periods. 3. Motions of the arms should be made in opposite and symmetrical directions and should be made simultaneously. 4. Hand motions should be confined to the lowest classification with which it is possible to perform the work satisfactorily. 5. Momentum should be employed to assist the worker whenever possible, and it should be reduced to a minimum if it must be overcome by muscular effort. 6. Smooth continuous motions of the hands are preferable to zigzag motions or straight-line motions involving sudden and sharp changes in direction. 7. Ballistic movements are faster, easier, and more accurate than restricted (fixation) or "controlled" movements. 8. Rhythm is essential to the smooth and automatic performance of an operation, and the work should be arranged to permit easy and natural rhythm whenever possible.	9. There should be a definite and fixed place for all tools and materials. 10. Tools, materials, and controls should be located close in and directly in front of the operator. 11. Gravity feedbins and containers should be used to deliver materials close to the point of use. 12. Drop deliveries should be used whenever possible. 13. Materials and tools should be located to permit the best sequence of motions. 14. Provisions should be made for adequate conditions for seeing. Good illumination is the first requirement for satisfactory visual perception. 15. The height of the workplace and the chair chould preferably be arranged so that alternate sitting and standing at work are easily possible. 16. A chair of the type and height to permit good posture should be provided for every worker. 17. The hands should be relieved of all work that can be done more advantageously by a jig, a fixture, or a foot-operated device.	18. Two or more tools should be combined whenever possible. 19. Tools and materials should be prepositioned whenever possible. 20. Where each finger performs some specific movement, such as in typewriting, the load should be distributed in accordance with the inherent capacities of the fingers. 21. Handles, such as those used on cranks and large screwdrivers, should be designed to permit as much of the surface of the hand to come in contact with the handle as possible. This is particularly true when considerable force is exerted in using the handle. For light assembly work the screwdriver handle should be so shaped that it is smaller at the bottom than at the top. 22. Levers, crossbars, and handwheels should be located in such positions that the operator can manipulate them with the least change in body position and with the greatest mechanical advantage.

Source: R. M. Barnes, *Motion and Time Study: Design and Measurement of Work,* 6th ed. (New York: Wiley, 1968).

of tools and equipment. Although there is nothing sophisticated or mysterious about the principles, they have been extremely beneficial in job design.

Labor Measurement

There are two basic techniques for determining labor standards: stopwatch and work sampling. Both are used extensively in the factory to determine the time a worker should take to accomplish a particular task.

Stopwatch Method

With this approach, a stopwatch is used to estimate the time it will take to complete a task. After timing a particular task an appropriate number of times, the times are averaged to arrive at a standard time. A weakness that has been associated with the **stopwatch method** is that workers often either speed up or slow down when they know that they are being timed.

stopwatch method

Work Sampling

An approach that has been used effectively in overcoming the deficiencies involved in the stopwatch method is **work sampling**. Workers are observed at random times to determine the proportion of their time that is being spent on different tasks. Statistical sampling techniques are used to determine the number of observations that are needed to obtain the degree of reliability desired.

work sampling

QUANTITATIVE TOOLS FOR PRODUCTION AND OPERATIONS MANAGEMENT

Our intent in discussing the quantitative tools should not be taken to mean that a manager is always expected to know the detailed mathematics of each approach. James F. Olson, manager, corporate strategic planning for General Mills, Inc., reinforced the authors' philosophy with regard to quantitative tools when he stated, "I would urge students to become as familiar as possible with all techniques but to remain enough detached from them to allow clear thinking to take place." A manager should at least have an appreciation of the following:

- the tools available
- the situation for which the tools are designed
- how the tools are used in business

This approach will be taken because of an apparent misconception that has evolved regarding the use of quantitative techniques by students of management. The myth is that these tools cannot be used without a total and complete theoretical and mathematical appreciation of the quantitative techniques. *This need not be the case!* A prudent manager wants to utilize his or her resources to their maximum. Thus, a manager must be capable of recognizing what tools are available and when they should be used. Once the manager has made this determination, the mathematician, statistician, or computer specialist may be called on to perform the actual calculation. These individuals are trained to implement a quantitative technique once the manager has made the decision as to which tool is appropriate and identified the factors that should be considered in the problem.

Another major point that should be made regarding the use of any quantitative tool is that the manager must still use his or her personal judgment

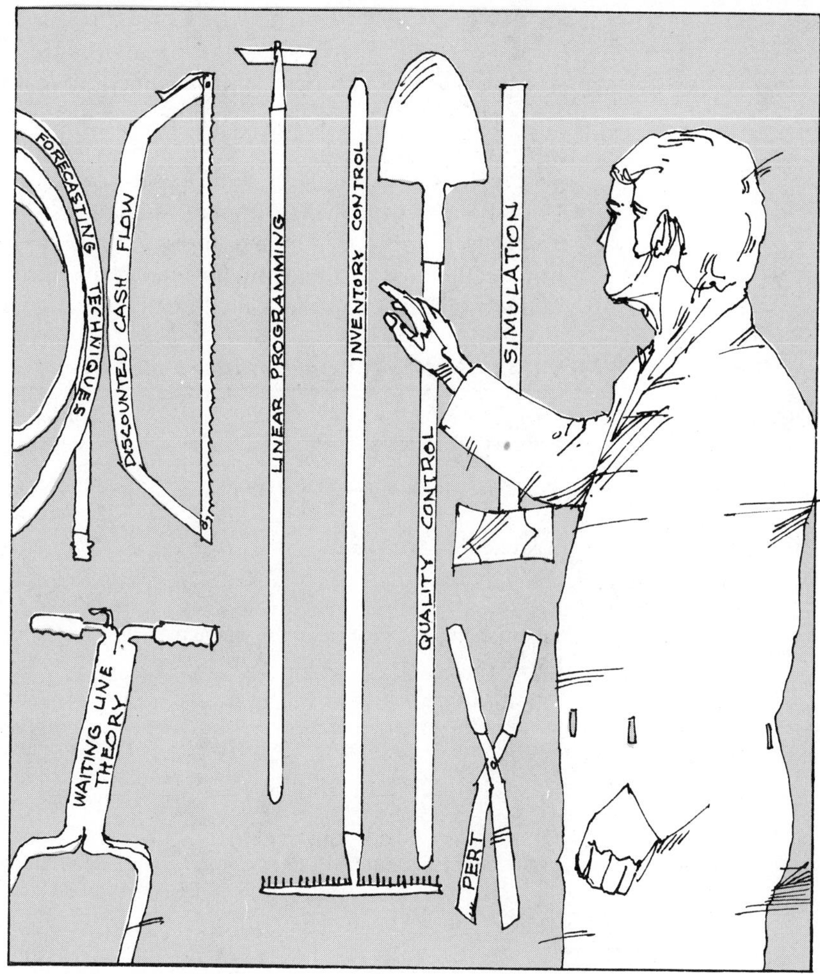

A manager needs to be capable of choosing the proper quantitative technique.

once an answer has been obtained. As D. E. Eckdahl, senior vice-president, engineering and manufacturing, of NCR Corp., stated:

> Since no mathematical model can satisfactorily emulate all aspects of most decision problems, it is essential that sound judgment is exercised in evaluating mathematical models rather than unquestioning reliance on simple quantitative results.

After all factors affecting a decision are considered, a manager must still exercise sound judgment in deciding whether to use solutions that have been derived from the use of quantitative techniques.

The importance of a specific production and operations management technique varies with time, project attention, business cycles, and performance achievement in various aspects of the business. The needs of the time dictate the techniques as well as the capabilities and understanding of the concepts by the project manager and his team.

MANAGERIAL USES FOR QUANTITATIVE TECHNIQUES

A major point for a student of management to realize is that many companies are making extensive use of various quantitative tools. The need may be different for each firm, but the fact remains they are being used. This was vividly illustrated when the authors surveyed a sample of major firms in the United States as to which primary quantitative tools they used (see Table 15-2). Each firm had a minimum of $250 million in sales annually. As you can see, their use of the quantitative tools apparently depended on the nature of the business and the specific desires of management.

TABLE 15-2. ***Use of Quantitative Techniques***

Primary Product of Firm	Primary Quantitative Techniques Used
Vehicle components and assemblies	Inventory control models Economic modeling
Railroad transportation	Discounted cash flow techniques PERT, CPM Simulation
Pharmaceuticals, proprietary remedies, confections, cosmetics and toiletries	Simulation
Petroleum	Simulation Mathematical programming Discounted cash flow techniques Probability theory (Bayesian statistics, payoff and risk analysis)
Construction, engineering, and real estate development	Simulation Mathematical programming PERT, CPM
Tires and tubes	Inventory control models Discounted cash flow techniques
Automobile accessories	Simulation Probability theory (Bayesian statistics, payoff and risk analysis) Inventory control models
Industrial and agriculture products	Inventory control models
Petroleum products	PERT, CPM Discounted cash flow techniques
Building products	Simulation Probability theory (Bayesian statistics, payoff and risk analysis) Inventory control models Discounted cash flow techniques
Steel	Inventory control models Mathematical programming Discounted cash flow techniques
Building products	Inventory control models PERT, CPM

TABLE 15-2 *(continued)*

Electrical equipment	Inventory control models PERT, CPM
Paper products	Discounted cash flow techniques Simulation Mathematical programming
Computers	PERT, CPM Simulation
Natural gas	Discounted cash flow techniques
Toiletries and grooming aids	Inventory control models Discounted cash flow techniques Simulation
Aircraft	Discounted cash flow techniques PERT, CPM
Computers	Discounted cash flow techniques Simulation
Tires	Inventory control models Discounted cash flow techniques
Heating and refrigeration equipment	Inventory control models Discounted cash flow techniques
Construction and engineering	PERT, CPM
Engines and trucks	Inventory control models Discounted cash flow techniques Mathematical programming
Petroleum	Discounted cash flow techniques
Catalog order and retail department store	Inventory control models Simulation
Beverages and food concentrates	Discounted cash flow techniques

The rest of this chapter and the next chapter concentrate on providing an overview of some of the production and operations management quantitative tools that have transcended the boundaries of traditional production. The discussion in this chapter is devoted primarily to the quantitative tools that have been found useful in the planning function. A person should remember, however, that although the tools have been beneficial in the planning stage, their use is not confined strictly to the planning function.

PLANNING TECHNIQUES

In this section, several techniques are presented that have been used effectively for business planning. As previously mentioned, their placement in the planning section should not be taken to mean that the technique is reserved solely for the planning function. The quantitative techniques may be appropriate for use in solving other management problems.

Words of Advice

I make many purchasing decisions. I learned early that different companies that sell the same product or service have different prices. Often, the grounds are that one company would claim to give better service after the sale.

Yes, it is important to have good service, but soon I decided I could get the good service without regard to where the item was purchased. More than ten years ago I made the decision that all purchases would be on a competitive bid basis and that is the way it has been done since. It has worked very much to the advantage of the company. It eliminates all charges of favoritism and the auditors like it because I keep copies of all competitive bids. It resolves many management problems where people think you should give them business even if the price is not right.

DOROTHY H. MOORE, Vice President and Corporate Secretary, Michigan General Corporation

Financial Models

One of the most valuable tools for a business planner is financial modeling. Factors relating to profit and loss are so vital to the growth and even survival of a firm, it is advantageous for any planner to understand the techniques that are available. In this section, several basic financial approaches will be discussed.

Break-even Analysis

break-even analysis

One approach to use to determine the amount of a particular product that must be sold if the firm is to generate enough revenue to cover costs is **break-even analysis.** In order to progress in a break-even study, the student of management must be capable of identifying the following items:

1. Fixed cost
2. Variable costs
3. Price of the item

fixed costs

variable costs

Fixed costs are costs that do not change with the level of output. Items that normally are considered fixed are the salaries of top management, rent, property taxes, and other similar expenses. **Variable costs** are those costs that are directly related to changes in output. Items that might be included as variable costs are direct materials and labor expenses that are used in manufacturing a particular product. However, these definitions are not always as clear-cut in reality as we would like them to be. There is often a gray area in which some costs can at times be considered either fixed or variable, but this should not deter the student of management from understanding and appreciating the concept.

Let us next work a break-even problem to gain a better understanding of the concept. Suppose that a product is priced at \$15, the variable cost is \$10 per unit, and total fixed costs are \$1,000. Using the following formula to determine the break-even point (BEP) in units of output we have:

$$\begin{array}{c}\text{Break-even point}\\ \text{in amounts}\end{array} = \frac{\text{Total fixed costs}}{\text{Price}-\text{Variable cost}} = \frac{\$1{,}000}{\$15-\$10} = 200.$$

Thus, according to break-even analysis, we would have to sell 200 units before we could begin making a profit.

We next show how to use break-even analysis through a graphical illustration. As seen in Figure 15-2, the vertical axis is designated as cost and revenue while the horizontal axis shows the units of output.

Since it is assumed that our \$1,000 fixed costs do not change, they are placed on the graph as a straight line. Our \$10 variable costs change with the level of production, and the cost line slopes upward. The variable cost line is drawn starting at the point where fixed costs intercept the vertical axis.

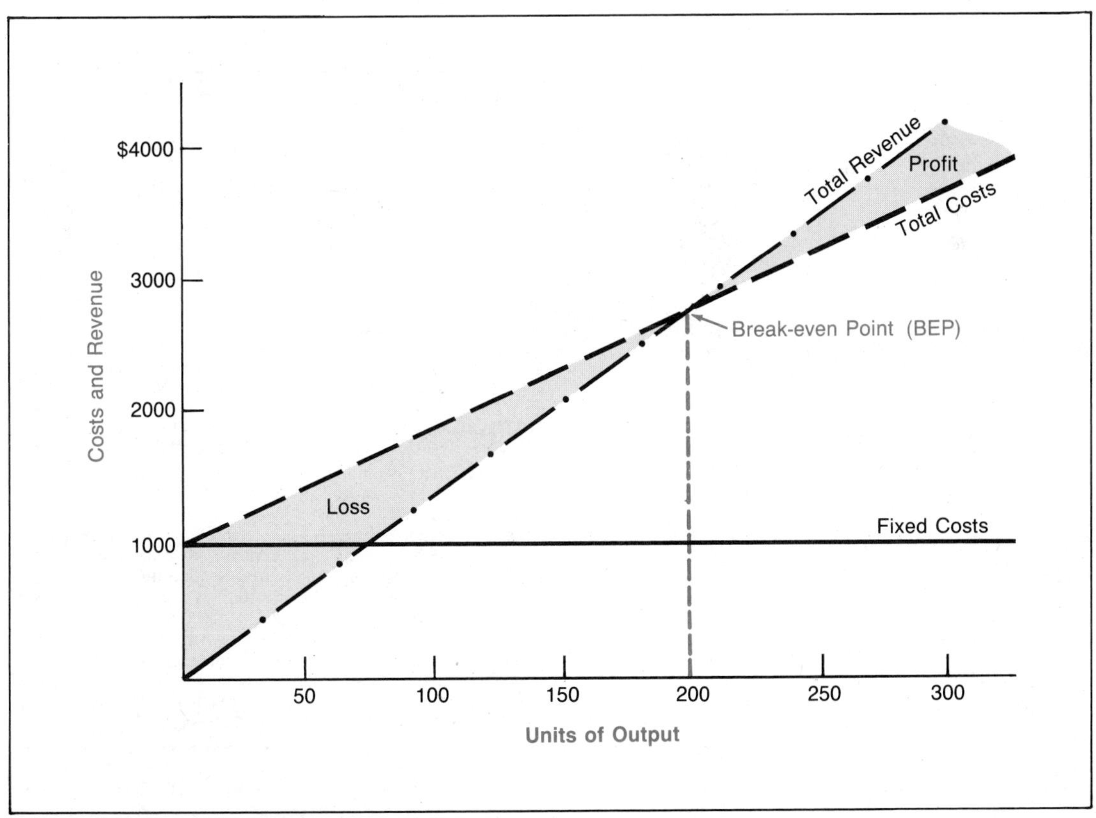

FIGURE 15-2 *Break-even Analysis*

The resulting line is total cost. Next, our total revenue line is drawn showing the total amount of revenue (price times number of units sold) at all possible combinations of production. When the total revenue line intersects the total cost line, the break-even point of 200 units has been reached.

But how reliable is this one point in space? Would you bet your firm's survival on its accuracy? Likely not, but its benefits are substantial if used with full appreciation of the weaknesses of the technique. If you drew a bead on the break-even point with a shotgun and fired, the pattern of the shots would spread out around the break-even point. This is about as accurate as you might expect because of the nature of identifying correctly fixed and variable costs. But the break-even analysis has been used effectively because it forces a manager to plan. An individual who plans is in a position to make better decisions than a nonplanner.

Discounted Cash Flow

A dollar earned today does not have the same value as a dollar that will be earned one year from today. This is because if you invest this dollar today, a year later it will be worth the dollar plus interest. Thus, the time value of money becomes quite important in business planning. Take for example the signing of a superstar professional athlete for over a million dollars. We are often awed by these large amounts and wonder how a team can afford

Touchdown Tony: What Price Glory?

Dorsett: *Sound Investment.*

There's really no need to feel sorry for the Tony Dorsetts of this world, but things aren't quite as rich as they seem. Headlines suggest that Dorsett's five-year Cowboy contract calls for $1.1-$1.2 million. A million dollars or so over five years is worth more than $200,000 a year? Right? Not really.

We checked with a well known local sports executive, who prefers to remain anonymous. Aided by his accountant, our executive gave us this "hypothetical" example of a Dorsett-like, million-dollar, superstar contract.

A five-year contract calls for a salary beginning the first year at $40,000, and increases by $20,000 each year until it reaches $120,000 in year five. Total salary over five years: $400,000.

Next, the contract adds $600,000 in deferred payments. The first payment begins 10 years after the contract is signed and payments continue at $20,000 a year for the next 30 years.

The trick here is a financial principle money wizards call "net present value." Ordinary folks call it common sense. Because the salary payments are spread over five years the superstar forfeits the right to earn interest from the beginning on the entire $400,000. He thus loses the interest he needs to cover the declining value of his dollar (the inflation pinch). In effect, that delay makes the $400,000 he eventually will receive in salary worth only $312,120 in today's money. Applying the same logic to the deferred payments, one finds the $600,000 spread out over 30 years worth only $104,291 in today's money. Total value of the million dollar contract: $414,411 in today's dollars.

Now, let's assume that a player such as Dorsett could draw 7,900 fans for each 1977 home game, not too far-fetched if you note the season ticket boom tony has triggered. The Cowboys' take from 7,900 extra tickets at 11 home games would be about $414,000. Invest that money at eight percent for 40 years and it will grow to nine million dollars. In today's dollars that would be $414,411, fully repaying the Cowboys for the "million dollar" contract. Meaning that Touchdown Tony would pay for himself — in just one season. Hypothetical, of course.

FIGURE 15-3

"Touchdown Tony: What Price Glory," *D Magazine,* August 16, 1977.

to stay in business by paying these salaries. But the managers of these clubs are usually business people and understand the time value of money. This was vividly illustrated in the signing of Tony Dorsett by the Dallas Cowboys, described in the article in Figure 15-3. As you can see, even though the contract was in excess of $1 million, this amount was paid back in one year when the time value of money was considered. The signing of a superstar or placing an order for new equipment have the same implications—the decision should take into consideration the time value of money.

discounted cash flow

In business planning the **discounted cash flow** technique is used extensively. As may be seen in Table 15-3, a wide diversity of firms are deeply involved in the use of discounted cash flow techniques for solving business problems, but most involve capital investment decisions. Taking into consideration the time value of money can mean the difference between a firm's achieving a profit or loss.

Let us help Brian Jones, vice-president of production for Marlboro Corporation, decide which machine he should purchase. Remember that Brian must make a choice from two machines that will be used to increase produc-

TABLE 15-3. *Uses of Discounted Cash Flow Techniques*

Company	Uses
AMF Inc.	Evaluation of strategic alternatives
Bendix Corporation	Plant expansion Machinery purchase
Carrier Corporation	Plant expansion Major capital expenditures
Crown Zellerbach	Make or buy decisions Lease or buy decisions Plant expansion decisions Alternative courses of action
Glidden Division, SCM Corporation	Capital expenditure request model—corporate-wide Capital investment analysis system New product planning
Inland Steel Company	Capital investment decisions Lease or buy Repair or replace
Kellogg Company	Project justification and decision making Justification of new technologies All capital expenditures
Kimberly-Clark	Maintenance analysis Project evaluation Lease/buy decisions
Lear Siegler	Capital equipment purchases Plant expansion Make or buy
Oscar Mayer & Co.	All major economic analyses Investment analysis Investment rish analysis

TABLE 15-3. *(continued)*

Company	Uses
Procter & Gamble Company	New product decisions Evaluation of capital appropriations Evaluation of engineering alternatives
The Signal Companies, Inc.	All major capital investment decisions (new plants, equipment) Lease vs. purchase Acquisitions
Southern Railroads	Investment decisions RR rate and pricing decisions Merger and acquisition analysis
The Southland Corp.	Building decisions
3M Company	Investment analysis Decisions for capital expenditures Make or buy and lease and buy

tion efficiency at Marlboro. One piece of equipment costs $200,000 and is capable of providing a savings of $50,000 a year over the next seven years. The other machine costs $150,000 but will generate $60,000 in savings over the next four years. If we assume an interest rate of 15 percent, let us see what choice Brian might make. Referring to Table 15-4, you can see that based upon the discounted cash flow method, Brian should purchase Machine B because cash savings would be $21,360 as compared to Machine A's savings of only $8,050. When time value of money is taken into consideration, decisions should be evaluated much more thoroughly.

TABLE 15-4. *Brian Jones's Purchase Decision*

Year	Savings per Year Machine A	Savings per Year Machine B	Present Value of $1	Machine A	Machine B
1	50,000	60,000	0.870	43,500	52,200
2	50,000	60,000	.756	37,800	45,360
3	50,000	60,000	.658	32,900	39,480
4	50,000	60,000	.572	28,600	34,320
5	50,000		.497	24,850	
6	50,000		.432	21,600	
7	50,000		.376	18,800	
				208,050	171,360
			Less cost of equipment	200,000	150,000
			Net discounted cash flow	8,050	21,360
			Difference in cash flow	$13,310	

Note: Machine A costs $200,000; Machine B costs $150,000.

Make/Buy Decisions

make/buy planning decision

When a **make/buy planning decision** is considered by a manager, he or she is concerned with evaluating the benefits of making the product *in-house* or going *outside* to another manufacturer. A prime factor that a manager should consider relates to whether the manufacturing costs in-house are lower than the cost to go outside. But this is not the only factor to consider. The manager must also ask whether the space that will be used to manufacture the product in-house could be used more advantageously. If the space could be used more effectively (make more money), through manufacturing other products, the decision might be made to produce the product outside the firm.

Purchase/Lease Decisions

purchase/lease decision

Another financial alternative that many business people are considering is whether to purchase or lease equipment. Such a decision is called a **purchase/lease decision**. Realistically, at times it is better to purchase and at other times it becomes more advantageous to lease. The answer may again be derived through evaluating the time value of money. If a manager were to purchase the equipment, such things as interest expense, depreciation, and salvage value must be evaluated to come up with a net discounted cash flow value. However, if a firm were to lease the equipment, only the lease payment could be used with regard to tax savings in computing a net discounted cash flow value. Under the leasing arrangement, there is no salvage value and although leasing may be attractive at times, the decision should certainly be evaluated as to which decision would be best for the firm.

Linear Programming

linear programming

With **linear programming**, we are attempting to allocate limited resources among competing demands in an optimum way. As may be seen in Table 15-5, linear programming is used for a variety of reasons in industry, but its use depends on the nature of the needs of the firm. Summarizing the uses presented in Table 15-5, and other uses, linear programming has been used effectively in industry to solve these and other types of problems:

- Locations and closures of plants, warehouses, and retail stores
- Product scheduling
- Distribution planning between factory and warehouse
- Product mix problems
- Optimizing use of transportation facilities
- Strategic and tactical planning
- Blending problems

Linear programming does have many uses in the business world. There are two basic areas that the manager must be able to define: the *objective*

TABLE 15-5. *Uses of Linear Programming*

Company	Uses
Bendix Corporation	Minimizing transportation costs for truck fleet Production scheduling
Glidden Division, SCM Corporation	Product formulation Analysis of competitors' products Capacity planning (long range)
Inland Steel Company	Evaluating energy impact of facility and policy decisions Allocating products to certain production facilities
Kaiser Steel Corporation	Proportioning of raw materials to satisfy quantitative constraints
Kellogg Company	Analyzing production capacity for budgets Long-range production planning Minimizing transportation costs for finished products
Kimberly-Clark	Distribution planning between multiple production locations New plant location-distribution cost comparison
Lear Siegler Inc.	Work-flow Transportation analysis
Oscar Mayer & Co.	Product formulation Identifying new plant locations Design of distribution transportation systems
Procter & Gamble Company	Allocations of material to suppliers and to manufacturing plants Warehouse and plant site selection Production planning
3M Company	Selection of manufacturing facility for new product

objective function

and *constraint* functions. The **objective function** is what the decision maker is attempting to maximize or minimize. For instance, in helping Barry Williams, the production manager for Ampex Corporation, we are attempting to determine the optimum number of tables and chairs to manufacture in order to maximize profits. We first must determine the contribution to profit of both items. Barry has determined that chairs will contribute \$5 (selling price of \$11 minus cost of \$6) and tables will contribute \$7 (selling price of \$17 minus cost of \$10). The objective function would be stated as:

$$\text{Maximize} = \$5\,(\text{chair}) + \$7\,(\text{table}).$$

constraint functions

Once the objective function has been identified, the manager must next determine what restrictions or **constraint functions** he or she will have. If the resources of personnel, material, and equipment were unlimited, there would be no need for linear programming. But since this is unlikely, managers must know what restrictions are placed on their ability to make decisions. For instance, Barry knows that there will be only sixty hours available in the machine shop to work on either tables or chairs. Also, there are only forty-eight hours available in the paint shop. If it takes four hours to machine a chair and two hours to machine a table and two hours to paint a chair and four hours to paint a table, we come up with the following constraint equations for Barry:

$$4\,(\text{chair}) + 2\,(\text{table}) \leq 60 \text{ (machine shop constraint).}$$

$$2\,(\text{chair}) + 4\,(\text{table}) \leq 48 \text{ (paint shop constraint).}$$

One should notice the inequality signs ($\leq$) in both equations. We are merely stating that the maximum amount of time in either the machine or paint shop does not have to be used. The inequality could also go the other direction ($\geq$), which means that a minimum amount of time must be used. Once the objective and constraint functions have been identified, the manager may turn the problem over to the analyst.

We will next use the graphical solution to linear programming to determine the optimum number of tables and chairs that Barry should produce. We have plotted the two constraints in Figure 15-4. Since the inequality signs

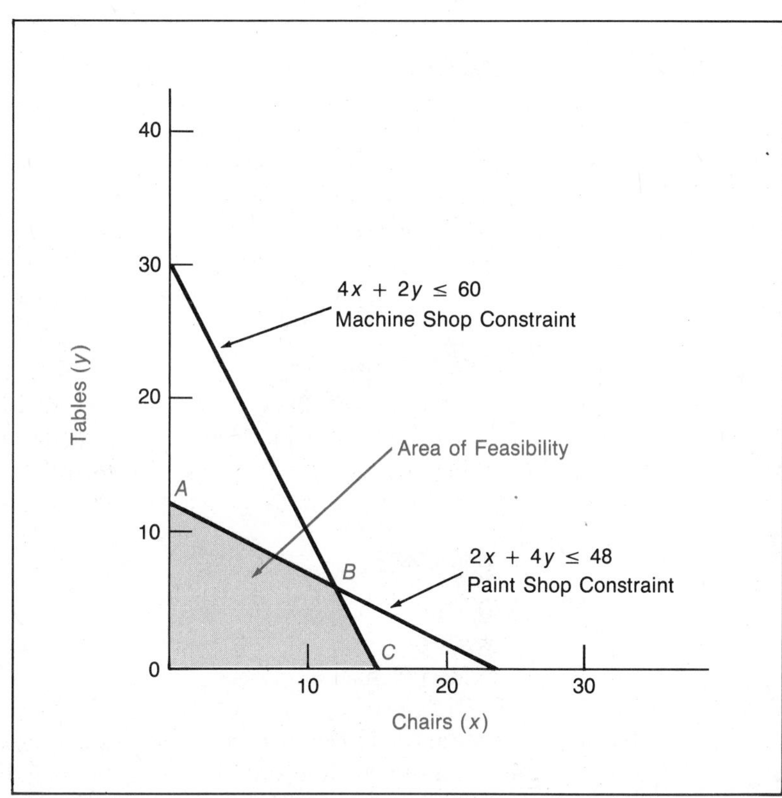

FIGURE 15-4

Linear Programming Example

are less than or equal to ($\leq$), our area of feasibility, where we could have a potential solution, is the shaded area. A characteristic of linear programming is that optimum solutions can occur only at extreme points. We have three in this problem (Points A, B, and C). Next, we must read from the graph to determine the solution points. They would be:

Point A: 0 chairs, 12 tables
Point B: 12 chairs, 6 tables
Point C: 15 chairs, 0 tables

When these values are substituted into the objective function, we can see that if we wish to maximize profits, six tables and twelve chairs should be produced, and a maximum profit of $102 will be achieved.

Point A: $0(5) + 12(7) = \$\ 84$
Point B: $12(5) + 6(7) = \$102$
Point C: $15(5) + 0(7) = \$\ 75$

In using linear programming, the manager's job is to develop the constraint and objective functions. The manager is the individual who is closest to the problem and best capable of providing this information. The actual mechanics of linear programming are often performed with the assistance of a computer.

Forecasting

An effective business planner must be capable of estimating with a certain degree of accuracy what will occur in the future. Naturally, we can never be completely correct in projecting the future, but a high *batting average* in accomplishing this task often separates the successful from the less successful manager. In this section, we concentrate on some of the forecasting techniques that have proved beneficial to business planners.

Terminology

A general overview of terminology used in forecasting will first be presented and is illustrated in Figure 15-5. An attempt to estimate the demand for a firm's product is referred to as **demand forecasting**. The four basic components to consider in demand forecasting are the following:

demand forecasting

- long-term trend
- cyclical
- seasonal
- random demand

trend

As you can see in Figure 15-5, the **trend** line projects the long-run estimate of the demand for the product being evaluated. Long-run projections are

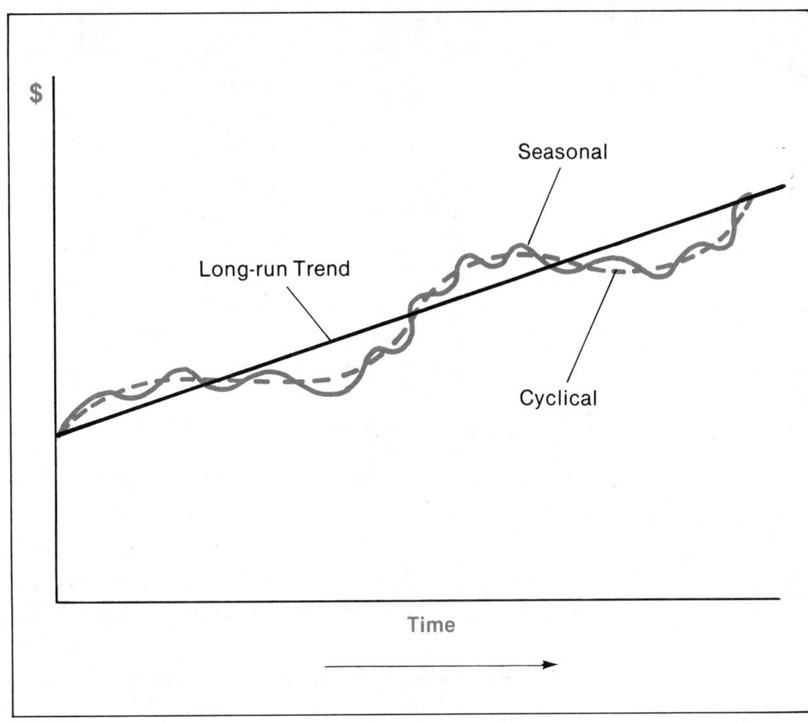

FIGURE 15-5
Forecasting

Note: Random patterns are not shown because we do not know when they will occur.

typically said to be five years or more into the future. In this instance, it shows that the long-run demand for this product is increasing.

cyclical

But a business planner needs more than just a long-run trend. **Cyclical** variation occurs around the trend line. A busiess recession may cause sales to go down or, on the other hand, demand may be above the trend line in a recovery period. A common view of cyclical variations is greater than one year but less than five, with the typical cyclical span being three years. Cyclical consideration is important because of the severe peaks and valleys associated with the demand for some products. Even though there is a trend for increased demand for the product, a firm may currently be in a valley in the business cycle, which may affect production, inventory, and labor requirements.

seasonal

A business person often needs to evaluate demand patterns in a shorter time frame than cyclical. This is known as **seasonal** demand, and the forecasted period is typically thought to be twelve months or less. During a twelve-month period the demand for many products fluctuates drastically. Electric shaver sales are concentrated heavily in the holiday seasons; swim suits are sold in the spring. Knowledge of these seasonal demand patterns is quite important to the business planner because of production, inventory, and labor requirements.

random Finally, **random** demand patterns are the ones that accelerate the early retirement of many business planners. With random demand there is no pattern. By definition, it occurs for reasons that the business manager cannot anticipate, even with the most sophisticated forecasting techniques.

With this brief discussion of business forecasting completed, it is now time to consider some specific tools available to the business forecaster. It should be remembered that forecasting tools are especially needed in the factory environment. For instance, it is important to forecast sales adequately because production forecasts, labor forecasts, material forecasts, and cash forecasts depend on the projection of sales. The following discussion should not be considered all encompassing but is presented to give the students of management an appreciation of some of the tools that are available.

Moving Averages

moving averages A simple technique for smoothing the effects of random variation is through the use of **moving averages**. Since we do not want to make a business decision based on a random occurrence that may never again happen, business people have attempted to remove this one-time occurrence through moving averages. As may be seen in Table 15-6, the different time periods are averaged to get both a three-month moving average and a five-month moving average. The greater the number of months that are averaged, the less effect the random variations will have on the demand estimation. To compute a three-month moving average, periods 1, 2, and 3 are averaged. This provides the first figure for the three-month moving average. To get the next month's estimate, the first month is dropped and the fourth month is added and again averaged. Through the use of moving averages, the effects of random variation are reduced, and the demand estimate is smoothed.

TABLE 15-6. *Moving Average Example*

Quarter	Actual Demand	Three-Quarter Moving Average	Five-Quarter Moving Average
Q 1	3000	—	—
Q 2	2350	2767	—
Q 3	2950	2758	3075
Q 4	2975	3342	3025
Q 1	4100	3275	3065
Q 2	2750	3133	3548
Q 3	2550	2533	2980
Q 4	2300	2683	2915
Q 1	3200	3092	3035
Q 2	3775	3442	—
Q 3	3350	—	—

Exponential Smoothing

exponential smoothing

One of the major difficulties associated with moving averages is that a large amount of historical data must be used. When the **exponential smoothing** technique is applied, the manager needs only three types of data:

- the forecast from the previous period
- the actual demand that resulted from this forecasted period
- a smoothing constant

While the first two pieces of data are relatively easy to obtain, determining the smoothing constant requires that the manager personally identify what he or she feels is a good response rate. This smoothing constant depends to a large extent on the past demand for the product. If it has been relatively stable, the smoothing constant will likely be small. However, if the product is experiencing rapid growth, the manager may wish to have a large smoothing constant to ensure that the firm is keeping up with the actual demand.

Exponential smoothing may be quite helpful to Lisa Thompson and Molly Holmes as they try to determine how much to increase production. Let us envision how exponential smoothing might be helpful through considering two entirely different products; one has a stable demand (much like the Super X product) and the other has experienced a rapidly increasing demand. A low smoothing constant (perhaps 0.05) might be chosen for the stable product and a high smoothing constraint (0.50) for the rapid-growth product. Let us assume that in both instances the previous forecast was 1,000 units and actual demand was 2,000 units. Two entirely different projections for future demand result, as may be seen below:

$$\text{New forecast} = \text{Past forecast} + \text{Smoothing constant}(\text{Actual demand} - \text{Past forecast})$$

$$\text{New forecast (Stable product)} = 1{,}000 + 0.05\,(2{,}000 - 1{,}000) = \underline{\underline{1{,}050}}\ \text{units of forecasted demand}$$

$$\text{New forecast (Rapid growth product)} = 1{,}000 + 0.5\,(2{,}000 - 1{,}000) = \underline{\underline{1{,}500}}\ \text{units of forecasted demand}$$

Both Lisa and Barry can use exponential smoothing to maintain a balance in planning activities. If the product has been relatively stable in demand, there is no reason to believe that a rapid surge in sales will occur through other than perhaps random fluctuation. However, when a high smoothing constant is chosen, the manager realizes that demand shifts rapidly and requires swift action in order for the business to be competitive. The identification of the proper smoothing constant represents the major difficulty in working exponential smoothing problems.

Regression Analysis

With the increased use of high-speed computers and sophisticated statistical packages, the manager has at his or her disposal a useful tool for forecasting—regression analysis. Its use has obtained respectability in accomplishing many forecasting functions ranging from estimating product demand to development of profiles of successful versus less successful employees within a particular firm.[1]

regression analysis

Regression analysis is used to predict one item (known as the dependent variable) through knowledge of other item(s). Your task as a manager would involve first determining what you would like to predict and then identifying the independent variables to determine if they actually are capable of predicting a particular outcome. Suppose, for instance, a manager would like to determine the relationship that advertising and size of the sales force has upon company sales. The basic equation that would develop is as follows:

$$\underset{\text{(dependent variable)}}{Y\text{ (company sales)}} = \underset{\text{(independent variable(s))}}{\text{Advertising } (X_1) + \text{ sales force size } (X_2)}$$

If there does exist a relationship the equation that might result is:

$$Y = 2\,(X_1) + 4\,(X_2).$$

Interpreted, the manager would determine that for each added dollar spent on adding to the sales force, total sales would increase by four dollars. However, for every dollar spent on advertising, total sales would increase by only two dollars. The manager might use this model to assist in developing a marketing plan to achieve the greatest company sales. Naturally, the manager must determine the reliability of the model, but we do not wish to take away from the enjoyment of a statistics class to learn the detailed mechanics associated with regression analysis.

TABLE 15-7. *Auto Sales*

Cars Sold	Year
400	1960
600	1961
1550	1962
1500	1963
1500	1964
2400	1965
3100	1966
2600	1967
2900	1968
3800	1969
4500	1970
4000	1971
4900	1972

Time Series Analysis

time series analysis

Another approach to the use of regression is **time series analysis**. Here the same mathematical approach is used except that the independent variable is expressed in units of time. For instance, we might like to project the number of car sales in a particular district for the coming year. In order to accomplish this projection, we would need the car sales for previous years as shown in Table 15-7. Given these data, the prudent manager turns the work over to the analyst, and the following equation is given to the manager:

$$Y\text{ (auto sales)} = -21{,}230 + 361\text{ (year)}$$

substituting 1973 into the equation we have:

$$Y = -21{,}230 + 361\,(73) = 4{,}762$$

Thus, the estimated number of cars that will be sold in this district for the coming year is 4,762. The −21,230 represents a constant that results from the calculation of the regression equation. As with the previous illustration, the manager must study the accompanying statistics to determine the reliability of the model. But it provides the manager with a valuable tool for planning and decision making.

Summary

Only a few years ago, production and operations management concentrated primarily on the factory environment. Today, production and operations management takes on a much broader application. Most of the quantitative techniques apply to both factory and service industries. There are, however, several concepts that at one time were used primarily in the manufacturing environment. Site selection, plant layout, work methods, operations charts, worker machine charts, principles of motion economy, and labor measurement are some examples of traditional techniques.

Many companies are making extensive use of various quantitative tools. One of the most valuable tools for a business planner is financial modeling. Two of the most commonly used financial models are break-even analysis and discounted cash flow analysis. Break-even analysis helps determine the amount of a particular product that must be sold if the firm is to generate enough revenue to cover costs. With discounted cash flow analysis, the time value of money becomes important. A dollar earned today does not have the same value as a dollar that will be earned in the future. Linear programming is used as a planning tool to assist management in allocating limited resources among competing demands in an optimum way.

An effective business planner must be capable of estimating with a certain degree of accuracy what will occur in the future. The basic components that should be understood in demand forecasting are long-term trend, cyclical demand, seasonal demand, and random demand. Some of the quantitative tools that are available to forecast demand include moving averages, exponential smoothing, regression analysis, and time series analysis. These forecasting tools will not provide the manager with all the answers concerning the future, but they do assist the manager in planning and decision making.

Review Questions

1. **Why do we currently refer to production and operations management as opposed to merely production? What changes in attitudes have brought this about?**
2. **What are the traditional production management concepts and techniques?**
3. **Distinguish by definition and an example among moving averages, exponential smoothing, times series analysis, and regression analysis. What is the purpose of each?**
4. **According to the text, what should a manager know when considering using each of the various quantitative techniques?**

5. Why is the time value of money so important to a manager?
6. Define:
   a. Break-even analysis
   b. Fixed costs
   c. Variable cost
   d. Discounted cash flow

Exercises

1. How might the discounted cash flow technique be used in the following instances?
   a. Purchase of a major league ball player
   b. Purchase of a fleet of trucks
   c. Decision by you to purchase or lease your business automobile
   d. A decision as to whether to go to college or go to work after completing high school
2. Think of five different types of businesses. How could the following quantitative planning techniques be useful in their operations?
   a. Moving averages
   b. Exponential smoothing
   c. Time series analysis
   d. Regression analysis

Case Study

Exponential Smoothing

Larry Smiler is the production manager for a firm that manufactures high-quality watches. His job is to maintain a smooth flow of production of these watches. In order to determine what levels of output to produce, Barry relies heavily on sales forecasts. If he produces too many watches, inventory will increase, and this can be extremely costly to a company in the quality watch business. Should inventory become excessive, workers may have to be laid off or terminated. On the other hand, if too few watches are produced, the sales force gets extremely unhappy since orders cannot be filled. Barry is aware of exponential smoothing and decides to use it to assist him in estimating next month's demand. He realizes that last month's sales forecast was for 10,000 watches, but actual demand for watches during the month was 12,000. Barry also realizes that demand changes rapidly so he decides to use a 0.5 smoothing constant.

QUESTIONS

1. What is the forecasted demand for next month?
2. If demand were relatively constant, what size smoothing constant would you recommend that Barry use?

Case Study

Break-Even Analysis

Phyllis Stevens, a junior management major at Midwestern State University, has been elected promotional manager for the Society for the Advancement of Management (SAM), a professional organization of which she is a member. She is thinking of recommending that SAM sell miniature flags of the university to the student body. Students can take these flags to football games and wave them to cheer their team on to victory! (The team is expected to have a winning season.)

Phyllis is aware of break-even analysis so she develops some cost figures for producing the flags. She estimates that the fixed cost for the project will be $200. The flags will be made by members and she estimates that the variable cost to make each flag is $0.50. They will sell them for $1.

QUESTIONS

1. How many flags must the organization sell in order to break even?
2. How many flags must the group sell to make a profit of $100?
3. If Phyllis thinks that the maximum number of flags that the group can sell is 500, do you feel that SAM should take on the project? Discuss.

Notes

1. R. Wayne Mondy and Frank N. Edens, "An Empirical Test of the Decision to Participate Model," *Journal of Management* 2 (1977): 11–16.

References

Adam, N., and Surkis, J. "Comparison of Capacity Planning Techniques in a Job Shop Control System." *Management Science* 23 (May 1977): 1011–1015.

Buffa, Elwood S. *Modern Production/Operations Management.* 6th ed. New York: Wiley, 1980.

Chase, Richard B., and Aquilano, Nicholas J. *Production and Operations Management: A Life Cycle Approach.* Homewood, Ill.: Irwin, 1981.

Clay, M. J. "Evaluating the Production Function." *Journal of Accountancy* 148 (May 1977): 82.

Cummings, L. L. "Needed Research in Production/Operations Management: A Behavioral Perspective." *Academy of Management Review* (July 1977): 500–504.

Green, T. B. "Why Are Organizations Reluctant to Use Management Science/Operations Research? An Empirical Approach." *Interfaces* 7 (August 1976): 59–62.

Harwood, G. G., and Hermanson, R. H. "Lease or Buy Decisions." *Journal of Accountancy* 147 (September 1976): 83–87.

Lebell, D., and Krasner, O. J. "Selecting Environmental Forecasting Techniques from Business Planning Requirements." *Academy of Management Journal 20* (July 1977): 373–383.

"Linear Programming Discovery." *Science* 206, November 30, 1979, p. 1022.

Miller, L. W. "Using Linear Programming to Derive Planning Horizons for a Production Smoothing Problem." *Management Science* 25 (December 1979: 1217–1231.

Morey, R. "Operations Management in Selected Non-manufacturing Organizations." *Academy of Management Journal* 19 (March 1976): 120–124.

Petry, Glenn H. "Effective Use of Capital Budgeting Tools." *Business Horizons* 18 (October 1975): 57–65.

Remick, Carl. "Robots: New Faces on the Production Line." *Management Review* 68 (May 1979): 27.

Robinson, S. M. "Characterization of Stability in Linear Programming." *Operations Research* 25 (May 1977): 435–447.

Schmenner, Roger W. *Production/Operations Management: Concepts and Situations.* Chicago: Science Research Associates, 1981.

Sprague, L. G., and Sprague, C. R. "Management Science?" *Interfaces* 6 (November 1976): 57–62.

Solomon, Eyra, and Pringle, John J. *An Introduction to Financial Management.* Santa Monica, Calif.: Goodyear, 1980.

Thomapoulis, Nick T. *Applied Forecasting Methods.* Englewood Cliffs, N.J.: Prentice-Hall, 1980.

KEY TERMS

simulation
waiting line theory
quality
statistical quality control
variable sampling
attribute sampling
control chart
inventory
ordering costs
carrying costs
ABC method
network
program evaluation and review technique (PERT)
critical path method (CPM)
event
activity
optimistic time
most likely time
pessimistic time
expected time
critical path

LEARNING OBJECTIVES

After completing this chapter you should be able to

1. Describe simulation and waiting line theory and explain how the two may be used in business.
2. Explain quality control and state the usefulness of control charts.
3. Define inventory, state the purposes of inventory, describe the costs involved in inventory, and explain the ABC method of inventory control.
4. Explain network models and describe how PERT can be used in planning and controlling.

16

Simulation, Waiting Line, and Control Techniques

In Chapter 15, our discussion was directed toward gaining an appreciation of some of the quantitative tools that are especially beneficial in planning. But as was previously mentioned, the fact that these tools are discussed as being useful in the planning function should not be thought to mean that they are beneficial only in that area. The same general theme is followed in this chapter. Concepts are presented that have been successful in helping managers solve problems. Simulation and waiting line theory are first discussed. These are followed by a brief presentation of the techniques that have been applied successfully to the control function of management. Included in these topics are inventory control, quality control, and network models (PERT and CPM). Again, their presentation follows the format of presenting the techniques from the standpoint of how managers can use them in their jobs.

SIMULATION

In front of a radarscope in the western United States sits a young officer with his eyes fixed on the scope. He is controlling an air force fighter jet whose target is a Russian bomber flying toward San Francisco. The conversation is progressing in the following manner:

The young controller: "Tango Papa Ol, this is Ringdove. You have a Russian bomber in your 12 o'clock position closing fast. Looks as if its target is San Francisco."

The fighter pilot: "Roger, Ringdove. I have a visual and am going in for the kill. Ringdove, Ringdove, my engine just flamed out. I am bailing out!"

Will San Francisco be destroyed? Will the fighter pilot be saved? These and other types of problems occurred daily to one of the authors when he was an Air Force aircraft controller. The Russian bomber was on the radar screen, but a real bomber was not attacking San Francisco. The pilot who bailed out was merely in another room simulating the problem. The purpose of this exercise was to train the young controller for possible real-life situations. A fighter pilot would hate to have to bail out and lose his plane in order for the controller to be trained. It was much better to simulate the occurrence, representing the real-life situation as much as possible. Businesses, as well as the military, have found simulation a valuable tool to assist in the planning and decision-making process.

simulation

We will define **simulation** as the use of computers to assist in performing experiments on a model of a real system.[1] In Chapter 5, a model was

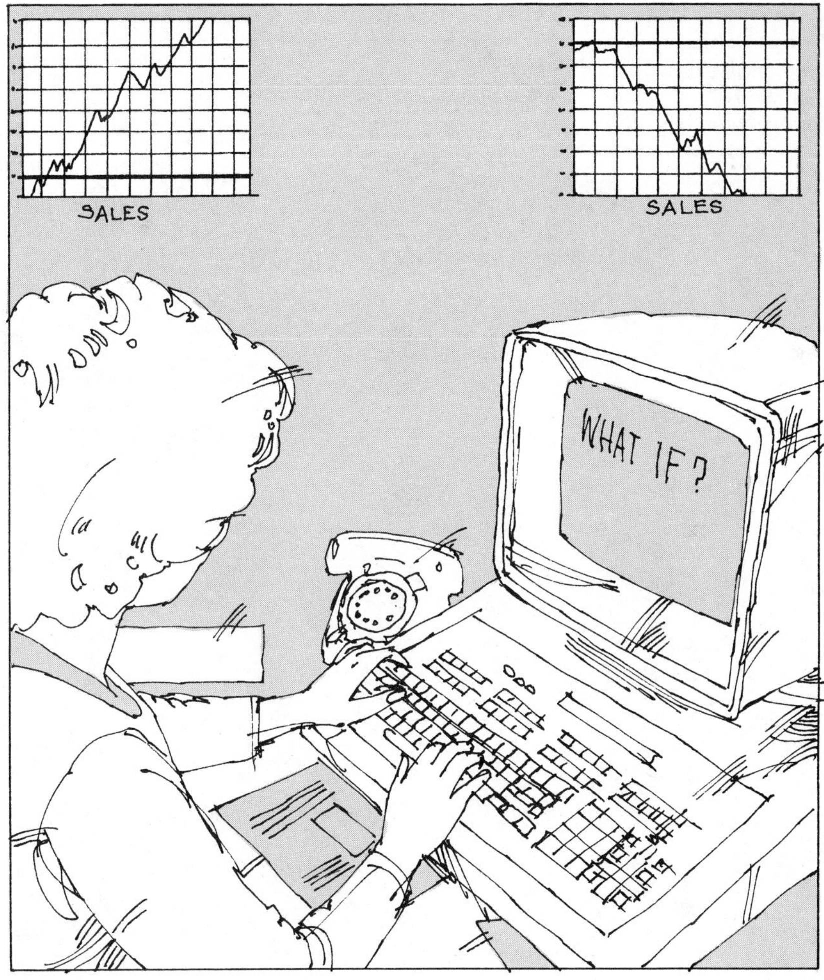

Simulation permits the manager to ask many "what if" questions before having to make the decision in the real world.

defined as an abstraction of the real world. Thus, a simulation model is an attempt to represent a real world situation through mathematical logic in an attempt to predict what will occur in an actual situation. Its uses are many and widespread.

As may be observed in Table 16-1, firms are using simulation for a variety of reasons ranging from "economic analysis of alternate hog cutting methods" by Oscar Mayer & Company to the calculation of locomotive fuel requirements by Southern Railway. In all instances simulation assists the manager by permitting him or her to ask many *what if* questions without having to make the decision in the real world.

A major factor that should be realized is that simulation transcends the boundaries of many of the other quantitative techniques that have been and will be discussed. As such, it is not a separate quantitative tool; rather it is a procedure that has been used effectively in conjunction with other

TABLE 16-1. *Uses of Simulation Techniques*

Company	Primary Uses
Bendix Corporation	Inventory control Production scheduling
Carrier Corporation	Energy modeling
Crown Zellerbach	Inventory control Production planning
Glidden Division, SCM Corporation	Price-profit analysis Production scheduling Capacity analysis system
Inland Container Company	Determine the impact of the number of pugh ladles on hot metal distribution Evaluate productivity effect of additional pollution control equipment
Kaiser Steel Corporation	Hot strip mill production rates under different conditions
Kimberly-Clark	Plant layout Inventory control Process system design
Lear Siegler, Inc.	Projecting results based on assumptions tied to math models to project economic impact on sales volumes, profits, and cash flow
Oscar Mayer & Company	Product layout within an order filling cooler Economic analysis of alternate hog cutting methods Plant design problems
Procter & Gamble Company	Design of manufacturing facilities Design of communication facilities Understanding of chemical processes
The Southland Corporation	Analysis of operations EDP teleprocessing system Distribution center layout Vehicle delivery programs
3M Company	Distribution system Inventory control

mathematical tools such as inventory control, quality control, waiting line theory, and mathematical modeling. When a manager operates in an uncertain environment, simulation may be considered.

Simulation is a quantitative approach that many students of management often shy away from because they believe it is too sophisticated for them to use. They apparently reason that they must know computer programming and how to operate the computer to use simulation. This certainly need not be the case, for many firms have their own in-house programmers capable of interpreting the needs of the user and developing the necessary computer programs.

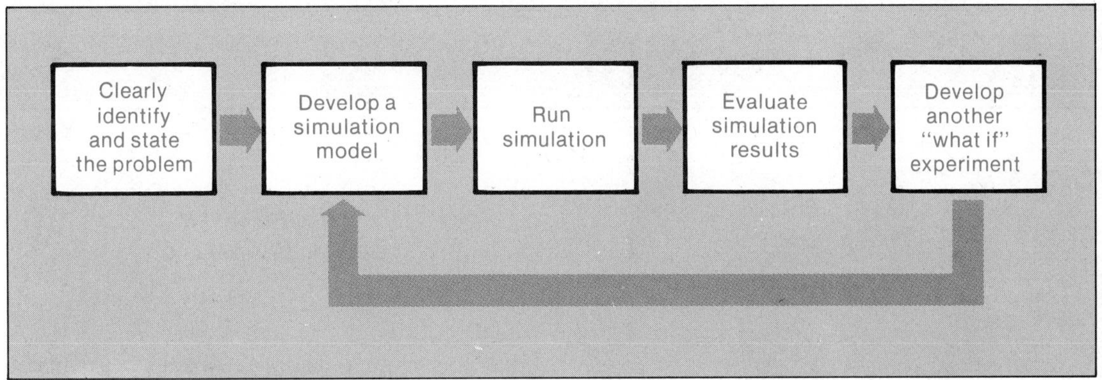

FIGURE 16-1 *Steps in Simulation*

On the other hand, this does not mean that the manager has nothing to do. He or she must be capable of clearly defining the problem that needs solving and identifying the factors that may be associated with the problem. The general steps associated with developing a simulation model are presented in Figure 16-1. Once the problem has been identified, a simulation model is developed and run. The results are analyzed and then if the manager again desires to ask other *what if* questions regarding the problem, they can be asked. The manager is in a position to ask many questions regarding the other factors that could affect the problem.

Assume for a moment that you are employed by Oscar Mayer and you are attempting to determine the optimum manner to cut up a hog to maximize profits. The problem has not been defined, but what are some of the possible factors that could affect obtaining optimum results? Perhaps the manager desires to determine whether to automate a production line or hire additional workers. What happens as the size of the hogs varies? The hog-cutting methods may have to be changed. Through simulation a person is once again able to see that there is more than one way to skin a hog!

Railroads also have found simulation quite beneficial. Have you ever wondered why more trains don't arrive at the same time on a single track? Trains are different lengths and weights; they travel at different speeds and typically must share a common track to get from one place to another. At times there are two or more tracks that the cars could travel, but the majority of the time there is only one. Simulation provides the manager with the ability to recognize the many variables that are involved and ask questions regarding solutions to the problem.

Procter & Gamble Company also utilizes simulation to assist in solving some unusual problems. Gary O. Walla, management science manager for Procter & Gamble Company, provides the following example of how they use simulation.

> Pulp forms the basic raw ingredient for manufacturing paper and can be made in a variety of grades that are dependent on the chemical

• CAREER PROFILE •

JAMES A. SILBAUGH
Vice-President
Geo. A. Hormel & Co.

Hormel

James A. Silbaugh began his career with Hormel after graduating from Carleton, a prestigious liberal arts college, with a B.A. in mathematics and a minor in economics. His employer, Geo. A. Hormel & Company, one of the nation's largest meat processors, has its corporate offices and largest plant in Austin, Minnesota.

Although Silbaugh worked in the plant part-time and during vacations prior to a stint in the U.S. Navy, he started in sales after graduating from college. He feels that sales is an excellent way to get into management and that sales provides a way to learn about the company's lifeblood—its products and its customers. He points out that sales usually means a number of different assignments and physical moves—not exactly the cup of tea for one

processing and the blend of wood species. Procter & Gamble refines pulp from trees and they use simulation to aid in the design of a woodyard, assuring maximum operating efficiency with a minimum of capital investment.

A woodyard serves as a surge area for wood arriving from various sources by unscheduled rail cars and trucks. The wood is in the form of short and long logs and must be stored until used in the pulp mill. Naturally, rail cars require different unloading equipment than trucks and the simulation helps determine the optimum number of unloading stations for both. Additionally, different equipment is needed to handle long logs than short logs for both railcars and trucks. After long logs are unloaded, they are cut into short logs before they can be stored, an operation that requires other special equipment. Finally, the operation of the pulp mill needs a constant feed of a well-controlled blend of wood species to be efficient. Wood must be stockpiled sufficiently to assure a constant feed regardless of the weather, which can bring the tree cutting operations to a standstill for a couple of weeks, or equipment failures in the woodyard. In net, the simulation of the flow of materials through interested in putting down roots early in the game. In his case, it was Texas, Tennessee, Nebraska, Wisconsin, and California before the corporate offices in Minnesota. During this eighteen-year span, he held all of the sales positions in the company's grocery products division from sales trainee to national sales manager. These assignments led to the position of vice-president of that division with responsibilities for production, marketing, sales, and distribution.

He points out that, whereas at one time many heads of corporations had legal or financial background, the trend has changed, and today people with marketing backgrounds are well represented at the top. The challenge in sales and marketing is to develop strong market shares for the company's products, while at the same time keeping an eye on the bottom line by maximizing return on investment. Hormel's corporate mission says in part that it will be a leader in the food field and, of course, that means many things, including strong market shares, quality products, and a respectable return on the stockholders' investment.

Silbaugh says that one of the most difficult periods was during price controls when Hormel selling prices were controlled by the Wage Price Council, but raw agricultural commodities were allowed to fluctuate. This meant that the price of livestock was not controlled, but the prices Hormel received for its products were controlled. This situation taxed the talents of management, but a dedication to the challenge enabled Hormel to emerge from this period stronger than ever.

Silbaugh offers the following advice to people interested in a management career: "Consider sales as an entry-level position because of the opportunity to learn about a company's products, customers, strategy, and philosophy. Establish some personal goals that are consistent with those of the corporation. Pursue these goals diligently with periodic measurement of progress." The rewards can be exciting, not only from the satisfaction of accomplishment, but financially as well. Public companies publish data on executive compensation. You will find that six-figure salaries are not uncommon for managers who can deliver.

the woodyard helps size equipment and stockpiles of logs to assure constant availability of the proper wood species for input to the pulp mill.

Examples of how simulation has been used effectively in business are extensive. Its use is expected to receive additional attention by managers in the future. As the risk of making a particular decision increases, managers will need to evaluate many options prior to making a commitment to allocate resources. Simulation provides an excellent tool for evaluating alternatives and finding solutions to problems.

WAITING LINE/QUEUING THEORY

Friday is payday and you want to get to the bank to cash your check in time to do some shopping before the stores close. You know the main bank is closed, but the one-window, drive-in bank is still open. As you pull into the drive-in bank lane, your heart sinks; there are ten cars ahead of you and the line does not appear to be moving very fast. You may not realize it but you have now confronted a waiting line/queuing theory problem.

waiting line theory

A **waiting line theory** situation occurs when arrivals at a service facility want similar service. In the bank illustration, the service facility was the bank's drive-in window, and the people who want service are all the car drivers who want banking service. The problem that exists is that all customers do not require the same type of service (some may want merely to cash a check and others want to deposit an entire week's receipts) and customers do not arrive at regular intervals (at times it has appeared that everyone arrives at once and you are a second too late). The solution of a waiting line problem via simulation involves a trade-off or balance of costs. If the line is constantly too long, some customers may get angry and change banks; this results in lower deposits and lost revenue for the bank. But there is another cost that must be considered. It also costs to add another drive-in window and pay the salary of another teller. From a managerial standpoint, waiting line theory assists the manager in determining if it is worth the additional investment to add the new drive-in window.

Most Important Reasons for Success and Effectiveness as a Manager

- **Ability to make decisions**
- **Able to delegate responsibility to subordinates**
- **Capable of creating and maintaining a sense of direction**
- **100 percent sold on the free enterprise system**
- **Able to be a good listener when necessary**
- **A good judge of people**
- **Approach each project enthusiastically**

WARREN E. McCAIN, Chairman of the Board, Albertson's, Incorporated

Another illustration of a waiting line problem that virtually everyone has seen relates to the number of checkout counters at a grocery store. Just how many should be kept open at a given time? Customers may get quite angry if they have to wait an excessive amount of time to be checked out. But it also costs the store if checkers are behind the cash registers with nothing to do. Again, a balance must be achieved. When the store was built, a waiting line problem should also have been considered. The store developer must consider how many checkout counters to install initially. Every checkout counter costs money because store space is valuable. However, if insufficient counters are included, lost revenue may result.

Businesses have found that waiting line or queuing theory can assist in the solution of a variety of problems. As may be seen in Table 16-2, the uses

TABLE 16-2. *Uses of Waiting Line/Queuing Theory*

Company	Uses
Bendix Corporation	Maintenance Skilled trades study
Kimberly-Clark	Process systems layout Process design capacities of component units
Southern Railroads	Shop assembly line procedures Scheduling locomotive maintenance
Oscar Mayer & Company	Production line balancing Plant design problems Production scheduling
The Southland Corporation	EDP system
Glidden Division, SCM Corporation	Queuing theory developing industrial engineering standards Line balancing developing industrial engineering standards
Proctor & Gamble Company	Design of communication facilities Design of manufacturing facilities
Crown Zellerbach	Maintenance evaluation
Kaiser Steel Corporation	Hot Metal Delivery System Study

are quite widespread but differ depending on the specific needs of the firm. A major petroleum firm uses queuing theory to determine if they need to construct additional docking facilities. A ship delayed in unloading costs the firm a certain amount per day. The ship cannot make money for the firm if it is not transporting petroleum. But constructing additional docks is also expensive. Again, a balance must be achieved.

The mathematics of waiting line problems is often quite complicated. But as with the other quantitative tools, this should not keep the manager from using the approach. He or she must first recognize that queuing theory is appropriate to solve the problems and be able to identify the costs that are involved in the balancing process. At this point the quantitative expert may again be brought in to accomplish the mathematical manipulation.

QUALITY CONTROL

Quality is likely to be in the vocabulary of the majority of Americans. When a buyer states that he got a "lemon," the immediate impression is that the product purchased was of inferior quality. As was mentioned in Chapter 14, quality of a product is the combination of several factors such as form, dimension, composition, and color. For a particular product, all of these factors may have to be considered with regard to quality.

quality

But what exactly is meant when the term *quality* is mentioned? **Quality** is the degree of conformity to a certain predetermined standard. Standards result ultimately from the establishment of objectives. If the company has an objective of gaining a reputation for manufacturing a high-quality product, standards will have to be high. In order to meet these high standards, there would have to be a very rigid quality control program. On the other hand, another firm may not have as its objective such a high quality product. Increased quality generally results in higher prices. Therefore, some firms may target their appeal to a market that desires lower prices and will accept lower quality. Certain standards remain, but they are not as rigid as with the high-quality product.

There are numerous ways to maintain quality of a product. A company could make the decision to have a 100 percent inspection of all items manufactured, but even with a total inspection program, some defects will not be discovered. When you insert the human element into a quality control environment, mistakes will occasionally be made. Some items that are good may be rejected and other items that are bad will be accepted.

In many instances it is impossible to have a 100 percent inspection. For instance, if the standard for the life of a light bulb were 200 hours, you would have to burn the light for the assigned number of hours to determine if it met standards. Naturally, you would have no product to sell in this situation. Tire manufacturing companies set standards for their tires in order that they will be capable of being driven a certain number of miles. If each tire were placed on a machine and run the assigned number of miles to determine if they can meet standards, there would be no product to market. In still other instances, the cost to inspect each item to determine if they conform to standard is prohibitive. If each nail in a keg were inspected separately, the cost to inspect might be higher than the price of the nails.

statistical quality control

The technique that is available to overcome the above deficiencies is known as **statistical quality control**. In statistical quality control, a portion of the total number of items is inspected. For instance, five out of one hundred items may be selected and an estimate made as to the characteristics of the other ninety-five. Naturally, some degree of error exists. For instance, if out of one hundred items only five are defective (this amount of error may be perfectly acceptable), it is conceivable that all five defectives might be selected, and the entire lot would be rejected. On the other hand, there might be only five good parts out of the one hundred parts manufactured. These five good parts might be the ones drawn and the batch would be accepted. With sampling there is risk, but the benefits of sampling are far superior to other procedures in many instances.

There are two basic types of sampling plans: sampling by variables and sampling by attributes. Both are appropriate for use but under different circumstances.

Sampling by Variables

variable sampling

A plan developed for **variable sampling** consists of determining how closely an item conforms to an established standard. In essence, degrees of goodness and degrees of badness are permitted. For instance, a stereo speaker is designed to project a certain tone quality. All speakers will not project precisely the same tone quality. Some speakers will have quality that is above the established standard, and some will have tone quality that is below standard. This does not necessarily mean that the speaker will be rejected. Only when the quality is outside a certain established limit will it be rejected.

Sampling by Attributes

attribute sampling

With sampling by variables, degrees of conformity are considered; with **attribute sampling**, the item is either acceptable or unacceptable. The product is either good or bad; there are no degrees of conformity to consider. For instance, if a keypunch operator makes only one off-punch in a general purpose computer card, that card is rejected; it is not 99 percent correct; it is considered incorrect.

Control Charts

control chart

A procedure that measures the process during actual operations is referred to as a **control chart**. It is used with both variable and attribute sampling, although the statistical procedure for developing the charts is different. In both instances, the standard is determined (see Figure 16-2). A variable sampling plan in the manufacture of tire treads might have standards that test thickness, weight, length, and width. The company creates a desired level of acceptability through the standards. In the example of the keypunch operator, a certain percentage of defects would constitute the standard.

Once the standard has been established the manager must determine the amount of deviation that will be acceptable. The amount of deviation that will be acceptable above the standard is referred to as the *upper control limit* (UCL) and the amount of deviation below the standard is referred to as the

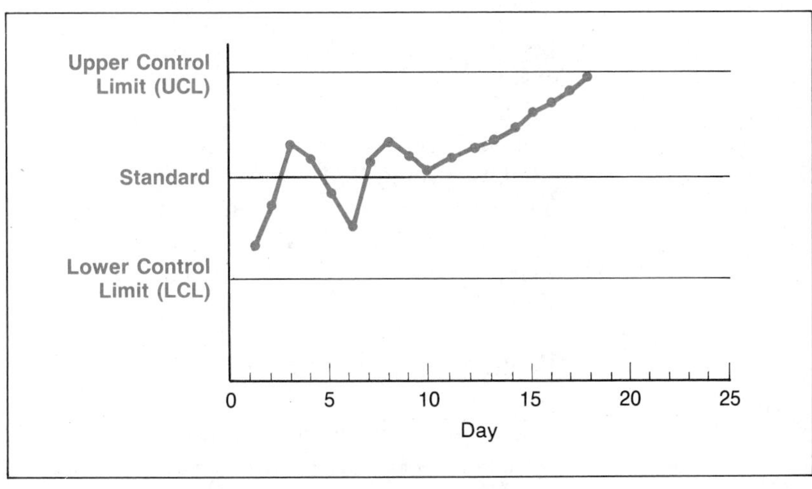

FIGURE 16-2
Example of Control Chart

lower control limit (LCL). If a product that is being evaluated falls within the two extremes between the UCL and the LCL, it will be accepted. If it falls outside the limit, it will be rejected. Although the statistics involved in the development of control charts are beyond the scope of this text, the concept is nevertheless sound.

Another benefit that accrues through the use of control charts is that potential problems may be recognized prior to their actual occurrence. As may be seen in Figure 16-2, from day 10 until day 17 the quality of a product is progressively getting worse. Although still within the limits of acceptability, if the problem is not corrected, the process may very shortly go above the upper control limit. When a manager sees this pattern developing, he or she is in a position to take corrective action.

What a Manager Should Know about Quality

Through an understanding of the objectives of the firm, a manager establishes standards and levels of quality that are in line with these goals. He or she realizes that as quality increases, costs go up. Quality represents a cost! There is an optimum level of quality for each product consistent with maximizing profits. The manager, working in conjunction with statistical and accounting personnel, will be able to develop a plan that is consistent with attaining these goals. The primary task of a manager at upper levels is determining the quality level that is appropriate. A lower-level supervisor monitors the quality on a day-to-day basis to ensure that the stated level of quality is being maintained.

INVENTORY CONTROL

inventory

Inventory refers to the goods or materials that are available for use by a business. Our exposure to inventory occurs almost daily. You hear that a car dealer has excessive inventory and they will offer you a special deal to buy a car. A furniture dealer provides you with a similar offer. While there may be a bit of sales promotion in these offerings, inventory does represent a cost that must be controlled. A product in inventory constitutes an idle but valuable resource. Suppose that the car dealer mentioned above keeps a million dollars in extra inventory for one year. At a 10 percent interest rate, $100,000 would be lost because items in inventory do not draw interest. Much of the resources of some major companies are in inventory, yet failure to control inventories can mean the difference between a profit or a loss to a firm.

Purposes of Inventory

One of the major purposes of inventory is that it permits independence of operations between two activities. For instance, if Machine A makes a product that will be used in a later stage by Machine B and Machine A breaks down, Machine B will have to cease operation unless inventory of the product has been previously built up.

Inventories also provide for continuous operations when demand for the product is not consistent. Electric razors are sold primarily during the Christmas holiday season, but a manufacturer of electric razors typically keeps production going through the entire year. Stability is assured in that a skilled work force can be maintained and equipment usage can be kept at an optimal level.

Another purpose of inventory is to be capable of filling orders when they are received, thereby maintaining customer satisfaction. If orders arrived on a constant basis, there would be no need to maintain inventory. But if five orders come in this month and a hundred are processed the next month, a company might be hard pressed to fill the hundred requests unless an inventory had been maintained.

Costs Involved

ordering costs
carrying costs

As with several of the quantitative techniques, inventory control involves a balancing of two general types of costs: ordering costs and carrying costs. **Ordering costs** relate to the clerical expenses associated with preparing the order. **Carrying costs** include all of the expenses that would be asso-

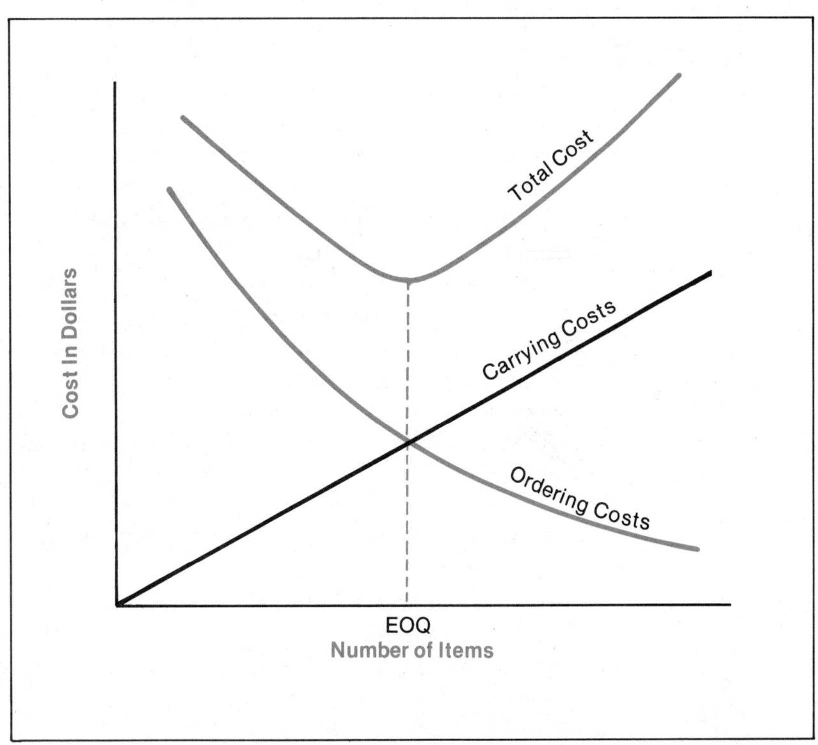

FIGURE 16-3

Economic Order Quantity Illustration

ciated with maintaining the product before it is sold or used. Taxes, insurance, interest on capital invested, storage, electricity, and spoilage are some of the items associated with carrying costs. The purchase cost is the price of the product multiplied by the number of items ordered.

Thus, the total cost associated with a particular order follows the following general formula:

$$\text{Total cost} = \text{Ordering cost} + \text{carrying cost} + \text{purchase cost.}$$

It is the task of the manager to purchase in amounts that will minimize total cost (economic order quantity, EOQ). You realize that if you order less frequently, ordering costs will go down but carrying costs go up. On the other hand, if you submit frequent orders, ordering costs go up but carrying costs are reduced. This balancing process is graphically presented in Figure 16-3. The optimum number of items to order at any one time is at the lowest point on the total cost curve. The lowest point would be where carrying costs and ordering costs intersect.

In order to determine the EOQ, calculus is used in the development of the mathematical model. Again, the manager does not have to be a quantitative wizard to determine EOQ. A manager, however, must be capable of identifying two primary costs: carrying (C) and ordering (O). Through the power of calculus, an EOQ formula is then determined from the total cost equation. The basic equation for EOQ is presented below:

$$\text{EOQ} = \sqrt{\frac{2\begin{pmatrix}\text{ordering}\\ \text{cost}\end{pmatrix}\begin{pmatrix}\text{annual}\\ \text{demand}\end{pmatrix}}{\text{carrying costs}}} = \sqrt{\frac{2(O) \times (D)}{C}}.$$

If we assume that annual demand is 1,000 units, carrying cost is \$2 per unit and ordering cost is \$4, we will determine that optimum number to order is 63.25, or 63 when rounded to the nearest unit. We cannot choose another order quantity that would lower the total cost.

It should be remembered that the model described above is one of the simplest to develop. The sophistication level of the model depends on the actual need of the company and the demands of the environment. The manager must be capable of realizing when inventory control procedures may be useful and must identify what costs may be associated with the problem. Then specialists such as accountants and mathematicians are called upon to assist in the development of the model. The manager provides the guidelines and ensures that necessary output is received.

The ABC Method of Inventory Control

There are times when it is impractical to monitor every item that is in inventory with the same degree of intensity. A procedure that permits the manager to determine which items should be under close scrutiny relates to the ABC

ABC method method. With the **ABC method**, inventories are classified into three groups according to cost.

- A Category—Small number of items but large dollar value
- B Category—Moderate number of items and cost
- C Category—Large number of items but low dollar value

Through the ABC classification, a manager is able to develop a sophisticated system to monitor the Category A items. Items in the category might include automobiles, machinery, and tractors. Category B items would have a less sophisticated inventory control system. Category C items might not even be controlled if the cost associated with monitoring the items would be prohibitive, such as pencils and paper. Through the ABC method, a manager is capable of monitoring inventory in an optimum manner.

NETWORK MODELS

The number of separate tasks that must be accomplished to build a skyscraper or a dam across a river are almost impossible to conceive for the average person. We are often fascinated at how the construction manager in charge of a project of this magnitude is able to coordinate all the tasks and arrive at a finished product. When the project is nonrecurrent, large, complex, and involves multiple organizations, the manager needs a tool that will assist in coordinating this complicated **network** of interdependencies. He or she needs to be able to think through the project in its entirety and see where resources can be shifted or rescheduled to ensure that the project is completed within the time and cost constraints.

network

The primary techniques available to accomplish the above mentioned tasks are **program evaluation and review technique** (PERT) and **critical path method** (CPM). PERT was developed to assist in the rapid development of the Polaris submarine program. During approximately the same time period (1957–1958), researchers for E. I. DuPont de Nemours and Company and computer specialists from what was the Remington Rand's Univac division combined their talents to develop a method to schedule and control all activities involved in constructing chemical plants. The result of their effort was a network model termed *critical path method.*

program evaluation and review technique
critical path method

Both PERT and CPM have received widespread acceptance since their beginning in 1957–1959. The manner in which some firms have used the techniques may be seen in Table 16-3. As may be seen, their use primarily involves construction projects, but some firms such as 3M Compay even use the technique to assist in the development of new products. Firms that do major construction work for the government are required by contract to use PERT.

TABLE 16-3. *Uses of PERT or CPM*

Company	Uses
Bendix Corporation	Plant construction Project work
Carrier Corporation	Plant construction Government projects
Kimberly-Clark	Control of major projects Systems design
The Signal Companies, Inc.	Petroleum process unit construction Industrial building construction
Southern Railway	Major plant construction project Installation of new MIS system at major RR yards Time schedule for preparing five-year plan
3M Company	Construction projects Introduction of new products Marketing plans
Oscar Mayer & Company	Plant construction New product development and production startup Allocation of craft personnel
The Southland Corporation	Facility construction Establishment of a new operation
Glidden Division, SCM Corporation	Plant construction
Lear Siegler	New product development Major program control (particularly government contracts)
Procter & Gamble Company	Facilities construction New product introduction
Kellogg Company	New product development Construction project control Forecasting New plant construction
Crown Zellerbach	Construction Most capital projects Planning inputs
J. Ray McDermott & Co., Inc.	Plant construction
Kaiser Steel Corporation	Construction of new facilities

PERT

Network analysis is common to both PERT and CPM. Because of their similarity only PERT will be discussed in its entirety. Two definitions are first needed: an event and an activity.

event An **event** is a meaningful specified accomplishment (physical or intellectual) in the program plan, recognizable at a particular instance of time.

It does not consume time or resources. A circle or node provides the representation of an event.

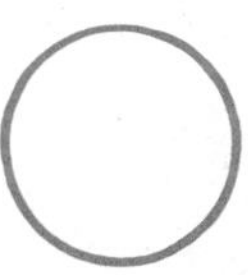

activity

An **activity** is the time-consuming element of the program. It is represented by an arrow.

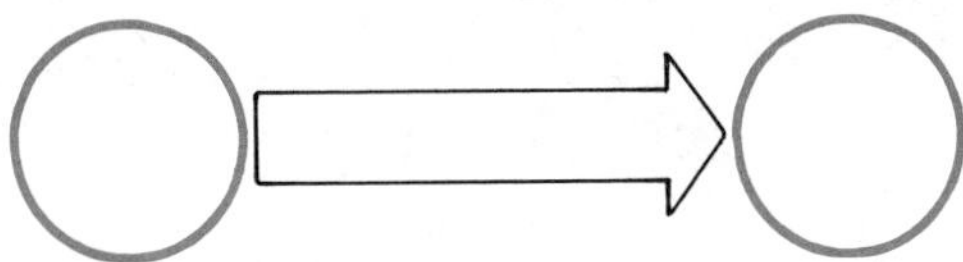

In order to assist in the understanding of PERT, a project will be developed. The project entails obtaining a production contract award for an aircraft. The principal steps to be taken by a project manager in this problem are described below.

1. Define the objective of the project and specify the factors (time, cost) that must be considered as the variables to be controlled—for instance, how quickly the project must be completed or how much money is allocated for completion of the project.
2. List all of the significant activities that must be performed for the project objectives to be achieved. These are as follows:

   Preparing specifications
   Establishing quantity requirements
   Negotiating contract
   Preparing test facilities
   Developing airframe
   Developing engine
   Assembling airframe
   Installing engine
   Preparing test
   Testing
   Obtaining headquarters approval
   Evaluating by contractor
   Negotiating contract

3. Develop a statement of the relationship among project activities. The order in which each task is to be accomplished is also specified. A PERT network is then developed through this information. (See Figure

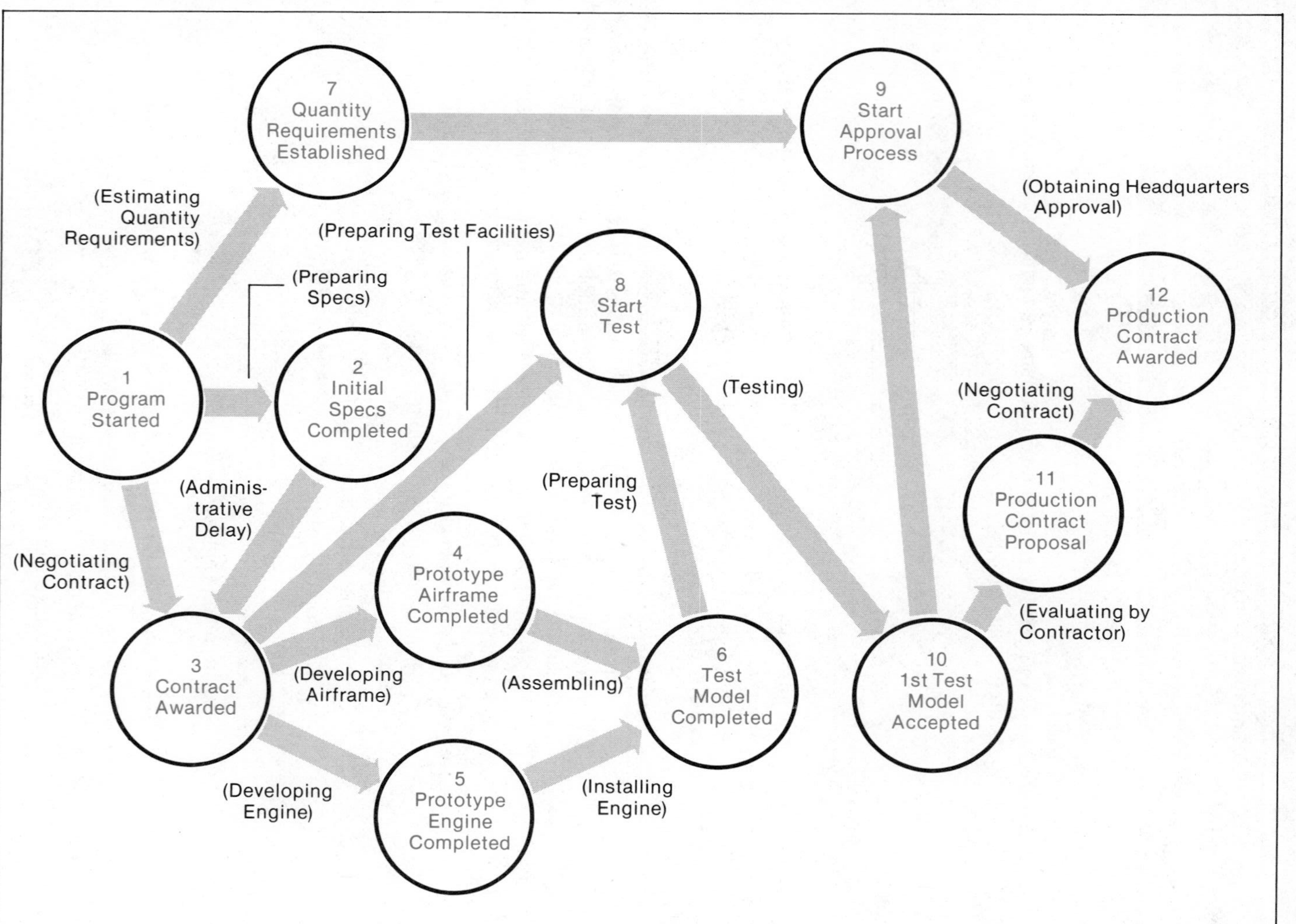

FIGURE 16-4 *PERT Network with Activities and Events*

16-4). As may be seen, the prototype airframe and the prototype engine must be completed before the test model is completed.

4. Determine the expected times that will be required to complete each activity. PERT requires that three time estimates be provided.

optimistic time

Optimistic time—If everything goes right and nothing goes wrong, the project can be completed in this amount of time.

most likely time

Most likely time—The most realistic completion time for the activity.

pessimistic time

Pessimistic time—If everything goes wrong and nothing goes right, the project will be completed in this amount of time.

The expected time for the completion of each activity may be seen in Figure 16-5. For instance, the optimistic time for the activity "developing airframe" is 36 weeks, the pessimistic time is 56 weeks, and the most likely time is 40 weeks. Inserting these figures into the expected time formula, we determine that 42 weeks is the expected time to complete the activity.

expected time

Expected time is then computed by applying the three time estimates to the following formula:

$$\text{Expected time (te)} = \frac{\text{Optimistic time} + 4(\text{most likely time}) + \text{pessimistic time}}{6}.$$

critical path

5. Determine the **critical path,** that is, the longest path from start to finish of the project. (The actual work of the manager terminates once the three time estimates have been obtained.) There are numerous computer programs that are available to perform the mechanics of this task. The critical path for this project is represented by the broken line seen in Figure 16-6. If any activity along the critical path is a week late, the entire project will be delayed an additional week.

6. Determine the probability of completing the entire project or a particular activity on time. This in itself is a major feature of PERT. Because of the three estimates, the manager is able to obtain an estimate of whether the project will be completed on schedule. The optimistic and pessimistic times have been determined to assist in this operation. If there were but one time estimate—the most likely time—probabilities could not be computed.

   A manager usually finds it beneficial to compare the optimistic and pessimistic times to the most likely time. For instance, the activity "developing engine" would likely cause greater concern to the manager than the activity "developing airframe." The difference between the optimistic time and pessimistic time for "developing engine" is 30 weeks (54 – 24) while the difference for the activity "developing airframe" is but 20 weeks (56 – 36). A manager will likely monitor the activities that have the greatest difference between optimistic and pessimistic time because they provide the greatest potential for not meeting the completion date.

Once the critical path has been identified, the manager is able to quickly determine what activities must be carefully monitored. If an activity along

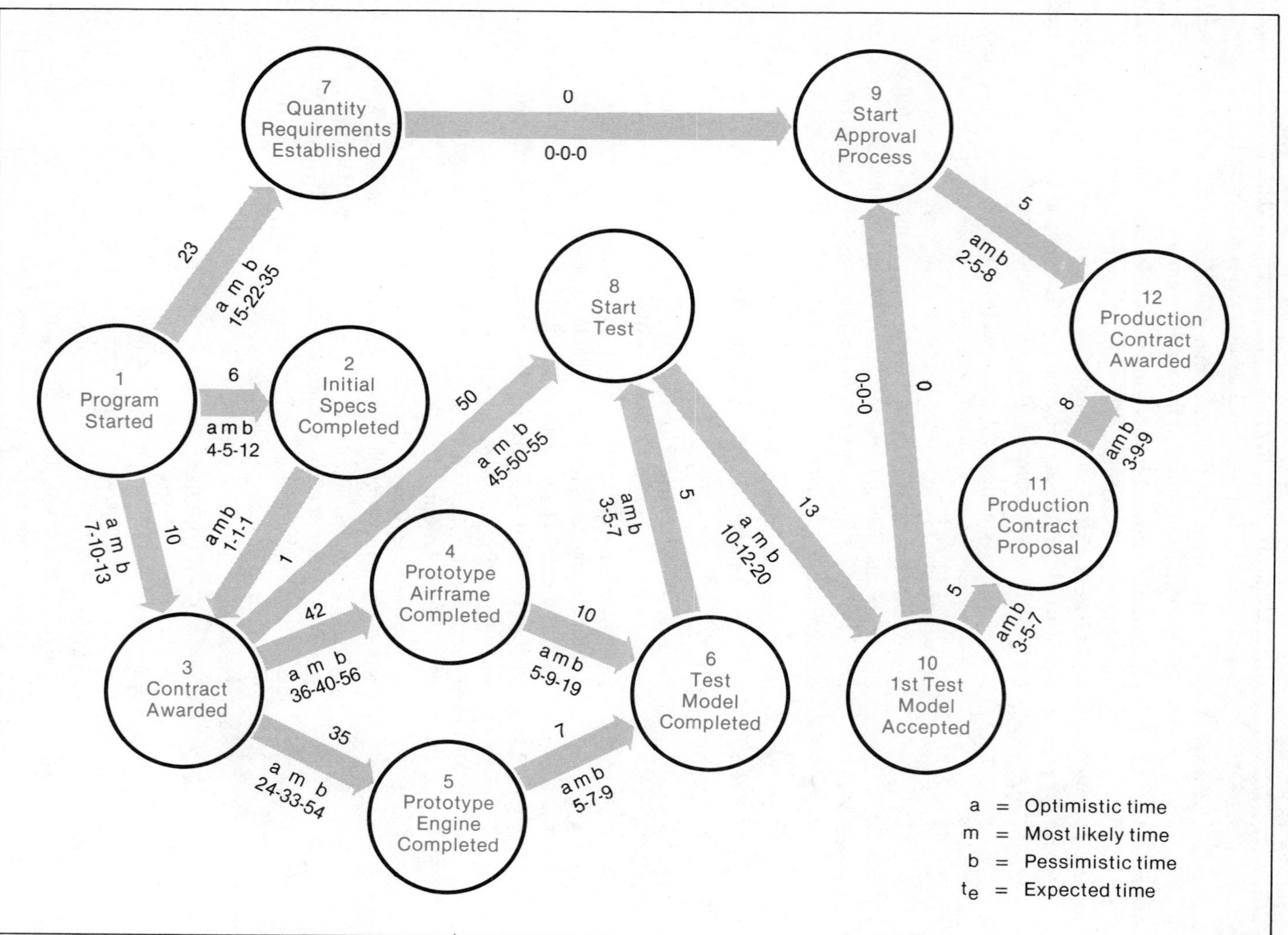

FIGURE 16-5 *Expected Times to Complete Each Activity*

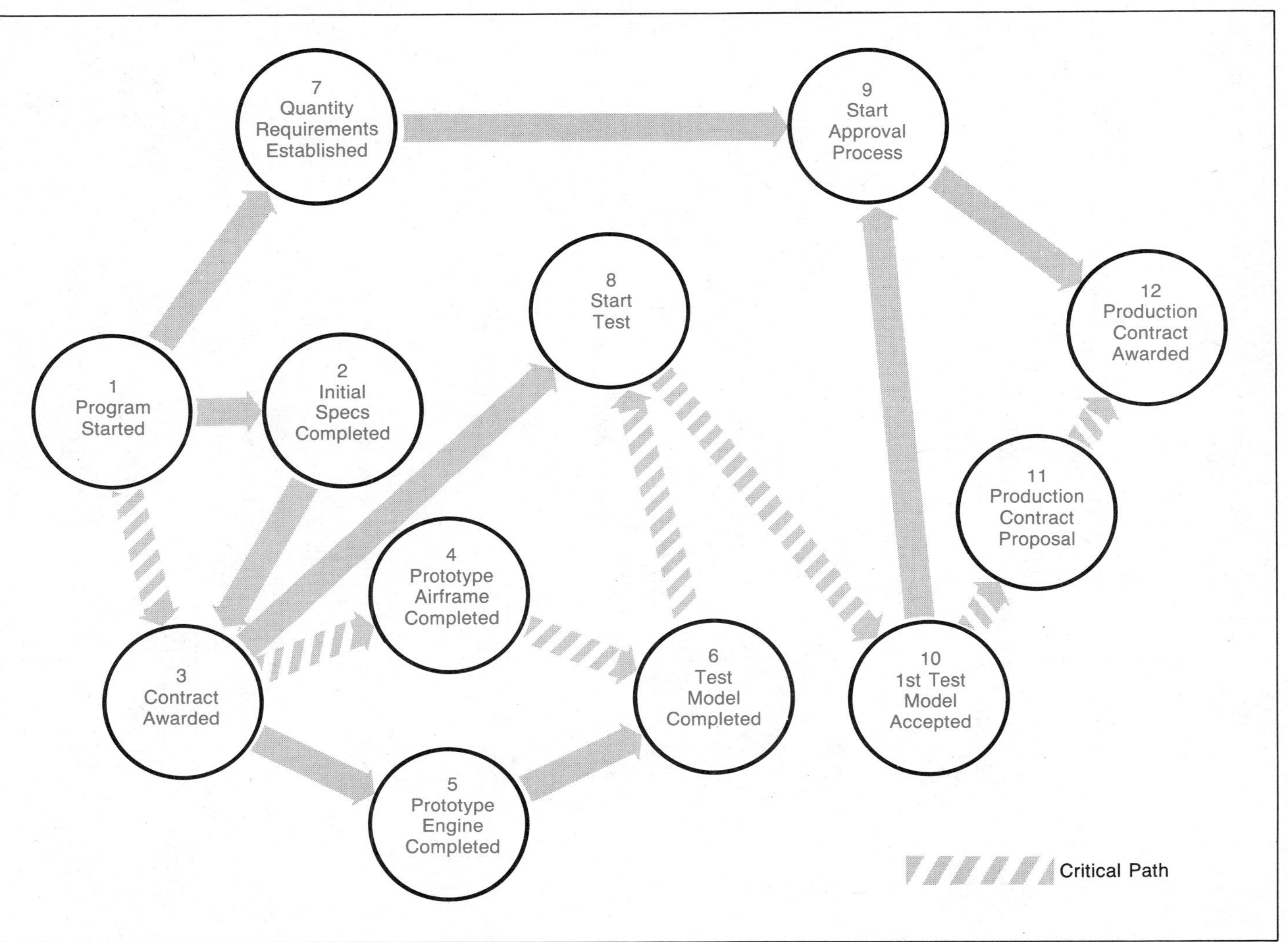

FIGURE 16-6 *Critical Path for Project*

the critical path slips one day, the entire project will be delayed one day. Activities that are not on the critical path may not have to be monitored as carefully as those on the critical path. The manager is also in a position to determine which activities are not likely to be completed on time and carefully monitor them.

PERT may serve both as a planning and a control function. It *forces* a manager to think thoroughly through a project and identify the tasks that must be accomplished and how they interrelate in the completion of the project. It serves as a control function in that a critical path (the longest path from start to finish of the project) is identified. Thus, a manager is able to work with extremely complex projects and still maintain control over the project.

Critical Path Method

The developers of CPM were dealing with projects for which the time and cost of tasks (activities) required to complete the project were known. In CPM the points or nodes of the CPM network represent activities rather than events. Also, there is but one time estimate in CPM because it was designed to accommodate situations in which sets of standardized activities were required for the completion of a complex project. Time for completion of a task was relatively easy to determine accurately. Because there was but one time estimate, probabilities of completing the project on time were not available. With these minor exceptions, PERT and CPM provide for accomplishment of similar functions.

PRODUCTION AND OPERATIONS MANAGEMENT: A WRAP-UP

The quantitative techniques discussed in this and the previous chapter were provided to stimulate the student to gain further insight into what planning tools are available to managers. A person should not be led into believing that these techniques are the only ones that managers have at their disposal. A course in statistics should dispel this notion. But managers should always remember that these are but tools to be used, just like a calculator or a piece of machinery. You yourself need not know the inner workings of either—you will hire experts for that. Your primary concern is the end result. Thus, managers need to be able to select the correct tool that will solve the problem at hand and not become overly concerned with the details of each technique. When this has been achieved, the production and operations tools become a valuable part of a manager's repertoire of knowledge.

Summary

Additional quantitative concepts and techniques that have proven successful in assisting managers solve problems are simulation and queuing theory.

Simulation is a technique that permits managers to ask many "what if" questions without having to make the decision in the real world. With the advent of high-speed electronic computers, simulation has come of age. A simulation model is used to represent a real world situation through mathematical logic in an attempt to predict what will occur in an actual situation.

Queuing or waiting line theory is used by management to determine how much service to provide at the time of greatest need. Although the mathematics of a waiting line problem is often quite complicated, businesses have found that the technique can assist in the solution of a variety of problems.

There are numerous control techniques available for use by managers. Four approaches are quality control, inventory control, Program Evaluation and Review Technique (PERT) and the Critical Path Method (CPM). When a manager uses quality control, a product is evaluated regarding the degree of conformity to a certain predetermined standard. If a firm has an objective of gaining a reputation for manufacturing a high-quality product, standards will have to be high. There are two basic types of sampling plans: sampling by attributes and sampling by variables. A plan developed for variable sampling consists of determining how closely an item conforms to an established standard. With sampling by attributes, the item is either acceptable or unacceptable. A procedure that measures the quality control process is referred to as a control chart.

Inventory control is a vital technique that can mean the difference between a profit or a loss to a firm. Inventory control involves the balancing of two general types of costs: ordering costs and carrying costs. It is the job of the manager to use inventory control as a means to minimize total cost. A procedure that permits the manager to determine which items warrant careful control is referred to as the ABC method of inventory control.

When a project is nonrecurrent, large, complex, and involves multiple organizations, the manager needs a tool that will assist in coordinating this complicated network. The primary techniques available to accomplish this task are PERT and CPM. Both serve as planning and control devices.

Review Questions

1. Define simulation. Why does the technique have so much potential to a business person of today?

2. Give the sequence that should be followed in developing a simulation problem.

3. Why is a waiting line or queuing theory problem called a process of balancing? When would this technique be used?

4. What are the costs that are involved in developing an inventory control problem? Define each.

5. Why do we often use sampling techniques in quality control?

6. In terms of quality control define the following:

a. Standard

b. Upper confidence limit

c. Lower confidence limit

7. Distinguish between sampling by attributes and sampling by variables. Give an example of each.
8. Distinguish between PERT and CPM.
9. Define the following:
   a. Optimistic time
   b. Most likely time
   c. Pessimistic time
   d. Expected time

Exercises

1. Assume that ordering costs are $6.00 per order, carrying costs are $1.50 per unit per year, and the annual demand is 1,000 units. What would be the economic order quantity (EOQ) for this situation?
2. Assume that you are responsible for monitoring inventory control for the following types of firms:
   a. Fancy restaurant
   b. Automobile dealership
   c. Bookstore

   Using the ABC method of inventory control, identify inventory items that would be in each class.
3. Develop a small PERT network for a task with which you are very familiar. The task that is chosen should have at least two people performing different tasks at the same time.

Case Study

Production Applications

Robert Channell is vice-president of operations for a firm that manufactures minicomputers. Robert works in an industry that is quite dynamic and constantly changing. A product that is in the forefront today may be out of date tomorrow because of the rapid technological changes that take place in the minicomputer industry. The firm that Robert works for is known for quality equipment and delivery that is on time. The environment in which the company operates is constantly changing. This makes it very difficult to forecast market demand and schedule production. Robert believes in using the quantitative tools that are at his disposal. Although he does not have a math background, he has experts who can be called upon when needed.

Assume for a moment that you are Robert Channell, vice-president of operations. Answer the following questions.

QUESTIONS

1. Comment on the usefulness of the quantitative technique(s) discussed in Chapters 15 and 16. Which of these tools do you feel would be the most beneficial for you? Explain.

2. What information should you provide your experts in order to use these techniques?

Notes

1. Richard B. Chase and Nicholas J. Aquilano, *Production and Operations Management: A Life Cycle Approach,* rev ed. (Homewood, Ill.: Irwin 1977), p. 269.

References

Backes, Robert W. "Cycle Counting—A Better Way for Achieving Accurate Inventory Records." *Production and Inventory Management* 21 (Second Quarter 1980): 36–44.

Brennan, J. M. "Up Your Inventory Control." *Journal of Systems Management* 28 (January 1977): 39–45.

Buffa, Elwood s. *Modern ProductionsOperations Management.* 6th ed. New York: Wiley, 1980.

Chase, Richard B., and Aquilano, Nicholas J. *Production and Operations Management: A Life Cycle Approach.* 2nd ed. Homewood, Ill.: Irwin, 1981.

Gullapelli, S. M. "Simulating a Cash Budget for a Small Manufacturer." *Management Accounting* 61 (November 1979): 25–29.

Hostage, G. M. "Quality Control in a Service Business." *Harvard Business Review* 53 (July–August 1975), 98–106.

Mittelstaedt, Arthur H., and Berger, Henry A. "The Critical Path Method: A Management Tool for Recreation." *Parks and Recreation* 7 (July 1972): 14–16.

Plossl, G. W., and Welch, W. Evert. *The Role of Top Management in the Control of Inventory.* Reston, Va.: Reston Publishing, 1979.

Reuter, Vincent G. "ABC Method of Inventory Control." *Journal of Systems Management* 27 (November 1976): 26–33.

Schenner. Roger W. *ProductionsOperations Management.* Chicago: Science Research Associates, 1981.

Smith, Martin R. "A 10-point guide to Making Quality control Management Effective." *Management Review* 64 (April 1975): 52–54.

Solomon, S. L. "Building Modelers: Teaching the Art of Simulation." *Interfaces* 10 (April 1980): 65–72.

Wiley, J. M. "Just Enough Queuing Theory." *datamation* 23 (February 1977): 87.

CASE STUDY FOR PART VI

Atlas Aircraft

OBSERVATIONS

"It's sure too bad about Willis, Ball, and Conrad," Bob Harris said to George Mathews, who was stirring his coffee when Bob joined him on a Friday afternoon break. George shook his head in apparent disbelief at the news. The three managers mentioned had just been fired as a result of a disastrous bid on a proposal they had worked on. Mathews then asked, "What do you suppose really went wrong on that bid?" It was now Harris's turn to shake his head. "We'll probably never know the whole story," he said. "Oh sure, somebody has to be responsible for goofs, but it really shakes you up to think of those guys, all of them with over twenty years here, and all at once out on their butts!" Nodding his head in agreement, George said, "Boy, we really gotta watch what the hell we're doing from now on!"

BACKGROUND

Atlas had been a successful airframe manufacturer—one of the five largest—for forty years. The firm took pride in the fact that 85 percent of its managers were engineers. This feeling seemed to stem from the idea that such a manager could better cope with the technical aspects of airplane manufacture than could a nonengineer manager.

TROUBLE

The Cargo Plane

About one year prior to the above conversation, Atlas had submitted a bid on a giant cargo plane for the U.S. Air Force. At the time of the bid, the engineering was not yet complete on the internal materials-handling equipment that

The case history was written by Edgar A. Wiley, Professor of Management Emeritus, California State University, Fullerton, as the basis for class discussion. Names and incidents have been disguised at the request of the participants. Presented at a Case Workshop and distributed by the Intercollegiate Case Clearing House, Soldiers Field, Boston, Mass. 02163.

would be used to load a wide variety of cargoes. Cargoes would range from heavy tanks or trucks to the bulk-loading of small, irregularly shaped packages. To ensure submission of the bid on time, the Atlas executive committee insisted on getting a "safe but competitive" price from engineering on the loading system.

Atlas was awarded the contract on the cargo plane, but the estimated costs on the loading system were nowhere near the actual costs. The additional R & D needed to make the loading system operational and efficient ran to about $160,000, compared to the $20,000 estimate. Also, the production costs of the system were over $135,000 per plane, in contrast to the $27,000 per unit estimate. These increased costs amounted to nearly $1.5 million for the twelve-plane contract, and the air force admitted only $600,000 for additional billing on this system. This meant that Atlas' potential profit on the contract was reduced by nearly $1 million.

Henry Murphy, the president, was furious at this result, which he blamed on poor engineering and on irresponsibility on the part of those who put the loading-system estimate together. In order to shake up the entire management and to force the managers and staff to accept responsibility, Murphy insisted on seeing "some heads roll." Consequently, the chief of R & D was fired, along with the chief of production engineering and the manager of manufacturing.

Murphy was correct in expecting management to be shaken, but the event did not seem to be followed by any noticeable improvement in decision making.

The Fighter Plane

It has been the practice among U.S. planemakers for a prime contractor* to subcontract 40 percent to 60 percent of the contract value to other manufacturers. In keeping with this practice, Atlas prepared plans and requested proposals for various subcontracts on a new fighter plane—the NFX-3. The total amount of electronic gear on this sophisticated plane was considerably greater than had appeared on any previous Atlas plane. The electronics manufacturers who commonly subcontracted for Atlas were not able to handle the physical volume required by the NFX-3 schedule. Consequently, Atlas was forced to seek new electronics manufacturers for this purpose. The usual "Requests for Bids" were sent out, and several companies responded with proposals. After

*Holder of the airplane contract from the customer.

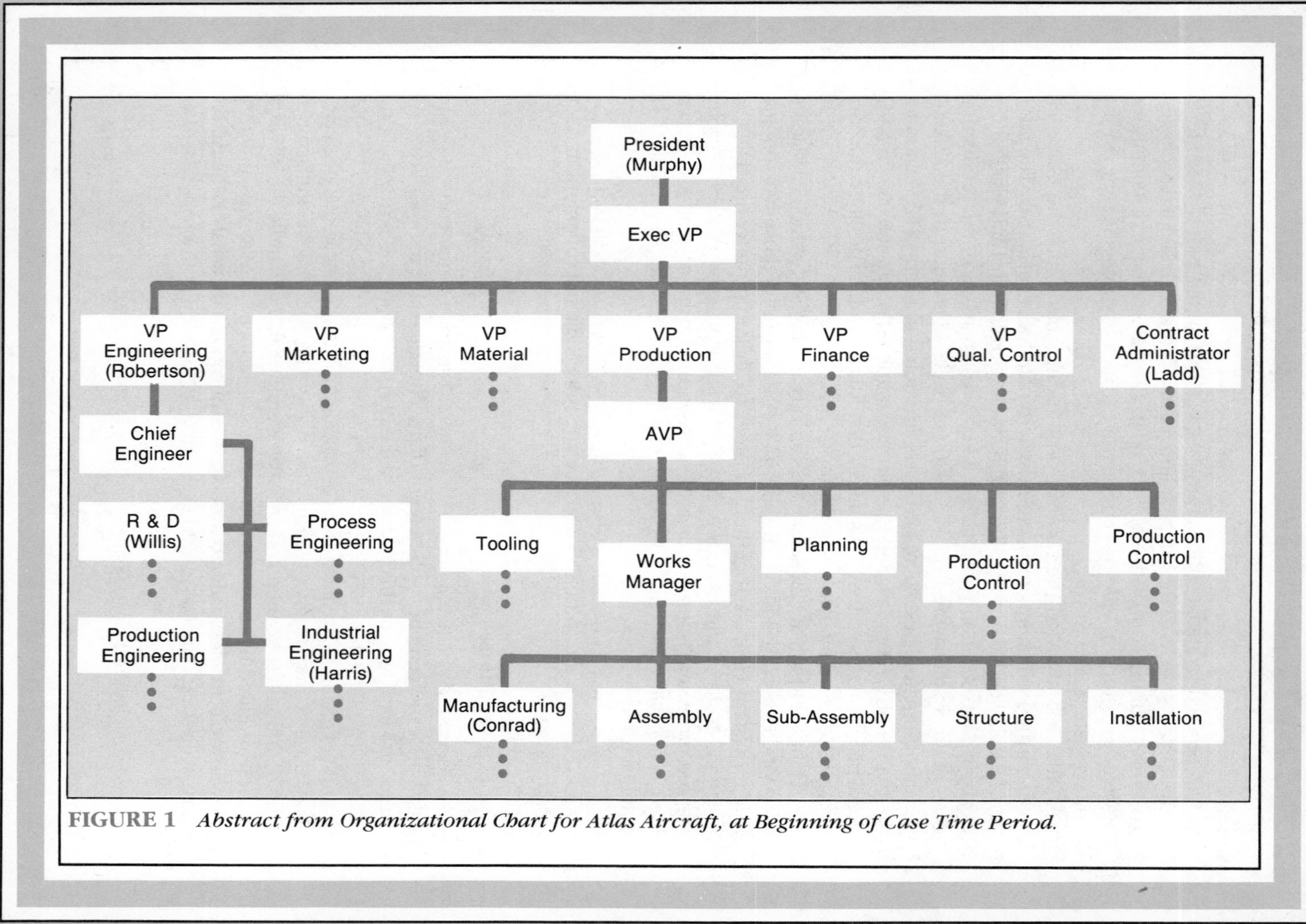

FIGURE 1 *Abstract from Organizational Chart for Atlas Aircraft, at Beginning of Case Time Period.*

correspondence regarding specifications and costs, Atlas dispatched some electronics engineers and production coordinators to evaluate physically the potentialities of the interested electronics firms. Out of the five firms evaluated, the team determined that two of the five were fully qualified as subcontractors and wrote their report to that effect. They had found that both firms were currently in production of sophisticated army and navy electronics, and that their production lines were not "contaminated" with civilian consumer items. The investigation suggested a highly satisfactory on-time delivery record.

After the scheduling was completed and all subcontracts had been let for the NFX-3, the manufacturing and the assembly operations were begun. These, and the subcontracting and purchasing deliveries, were closely observed and checked with the PERT charts. The first deliveries of the electronic equipment from the two new subcontractors were due in the 38th week of the NFX-3 schedule. Delivery from Firm A came in, a few days early, while Firm B's delivery missed the deadline. Following the PERT schedule, Production Control had checked with Firm B two weeks before the scheduled delivery. Production Control was told that some purchased component parts had been unacceptable and had been returned to the maker, who had promised immediate replacement. Since the PERT dates for these items included some slack, the delay seemed to be relatively minor, and quickly correctible, with rush work on the part of Firm B.

Unfortunately, Week 42 went by with still no delivery from Firm B. Now, things began looking a little hairy; by Week 44, additional equipment would have to be installed, which could go in only after the gear from Firm B had been installed. This meant that a real possibility existed that a line-stoppage would occur unless the delayed electronics arrived almost immediately.

An electronics engineer and a production planner were dispatched to Firm B to get an actual look at the situation and to try to devise means to accelerate deliveries.

The subsequent report was grim; according to the troubleshooters, Firm B's production line was very primitive, and an educated guess would put earliest delivery at around Week 58!

Murphy really blew his top. As after the loading-system fiasco, he thought that drastic action was necessary. Therefore, the senior electronics engineer and the production control chief were fired. Again, the reason was to inspire the remaining managers and staff to approach the decision making more seriously and to accept responsibility more completely.

A couple of days later, George Whyte, board chairman of Atlas, called Murphy. "I hear that heads have rolled again," he said, "I'm afraid so," replied Murphy, as the weight in his stomach seemed to get heavier. "You may have good reason to be afraid," said Whyte, "if this action doesn't start bringing in some answers. I hope that you haven't lost control."

The Swing-Wing

In the following year, nearly all production seemed to slow, although almost imperceptibly. Schedules became more difficult to maintain; new development, bids, and proposals seemed excruciatingly slow. Several times, requests for extensions in bidding deadlines were forwarded by Atlas because of behind-schedule conditions. Investigations into the reasons for such delays seemed to always suggest a nearly unanimous feeling among managers that the increasingly complex technology in nearly every aspect of airframe design and manufacture seemed to require greater precision and certainty in decision making. This, of course, would require more research, more data, and more time to come up with optimum decisions and their implementing plans.

Since *time* was one thing which Atlas surely could not spare, the only solution occurring to top management was an increase in the number of managers and staff experts to get the work out.

The resulting organizational structure turned out to have nearly one manager or staff person for each three hourly workers at Atlas. This is in contrast to the two-year earlier proportion of one manager/staff member to each 3.46 hourly workers (at the start of this case history). This can be seen as an increase of almost one-seventh in administrative salaries.

In the meantime, the air force was soliciting bids for a swing-wing fighter. Atlas was very eager to get such a contract. In fact, overhead expenses were so high that new contracts seemed imperative to maintain an acceptable cash flow.

As the swing-wing bid deadline approached, no proposal from Atlas had been finalized. The president called in his top-level people and asked, "Why the delay?" All reasons suggested were centered on new technology and the need for more data. Murphy emphasized the need for a timely bid and suggested an all-out effort.

Five days before the deadline, the bid was still not finished, and the need for more data was again insisted on. Through political contacts, Murphy was able to get a two-week extension on the deadline, but at the cost of some strained friendships. Upon receiving the extension, Murphy put out the word that the proposal *must* be ready, this time.

Three days before the extended deadline, President Murphy received a copy of a report sent to Contracts Administration by the group responsible for the proposal figures. The third paragraph caught his eye; it read:

> 3. The production technology for the swing-wing hinge is in flux at this time. It is necessary to combine great strength with optimum weight. There are two or three firms which might be able to make the hinges with a forging-press. The tooling for this may run to $180,000, but we have no firm commitment as to the cost of tooling, the unit cost, or delivery schedule.
>
> There are several firms interested in the carbon-filament technique, but time has not permitted the necessary stress-analyses to determine optimum size and weight. Here, the cost of tooling is estimated at from $40,000 to $115,000.
>
> If neither of these processes is available and appropriate, we can hang the hinges from 8″ titanium stock. The tooling here would probably be below $20,000, but there is a great waste in scrap, from which there is little salvage.
>
> If we are able to get a forging for the hinges, we can produce the hinges for about $17,000 (direct cost) per plane. If we could seek a manufacturer to produce them from carbon-filament, we can expect about $29,000 per plane. If neither of these techniques is available, we shall have to machine them from titanium plate, at about $48,000 per set.

After a very deep sigh, Murphy murmured to himself, "What the hell kind of a proposal is this?"

A few minutes later, Murphy rang his secretary and told her, "Cancel all of my appointments. Get hold of Ladd* and Robertson†—tell them to cancel *their* appointments and to plan to spend the next forty-eight hours with me, to get this proposal finalized."

Shortly thereafter, Chairman Whyte called Murphy. "How's the proposal?" Murphy explained the situation as briefly as possible. Whyte responded with, "You'd better meet that deadline!"

*Contract administrator.
†VP, engineering.

Hanging up, Murphy heaved another sigh, as his ulcers burned, then sat motionless for five minutes. "Where did I go wrong?" he thought. "What have I solved?" He then phoned a nationally known management consulting firm and talked with one of the partners. "We seem to have lost our capability for making decisions," Murphy said. "Can you help me?"

QUESTION

What would you do in this situation?

PART VII

Situational Applications

KEY TERMS

social responsibility

economic function

iron law of responsibility

Friedman's view of social responsibility

social audit

ethics

Kodak's SPICE concept

ethical dilemmas

managerial code of ethics

LEARNING OBJECTIVES

After completing this chapter you should be able to

1. Describe corporate social responsibility.
2. Explain the role of business in society.
3. Identify the arguments both for and against social responsibility.
4. State some of the current corporate practices regarding social responsibility and explain what is meant by a social audit.
5. Define business ethics and describe why it is important for an industry and/or company to establish ethical codes of behavior.

17

Social Responsibility and Business Ethics

Paper mills have a universal problem—paper production is a smelly and polluting process and offends the residents of areas surrounding the plant. Today, the Southern Paper Corporation faces a dilemma not uncommon to other businesses that pollute the environment. Top-level management at Southern is considering three choices: (1) install an air pollution control system that is considered so costly that some board members say that the cost would outweigh its benefits, or (2) agree to continue to pay the regular (but affordable) air quality violation fines and look for another solution, or (3) face plant closure.

Management at Southern is comprised of a number of people with long tenure with the family-held business. They feel a strong commitment to their employees and to the local economy of the community where the plant is located. They must balance these feelings against the prohibitively expensive investment in the air pollution control devices. The costs of this would have to be absorbed by the stockholders and purchasers of the products of the plant. This could drastically affect the economic stability of Southern Paper Corporation.

Payment of the fines on a regular basis almost seems the best answer, for it avoids closure of the plant and dodges the expensive investment in air control devices. However, it does nothing to alleviate the original problem—air pollution.

Bill Smith, manager of purchasing with the Allied Wholesale Company, was offered expensive gifts including an expense-paid vacation to Hawaii for himself and his wife, by a sales representative of one of his firm's major suppliers. In return for these gifts, Bill realized he would be expected to show favoritism toward this supplier by purchasing from him.

Southern Paper Corporation is confronted with a social responsibility dilemma that many of today's organizations constantly face. While striving to earn a satisfactory profit, it must also balance the needs of its employees with the needs and interests of society. Bill Smith is faced with a decision that involves determining what is ethically right or wrong. Bill's ethics may be severely tested as he decides whether to accept the gifts and give the vendor preferential treatment.

Often in the area of social responsibility and business ethics, there are no clear-cut answers of "right" or "wrong" but rather "best" solutions for the situation at hand. Management is faced with a juggling act to meet the demands of employees, produce profits for stockholders, remain within government regulation, and provide a product to consumers at a cost that will not contribute to inflation. In this chapter we will examine a number of basic issues of social responsibility and business ethics.

CORPORATE SOCIAL RESPONSIBILITY

social responsibility

Social responsibility is concerned with how organizations deal with the issues and problems confronting society. Corporate **social responsibility** can be defined as "a firm's obligation to constituent groups in society other than stockholders and beyond that prescribed by law or union contract."[1] Acceptance of the social responsibility concept means that a primary obligation of an organization is to ensure that its decisions and operations meet the needs and interests of society.

In the past, some practices of corporations may have been questionable with regard to social responsibility. During the late 1960s and throughout the 1970s, managers and the corporations they worked for were subjected to considerable criticism and received low levels of approval from the public. Hardly a week passed without news headlines of corporate bribery, illegal political contributions, or price-fixing practices being alleged about some of America's largest and best-known corporations. The impression was that almost all business people engaged in illegal and/or unethical practices. Nothing could have been further from the truth, then or now. Nevertheless, there has been and currently is a certain amount of corruption in businesses and in most other areas of society. The public's mistrust of business and business executives is exemplified by surveys of public opinion, indicating a decline in the public's confidence in business. In one study, over 50 percent of the respondents believed that the "bad" features of our business system either equal or outweigh the "good."[2] Another survey indicated that the public confidence in the executives who manage major corporations had declined drastically from 55 percent in 1968 to 16 percent in 1978. In another survey, 87 percent of those interviewed agreed that most business people are more interested in profits than in serving the public's needs, and 53 percent felt that many major companies should be dismantled.

Other surveys have revealed that the public's estimate of the profits of business is considerably out of line with reality. For example, the public's estimate of the level of after-tax profits per dollar of sales for the typical business is between twenty-five and thirty cents; the actual amount was about five cents in 1982. Also, surveys have pointed out that the general public has a relatively low opinion of the caliber of the business executive's ethics. While surveys have also found that a substantial majority of the public contend that business firms have an obligation to help society even if it means making less profit, fewer than half of those surveyed accept the notion that executives have a social conscience. Many people believe that business executives do everything within their power to earn a profit, even if it means ignoring the public's needs.

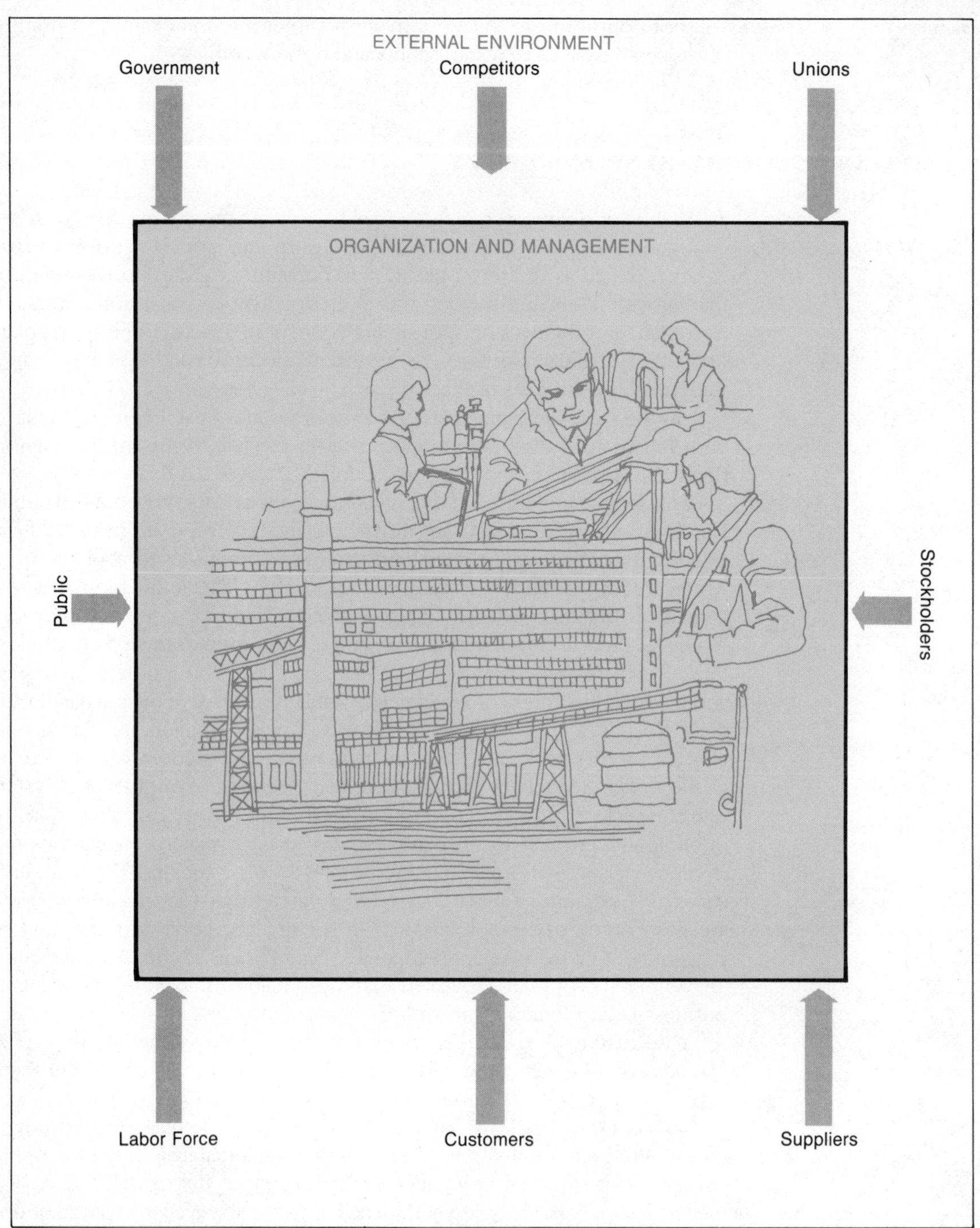

FIGURE 17-1 *Relationship of the Firm to Groups in Society*

Socially responsible decision makers within corporations consider both the economic and social impact of their decisions and the firm's operations on the various groups in society. Keith Davis believes that in meeting its responsibilities to society, a firm must be concerned with more than the narrow technical and legal requirements.[3] It should recognize that an obligation exists to protect and enhance the interests and welfare of not only the corporation but also those of society.

In today's environment, business organizations are being expected to assume broader and more diverse responsibilities to the various groups within society. There is little doubt that there is an increasing amount of attention directed to the social responsibilities in business firms. However, critics argue that there is more lip-service than action, more public relations programs than concrete social responsibility activities. Nevertheless, social responsibility is an area in which the modern business firm must develop a stance, accompanied by appropriate policies and activities.

The factors that affect corporate social responsibility are illustrated in Figure 17-1, which depicts the relationship of a business firm to its environment. How business conducts itself with regard to each of these groups will greatly affect its opportunities for survival, growth, and profitability. Labor unions and governmental units are among the most powerful groups in the external environment in terms of the potential effects on the firm. Consumer groups are gaining increased power, as have special interest groups such as the Urban League and the National Organization for Women. On occasion, even stockholders have organized to alter or overthrow the existing management of an organization when the firm has not conducted business in a socially responsible manner.

Managers must assess the power of each group and its potential threat to the organizational activities. They should pursue what they deem to be the primary goals of the enterprise, but always with an eye out for constraints imposed by forces in the external environment. When managers go too long without responding or when they fundamentally disagree with actions demanded by various groups, they risk the possibility of boycotts, picketing, new legislation, government hearings, proxy contests, and strikes. However, demands made by groups in society will keep the organization from becoming too selfish and irresponsible. Actions by these groups, rather than profits or conscience, have often led a firm to pursue socially responsible actions.

THE ROLE OF BUSINESS IN SOCIETY

Traditionally, the responsibility of the business firm has been to produce and distribute goods and services in return for a profit. Businesses have performed this function extremely effectively. Largely as the result of our economic system and the important contributions of business firms, the United States enjoys one of the highest overall standards of living in the world. Rising standards of living in the United States have enabled a high percentage

• CAREER PROFILE •

WILLIAM E. WINTER
President and Chief Executive Officer
The Seven-Up Company

William E. Winter, president and chief executive officer of The Seven-Up Company, has played a key role in pacing the steady expansion of the St. Louis, Missouri, firm, which currently markets the third-largest-selling soft drink in the world. Winter gained his first experience in the bottling business as a part-time employee. He worked during summer vacations at the Madison, Illinois, Seven-Up plant where his father was sales manager of one of the earliest Seven-Up bottling operations. Bill performed production-line assignments and case-stocking chores in the warehouse and worked as an extra hand on Seven-Up route trucks. He graduated from the University of Illinois where he received his Bachelor of Science degree in labor

of the population to have their basic needs for food, clothing, shelter, health, and education reasonably well satisfied. Businesses can take pride in these accomplishments because they had a great deal to do with making the higher standards of living possible.

Business has been able to make significant contributions to the rising living standards primarily because of the manner in which the free enterprise economic system operates. The profit motive provides incentive to business to produce products and services as efficiently as is possible. Business firms try to improve the quality of their products and services, reduce costs and prices, and thereby attract more customers to buy from the firm. By earning profits, the successful firm pays taxes to the government and makes donations to provide financial support for charitable causes. Because of the efficient operations of business firms, an ever increasing number of people have the means and the leisure time to enjoy the "good life."

But businesses operate by public consent with the basic purpose of satisfying the needs of society. Despite significant improvements in standards

economics (and was elected to membership in Phi Beta Kappa).

In 1946, Winter joined the world headquarters of the Seven-Up Company in St. Louis. He began as a sales training instructor, then moved into sales counseling activities in the field. By 1950, Winter's successful promotional record rated him a transfer, and he was brought into the main offices in St. Louis as a sales promotion assistant. Within four years, a department of his own had grown up around him, and he was officially appointed sales promotion manager. Through innovation and general company growth, new responsibilities were assigned to the sales promotion department, and in 1965 Winter was made vice-president and manager over a fully integrated marketing department. In January 1969, Winter was appointed director of marketing with the responsibility for supervising departments in advertising and promotion, field sales operations, fountain syrup sales, marketing planning services, and public relations. With his appointment as executive vice-president in 1971, and president and chief operating officer in July 1974, Winter assumed additional administrative duties with overall responsibility for attainment of total corporate marketing objectives of The Seven-Up Company. Winter was appointed president and chief executive officer of The Seven-Up Company in July 1976. Domestic and international subsidiaries reporting to Winter include: Seven-Up U.S.A.; Seven-Up Canada Limited; Seven-Up International; Ventura Coastal Corporation; Warner-Jenkinson Company; and Golden Crown Citrus Corporation.

Mr. Winter believes that it takes hard work that is performed on a highly ethical and moral level to be successful today. He has always set high standards for himself, and this philosophy carries over into his expectations of employees at Seven-Up. He believes nothing should be submitted to him unless it is in the best final form and accompanied by a recommendation. Concerning decision making, Mr. Winter says, "There comes a time for 'gut instinct.' At times, decision making is fun and at other times it is frightening." He realizes, however, that a president and chief executive officer doesn't get paid for easy decisions.

of living in recent years, society has begun expecting—even demanding—more of all of its institutions, particularly large business firms. Goals, values, and attitudes in society are changing to reflect a greater concern for improvements in the quality of life. An indication of these concerns would include such goals as the following:[4]

- Elimination of poverty and provision of quality health care
- Preservation of the environment by reducing the level of pollution
- Providing equal employment and educational opportunities regardless of race, color, creed, or sex
- Providing a sufficient number of jobs and career opportunities for all members of society
- Improving the quality of working life of employees
- Providing safe, livable communities with good housing and efficient transportation.

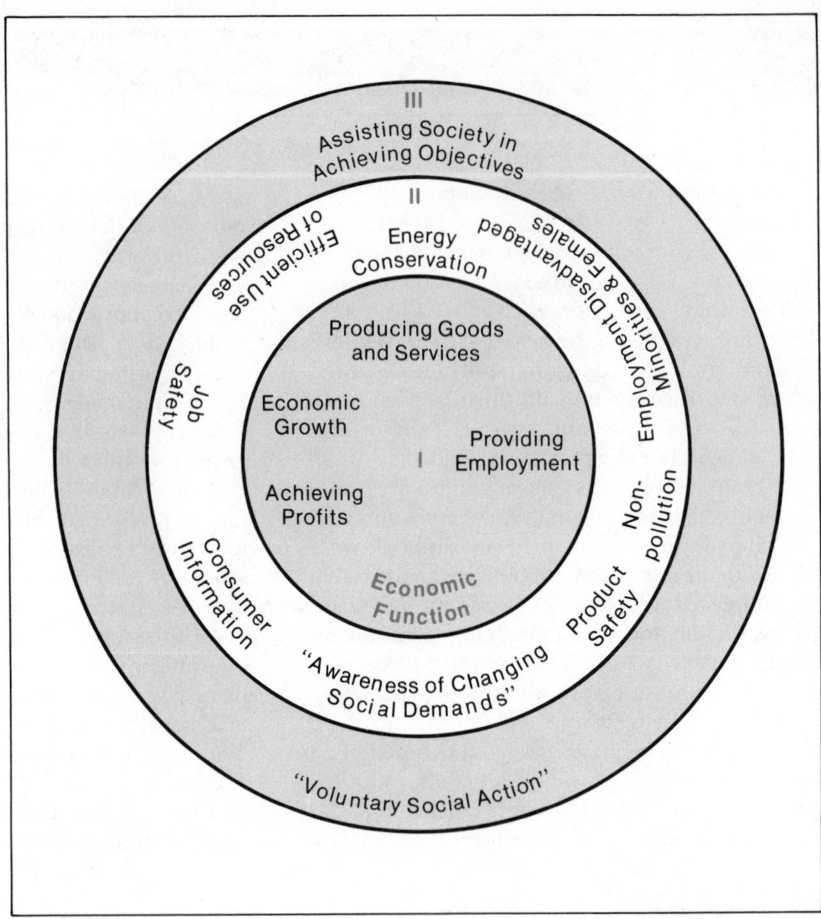

FIGURE 17-2
Primary Roles of Business

Society's expectations of business have broadened considerably in recent years to encompass more than the traditional economic function. This is illustrated in Figure 17-2. Inner circle I represents the traditional economic functions of business. The **economic function** is the primary responsibility of businesses to society. In performing the economic function, businesses produce needed goods and services, provide employment, contribute to economic growth, and earn a profit. Level II represents the responsibility of business to perform the economic functions with an awareness of changing social goals, values, and demands. Management must be aware of such concerns as: the efficient utilization of resources, reducing environmental pollution, employing and developing disadvantaged minorities and females, providing safe products, and providing a safe working environment. In Level III, the outer circle is concerned with the corporation's responsibility for assisting society in achieving such broad goals as the elimination of poverty and urban decay through a partnership of business, government agencies, and other private institutions. While the responsibilities in Level III

economic function

are not primary obligations of businesses, there is increasing interest by business in voluntary social action programs.

VIEWS FOR AND AGAINST SOCIAL RESPONSIBILITY

As in every other controversial area there are always at least two opposing views. This is the case with regard to the acceptance of social responsibility of businesses.

Arguments Favoring Social Responsibility

Numerous associations and groups of respected business leaders including the American Management Association and the Committee for Economic Development have encouraged corporations and managers to become involved in socially responsible activities. These groups have stressed such programs as providing better jobs and promotion opportunities to minorities and women; financial support for education; financial and managerial support for improving health and medical care; a safer working environment; leadership and financial support for urban renewal; and means to reduce environmental pollution.

The major arguments for the acceptance of social responsibility by business can be summarized below:

1. People expect businesses and other institutions to be socially responsible.
2. It is in the best interest of the business to pursue socially responsible programs.
3. It improves the image of the firm.
4. Business should be involved in social projects because it has the resources.
5. Corporations must be concerned about society's interests and needs because society, in effect, sanctions business operations.
6. If the business is not responsive to society's needs, the public will press for more governmental regulation requiring more socially responsible behavior.
7. Socially responsible actions may increase profits in the long run.

iron law of responsibility

Keith Davis summarizes these arguments with what he terms the **iron law of responsibility**. The *law* states that "in the long-run, those who do not use power in a manner in which society considers responsible will tend to lose it." Thus, if business firms are to retain their social power and role, they must be responsive to society's needs.[5]

Arguments Against Social Responsibility

There are numerous arguments against businesses' assuming an active role of social responsibility. A leading opponent of businesses' assumptions of social responsibilities is Dr. Milton Friedman, a Nobel Prize-winning economist. **Friedman's view of social responsibility** can be stated as follows:

Friedman's view of social responsibility

> There is one and only one social responsibility of business—to use its resources and engage in activities designed to increase its profits so long as it stays within the rules of the game, which is to say, engages in open and free competition without deception and fraud. . . . Few trends could so thoroughly undermine the very foundations of our free society as the acceptance by corporate officials of a social responsibility other than to make as much money for their stockholders as possible.[6]

Friedman goes on to assert that social responsibility is a "fundamentally subversive doctrine." He argues that managers are agents of the owners of the enterprise and that to engage in any activities not related to earning profits may be illegal. Diverting funds to social projects without stockholders' approval is, in effect, "taxation without representation." He says that business performance is economic not social.

Concentrating resources in the social area could lead to less economic efficiency and therefore actually be detrimental to society. Friedman and others who argue against the assumption of social responsibility by business believe that government should deal with the social demands of society.

The major arguments against social responsibility may be summarized as follows:

1. Violates sound economic business decision making that should rightfully concentrate on earning profit.
2. Might be illegal—executives do not have the legal right to use corporate resources to pursue social responsibility.
3. *Costs* are excessive compared to the *benefits* to society and would tend to raise prices to excessive levels.
4. Managers aren't trained nor do they possess the skills or resources to determine which socially desirable projects to support.
5. Concentrates too much power in the hands of business executives.
6. Leads to the deterioration of the free enterprise system.

An Evaluation of the "Pros" and "Cons" of Social Responsibility

Both the positions for and against the assumption of social responsibility by business make logical arguments to support their case. What we often find is that business and executives themselves are very "pro" social responsibility when profits are high or social conditions unfavorable, and "anti" social responsibility when the economy is under great pressure, when the company is in financial difficulty, or when social conditions do not warrant a great deal of concern.

Friedman's arguments against the assumption of social responsibility by business firms have been criticized on a number of grounds. First, Friedman implies that business should engage in "open and free competition" as part of the "rules of the game." However, open and free competition in most sectors of our economy does not exist. A second and more fundamental counterpoint to Friedman's position is that business firms (particularly large ones) cannot ignore their social responsibilities. Almost every major decision made in a corporation affects various groups in and outside the organization. Problems confronting society—employment discrimination, environment pollution, unsafe products, corporate bribery, illegal political contributions, and price fixing—are all past practices of some companies not in the best interest of society.

Because of the social undesirability of many acts of managers, there has been an increasing amount of governmental regulation. Some managers have concluded that "if it's legal, it's ethical," i.e., if it is not in violation of the law, one is free to do as one wishes. This managerial philosophy will tend to invite more and more outside regulatory attempts and may be self-defeating in the long run. Being socially responsible means more than just following the law. It means considering the *consequences* of one's actions and asking if such actions are socially responsible. *Social responsibility starts where the law ends.* Keith Davis stresses this point by the following statement:

> A firm is not being socially responsible if it merely complies with the minimum requirements of the law, because this is what any good citizen would do. A profit maximizing firm under the rules of classical economics would do as much. Social responsibility goes one step further. It is a firm's acceptance of a social obligation beyond the requirements of the law.[7]

MANAGEMENT'S REACTION TO GOVERNMENT LAWS AND REGULATIONS

Business is regulated by a large number of federal, state, and local laws and agencies. In recent years, there has been considerable discussion on the issue of whether there is excessive and unnecessary regulation of business by government. The sheer volume and complexity of government laws and regulations creates a great deal of frustration for many managers. All levels of government have played an increasingly active role in business operations. The laws and regulations affect managers and organizations because they add a degree of uncertainty to the organization and limit the decision-making freedom of managers.

While most managers accept some degree of government regulation of business, many people believe that excessive controls prevent the business

Qualities Needed for Success as a Manager in Your Organization

- Basic honesty
- Loyalty
- Dedication to the job
- Eagerness to learn
- Humility
- Ability to communicate effectively

CHARLES W. MERRITT, Chairman of the Board, Emeritus, Commercial Metals Company

from operating efficiently and effectively. They argue that the costs of many government regulations are far greater than the benefits to society. Practicing managers often cite several complaints about laws and regulations such as:

1. Lack of understanding on precisely how to comply with the laws and regulations
2. The excessive reporting load created
3. The difficulties of accurate record keeping
4. Duplication of regulations
5. The costs incurred in implementing laws and regulations
6. Inconsistency in the application of laws and regulations
7. The dilution of managerial decision-making authority brought about by government intervention.

Consumer groups and others insist that government plays an essential role in protecting society from business practices that are not in the best interests of all people.

CORPORATE PRACTICES

Many firms are doing more than just complying with the law. A survey of 232 large corporations revealed that approximately two-thirds have established definite policies regarding social responsibilities and have created special organizational units to deal with these areas.[8] The most common unit is headed by a vice-president reporting to the chief executive officer or president. It appears that the larger the number of stockholders for a corporation, the more committed the management is to a sense of social responsibility. Allied Chemical, for example, has set up an Environment Service Department concerned with air and water pollution control, occupational health, and product safety. Its manager reports directly to the company's president. Some firms have approached the task through the boards of directors to ensure a greater concern for social responsibility. Koppers Company established two board committees composed of four outside directors each. One committee is concerned with the environment and the other with human resources. At least twice each year, the management of Koppers will account to these two committees concerning their efforts in this regard.

Other companies feel that the responsibility cannot be segmented and compartmentalized. When its treatment of migrant field workers was brought rather forcefully to the attention of the Coca-Cola Company, a special project was established at the direction of the president of Coca-Cola's food division. Expenditures on housing, education, and health services for migrant workers have now been integrated into the company's regular activities.

With respect to specific activities by particular companies, in one year Dow Chemical invested $20 million in pollution control equipment. At a 9 percent depreciation rate, the yearly cost came to $1.8 million, to which was added $10.5 million to run the equipment. The environmental clean-up cost came to $12.3 million for the year, but Dow claims to have recovered at least that much in terms of reduced corrosion on cooling towers and the saving of valuable chemicals previously pumped out as waste. In three years' time, over $6 million was saved in recovery of these wasted chemicals alone. Although this attempt at a Michigan plant was quite successful, Dow still has serious air and water pollution problems to be solved in other plants it owns. But this case indicates that both economic and social values can at times be coaligned in the short run.

In recent years, *Business Week* has given awards for private company efforts in the two major areas of (1) improving the physical environment and (2) developing human resources. The process of selecting companies for these awards has brought to light many examples of specific company actions in these two fields. Among these are:

- an educational program to combat drug abuse
- provision of seed money to minority suppliers
- urban rehabilitation
- loans to construct low-cost housing
- providing managerial training to minority groups
- establishing manufacturing plants in ghetto areas

International Business Machines Corporation located a new plant in the Bedford-Stuyvesant neighborhood of Brooklyn in 1968. After a financially disastrous beginning, the facility became profitable in 1970. The plant probably could have been immediately profitable if located elsewhere, but the economic decision to build the plant in Brooklyn was affected by a felt responsibility for providing jobs in an area that probably had the largest con-

Rather than introducing specific programs such as job enrichment and decision participation, the U.S. Eaton Corporation proposed to improve the general climate and quality of work life in all new plants built since 1968. Some thirteen plants involving over 5,000 personnel now work within climates characterized by:

1. Counseling rather than a rule-penalty process in altering undesirable behavior.
2. Hiring as a two-way exchange process. Procedures normally accorded only to managers and white-collar employees are now extended to all.
3. Abolition of probationary periods.
4. Abolition of time clocks and buzzers.
5. The same fringe benefit package for both factory and office personnel.
6. Biweekly departmental meetings to discuss work problems.
7. Periodic plant manager roundtables with chosen representatives from departments.
8. Staff specialists conducting most business at the work site rather than within their offices.
9. More employee participation in a variety of managerial staff meetings.

As a consequence, some employees asked for job enlargement and enrichment, while others did not. The company responds to these initiatives, rather than pushing a standard program for all. Major concrete results thus far are: (1) new plants have an absenteeism rate ranging from .5 to 3 percent, compared to 6 to 12 percent for older installations, (2) new plants have annual turnover rates under 4 percent, as compared to up to 60 percent in other plants, (3) hourly outputs for identical products range up to 35 percent more in the new plants, and (4) scrap and rework range up to 15 percent less for the new installations. The only negative for the new plants is a poorer safety record, presumably caused by personnel striving harder to improve output.

FIGURE 17-3

Changes in the Quality of Life at U.S. Eaton

For greater details, see Donald N. Scobel, "Doing Away with Factory Blues," *Harvard Business Review* (November–December 1975): 132–142.

centration of hard-core unemployed in the United States at the time. An example of a systematic effort at improving the quality of worker life is described in Figure 17-3 outlining changes in the quality of work life at the U.S. Eaton Company.

THE SOCIAL AUDIT

social audit

A **social audit** is defined as a commitment to systematic assessment of and reporting on some meaningful, definable domain of a company's activities that have social impact. Some firms have demonstrated their concern for the area of social responsibility by periodically surveying and assessing their activities. This practice, when formalized, has become known as *social auditing*. Systematic social auditing is only in its infancy, and relatively few firms have undertaken a periodic appraisal process.[9] Its uses are to provide internal information to management, which aids in decision making, and to provide external information to the public in response to pressures on the enterprise.

Four possible types of audits are currently being utilized: (1) a simple inventory of activities, (2) compilation of socially relevant expenditures, (3) specific program management, and (4) determination of social impact. The inventory is generally the place where one would start. It would consist of a simple listing of activities undertaken by the firm over and above what is required. For example, firms have itemized the following types of social activities: (1) minority employment and training, (2) support of minority enterprises, (3) pollution control, (4) corporate giving, (5) involvement in selected community projects by firm executives, and (6) a hard-core unemployed program. The ideal social audit would involve determination of the true *benefits* to society of any socially oriented business activity.

BUSINESS ETHICS

Our previous discussion has been concerned with the issue of social responsibility as it relates to the decisions made by managers within organizations. Whereas social responsibility is primarily concerned with the overall operation of the corporation, **ethics** are contemporary standards or principles of conduct that govern the actions and behavior of individuals within the organization. They provide a basis for determining what is *right* or *wrong* in terms of a given situation. Defining what is ethical or unethical is complicated because social values—moral concepts—tend to change over time. Different groups within society may have divergent views of acceptable conduct.

ethics

A distinction between laws and ethics should be made. While laws provide an overall framework of restrictions, they should not be confused with ethics. What is within a literal interpretation of the law may not be ethical. If a practice is defined by the law as illegal, then it is not a matter of ethical or moral standards but a legal requirement. Society, through its government representatives, may pass laws to stop harmful practices where the ethical standards of individuals in the industry have been unsuccessful in preventing such practices.

As illustrated in Figure 17-4, ethical norms are established by society and govern the development of ethical standards for an industry, a business firm, or an individual manager. Each industry develops its own ethical standards, and the firms and individual managers in the industry are expected to adhere to these codes of behavior.

The ethical norms provided by society in general are not so specific and long lasting that they always give clearly defined guidelines for everyone to follow. The difference between conduct that is just barely tolerated and that

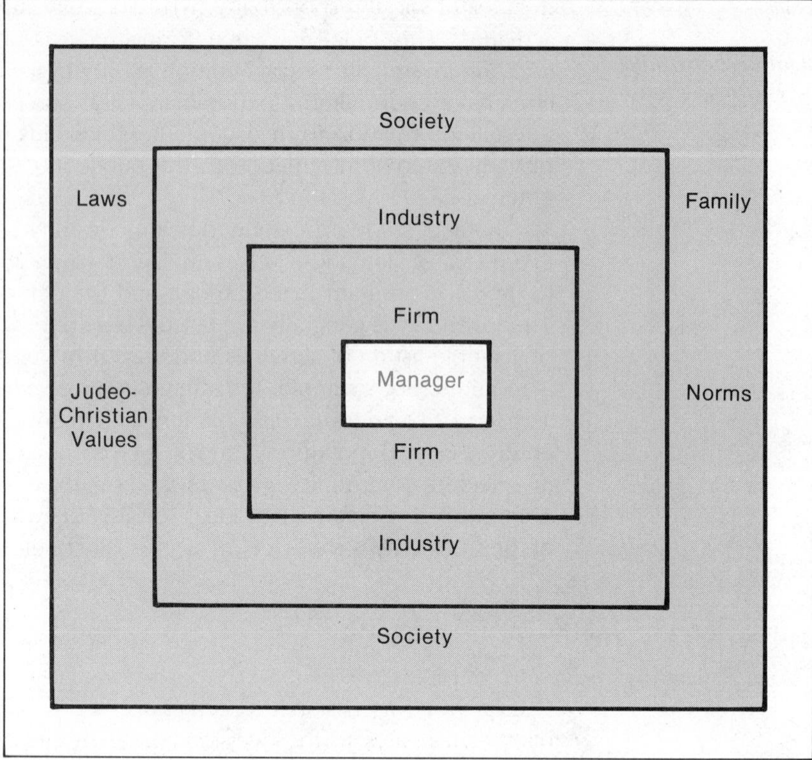

FIGURE 17-4

Frames of Reference for Ethical Standards for Managers

which is clearly indefensible is often difficult to identify. Our elected federal representatives often take lavish foreign trips on taxpayers' money to investigate some phenomena that have low probabilities of affecting future legislation. Highly respected members of society hire professional lawyers to look for loopholes in tax laws.

EXAMPLES OF ILLEGAL AND UNETHICAL PRACTICES

Reading the newspapers or watching the evening news provides ample illustrations of illegal and/or unethical practices of individuals within large corporations. While ethics are our primary consideration, there are numerous examples of illegal practices engaged in by managers. How widespread are these illegal activities? An article in *The Wall Street Journal* indicated that the Internal Revenue Service was investigating 111 companies concerning their political gifts. These "political gifts" involved most of the top-level executives of the companies. The executives involved allegedly either falsified expenses to obtain reimbursement for "contributions" or brought "laundered money" back from Europe, or stashed money in secret safes in their offices.

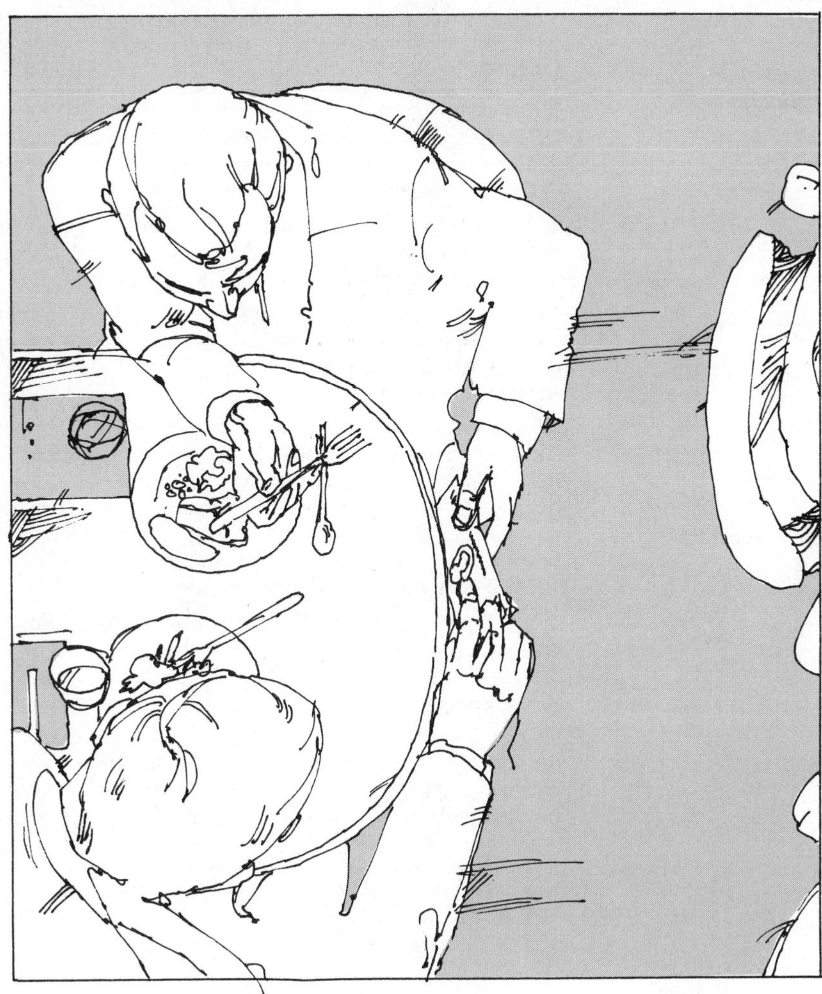

Where ethics are concerned, actions speak louder than words.

A study of 1,043 major corporations during the period 1970–1979 revealed that 117 or 11 percent had been involved in at least one major criminal scandal. A total of 188 citations were involved covering 163 separate offenses, including 98 antitrust violations, 28 cases of kickbacks, bribery, or illegal rebates, 21 illegal political contributions, 11 cases of fraud, and 5 income tax evasion cases.[10] Examples of some of these illegal activities are presented in Table 17-1.

While having 11 percent of America's largest corporations involved in some form of illegal activity is perhaps shocking, the figures do not include the illegal misdoings of small or medium-sized firms. Bribing purchasing agents and "skimming" cash are often considered usual occurrences in some small enterprises. Large corporations and their executives are more closely scrutinized than are smaller firms; thus managers in large companies are

TABLE 17-1. *Examples of Illegal Activities of Large U.S. Business Firms*

Offense	Company
Illegal compaign contributions in 1973 of $55,000. Plea Guilty. 1975—CAB charges related to slush fund contributions. Settlement. 1977—SEC charges related to same. Consent decree.	American Airlines
1977—SEC charges concerning $2.7 million in payments to customers. Consent decree. 1978—Treasury Dept. charges about some matter. Settlement and $750,000 fine.	Anheuser-Busch
1973-1974—Two cases of fixing prices of steel reinforcing bars. Company and one employee pleaded nolo; another convicted after trial. 1980—Mail fraud related to bribes paid for ship-repair business. Guilty plea.	Bethlehem Steel
1973— Illegal political contributions of $100,000. Company and executive pleaded guilty. 1975—SEC charge about $10 million slush fund used for political contributions. Consent decree. 1977—Company and two employees charged with giving illegal gifts to an IRS agent. Company pleaded guilty, one employee pleaded nolo, the other convicted after trial. 1978—Fixing prices of uranium. Pleaded guilty.	Gulf Oil
1973—Illegal campaign contributions of $30,000. Company and chairman pleaded guilty. 1975—SEC charges related to $634,000 slush fund for contributions. Consent decree.	3M
1977—SEC charges related to over $1 million in allegedly illegal rebates to customers and political contribution. Consent decree. 1978—Seagram Distillers, three subsidiaries and four executives charged with bribery of a state liquor official. All pleaded guilty. 1979—Illegal payments to members of a state liquor-control board. Guilty plea. Fined $1.5 million.	Joseph E. Seagram

Source: Adapted from Irwin Ross, "How Lawless Are Big Companies?" *FORTUNE,* December 1, 1980, p. 57.

probably less prone to be engaged in illegal activities than those managers in small companies or even many individual taxpayers.

While there are many practices that are clearly illegal, deciding what is unethical is much more difficult. The following provide examples of unethical behavior or activities of managers:

- Padding expense accounts to obtain reimbursement for questionable business expenses
- Divulging confidential information or trade secrets
- Using company property and/or materials for one's own personal use
- Giving or receiving "gifts"
- Terminating employment without giving sufficient notice
- Downgrading fellow employees or managers
- Being severely critical of competitors

Factors Affecting Managerial Ethics

At least five factors significantly affect decisions made by managers involving ethical issues. These factors will be discussed next.

Legislation

Laws may be viewed as the results of a trend of what society expects in terms of acceptable behavior. A practice can be made illegal if society views it as being excessive or unethical. The law defines and clarifies acceptable standards or practices in a given area. For example, if contributions to political candidates from corporations are illegal, then one either obeys the law or violates it. However, in either case the guidelines or standards are clear, and the violator may be punished for engaging in the illegal activity. Laws are often passed as a result of low ethical standards or the failure to recognize social responsibilities.

Government Regulations

These rules or standards define acceptable and unacceptable practices. For example, government regulations in the areas of minimum product safety, acceptable level auto emissions, safe working conditions, and nondiscriminatory employment practices are all supported by federal and state laws. However, the interpretation of the laws by the courts and the development of guidelines by government agencies assist managers in understanding what are acceptable practices.

Industry and/or Company Ethical Codes of Behavior

Many industries and individual companies have formal, written codes of ethics that provide specific guidelines for managers and other employees to follow. The key question in this regard is whether individuals within organizations are truly governed by the code of ethics or simply give lip-service to the guidelines. Another issue is whether the company or industry *enforces* the code if individuals or companies violate it. In any event, these *codes of ethics* define or clarify the ethical issues and allow the individual to make the final decision.

Kodak's SPICE concept

As mentioned above, companies have developed specific codes of ethics. Eastman Kodak and Texas Instruments provide excellent examples. **Kodak's SPICE concept** provides guidelines for company practices (see Figure 17-5) and as such is dynamic and flexible. Kodak intends for SPICE to reflect the needs in the marketplace and to anticipate legal changes.

Throughout the history of Eastman Kodak Company, the principal factor in its growth has been the conviction that fulfilling customer needs and desires is the only road to corporate success. Such clichés as "share of the market," when used to explain performance, gloss over the fact that the consumer is supreme in a free economy and that all ingredients contributing to corporate success rest ultimately with him.

Kodak recognizes that it has to meet many responsibilities to assure successful operations. Our concern for Shareowners, the Public Interest, Customers, and Employees has come to be known throughout the Kodak organization as the "SPICE" concept.

A review for management of each element in the SPICE concept reveals how its combined approaches to influencing business operations apply to the company's growth and success.

Shareowners

Currently there are more than 222,000 shareowners of Eastman Kodak Company—an increase from 210,000 a year ago and from fewer than 121,000 in 1960. Kodak investors now own more than 161,000,000 common shares. These figures indicate that investors expect continued good performance from Kodak.

Men, women, and institutions have used their savings to invest in Kodak, and the Company has a primary obligation to satisfy their fair interests. Their judgment of Kodak and their confidence in the Company rest on the prospects of dividends and growth from their investments. In response to shareowners' interest in the Company, it is necessary to produce profits and provide an adequate return on investment. Today, the shareowners' judgment also is based increasingly on the ability of Kodak to meet its responsibilities to employees and the public interest.

In this respect, the concern of investors and employees should be parallel, serving each other for mutual benefit.

Public Interest

Our corporate social responsibility may take diverse forms, but in essence it reflects concern for the well-being of the communities and countries in which Kodak carries on its activities. Examples of Kodak's activities in the public interest can be found in the improvement of communities through special training programs to upgrade the disadvantaged; clean air and water (healthful environment) programs, aid to education and numerous other projects for civic betterment. This concern also is reflected in Kodak's encouragement of employee participation in civic, community, political, and other similar individual pursuits. It is exhibited, too, in the constant, substantial research and development efforts to produce new and improved products and services. Although often overlooked, corporate profits are essential to finance public interest projects. Kodak's 114,000 people are, of course, members of the public that renders judgment of performance in the public interest. While this judgment of accomplishment obviously varies among Kodakers, collectively it will have a substantial influence on public opinion about the Company.

FIGURE 17-5
"SPICE" Concept Guides Kodak Business Practices

Customers

Kodak must sell products and services—and continue to sell them in volume. Only satisfied customers will come back again and again. Thus, customer satisfaction is both a short- and a long-term goal. To reach this objective, the Company must produce and offer—at fair prices—high-quality products and services containing the features and capabilities that customers desire. This requires all the inventive genius we can muster in research and development leading to new and improved products and services; better ideas and greater efficiency in production, purchasing, distribution, marketing, and every other area of the Company's activities. This also means continued attention to the informative quality and scope of advertising and promotion; better exercise of personal and collective skills and capabilities; improved training programs for product users and for Kodak people as well as for our intermediate customers, the dealers and distributors.

Employees

Each Kodak man and woman is likely to judge the Company's overall performance in a different way; perhaps in terms of wages and salaries, opportunity for advancement, or direct and indirect benefits such as the Wage Dividend, hospital and medical care benefits, and work environment. There are also intangibles that he may consider, such as pride in the Company, opportunity through his job to make contributions to improving products or services and personal recognition for his accomplishments. The interests of Kodak people, Kodak shareowners, and Kodak customers are not mutually exclusive as one might initially be inclined to believe. During the past 10 years, 31,000 Kodak people have shown their faith in the future of the Company by deferring $146,000,000 in Wage Dividend payments for investment in the Savings and Investment Plan. Their interests merge with those of other shareowners in renewed appreciation for achieving profits and growth.

This, then, is a summary of the SPICE concept. It emphasizes that concern for shareowners, public interest, customers, and employees must motivate any successful business. Companies that are dedicated to satisfying the fair needs of these elements to the exclusion of all others are indispensible for the continued health of our society and the survival of the free enterprise system.

FIGURE 17-5
(continued)

Kodak communicates this concept to its employees in meetings and discussion groups by members of management.

Texas Instruments published a handbook entitled "Ethics in the Business of T.I."[11] The company's overall philosophy of business can be summarized as follows:

> It is fundamental to TI's philosophy that good ethics and good business are synonymous when viewed from moral, legal and practical standpoints. The trust and respect of all people—fellow workers, customers,

consumers, stockholders, government employees, elected officials, suppliers, competitors, neighbors, friends, the press, and the general public—are assets that cannot be purchased. They must be earned. This is why all of the business of TI must be conducted according to the highest ethical standards.

In the handbook, TI has statements establishing guidelines for ethical decision making in business. Areas covered include: truthfulness in advertising, gifts and entertainment, improper use of corporate assets, political contributions, payments in connection with business transactions, conflicts of interest trade secrets and proprietary information, and other matters.

There are advantages for organizations to form industry associations to develop and promote improved codes of ethics. It is difficult for a single firm to pioneer ethical practices if its competitors undercut them by taking advantage of unethical shortcuts. For example, U.S. companies must comply with the Foreign Corrupt Practices Act of 1977 with respect to bribes of foreign government officials or business executives. Obviously this law does not prevent foreign competitors from bribing government or business officials to achieve business.[12] Perhaps the best hope would be for the major multinational enterprises to agree jointly to such a prohibition. When codes are not voluntarily followed, a society usually resorts to specific laws and penalties. In the case of international bribes, there is no international law. Should the United States declare the practice illegal, its multinational companies may find it difficult to compete with firms based in nations that do not disapprove. In this case, a voluntary code adopted by the leading firms of the world is likely to be the most effective method of handling the situation.

Social Pressures

Social forces and pressures have considerable impact on ethics or acceptable standards of behavior. Examples of pressure groups seeking to make organizations more responsive to the needs and desires of society are numerous. Groups have demonstrated for more employment of blacks or other minorities, boycotted products, and complained and threatened action to prevent the construction of nuclear power plants. Such actions by pressure groups may, in fact, cause management to alter certain decisions by taking a broader view of the environment and the needs of society.

Conflicts Between a Manager's Personal Standards and the Needs of the Firm

The needs and goals of the firm may conflict with the values and ethical standards of a manager. This dilemma between organizational goals and personal ethics or values greatly complicates the life of the typical manager.

There is often considerable pressure on managers to increase performance and generate higher profits. At times, this may create pressures to compromise personal ethics for the goals of the company. A study by Archie Carroll found that managers feel a great deal of pressure to compromise their personal ethical standards in order to achieve organizational goals.[13] Carroll's study, representing the response of 258 managers, revealed that 50 percent of top-level managers, 65 percent of middle-level managers and 84 percent of lower-level managers felt "under pressure to compromise personal standards to achieve company goals."

ETHICAL DILEMMAS FACED BY MANAGERS

ethical dilemmas

Today's managers are confronted by many ethical dilemmas. The following are examples of legal but perhaps **ethical dilemmas** faced by managers in business today:

- The vice-president of a California industrial manufacturer "being forced as an officer to sign corporate documents that I knew were not in the best interests of minority stockholders."
- A manager of product development from a computer company in Massachusetts "trying to act as though the product [computer software] would correspond to what the customer had been led by sales to expect, when, in fact, I knew it wouldn't."
- A manager of corporate planning from California "acquiring a non-U.S. company with two sets of books to evade income taxes—standard practice for that country. Do we (1) declare income and pay taxes, (2) take the 'black money' out of the country (illegally), or (3) continue tax evasion?"
- The president of a real estate property management firm in Washington "projecting cash flow without substantial evidence in order to obtain a higher loan than the project can realistically amortize."
- A young Texas insurance manager "being asked to make policy changes that produced more premium for the company and commission for an agent but did not appear to be of advantage to the policyholder."[14]

CHANGES IN THE ETHICS OF BUSINESS

As we have discussed, concern over ethical issues is not new. Brenner and Molander compared views of over twelve hundred 1976 *Harvard Business Review* readers with a similar survey done in 1961.[15] The survey was concerned with determining if business ethics had changed since the early 1960s and if so, how and why? Also the study investigated the relationship between ethical issues and the dilemma of corporate social responsibility. The highlights of this study can be summarized as follows:

1. There is substantial disagreement among respondents as to whether ethical standards in business today have changed from what they were.
2. Respondents are somewhat more cynical about the ethical conduct of their peers than they were.
3. Most respondents favor ethical codes, although they strongly prefer general precept codes to specific practice codes.
4. The dilemmas respondents experience and the factors they feel have the greatest impact on business ethics suggest that ethical codes alone will not substantially improve business conduct.
5. Most respondents have overcome the traditional ideological barriers to the concept of social responsibility and have embraced its practice as a legitimate and achievable goal for business.
6. Most respondents rank their customers well ahead of shareholders and employees as the client group to whom they feel the greatest responsibility.

TABLE 17-2. *Percentage of Companies (Overall and by Size) Reporting Various Practices Related to Corporate Codes of Conduct*

Question	Overall Response	Size Categories[a] 1	2	3	4	5	6	7	8	9	10
Does your company have a code of conduct?	(N = 611)										
Yes	77%	40	57	74	75	72	90	85	87	92	97
Who receives a copy?	(N = 486)										
Officers/key employees	97%	83	97	94	98	100	100	98	96	100	100
Other employees	55%	46	60	35	54	58	42	60	46	70	68
Who signs it periodically?	(N = 481)										
Officers/key employees	85%	75	62	80	87	80	85	91	86	91	90
Other employees	(N = 451) 27%	23	27	12	17	30	25	23	31	47	39
Are procedures specified for handling violations of the code's provisions?	(N = 478)										
Yes	63%	41	46	38	54	58	55	66	75	85	83
Have procedures been enforced in the last several years?	(N = 463)										
Yes	62%	42	43	30	48	48	64	63	77	83	91

Source: Bernard J. White and B. Ruth Montgomery, "Corporate Codes of Conduct," *California Management Review* 23 (Winter 1980): 82.

[a]The overall sample of 673 was broken into deciles by size. Category 1 is $0–60 million; category 2 is $60–132 million; category 3 is $132–207 million; category 4 is $201–300 million; category 5 is $300–467 million; category 6 is $467–717 million; category 7 is $717–1,150 million; category 8 is $1,150–1,900 million; category 9 is $1,900–4,000 million; category 10 is $4,000 million and above.

According to Raymond C. Baumhart, author of a 1961 study on the ethics of businessmen,

> Business behavior is more ethical [in 1976] than it was 15 years ago [1961], but the expectations of a better educated and ethically sensitized public have risen more rapidly than the behavior.[16]

The study also found that respondents thought that they were more ethical than the average manager and that their department and company were more ethical than others. The respondents suggested that a written code of ethics would help to improve business practices.

Apparently the use of formalized corporate codes of ethics is increasing in American businesses. In a 1980 survey of 611 companies, it was found that 77 percent of the firms had a code of conduct. As can be seen in Table 17-2, 97 percent of the largest companies (those with $400 million or more in sales) had corporate codes of conduct.

A MANAGERIAL CODE OF ETHICS

The medical and legal professions have established codes of ethics that provide guidelines and standards for conduct. These "codes" are known to everyone in the profession but may or may not be practiced to the letter. Managers do not have an established code of ethics, but in recent years there have been numerous attempts to develop and promote one. The following list provides an example of such an attempt to formulate a **managerial code of ethics:**

managerial code of ethics

- I will recognize that management is a call to service with responsibilities to my subordinates, associates, supervisors, employer, community, nation, and world.
- I will be guided in all my activities by truth, accuracy, fair dealings, and good taste.
- I will earn and carefully guard my reputation for good moral character and citizenship.
- I will recognize that, as a leader, my own pattern of work and life will exert more influence on my subordinates than what I say or write.
- I will give the same consideration to the rights and interests of others that I ask for myself.
- I will maintain a broad and balanced outlook and will look for value in the ideas and opinions of others.
- I will regard my role as a manager as an obligation to help subordinates and associates achieve personal and professional fulfillment.
- I will keep informed on the latest developments in the techniques, equipment, and processes associated with the practice of management and the industry in which I am employed.

- I will search for, recommend, and initiate methods to increase productivity and efficiency.
- I will respect the professional competence of my colleagues in the ICPM and will work with them to support and promote the goals and programs of the Institute.
- I will support efforts to strengthen professional management through example, education, training, and a lifelong pursuit of excellence.[17]

Summary

Managers in today's organizations have the difficult job of trying to meet the demands of employees, stockholders, government, customers, the public, and other groups. Social responsibility is concerned with how organizations and managers deal with the issues and problems confronting society.

Although a universally acceptable definition of social responsibility has not been developed, we define it as the basic obligation of an organization to constituent groups in society other than stockholders and beyond that prescribed by law or contract. Full acceptance of this definition means that a firm ensures that its decisions and operations meet the needs and interests of society. While business firms have contributed greatly to the high standards of living enjoyed in the United States, they are being expected by many people to do more. But how much responsibility for society's problems should business assume? Those favoring increased corporate social responsibility advance arguments that: (1) it is in the best interest of the firm to pursue socially responsible programs, (2) they have the resources to do so, (3) society expects business to be socially responsible, (4) long-run profits for the business may increase, and (5) if business is not responsive to society's needs, the public may press for more government regulation.

There are several arguments against business assuming social responsibility. Dr. Milton Friedman, a leading opponent of business assumption of social responsibility, asserts that there is one and only one social responsibility of business and that is to generate profits so long as it stays within the rules of the game by engaging in open and free competition without deception and fraud. The major arguments against social responsibility include these: it misdirects resources and violates sound business decision making that should concentrate on making profits; costs are excessive relative to benefits and therefore may cause prices to increase; managers do not have the resources or skills to engage in social projects; it concentrates too much power in the hands of business executives; and it may lead to the deterioration of the free enterprise system. What has been the response of business? Many large corporations are engaged in numerous socially responsible programs such as minority employment and training, pollution control, job and product safety programs, energy conservation, quality of life, and the elimination of poverty.

While social responsibility is primarily concerned with the overall operation of the corporation, ethics are contemporary standards or principles of conduct that govern the actions and behavior of individuals within the organization. Ethics provide a basis for determining what is right or wrong. What is ethical or unethical is complicated because societal values and moral concepts tend to change over time. Acceptable practices are established by society and govern the ethical standards for an industry, a business firm, or an individual manager. Laws, government regulations, industry ethical codes, social pressures, and conflicts between the manager's personal standards and the needs of the firm all affect decisions made by managers involving ethical issues.

Review Questions

1. In general, how is American business viewed by the general public? Provide examples. Is the perception accurate? Why or why not?
2. What is meant by social responsibility? Define and describe the relationships a firm has with groups in society.
3. What is the primary role(s) of business in society? Explain. Should the role(s) change? Why?
4. Compare and contrast two opposing views of social responsibility (arguments for and against). Which, in your view, is more correct or appropriate?
5. Can social responsibility be legislated? If so, give examples of laws.
6. What are some examples of current practices of companies engaging in social responsibilities? Be specific. Are there others you are aware of from your own experience or reading?
7. What is meant by the term *ethics*? How ethical are business people, and what determines ethical norms for managers?
8. Briefly discuss several examples of unethical practices by business managers. What factors affect managerial ethics?
9. What is Kodak's "SPICE" concept? How does the company use it?
10. What are some examples of ethical dilemmas faced by managers? How can they cope with these dilemmas?
11. Are the ethics of business/managers changing?

Exercises

1. Visit two local companies that have formal codes of ethics. Compare the codes of ethics with our discussion of ethics in this chapter.
2. Select what you consider to be a local social or environmental problem—such as water or air pollution. Make a list of the groups or businesses within the community that are concerned about the problem. Analyze the impact of the problem on the various segments of the community. Develop a proposal for solving the problem giving consideration to the benefits and costs of your solution.

Case Study

An Ethical Dilemma

James Young is marketing manager for a large heavy equipment manufacturer. He has a staff of twenty sales representatives who report directly to him. Business has been rather poor lately. Another firm in the industry has developed a product that is slightly lower in price and Mr. Young's sales force has been having a rather difficult time competing with this new product. James recognizes that production will likely have to be reduced and personnel terminated unless sales improve. This bothers James quite a bit as some of his close friends are employed in the production department.

One of James's top salesmen is Bob Trezivant. Bob has had the reputation for obtaining sales when no one else could. But James has become extremely concerned of late because of rumors that have come to his attention regarding Bob. James has heard that Bob has been giving kickbacks to purchasing agents for recommending the company's product. James calls Bob in to speak with him regarding the kickback rumors and the conversation goes as follows:

James: Bob, I realize your sales are tops in the firm. We really appreciate your efforts. However, a very difficult subject has come to my attention lately. I have heard that you are providing inappropriate payoffs to certain purchasing agents when they helped you out. Is this so?

Bob: You are darn right it is! Our products aren't selling well now. That's the only way to compete with that new, lower-priced product. Some of my best friends are in production. I don't want them to be laid off.

James: ?

QUESTIONS

1. What should James tell Bob?
2. Is what Bob is doing ethical?
3. What controls should be initiated to reduce this practice in the future?

Case Study

The Hiring of a Friend's Daughter

Marcie Sweeney had recently graduated from college with a degree in general business. Marcie was quite bright, although her grades might lead a person to think otherwise. She had thoroughly enjoyed school—dating, tennis, swimming, and similar stimulating academic events. When she graduated from the university she had not found a job. Her dad was extremely upset when he discovered this and he took it on himself to see that Marcie became employed.

Her father, Allen Sweeney, was executive vice-president of a medium-sized manufacturing firm. One of the people he contacted in seeking employment for Marcie was Bill Garbo, the president of another firm in the area. Mr. Sweeney purchased many of his firm's supplies from Garbo's company. On telling Bill his problem, Allen was told to send Marcie to his office for an interview. Marcie did as instructed by her father and was surprised that before she left that day she had a job in the accounting department. Marcie may have been lazy but she certainly was not stupid. She realized that this job was obtained because of the hope of future business from her father's company. Although the work was not challenging, it paid better than the other jobs in the accounting department.

It did not take long for the employees in the department to discover the reason she had been hired—Marcie told them. When a difficult job was assigned to Marcie, she normally got one of the other employees to do it, inferring that Mr. Garbo would be pleased with them by helping her out. She developed a pattern of coming in late, taking long lunch breaks, and leaving early. When the department manager attempted to reprimand her for these unorthodox activities, Marcie would bring up the close relationship that her father had with the president of this firm. The department manager was at his limits when he asked for your help.

QUESTIONS

1. From an ethical standpoint, how would you evaluate the merits of Mr. Garbo employing Marcie? Discuss.
2. Now that she is employed, how would you suggest that the situation be resolved?
3. Do you feel that a firm should have policies regarding such practices? Discuss.

Notes

1. Thomas M. Jones, "Corporate Social Responsibility, Revisited, Redefined," *California Management Review* 22, no. 2 (Spring 1980): 59, 60.
2. Thomas Benham, "The Factual Foundation," in Clarence H. Danhof and James C. Worthy, eds., *Crisis in Confidence 11: Corporate America* (Springfield, Ill,: Sagamon State University, 1975), pp. 21–53.
3. Keith Davis, "The Case for and against Business Assumption of Social Responsibilities," *Academy of Management Journal* (June 1973). Reprinted in Archie B. Carroll, *Managing Corporate Social Responsibility* (Boston: Little, Brown, 1977) p. 35.
4. Adapted from the Committee for Economic Development and from Sandra L. Holmes, "Corporate Social Performance and Present Areas of Commitment," *Academy of Management Journal* 20 (1977): 435.
5. See Davis, "Case for and against," p. 36.
6. Milton Friedman, "The Social Responsibility to Business Is to Increase Its Profits," *New York Times Magazine,* September 1970, pp. 33, 122–126.
7. Davis, "Case for and against," p. 36.
8. Vernon M. Buehler and Y. K. Shetty, "Managerial Response to Social Responsibility Challenge." *Academy of Management Journal* 19 (March 1976): 69.
9. Raymond A. Bauer and Dan H. Fenn, Jr., "What Is a Corporate Social Audit?" *Harvard Business Review* 51 (January–February 1973): 38.
10. Irwin Ross, "How Lawless Are Big Companies?" *Fortune* (December 1980): 57.
11. Texas Instruments, "Ethics in the Business of T.I." (Dallas, 1977).
12. Bernard J. White and B. Ruth Montgomery, "Corporate Codes of Conduct," *California Management Review* 22, no. 2 (Winter 1980): 80.
13. Archie B. Carroll, "Managerial Ethics: A Post Watergate View," *Business Horizons* (April 1975): 77. See also Archie B. Carroll, "A Survey of Managerial Ethics:

Is Business Morality Watergate Morality?" *Business and Society Review* (1976): 58–63.

14. Steven N. Brenner and Earl A. Molander, "Is the Ethics of Business Changing?" *Harvard Business Review* (January–February 1977): 60.
15. Ibid., pp. 58–73.
16. Ibid., p. 68.
17. Code of Ethics of the Institute of Certified Professional Managers.

References

Armandi, B. R., and Tuzzolino, F. "Need Hierarchy Framework for Assessing Corporation Social Responsibility." *Academy of Management Review* 6 (January 1981): 21–28.

Carroll, Archie E. "A Three-Dimensional Conceptual Model of Corporate Performance." *Academy of Management Review* 4, no. 4 (October 1979): 497–505.

Clutterbuck, D. "Blowing the Whistle on Corporate Misconduct." *International Management* 35 (January 1980): 14–16.

Dhir, K. "American Corporate System." *Management International Review* 19 (1979): 13–20.

Drory, Amos, and Gluskinos, Uri M. "Machiavellianism and Leadership." *Journal of Applied Psychology* 64, no. 1 (February 1980): 81–86.

Greenough, William Croan. "Keeping Corporate Governance in the Private Sector." *Business Horizons* 23, no. 1 (February 1980): 71–81.

Grunig, James E. "A New Measure of Public Opinions on Corporate Social Responsibility." *Academy of Management Journal* 22, no. 4 (December 1979): 738–764.

Henderson, H. "Changing Corporate-Social Contract in the 1980s: Creative Opportunities for Consumer Affairs Professionals." *Public Relations Quarterly* 24 (Winter 1979): 7–14.

Hipp, H. "Business Ethics and Society's Future." *National Underwriter* 3 (property ed.) (September 14, 1979) pp. 7–14.

"How Business Treats Its Environment." *Business and Society Review* 33 (Spring 1980): 56–65.

Jones, T. M. "Corporate Social Responsibility Revisited, Redefined." *California Management Review* 22 (Spring 1980): 59–67.

Lippin, P. "When Business and the Community Cooperate." *Administrative Management* 42 (February 1981): 34– 35.

Marusi, A. R. "Balancing Power Through Public Accountability." *Public Relations Journal* 35 (May 1979): 24–26.

"Privacy Issue Arouses Concern about Ethics in Marketing Research." *Sales and Marketing Management,* December 8, 1980, pp. 88–89.

Rosen, G. R. "Can the Corporation Survive." *Dun's Review* 114 (August 1979): 40–42.

Shapiro, I. S. "Accountability and Power: Whither Corporate Governance in a Free Society?" *Management Review* 69 (February 1980): 29–31.

Sonnenfeld, Jeffrey, and Lawrence, Paul R. "Why Do Companies Succumb to Price Fixing?" *Harvard Business Review* 56, no. 4 (July–August 1978): 145–156.

Waters, James A. "Catch 20.5: Corporate Morality as an Organizational Phenomenon." *Organizational Dynamics* 6, no. 4 (Spring 1978): 3–19.

White, B. J., and Montgomery, B. R. "Corporate Codes of Conduct." *California Management Review* 22 (Winter 1980): 80–87.

KEY TERMS

Small Business Act	entrepreneur	procurement assistance
small business	nepotism	management assistance
Small Business Administration	financial assistance	Small Business Institute

LEARNING OBJECTIVES

After completing this chapter you should be able to

1. Describe what is meant by a small business and identify why some people want to have their own business.
2. Describe some of the factors affecting the management of small business.
3. State some of the pitfalls to starting a small business.
4. Describe the types of assistance available to small businesses from the U.S. Small Business Administration.

18

Managing Small Businesses

Amy Wells talks with much emotion about the three months since her husband died unexpectedly and she took over his quite successful gift shop. Coping with the loss of her husband as well as rearing her fourteen-year-old son has been mixed with learning about buying merchandise, conducting inventory, paying the sales staff, and paying the firm's suppliers. This is Amy's first experience with the working world, and she chose to throw herself into it. Along with the help of her husband's lawyer and accountant, she personally contacted the over five hundred suppliers her husband dealt with, assuring them that she would be taking over the business and that they would get paid.

Some of her know-how about merchandising she had picked up without much effort simply by listening to her late husband talk about the shop at home or occasionally helping him at the store. The remainder of the skills she is developing came from the advice of friends and business associates–and from a real determination to keep the gift shop as successful as her husband would have wanted it to be.

Jack Wilson smiled as he punched the time clock in the electronic parts assembly plant. It was his last time to walk through the doors of a business he couldn't call his own—or so he hoped. Jack had always been talented with his hands; there was even talk of art school scholarships when he won some sculpting competitions in high school. But his family was poor, so he soon joined the work force, and Jack probably would have died in its ranks had he and his wife Lois not recently inherited a small upstate farm belonging to her grandparents.

After settling the estate and selling the farm, Jack and Lois were investing every cent in a small jewelry store that had been on the market for some time. Previously, all merchandise had been handled on consignment, but Jack had plans to purchase all merchandise and, in addition, create his own original designs. At first, he would have to depend on watch and other repair work to supplement sales. Jack had no skills in management, sales, inventory, or retailing, but he vowed that his desire to be his own boss would carry him through.

In this chapter, we will define and describe the role of small businesses in our society, discuss the reasons why people want to own a small business, the factors affecting the management of small businesses, the pitfalls or problems of small businesses, and the types of assistance available to small business owners. At times in the chapter, readers might sense the authors are being unduly pessimistic with regard to recommending that individuals start their own small businesses. This is certainly not the case. But individuals should be fully aware of the difficulties they may encounter if a decision is made to start a small business. Successfully starting and continuing profitable operations of a small business requires knowledge and application of the basic fundamentals of business and management. The potential small business owner should be aware of the pitfalls or possible causes of failure, as well as the types of assistance available to help them avoid becoming part of the failure statistics.

THE SMALL BUSINESS

Every year thousands of individuals motivated by a desire to "be their own boss," to earn a better income, and to realize the American dream, launch a new business venture. These individuals, often referred to as entrepreneurs, have been essential to the growth and vitality of the American free enterprise system. Entrepreneurs develop or recognize new products or business opportunities, secure the necessary capital, and organize and operate the business. Most people who start their own business get a great deal of satisfaction from owning and managing their own firm.

Small Business Act

Believing that the development of the small busiess is vital to the success of our economic system, Congress passed the **Small Business Act** in 1953. The intent of the act is summarized below:

> It is the declared policy of the Congress that the Government should aid, counsel, assist and protect, insofar as is possible, the interests of small business concerns in order to preserve free competitive enterprise . . . to maintain and strengthen the overall economy of the nation.[1]

Even with the assistance provided by the U.S. government, the failure rate of small businesses continues at an extremely high rate. Statistics reveal that 50 percent of all new businesses fail within the first two years of operation, and 70 percent fail within five years. According to Dun and Bradstreet, most businesses fail because of ineffective management. However, in spite of high failure rates, a large number of people each year decide to challenge the odds. Several hundred thousand new businesses are started each year.

Beginning and managing one's own business continues to be a prime motivator for many people. There are approximately 14 million businesses in the United States, including nearly 3 million corporations; almost 97 percent of these are classified as small businesses. As shown in Figure 18-1, approximately 77 percent of all business establishments in the United States have nine or fewer employees. Small businesses provide income to millions of families in the United States.

What Is a Small Business?

Almost every large corporation began as a small business. Thousands of small businesses are so successful that they become a big business. For instance, after six years in the computer industry, Sam Wyly decided that he was tired of working for the "other guy." So in 1963 he purchased a used computer

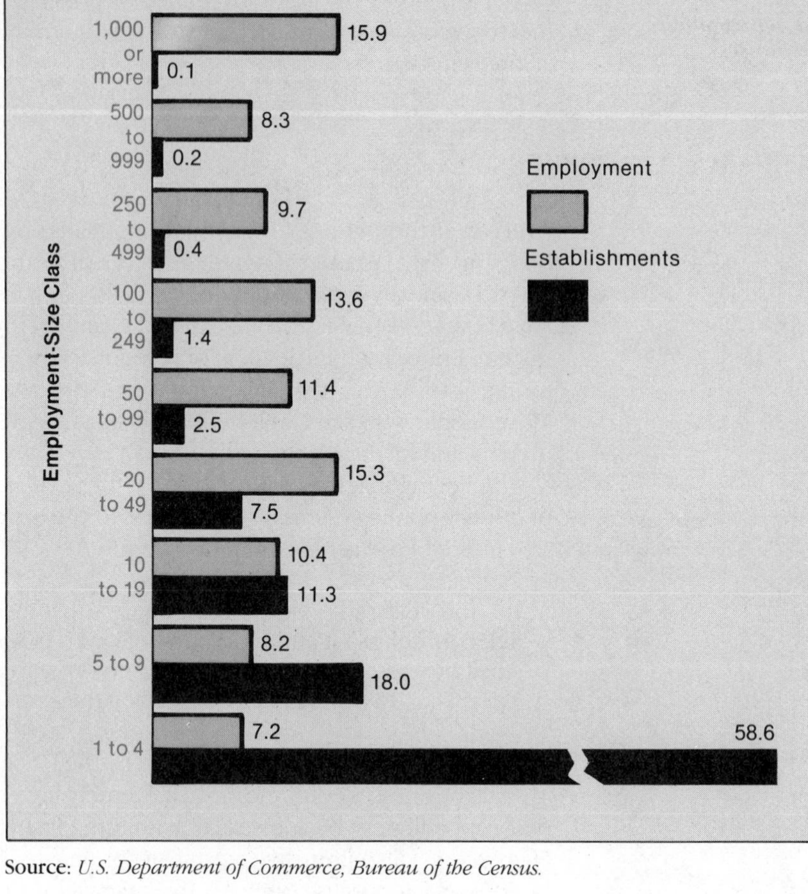

FIGURE 18-1

Distribution of Employment and Establishments by Employment-Size Class (in percent)

Source: *U.S. Department of Commerce, Bureau of the Census.*

and started his own business, University Computing Company. From this meager beginning, UCC evolved in a period of just ten years into a multinational organization. Wyly's success story proves once again that the American dream of developing a successful small business can be realized.

Despite the fact that there are millions of small businesses, there is no commonly agreed-on definition of what constitutes a small business. The Small Business Act of 1953 defines a **small business** as one that is (1) independently owned and operated and (2) not dominant in its field.[2] The act created the **Small Business Administration** (SBA), an agency empowered to set more specific criteria in conjunction with the number of employees and the dollar volume of business. For the purpose of determining who may receive special financial assistance under the act, the SBA has established the guidelines as presented in Table 18-1.

small business

Small Business Administration

The flexibility of the SBA in classifying small businesses is demonstrated by the fact that in 1966, the nation's sixty-third largest company was identifiied as a small business for the purpose of providing assistance to the

TABLE 18-1. *SBA Classification of Small Businesses*

Types of Business	Classification Standards
Manufacturing	1. Up to 1,500 employees (varying industrial standards may be applied)
Retailing	2. Up to $7.5 million in annual sales
Wholesaling	3. Up to $22.5 million in annual sales
Services	4. Annual receipts up to $8 million
Construction	5. Annual receipts up to $9.5 million
Agriculture	6. Annual receipts not exceeding $275,000

Source: U.S. Small Business Administration.

company in obtaining government contracts. The firm was American Motors, and the key characteristic was its marginal standing in the automobile industry. Though this company had approximately 28,000 employees, its sales comprised less than 4 percent of total industry output.

Most Important Reasons for Success and Effectiveness as a Manager

The industrial background I had in the engineering and construction field gave me early exposure to so many different and and varied managerial problems in a true growth situation from 8 employees to over 1,000.

HENRY C. GOODRICH, Chairman and CEO, Southern Natural Resources, Inc.

The Committee for Economic Development (CED) has also developed a definition of a small business. To qualify as a small business, the CED stated that a firm must meet at least two of the following:

- Management of the firm is independent. Most often the managers are also the owners.
- Capital is supplied and ownership is held by an individual or small group.
- The firm's primary area of operations is local. Markets need not be local, but the owners and workers are in one home community.
- The business is small compared to the largest firms in its field. This would vary according to the industry. A large firm in one industry might seem small in another.[3]

As noted in the above CED definition, the small enterprise is one in which the owner-operator knows personally the "key" personnel. In most

•CAREER PROFILE•

JAMES E. WATSON
President
WAR Terminals, Inc.

WAR Terminals, Inc. The name of Jim Watson's company may sound imposing until he tells you it stands for Watson and Ray (WAR). In 1981, Mr. Jim Watson left Alsco-Anaconda Aluminum Division, where he had held a position as vice-president of marketing, to return to his hometown, Baton Rouge, Louisiana. "It was a difficult period," he said, "but one has to go forward without looking back." At Alsco-Anaconda, Jim headed up a sales distribution organization of 225 individuals, including 3 regional managers and 28 branch managers. "Moving from corporate life to organizing a company in which I had equity was a major change, but I believe my present endeavor is even more challenging and rewarding," Jim said. "I had never organized a company from the ground up." The company was

small businesses, this key group would ordinarily not exceed twelve to fifteen people. Regardless of the specific definition of a small business, it is a certainty that this category makes up the overwhelming majority of business establishments in this country.

Why Some People Want to Have Their Own Business

As discussed previously, many thousands of people start their own business each year. Why? While there are probably dozens of reasons, some of the more common ones may be seen in Figure 18-2 and are discussed below.

1. A strong desire to be one's own boss—to be independent, able to set one's own direction, relying on one's own talents, skills, and hard work.
2. The opportunity to work at something enjoyable instead of settling for, perhaps, a more secure job in a large organization. (This was the case

immediately highly successful, and Jim looks to even more successful endeavors in the future.

Jim classifies himself as an entrepreneur. He said, "I need my independence. I don't like to be in a situation where I cannot control my own destiny." Jim credits hard work and dedication as a primary reason for his success. He began selling newspapers when he was six years old and worked in various part-time sales jobs until he obtained his B.S. in marketing in 1960. Upon completion of military service in 1962, he took a position as a sales representative with a building products company. Although Jim achieved a highly successful "track record," he realized that additional education would help him. In 1967, Jim quit his job and entered graduate school as a full-time student, receiving his M.B.A. in 1968. After graduation, he took a position with a major hardboard manufacturer, and one year later he was promoted to sales manager. In 1973, he accepted the position of product manager for three hardboard plants. Jim went to work for a manufacturer and wholesaler of forest products in 1975 and progressed rapidly from sales manager to general manager to president. In 1978, Jim was contacted by an executive search firm and, as a result, joined Alsco-Anaconda as vice-president of marketing.

Jim attributes much of his success to establishing goals and determining the means for them to be accomplished. He says that his return to graduate school to obtain an M.B.A., after having obtained actual business experience, provided him with the tools and techniques that have been invaluable.

Jim expressed his view of the planning process very concisely when he said, "Planning is examining where you have been, where you are today, where you want to go, and what you must do to get there." He believes that too many business people get so wrapped up in day-to-day operations that they forget their end objective. Successful business people must have a clear picture of what is to be accomplished and then react to changing conditions, as well as to accomplish their goals.

---

with Jack Wilson, the entrepreneur mentioned at the beginning of the chapter who is starting a jewelry store.)

3. Achieving a goal of financial success and desire for and expectations of future profits and wealth. Earning a profit is a primary motivator for wanting to own a business.
4. An ego identification with their business. Most small business owners have a close identification with their business and demonstrate a pride of ownership. The business often represents an extension of themselves and their ideals and values. Or a business may allow a family to maintain a historic tradition of ownership of a particular business firm. For example, the owners of a large Southwest U.S. bakery firm continually stress that their bread is "baked with family pride."
5. A strong motivation for recognition and prestige. A business owner may gain considerable prestige or status from owning and operating a small business. A small business gives the owner a base of power in the community and an opportunity for political and economic influence.

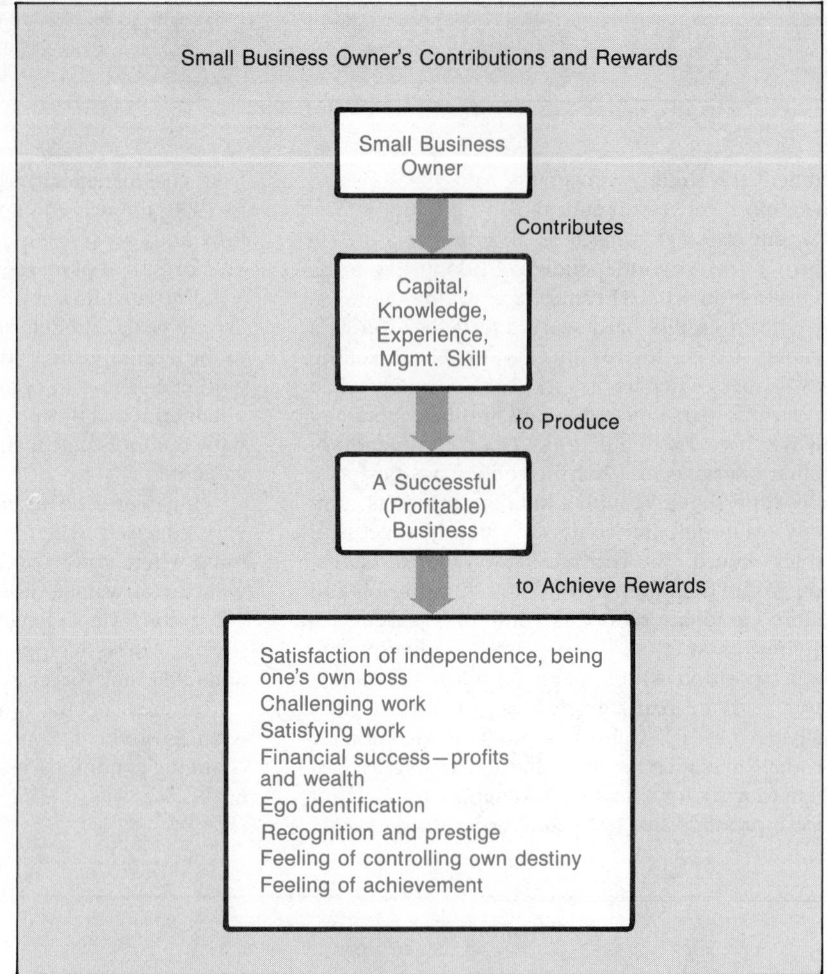

FIGURE 18-2

Small Business Owner's Contributions and Rewards

6. A feeling they are controlling their own destiny. To many individuals, controlling their own firm is tremendously rewarding.
7. A desire for achievement. One of the most prevalent characteristics of the entrepreneur is a strong drive for achievement. Most studies of the motives of individuals who own their own firm indicate that they are achievers—they prefer to set their own goals and like to control their future.

FACTORS AFFECTING THE MANAGEMENT OF SMALL BUSINESSES

The small business enterprise offers unique challenges and opportunities—and considerable difficulties—that differ from those encountered by large businesses. In fact, a number of factors may have a greater impact on small businesses than on large companies, i.e., a large firm usually has the resources to weather adverse conditions. Several factors affecting the management of small businesses are discussed below.

Economic Environment

Unlike the large corporation, the small business can concentrate on a restricted economic market in one locale or in one segment of an industry. But this condition is a two-edged sword. If economic conditions become depressed in one portion of the industry, the small business may suffer severely, whereas the large, diversified firm may be capable of relying on other segments of the firm to offset the adverse conditions. However, in some situations the small business may be able to choose a more favorable economic environment in which to operate.

In numerous instances a small business may find itself in competition with a large enterprise. When it does, it often will seek to protect itself by serving a particular market segment. Microcomputer and minicomputer manufacturers competing against IBM often decide not to go "head-to-head" against the "giant's" strength. Rather, they might direct their effort at a market segment IBM hasn't pursued. The same situation exists for a small grocery store competing for sales against the major chains such as Safeway and Kroger. Because of the volume sales of the giants, the small stores may find it very difficult to engage in strong price competition. Factors such as staying open late, offering shorter service lines, and allowing customers to charge their purchases frequently provide the means for the small business to survive.

The flexibility of being small is somewhat offset by weaker power because of limited resources. On occasions, a major customer can take advantage of the small company by insisting on excessively favorable terms in price, quality, or delivery. It is difficult to push around a supplier larger than the small firm itself. Small businesses often find it more difficult to secure adequate financing from institutional lenders because of their size. Lenders are aware of the fact that the small business has less depth in management. They are also aware of the statistics with respect to small business failure—one of the major reasons for the establishment of special loans under the Small Business Act of 1953. However, many small businesses are able to secure a loan simply on the basis of personal reputation of the owner.

Unlike many large enterprises, the small business is typically unable to exert a major influence on the economic environment. Whereas some suggest that large enterprises are engaged in *closed enterprise,* there is usually little doubt that the small firm is involved in a highly competitive *free enterprise system.* In this environment the small business that is able to maintain lower operational costs will be the most profitable and have the greatest chances of remaining in business.

Political and Legal Environment—Government Regulation

It would seem that the political and legal environment for small businesses would be no different from that of large enterprises. One could also contend that this aspect of the environment would be considerably simpler for the small business since it is unlikely to be subject to prosecution under such laws as the Sherman Antitrust Act or the Employees Retirement Income Security Act. Since over 75 percent of the small businesses employ fewer than ten people, many federal laws do not apply to them.

There are, however, many laws that apply equally to small and large enterprises and that require considerable expertise and resources. Though the effort is burdensome, the large enterprise can utilize its staff of specialists

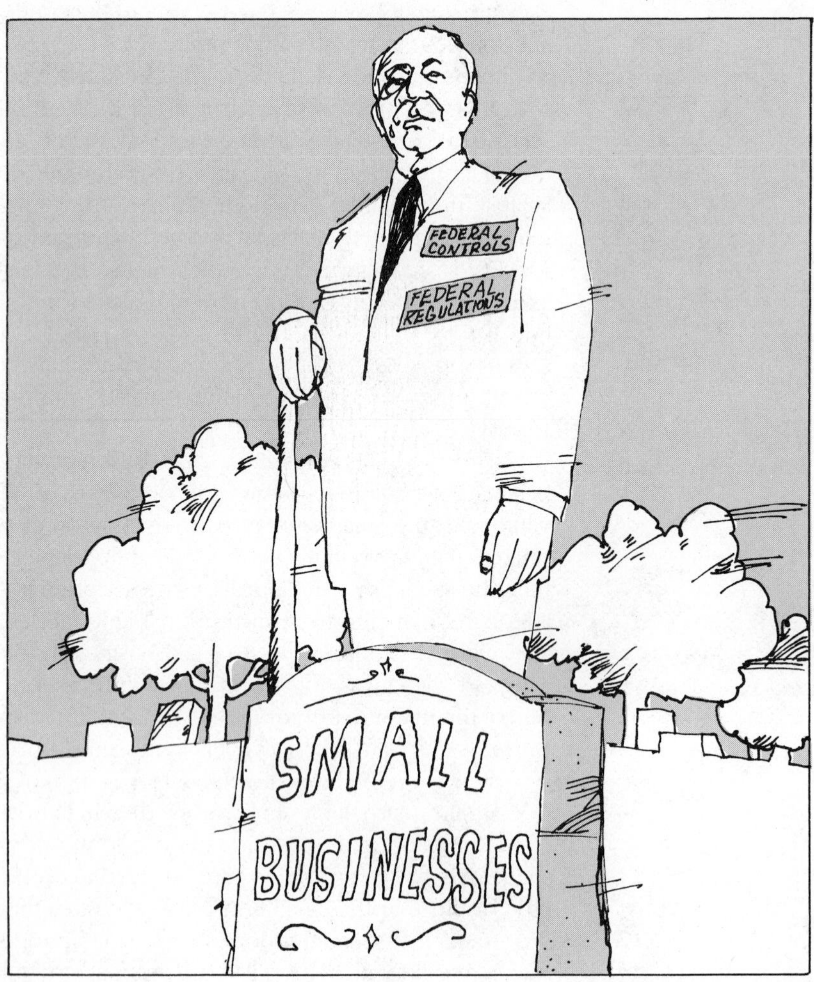

Federal Legislation Places Major Burdens on Small Businesses

and larger capital resoures to meet legal and/or administrative requirements. The small business, on the other hand, often has few, if any, staff experts and may experience difficulty in complying with government regulations. For example, a firm with fifty or sixty employees may be required to complete as many as seventy-five to eighty government report forms a year.

As a tangible example of this problem, the Occupational Safety and Health Act applies to all firms with one or more employees (in addition to the owner). Basically, the approach in this revolutionary law is one of setting comprehensive and specific standards, governmental regulation of company practices and work places, and enforcement by citations and fines. Standards governing physical conditions and work practices are published in a voluminous *Federal Register*. Some have stated that if small businesses are required to adhere rigorously to these detailed specifications, many would be forced into bankruptcy. However, considering the millions of business establishments as compared with the hundreds of OSHA inspectors, the odds of receiving a surprise inspection are quite low.

Another major factor that must be considered is that of ecology. Many small firms have been charged with excessively polluting sewer systems, waterways, and the air. Prevailing winds can carry animal and waste odors generated from hog and cattle feedlots as far as two miles. Small laundries that bleach blue jeans have added blue water and sludge to municipal sewer systems. Most small businesses operate on "thin" margins and have reduced their operating costs by pouring wastes into available streams, air, land, and sewers. This, combined with the lack of expert staff and alternative production facilities, makes coping with new ecological demands a very critical problem.

In a few instances, the owner-manager of small businesses has found means to cope with environmental problems and to do so at a profit. For example, animal waste solids from feedlots have been collected, sterilized, and sold as organic fertilizer or converted to gas to be used to heat a home. Some laundry managers who were forced to buy a special tank truck to remove excessive sludge have expanded into the septic tank drainage business. The pressing necessity for ecological cleanup applies to both small and large enterprises.

Social Environment

The small business typically has fewer problems in coping with the social environment than does the large corporation. First, the small firm typically has only one community with which to deal. Also, the small firm's manager, being part of the local community, is better able to understand its customs and mores than is the manager of a large corporation. Customers in the community may patronize the business because they know the owners. A small grocery store may find that some of its customers will pay a higher price for their groceries because they know and trust the owner.

Owner-Entrepreneur

entrepreneur

The key individual in most small businesses is the owner. Because of the nature of the factors in establishing small businesses, the small business owner is often referred to as an **entrepreneur.** In fact, the small business is a natural haven for the entrepreneur. The entrepreneur is a unique person whose major characteristic is the ability to create an ongoing enterprise where none existed before. He or she performs the act of bringing ideas, skills, money, equipment, and markets together into a profitable combination. It has been suggested that this type of person strongly feels that security cannot be found in working for others in a well-structured situation. Rather, security is found only in working for oneself with minimum external restraints.

Entrepreneurs desire to control their own destiny and have a tremendous need for independence. There is a constant drive to remove all restrictions and threatening figures. Any other person in the small firm who appears to aspire for power will be quickly removed. It is for this reason that some small businesses fail when their owners die or retire; no one has been developed to take their place.

This yearning for security by independence demands a great deal of self-confidence. An entrepreneur finds it exceedingly difficult to accept leadership from others. Such a person often makes a relatively poor member of a large enterprise. In addition, entrepreneurs have little fear of failure; they seek risks eagerly. Venturesomeness is almost an obsession; their level of activity is steadily high. Entrepreneurs are ardent believers in a truly competitive system and take great joy in winning.

The management style of the entrepreneur is not one that fits well into structured and orderly organizations. The entrepreneur shows great reluctance to formalize structure and processes. Leadership is primarily based on charismatic attraction. Entrepreneurs are organization "starters" rather than organization "builders." As a consequence, their level of mobility is great. They move from one "deal" to another, all of which are rationalized in the name of profit. They have few qualms about severing relationships with people or with organizations. They would rather leave intolerable situations than stay and resolve problems. Entrepreneurs provide a highly dynamic and innovative element in our economic system.

Objectives

The objectives of a small business are typically no different from those of a large enterprise, although the priorities that the owner may place on them may be different. As we discussed in Chapter 3, the major objectives that a firm may have are survival, profit, service, and growth.

For a small business, survival of the enterprise is often most crucial and difficult to attain. A significant percentage of new business ventures fail in the first year of existence. Earning a profit is absolutely essential to long-term business survival. But a newly formed small business must be prepared financially and psychologically not to earn a profit during the early phases of operation. The profit objective provides incentive to assume business risks, and without the profit motive, few people would start their own business. It is apparent that the survival objective constantly haunts the small business. Because of its very nature, the small business is limited, short on capital, subject to competitive destruction, and often operates on a hand-to-mouth existence. With respect to the service objective, the typical small business is highly customer oriented. Whereas the large enterprise can manipulate and control products and markets with its vast resources, the small firm must be attuned to specific customer wishes and requirements. In this way, a unique market niche can be gained.

The small business has the advantage of specialization by concentrating on a limited number of services. Though real estate agents often concentrate on a particular type of property, such as residential or commercial, one particular agency carved out a niche by concentrating solely on providing faculty housing in a city that contained a major university. A retail supermarket may develop special excellence in providing unusually good meat products. One small pharmaceutical company prospered in competition with larger firms by concentrating on the needs of one type of medical specialty—the ophthalmologic surgeon. The large enterprise must also adapt to customer requirements, but such adaptions are not usually as specific or as rapid.

Another basic objective of most small businesses is growth. However, there are certain limitations to growth that must be considered. Unlimited growth cannot be an objective of the small business if—

1. the owner-manager seeks to retain direct and personal control of the firm;
2. the firm wishes to remain in certain selected products or services;
3. management wants the firm to remain highly flexible; or
4. the owner does not value growth.

The personal values and stage in life of the owner of a small business have a significant effect on the goal of growth. This point has been vividly illustrated to one of the authors by his father-in-law on numerous occasions. The father-in-law owns and operates a highly successful photography studio in a large city. The father-in-law's lack of interest in growth of his business has often perplexed the author. Despite the author's "good suggestions" as to how to increase overall revenues and profits, the father-in-law has not shown an interest in growth. The author's father-in-law is sixty, is an excellent and avid golfer, and operates a ranch during his spare time. He values time for these activities and realizes that if the volume of business increases, he will probably have to work longer and harder or hire additional personnel. He chooses to do neither. He prefers to "pioneer the two-day work week" and thus is not interested in, nor does he need, the greater income that could be generated if he pursued a growth strategy. The quality of his studio's work is so exceptional that the firm has continued to do well and he has been able to increase his prices at least enough in recent years to offset the effects of inflation. Thus, in a small business it is virtually impossible to separate the values and objectives of the owner from those of the business.

Technology

Technology exerts a significant impact on the types of products and services provided by small business firms. These products and services tend to possess characteristics that distinguish them from those of larger enterprises. These include the following:

- The technology needed to create these products and services is characterized by shorter processing cycles. This enables promptness of service and does not require extensive investment in facilities.
- The demand for products and services of many small businesses tends to show greater seasonal variations.
- Small businesses are often in a better position to produce higher-quality products than are larger firms.
- The technology used to produce the products and services tends to be relatively stable. The small firm does not have the resources to be constantly bringing out new products as markets for old products disappear.

Because of these technological characteristics, there will always be a place for small business to provide products and services uniquely adapted to their capabilities. With over 70 percent of small businesses being engaged in retailing, wholesaling, and services, it has been suggested that the most commonly needed technology is that of dealing directly with customers. Because customers are not completely controllable, this would demand greater flexibility and freedom.

Many small businesses were started because of one technological innovation by its owner. As the owner begins to deal with the day-to-day operations of the business, there often is not sufficient time to devote to continued research and development. The reason that caused the small business to be created may also be the cause of its failure. Should the competition develop a superior product, the small business may find itself in severe difficulties.

Organizational Structure

The major characteristics of small business organizational structure are: (1) an emphasis on informality, (2) the critical importance of the owner and/or manager; and (3) the necessity for increased departmentalization with growth. Small firms tend to operate in a somewhat informal manner. The small size permits it; the need for flexibility demands it. High degrees of formalization, in terms of organizational charts, job descriptions, and procedures, do not encourage creativity and change. The large organization must formalize in order to effect coordination and control.

Because of the size of the small business, its owner and/or operator is of critical importance. There has been a tendency for operators of successful small firms to remain in the position for long periods of time—sometimes as much as twenty to forty years. In large enterprises, a president remains for a much shorter period, typically fewer than ten years. Heads of small businesses almost always wear two or more hats—they must perform several important functions. Not only do they manage the total enterprise, but almost always perform a second or third function, frequently the finance function. In some small manufacturing firms, owners personally handle the big "bread-and-butter" sales, placing themselves in competition with subordinate sales representatives. If a labor union is present, the owner-manager often handles the negotiations personally. If the owner has an engineering degree, he or she may be the firm's only machine maintenance person. Management problems will just have to wait until the machine is back in operation.

As the small business grows, the variety, number, and complexity of functions and relationships will increase. The typical span of control in the small firm ranges from four to seven subordinates, whereas in the large company ranges from five to over eleven. Thus, in the small business, communication distances are short and personal contacts frequent.

Not only do the typical small business manager and virtually all personnel wear two or more hats, they are expected to perform many activities that would normally be handled by a staff of experts in a large organization. For example, there may be only six people in a small business. One day all six may be sales personnel, the next day they may spend seeking financing, and the next day they all may be on the production line. The limited number of different departments and specialization of personnel enables the small business to operate with speed and flexibility.

There also tend to be fewer rigid or formal rules to follow in small firms. Employees may leave assigned work places without permission, have more flexible starting and quitting times, and have a more flexible dress code. The climate of the organization is more personalized. Names are more important than time clock numbers. It is likely that there are neither time clocks nor codified rule books. When instances calling for disciplinary action do arise, there is more individualized handling of the case. The less-rigid scheduling of tasks permits greater degrees of interaction among employees.

The nature of the job assignment combined with the friendly climate that can be developed in a small business leads to greater employee identification with the enterprise. There is an excitement in being in on things, of having personal contact with managers and customers. Individual impact upon the total organization is greater, and one can see what has been personally accomplished. Absence rates are often significantly lower in the small firm. There is considerably less likelihood that an organized labor union will be present.

Personnel

There are many noneconomic reasons for a person to prefer to work in a small business. While work in a large organization is often highly specialized, the typical task assignments in the small firm offer variety, challenge, and greater degree of self-control. This is why many recent graduates are beginning to seek jobs with small businesses. At times, an employee has an opportunity to carry a job through from the original idea to its introduction into the market. Experience is gained at an accelerated pace. Such opportunities provided by a small business are very important to many people.

Although there are exceptions, larger organizations usually pay their employees higher salaries than do most small businesses. Most small firms have a tendency to view salary as an expense rather than the employee as an asset. If the owner of a small business had to choose between a $25,000 accountant and one costing $35,000, the odds are heavily in favor of the former. If the owner were choosing between a $25,000 piece of machinery and one costing $35,000, considerably more deliberation would go into the decision. The owner may be aware that the more expensive machine might have certain advantages over the less expensive one, which would make the additional expenditure worthwhile.

A type of employee that is sometimes characteristic of small firms is a member of the owner-manager's family. The practice of hiring one's own relatives is known as **nepotism.** In the past this has been the son or son-in-law of the owner. More recently, a number of daughters of successful small business owners have gone to work in the family business. One writer states that the most lethal of all deadly triangles in small businesses is where all three—father, son, and son-in-law—are key people in the enterprise.[4]

nepotism

Using family members has some advantages to the concern. Identification with "our business" should be great, thereby leading to increased effort and dedication. In addition, family members may constitute sources for funds to finance the enterprise. Bringing the son or daughter into the firm enables retention of control by the family in the years ahead. However, if a firm rigidly follows a policy of nepotism in its hiring or promotion practices, competent nonfamily personnel may leave the firm because they see little opportunity for advancement.

Employing family members can cause a number of interpersonal problems. Family quarrels can and do spill over into the everyday operations of the firm. In one instance, the introduction of the son initially caused few problems in a small hardware business. As the firm prospered, the standard of living of the son's family exceeded that of the daughter and her husband. The daughter brought pressure on the father to bring the son-in-law into the firm. After this was done, head-on competition began to develop between the son and the son-in-law as the daughter used the firm to increase her family status. Ultimately the father was forced to dissolve the firm because of family warfare.

PITFALLS TO STARTING A SMALL BUSINESS

A person who desires to start a small business should be aware of a number of limitations or pitfalls. Dun and Bradstreet has prepared a list of potential problems that small businesses often encounter.[5] Most of them relate to ineffective management. An awareness and understanding of the possible pitfalls discussed below should be of value to the small business manager.

Lack of Experience in the Business

A good rule of thumb is: "You don't enter a business that you know nothing about." Much more experience is needed than merely a knowledge of the product or service that will be provided. Experience relates also to areas such as purchasing, marketing, and finance. It is because of lack of balanced experience that many small businesses fail. The old adage that said, "Build a better mousetrap and the world will beat a path to your door" is not necessarily so when discussing small business. For instance, an engineer who has a tremendous idea for a new product will likely discover that the above statement is correct. Before the product can be manufactured, capital must be available to secure parts required to produce the item. The engineer must determine what quantities and quality levels are needed. Once the item has been manufactured, it must be marketed. A certain amount of personal selling is necessary. Thus, in order to go into business for oneself, a person should ask if he or she has the "package" of experience that is necessary to operate the business on a sound basis.

Lack of Capital

A good idea does not guarantee success of a small business. A person should also evaluate carefully the amount of capital that will be required to start and maintain a business. Often these calculations are much too low, and a person can actually fail before the business has opened. For instance, an individual decided to take over the operation of a small convenience store. All expenses were carefully calculated: salaries, rent, utilities, and advertising. The only thing that was forgotten was that additional inventory had to be purchased for the successful operation of the business because the previous owner had reduced inventory to a very low level prior to selling the store. The new owner was not aware of this and did not have funds to purchase the inventory required. The store was never opened.

Lack of a Good Location

A large percentage of small businesses are retail store operations. As such, a major factor that should be considered is the selection of the proper location. Low rent in the wrong location may be high; high rent in the right location may be low. Factors that should be considered might be the following:

- **Population.** What is the traffic volume surrounding the store? Are the types of customers who will potentially purchase the product located within the trading area? For instance, approximately 70 percent of all convenience store customers reside within one mile of the store.
- **Accessibility.** Do cars have to cross traffic to get to the location? How fast is the traffic generally moving past the location?
- **Competition.** Are there a large number of similar types of businesses in the marketing area? The question that must be answered is, "How will the competition affect the proposed location?"
- **Economic stability.** The site must be considered not only from its current location potential but also from future potential considerations. The anticipated move of a large supermarket across the street may have a detrimental effect on some businesses.

Lack of Adequate Inventory Management

Inventory represents a debt for management; it ties up funds that could be used for other purposes. Inventory mismanagement may be thought of as a double-edged sword. If a person attempts to get by on only minimum inventory, customers may begin shopping at other locations because all of the items that are wanted are not available. On the other hand, if excessive inventory is carried, funds cannot be used for other purposes. Also, if the items cannot be sold, they represent a complete loss for the business.

Another major factor related to inventory mismanagement is internal theft. Often the greatest number of thefts are committed by "in-house" personnel. Managers of small businesses often become so closely involved with their personnel that they never believe that they would steal. There have been numerous instances where the employee was making more than the owner because of internal theft. An inventory control system should be established to discover shortages before they become excessive.

Excessive Capital Investment in Fixed Assets

Fixed assets such as buildings and equipment cannot be converted into cash easily, if at all. Sales may be increasing so the owner decides to purchase additional equipment. Additional personnel are then hired to use the equipment. If a decline in sales is experienced, payment on the equipment may prove difficult. Because of this, the business may be forced into bankruptcy even though it had an excellent chance for success. The small business owner must consider this factor much more carefully than do large established firms.

Poor Credit Policies

One sure way to make a sale is to give credit. But small business owners have discovered that one of the fastest ways to go out of business is to give excessive credit. In many instances, credit is granted based on whether the owner "likes" a person. The owner has not determined if the individual is a poor credit risk. With this approach, an owner may find that sales are increasing but there is little cash inflow. Because the owner may feel uncomfortable in asking people to pay their debts, the debt owed by the customer may not be collected.

The Owner Taking Too Much Cash Out of the Business

Money that is spent by the owner cannot be used to make the business grow. When a small business is just starting to develop, it is likely that a major problem relates to securing sufficient capital. If the owner takes too much cash out of the business to maintain a high life-style, growth may be stymied. Sacrifices must be made at first to enjoy future success.

Unplanned Expansions

If one store is doing fine, there may be the temptation to add an additional store and do twice as well. This growth by acquisition has often caused major problems for owners of small businesses. When rapid expansions occur, difficulties are often experienced. The manager will likely discover that running two locations is much more difficult than one. He or she may not be accustomed to delegating authority, and this must be done if there is more than one location. If the owner has been making all the decisions, efficiency may drop when additional locations are involved.

Having the Wrong Attitude

Let's face it; starting your own business is difficult. There is a good possibility of failure. It is certainly not a nine-to-five job where you can leave the problems of the job behind at quitting time. If a business is to be successful, it will take a lot of hard work. The responsibilities of the business will likely mean that many outside interests will have to be reduced. When an outside activity is considered, the question that must be raised is, "Can I afford it?" The answer is not merely in terms of money. Personal decisions may need to be made in light of how they will affect the business. If the owner decides to go fishing, this decision could even affect the business. Sacrifices will be necessary, but to see a business survive and grow is worth the effort. The business is yours and you are answerable to no one but yourself.

Qualities Needed for Success as a Manager in Your Organization

- **Imagination**
- **Early responsiveness**
- **Ability to identify proper niche for involvement of our small and now medium-size company**

K. B. WATSON, President & C.E.O., Pioneer Corporation

ASSISTANCE PROVIDED BY THE SMALL BUSINESS ADMINISTRATION

Given the pitfalls described above, where can a small business owner obtain assistance? As previously mentioned, the Small Business Act of 1953 created the Small Business Administration (SBA) to provide assistance to prospective, new, and established small businesses. The SBA provides financial assistance, management training and counseling, and helps small firms obtain government contracts. The types of assistance provided by the SBA are discussed below.

Financial Assistance

financial assistance

The SBA offers a variety of programs of **financial assistance** for small businesses that need money and cannot borrow it on reasonable terms from conventional lenders. The SBA, individually or working with a local financial institution, may make or guarantee loans for small businesses. The typical practice is for the SBA to guarantee up to 90 percent of a loan that a bank or other lender agrees to make to a small business. The SBA is permitted to make direct loans to small businesses only if local financial institutions are unable or unwilling to provide the funds. SBA loans may be used for these purposes:

- business construction, expansion, or conversion
- purchase of machinery, equipment, facilities, supplies, or materials
- working capital

Procurement Assistance

procurement assistance

Each year the U.S. government purchases billions of dollars worth of goods and services from thousands of businesses in the United States. In recent years, about one-third of the total government purchases have been from small businesses. The SBA provides **procurement assistance** and counseling to small businesses on how to obtain government contracts. Specific services offered by the SBA include: counseling on how to prepare bids and obtain contracts, help in getting the name of the business placed on the bidders' lists, and advice on research and development projects and new technology.

Management Assistance

management assistance

More than 90 percent of the business failures each year are due to ineffective management. To prevent business failure, an important service provided by the SBA is **management assistance,** which takes the form of counseling and management training. The Management and Technical Assistance Programs offer such extensive and diversified services as the following:

- Free individual counseling by retired and active business executives, university students and other professionals
- Courses, conferences, workshops, and problem clinics
- Wide range of technical and management publications

Small Business Institute

Free counseling is provided by SBA Management Assistance staff and by members of the Service Corps of Retired Executives (SCORE) and the Active Corps of Executives (ACE) and many professional organizations that offer volunteer services to small businesses. Another program that has gained considerable recognition in recent years is the counseling provided through the **Small Business Institute** (SBI) program. The SBI, using senior and graduate students of leading business schools throughout the country, provides on-site management counseling to small businesses. More than 450 colleges and universities have SBI programs. Supervised by a faculty member, students provide consultant services to the small business and receive academic credit for their work.

In addition to the above forms of management assistance, the SBA pays for management and technical assistance provided by professional consultants and offers short courses, conferences, and workshops for small business operators. Finally, the SBA publishes hundreds of management, technical, and marketing publications that provide valuable information to small businesses. Most of these publications are free and can be obtained from the nearest SBA office.

CHECKLIST FOR GOING INTO BUSINESS

A person considering starting a business should carefully and critically evaluate a number of factors. The SBA has developed a comprehensive checklist of questions that assist in this evaluation process (see Table 18-2). As can be seen, these questions are organized under such topics as: "Before You Start," "Getting Started," and "Making It Go."

Once you have carefully answered the questions posed in Table 18-2, you have done some hard work and serious thinking. That's good! But you have probably found some things you still need to know more about or do something about.

Do all you can for yourself, but don't hesitate to ask for help from people who can tell you what you need to know. Remember, running a business takes guts! You've got to be able to decide what you need and then go after it.

Good luck!

TABLE 18-2. *Checklist for Going into Business*

BEFORE YOU START

How about You?

- Are you the kind of person who can get a business started and make it go?
- Think about why you want to own your own business. Do you want it badly enough to keep working long hours without knowing how much money you'll end up with?
- Have you worked in a business like the one you want to start?
- Have you worked for someone else as a foreman or manager?
- Have you had any business training in school?
- Have you saved any money?

How about the Money?

- Do you know how much money you will need to get your business started?
- Have you counted up how much money of your own you can put into the business?
- Do you know how much credit you can get from your suppliers—the people you will buy from?
- Do you know where you can borrow the rest of the money you need to start your business?
- Have you figured out what net income per year you expect to get from the business? Count your salary and your profit on the money you put into the business.
- Can you live on less than this so that you can use some of it to help your business grow?
- Have you talked to a banker about your plans?

TABLE 18-2 *(continued)*

How about a Partner?

- If you need a partner with money or know-how that you don't have, do you know someone who will fit—someone you can get along with?
- Do you know the good and bad points about going it alone, having a partner, and incorporating your business?
- Have you talked to a lawyer about it?

How about Your Customers?

- Do most businesses in your community seem to be doing well?
- Have you tried to find out whether stores like the one you want to open are doing well in your community and in the rest of the country?
- Do you know what kind of people will want to buy what you plan to sell?
- Do people like that live in the area where you want to open your store?
- Do they need a store like yours?
- If not, have you thought about opening a different kind of store or going to another neighborhood?

GETTING STARTED

Your Building

- Have you found a good building for your store?
- Will you have enough room when your business gets bigger?
- Can you fix the building the way you want it without spending too much money?
- Can people get to it easily from parking spaces, bus stops, or their homes?
- Have you had a lawyer check the lease and zoning?

Equipment and Supplies

- Do you know just what equipment and supplies you need and how much they will cost?
- Can you save some money by buying secondhand equipment?

Your Merchandise

- Have you decided what things you will sell?
- Do you know how much or how many of each you will buy to open your store with?
- Have you found suppliers who will sell you what you need at a good price?
- Have you compared the prices and credit terms of different suppliers?

Your Records

- Have you planned a system of records that will keep track of your income and expenses, what you owe other people, and what other people owe you?
- Have you worked out a way to keep track of your inventory so that you will always have enough on hand for your customers but not more than you can sell?
- Have you figured out how to keep your payroll records and take care of tax reports and payments?
- Do you know what financial statements you should prepare?
- Do you know how to use these financial statements?
- Do you know an accountant who will help you with your records and financial statements?

TABLE 18-2 *(continued)*

Your Store and the Law

- Do you know what licenses and permits you need?
- Do you know what business laws you have to obey?
- Do you know a lawyer you can go to for advice and for help with legal papers?

Protecting Your Store

- Have you made plans for protecting your store against thefts of all kinds—shoplifting, robbery, burglary, employee stealing?
- Have you talked with an insurance agent about what kinds of insurance you need?

Buying a Business Someone Else Has Started

- Have you made a list of what you like and don't like about buying a business someone else has started?
- Are you sure you know the real reason why the owner wants to sell the business?
- Have you compared the cost of buying the business with the cost of starting a new business?
- Is the stock up to date and in good condition?
- Is the building in good condition?
- Will the owner of the building transfer the lease to you?
- Have you talked with other businesspeople in the area to see what they think of the business?
- Have you talked with the company's suppliers?
- Have you talked with a lawyer about it?

MAKING IT GO

Advertising

- Have you decided how you will advertise? (Newspapers—posters—handbills—radio—by mail?)
- Do you know where to get help with your ads?
- Have you watched what other stores do to get people to buy?

The Prices You Charge

- Do you know how to figure what you should charge for each item you sell?
- Do you know what other stores like yours charge?

Buying

- Do you have a plan for finding out what your customers want?
- Will your plan for keeping track of your inventory tell you when it is time to order more and how much to order?
- Do you plan to buy most of your stock from a few suppliers rather than a little from many, so that those you buy from will want to help you succeed?

Selling

- Have you decided whether you will have salesclerks or self-service?
- Do you know how to get customers to buy?
- Have you thought about why you like to buy from some sales representatives while others turn you off?

TABLE 18-2 *(continued)*

Your Employees

- If you need to hire someone to help you, do you know where to look?
- Do you know what kind of person you need?
- Do you know how much to pay?
- Do you have a plan for training your employees?

Credit for Your Customers

- Have you decided whether to let your customers buy on credit?
- Do you know the good and bad points about joining a credit-card plan?
- Can you tell a deadbeat from a good credit customer?

A FEW EXTRA QUESTIONS

- Have you figured out whether you could make more money working for someone else?
- Does your family go along with your plan to start a business of your own?
- Do you know where to find out about new ideas and new products?

Summary

An American dream for millions of people is to own and manage their own business—"to be my own boss." This dream has been realized by many people in the nearly 14 million small businesses that exist in the United States. While the freedom to start and manage one's own business is available to everyone, each year thousands of businesses fail. In fact, statistics reveal that half of all new businesses fail within the first two years of operation and 70 percent fail within five years. Despite the grim statistics, virtually every large, successful business began as a small business. Also, it is important to note that small businesses make significant contributions to the health and vitality of our economy. The U.S. government, in an effort to provide financial and managerial assistance to small businesses, created the U.S. Small Business Administration (SBA) in 1953.

The small business enterprise offers unique challenges and opportunities—and considerable problems—that differ from those encountered by large businesses. The large firm usually has the resources to withstand adverse circumstances. Limited resources may make it difficult for the small business to exert a major influence on the economic or political legal environment. However, in certain respects, a small business, because of its size, may be more flexible and responsive to changing conditions. For example, a small firm may be able to offer more personalized service, maintain lower operational costs, be less susceptible to some federal regulations, and often is not unionized.

As noted above, the failure rates for small businesses are very high. Why do failures occur? Failures are caused primarily by ineffective management. Some of the major pitfalls or problems that small businesses often encounter include lack of experience in the business, lack of capital, lack of a good location, lack of adequate inventory management, excessive capital investment in fixed assets, poor credit practices, the owner taking too much cash out of the business, unplanned expansions, and having the wrong attitude. To help prospective, new, and established small businesses avoid and/or overcome problems that might cause failure, the SBA provides financial, procurement, and management assistance.

Review Questions

1. What was the purpose of the Small Business Act of 1953?
2. What is considered to be a small business in manufacturing, retailing, and wholesaling?
3. What situational factors affect the management of small businesses? Do each of these factors affect small firms more than large companies?
4. What are the failure rates for small businesses? Why? Discuss briefly.
5. What are the basic objectives of the typical small business? Is *growth* always an objective of a small business? Why or why not?
6. Products and services of small businesses tend to possess characteristics that distinguish them from those of larger enterprises. Discuss any three of these characteristics.
7. What are the major characteristics of small business organization structures?
8. What is meant by nepotism? Briefly discuss how the practice can affect a small business.
9. What is an entrepreneur? What are the major personality characteristics of entrepreneurs?
10. List and briefly discuss five of the more important "pitfalls" often encountered in starting a small business.
11. Review the Checklist for Going into Business. What areas covered in the checklist are most significant?
12. Briefly describe the various types of assistance available to small businesses from the U.S. Small Business Administration.

Exercises

1. Using Table 18-2, Checklist for Going into Business, evaluate the feasibility of starting your own restaurant specializing in steak and seafood entrees.
2. Visit three successful small businesses in your local area. Discuss with the owners-managers of each business the reasons for success of their business. Ask them if they would advise a person to begin his or her own small business.

3. Visit or call the local office of the Small Business Administration (or use library sources if the SBA does not have an office near you) to determine the types of financial and managerial assistance available to small businesses. How does a business qualify for SBA assistance?

Case Study

Management Incident
*Ole Miss Inn**

For many years, John Goodson had thought that Oxford, Mississippi, a town of 10,000 population, needed a first-class motel, restaurant, and private club. Although there was limited industry in the city, Oxford was the home of the University of Mississippi. The building of a quality motel, restaurant, and club facility in Oxford had long been a dream of Goodson. He became particularly enthusiastic about the potential success of the motel facility after discussing his plans with local business people and university officials. The business and university leaders pledged their support and encouraged Goodson to continue with plans for the creation of the facility. Goodson, the president of a local bank, was able to interest his brother-in-law, Charles Jones, and two of Jones's business associates, Paul Prince and Bob Johnson, in the venture. Jones was a vice-president with World Book Encyclopedia and Prince and Johnson were highly successful sales managers. All three men lived in Memphis, some eighty miles from Oxford and traveled extensively.

After considerable discussion, the four men—Goodson, Jones, Prince, and Johnson—formed a partnership and began serious preparations for entering the motel business. While none of the partners had any previous experience in the motel, restaurant, or club business, each was considered a successful businessman. The partners hired a nationally known consulting firm, specializing in hotel/motel operations, to conduct a study to determine the feasibility of the project. Prior to engaging the consulting firm, the four men agreed on the location and size of the proposed facility. The consulting firm recommended the creation of the proposed motel, restaurant, and club facility on the location specified by the partners. The study was completed in ten days at a cost of $5,000 to the partners. The consultants based their recommendation of the project on the following factors:

1. Favorable general business conditions and projected growth of Oxford and the university.
2. Supply of and demand for motel rooms seem to be favorable.
3. There was a lack of "quality" motel and/or restaurant facilities in Oxford.
4. Financial projections appeared excellent—a forecast of $50,000 net income during the first year of operation.
5. The proposed site was excellent because of its location on a major state highway and its proximity to the university.

*This is a condensed version of the Ole Miss Inn, #9-377-710 case written by Robert E. Holmes and R. Dean Lewis and listed in the Intercollegiate Bibliography, Intercollegiate Case Clearing House, 1977.

Much of the consultants' study consisted of interviewing business and university leaders to obtain their estimate of the potential for such a venture.

After reviewing the feasibility study, the partners decided to proceed immediately with plans for the facility, which was to be named "Ole Miss Inn." An architectural firm completed plans for the facility and construction began in September, and the motel opened for business the next September, with sixty rooms, a restaurant, and a private club. The total capital invested in the facility was $800,000 with $100,000 being contributed directly by the partners. A $700,000, twenty-year loan at 9 percent annual interest provided the remainder of the capital.

Almost immediately on opening, Ole Miss Inn began experiencing operational and financial difficulties. None of the partners was interested in managing the facility, so a professional manager was hired, as well as a staff of several full and part-time personnel. During the first two years of operation, Ole Miss Inn had five managers and experienced losses totaling over $200,000. The occupancy rate was much lower than the level predicted by the feasibility study, and expenses for food and salaries were far out of line.

When questioned about the lack of success of Ole Miss Inn, Mr. Goodson stated, "Our poor results during the first two years of operation were due to poor management—particularly in the areas of control of salaries and food expenses. Also, we haven't had the business we were promised from the university, particularly the Division of Continuing Education, or from local towns people. We've also had a tough time finding competent managers."

QUESTIONS

1. What were the primary problems being experienced by Ole Miss Inn? What were the causes of these problems?
2. Do you think that Goodson and his partners should have entered the business? Discuss.
3. Do you spot any apparent weaknesses in the consultants' feasibility study? If so, what are they?
4. What do you predict in the future for Ole Miss Inn?

Case Study

Harrison Photography Studio

The Harrison Photography Studio located in Atlanta, Georgia, has an excellent reputation for high-quality photography. The studio specializes in bridal, family, and executive portraits. In addition, the studio is very active in photographing weddings. John Harrison is the owner and manager of the studio. He started the business in his garage thirty years ago, and it has since grown to become one of the leading photography studios in Atlanta with revenues in excess of $150,000 annually and five full-time employees. Mr. Harrison has earned the reputation as a highly creative and innovative photographer.

One example of this is the fact that he was the first portrait photographer to take outdoor garden color portraits some fifteen years ago. Most of his bridal portraits and many of the individual and/or family portraits are taken in his outdoor garden studio. Because of the unique features of the studio's portraits, the studio has as much business as Mr. Harrison believes he wants. He has never advertised in any form—depending on "word-of-mouth" to carry his message of quality photography. Throughout the history of the business, Mr. Harrison's goal has been to be a high-quality photographer. In recent years, he has raised prices considerably, but has noticed no overall decrease in revenues.

There are five key employees in the business. Mr. Harrison; his wife, Joan, who handles customers and manages the office; Mr. Harrison's son, Ken, who is also a professional photographer; Hilda, a professional spotter (touch-up work on negatives and prints); and Cathy, who performs such duties as framing pictures and working with customers. Ken, thirty-two, is one of Harrison's three sons. He is very interested in someday owning the business. Ken has had a history of instability and unpredictability, especially with regard to work. He has either quit or been fired by his father several times and has not always been a very conscientious employee. Recently, however, he seems to have taken a more responsible attitude. Mr. Harrison's others sons have never been interested in the photography business.

In recent years, Mr. Harrison has been spending less and less time in the business. Several years ago, he decided to close the studio on Mondays—which meant that the business was open from 9–5 Tuesday through Friday and from 9–noon on Saturday. Although the studio is currently operating on this schedule, Mr. Harrison, who is sixty, and is interested in retiring from the business, has chosen to work a fewer number of days. His typical work week is as follows:

Wednesday: 9–5
Thursday: Plays golf
Friday: 9–5
Saturday: 9–Noon (He actually works every other Saturday)

While not at the studio, Mr. Harrison spends most of his time at his ranch located about ninety miles from Atlanta. Six years ago, he bought 150 acres of land and built a large, beautiful "retirement" home. He has twenty-five head of cattle on the ranch and enjoys having a garden. Mr. Harrison and his son-in-law, Bob Shroeder, have frequent discussions about the future of the Harrison Photography Studio. One of their recent conversations was as follows:

Bob: "John, how are your plans for retirement coming along? Do you think that Ken is ready to take over the business?"

John: "I'm ready to get out now, but I don't believe that Ken can handle the business on his own yet. He is doing a good job, but if Joan and I leave the studio, I'm not sure he could make it. Ken wants to buy the business but I think that he would have a difficult time making the payments. Just the other day I was offered $300,000 for the studio property by a group of investors who want to build condominiums on the land. That's an excellent price, don't you think?"

Bob: "The $300,000 offer sounds good to me, especially when you consider the interest income from that amount of money. However, your annual earnings from the business are more than the interest on the $300,000."

John: "I want out of the big city and the pressures of the business. However, I have been able to work two or three days a week now for two years and still earn almost what I earned when I was spending five days in the studio. Our business has declined some during the past year, but not drastically. Besides, I enjoy my golf day on Thursdays with the boys and Joan likes to come in to Atlanta to visit friends—so I'll probably continue the two or three day schedule for a while longer."

QUESTIONS

1. What are the present goals of Mr. Harrison as a small business person? Have they changed over time?
2. Why has the Harrison Photography Studio been successful in the past? Do you believe its current goals ensure continued success in the future?
3. In view of what we discussed in this chapter, evaluate the effectiveness of Mr. Harrison as an owner-manager.
4. Since Mr. Harrison wants to retire, would you advise that he accept the $300,000 offer for the studio property?
5. Why do you think he does not have much confidence in his son Ken's ability to run the studio when he retires?

Notes

1. U.S. Congress, Reconstruction Finance Corporation Liquidation Act; Small Business Act of 1953, Public Law 163, 84th Cong., 1st sess., 1953.
2. Ibid.
3. Hal B. Pickle and Royce L. Abrahamson, *Small Business Management,* 2d ed. (New York: Wiley, 1981), p. 10.
4. Howard J. Klein, *Stop! You're Killing the Business* (New York: Mason & Lipscomb, 1974).
5. *Pitfalls of Starting a Small Business* (New York: Dun and Bradstreet, 1980).

References

Bruckman, J. C., and Iman, S. "Consulting with Small Business: A Process Model." *Journal of Small Business Management* 18 (April 1980): 41–47.

Charan, Ram; Haber, Charles W.; and Mahan, John. "From Entrepreneur to Professional Manager: A Set of Guidelines." *Journal of Small Business Management* 18 (January 1980): 1–10.

Clute, R. C. "How Important Is Accounting to Small Business Survival?" *Journal of Commercial Bank Lending* 62 (January 1980): 24–28.

Gilbreath, J. D., and Humphries, N. J. "Aggressive Contracting Strategies for Small Business Owners." *Journal of Small Business Management* 17 (October 1979): 30–36.

House, W. C. "Dynamic Planning for the Smaller Company—A Case History." *Long Range Plan* 12 (June 1979): 38–47.

"How to Start a Sideline Business." *Business Week,* August 6, 1979, pp. 94–95.

McKenna, J. F., and Oritt, P. L. "Small Business Growth: Making a Conscious Decision." *Advance Management Journal* 45 (Spring 1980): 45–53.

Petrof, J. V. "Small Business and Economic Development: The Case for Government Intervention." *Journal of Small Business Management* 18 (January 1980): 51–56.

Robinson, R. "Forecasting and Small Business: A Study of the Strategic Planning Process." *Journal of Small Business Management* 17 (July 1979): 19–27.

"Small Business Process a Passport to Profits." *Nation's Business* 67 (April 1979): 48.

"Study Shows Companies in Trouble Invariably Lack Planning and Control." *Management Review* 70 (February 1981): 38–39.

Timmins, S. A. "Large-Firm Forecasting Techniques Can Improve Small Business Decision-Making." *Journal of Small Business Management* 17 (July 1979): 14–18.

Walker, Gene C. "Starting a New Business—Pitfalls to Avoid." *U.S. News & World Report,* July 13, 1981, pp. 75–76.

KEY TERMS

multinational company (MNC)

multinational

parent country

host countries

less developed countries (LDC)

parent country nationals

host country nationals

third country nationals

godfather system

repatriation

LEARNING OBJECTIVES

After completing this chapter you should be able to

1. Describe the characteristics of a multinational enterprise and briefly explain the history and development of multinationals.
2. Explain how the external environment, objectives, and technology affect managing international operations.
3. State how the organization structure may change when firms are engaged in international operations.
4. Describe personnel requirements and management approaches for a multinational company.

19

Managing the Multinational Enterprise

Dan Shelton, a production manager for Axton International Corporation, a multinational organization operating primarily in developing countries, has been on his present assignment in a foreign country for only two months. During these two months, he has learned a great deal about the country's culture, and today he is being further educated. Dan has been very dissatisfied with the performance of one of his production foremen (a national of the country where Dan is working). When he told his assistant to terminate the foreman, he was told, "You can't fire that person. The government will not permit the dismissal of an employee unless the company agrees to continue paying his salary."

As the new manager for the Mideast division office of Dester International, Beth Adams is experiencing a bit of adjustment. Beth is a hard-working manager and was selected for her new assignment while working in the corporate headquarters in New York. There is one highly efficient and productive worker in Beth's office. When Beth requested a pay increase for this individual, she was told by her supervisor that merit increases are not permitted in this country. All employees must receive equal salary increases.

Salama Saloma is a foreign national of a developing country who has come to the United States to train as a manager in the firm's Chicago headquarters. After two years of training with Bedford International, Salama will return to his country to work in one of Bedford's offices. Salama is currently experiencing "management shock." He is unaccustomed to the freedom that is given him in accomplishing his job. In the United States, when a task is assigned, he has the responsibility for completing the project; no one is constantly standing around him to tell him precisely what to do. For Salama, it is quite a new experience.

multinational company (MNC)

As the above illustrations indicate, there are problems associated with conducting business in foreign countries. However, few developments have had the overall impact of multinationals. These firms have caused the countries of the world to be more closely related to each other. A firm engaged in business in two or more countries is referred to as a **multinational company (MNC).** These firms typically have sales offices and sometimes manufacturing plants in many different countries. These organizations are not only instrumental in improving the world economy and standards of living of many people but also significantly affect the technology, culture, and customs of the countries in which they operate. Peter Drucker refers to the multinational company as "the outstanding social innovation of the period since World War II."[1]

Many people believe that with resources, technology, food, and trained personnel unevenly distributed throughout the world, the multinational enterprise has the potential for bringing about a more equitable distribution of goods and services and improved living standards. The complexities and challenges of managing in the international environment are illustrated by the following comments from practicing executives of multinational firms.

> In general, the fundamental challenge in international management is to understand new sets of economic and business factors, their relationships, their interconnectedness in the world, their impacts on business strategy, and develop responses to these factors consistent with particular business goals.
>
> W. W. HAMILTON
> Manager—International Communications
> General Electric Company

> While many problems have existed in managing in the international environment, one of the more troublesome areas is in establishing the limits of authority for the foreign operation so that the manager at that location has sufficient control and power, that the decision-making process and operation of the business is not delayed by the necessity of frequent consultations through the normal chain of corporate command. Also, in the last few years, the incidence of terrorism in some countries has placed stress on managers, handicapping the normal management function and limiting the effectiveness of the person in the assignment.
>
> D. A. GULLETTE
> Director, Administration
> International Division
> A. E. Staley Manufacturing Company

In this chapter we begin by describing the characteristics, history, and development of multinational enterprises. Next we identify and describe the factors that should be considered in managing multinationals. Finally, we describe the personnel and managerial problems that are unique to the multinational company.

WHAT IS A MULTINATIONAL?

multinational A **multinational** is a company conducting business in two or more countries. However, this definition is far too simplistic because it does not give adequate recognition to the size and scope of operations of many such organizations. Some experts in the field of multinational enterprises believe that organizations designated as multinationals should meet the following criteria:

1. Conduct operations in at least six different countries
2. Have at least 20 percent of the firm's assets and/or sales from business in countries other than that where the parent company is located

•CAREER PROFILE•

DR. ARMAND HAMMER
Chairman of the Board and
Chief Executive Officer
Occidental Petroleum Corporation

OXY

Dr. Armand Hammer is chairman of the board and chief executive officer of the Occidental Petroleum Corporation. He took over the company in 1958 when it was almost bankrupt and has since built Oxy into the tenth largest oil company in the U.S. with annual sales of more than $6 billion. Dr. Hammer, who was 84 on May 21, 1982, has continued to work twelve-to-fourteen-hour days and has traveled an average of 250,000 miles per year for many years. Dr. Armand Hammer, who was born and grew up in New York, became a millionaire while attending medical school at Columbia University.

While Dr. Hammer has never practiced medicine, he has become one of the most successful entrepreneurs and managers in U.S. history. His business accomplishments include building pencil factories in Russia, cattle breeding, drug manufacturing, distilling whiskey, asbestos mining, and the oil business. He currently serves on the board of dozens of organizations, and also has one of the most extensive art collections in the world, valued in excess of $30 million. Many people know Dr. Hammer as the "Russian Connection"—the man who developed the first foreign business contacts with Russia. He forged a personal relationship with Lenin and has since negotiated the sale of over $20 billion worth of fertilizer to the Russians.

Dr. Hammer made the following statement in regard to his success as an entrepreneur and manager:

> Well I suppose I have a natural flair for business. It really doesn't make much difference to me what business I'm in; I always seem to find a way to make it pay, to make it profitable. I suppose people say luck plays a big role. But I think to a large extent you make your own luck. Some people have the same opportunities as others and they don't take advantage of them. When you work fourteen hours a day, seven days a week, you get lucky.

Dr. Hammer had the following advice for managers:

- Never lose your enthusiasm. No matter what you do, do it with enthusiasm.
- People should try to do a better job than anyone else has done before and to do it with zest. I suppose my ambition in life is to leave the world a little better than when I found it.

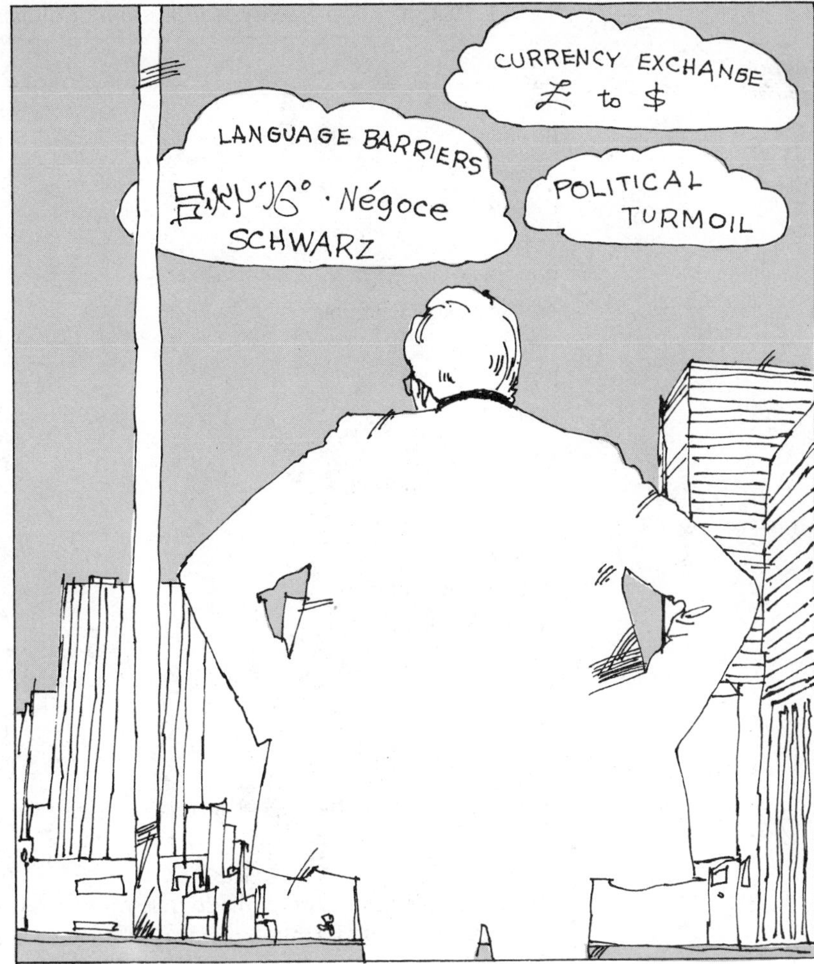

Although there are many difficulties associated with multinational operations, the benefits often outweigh the risks.

3. Have and demonstrate an integrated, global managerial orientation
   a. Resources of the enterprise are allocated without regard to national boundaries.
   b. National boundaries are merely a constraint that enters into the decision-making process; they are not part of the definition of the company itself.
   c. The firm's organization structure cuts across national boundaries.
   d. Personnel are transferred throughout the world.
   e. Management takes on a broad, global perspective—they view the world as interrelated and interdependent.

A list of the largest twenty multinational companies is presented in Table 19-1. As shown in the table, twelve of those are based in the United States. To illustrate the impact of the multinational, a Massey-Ferguson executive

TABLE 19-1. *The Top Twenty Multinational Companies*

Company	Home Country
Exxon	USA
Royal Dutch/Shell Group	Netherlands/GB
Mobil	USA
General Motors	USA
Texaco	USA
British Petroleum	GB
Standard Oil of California	USA
Ford Motor	USA
ENI	Italy
Gulf Oil	USA
IBM	USA
Standard Oil (Indiana)	USA
Fiat	Italy
General Electric	USA
Francoise des Petroles	France
Atlantic Richfield	USA
Unilever	GB/Netherlands
Shell Oil	USA
Renault	France
Petroleos de Venezuela	Venezuela

Source: Adapted from "The Largest Industrial Companies in the World," *Fortune,* August 10, 1981, p. 205.

states, "We combine French-made transmissions, British-made engines, Mexican-made axles, and United-States-made sheet metal parts to produce in Detroit a tractor for sale in Canada."[2]

HISTORY AND DEVELOPMENT OF MULTINATIONALS

The first multinational corporation (MNC) established with a global orientation grew out of a merger in 1929 between Margarine Unie, a Dutch firm, and Lever Brothers, a British company. The company became Unilever, and it has since become one of the largest companies in the world with approximately 500 subsidiaries operating in about sixty nations. Unilever even has two headquarters units, one located in Rotterdam and the other in London.

Multinationals usually operate through subsidiary companies in countries outside their home nation. Some of the names of the largest multinationals have become household words including such companies as General Motors, Ford, IBM, General Electric, Gulf Oil, and Exxon. The worldwide impact of these companies is very significant. Their operations create interrelationships

Insights to Success

Get where the action is. If it's sales—sell. If it's manufacturing—run a production line. Get to know the product and the people and process for producing that product. Learn how to listen to and communicate with people.

BILL HANSON, Vice-President, Digital Equipment Corporation

between countries and cultures, as well as between economic and political systems.

The economic output of MNCs contributes a significant portion of the total economic output of the world. Some economists have estimated that by the year 2000, about 200 to 300 multinationals will account for one-half of the world's total output of goods and services. In recent years, there has been a rapid growth of direct investment by multinational firms averaging about 10 percent per year. MNCs based in the United States account for more than half of this worldwide investment.

FACTORS TO BE CONSIDERED IN MANAGING INTERNATIONAL OPERATIONS

As noted previously in this chapter, multinational management requires careful consideration of several factors, including the external environment, objectives, technology, structure, personnel, and management approaches of multinational corporations.

External Environment

parent country
host countries

The external environment that confronts multinational enterprises is diverse and complex. The success or failure of the MNC is determined largely by how they respond to this environment. As portrayed in Figure 19-1, the MNC must deal with the environment not only of the **parent country** (location of headquarters) but of all **host countries** (location of operational unit) as well. A diversity of problems exists in managing a multinational. The majority of the problems can be summarized under the topics of (1) economics, (2) political-legal, and (3) social. When we add the barriers of distance and national boundaries, we can visualize an external environment characterized by great complexity, variety, and uncertainty. Such a situation requires that managers develop sophisticated skills to deal effectively with this environment.

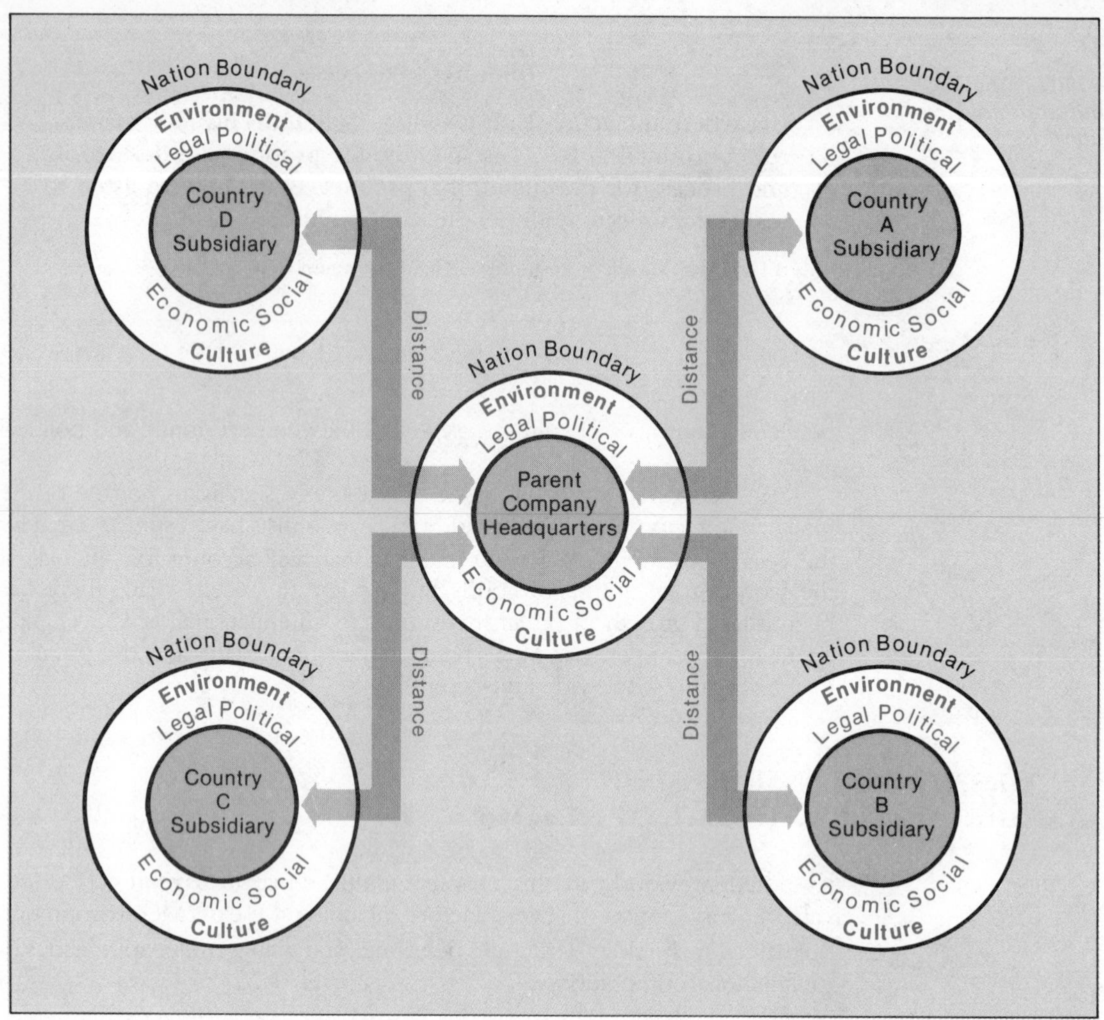

FIGURE 19-1 *The Multienvironments of MNCs* [*Source: Edwin B. Flippo and Gary M. Munsinger,* Management, *4th ed. (Boston: Allyn and Bacon, Inc., 1978), p. 583.*]

Economic Environment

The economic environment of the various host countries is of prime importance to the management of multinational companies. A number of crucial questions must be answered.

- What are income levels, growth trends, inflation rates, balance of payments, gross national product, and the number and nature of economic institutions?
- Is there a local banking and financial resource that can be tapped?

- Are there organized labor unions, economic planning agencies, and the necessary service structures for power, water, housing, communication, and the like?
- How politically stable is the country, and what about the stability of the currency?

A major economic problem that affects multinationals is the stability of currency of the host country. The comments of T. P. Townsend, group vice-president of Daniel International, illustrated this point when he said, "A quick change in government directions can cause a fluctuation in currency exchange rate and cause difficulties in repatriating profits." A multinational must be constantly aware of the economic stability as reflected by the country's rate of inflation and the degree of stability of the host country's currency.

less developed countries (LDC)

On a general basis, the countries of the world are classified as either developed countries or **less developed countries (LDC).** An LDC lacks modern industry and the supporting services. The output per person is low. There is usually an unequal distribution of income, with a few very rich, a small middle class, and a great number of poor. The MNC provides an opportunity for a fast start in the building of an economy. The objective is to reach a level where the economy can grow on a self-sustaining basis. A substantial percentage of the MNC's total investment is located in LDCs. Often, the LDC has an identity problem, which is shown in strong feelings of nationalism. Though they need the MNC to exploit their national resources, they perceive it as a threat to their soverignty. When they feel that they have effected sufficient transfer of skills in a particular technology, they are likely to expropriate or confiscate the business organization. The MNC must consider this risk in making an investment decision.

The fact that so much of total foreign investments is in LDCs is evidence that possible returns are worth the risk. If the most important resources of a multinational are technological and managerial skills rather than property and goods, some companies can reduce the risk of expropriation or host country take-overs by one or more of the following means: (1) licensing agreements, (2) contracts to manage host country-owned installations, and (3) turnkey operations (constructing and developing the unit to the point where the key can be turned over to ownership by nationals of the host country). It is far more difficult to expropriate skills of persons than property. There are also far fewer conflicts of interests between this type of MNC and the various countries.

Political-Legal Environment

"Local laws that restrict imports and/or repatriation of profits and royalties" constitutes a major political-legal barrier that confronts many multinationals according to L. R. Flandeau, vice-president international, for Signode Corporation. The MNC must assess the stability of the existing government through careful analysis of conditions existing within the countries. Such analysis should consider competing political philosophies, how recently political independence was obtained, and the amount of social unrest and violence. The impact that violence has on the operations was highlighted by D. A. Gullette, director for administration—International Division, of A. E. Staley Manufacturing Company, when he said, "In the last few years, the incidence of terrorism in some countries has placed stress on managers, handicapping normal management and limiting the effectiveness of the person in the assignment." During the summer of 1981, a Goodyear Tire and Rubber Company executive was murdered after being held hostage for six months in Guatemala. Numerous examples such as this have caused company executives to become reluctant to accept an assignment in certain countries.

Because there is no comprehensive system of international law or courts, the MNC must become acquainted in detail with the laws of each host country. The United States, England, Canada, Australia, and New Zealand have developed their legal requirements by means of English *common law.* Judges and courts are extremely important, for they are guided by principles declared in previous cases. In most of continental Europe, Asia, and Africa, the approach is one of *civil law.* The judges play a lesser role because the legal requirements are codified. The civil servant or bureaucrat has greater power under the civil law than under the common law.

Managers of MNCs must be highly interested in:

1. Laws governing profit remission to the parent country
2. Import and export restrictions and investment controls
3. Degree of foreign ownership permitted

Though the United States is a highly legalistic country and MNCs tend to "carry" American law with them, executives must realize, for example, that the Japanese dislike laws, lawyers, and litigation. In France, lawyers are prohibited from serving on boards of directors by codes of the legal profession. The vastness and sheer complexity of varying legal systems throughout the world demonstrate quite clearly the intricate and demanding environment of the MNCs.

Social and Cultural Environment

It is apparent that the culture of one nation will differ to some extent from the cultures of all other countries. As Robert J. Sweeney, president of Murphy Oil, said, "A major problem exists because we are not citizens of the various host countries and tend to superimpose our ethics on a foreign environment." Customs, beliefs, values, and habits will vary. If the MNC is to operate in many nations, it will of necessity be required to adapt some of its managerial practices to the specific and unique expectations and situations of each nation. Attitudes will differ concerning such subjects as work, risk taking, change introduction, time, authority, and material gain. It is dangerous to assume that the attitudes within the parent country will be similar in all other countries.

As described by a high-ranking marketing executive with a multinational company, one must learn to "do as the Russians do when in Russia." In describing the process of doing business with Russian counterparts, he said, "One must establish a personal relationship with the Russian businessman by toasting one another with vodka. If you don't like vodka, you are in trouble because it is offensive and appears rude to the Russian not to drink heartily and return toast for toast." Before he finalized a deal in that country, he had spent three consecutive evenings "socializing" with vodka and the Russian businessman.

In some nations, authority is viewed as a natural right and is not questioned by subordinates. In other cultures, authority must be earned and is provided to those who have demonstrated their ability. In some cultures, work is good and moral, whereas in others it is to be avoided. Building up wealth in some nations is indicative of good and approved behavior. In others, riches are to be avoided. David McClelland has discovered that the fundamental attitude toward achievement is somewhat correlated with rates of economic development. If a nation's citizens are willing to commit themselves to the accomplishment of tasks deemed worthwhile and difficult, a country will benefit economically. As previously discussed in Chapter 10, McClelland contends that the achievement motive can be taught.[3] Certainly, cultural beliefs concerning one's ability to influence the future will have impact upon the behavior of a country's work force. If the basic belief is one of fatalism—what will be, will be—then the importance of planning and organizing for the future is downgraded. Cultures also vary as to interclass mobility and sources of status. If there is little hope of moving up to higher classes in a society, then fatalism and an absence of a drive for achievement are likely.

In many instances, the MNC will have to adapt and conform to the requirements of the local culture. A multinational must introduce new technology and skills into a host nation's culture if economic development is to occur. Some changes proposed are revolutionary. There must be one common language and system of measurements when communicating between subsidiaries and headquarters of the MNC. Engish and French are the two most commonly chosen MNC languages. Despite the slowness of the United States to adapt, the metric system will be the common method of measurement.

Thus, a review of the bare outlines of differences in the economic, political-legal, and social environments of a variety of nations in the world serves to highlight the enormous complexity of the task of managing an MNC. It is apparent that sophisticated and unique approaches to managing are necessary for survival and growth.

Objectives of the Multinational

On first glance, the objectives of multinational companies would not appear to be any different from the objectives of businesses operating exclusively

What in the World Is Owens-Illinois?	A manufacturer and marketer of glass, plastic, paper, and metal packaging materials; Kimble® brand glass and plastic laboratory ware and health-care products. Libbey® glass tableware; Lily® paper and plastic convenience products; television bulbs and faceplates. We are the world's largest manufacturer of glass containers, and among the world's largest manufacturers of corrugated boxes and blow-molded plastic containers. Our consolidated sales are currently in excess of $2.6 billion, and we employ more than 84,000 individuals. We are big, diversified,and growing.
Where in the World Is Owens-Illinois?	Internationally, you'll find O-I operations in Europe, Latin America, the Middle East, South Africa, the Pacific, and the Far East. O-I is involved with more than 124 production facilities in 29 countries, manufacturing most of the items we produce domestically, and a few we don't such as flat glass and glass block. And O-I exports American products to more than 90 foreign countries.
And What Do We Do Internationally?	Owens-Illinois is enthusiastically involved with the global marketplace, and reaches international customers in one of three basic ways. Through partially or wholly owned affiliates, through technical assistance and licensing agreements, and through exports. Each of our affiliates and licensees is an experienced manufacturer and marketer in its own respective market areas. Through our corporate headquarters in Toledo, Ohio, and our European office in Geneva, Switzerland, we can help coordinate or guide our various operations when needs extend beyond country or even international boundaries. And we can assist customers who may be facing shortages or who may be entering a foreign marketplace for the first time. Of course, the concept of an international marketplace doesn't mean that individual nations are losing their traditions, their local color or their identity. We recognize that international business is not simply

FIGURE 19-2 *International Operations of Owens-Illinois. [Used with permission of Owens-Illinois.]*

within the United States. The typical goals of survival, profit, and growth are indeed similar to companies operating in the United States. An MNC seeks to produce and distribute products and services throughout the world in return for a satisfactory return on its invested capital. It seeks to survive and grow by maintaining its technological advantages and minimizing risks. As may be seen in Figure 19-2, the objectives of Owens-Illinois illustrate the diverse goals and operations of a large multinational company.

However, the MNC differs from the firm that operates only within the United States because of the potential clash of its goals with the objectives of the economic and political systems of the various countries within which they operate. Some of the objectives of countries may coincide with the objectives of the MNC and some may not. Most countries want improved a matter of selling the same products in different foreign locations. The people, the markets, the rules, the regulations must all be carefully considered in any given situation.

From a relatively modest beginning in 1956, O-I International Operations has expanded and diversified to the point where it now accounts for one-fourth of O-I's total sales and earnings, and employs some 32,000 individuals overseas—of whom less than 40 are U.S. citizens.

In management philosophy, O-I International Operations naturally seeks a fair return on investment, but our success is founded on long-term relationships that are mutually beneficial, rather than on short-term policies. National managers are developed not only to operate affiliates in their own countries but also to take an active part in the O-I International management team.

Working abroad carries with it responsibilities and obligations—obligations that touch people at all levels in the host countries: government, customers, the general public, employees, and partners. By meeting those obligations fairly and honestly, by exercising in our operations overseas the same good corporate citizenship which we stress in the U.S., O-I extends the benefits of the free enterprise system in the best economic, political, and social interests of both the U.S. and the host countries.

It is indeed one world, and through its International Operations, Owens-Illinois is very much a part of it.

W. F. Spengler

William F. Spengler
President and Chief Operating Officer
International Operations

standards of living for their people and such goals as: a trained labor force, full employment, reasonable price stability, a favorable balance of payments, and steady economic growth.

In achieving some of these goals, there is an overlapping of interests between the MNC and the host country (as shown in Figure 19-3). For example, a new MNC in a country will usually create new jobs, thereby contributing to a higher level of employment, increased income, and economic growth. While the company contributes to the accomplishment of these goals, it may not do so at the rate expected by the host country.

In some areas, there will be conflicts of interest. A multinational may close a plant in one country to streamline its worldwide production facilities. A company may subsidize a beginning assembly operation in Country A by

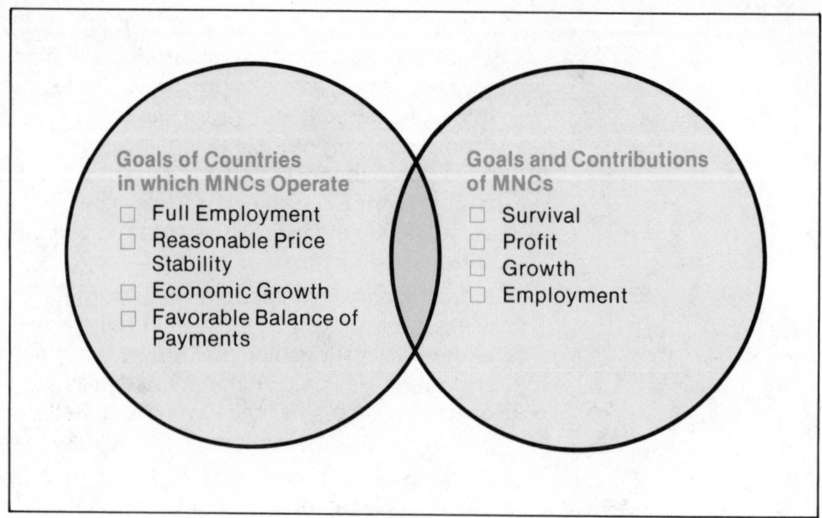

FIGURE 19-3

Overlapping Interest of MNC and Host Countries

underpricing component parts produced in Country B. Country B's economy in effect is required to make a sacrifice to enable the plant in Country A to get started.

If the MNC is to achieve its return-on-investment objective, some portion of subsidiary earnings must be returned to headquarters in the parent country. This could adversely affect the host country's balance of payments, particularly if the subsidiary unit does no exporting of its products. Funds may be shuffled among various countries so that profits are maximized in countries having the most stable political systems and the lowest tax rates.

Some of the complaints various countries have regarding multinationals are that MNCs:

- Restrict or allocate markets among subsidiaries and do not allow manufacturing subsidiaries to develop export markets.
- Are able to extract excessive profits and fees because of their monopolistic advantages.
- Enter the market by taking over existing local firms rather than developing new productive investments.
- Finance their entry mainly through local debt and maintain a majority or up to 100 percent of the equity with the parent.
- Divert local savings away from productive investments by nationals, hire away the most talented personnel, exhaust resources, and so on.
- Restrict access to modern technology by centralizing research facilities in the home country and by licensing subsidiaries to use only existing or even outmoded technologies.
- Restrict the "learning-by-doing" process by staffing key technical and managerial positions with expatriates.

- Fail to do enough in the way of training and development of personnel.
- Affront the country's social customs or frustrate the objectives of the national plan.
- Contribute to price inflation.
- Dominate key industrial sectors.
- Answer to a foreign government.[4]

In response to the type of complaints noted, there have been moves toward applying restrictions upon the operations of multinationals. For example, one of the guides in the Andean Common Market (Bolivia, Chile, Colombia, Ecuador, and Peru) is that 51 percent of the stock in manufacturing subsidiaries should be held by nationals of the host country within fifteen to twenty years of start-up. When extremely discontented with the MNC or in response to the rising tide of nationalism, subsidiaries may be expropriated or confiscated by the host country. France gained control over its telephone system by purchasing a controlling interest from International Telephone & Telegraph Corporation of the United States and Sweden's L. M. Ericsson Group.[5] In other instances, the host country has seized the subsidiary unit without compensation, for example, the Anaconda and Kennecott Copper units in Chile and all subsidiary units in Cuba.

Though the host country has power as a result of national sovereignty, the multinational is not helpless. Its power lies in its ability to grant or withhold needed economic resources and technological knowledge. Other MNCs will observe the nature of treatment accorded by the host country, and this will affect their decision to invest in that country. Should the host country have enterprises with investments in the parent country, retaliation can be threatened. If the parent country provides foreign economic aid, this can also be used as leverage in promoting equitable treatment for the MNC subsidiary.

In most instances, the economic power of the MNC and the political power of the host country will lead to accommodations whereby both parties can achieve some of their goals. The intense emotions of national sovereignty do not always coincide with long-term national interests. The MNCs will have to alter objectives to suit minimum requirements of the host countries if operations are to be conducted in that country. If such requirements do excessive damage to global objectives, the MNC may choose to conduct its business elsewhere in the world.

To head off a possible effort by LDCs to ram through the United Nations a tough set of restrictions upon MNCs, the governments of twenty-four of the most highly developed noncommunist nations have developed a proposed code of ethics. Important aspects of the Code of Ethics are listed as follows:

1. MNCs are not to meddle in the political processes of the countries in which they operate.
2. No bribes are permissible under any conditions.

3. No donations to political parties are proper unless national laws allow them.
4. MNCs should make full disclosure of local sales and profits, number of employees, and expenditures for research and development for major regions of the world.
5. MNCs should refrain from participating in cartels and avoid "predatory behavior toward competitors."
6. The proper amount of taxes in the countries in which they are earned should be paid. One should not seek to avoid taxes by switching money from high-tax to low-tax countries.
7. MNCs should respect the right of their employees to organize into unions.[6]

Technology and Multinationals

Technological expertise is the primary advantage of the multinational enterprise. Many of the MNCs operate in such high-technology industries as oil, tires, pharmaceuticals, electronics, and motor vehicles. There are fewer MNCs in such fields as cotton, textiles, and cement. It is this technological gap in other nations that provides the unique opportunity for the MNC to transfer high technology from the parent country. The simpler industries are likely to be developed by each country for itself.

The more important the economies of scale to be derived from a particular technology, the greater the opportunity for an MNC to transfer knowledge to other countries. If the market size of a particular country is not such that it can absorb the output of an advanced economic unit, then many nations must be interlocked. MNCs in the many small European countries started before those in the United States for just this reason. The development of the European Common Market constituted an attempt to develop a wide market area.

The situation existing within a country will dictate the nature of the technology required to accomplish work. There is obviously a wide range of environments, objectives, and technologies that would preclude any significant general statements that would apply to all multinationals. It should be noted, however, that the strength of most MNCs lies in their ability to operate highly complex technologies.

Multinational Organizational Structures

The organizational structure of a multinational firm must be designed to meet the needs of the international environment. Normally the first effort of a firm to become a multinational is the creation of an export unit in the domestic marketing department. At some point, the firm may perceive the necessity of locating manufacturing units abroad. After a time, these various foreign units are grouped into an international division. This is the typical structure for the United States multinational.

The international division becomes a centralized profit center with equal status with other major domestic divisions. It is typically headed by a vice-president and operates on a fairly autonomous basis from the domestic operations. The reasons for this approach are: (1) the necessity of obtaining managerial and technical expertise in the diverse environments of many countries and (2) the reduction of control from the often larger domestic divisions. Of course, this approach to organization has the disadvantage of decreased coordination and cohesion of the international division with the rest of the company.[7]

As the international division grows, it usually becomes organized on either a geographical or product base of specialization. In giant MNCs the international division is often a transitional stage in moving toward a worldwide structure that discounts the importance of national boundaries. As portrayed in Figures 19-4, 19-5, and 19-6, any such global structure requires a careful balance of three types of specialization: functional, geographical, and product. When the primary base is any one of the three, the other two must be present in the form of specialized staff experts or coordinators. A clear-cut decision that is heavily in favor of any one base is usually inappropriate.

Figure 19-4 illustrates a functional organizational structure for a multinational. The executive in charge of the production function has a world-

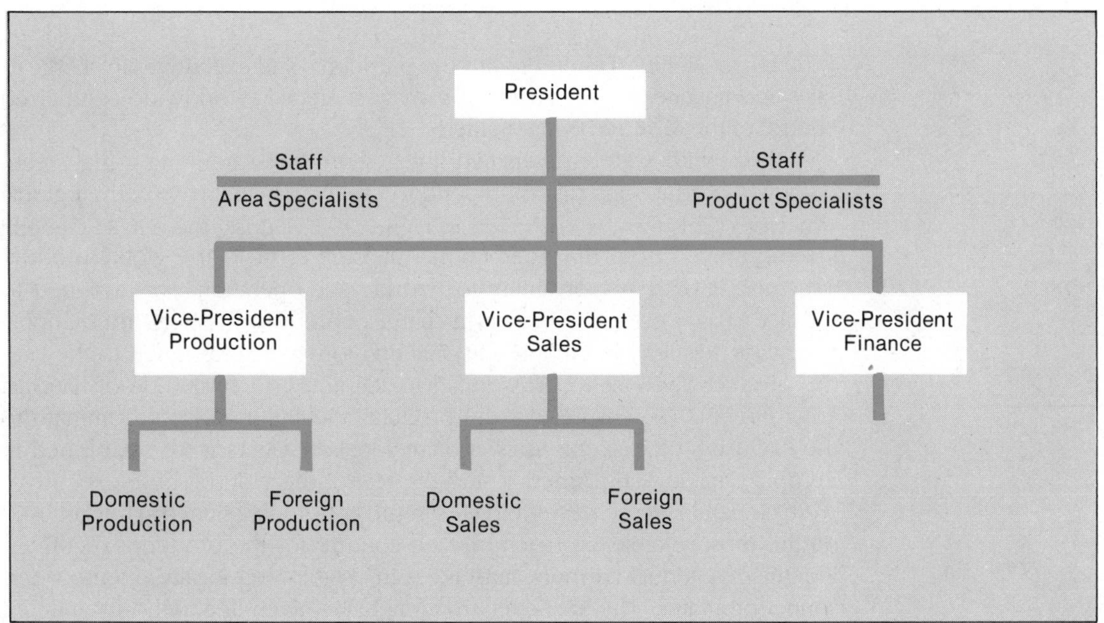

FIGURE 19-4 ***MNC: Global-Functional Structure*** [*Source: Edwin Flippo and Gary M. Munsinger,* Management, *4th ed. (Boston: Allyn and Bacon, Inc., 1978), p. 588.*]

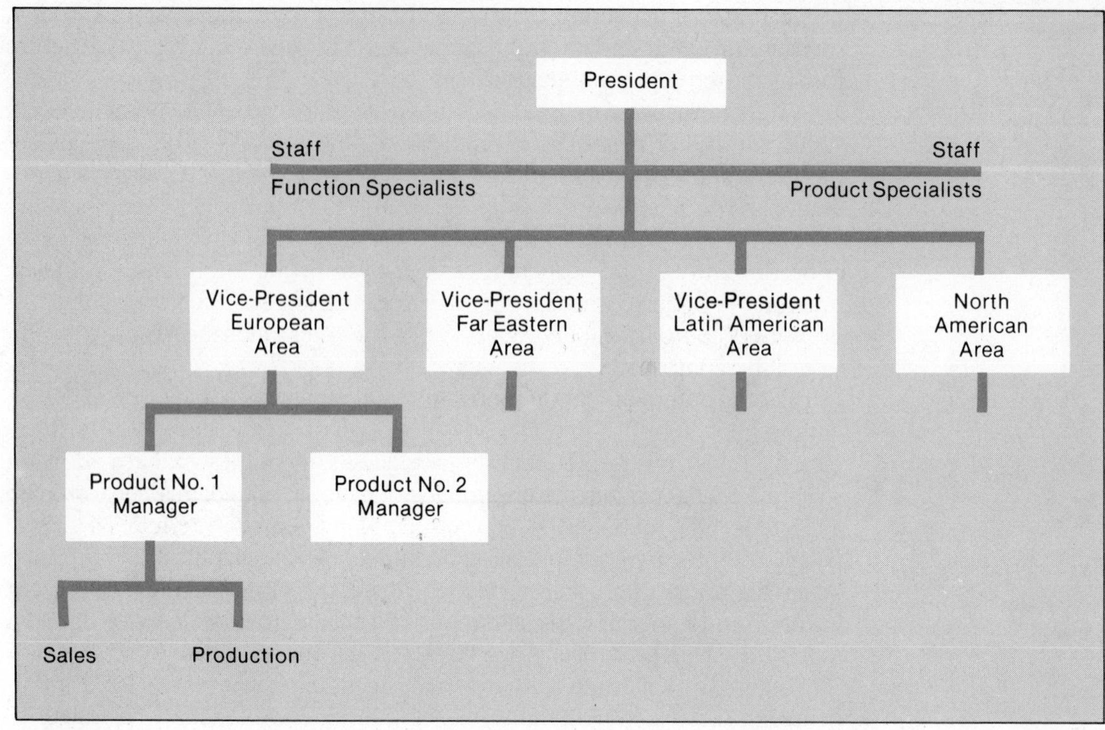

FIGURE 19-5 ***MNC: Global-Area Structure*** [*Source: Edwin B. Flippo and Gary M. Munsinger,* Management, *4th ed. (Boston: Allyn and Bacon, Inc., 1978) p. 589.*]

wide responsibility. Together with the presidents and executives in charge of sales and finance, a small group of managers enables worldwide centralized control of the MNC to be maintained.

MNCs with widely diversified lines of products requiring a high technology to produce and distribute tend to use the product base in their global structures. This form is portrayed in Figure 19-5. During the 1960s, General Electric moved from the international division form to the global product structure. Primary responsibility for world-wide operations was assigned to the fifty to sixty general managers in charge of product divisions. International specialists, formerly in the international division, were reassigned to the various product divisions to provide aid in adapting to a multitude of national environments. To ensure that the product orientation did not dominate to the exclusion of area emphasis, four regional managers were established in Europe, Canada, Latin America, and the rest of the world. These executives were General Electric's eyes and ears in the countries assigned. They advised on the most suitable approach in each country for the product executives, identified potential partners, and aided in establishing locally oriented personnel programs. The area executive might be given line authority when a product division had not yet sufficient skill in the region or when a subsidiary unit reported to many product divisions. Though the basic emphasis

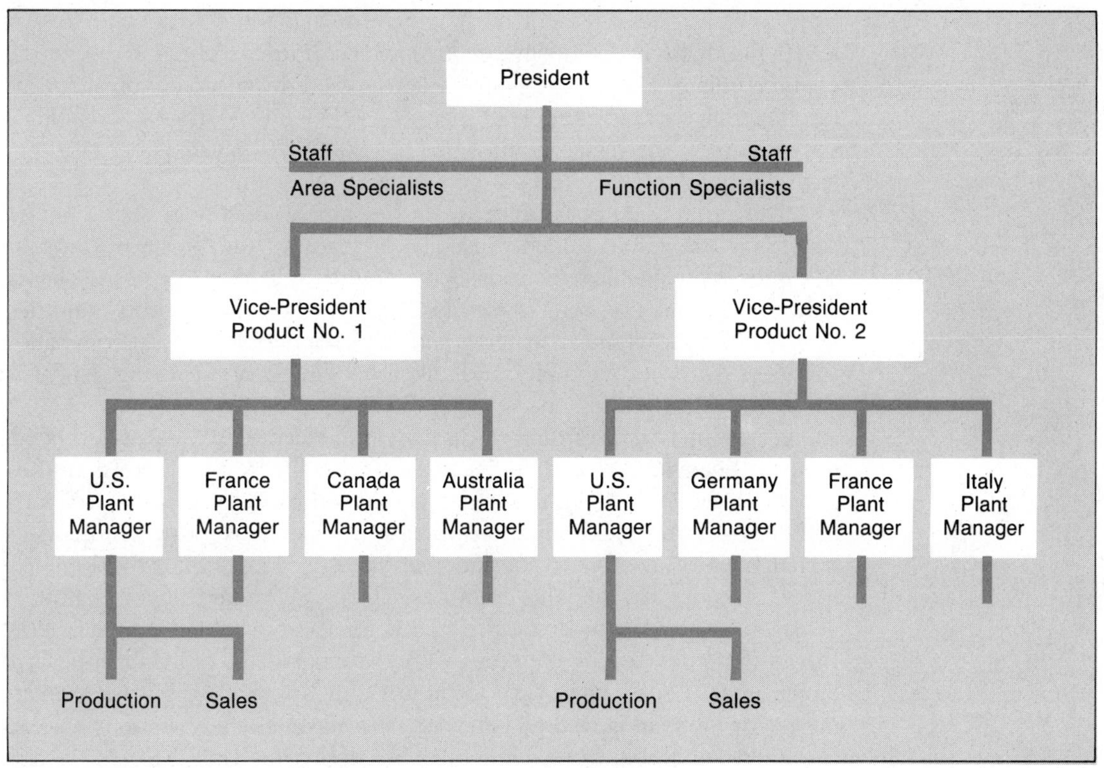

FIGURE 19-6 *MNC: Global-Product Structure* [*Source: Edwin B. Flippo and Gary M. Munsinger,* Management, *4th ed. (Boston: Allyn and Bacon, Inc., 1978) p. 588.*]

is on product, the addition of the geographical concept produced a type of matrix organizational structure.

Finally, when the range of products is somewhat limited or when the product is highly standardized, MNCs tend to use the global product structure, as shown in Figure 19-6. Executives with true line authority are placed over major regions throughout the world. This type of structure is used by international oil companies (limited variety of products) and soft-drink producers (highly standardized product). As in the other instances, some supporting staff is necessary in the product and functional areas. In all forms of MNC structures, one makes sure (1) that the product is properly managed and coordinated throughout the world, (2) that the functional processes of production, sales, and finance are executed efficiently, and (3) that proper and efficient adaptations are made in response to the environments in the host country.

Personnel

Successful management of an MNC requires that the manager understand the needs, values, and problems of personnel in the countries where the company operates. Management must recognize that there is no one style of leadership that will be equally effective in all countries. People in the various countries have widely divergent backgrounds, education, cultures, and religions and live within a variety of social conditions and economic and political systems. All of these factors must be considered by managers because they have a rather dramatic effect on the working environment.

The requirements for effective leadership of personnel in the United States, Canada, Great Britain, Australia, or many of the Western European countries differ significantly from such countries as Turkey, Mexico, Malaysia, Taiwan, Thailand, or certain African, Asian, or South American countries. Research has shown that the needs and values of people do vary from nation to nation. This is often the result of differences in economic living standards, cultural or religious inflluences.

As you may recall from our discussion in Chapter 10, unsatisfied needs motivate behavior. In the United States and other highly developed countries, people's basic needs—physiological, security, and social—are fairly well satisfied. Research on the application of Maslow's hierarchy of needs theory of human behavior has shown considerable differences concerning the dominant needs of people in different countries. Thus, in some advanced countries, managers must try to satisfy the needs for esteem and self-actualization. However, in developing countries with lower standards of living, appeals to basic human needs may prove to be not only appropriate but the primary means for motivating desired behavior. The Maslow need hierarchy appears to be very applicable when conducting business in the United States, Canada, United Kingdom, or Australia. We may well have to ignore it or be somewhat cautious with it in dealing with employees in other nations.

Types of MNC Employees

parent country nationals
host country nationals
third country nationals

In filling key managerial, technical or professional positions abroad, multinationals can choose among three basic types of personnel: (1) **parent country nationals** (PCN), (2) **host country nationals** (HCN), and (3) **third country nationals** (TCN). Until the 1950s, it was very common for MNCs to fill their foreign key posts with trusted and experienced personnel from home (PCNs). Recently, stronger nationalistic feelings have led countries to alter their policies and employ more people from host countries (HCNs). Additionally, some firms have used personnel from countries other than the parent country or host country. Such personnel are known as third country nationals (TCNs); for example, one U.S.-based firm received a contract to build highways in Saudi Arabia using personnel from Turkey and Italy. Still, many companies attempt to keep parent country personnel in at least half of the identified key positions, particularly in the financial function.

Using personnel from the parent nation of the multinational ensures a greater degree of consistency and control in the firm's operations around the world. This is not without its costs because these personnel may experience considerable difficulty in understanding cultural differences. In an attitude survey of personnel in forty-nine multinationals, personnel from the host country contended that parent country personnel tended not to question orders from headquarters even when appropriate to do so.[8] This enabled them to advance their own long-term interests in the firm by getting better headquarter evaluations and facilitating repatriation at the end of their tour of duty. In addition, the common practice of frequent rotation of key personnel intensified the problem of understanding and adapting to local cultures. However, employing the PCN does facilitate communications with headquarters because both parties are of the same culture.

Utilizing personnel from the host country in key positions will improve the MNC's relations with the host country government. It will also enable a quicker and more accurate adaptation to requirements of the local culture. Disadvantages would include a lessened degree of central control and increased communication problems with headquarters. In addition, if the HCNs perceive that the opportunity for higher positions is blocked for ethnic reasons, they will use the MNC to gain experience so they may transfer to local national firms at higher positions.

Personnel Problems in Sending Parent Company Nationals Abroad

One of the most difficult personnel problems for the multinational is that of selecting the appropriate people to be sent on foreign assignments. Careful plans should be made to assure that selectees possess certain basic characteristics. Among these are the following:

- a very real desire to work in a foreign country
- spouses and families who have actively encouraged the person to work overseas
- cultural sensitivity and flexibility
- high degree of technical competence
- a sense for politics

Several surveys of overseas managers have revealed that the spouse's opinion and attitude should be considered the number one screening factor. Cultural sensitivity is also essential if we are to avoid antagonizing host-country nationals, unnecessarily.

Comments from top-level executives of multinationals provide insight as to how their companies select managers for international assignments.

Daniel International Corporation	T. P. Townsend, Jr. Group Vice-President	Train and observe in a domestic position. Because of the high cost and high risk, we use only proven and tried people in our international operations.
General Electric Company	W. W. Hamilton Manager International Communications	Managers are selected internationally by the same criteria as in the United States, leadership ability, effectiveness in teaching

		and developing people, appropriate priority on long- and short-term goals, understanding of the business, etc. In sending a United States national to a foreign country, or a foreign national to the United States, it is extremely important that the individual be outstanding in his field, because he will be perceived as representative of his country's best qualifications.
Signode Corporation	L. R. Flandreau Vice-President International	Selected mostly from within the company, and local to the operation to be managed if possible. New hires are looked at from standpoint of marketing skills, language skills, desire for international environment, logic, personality (sensitive, flexible yet tough minded).
A. E. Staley Mfg. Co.	D. A. Gullette Director Administration International Division	With the qualities of leadership, mental and physical endurance, and a broad knowledge of parent company operations and products, we would then first screen our international managers for the skills or potential talent for these skills. Our selection process would not be limited to U.S. nationals, but would also include our foreign nationals who had or could develop the necessary skills and were culturally acceptable for the new position.

The comments of these executives suggest that managers given international assignments possess considerable education concerning the culture, history, politics, language, and business setting of the country where the operations are located.

A second major problem that confronts MNCs is the establishment of equitable compensation systems for personnel given international assignments. Typically, personnel from the parent country receive a salary plus an overseas premium of up to 50 percent plus moving expense allowances and certain living allowances. Personnel from the parent country of the MNC receive a higher pay than personnel employed from the local country. This tends to create resentment and reduce cooperation. Many Americans have found their standard of living and social class to be considerably improved in foreign countries over what it had been in the United States. This may make for some difficulties when they return. An important incentive for U.S. citizens to accept assignments in foreign countries is the opportunity to exclude a portion of their income earned in the foreign country from U.S. income taxes. Internal Revenue regulations allow U.S. citizens to exclude up to $75,000 of income earned while working in a foreign country provided that the individuals are bona fide residents of a foreign country for twelve months or longer. In addition to financial rewards, the assignment often provides career advancement opportunities.

godfather system

repatriation

Despite the company's intention to provide career advancement opportunities, there is still some danger that skilled personnel will come to feel that their career progress has suffered by leaving their home country. Some personnel have returned from foreign assignments to find no job available, or they are given jobs that do not utilize skills obtained during the overseas service. To solve ths problem, a **godfather system** has been set up in companies such as Control Data Corporation.[9] Before the person leaves on the assignment, a specific executive is appointed as the godfather to look after the person's interest while in a foreign country and to assist the executive in achieving a smooth transition when the manager returns home. A **repatriation** plan is worked out including how long the assignment is to be and to what job the appointee will return. Ordinarily, the godfather is the person's future boss upon return to the parent country. During the assignment, the individual is kept informed of major ongoing events occurring in the unit of future assignment. In this way, not only is there a logical career plan worked out, there is no feeling of being lost in the vast international shuffle of the company.

Management Approach

As noted previously in this chapter, managing in an international environment requires careful consideration of significant factors. This point is vividly illustrated by the following remarks of a multinational executive in describing the unique qualities necessary for a manager to possess in managing in the international environment.

- **History**. A knowledge of basic history, particularly in countries of old and varied cultures.
- **Sociology and Economics**. A social background in basic economics and sociological concepts, which differ from country to country.
- **Languages**. A working knowledge of languages and willingness to learn and practice a language to a level of perfection needed to carry on business conversations.

- **Cultural Nuances.** A genuine respect for different philosophical and ethical approaches.

The multinational company by definition is faced with a wide variety of situations—differing cultures, economic and political systems, and religions. Management must capitalize on its unique strength of being able to make worldwide decisions in the selection of markets and allocation of resources. Yet in each market, there are different environmental constraints. Thus, multinational managers must adapt to and work with the varying cultures of a multiplicity of nations throughout the world. W. W. Hamilton, manager for international communications with General Electric, indicated the importance of the type of qualities needed by management in the international environment with the following comments:

> Leadership ability, effectiveness in teaching and developing people, appropriate priority on long- and short-term goals, and an understanding of the business. Also, a degree of self-sufficiency and willingness to understand though not necessarily adapt to local cultures and problem-solving approaches.

The chief executive officer of each foreign subsidiary is confronted by opposing flows of corporate uniformity and cultural fragmentation. If the officer is from the parent country, uniformity is likely to be emphasized. If the manager is from the host country, cultural adaptation may take precedence. Because of growing nationalistic tendencies of many countries, there is an increased chance that the top manager will be from the host country. In Germany, for instance, the chief executive officer must have an engineering degree to be accepted and respected. In France, graduates of the Grandes Ecoles are favored. If third-country nationals are to be used as chief executive officers, varying mobilities must be considered. A married Frenchman living in Paris is almost unmovable. However, most German managers are quite enthusiastic about working in other countries. The English and Scandinavians are typically willing to relocate, but they require assurance of return to their native lands.

Adaptation is not all one way. Local nationals will have to try to understand and adapt to the culture of the MNC, which inevitably requires some understanding of the culture of the parent country of the MNC. This learning, too, will require considerable effort and time. In dealing with headquarters executives of an American MNC, the local national will have to learn to get to the point quickly. Americans are notoriously impatient with lengthy and expanded explanations. Nationals must be basically positive in approach, and they must avoid constant criticism. However, they must also learn to argue with the American executive, but know just how far they can go.

Effective managers of multinational operations must develop a style of leadership consistent with the needs of the situation existing in the host country. The appropriate managerial style of leadership can be determined only after a careful assessment is made of the external environment of the host country, the type of and personnel to be managed, the level of existing technology, and the specific goals and operational requirements of the company.

Summary

We are now in the age of the multinational corporation (MNC). Few other developments have had the overall impact of multinationals. These firms have caused the countries of the world to become more closely related to each other. An MNC is a firm engaged in business in two or more countries. These firms typically have sales offices and sometimes manufacturing plants in many different countries. The MNCs are not only instrumental in improving the world economy and thereby standards of living of many people but also significantly affect the technology, culture, and customs of the countries in which they operate.

The multinational corporation is the type of enterprise that provides a special challenge to managers. Effectiveness in managing in an international environment requires the manager to give careful consideration to such factors as the external environment, objectives, technology, structure, personnel, and the management approach. The external environment that confronts multinational enterprises consists primarily of the economic, political-legal, and social-cultural system of the various countries in which the MNC operates. This external environment characterized by complexity, variety, and uncertainty requires that managers develop sophisticated skills to deal effectively with these conditions. Objectives of the MNC would not seem to be any different from the objectives of businesses operating exclusively within the United States. However, the MNC differs from domestic firms because of the potential clash of its goals with the objectives of the economic and political systems of the various countries within which they operate.

Technological expertise is the primary advantage of the MNC. Many MNCs operate in such high-technology industries as computers, oil, pharmaceuticals, electronics, and motor vehicles. Another major factor to be considered in managing the MNC is the organization of the firm. The organizational structure of an MNC must be designed to meet the needs of the international environment. Such a structure may differ significantly from the company's domestic operations.

Successful management of an MNC requires that the manager understand the needs, values, and problems of personnel in the countries where the company operates. Management must recognize that there is no one style of leadership that will be equally effective in all countries. People in the various countries have widely divergent backgrounds, educations, cultures, and religions and live in a variety of social conditions and economic and political systems.

Effective managers of MNCs must develop a style of leadership consistent with the needs of the situation existing in the host country. The appropriate managerial style of leadership can be determined only after a careful assessment is made of the external environment of the host country, the type of personnel to be managed, the level of existing technology, and the specific goals and operational requirements of the company.

Review Questions

1. What is a multinational corporation? List three of the major criteria used to classify multinationals.
2. Name four of the largest multinational corporations (MNC).
3. "The success or failure of the MNC is determined largely by how they respond to the external environment." Comment.
4. List the major factors affecting the management of multinationals.
5. Describe two major economic problems that often confront multinationals.
6. Distinguish between developed and less developed countries.
7. How does the political-legal environment affect the MNC?
8. What specific types of laws or local regulations must a multinational corporation be concerned with?
9. How may the objectives of the MNC differ from domestic firms?
10. Identify *five* of the more typical complaints host countries have against MNCs.
11. Is a code of ethics needed to MNCs? Why or why not? Give examples of what might be included.
12. "Technological expertise is the primary advantage of the multinational enterprise." Explain.
13. Describe the types of personnel used by MNCs and any potential problems with these personnel.

Exercises

1. Assume that you have agreed to accept a position in the international division of General Electric and have been assigned to the Helsinki, Finland, office effective in sixty days. You are married and have a six-year-old daughter. What would you do to prepare yourself and your family for this assignment?
2. **A.** If you were selecting personnel to be sent on international assignments, what qualities, experience, and characteristics would you look for in prospective personnel?

   B. Review two current journal articles on the problems multinational companies have in recruiting and placing U.S. managers and/or technical personnel in assignments in foreign countries. Make a list of the problems and how the companies are able to overcome them.

Case Study

The Case of the Missing Ads

When several Americans came to work as department heads at one of the largest Japanese automotive firms in the United States, they had all been reading extensively on Japanese methods. Most of them had come from a major American automotive company, and all had had long experience in the industry. Inevitably, under the pressure of business in this fast-growing organization, they turned instinctively to their accustomed Western management techniques. They looked to the Japanese nationals at the top levels of the organization to give them direction, objectives, and priorities. But nothing was forthcoming; the Japanese were waiting patiently for initiatives from them.

After a time, on the Americans' initiative, an organization chart was drawn up in an effort to settle where the authority and responsibility for decisions rested. It was a thoroughly American document, showing in neat boxes the various departments—parts, service, sales, marketing, planning, and so on—and the vertical relationships, with the Japanese president at the top and the lowest subdepartment on the bottom. The Japanese, who rarely draw up organization charts (and who, if they do, invariably make them read horizontally, like a flow chart), tolerated the American version as a "when in Rome" accommodation. But the chart did not solve the problems; the organization was not functioning well, and decisions were not being made.

For example, there was the simple problem of timing the availability of advertising media for the introduction of new models each year. In the U.S. market this occurs in October; in Japan, new models are introduced in January. From the parent company in Japan, the advertising materials consistently arrived two to three months late for the introduction of new models. Year after year, the U.S. distributors complained about the delay. The American heads of the sales and advertising departments took the problem up the chain of command and requested their Japanese president to contact Japan and straighten the matter out. The president did contact Japan—but the problem remained.

By chance, other developments in the organization provided an opportunity for overcoming the difficulty. Beginning in the early 1970s top management began to assign a Japanese "coordinator" to each American department head. The coordinators, usually promising young executives in training for international assignments, were to become acquainted with U.S. business practices. It was not long before they began observing with dismay that the American managers tended to concentrate on their functional roles and to expect coordination between functions to occur at the senior management levels—as is the practice in many U.S. companies. To the Japanese, it appeared, as one put it, "as if the various departments were separate companies, all competing against each other."

As inveterate communicators, some coordinators began to pick up problems that cropped up in one department and share them with their counterparts in other departments. In this roundabout way, the Americans learned what their colleagues were doing. Coordination between departments improved.

Soon the Japanese coordinators became aware of the difficulties typified by the late arrival of the advertising materials. True to their training in U.S. compa-

Source: Richard Tanner Johnson and William G. Ouchi, "Made in America (under Japanese Management)," *Harvard Business Review* 52 (September–October 1974): 67–68.

nies, the Americans were sending a report on every problem up the chain of command. Japanese top management in the United States would listen to each complaint, then send the American manager back for "more information." Translated, this meant "Come back with a proposal." Not comprehending, the Americans became increasingly impatient and frustrated. Occasionally, as in the case of the ads, the problems became so serious that the Americans insisted they be reported to Japan. The Japanese president obliged them, but the parent company remained unresponsive. The reason was simple: since Japanese organizations are unaccustomed to dealing with problems from the top down, the Tokyo organization did not know how to handle a letter from the president of the Japanese subsidiary in the United States to the president of the parent company in Japan.

Once the coordinators understood the nature of the difficulty, remedying the advertising materials lag and similar problems was easy. A coordinator would simply pick up the telephone and call somebody at his managerial level in Tokyo. In a few days an answer would come back—and in this manner the matter of the ads was resolved.

The coordinators took some time—and the American department heads a somewhat longer time—to realize that the neat boxes in the organization chart were not interacting. By U.S. standards, the Americans were doing a good job. But without American superiors to make decisions and weave the organization together, they found that their effectiveness was diminished. To bridge the gap in managerial styles, the coordinators created a shadow organization. In this manner they not only solved the coordination problem but also involved the parent organization.

QUESTIONS

1. Identify the major factors that affect American managers working for a foreign company.
2. Why do you believe the informal organization was so important in the solution of this problem?

Case Study

Mark Is Transferred Overseas

In college, Mark Hammer majored in industrial management and was considered by his teachers and peers to be one of the best all around students to graduate from Midwest State University. Mark not only took the required courses in business, but he also acquired a minor in foreign language. The language that Mark concentrated on the most was French, and he became quite fluent in the language.

After graduation, Mark took an entry-level management training position with Tuborg International, a multinational corporation with offices and factories in thirty countries, including the United States. Mark's first assignment was in a plant in New York. His supervisors quickly identified Mark for his ability to get the job done and still maintain excellent rapport with subordinates, peers, and superiors. In only three years, Mark had advanced from a manager trainee to the position of assistant plant superintendent.

After two years in this position, Mark was called into the superintendent's office one day and told that he had been identified as being ready for a foreign assignment. The move would mean a promotion and the location of the plant was in a small industrialized region in France. One of the reasons that Mark had been chosen for France was due to his knowledge of French he had gained in college. Mark was excited and he wasted no time in making the necessary preparations for the new assignment.

Prior to arriving at the plant in France, Mark took considerable time to review his books in the French language. He was surprised at how quickly the use of the language came back to him. He thought that there wouldn't be any major difficulties in making the transition from the United States to France. But on arriving, Mark rapidly discovered that there were to be problems. The small industrialized community where Mark's plant was located did not speak the "pure" French that he had learned. There were many slang expressions that meant one thing to Mark but had an entirely different meaning to the employees of the plant.

While meeting with several of the employees a week after arriving, one of the workers said something to Mark that he interpreted as very uncomplimentary (in actuality, the employee had greeted him by saying a rather risque expression but in a different tone that he had known before. All of the other employees interpreted the expression to be merely a friendly greeting). Mark's disgust was evident and as time went by, this type of instance occurred a few more times, and the other employees began to limit their conversation with Mark. In only one month, Mark managed to virtually completely isolate himself from the workers within the plant. He became disillusioned and thought about asking to be relieved from the assignment.

QUESTIONS

1. What problems had Mark not anticipated when he took the assignment?
2. How could the company have assisted Mark to reduce the difficulties that he confronted?
3. Do you believe the situation that Mark confronted is typical of an American going to a foreign assignment? Discuss.

Notes

1. Peter F. Drucker, *Management* (New York: Harper, 1973), p. 729.
2. Robert W. Stevens, "Scanning the Multinational Firm," *Business Horizons* 14 (June 1971): 53.
3. David C. McClelland, *The Achieving Society* (Princeton, N.J.: Van Nostrand, 1961).
4. R. Hal Mason, "Conflicts between Host Countries and Multinational Enterprise." Copyright © 1974 by the Regents of the University of California. Reprinted from *California Management Review,* volume XVII, no. 1, pp. 6 and 7, by permission of the Regents.
5. "France Seizing Control of Technical Industries," *Business Week,* May 17, 1976, p. 47.
6. United Nations information.
7. Rodman, L. Drake and Lee M. Caudill, "Management of Large Multinationals: Trends and Future Challenges," *Business Horizons.*
8. Yoram Zeira, "Overlooked Personnel Problems of Multinational Corporations," *Columbia Journal of World Business* 10 (Summer 1975): 96–103.
9. David M. Noer, "Integrating Foreign Service Employees to Home Organization: The Godfather Approach," *Personnel Journal* 53 (January 1974): 45–50.

References

Alpander, Guvenc G. "Multinational Corporations: Home-based Affiliate Relations." *California Management Review* 20, no. 3 (Spring 1978): 47–56.

Capstick, R. "The Perils of Manufacturing Abroad." *International Management* 33 (March 1978): 43–46.

Davis, S. M. "Trends in the Organization of Multinational Corporations." *Columbia Journal of World Business* 11 (Summer 1976): 54–71.

Davis, Stanley M., and Lawrence, Paul R. "Problems of Matrix Organizations." *Harvard Business Review* 56, no. 3 (May–June 1978): 131–142.

Duncan, Robert. "What Is the Right Organization Structure?" *Organizational Dynamics* 7, no. 3 (Winter 1979): 59–80.

Galbraith, J. K. "The Defense of the Multinational Company." *Harvard Business Review* 56 (March 1978): 83–93.

————, and Edstrom, A. "International Transfer of Managers: Some Important Policy Considerations." *Columbia Journal of World Business* 11 (Summer 1976): 100–112.

Ghymn, K. I., and Bates, T. H. "Consequences of MNC Strategic Planning: An Empirical Case Study." *Management International Review* 17 (1977): 83–91.

Lawrence, Paul R.; Kolodny, Harvey F.; and Davis, Stanley M. "The Human Side of the Matrix." *Organizational Dynamics* 6, no. 1 (Summer 1977): 43–61.

May, W. F. "Between Ideology and Interdependence." *California Management Review* 19 (Summer 1977): 88–90.

Mitchell, J., and Shawn, A. "All Multinationals Aren't the Same." *Financial World,* January 1, 1977, p. 36.

Morris, James H.; Steers, Richard M.; and Koch, James L. "Influence of Organization Structure on Role Conflict and Ambiguity for Three Occupational Groupings." *Academy of Management Journal* 22, no. 1 (March 1979): 58–70.

Paulson, Steven K. "Organizational Size, Technology, and Structure: Replication of a Study of Social Service Agencies among Small Retail Firms." *Academy of Management Journal* 23, no. 2 (June 1980): 341–346.

Pohlman, R. A. "Policies of Multinational Firms: A Survey." *Business Horizons* 19 (December 1976): 14–18.

Prahalad, C. K. "Strategic Choices in Diversified MNC's." *Harvard Business Review* 54 (July 1976): 67–78.

Sparkman, J. "Economic Interdependence and the International Corporation." *California Management Review* 20 (Fall 1977): 88–92.

Vernon, R. "Multinational Enterprises and National Governments: An Uneasy Relationship." *Columbia Journal of World Business* 11 (Summer 1976): 9–16.

Zeira, Y. "Management Development in Ethnocentric Multinational Corporations." *California Management Review* 18 (Summer 1976): 34–42.

————, and Harari, E. "Managing Third Country Nationals in Multinational Corporations." *Business Horizons* 18 (October 1977): 83–88.

CASE STUDY FOR PART VII

Damned if You Do and Damned if You Don't

"Recycle those by-products—reduce that waste—save that scrap! Preserve our natural resources by conserving any and everything possible!"

"That's exactly what we've been doing," exclaimed James R. Piedmont, fiery founder and chairman of the board of Piedmont Poultry Processors (PPP). "I've built this company from a one-man operation in a ramshackled warehouse to one of the finest poultry processing operations in the Southwest with over 400 employees on the payroll. And conservation of resources has always been our byword. Even the chicken litter from the commercial egg farm is recycled for both fertilizer and chicken feed.

"And now the citizens of Claridge are complaining about a little cooking odor? It looks to me like it's damned if you do and damned if you don't around here!"

AIR POLLUTION PROBLEMS AIRED

The first inkling of serious action came when Piedmont processing plant manager Franklin Ross was called before the regular city commission meeting in June. At that meeting commissioners called Ross's attention to continued complaints from Claridge citizens over the odor being emitted from the plant.

Ross's reply attributed the odor to rendering equipment in that part of the plant where chicken by-products were processed to make cat food. By-products were used from the Claridge plant, a company-owned plant in nearby Mansfield, and two noncompany plants in distant locations. By-products were hauled by uncovered company trucks from the distant locations to the Piedmont Plant.

Ross assured the commissioners at the June meeting that new cookers and air scrubbers were currently being installed. The project would be com-

This case prepared by Prof. Janelle C. Ashley of Stephen F. Austin State University, Nacogdoches, Texas, as a basis for class discussion rather than to illustrate either effective or ineffective handling of an administrative situation.

plete by August 1 and as of that date the "malodor" should be eliminated. Ross left the meeting feeling confident that his pollution worries were over.

TWO-FOLD VIOLATION CITED

No such luck! Ten days after the regular commission meeting Ross was again summoned—this time to appear before an emergency meeting of the Claridge City Commission. Expecting just an interrogation over Piedmont's progress in the air pollution problem, plant manager Ross ran head-on into the city commissioners armed with pictures, a five-page report, the city health inspector, and the pollution control officer. Not only did the commissioners cite Piedmont for polluting the air with cooking process odor, but they added a citation for polluting nearby Anson Creek.

Based on a series of complaints from citizens of Claridge regarding the odor being emitted from the plant and a second complaint that PPP was polluting Anson Creek with chicken by-products, city officials had gathered sufficient information for the emergency meeting to issue specific demands that Piedmont "either clean up the operation or answer an injunctive relief suit by the city that would mean, at the least, a mandatory temporary shutdown of the plant."

Four of the five city commissioners were present for the meeting and voted three to one to give Piedmont and Ross one week to make significant on-site improvements of water pollution, sanitary conditions, and air pollution. If this were not accomplished to the satisfaction of city inspectors, injunctive relief was to be sought through state agencies as outlined by the city attorney. The one female commissioner voted against the one-week reprieve. The proposal, she felt, was not stringent enough. "Since the last meeting there apparently has been no improvement," she said, "especially since a whole chicken was found in the sewer. I favor a shutdown of the plant until the sanitary conditions are met."

CASE AGAINST PIEDMONT

Commissioners had no qualms over the August deadline for the air pollution problem in the rendering plant. They had, however, grave concern over a matter of water pollution and sanitary conditions at the plant site. Pictures had been taken on two occasions after the first commission meeting showing chicken by-products in a ditch flowing from Piedmont into a nearby creek and then into the larger Anson Creek. Chicken by-products were stacked outside the plant accumulating flies, and a truckload of chicken cleanings was parked, uncovered, near the plant.

Claridge city manager reported that when the truck dumped the by-products, blood and water ran off onto the ground and around the building. "That eventually contaminates our waterways," he noted. Water samples taken by the city pollution control officer showed extreme contamination of the water. The water tests registered 450 parts per million of biochemical oxygen demand. The state allowable was 20 parts per million. Total suspended solids measured 35 parts per million with 10 allowable. Oil and grease content was 36, while state allowable was 10.

Ross said the water contamination was due to a breakdown of a main separator in the plant. "All the water had to be let out of the processing equipment. There was nothing else we could do," he said. Three days after the spillage from the plant breakdown, however, the water tests still registered high contents of the noted pollutants, according to the pollution control officer.

The city health inspector had further fuel to add to the fire. Answering a complaint registered against Piedmont on June 9, the inspector found chicken parts and other waste in the creek near the plant. He also saw piles of chicken by-products, which he classified as "choice media for fly larva, and extremely bad odor." In the health inspector's opinion, the only way to eliminate the long-standing malodor and bad sanitary condition would be to concrete the entire area. "You just can't clean dirt," he added.

After hearing the city attorney report on a conversation with the state attorney general's office, the commissioners went into executive session to discuss the legal aspects of the issue. According to the state office, commissioners could instruct the city attorney to file suit for injunctive relief. The result of the suit would be that the plant would either be closed or it would stay open. The suit would be filed in district court, and the state would be involved in the hearings.

The commissioners' decision came in the form of the following motion:

> That offenders be notified in writing that relief will be sought through injunctive waste ordinances of the state and daily on-site inspection by city officials will be made, and if progress is not made within one week from Monday, and if said offenders do not show signs of complying, injunctive relief will be sought.

MONITORING VISITS CONTINUED

At the conclusion of the one week clean-up period, Claridge commissioners met in special session to determine if injunctive relief against PPP should be sought. Representing Piedmont in addition to plant manager Ross was Vice-President Sam Smithart.

Smithart listed air pollution control being made by his firm and added, "We welcome suggestions and will do anything in our power to carry out these suggestions. I will be disappointed if, in ninety days, anybody knows there is a chicken processing plant in Claridge." When questioned by the commissioners about the August 1 date (the date formerly agreed upon for the end of the odor), Smithart assured, "We are going to meet that deadline. But sometimes it takes a little time to get new equipment adjusted, to get the proper mix of controls. We are planning to beautify the area, and we have drawings to expand the plant."

Sanitary superintendent for Claridge then read the following report, made from frequent visits to both Piedmont and Carsons (a competing poultry processor in Claridge):

> After having observed the operation of the two poultry processing plants for the prescribed time and at the direction of city commission, the following observations and recommendations are made:
>
> - General cleanup has progressed and noticeable improvement was observed.
> - Trucks are now draining waste liquids onto the wash ramp which is washed and drained well.
> - The baffle height was raised and a screen is being installed. This should be a satisfactory temporary arrangement to alleviate the problem until permanent renovation is completed.
> - Pipes discharging water into the drainage ditch that eventually ends in Anson Creek have been rerouted to discharge into the city sewer.
> - A dike was erected across the drainage ditch to trap water draining from the plant area. This ditch has been cleaned with a backhoe and pumped once with a suction pump truck and is now filled with clean rain water.
> - Truck scheduling has minimized the waiting time for loaded trucks. Very few have been noted sitting.

- Covers for the trucks have been ordered and should arrive shortly for all trucks; some new trucks have arrived equipped with enclosed blood tanks.
- Employees are more aware of sanitation, cleaning up spills and keeping solids out of the sewage system, as witnessed by the drop of foreign material at the sewage plant and the cleanup in the yard, also the covering of spillage, etc.
- The Carsons plant was inspected every time the Piedmont plant was. Several recommendations were made, and corrective action was taken at once, with the biggest improvement noted when the large door in the rendering plant was shut and welded.

Claridge commissioners accepted the recommendation "that the current inspection program be continued until such time as the renovations are completed."

Discussion Questions

1. Was the action of the Claridge city commission precipitous?
2. Was it unreasonable to expect PPP to use covered trucks to haul the chicken by-products to the rendering plant?
3. What is your reaction to Ross's comment that the water contamination was due to a breakdown of a main separator in the plant? Evaluate his statement, "All the water had to be let out of the processing equipment. There was nothing else we could do."
4. Can you suggest a way to prepare for a recurrence of the problems mentioned in the previous question?
5. If you were in Smithart's position, what else would you do to meet the city commission's mandate?

Glossary

ABC method An inventory technique in which inventory is classified into groups according to cost.

accountability Final responsibility for results that a manager cannot delegate to someone else.

action planning Establishment of performance objectives and standards for individuals. Requires that challenging but attainable standards be developed for the purpose of improving individual or group performance.

activity In PERT it is the time-consuming element of a network.

activity trap Exists when managers and employees become so enmeshed in performing assigned functions that they lose sight of the goal or reasons for their performance.

Adult The ego state of transactional analysis that identifies the person who tends to evaluate the situation and attempts to make decisions based on information and facts.

analytical skill The ability of the manager to use logical and scientific approaches or techniques in the analysis of problems and business opportunities.

aptitude tests Used to determine a person's probability for success in a selected job.

arbitration Calls for outside neutral parties to assist in resolving the conflict. The arbitrator is given the authority to act as a judge in making a decision.

attribute sampling Sampling plan in which there are no degrees of conformity to consider. The product is either good or bad.

authority The right to decide, to direct others to take action, or to perform certain duties in achieving organizational goals.

bankruptcy The financial failure of a firm.

barriers to communication Factors that can reduce communication effectiveness between the sender and the receiver.

behavior Goal-oriented actions of individuals.

body language A nonverbal method of communication in which physical actions such as motions, gestures, and facial expressions convey thoughts and emotions.

break-even analysis Approach used to determine the amount of a particular product that must be sold if the firm is to generate enough revenue to cover costs; the point at which revenues and costs are equal.

budget Formal statement of financial resources—planned expenditures of money for personnel, time, space, or equipment.

budgetary standard Concerned with the comparison of actual to planned expenditures.

capital Money used to finance business operations. Primary sources of capital are from owners or creditors or funds generated internally within the business.

capital budget Indicates planned capital acquisition, usually for the purpose of purchasing additional facilities or equipment.

career objectives A determination of the specific type of career that an individual desires to pursue.

carrying costs Expenses that would be associated with maintaining the product in inventory before it is sold or used.

cash budget Summarizes planned cash receipts and disbursements.

centralized The type of situation in which decision-making authority is concentrated at the upper levels of the organization.

chain of command Means by which authority flows from top to bottom in the organization.

change agent The person who is responsible for ensuring that the planned change in OD is properly implemented.

Child The ego state of transactional analysis that identifies the person who bases decisions primarily on personal satisfaction.

coercive power The leader's ability to administer and control punishments (such as the power to fire, demote, or reprimand) to others for not following the leader's requests.

cohesiveness The degree of attraction that the group has for each of its members.

communication The achievement of meaning and understanding between people through verbal and nonverbal means in order to affect behavior and achieve desired results.

communication overload Exists when the sender attempts to present too much information to the receiver at one time.

communication skill The ability to provide information orally and in written form to others in the organization for the purpose of achieving desired results.

comparison controls Used to determine whether deviations from plans have taken place and, if necessary, to bring them to the attention of the responsible managers.

compensation All rewards individuals receive as a result of their employment.

conceptual skill Ability of the manager to understand the complexities of the overall organization and how each department or unit fits into the organization.

conflict management A facilitator to communication. Has the ability to resolve disagreements between individuals within the organization that could have an adverse effect on attainment of organizational goals.

consideration The extent to which leaders have relationships with subordinates characterized by mutual trust, respect, and consideration of employees' ideas and feelings.

constraint function In linear programming, it is a restriction placed on solving the problem.

contact chart Identifies the connections that an individual has with other members of the organization.

control The process of comparing actual performance with established standards for the purpose of taking action to correct deviations.

control charts Procedure that measures the progress against actual performance during operations.

control process Involves establishment of standards, comparison of performance to standard, and taking corrective action.

critical path In PERT and CPM it is the longest path from start to finish of a project.

critical path method (CPM) A network technique developed by industry. Only one time estimate is used, thereby making the network a deterministic model.

cyclical Variations in demand that fluctuate around the long-run trend line. A cycle typically is two to three years in duration.

decentralized The type of situation in which decision-making authority has been delegated to lower levels in the organization.

decision maker The person who has the responsibility for choosing the course of action that will solve the problem within the area for which he or she is accountable.

decision making The process by which we evaluate alternatives and make a choice among them.

decision-making skill The manager's skill in selecting a course of action designed to solve a specific problem or set of problems.

delegation The process of making specific work assignments to individuals within the organization and providing them with the right or power to perform these functions.

demand forecasting An attempt to estimate the demand for a firm's products.

departmentation The grouping of related functions or major work activities into manageable units to achieve more effective and efficient overall coordination of organization resources.

disciplinary action The process of invoking a penalty against an employee who fails to adhere to standards.

discounted cash flow A procedure of analyzing economic alternatives that takes into consideration the time value of money.

downward functional differentiation Adding workers to perform certain functions. It is usually the first growth in a firm.

E-R-G Theory Theory developed by Clayton Alderfer that is an attempt to make Maslow's theory more consistent with knowledge of human needs. Alderfer's classification of needs is existence, relatedness, and growth.

economic function Businesses' production of needed goods and services, provision of employment, contribution to economic growth, and earning of profit.

economic objectives Goals of the firm that are associated with survival, profit, and growth.

empathy The ability to identify with the various feelings and thoughs of another person.

employment application Form that collects objective, biographical information about an applicant, such as education, work experience, special skills, general background, marital status, and references.

entrepreneur A person who has the ability to create an ongoing enterprise where none existed before.

equity Involves an individual's comparing his or her performance and the rewards received with the performance and rewards others receive for doing similar work.

ethical dilemmas Ethical situations that confront managers and that are often difficult to resolve or avoid.

ethical responsibility Concern for personal and corporate integrity and honesty.

ethics Contemporary standards or principles of conduct that govern the actions and behavior of individuals within the organization.

event In PERT it is a meaningful specified accomplishment (physical or intellectual) in the program plan, recognizable at a particular instance of time.

executive burnout A person who is in a state of fatigue or frustration brought about by devotion to a cause, way of life, or relationships that failed to produce the expected reward.

expatriate A person who is out of his or her native country.

expectancy An individual's perception of the chances or probability that a particular outcome will occur as a result of certain behavior.

expected time In PERT it is calculated by using a formula consisting of three time estimates: optimistic, most likely, and pessimistic.

expert power Based on the special knowledge, expertise, skill, or experience possessed by the leader.

exponential smoothing Technique using the forecast from the previous period, the actual demand that resulted from this forecasted period, and a smoothing constant.

external environment Anything outside the organization (legal, social, political, and economic) that can affect the firm.

Fiedler's contingency model Suggests that there is no one most effective style that is appropriate to every situation.

filtering Attempts to alter and color information to present a more favorable image.

financial assistance Refers to programs offered by the Small Business Administration designed to provide aid for small businesses that need money and cannot borrow it on affordable terms from conventional lenders.

financial budget Indicates the amount of capital the organization will need and where it will obtain the capital.

fixed costs Costs that do not change with the level of output.

flow process chart A production method using symbols to depict the flow of a job.

forecasting An attempt to project what will occur in the future.

formal power Derived from authority or legitimate position in the firm.

Friedman's view of social responsibility There is one and only one social responsibility: to earn maximum profits while following the rules of the game.

functional authority A staff position that has direct-line authority over specialized functions or activities.

functional organizations Structure in which specialists are given authority to issue orders in their own names in designated areas of work.

functionalization The process of splitting and differentiating functions as the organization grows.

functions Work that can be identified and distinguished from other work, such as production, marketing, and finance.

godfather system A program in which an experienced executive is assigned to assist a manager in his or her development when on an international assignment.

grapevine The informal means by which information is transmitted in an organization.

group Two or more people who join together to accomplish a desired goal.

Hersey/Blanchard's situational leadership theory Theory based on the notion that the most effective

leadership style varies according to the level of maturity of the followers and the demands of the situation.

hierarchy of needs Maslow's theory that human needs such as psychological, safety, social, esteem, and self-actualization are arranged in a hierarchy.

host country Country where the multinational company is operating.

host country nationals Personnel from the host country.

human resources All personnel, both managerial and operating, who perform work of the organization.

human skill The ability of a manager to understand, work with, and get along with other people.

human social responsibility A firm's concern for people.

hygiene factors According to Frederick Herzberg, the factors include such items as pay, status, working conditions, and so on.

hypothesis A tentative statement of the nature of the relationships that exist.

influencing Motivating and leading personnel.

informal relationships Relationships that are created, not by officially designated managers, but by any and all organizational members.

informal work group A group of people who join together to accomplish mutually satisfying goals.

initial controls Attempt to monitor the resources—material, human, and capital—that come into the organization for the purpose of ensuring that they can be used effectively to achieve organizational objectives.

initiating structure The extent to which leaders establish goals and define and structure their roles and the roles of subordinates toward the attainment of the goals.

innovative objectives Concerned with unique or special accomplishments, such as the development of new methods or procedures.

inputs Human (employees to run the plant) or nonhuman (fuel for the factory) energies, supplies, and information. Processed within the organization to create desired outputs.

interest tests Assists a person in identifying career fields.

interview Method of assessing the qualifications of job applicants.

intuition Acquired through experience and accomplishment rather than through a formal decision-making process.

inventory Goods or materials available for use by a business.

iron law of responsibility States that if business firms are to retain their social power and role, they must be responsive to society's needs.

job analysis Process of determining the responsibilities and operations of a job leading to the development of a job description.

job description Summarizes the purpose, principal duties, and responsibilities of a job.

job enlargement Provides a horizontal expansion of duties. An approach that involves an increase in the number of tasks employees are required to perform.

job enrichment Refers to basic changes in the content and level of responsibility of a job so as to provide for the satisfaction of the motivation needs of personnel.

job specification Statement of the minimum acceptable human qualities necessary to perform the job.

leader-member relations According to Fiedler, the degree to which the leader feels accepted by the subordinates.

leadership The process of influencing the behavior and actions of others toward the accomplishment of goals.

leadership continuum As developed by Tannenbaum and Schmidt, suggests that choosing an effective leadership style depends on the demands of the situation. The continuum ranges from boss-centered, autocratic management to subordinate-centered, participative management.

less developed countries A country lacking modern industry and the supporting services.

Likert's system of management Universal theory of leadership consisting of a continuum of styles ranging from autocratic to participative.

likes/dislikes analysis Provides a person with the ability to assess certain situational factors that could have an impact on successful accomplishment of a job.

line and staff organization Type of structure that makes provision for the use of staff specialists who provide advice to line managers.

line organization Structure that shows the direct, vertical relationships between different levels within the firm.

linear programming Method used in attempting to allocate limited resources among competing demands in an optimum way.

listening One of the most effective tools to facilitate

communication. Entails actively participating in hearing what type of communication the sender is attempting to transmit.

lower-level managers Usually referred to as supervisors or foremen. Responsible for managing employees in the performance of the daily operations.

make/buy decisions Process through which a manager evaluates the benefits of making a product in-house or going outside to another manufacturer.

management The process of planning, organizing, influencing, and controlling to accomplish organizational goals through the coordinated use of human and material resources.

management assistance Service provided by the Small Business Administration that offers counseling and management training in an attempt to prevent business failures.

management by objectives A systematic and organized approach that allows management to attain maximum results from available resources by focusing on achievable goals.

management development programs Technique used to help managers learn more effective approaches to management.

management information system A means that facilitates managers in obtaining timely, accurate, and useful information.

management training program Through this program, a college graduate is provided formal training, which lasts from three months to two years, for the job he or she will ultimately be filling.

managerial code of ethics Provides guidelines and standards for conduct of managers.

managerial grid Leadership theory developed by Blake and Mouton that depicts five primary styles of leadership described according to the leader's concern for people and production.

mathematical models An equation or set of equations that defines and represents the relationship among elements of a system.

mediation Calls for outside neutral parties to enter the situation to assist in resolving the conflict. Suggestions and recommendations are given in the hope that the two parties in conflict will reach a solution.

methods and procedures Guidelines developed to assist in the implementation of plans. Includes policies, procedures, rules, and standards.

microcomputer The smallest computers.

middle managers Concerned primarily with the coordination of programs and activities that are necessary to achieve the overall goals of the organization as identified by top management.

minicomputers Computers that are a step above microcomputers because they are larger and more powerful.

model An abstraction of a real-world situation.

most likely time In PERT, it is the most realistic completion time for the activity.

motivation The process of influencing or stimulating a person to take action by creating a work environment wherein the goals of the organization and the needs of people are satisfied.

motivators According to Frederick Herzberg, these consist of factors intrinsic to the job, such as recognition, responsibility, achievement, and opportunities for growth and advancement.

motives Explain why people engage in certain behavior. They are the drives or impulses within an individual that cause behavior.

moving averages Technique for smoothing the effects of random variation.

multinational company A firm engaged in business in two or more countries.

need for achievement According to David McClelland, the need for achievement is concerned with an individual's desire for excellence.

need for affiliation According to David McClelland, this need is concerned with the desire for affection and establishing friendly relationships.

need for power According to David McClelland, this need is concerned with an individual's desire for influence and control over others.

nepotism The practice of hiring one's own relatives.

network An approach through which the various interdependencies of a project may be studied.

nonroutine decisions Those decisions that are designed to deal with unique problems or situations.

norms Standard of behavior that is expected from group members.

objective function In linear programming, what the decision maker is attempting to maximize or minimize.

objectives Describes the end results a person desires to accomplish.

Ohio state leadership studies In-depth studies of the behavior of leaders in a wide variety of organizations.

operating budget Indicates the revenues and expenses the business expects from producing goods and services during a given year.

operations chart Used to analyze the movement of the right and left hand in production operations.

optimistic time In PERT, it is the time that if everything goes right and nothing goes wrong, the project can be completed in this amount of time.

ordering costs Relate to the expenses associated with preparing an inventory order.

organization Two or more people working together in a coordinated manner to achieve group results.

organizational behavior modification Rests on the concepts that people act in ways they find most personally rewarding and by controlling the rewards, people's behavior can be shaped and determined.

organizational climate The psychological environment of the firm.

organizational development A planned and calculated attempt to move the organization as a unit from one state to another, typically to a more participative environment.

organizational structure Framework for providing a pattern for organizing the formal relationships of responsibility, authority, and accountability.

organizing Allocation of resources and establishment of the means to accomplish plans.

outputs The products and/or services that are the end result of the conversion process.

outward differentiation A splitting out of functions forming horizontal levels in the organization.

overseeing controls Monitor the actual creation of products or services. Accomplished largely by observation and by conference between supervisor and subordinate while the actual work activities are being performed.

Parent The ego state in transactional analysis that identifies the person who bases decisions primarily on what the individual has heard or learned in the past.

parent country Home base or headquarters for multinational firms.

parent country nationals Personnel from the parent country.

participative climate An open type of climate characterized by trust in subordinates, openness in communication, considerate and supportive leadership, group problem solving, worker autonomy, information sharing, and establishment of high output goals.

Path-Goal Leadership Theory Developed by Robert House. Stresses that managers can facilitate job performance by showing employees how their performance directly affects them in receiving desired rewards.

patterned interview Method in which an interviewer follows a predetermined series of questions in interviewing applicants.

payoff relationships The ability to measure the costs or profits of various courses of action and benefits than may be obtained.

perception sets Differences in individuals' background and experience that may result in different meanings and interpretations being associated with various words or phrases.

performance results standards Standards used when it is relatively simple to specify what end results are desired.

personal development objectives Provide the opportunity for each individual to state their personal goals and action plans for self-improvement and personal growth and development.

personal objectives Goals of individuals who are employed by the firm.

personality tests Assist in determining if a person possesses the proper personality for a particular job.

personnel planning Determining in advance how many workers and what kinds of skills are needed to accomplish the firm's objectives.

pessimistic time In PERT it is the time that if everything goes wrong and nothing goes right, the project will be completed in this amount of time.

physical models Models that look like the system they represent.

physical resources Materials, equipment, and money required to accomplish the objectives of the organization.

planning process Determining objectives and the courses of action needed to obtain these objectives.

planning-programming budgeting system Aids management in identifying and eliminating costly programs that were duplicates of other programs and to provide a means for the careful analysis of the benefits and costs of each program or activity.

plans Specify the manner in which objectives are to be accomplished.

policies A predetermined, general course or guide established to provide direction in decision making.

politics A network of interaction by which power is acquired, transferred, and exercised when dealing with others.

position power of the leader According to Fiedler, the degree of influence over rewards and punishments as well as by his or her official authority.

power The ability of one person to influence the behavior of another person.

preliminary screening interview Used to eliminate obviously unqualified applicants for reasons such as excessive salary requirements, inadequate education, inability to speak coherently, lack of job-related experience, or other reasons.

problem content Includes the environment within which the problem exists, the decision maker's knowledge of that environment, as well as the environment that will exist after a choice is made.

problem-solving objectives Goals that are established to deal with special projects or situations that need management attention.

procedures A series of steps established for the accomplishment of some specific project or endeavor.

process layout A type of plant layout in which pieces of equipment that perform virtually the same function are grouped together.

process standards Standards used when attempting to evaluate a function for which specified standards are difficult or impossible to formulate.

procurement assistance Program sponsored by the Small Business Administration designed to provide assistance and counseling to small businesses on how to obtain government contracts.

product layout A type of plant layout in which equipment is sequenced to permit a product to go from start to finish through the use of automated equipment and assembly lines.

professional decision maker A person who uses the best features of both the intuitive and research approach in the decision-making process.

professional decisions Encompass the best features of both the intuitive and research approach in the decision-making process.

Program Evaluation and Review Technique (PERT) A network technique developed by the U.S. Navy that is used to think through a project in its entirety. Three time estimates are used, which permits the user to develop probabilities of occurrences.

progressive discipline Efforts made to make the penalty appropriate to the violation or violations.

project organization Temporary organizational structure designed to achieve specific results by using a team of specialists from different functional areas within the organization.

purchase/lease decisions Process through which a manager decides whether to purchase the product outright or lease the use of the product.

quality The degree of conformity to a certain predetermined standard.

quality control Measures the degree of conformity according to form, dimension, composition, and color.

quantity control Established standard in terms of volume or numbers.

random No pattern. Occurs for reasons that the manager cannot anticipate.

reactive planning Flexibility of the planner to be able to respond to changing external and internal conditions.

receiver Individual who interprets the communication signals from the sender through means such as listening, observing, and reading.

recruiting Involves encouraging individuals with the needed skills to make application for employment with the firm.

referent power Based on the leader's possession of personal characteristics that make him or her "attractive" to other people.

regression analysis A quantitative technique that is used to predict one item through knowledge of other variables.

reinforcement theory Concerned with the way in which behavior is learned. Is the result of either positive or negative consequences.

reinforcers Rewards used in organizational behavior modification.

relationship behavior Consideration of people; level of socioemotional support.

reliability Concerned with the degree of consistency of test results.

resources Personnel, machines, material, and capital necessary to produce outputs.

responsibility An obligation of personnel to perform certain work activities.

resume A written description that a job applicant provides to a prospective employer with information such as career objectives, education, work experience, and other biographical data.

reward power Based on the leader's ability to administer and control rewards (such as pay, promotions, and praise) to others for complying with the leader's directions.

risk The probability of a particular decision's having an adverse effect on the company.

role The total pattern of expected behavior, interactions, and sentiments of an individual.

routine decisions Daily decisions made by managers that are governed by policies, procedures, and rules of the organization, as well as the personal habits of the manager.

routine objectives Represent recurring day-to-day activities that are expected to be performed. They represent standards of performance.

rule A very specific and detailed guide to action that is set up to direct or restrict action in a fairly narrow manner.

schematic models Line drawings, flow charts, graphs, maps, organizational charts, and similar items that represent the major features of a particular system.

scientific approach Based on a systematic formal approach to decision making.

seasonal Demand patterns in a shorter time frame than cyclical, typically twelve months.

selection The process of identifying those recruited individuals who will best be able to assist the firm in achieving organizational goals.

self-assessment Assists people in developing a realistic understanding of themselves. Individuals attempt to gain critical insight into who they are and what they desire out of life.

self-fulfilling prophecy What one expects to happen actually occurs. A manager's expectations often determine employee performance.

semantics Breakdowns in communication resulting from language barriers and different meanings being applied to the same word.

sensitivity training Technique used to develop awareness of sensitivity to oneself and others.

service objectives The reason that a firm is in business as viewed by society.

signal Medium by which the message is transmitted from sender to receiver.

simulation The use of a computer to assist in performing experiments on a model of a real system.

single accountability Each person should be answerable to only one immediate supervisor—one boss to each employee.

situational approach The ability to adapt to meet particular circumstances and constraints that a firm may encounter.

small business A business that is independently owned and operated and is not dominant in its field.

Small Business Administration (SBA) The federal agency that provides financial, managerial, and procurement assistance to small businesses.

Small Business Institute (SBI) Program using senior and graduate students of leading business schools throughout the country to provide on-site management counseling to small businesses.

social audit A commitment to systematic assessment of and reporting on some meaningful, definable domain of a company's activities that have social impact.

social responsibility A firm's obligation to constituent groups in society other than stockholders and beyond that prescribed by law or union contract.

source (sender) The person who has an idea or message to communicate to another person(s).

span of management There is a limit to the number of employees a manager can effectively supervise.

specialization of labor Division of functions into small work activities.

staffing process Involves planning for future personnel requirements, recruiting individuals, and selecting from those recruited individuals employees who fulfill the needs of the firm.

standards A norm, or criterion, to which something can be compared.

state of nature Refers to the various situations that could occur and the probability of this happening.

statistical quality control Technique that allows for a portion of the total number of items to be inspected.

status A person's rank or position in a group.

status symbol A visible, external sign of one's social position.

stockholders Individuals who share in a corporation's profit (or loss).

stopwatch method Method using a stopwatch to estimate the time it will take to complete a task.

strategic control points Critical areas that must be monitored if the organization's major objectives are to be achieved.

strategic planning The determination of how the organizational objectives will be achieved. Primarily accomplished by top-level management.

strength/weakness balance sheet Technique to identify what change in career objectives should be undertaken. Involves identifying all strengths and weaknesses.

stress The nonspecific response of the body to any demands made upon it.

structure The manner in which the internal environment of the firm is organized or arranged.

survey feedback The systematic collection and measurement of subordinate attitudes by anonymous questionnaires.

synergistic effect Sum of the parts is greater than the whole.

system An arrangement of interrelated parts designed to achieve objectives.

systems approach A concept that facilitates a manager's ability to perform the major functions of management and to respond effectively to environmental factors. Through the systems approach, a manager is better able to understand and work with the various units within the organization to interrelate and coordinate the accomplishment of the goals of the firm.

task behavior Behavior of the manager designed to provide direction and emphasis on getting the job done.

task-relevant maturity Defined in terms of the follower's desire for achievement, level of education and skills and his or her willingness and ability to accept responsibility.

team building A conscious effort to develop effective work groups throughout the organization.

team objectives Established in group meetings to provide overall direction and coordination of action of a group or division.

technical skill Ability to use specific knowledge, methods, or techniques in performing work.

technology All of the skills, knowledge, methods, and equipment required to convert resources into desired products and/or services.

telecommuting Computer hookups from office to home.

testing Process of screening job applicants in terms of skills, abilities, aptitudes, interests, personality, and attitudes.

Theory X Traditional philosophy of human nature. Suggests that motivation of employees requires managers to coerce, control, or threaten employees in order to achieve maximum results.

Theory Y A theory of human nature that provides an alternative to Theory X. Theory Y suggests that people are capable of being responsible and mature.

third country nationals Personnel from countries other than the parent or host countries.

time series analysis Mathematical approach in which the independent variable is expressed in units of time.

time standard Monitor the time required to complete the project.

timing Selecting the most appropriate time to transmit a message.

top management Referred to by such titles as president, chief executive officer, vice-president, or executive director. Responsible for providing the overall direction of the firm.

trade journals Publications written primarily for individuals who are associated with a particular type of industry or business.

training and developing Programs designed to assist individuals, groups, and the entire organization to become more efficient.

trait approach Study of leadership that focuses on leader's physical, intellectual, and personal characteristics.

transactional analysis (TA) A method that assists individuals in understanding both themselves and the people with whom they work. TA consists of three ego states that are constantly present and at work within each individual: the Parent, the Adult, and the Child.

trend Projects the long-run estimate of the demand for the product being evaluated.

unethical practices Practices that are legal but questionable in terms of ethical standards, honesty, or personal integrity.

unions Employees who have joined together for the purpose of presenting a united front in dealing with management.

valence How much value an individual places on a specific goal or result he or she is seeking.

validity Concerned with the relationship between the score on the test and performance on the job. Questions whether the test measures what it was intended to measure.

variable costs Costs that are directly related to changes in output.

variable sampling A sampling plan developed to determine how closely an item conforms to an established standard. Degrees of goodness and badness are permitted.

waiting line theory A quantitative technique that involves determining the optimum number of stations or queues to operate.

work sampling Method in which workers are observed at random times to determine the proportion of time spent on different tasks.

work simplification Organizes jobs into small, highly specialized components.

worker machine charts Used to determine if there is excessive idle time associated with either the worker or the machine.

work-force analysis Process of identifying the skills of current personnel to determine if work loads can be accomplished by these employees.

work-load analysis Process of estimating the type and volume of work that needs to be performed if the organization is to achieve its objectives.

zero base budgeting Requires management to take a fresh look at all programs and activities each year rather than merely building on last year's budget.

INDEX